D1710842

MCSA 70-697 and 70-698 Cert Guide

Don Poulton, Harry Holt, Randy Bellet

800 East 96th Street
Indianapolis, Indiana 46240 USA

MCSA 70-697 and 70-698 Cert Guide

ISBN-13: 978-0-7897-5880-4

ISBN-10: 0-7897-5880-6

Library of Congress Control Number: 2017943881

Printed in the United States of America

1   17

Trademarks

All terms mentioned in this book that are known to be trademarks or service marks have been appropriately capitalized. Pearson IT Certification cannot attest to the accuracy of this information. Use of a term in this book should not be regarded as affecting the validity of any trademark or service mark.

Warning and Disclaimer

Every effort has been made to make this book as complete and as accurate as possible, but no warranty or fitness is implied. The information provided is on an "as is" basis. The authors and the publisher shall have neither liability nor responsibility to any person or entity with respect to any loss or damages arising from the information contained in this book.

Special Sales

For information about buying this title in bulk quantities, or for special sales opportunities (which may include electronic versions; custom cover designs; and content particular to your business, training goals, marketing focus, or branding interests), please contact our corporate sales department at corpsales@pearsoned.com or (800) 382-3419.

For government sales inquiries, please contact governmentsales@pearsoned.com.

For questions about sales outside the U.S., please contact intlcs@pearson.com.

Editor-in-Chief
Mark Taub

Product Line Manager
Brett Bartow

Acquisitions Editor
Michelle Newcomb

Development Editor
Christopher Cleveland

Managing Editor
Sandra Schroeder

Senior Project Editor
Tonya Simpson

Copy Editor
Barbara Hacha

Indexer
Ken Johnson

Proofreader
Chuck Hutchinson

Technical Editor
Vince Averello

Editorial Assistant
Vanessa Evans

Cover Designer
Chuti Prasertsith

Compositor
Studio Galou

Contents at a Glance

Table of Contents

About the Authors

Don Poulton (A+, Network+, Security+, MCSA, MCSE) is an independent consultant who has been involved with computers since the days of 80-column punch cards. After a career of more than 20 years in environmental science, Don switched careers and trained as a Windows NT 4.0 MCSE. He has been involved in consulting with a couple of small training providers as a technical writer, during which time he wrote training and exam prep materials for Windows NT 4.0, Windows 2000, and Windows XP. Don has written or contributed to several titles, including *Security+ Lab Manual* (Que, 2004); *MCSA/MCSE 70-299 Exam Cram 2: Implementing and Administering Security in a Windows 2003 Network* (Exam Cram 2) (Que, 2004); *MCSE 70-294 Exam Prep: Planning, Implementing, and Maintaining a Microsoft Windows Server 2003 Active Directory Infrastructure* (Que, 2006); *MCTS 70-620 Exam Prep: Microsoft Windows Vista, Configuring* (Que, 2008); *MCTS 70-680 Cert Guide: Microsoft Windows 7, Configuring* (Que, 2011); *MCTS 70-640 Cert Guide: Windows Server 2008 Active Directory, Configuring* (Que, 2011); *MCTS 70-642 Cert Guide: Windows Server 2008 Network Infrastructure, Configuring* (Que, 2012); and *MCSA 70-687 Cert Guide Configuring Microsoft Windows 8.1* (Que, 2015).

In addition, he has worked on programming projects, both in his days as an environmental scientist and more recently with Visual Basic to update an older statistical package used for multivariate analysis of sediment contaminants.

When not working on computers, Don is an avid amateur photographer who has had his photos displayed in international competitions and published in magazines such as *Michigan Natural Resources Magazine and National Geographic Traveler*. Don also enjoys traveling and keeping fit.

Don lives in Burlington, Ontario, with his wife, Terry.

Harry Holt started his technology career in the early 1980s while working in trust accounting, where he discovered the advantages of Lotus 1-2-3 over paper spreadsheets, and how much better D:Base was at tracking transactions than a cabinet full of 3×5 index cards. That prompted a career change, and Harry took advantage of the burgeoning IT program at Virginia Commonwealth University's prestigious School of Business to hone his knowledge.

Harry gained experience over the years in most technical roles in the industry—from computer operator, programmer, and LAN administrator, to network engineer, DBA, and project manager, among others. He has used his skills to improve efficiencies in a range of organizations, including Fortune 500 companies, financial institutions, government agencies, and even small partnerships and sole proprietorships.

Exploring aspects of the computer industry and evolution of technology both professionally, as a hobby, and as a volunteer for various nonprofit organizations, Harry gained a working knowledge of many types of systems from large IBM z/OS mainframes, VAX systems, and UNIX platforms, to Windows, Macintosh, and Linux systems. He can program in a variety of development languages and platforms and enjoys collaborating in open source projects.

Harry has a bachelor's degree in IT and PMP certification and is currently working as a cyber applications manager in Richmond, Virginia. He lives with his wife, Donna, and enjoys going for meals prepared by his son and Master Chef, Alex, at fine dining restaurants in Richmond, Virginia.

Randy Bellet: After establishing himself as a retailer in Richmond, Virginia, curiosity about the fledgling small computer industry brought Randy Bellet into the IT field in 1981. Beginning with the TRS-DOS operating system on a Radio Shack Model III and "sneaker-net," he automated his own and other businesses, initially programming spreadsheets using one of the original versions of VisiCalc. Hardware consisted of 32 K of RAM, monochrome monitors, and no hard drives. Data was stored on floppy disks that really flopped. After the PC-XT and its clones arrived, he followed the market and extended his skills into the networking of PCs and XENIX servers and wrote applications for the retail and pager industries.

As PCs became commonplace and their connectivity a necessity, Randy configured Windows client/server networks for small- and medium-sized businesses, and wrote n-tier applications on various Windows platforms ranging from Windows 3.1 through Windows Server 2008 for the medical, insurance, food, and leisure industries. As organizations expanded and scaled their uses of PCs, extracting data from mainframes for use in Windows applications became a specialty.

Since 1999, Mr. Bellet has been on the faculty of ECPI University, delivering and developing curriculum in Network Security and Software Development and writing ancillary instructor materials. Certifications include CompTIA Network +, MCSE, MCSD, and MCDBA. He holds a bachelor's degree in economics and marketing from New York University and a master's degree in IT from Virginia Tech.

Dedication

This book is dedicated to my newest grandson, Ryan, who arrived in this world just as this project was getting underway. Like his older brother, Blake, he holds a world of international love in his future with his Chinese/Canadian heritage.
—Don Poulton

This book is dedicated to my family. I love you.
—Harry Holt

Dedicated to my wife, Evelyn, and daughters Rachel and Sarah, all of whom supported my career choices at every turn.
—Randy Bellet

Acknowledgments

I would like to thank all the staff at Pearson IT Certification and, in particular, Michelle Newcomb, for making this project possible. My sincere thanks goes out to Vince Averello for his helpful technical suggestions, as well as development editor, Chris Cleveland, for their improvements to the manuscript. Thanks especially to Randy Bellet and Harry Holt for their contributions, without which this entire project would never have been possible.

—Don Poulton

I want to especially thank the small army of individuals at Pearson who helped to make this book possible. Michelle Newcomb, for her introduction to and guidance through the process. Chris Cleveland, for his patience with me and thoroughness in review. Vince Averello, for his invaluable and detailed feedback. Tonya Simpson, for her highly expert work as project editor. Thanks goes especially to Don Poulton for helping with his long experience and arranging all the legacy material and organizing it all into a form ready for update. This book would have been a much longer effort without his contributions. Thank you as well to all of the additional people at Pearson whose hard work is reflected in these pages. This book is very much a collaborative effort and exists as such a valuable resource only due to their dedication and input.

—Harry Holt

Thanks to everyone at Pearson, including Michelle Newcomb, Chris Cleveland, and Vanessa Evans. And to Vince Averello and Tonya Simpson. Thanks especially to Don Poulton, who has set the standards, and to Harry Holt, whose tireless efforts and research into the always-changing technology made this something special.

—Randy Bellet

About the Technical Reviewer

Vince Averello has been a professional geek for more than 30 years. During those often funny, sometimes frightening, but always interesting years, he's worked for more than 10 organizations, lending his expertise to a variety of projects. Every one of them has been a learning experience, so now he knows a little bit about a lot of things ranging from the Internet to garment trucking. Vince lives in lovely midtown Bayonne, New Jersey, with his loving wife, daughter, and two cats with delusions of grandeur.

We Want to Hear from You!

As the reader of this book, you are our most important critic and commentator. We value your opinion and want to know what we're doing right, what we could do better, what areas you'd like to see us publish in, and any other words of wisdom you're willing to pass our way.

We welcome your comments. You can email or write to let us know what you did or didn't like about this book—as well as what we can do to make our books better.

Please note that we cannot help you with technical problems related to the topic of this book.

When you write, please be sure to include this book's title and author as well as your name and email address. We will carefully review your comments and share them with the author and editors who worked on the book.

Email: feedback@pearsonitcertification.com

Mail: Pearson IT Certification
            ATTN: Reader Feedback
            800 East 96th Street
            Indianapolis, IN 46240 USA

Reader Services

Register your copy of *MCSA 70-697 and 70-698 Cert Guide* at www.pearsonitcertification.com for convenient access to downloads, updates, and corrections as they become available. To start the registration process, go to www.pearsonitcertification.com/register and log in or create an account*. Enter the product ISBN 9780789758804 and click Submit. When the process is complete, you will find any available bonus content under Registered Products.

*Be sure to check the box that you would like to hear from us to receive exclusive discounts on future editions of this product.

Introduction

MCSA 70-698: Installing and Configuring Windows 10 is designed to prepare you to implement and administer Windows 10 computers in environments ranging from a few computers to enterprise-level deployments. It is structured around the objectives and topics published by Microsoft for Exam 70-698. With this book, you get a direct and hands-on approach to installing, configuring, and supporting deployments of Windows 10 computers. This is the first of two exams required to complete your MCSA certification in Windows 10. The exam is designed to measure your skill and ability to implement, administer, and troubleshoot computers running all editions of Windows 10. Microsoft not only tests you on your knowledge of the desktop operating system, but also has purposefully developed questions on the exam to force you to problem solve in the same way that you would when presented with real-life problems.

MCSA 70-697: Configuring Windows Devices is designed to build upon the foundations laid by the 70-698 exam, including the management and supporting of devices on the network, configuration of devices, applications, and security features, as well as the recovery of computers from various types of failures. It is structured around the objectives and topics published by Microsoft for Exam 70-697. This exam is the second of two exams required to complete your MCSA certification in Windows 10.

Both exams rely heavily on use-case scenarios and real-world situations. These questions test your knowledge of the proper way to deploy, configure, and troubleshoot Windows 10 when faced with challenges that are common when operating Windows computer networks in the real world. Not only will this book help to prepare you for the certification exams, it will ensure you have a fundamental understanding of the way in which you can leverage these powerful tools regardless of the size or complexity of your organization.

This book covers all the topics listed in Microsoft's exam objectives, and each chapter includes key topics and preparation tasks to assist you in mastering this information. It covers all the objectives that Microsoft has established for exams 70-697 and 70-698. It doesn't offer end-to-end coverage of the Windows 10 operating system; rather, it helps you develop the specific core competencies that you need to master as a desktop support specialist. You should be able to pass the exam by learning the material in this book, without taking a class.

About the 70-697, Configuring Windows Devices and 70-698, Installing and Configuring Windows 10 Exams

The 70-697, Configuring Windows Devices and 70-698, Installing and Configuring Windows 10 exams compose the two exams required to complete your MCSA certification in Windows 10. They have been designed for individuals who already have experience administering Windows 10 client computers in an enterprise environment and want to transition their responsibilities to the next career level. These exams test the candidate's understanding of the functionality and technical support of enterprise-level networks of Windows 10 computers together with Windows Server computers, with a particular focus on best-practices solutions to real-world challenges. They assume a high degree of familiarity with the functionality of Windows computer networks and support components.

These exams are computer-based tests that have 50 to 60 questions and a 120-minute time limit. All exam information is managed by Microsoft and is always subject to change, so candidates should monitor the Microsoft certification sites for any exam updates at https://www.microsoft.com/en-us/learning/exam-70-697.aspx and https://www.microsoft.com/en-us/learning/exam-70-698.aspx.

You can take these exams at Pearson VUE testing centers. You can register with VUE at www.vue.com/microsoft.

70-697 Exam Topics

Table I-1 lists the topics of the 70-697 exam and indicates the chapter in the book where they are covered.

Table I-1   70-697 Exam Topics

Exam Topic	Chapter
Manage identity (10–15%)	
Support Windows Store and cloud apps: Install and manage software by using Microsoft Office 365 and Windows Store apps, sideload apps by using Microsoft Intune, sideload apps into online and offline images, deeplink apps by using Microsoft Intune, integrate Microsoft account including personalization settings.	Chapter 5
Support authentication and authorization: Identifying and resolving issues related to the following: Multi-factor authentication including certificates, Microsoft Passport, virtual smart cards, picture passwords, and biometrics; workgroup vs. domain, Homegroup, computer and user authentication including secure channel, account policies, credential caching, and Credential Manager; local account vs. Microsoft account; Workplace Join; Configuring Windows Hello.	Chapter 7
Plan desktop and device deployment (10–15%)	
Migrate and configure user data: Migrate user profiles; configure folder location; configure profiles including profile version, local, roaming, and mandatory.	Chapter 9
Configure Hyper-V: Create and configure virtual machines including integration services, create and manage checkpoints, create and configure virtual switches, create and configure virtual disks, move a virtual machine's storage.	Chapter 10
Configure mobility options: Configure offline file policies, configure power policies, configure Windows To Go, configure sync options, configure Wi-Fi direct, files, powercfg, Sync Center.	Chapter 10
Configure security for mobile devices: Configure BitLocker, configure startup key storage.	Chapter 8

Exam Topic	Chapter
Plan and implement a Microsoft Intune device management solution (10–15%)	
Support mobile devices: Support mobile device policies including security policies, remote access, and remote wipe; support mobile access and data synchronization including Work Folders and Sync Center; support broadband connectivity including broadband tethering and metered networks; support Mobile Device Management by using Microsoft Intune, including Windows Phone, iOS, and Android.	Chapter 12
Deploy software updates by using Microsoft Intune: Use reports and In-Console Monitoring to identify required updates, approve or decline updates, configure automatic approval settings, configure deadlines for update installations, deploy third-party updates.	Chapter 13
Manage devices with Microsoft Intune: Provision user accounts, enroll devices, view and manage all managed devices, configure the Microsoft Intune subscriptions, configure the Microsoft Intune connector site system role, manage user and computer groups, configure monitoring and alerts, manage policies, manage remote computers	Chapter 13
Configure networking (10–15%)	
Configure IP settings: Configure name resolution, connect to a network, configure network locations.	Chapter 6
Configure networking settings: Connect to a wireless network, manage preferred wireless networks, configure network adapters, configure location-aware printing.	Chapter 6
Configure and maintain network security: Configure Windows Firewall, configure Windows Firewall with Advanced Security, configure connection security rules (IPsec), configure authenticated exceptions, configure network discovery.	Chapter 16
Configure storage (10-15%)	
Support data storage: Identifying and resolving issues related to the following: DFS client including caching settings, storage spaces including capacity and fault tolerance, OneDrive.	Chapter 9
Support data security: Identifying and resolving issues related to the following: Permissions including share, NTFS, and Dynamic Access Control (DAC); Encrypting File System (EFS) including Data Recovery Agent; access to removable media; BitLocker and BitLocker To Go including Data Recovery Agent and Microsoft BitLocker Administration and Monitoring (MBAM).	Chapter 8

Exam Topic	Chapter
Manage data access and protection (10–15%)	
Configure shared resources: Configure shared folder permissions, configure HomeGroup settings, configure libraries, configure shared printers, configure OneDrive.	Chapter 14
Configure file and folder access: Encrypt files and folders by using EFS, configure NTFS permissions, configure disk quotas, configure file access auditing, configure authentication and authorization.	Chapter 14
Manage remote access (10–15%)	
Configure remote connections: Configure remote authentication, configure Remote Desktop settings, configure VPN connections and authentication, enable VPN reconnect, configure broadband tethering.	Chapter 15
Configure mobility options: Configure offline file policies, configure power policies, configure Windows To Go, configure sync options, configure Wi-Fi direct.	Chapter 11
Manage apps (10–15%)	
Deploy and manage Azure RemoteApp: Configure RemoteApp and Desktop Connections settings, configure Group Policy Objects (GPOs) for signed packages, subscribe to the Azure RemoteApp and Desktop Connections feeds, export and import Azure RemoteApp configurations, support iOS and Android, configure remote desktop web access for Azure RemoteApp distribution.	Chapter 17
Support desktop apps: The following support considerations including: Desktop app compatibility using Application Compatibility Toolkit (ACT) including shims and compatibility database; desktop application co-existence using Hyper-V, Azure RemoteApp, and App-V; installation and configuration of User Experience Virtualization (UE-V); deploy desktop apps by using Microsoft Intune.	Chapter 18
Manage updates and recovery (10–15%)	
Configure system recovery: Configure a recovery drive, configure System Restore, perform a refresh or recycle, perform a driver rollback, configure restore points.	Chapter 20
Configure file recovery: Restore previous versions of files and folders, configure File History, recover files from OneDrive.	Chapter 21
Configure and manage updates: Configure update settings, configure Windows Update policies, manage update history, roll back updates, update Windows Store apps.	Chapter 1

70-698 Exam Topics

Table I-2 lists the topics of the 70-698 exam and indicates the chapter in the book where they are covered.

Table I-2 70-698 Exam Topics

Exam Topic	Chapter
Implement Windows (30–35%)	
Prepare for installation requirements: Determine hardware requirements and compatibility; choose between an upgrade and a clean installation; determine appropriate editions according to device type; determine requirements for particular features, such as Hyper-V, Cortana, Miracast, Virtual Smart Cards, and Secure Boot; determine and create appropriate installation media.	Chapter 2
Install Windows: Perform clean installations, upgrade using Windows Update, upgrade using installation media, configure native boot scenarios, migrate from previous versions of Windows, install to virtual hard disk (VHD), boot from VHD, install on bootable USB, install additional Windows features, configure Windows for additional regional and language support.	Chapter 2
Configure devices and device drivers: Install, update, disable, and roll back drivers; resolve driver issues; configure driver settings, including signed and unsigned drivers; manage driver packages; download and import driver packages; use the Deployment Image Servicing and Management (DISM) tool to add packages	Chapter 3
Perform post-installation configuration: Configure and customize Start menu, desktop, taskbar, and notification settings, according to device type; configure accessibility options; configure Cortana; configure Microsoft Edge; configure Internet Explorer; configure Hyper-V; configure power settings.	Chapter 3
Implement Windows in an enterprise environment: Provision with the Windows Imaging and Configuration Designer (ICD) tool; implement Active Directory–based activation; implement volume activation using a Key Management Service (KMS); query and configure activation states using the command line; configure Active Directory, including Group Policies; configure and optimize user account control (UAC).	Chapter 4
Configure and support core services (30–35%)	
Configure networking: Configure and support IPv4 and IPv6 network settings; configure name resolution; connect to a network; configure network locations; configure Windows Firewall; configure Windows Firewall with Advanced Security; configure network discovery; configure Wi-Fi settings; configure Wi-Fi Direct; troubleshoot network issues; configure VPN, such as app-triggered VPN, traffic filters, and lockdown VPN; configure IPsec; configure Direct Access.	Chapter 6
Configure storage: Configure disks, volumes, and file system options using Disk Management and Windows PowerShell; create and configure VHDs; configure removable devices; create and configure storage spaces; troubleshoot storage and removable devices issues.	Chapter 9

Exam Topic	Chapter
Configure data access and usage: Configure file and printer sharing and HomeGroup connections; configure folder shares, public folders, and OneDrive; configure file system permissions; configure OneDrive usage; troubleshoot data access and usage.	Chapter 14
Implement apps: Configure desktop apps, configure startup options, configure Windows features, configure Windows Store, implement Windows Store apps, implement Windows Store for Business, provision packages, create packages, use deployment tools, use the Windows Assessment and Deployment Kit (ADK).	Chapter 18
Configure remote management: Choose the appropriate remote management tools; configure remote management settings; modify settings remotely by using the Microsoft Management Console (MMC) or Windows PowerShell; configure Remote Assistance, including Easy Connect; configure Remote Desktop; configure remote PowerShell.	Chapter 15
Manage and maintain Windows (30–35%)	
Configure updates: Configure Windows Update options; implement Insider Preview, Current Branch (CB), Current Branch for Business (CBB), and Long Term Servicing Branch (LTSB) scenarios; manage update history; roll back updates; update Windows Store apps.	Chapter 1
Monitor Windows: Configure and analyze Event Viewer logs, configure event subscriptions, monitor performance using Task Manager, monitor performance using Resource Monitor, monitor performance using Performance Monitor and Data Collector Sets, monitor system resources, monitor and manage printers, configure indexing options, manage client security by using Windows Defender, evaluate system stability using Reliability Monitor, troubleshoot performance issues.	Chapter 19
Configure system and data recovery: Configure a recovery drive, configure a system restore, perform a refresh or recycle, perform a driver rollback, configure restore points, resolve hardware and device issues, interpret data from Device Manager, restore previous versions of files and folders, configure File History, recover files from OneDrive, use Windows Backup and Restore, perform a backup and restore with WBAdmin, perform recovery operations using Windows Recovery.	Chapter 20
Configure authorization and authentication: Configure Microsoft Passport, configure picture passwords and biometrics, configure workgroups, configure domain settings, configure HomeGroup settings, configure Credential Manager, configure local accounts, configure Microsoft accounts, configure Device Registration, configure Windows Hello, configure Device Guard, configure Credential Guard, configure Device Health Attestation, configure UAC behavior.	Chapter 7
Configure advanced management tools: Configure services, configure Device Manager, configure and use the MMC, configure Task Scheduler, configure automation of management tasks using Windows PowerShell.	Chapter 19

About the *MCSA 70-697 and 70-698 Cert Guide*

This book maps to the topic areas of the 70-697 and 70-698 exams and uses a number of features to help you understand the topics and prepare for the exams.

Objectives and Methods

This book uses several key methodologies to help you discover the exam topics on which you need more review, to help you fully understand and remember those details, and to help you prove to yourself that you have retained your knowledge of those topics. So, this book does not try to help you pass the exams only by memorization, but by truly learning and understanding the topics. This book is designed to help you pass the 70-697 and 70-698 exams by using the following methods:

- Helping you discover which exam topics you have not mastered

- Providing explanations and information to fill in your knowledge gaps

- Supplying exercises that enhance your ability to recall and deduce the answers to test questions

- Providing practice exercises on the topics and the testing process via test questions on the companion website

Book Features

To help you customize your study time using this book, the core chapters have several features that help you make the best use of your time:

- **"Do I Know This Already?" quiz:** Each chapter begins with a quiz that helps you determine how much time you need to spend studying that chapter.

- **Foundation Topics:** These are the core sections of each chapter. They explain the concepts for the topics in that chapter.

- **Exam Preparation Tasks:** After the "Foundation Topics" section of each chapter, the "Exam Preparation Tasks" section lists a series of study activities that you should do at the end of the chapter. Each chapter includes the activities that make the most sense for studying the topics in that chapter:

  - **Review All the Key Topics:** The Key Topic icon appears next to the most important items in the "Foundation Topics" section of the chapter. The Review All the Key Topics activity lists the key topics from the chapter, along with their page numbers. Although the contents of the entire chapter could be on the exam, you should definitely know the information listed in each key topic, so you should review these.

  - **Complete the Tables and Lists from Memory:** To help you memorize some lists of facts, many of the more important lists and tables from the chapter are included in a document on the companion website. This document lists only partial information, allowing you to complete the table or list.

- **Define Key Terms:** Although the exam may be unlikely to ask a question such as "Define this term," the Microsoft MCSA exams do require that you learn and know a lot of Windows computer administration terminology. This section lists the most important terms from the chapter, asking you to write a short definition and compare your answer to the glossary at the end of the book.

- **Web-based practice exam:** The companion website includes the Pearson Test Prep practice test software that allows you to take practice exam questions. Use these to prepare with a sample exam and to pinpoint topics where you need more study.

How This Book Is Organized

This book contains 21 core chapters—Chapters 1 through 21. Chapter 22 includes some preparation tips and suggestions for how to approach the exam. Each core chapter covers a subset of the topics on the 70-697 and 70-698 exams. The chapters cover the following topics:

- **Chapter 1, "Introducing Windows 10,"** covers the basics of Windows 10, a history of the Windows operating system, new features introduced with Windows 10, and provides a brief tour of Windows 10. It also covers how to work with application updates and Windows Update.

- **Chapter 2, "Implementing Windows,"** covers installation of Windows 10, upgrades to Windows 10 from older versions of Windows, how to install or upgrade Windows using various media and techniques, and installing Windows features. This chapter also covers using virtual hard disks (VHDs) to install and run Windows 10 and maintaining Windows 10 images.

- **Chapter 3, "Post-Installation Configuration,"** covers configuring and customizing the Windows user interface for the many device types that Windows 10 supports, configuring Windows options, and configuring devices and device drivers.

- **Chapter 4, "Managing Windows in an Enterprise,"** covers Active Directory and the many tools and systems available for managing and deploying large numbers of Windows servers and workstations in an organization.

- **Chapter 5, "Installing and Managing Software,"** covers the use of a Microsoft Account for logging in and keeping user information in sync, the Windows Store, and how to work with Universal Windows Platform apps.

- **Chapter 6, "Windows 10 Networking,"** covers the basics of TCP/IP networking, and the network capabilities available in Windows operating systems. It also covers various Windows network settings for VPN, Bluetooth, wireless, and other networking features.

- **Chapter 7, "Windows 10 Security,"** covers basic Windows security features for authentication and authorization. It also covers NTFS permissions and access control lists (ACLs), credential storage and management, and User Account Control (UAC) features and configuration.

- **Chapter 8, "Windows 10 Data Security,"** covers Windows features available for securing data at rest, including NTFS security, BitLocker and BitLocker To Go, Data Access Control (DAC), and Encrypting File System (EFS). This chapter also covers Windows policies that can be used to enforce good data security standards.

- **Chapter 9, "Managing User Data,"** covers data storage technologies available in Windows, working with disks and volumes, Storage Spaces, Distributed File System (DFS), and OneDrive cloud storage. It also covers managing user profile data and migrating user data from one system to another.

- **Chapter 10, "Windows Hyper-V,"** covers some virtualization concepts and configuring and working with virtualization in Windows, including virtual hard disks (VHDs), native boot, Microsoft client Hyper-V, creating and configuring Hyper-V virtual machines, checkpoints, and Hyper-V virtual switches.

- **Chapter 11, "Configuring and Securing Mobile Devices,"** covers technologies useful for Windows mobile devices, including offline files and Sync Center, power policies, Windows To Go, and Wi-Fi Direct.

- **Chapter 12, "Managing Mobile Devices,"** covers tools for managing mobile devices, which includes mobile device policies, data synchronization, and Work Folders, and technologies for managing broadband connectivity.

- **Chapter 13, "Microsoft Intune,"** covers Intune, Microsoft's cloud-based mobile device management (MDM) solution for organizations. It includes coverage for Intune administration, monitoring, and deployment of software updates for managed devices.

- **Chapter 14, "Configuring File and Folder Access,"** covers data encryption using Encrypting File System (EFS), disk quotas for limiting user storage, file access auditing, and configuration of shared resources such as file and printer sharing.

- **Chapter 15, "Configuring Remote Access,"** covers remote authentication technologies, Remote Desktop settings, VPN authentication and configuration, and configuration and use of remote management technologies.

- **Chapter 16, "Configuring and Maintaining Network Security,"** covers the configuration of Windows Firewall, IPsec security, and network discovery in Windows 10.

- **Chapter 17, "Managing Mobile Apps,"** covers the server-based services Remote Desktop Services (RDS), RemoteApp, and the use of Azure RemoteApp.

- **Chapter 18, "Managing Desktop Applications,"** covers the Windows Store for Business, desktop application compatibility for older applications, Windows Installer, App-V, and User Experience Virtualization (UE-V). This chapter also covers the use of Microsoft Intune for managing desktop applications for Intune-managed client computers.

- **Chapter 19, "Monitoring and Managing Windows,"** covers tools available for Windows 10 to monitor the use and performance of Windows 10 clients and the configuration of advanced management tools, including Microsoft Management Console (MMC), the Services applet, Task Scheduler, and Windows PowerShell management cmdlets.

- **Chapter 20, "Configuring System Recovery Options,"** covers how to create and use a USB recovery drive, and using System Restore and restore points. It also covers how to use Device Manager to resolve driver problems and conflicts, and the use of Driver Rollback capabilities.

- **Chapter 21, "Configuring File Recovery,"** covers using File History and Windows Backup and Restore to restore previous versions of files and folders, how to configure File History, and how to recover files from OneDrive.

- **Chapter 22, "Final Preparation,"** identifies tools for final exam preparation and helps you develop an effective study plan. It contains tips on how to best use the web-based material to study.

- **Appendix A, "Answers to the 'Do I Know This Already?' Quizzes,"** includes the answers to all the questions from Chapters 1 through 21.

- **Glossary:** Provides the list of key terms and their definitions as listed at the end of Chapters 1 through 21.

- **Appendix B, "Memory Tables,"** (a website-only appendix) contains the key tables and lists from each chapter, with some of the contents removed. You can print this appendix and, as a memory exercise, complete the tables and lists. The goal is to help you memorize facts that can be useful on the exams. This appendix is available in PDF format on the book's website; it is not in the printed book.

- **Appendix C, "Memory Tables Answer Key,"** (a website-only appendix) contains the answer key for the memory tables in Appendix B. This appendix is available in PDF format on the book's website; it is not in the printed book.

- **Appendix D, "Study Planner,"** is a spreadsheet, available from the book's website, with major study milestones, where you can track your progress through your study.

Companion Website

Register this book to get access to the Pearson Test Prep practice test software and other study materials plus additional bonus content. Check this site regularly for new and updated postings written by the authors that provide further insight into the more troublesome topics on the exams. Be sure to check the box that you would like to hear from us to receive updates and exclusive discounts on future editions of this product or related products.

To access this companion website, follow these steps:

1. Go to www.pearsonITcertification.com/register and log in or create a new account.

2. Enter the ISBN: **9780789758804.**

3. Answer the challenge question as proof of purchase.

4. Click the **Access Bonus Content** link in the Registered Products section of your account page to be taken to the page where your downloadable content is available.

Please note that many of our companion content files can be very large, especially image and video files.

If you are unable to locate the files for this title by following the preceding steps, please visit www.pearsonITcertification.com/contact and select the "Site Problems/Comments" option. Our customer service representatives will assist you.

Pearson Test Prep Practice Software

This book comes complete with the Pearson Test Prep practice software containing two full exams. These practice tests are available to you either online or as an off-line Windows application. To access the practice exams that were developed with this book, please see the instructions in the card inserted in the sleeve in the back of the book. This card includes a unique access code that enables you to activate your exams in the Pearson Test Prep software.

NOTE The cardboard case in the back of this book includes a paper that lists the activation code. On the opposite side of the paper from the activation code is a unique, one-time-use coupon code for the purchase of the Premium Edition eBook and Practice Test.

Accessing the Pearson Test Prep Software Online

The online version of this software can be used on any device with a browser and connectivity to the Internet, including desktop machines, tablets, and smartphones. To start using your practice exams online, follow these steps:

1. Go to http://www.PearsonTestPrep.com.
2. Select **Pearson IT Certification** as your product group.
3. Enter your email/password for your account. If you don't have an account on PearsonITCertification.com, you will need to establish one by going to PearsonITCertification.com/join.
4. In the **My Products** tab, click the **Activate New Product** button.
5. Enter the access code printed on the insert card in the back of your book to activate your product.
6. The product will now be listed in your My Products page. Click the **Exams** button to launch the exam settings screen and start your exam.

Accessing the Pearson Test Prep Software Offline

If you want to study offline, you can download and install the Windows version of the Pearson Test Prep software. There is a download link for this software on the book's companion website, or you can enter this link in your browser:

http://www.pearsonitcertification.com/content/downloads/pcpt/engine.zip

To access the book's companion website and the software, follow these steps:

1. Register your book by going to PearsonITCertification.com/register and entering the ISBN: **9780789758804.**

2. Respond to the challenge questions.

3. Go to your account page and select the **Registered Products** tab.

4. Click the **Access Bonus Content** link under the product listing.

5. Click the **Install Pearson Test Prep Desktop Version** link under the Practice Exams section of the page to download the software.

6. After the software finishes downloading, unzip all the files on your computer.

7. Double-click the application file to start the installation, and follow the onscreen instructions to complete the registration.

8. After the installation is complete, launch the application and select the **Activate Exam** button on the My Products tab.

9. Click the **Activate a Product** button in the Activate Product Wizard.

10. Enter the unique access code found on the card in the sleeve in the back of your book, and click the **Activate** button.

11. Click **Next** and then the **Finish** button to download the exam data to your application.

12. You can now start using the practice exams by selecting the product and clicking the **Open Exam** button to open the exam settings screen.

Note that the offline and online versions will sync together, so saved exams and grade results recorded on one version will be available to you on the other as well.

Customizing Your Exams

When you are in the exam settings screen, you can choose to take exams in one of three modes:

- Study Mode
- Practice Exam Mode
- Flash Card Mode

Study Mode enables you to fully customize your exams and review answers as you are taking the exam. This is typically the mode you would use first to assess your knowledge and identify information gaps. Practice Exam Mode locks certain customization options, because it is presenting a realistic exam experience. Use this mode when you are preparing to test your exam readiness. Flash Card Mode strips out the answers and presents you with only the question stem. This mode is great for late-stage preparation when you really want to challenge yourself to provide answers without the benefit of seeing multiple-choice options. This mode will not provide the detailed score reports that the other two modes will, so it should not be used if you are trying to identify knowledge gaps.

In addition to these three modes, you will be able to select the source of your questions. You can choose to take exams that cover all the chapters, or you can narrow your selection to a single chapter or the chapters that make up specific parts in the book. All chapters are selected by default. If you want to narrow your focus to individual chapters, deselect all the chapters and then select only those on which you want to focus in the Objectives area.

You can also select the exam banks on which to focus. Each exam bank comes complete with a full exam of questions that cover topics in every chapter. You can have the test engine serve up exams from all four banks or just from one individual bank by selecting the desired banks in the exam bank area.

You can make several other customizations to your exam from the exam settings screen, such as the time of the exam, the number of questions served up, whether to randomize questions and answers, whether to show the number of correct answers for multiple-answer questions, or whether to serve up only specific types of questions. You can also create custom test banks by selecting only questions that you have marked or questions on which you have added notes.

Updating Your Exams

If you are using the online version of the Pearson Test Prep software, you should always have access to the latest version of the software as well as the exam data. If you are using the Windows desktop version, every time you launch the software, it checks to see if there are any updates to your exam data and automatically downloads any changes that were made since the last time you used the software. This requires you to be connected to the Internet at the time you launch the software.

Sometimes, due to many factors, the exam data may not fully download when you activate your exam. If you find that figures or exhibits are missing, you may need to manually update your exams.

To update a particular exam you have already activated and downloaded, select the **Tools** tab and select the **Update Products** button. Again, this is an issue only with the desktop Windows application.

If you want to check for updates to the Pearson Test Prep exam engine software, Windows desktop version, select the **Tools** tab and select the **Update Application** button. This ensures that you are running the latest version of the software engine.

This chapter covers the following topics:

- **A Brief History of Windows:** Windows 10 is the latest in a long hierarchy of Microsoft operating systems. This section traces the history of Windows as it has unfolded in the past 30-plus years.

- **New Features of Windows 10:** This section provides an overview of the restyled user interface in Windows 10, along with its many new and improved features designed to help users work smartly and securely.

- **A Quick Tour of Windows 10:** This section introduces the Windows 10 Start menu and desktop. It also provides a brief introduction to the features of the Settings app and Control Panel.

- **Configuring Windows Updates:** This section shows you how to configure Windows Update from both Control Panel and the new Windows Update app on the Start screen. It also introduces you to Group Policy settings that provide a series of settings which govern the use of Windows Update, both on the local computer and within an Active Directory domain.

- **Configuring Updates:** Administrators managing multiple Windows devices in an enterprise need to understand Windows as a service model and how to deploy updates to clients. This section introduces servicing branches and deployment rings and covers enrolling devices for Insider Preview, Current Branch (CB), Current Branch for Business (CBB), and Long Term Servicing Branch (LTSB).

This chapter covers the following objectives for the 70-697 and 70-698 exams:

  Configure and manage updates: Configure update settings, configure Windows Update options and policies, manage update history, roll back updates, update Windows Store apps.

 Configure updates: Implement Insider Preview, Current Branch (CB), Current Branch for Business (CBB), and Long Term Servicing Branch (LTSB) scenarios.

CHAPTER 1

Introducing Windows 10

In recent years, more and more individuals have been attracted to mobile devices such as smartphones and tablets marketed by manufacturers such as Apple, Samsung, and Android, equipped with touchscreens that have become increasingly simple to use and navigate. Accompanying these devices is an increasing number of simple applications (known simply as apps) that enable the user to perform such tasks as locating restaurants while in a strange city, or knowing when her kids arrive home from school. At the same time, computer manufacturers have come out with laptops and mobile devices equipped with touch-sensitive displays; additionally, touch-sensitive monitors have become available for the still ubiquitous desktop computer.

Windows 7 brought with it significant enhancements in the usability and security of Microsoft's flagship operating system. Included was an array of touch-sensitive options, but these lagged considerably behind those being offered by competitors in the mobile device business. Windows 8 brought a new Start screen-based desktop environment that was not accepted by the majority of Windows users, prompting Microsoft to bring back many of the discarded features into the Windows 8.1 update. Windows 10 improves the desktop experience even further by combining the familiar feel of older Windows desktops with the ease of locating and running apps from its redesigned Start menu, accompanied with the same right-click Start menu (also known as the Quick Access Menu) from Windows 8.1, which facilitates the execution of most of the tools that desktop support staff and administrators rely upon in the performance of their daily tasks.

Microsoft has stated that Windows 10 will be the "last version of Windows." That doesn't mean that it will not be updating the operating system; it means that Windows 10 becomes the first of the new "Windows as a service" delivery model for the OS. Instead of a major update every few years, Microsoft will push out minor and major updates to Windows on a frequent basis. They may decide to brand it Windows 11 or Windows 12 in the future, but it will be delivered the same way that regular OS updates are delivered: via Windows Update.

There are now just two release types for Windows, eliminating the major version releases such as Windows 8.1, Windows 8, and so on. Instead, there will only be feature updates, delivering new functionality two to three times per year, and quality updates that provide security and reliability fixes at least once per month. So instead of purchasing an upgrade or new computer every 3 to 5 years, feature updates will come from Microsoft much more frequently—two to three times per year—in bite-sized chunks, making it easier for users to become familiar with new features.

As with past Windows versions, Microsoft continues to release frequent updates to its operating systems, still relying on the popular series of "Patch Tuesday" updates, but delivered as monthly cumulative updates instead of individual patches. Many of these are directed at fixing bugs and intrusions as cracks and vulnerabilities surface. Further, hardware manufacturers provide driver updates from time to time; so do third-party software providers. This chapter also introduces you to the Windows Update feature that enables users to download and install all available updates from the Windows Update website. For the 70-697 exam, Microsoft expects you to know how to use Windows Update to provide the proper updates to drivers, software programs, and operating system files.

"Do I Know This Already?" Quiz

The "Do I Know This Already?" quiz allows you to assess whether you should read this entire chapter or simply jump to the "Exam Preparation Tasks" section for review. If you are in doubt, read the entire chapter. Table 1-1 outlines the major headings in this chapter and the corresponding "Do I Know This Already?" quiz questions. You can find the answers in Appendix A, "Answers to the 'Do I Know This Already?' Quizzes."

Table 1-1   "Do I Know This Already?" Foundation Topics Section-to-Question Mapping

Foundation Topics Section	Questions Covered in This Section
A Brief History of Windows	1
Features Tour of Windows 10	2
A Quick Tour of Windows 10	3–5
Configuring Windows Updates	6–10
Configuring Updates	11–12

CAUTION   The goal of self-assessment is to gauge your mastery of the topics in this chapter. If you do not know the answer to a question or are only partially sure of the answer, you should mark that question as wrong for purposes of the self-assessment. Giving yourself credit for an answer you correctly guess skews your self-assessment results and might provide you with a false sense of security.

1. In what way is Windows 10 Education different from Windows 10 Enterprise?

   a. Windows 10 Education does not provide for joining an Active Directory Domain Services (ADDS) domain.

   b. Windows 10 Education does not include advanced security features, such as BitLocker, Credential Guard, Trusted Boot, or Encrypting File System.

   c. Windows 10 Education does not include the ability to use Remote Desktop or Remote Assistance.

   d. Windows 10 Education includes all features of Windows 10 Enterprise and differs only in that it is available with Microsoft's Academic Volume Licensing for schools, universities, and colleges.

2. Which of the following actions requires that you install Windows 10 Pro, Windows 10 Education, or Windows 10 Enterprise, in contrast to Windows 10 Home? (Choose all that apply.)

   a. Joining a Windows Server domain

   b. Using Windows Firewall to safeguard your computer

   c. Using more than one monitor on your computer

   d. Encrypting files using Encrypting File System (EFS)

3. Which of the following is *not* visible when you click Start on a Windows 10 computer?

   a. The desktop, together with shortcut icons

   b. A menu containing administrative utilities

   c. Tiles for Windows apps

   d. An alphabetical list of installed programs and apps

4. Which of the following tasks can you perform from the Windows Settings screen in Windows 10? (Choose all that apply.)

   a. Select lock screen, start screen, and wallpaper images

   b. Create new user accounts

   c. Specify time zone and language options

   d. Install hardware devices

   e. Configure accessibility options

   f. Create a new HomeGroup or join an existing HomeGroup

5. Which of the following categories of the Control Panel applet includes tools for managing File History and Backup and Restore?

   a. Network and Internet

   b. Programs

   c. System and Security

   d. Appearance and Personalization

   e. User Accounts

6. Microsoft has packaged a set of updates that is designed to fix problems with specific Windows components or software packages such as Microsoft Office. What is this package known as?

   a. A critical security update

   b. An optional update

   c. An update roll-up

   d. A service pack

7. Your Windows 10 Pro computer is shared among several users in your small office. Occasionally, others have informed you that the computer slows down and displays a message informing them to restart the computer to complete installing updates. This frequently occurs when they are performing important tasks that they do not want to interrupt. What should you do to ensure that all updates are installed but not until after business hours? Each correct answer represents a complete solution. Choose two answers.

   a. From the Windows Update app in Windows Settings, click **Change Active Hours** and then specify the start and end times when you normally use your computer.

   b. From the Windows Update app in Windows Settings, click **Advanced Options** and then select the **Defer Feature Updates** option.

   c. From the Windows Update app in Windows Settings, click **Choose How Updates Are Delivered** and then choose the **Updates from More Than One Place** option.

   d. In Group Policy, enable the Configure Automatic Updates policy and select the **2–Notify for Download and for Install** option.

   e. In Group Policy, enable the Configure Automatic Updates policy and select the **3–Auto Download and Notify for Install** option.

   f. In Group Policy, enable the Configure Automatic Updates policy and select the **4–Auto Download and Schedule the Install** option.

8. You are a desktop support specialist for your company. You have frequently found that updates received by Windows 10 computers from the Windows Update website cause problems with proprietary software, and you prefer that Patch Tuesday updates are not installed for a 30-day period after their initial release. Which of the following policies should you enable?

   a. In Group Policy, enable the **Automatic Updates Detection Frequency** policy, and set the detection frequency to 30 days.

   b. In Group Policy, disable the **Allow Automatic Updates Immediate Installation** policy.

   c. In Group Policy, enable the **Select When Feature Updates Are Received** option, and set the deferral interval to 30 days.

   d. In Group Policy, enable the **Select When Quality Updates Are Received** option, and set the deferral interval to 30 days.

9. You have installed Windows Server Update Services on a server on your network, and you want to ensure that computers on the network do not attempt to access the Internet for downloading updates. What policy should you configure?

   a. Allow Automatic Updates Immediate Installation

   b. Turn on Software Notifications

   c. Specify Intranet Microsoft Update Service Location

   d. Enable Client-Side Targeting

10. You would like to receive detailed information about an update that you think might be causing a problem on your Windows 10 computer. Which option should you select from the Update & Security Windows Settings app?

    a. Check for Updates

    b. Update History

    c. Restore Hidden Updates

    d. Recovery Options

11. How are Windows Store apps updated?

    a. Using Windows Automatic updates

    b. Using the Store app

    c. Either Windows Store or Automatic updates

    d. Using Group Policies

12. A user is having an issue updating an app from Windows Store. Where can you go to find more information on the error?

   a. The Store app Advanced Settings dialog

   b. The Control Panel apps manager

   c. The PowerShell Get-AppxLog command

   d. Viewing the Windows System Event log

Foundation Topics

A Brief History of Windows

Computers running some version of Microsoft Windows have been with us since the mid-1980s, when Windows 1.0 was first released. Most people first discovered Windows with versions 3.1 and Windows for Workgroups 3.11 in the early 1990s. As this decade progressed, Microsoft released Windows 95, which sported the first graphical user interface (GUI) that is the oldest original ancestor to the GUI used in much the same form as the more recent Windows 7.

At the same time, Microsoft developed an industrial-strength, 32-bit networking system known as Windows NT. Starting with Windows NT 3.1 and progressing to Windows NT 3.5 and Windows NT 3.51, this operating system used the same GUI as displayed by the consumer-oriented Windows versions. In 1996, Microsoft released Windows NT 4.0, which brought the Windows 95-style GUI to the NT system of Windows operating systems. Following soon afterward was Windows 2000 Professional. Also available were server versions of each of these operating systems.

At this point, Microsoft brought the home and corporate user versions together under the Windows NT kernel. The home user version became Windows XP Home Edition, and the corporate version was Windows XP Professional. These differed in that Windows XP Professional contained additional components (many of which had been present in Windows 2000) designed for integration into corporate, server-based networks.

During the early 2000s Microsoft was forced to work hard in enhancing the security of Windows XP as a result of numerous incursions. This delayed the next release of the Windows operating system, named Windows Vista, which was finally released to the public on January 30, 2007. But Windows Vista was plagued by numerous security and operational problems that resulted in large segments of the population having a negative opinion of the operating system. As a result, not many purchasers opted to upgrade, and many others used the downgrade license that was provided to run Windows XP, particularly within corporations.

So Microsoft placed high priority in readying a new version of its flagship operating system with the strong hope of alleviating these concerns and developing a secure, well-planned version of Windows that would be well accepted by individuals and corporations around the world. The result was Windows 7, which Microsoft released to manufacturers on July 22, 2009, and to the general public on October 22, 2009.

At the same time, cellular phone manufacturers were increasing the capability of their devices, turning them into miniature computers that could surf the Internet and run many applications that had previously been unthought of. Users became able to perform these actions with a mere touch of the screen. Although Windows 7 brought touch capabilities to computers equipped with the appropriate hardware, the usability of these devices lagged considerably behind the new smartphones. So, with these shortcomings in mind, as well as Microsoft's entry into the smartphone market with Windows Phone 7, work on Windows 8 progressed, including a total redesign of the user interface to realign with the touch-enabled devices and smartphones that were flooding the market. The result of this feverish activity was a new interface that replaced the familiar Start button with a completely new Start screen, including by default a large range of apps much similar to those on an Apple iPhone or iPad, BlackBerry, or Android device. Microsoft released a Consumer Preview (beta) of the new operating system on February 29, 2012, and released Windows 8 to public availability on October 26, 2012.

However, consumers reacted rapidly to modified features introduced in Windows 8—in particular, most users of the new operating system lamented the disappearance of the Start button and the fact that the computer now booted into an unfamiliar Start screen containing tiles rather than the familiar desktop and icons. Microsoft responded in early 2013 by beginning development on Windows 8.1, and upgrades would be free for existing users of Windows 8, with public availability of Windows 8.1 taking place on October 18, 2013. This brought back the Start menu in a somewhat modified fashion and enabled users to boot directly to the desktop, rather than the Start screen as occurred in Windows 8. Further changes were introduced with Windows 8.1 Update on April 8, 2014. This included a revision to the Start menu, which more closely aligned with the older Windows 7 Start menu and brought back long-lost functionality that users missed in the original Windows 8 and 8.1. Also added at this time was a new Start right-click menu that enabled rapid access to many management and configuration tools and utilities.

Windows 10

Even as Windows 8.1 was being finalized and released to consumers, Microsoft was working on the next upgrade to its flagship operating system. The desire was to unify the operating code for computers, tablets, Windows smartphones, and other devices such as Xbox One. Codenamed "Threshold," developers were working on further improvements to the Start menu and the capability to run Windows Store apps inside desktop windows rather than full screen, as was the case in Windows 8/8.1. In addition, developers worked to restore the functionality for users working with keyboard and mouse, compared to touch devices that had been emphasized in Windows 8/8.1.

Why not Windows 9? No real answer has ever been provided. Terry Meyerson of Microsoft rationalized the naming of the new operating system as Windows 10 rather than Windows 9 in saying that "based on the product that's coming, and just how different our approach will be overall, it wouldn't be right to call it Windows 9." A theory was also brought forward that the Japanese might think that the number 9 would be unlucky, so Microsoft skipped this number to maintain its customer base in Japan. Maybe it also helps it to distance itself from the problems that many individuals encountered in Windows 8. Whatever the true reason is, Microsoft wanted to emphasize the newness of its newest operating system and its multi-platform capabilities.

NOTE If you want to know more about Microsoft's reasoning behind calling the operating system Windows 10, take a look at "Why Is It Called Windows 10 and Not Windows 9?" at www.extremetech.com/computing/191279-why-is-it-called-windows-10-not-windows-9.

Windows 10 Editions

Windows 10 is available in the following eight editions:

- **Windows 10 Home:** Descended from the Home Basic and Home Premium editions of Windows 7 and the base edition of Windows 8/8.1, this edition is designed for home users who do not require domain membership or enhanced security features.

- **Windows 10 Pro:** The full-fledged version of Windows 10 that supports enterprise requirements, such as the need to join Active Directory domains.

- **Windows 10 Pro Education:** Introduced in July 2016, this edition is similar to Windows 10 Pro; it adds a Set Up School PCs app and removes Cortana and some Windows Store functionality.

- **Windows 10 Enterprise:** Similar to Windows 10 Pro and descended from Windows 8.1 Enterprise, this edition is available only to Software Assurance customers via the Volume License Service Center. It adds a few business-based features. You can also obtain evaluation versions by means of your TechNet Professional Subscription or MSDN Subscription.

- **Windows 10 Enterprise LTSB:** The Long Term Servicing Branch (LTSB) version removes several features from Windows 10 Enterprise, including Microsoft Edge, Cortana, Windows Store, Photo Viewer, and so on.

- **Windows 10 Education:** Similar to Windows 10 Enterprise; available with Microsoft's Academic Volume Licensing for schools, universities, and colleges.

- **Windows 10 Mobile:** Descended from Windows RT, this edition is designed for smartphones and small tablets.

- **Windows 10 Mobile Enterprise:** Similar to Windows 10 Mobile, but adds several features that assist in enterprise-based management of devices.

NOTE Throughout this Cert Guide, we use the term *Windows 10* to include all editions of Windows 10, only identifying the Pro/Enterprise/Education/Mobile editions as required when features specific to these editions are discussed.

Table 1-2 provides additional detail on the components included in the major editions of Windows 10. We introduce many of these features in the following sections.

Table 1-2   Components Included in Windows 10 Editions

Component	Windows 10 Home	Windows 10 Pro	Windows 10 Enterprise	Windows 10 Education
Microsoft Edge	x	x	x	x
Continuum	x	x	x	x
Cortana	x	x	x	
Hardware device encryption	x	x	x	x
Start menu and Live Tiles	x	x	x	x
Tablet Mode	x	x	x	x
Voice, pen, touch, and gesture	x	x	x	x
Trusted Boot	x	x	x	x
Windows Device Health Attestation service	x	x	x	x
Sideloading of Line-of-Business apps	x	x	x	x
Windows Defender	x	x	x	x
Windows Firewall	x	x	x	x

Component	Windows 10 Home	Windows 10 Pro	Windows 10 Enterprise	Windows 10 Education
Action Center	x	x	x	x
Task Manager	x	x	x	x
HomeGroup membership	x	x	x	x
Windows OneDrive	x	x	x	x
Windows Hello	x	x	x	x
Improved support for multiple monitors	x	x	x	x
Remote Desktop client	x	x	x	x
Remote Desktop host		x	x	x
Ability to join an Active Directory domain		x	x	x
Group Policy		x	x	x
Hyper-V		x	x	x
Enterprise State Roaming with Azure Active Directory		x	x	x
Windows Store for Business		x	x	x
Assigned Access		x	x	x
Dynamic Provisioning		x	x	x
BitLocker		x	x	x
AppLocker			x	x
BranchCache			x	x
Credential Guard			x	x
Device Guard			x	x
DirectAccess			x	x
User experience control and lockdown			x	x
Windows To Go			x	x
Long Term Servicing Branch (LTSB)			x	x
File encryption using Encrypting File System (EFS)			x	x
Application Virtualization (App-V)			x	x

Features Tour of Windows 10

Microsoft has designed Windows 10 to be dynamically updatable—in other words, they are providing updates to the operating system on an ongoing basis that will continue for the life of the product. In particular, the initial release on July 29, 2015, was version 1507, which was quickly updated to version 1511 on November 12, 2015. On the anniversary of the initial release, Microsoft provided a more comprehensive update to version 1607 (actually released on August 2, 2016). These updates have been delivered automatically to users via Windows Update; future updates will follow the same path. Additional minor updates to all versions are provided on an approximately monthly basis; for details on each update, refer to "Windows 10 Update History" at https://support.microsoft.com/en-us/help/12387/windows-10-update-history.

Improvements Provided in Versions 1507 and 1511

Windows 10 includes a number of new and updated features that are designed to improve the way users interact with their computers. The basic productivity enhancements included with most editions of Windows 10 include the following:

- **Windows Imaging and Configuration Designer (ICD):** Enables you to easily configure a device without the need to install a new image.

- **Support for Mobile Device Management (MDM):** This enables enterprise-level management of corporate and personal devices including phones, tablets, laptops, and desktops. Included is support for Microsoft Azure Active Directory accounts, virtual private network (VPN) configuration, use of the Windows Store, and so on.

- **Enhancements to AppLocker:** Additional Windows PowerShell cmdlets and the capability to configure AppLocker with the use of an MDM server.

- **Enhancements to BitLocker Encryption:** When used with an Azure Active Directory domain, you can enable automatic device encryption with the recovery key saved to Active Directory. Also added is support for the newer 128- and 256-bit XTS-AES encryption algorithm.

- **Credential Guard:** Enables protection of credentials stored in Credential Manager, including domain credentials.

- **Microsoft Passport:** New to Windows 10, enables you to deploy strong two-factor authentication consisting of an enrolled device and a Windows Hello biometric or PIN. Users can authenticate to a Microsoft account, an Active Directory or Azure Active Directory account, or a non-Microsoft service that supports Fast ID Online authentication. After the initial authentication,

Microsoft Passport enables the user to set up a gesture such as Windows Hello or a PIN, which the user can use for rapid authentication.

- **Enhanced Security Auditing:** Additional information has been added to several existing audit events, and two new audit subcategories have been added to the Advanced Audit Policy Configuration, as follows:
    - **Audit Group Membership:** Enables you to audit the group membership information within a user's logon token.
    - **Audit PNP Activity:** Enables you to audit when plug and play (PnP) detects an external device, enabling you to track changes to system hardware.
- **Enhancements to Trusted Platform Module (TPM):** Added functionality in TPM, including support for Microsoft Passport, Device Guard, and Credential Guard.
- **Device Health Attestation:** Enables you to set up a health attestation service enabling you to check security components on a device and allow or deny access to secure resources on the network. You can check Windows 10 devices for support and enabling of Secure Boot, BitLocker Drive Encryption, and Data Execution Prevention.
- **Enhancements to User Account Control (UAC):** Includes the capability to scan UAC elevation requests for malware and block such requests if malware is detected.
- **Mobile Device Management (MDM) Capabilities:** This enables enterprise-level management of phones, tablets, laptops, and desktops, whether corporate-owned or personal. You can enroll corporate-owned devices automatically using Azure Active Directory.
- **Device Unenrollment:** When a user leaves the organization, you can remove accounts from devices remotely, including personal devices. The latter enables removal of enterprise information such as certificates, VPN profiles, and enterprise apps.
- **Device Lockdown:** You can configure devices to perform only a single task or limited number of tasks—for example, kiosks in the lobby that provide product catalogs or employee lookups. Only specified apps will run when a given user account is logged on. You can also configure a customized Start menu layout on these devices.
- **Windows Store for Business:** Enables you to make volume purchases of apps for the organization. Included are purchases based on organizational identity, options for flexible app distribution, the ability to reuse licenses, and so on.

- **Windows Update for Business:** Enables you to keep devices up-to-date with the latest security and feature updates through the Microsoft Windows Update service. You can use Group Policy Objects (GPOs) to control which devices receive updates first, delivery of updates to remote sites with limited bandwidth, and the use of existing tools such as System Center Configuration Manager.

- **Microsoft Edge:** New in Windows 10, this Internet browser provides enhancements to active browsing of the Internet, including the following:

    - **Web Note:** Enables you to annotate, highlight, and call items out directly.

    - **Reading View:** Enables you to view and print online articles in an optimized layout that fits your screen size. You can also save web pages or PDF files for later offline reading.

    - **Cortana:** Automatically enabled on Microsoft Edge, enables you to search the Internet by asking questions by typing in the taskbar Search box or talking on a device equipped with a microphone. You can give yourself reminders to do things based on time, people, or places, and you can also sync notifications to a Windows phone or an iPhone or Android device equipped with Cortana.

    - **Compatibility and Security:** Enables you to continue to use Internet Explorer 11 for sites on your corporate intranet or safe site list, as well as sites using older technology, such as ActiveX controls.

Improvements Provided in Version 1607

The anniversary update, version 1607, added or enhanced several features of Windows 10, including the following:

- **Enhanced Windows Deployment, Configuration, and Upgrade Capabilities:** Windows Imaging and Configuration Designer (ICD) can run using just the configuration designer component, independently of the rest of the Windows 10 Assessment and Deployment Kit (ADK). In addition, Windows Upgrade Analytics facilitates the management of client computer upgrades in your organization.

- **Enhanced Control Over Windows Updates:** You can increase the time allowed for deferring updates to longer time periods; for example, you can defer quality updates up to 30 days and pause them for 35 days; you can defer feature updates for up to 180 days and pause them for 60 days; also, you can exclude drivers from updates.

- **Credential Guard and Device Guard:** Hyper-V now includes Isolated User Mode, so you don't need to install it separately.

- **Windows Hello for Business:** Version 1607 combines the Microsoft Passport and Windows Hello technologies together, enhancing the use of multi-factor authentication.

- **Windows Information Protection (WIP):** Formerly known as enterprise data protection, WIP helps to protect against accidental data leakage from personal devices by enabling you to set up policies and best practices. You can also use WIP to protect enterprise apps and data against accidental data leakage on devices without the need for changes to these apps or your security environment.

- **VPN Enhancements:** Version 1607 adds several security enhancements to VPN. The client can integrate with the Conditional Access Framework within Azure Active Directory. The client can also integrate with WIP for added security. Within Microsoft Intune, support for native VPN plug-ins is provided through VPN Profile (Windows 10 Desktop and Mobile and later).

- **Improvements to Windows Defender:** Version 1607 adds several enhancements, as follows:

  - **Enhanced Scanning Capabilities:** You can run Windows Defender offline directly without the need to create bootable media. You can also use PowerShell cmdlets to execute scans, and even run a scan from the command line.

  - **Block at First Sight:** Enables the near-instant protection against new malware.

  - **Enhanced Notifications:** Provide more information regarding detection and removal of threats.

  - **Detection of Potentially Unwanted Applications:** These can be detected and blocked during download and install actions.

- **Application Virtualization (App-V):** App-V enables you to deliver applications to users in Virtual mode, where applications are installed on centrally managed servers and deployed to users in real time or on an as-needed basis. Users can launch and run them from locations such as the Windows Store, and interact with them as if they were on a local machine.

- **User Experience Virtualization (UE-V):** Enables you to save user-customized Windows and program settings on a centrally managed network file share. Users logging on from any device can have these customized settings applied automatically.

■ **Additional Management Options:** Version 1607 enables users to connect to remote computers that are joined to Azure Active Directory. You can also apply Group Policy to create a standardized set of apps to the taskbar. In addition, additional device management settings have been added to the Windows 10 configuration service providers.

Chapter 2, "Implementing Windows," Chapter 3, "Post-Installation Configuration," Chapter 7, "Windows 10 Security," Chapter 10, "Windows Hyper-V," Chapter 12, "Managing Mobile Devices," Chapter 15, "Configuring Remote Access," and Chapter 18, "Managing Desktop Applications," provide details of many of these features.

NOTE   For more information on new and improved Windows 10 features, refer to "What's New in Windows 10, Versions 1507 and 1511" at https://technet.microsoft.com/itpro/windows/whats-new/whats-new-windows-10-version-1507-and-1511 and "What's New in Windows 10, Version 1607" at https://technet.microsoft.com/en-us/itpro/windows/whats-new/whats-new-windows-10-version-1607, as well as links provided in these documents. Also refer to "Windows 10 Release Information" at https://technet.microsoft.com/en-us/windows/release-info for information on the history of operating system builds for each version.

NOTE   As this book was in the final stages of completion, Microsoft brought out a new version, 1703, that includes enhancements to deployment, management, security, and mobile enhancements. You should be aware that you can no longer access Control Panel from the Start button right-click menu; instead, click **Start** and scroll the program list to click **Windows Features**. Then click **Control Panel** from the expanded list of features that appears. For more information on the enhancements included in version 1703, refer to "What's new in Windows 10, version 1703 IT pro content" at https://docs.microsoft.com/en-us/windows/whats-new/whats-new-windows-10-version-1703.

A Quick Tour of Windows 10

In contrast to the Start screen appearance shown when you started up a computer running Windows 8/8.1, Windows 10 presents a desktop display with several default taskbar icons, as shown in Figure 1-1. Here, you can place icons that provide shortcuts to programs or folders in much the same way as with previous versions of Windows.

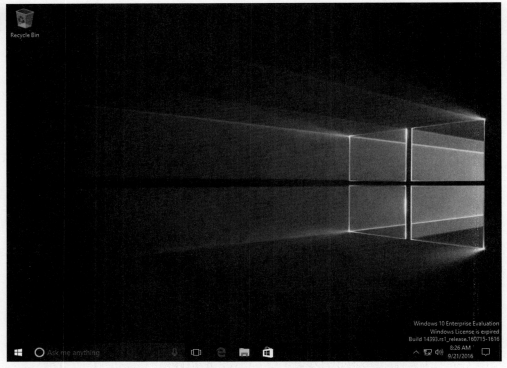

Figure 1-1 Windows 10 Desktop at First Installation of Windows 10

Click **Start** and you receive a modified Start screen that displays a list of all installed apps alphabetically arranged on the left side (with the most-used apps included at the top), as shown in Figure 1-2. Tiles for many of the default installed Windows apps appear on the right side of the menu. You can add additional tiles to the Start screen or move them around to arrange them in whatever fashion you prefer. Many programs, such as Microsoft Office, automatically add tiles to the Start screen when you install them.

On the far left of the Start menu, above the Start button, are several icons that permit you to do the following:

- The user icon at the top (which takes on the appearance of the users' default picture if you have specified one) enables you to change account settings from the accounts page of the Settings app (more about this later in this section), lock the computer (you then need to reenter your password to resume work), or sign out.

- The gear wheel icon enables you to access the Windows Settings app, described in the following section.

- The folder icon (not always seen) enable you to access File Explorer.

- The power icon enables you to enter Sleep mode, shut down, hibernate (if enabled), or restart your computer.

Figure 1-2 The Start Menu with Program List and Tiles

NOTE   Using a touchscreen device, you can tap any icon found on the Start screen to open the associated program or folder, or double-tap any icon found on the desktop. In the remainder of this Cert Guide, when we refer to clicking an icon or tile, this action also assumes you can tap the icon or tile when using a touchscreen device.

Right-click **Start** to display a menu list of administrative actions similar to those found in the previous Windows 8.1 Start right-click menu or the older Windows 7 Start menu. Shown in Figure 1-3, these actions permit you to perform many tasks discussed throughout this Cert Guide.

Figure 1-3   The Start Right-Click Menu Provides Shortcuts to Many Administrative Tasks in Windows 10

Cortana and the Windows 10 Search

Clicking in the **Search** field in the taskbar next to the Start button panel enables Cortana and brings up the new Windows 10 Search screen shown in Figure 1-4.

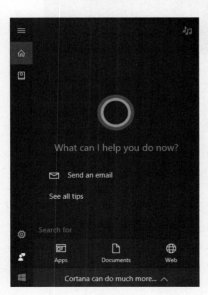

Figure 1-4   Use the Windows 10 Search Screen to Search for Apps, Settings, Folders, or Files on Your Computer or the Internet

Type any program, web page, or filename in the space provided. If you have a microphone connected to your computer, you can ask Cortana any question, and she will help you find an answer. You need to type only a portion of a name in the space, and Windows attempts to locate matches from your computer or the Internet. Click **See All Tips** to display a list of actions that Cortana can help you perform, such as play music, send emails, set reminders, display a calendar, and so on. You can also open a network share by typing the Universal Naming Convention (UNC) path to the share; for example, **\\server1\documents**.

The Get Started App

Type **get started** into the Search field to access the Get Started app. New to Windows 10, this app (see Figure 1-5) provides you with a series of items that enable you to become familiar with new and improved features, and it is updated automatically as new features are added or modified. You should browse this app and become familiar with everything contained within before preparing for your 70-697 exam.

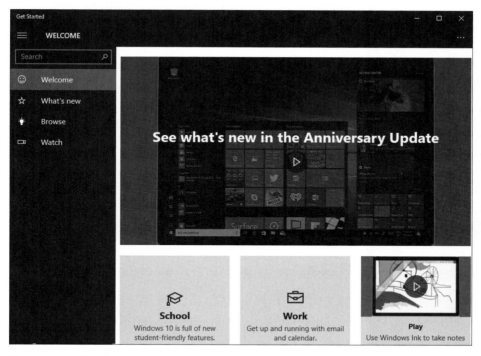

Figure 1-5 The Get Started App Provides Several Methods to Familiarize You with New and Updated Windows 10 Features

The Get Started app includes the following items:

- **Welcome:** As shown in Figure 1-5, this screen provides links to several items contained within the app. The upper portion starts a video that describes significant new features in the current update and is updated each time a new build of Windows 10 is released.

- **What's New:** Provides videos and informative text that describe new features in Windows 10. Items included at the time of writing include Cortana, Microsoft Edge, Windows Ink, the new Start menu, the improved Action Center, and improved features of the Lock screen. Items appearing here are continuously updated as new features evolve.

- **Browse:** Click any of these icons (see Figure 1-6) to obtain information and informative videos on the topic selected. Most icons provide a series of icons representing subtopics of the selected topic; click any of these to obtain additional help.

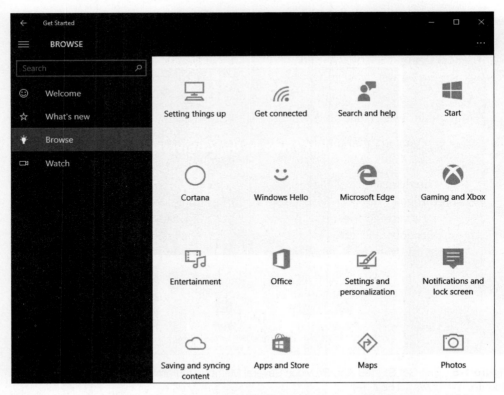

Figure 1-6 Browse Link with Active Icons That Provide Descriptive Information and Videos to Help You Become Familiar with Its Topic

- **Watch:** Provides a series of instructive videos on Windows 10 and the included Windows Store apps. As with everything else in the Get Started app, these are updated as new features evolve.

NOTE The Get Started app replaces the Windows Help feature found in previous Windows editions. Typing **help** into the Search field also leads you to this app.

Configuring the Windows 10 Taskbar

The Windows 10 taskbar is similar to the Windows 7/8/8.1 taskbar, combining features of the taskbar and Quick Launch area formerly present in older Windows versions. By default, when you first install Windows 10, the taskbar contains the revised Start button plus four buttons at the far left side, which represent Task View, Microsoft Edge, File Explorer, and the Windows Store. Each time you open an application, a button representing this application is added to the taskbar. You can add applications to the taskbar; find the desired application from the tiles on the Start screen (using Search if desired), right-click it, and choose **Pin to Taskbar**. These remain on the taskbar whether the program is running or not; if you want to remove a button from the taskbar later, right-click it and choose **Unpin from Taskbar**.

Taskbar buttons can take on any of the following three appearances:

- For a pinned program that is not running, a simple icon for the program appears. Click the button to open the program.

- If a single instance of the program (or a single File Explorer window or Microsoft Edge or other browser tab or page) is running, the button is enclosed by a single rectangular frame. Mouse over the button to view a thumbnail of the application; click it to bring it to the front. If the application is already in the front on your desktop, clicking its taskbar button minimizes the application.

- If multiple instances of the program (or of Explorer windows or Microsoft Edge tabs or pages) are running, the button takes on a pseudo-3D appearance that looks like stacked frames. If you mouse over the button, a series of icons representing each instance or tab appears; click the desired one to bring it to the front.

Windows 10 provides several options for configuring the properties of the taskbar. Right-click the taskbar and choose **Settings** to bring up the Taskbar Settings dialog box, which enables you to configure properties related to the taskbar and notification area. We describe the available settings later in this chapter.

Toolbars

Right-click the desktop and choose **Toolbars** to configure the taskbar to display toolbars for Address, Links, and the Desktop. These toolbars appear on the right side of the taskbar, next to the Notification area.

Windows 10 Apps

As already introduced, Windows 10 comes with a series of Start screen apps, which enable you to perform many simple tasks easily. These include mail, messaging, people, weather, music, photos, video, travel, maps, and so on (refer to Figure 1-2). If they do not appear within the set of tiles found on the right side of the Start menu, you can locate and open them from the program list on the left side of the Start menu. Windows 10 provides updates to most of these basic apps and adds several new ones. Unlike the case in Windows 8.1, each app appears in its own window; you can switch between them by pressing Alt+Tab or selecting its icon from the taskbar. You can obtain additional apps from the Windows Store; many of these are free, and most of the others are available for a small charge.

Libraries

Windows 10 continues the concept of libraries, first introduced in Windows 7 and continued in Windows 8/8.1. These are collections of Windows folders, such as Documents, Pictures, Saved Pictures, Camera Roll, Videos, and Music. These replace the special shell folders, such as My Documents, that were found in Windows versions prior to Windows 7 and provide access to files and folders with a common theme. Each library is simply a pointer that opens a window containing all subfolders and files within the library. By default, the following four libraries are shown in File Explorer:

- **Documents:** Includes the My Documents and Public Documents folders.

- **Music:** Includes the My Music and Public Music folders.

- **Pictures:** Includes the My Pictures and Public Pictures folders. You might also find two additional library folders, Camera Roll and Saved Pictures.

- **Videos:** Includes the My Videos and Public Videos folders.

To access your libraries in Windows 10, click the folder icon in the taskbar.

You can add additional folders to a library at any time. Right-click the desired library and choose **Properties** to display the dialog box shown in Figure 1-7. To add a folder, click **Add** and browse to the desired folder. To remove a folder, select it and click **Remove**.

Figure 1-7   The Library Properties Dialog Box Enables You to Perform Actions Such as Adding and Removing Folders Accessed from the Library

You can also create new libraries at any time. Right-click a blank area in the Libraries window and choose **New > Library**. Provide a name for the library and then follow the procedure in the preceding paragraph to add folders to your library.

By default, all libraries are shared when the computer is in a HomeGroup or workgroup. You can modify this behavior as desired. We discuss sharing of libraries and folders in more detail in Chapter 7, "Windows 10 Security."

Windows Settings

Clicking the gear wheel icon at the bottom left of the Start menu (refer to Figure 1-2) brings you to the new Windows Settings screen shown in Figure 1-8. From this screen, you can access a variety of utilities that enable you to configure various functions on your computer, as discussed in the following sections.

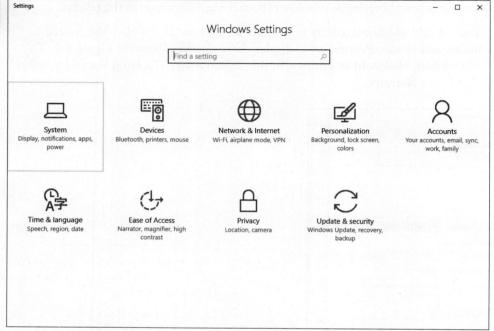

Figure 1-8 The Windows Settings Utility Enables You to Configure a Series of Settings on Your Computer

System

The System utility, shown in Figure 1-9, enables you to configure a series of options related to the use of the computer and the appearance of the desktop. The options enable you to perform the following tasks:

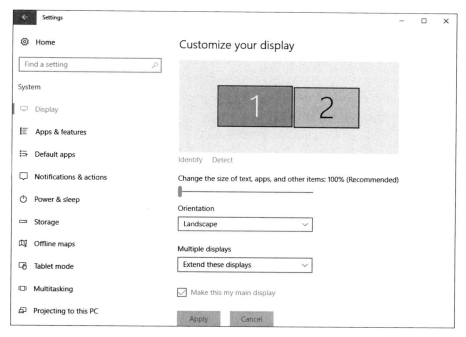

Figure 1-9   System Utility Enabling You to Perform Several System-Related Actions

- **Display:** Enables you to customize the appearance of your display, including setting the screen resolution and extending your desktop view to multiple monitors. When using multiple monitors, you can also select which monitor is your main display and choose to use only a specified display or to mirror your display on both monitors.

- **Apps & Features:** Provides a list of programs, Windows default apps, and additional features installed on your computer. You can search the list; sort it by name, size, or install date; and move or uninstall any app on the list. You can also configure advanced options for many of the apps on the list.

- **Default Apps:** Enables you to select default programs that are opened whenever you double-click a file of a given type. For example, for a music player you can select Windows Media Player or the new Groove Music app. You can also click **Look for an App in the Store** to search for additional programs from the Windows store.

- **Notifications & Actions:** Enables you to select the actions that will provide notifications appearing in the Action Center. You can also select third-party senders to receive notifications. For each available action, you can toggle its setting to On or Off.

- **Tablet Mode:** Available on laptops only, provides several options that enhance touch-friendly use when using your laptop as a tablet.

- **Battery Saver:** Available on laptops only or devices attached to a UPS; displays the battery charge level and provides several options for extending battery life by limiting background activity and push notifications.

- **Power and Sleep:** Enables you to specify the length of inactive time after which the computer will shut the screen off (10 minutes by default) and go to sleep (30 minutes by default). You can also click **Additional Power Settings** to access the Power Options control panel applet.

- **Storage:** Provides a list of internal and external hard drives and indicates the proportion of each that is used. You can also choose the drive to which new files of various types are saved by default.

- **Offline Maps:** Enables you to download maps using the Maps app, so that you can search for places and obtain directions without being connected to the Internet.

- **Multitasking:** Controls the appearance and arrangement of multiple windows when you have more than one program open. Also provides two options that govern which windows appear on virtual desktops.

- **Projecting to This PC:** Controls that ability of an external computer or Windows phone to project its image to your computer. You can also choose to require a PIN for pairing or whether the computer is discovered for projection only when it is plugged in.

- **Apps for Websites:** Enables you to select an alternative app (if installed) to open a website.

- **About:** Provides summary information on your computer, its operating system, current version, operating system (OS) build, and hardware configuration. You can also rename your computer and change the Windows product key, or upgrade your edition of Windows to a higher one (for example, Windows 10 Home to Windows 10 Pro).

Devices

As shown in Figure 1-10, this utility provides options for configuring hardware devices attached to your computer. Click **Add a Device** to enable Windows to search for new hardware devices. If using a metered Internet connection (where you pay according to the length of time connected to the Internet), you can toggle the Download Over Metered Connections option to Off to limit the connection time used for downloading updates, drivers, and so on.

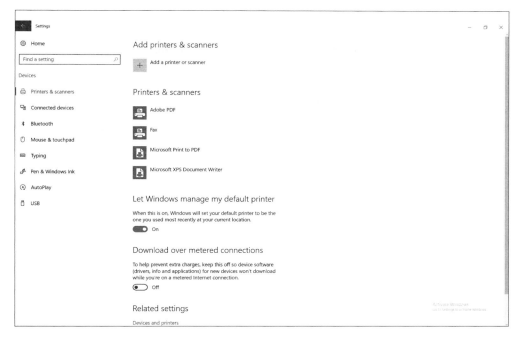

Figure 1-10   The Devices Utility Enables You to Configure Options with Various Hardware Devices

You have the following options:

- **Printers & Scanners:** Enables you to select default printers and add new printers, scanners, or faxes.

- **Connected Devices:** Displays other hardware devices connected to the computer and enables you to access several related Control Panel settings.

- **Bluetooth:** Enables your computer to search for and be discovered by Bluetooth devices. You can also configure several related Bluetooth options and send or receive files from another Bluetooth device. Available only on Bluetooth-enabled computers.

- **Mouse & Touchpad:** Enables you to configure the primary mouse button or the number of lines scrolled by the mouse wheel. Left-handed users can choose to use the right mouse button as the primary button from this utility. A link to the Control Panel mouse applet is provided for configuring additional mouse options.

- **Typing:** Enables you to highlight and autocorrect misspelled words as you type. By default, both options are turned on.

- **Pen & Windows Ink:** Appearing only on touchscreen devices, this option allows you to configure several options for your pen and how Windows Ink works, such as handedness (left or right), defaults for the pen shortcut button, and visual effects.

- **AutoPlay:** Enables you to use AutoPlay for all media and devices (turned on by default). This enables automatic startup of programs on devices such as CDs and DVDs to install programs, play music, watch videos, and so on. You can also choose AutoPlay defaults for removable devices and memory cards.

- **USB:** Enables you to provide a notification if issues occur when connecting to USB devices.

Network & Internet

As shown in Figure 1-11, this utility enables you to configure several network settings as described in the list that follows. We discuss network configuration in more detail in Chapter 6, "Windows 10 Networking," and Chapter 8, "Windows 10 Data Security."

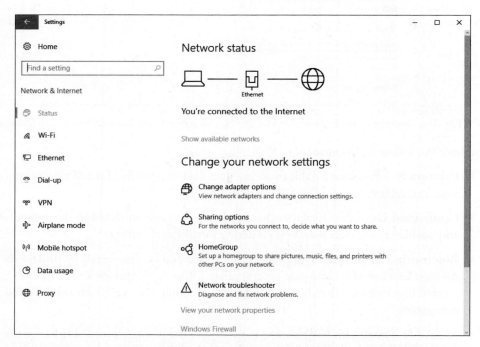

Figure 1-11   The Network Utility Enables You to Configure Several Networking Properties

- **Status:** As shown in Figure 1-11, you can configure several options related to your available network connections. Most of these options are discussed in later chapters of this Cert Guide.

- **Wi-Fi, Ethernet, Dial-up, and VPN:** These options enable you to view the properties of the respective type of network connection. All of them also provide links to configure options related to the specific type of network connection that you've accessed. Click **Add a VPN Connection** to set up a virtual private network (VPN) connection to a corporate network utilizing this service.

- **Airplane Mode:** Provides an option to stop all wireless communications to comply with air transport regulations.

- **Mobile Hotspot:** Enables you to share your Internet connection with other devices. You can also specify the network type that is shared, and edit the network name and password.

- **Data Usage:** Provides an overview of data usage from the previous 30 days. Click **Usage Details** to view a list of data usage from various apps that connect to the Internet. Click **Storage Settings** to view the same list previously described under the System section.

- **Proxy:** Enables you to specify automatic or manual setup for use of a proxy server for Ethernet or Wi-Fi connections.

Personalization

As shown in Figure 1-12, you can configure a series of options related to the use of the computer and the appearance of the desktop. The options provided enable you to perform the tasks described in the list that follows.

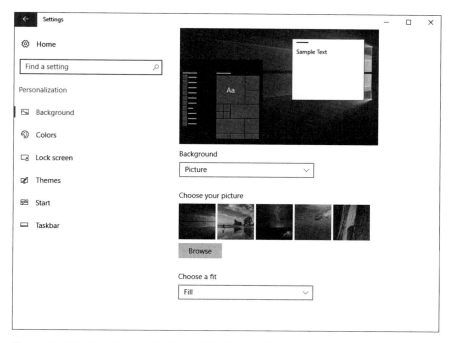

Figure 1-12   The Personalization Utility Enables You to Perform Several Desktop Personalization Actions

- **Background:** Enables you to select a background picture or slide show. You can specify several slide show options if you select this choice.

- **Colors:** Enables you to choose an accent color that appears on various places such as window borders. You can also choose from several options that determine where this accent color appears. Click **High Contrast Settings** to choose from several high contrast themes that improve readability for vision-impaired users.

- **Lock Screen:** The Lock screen is the image that appears before you log on or after you have logged off. By default, the Lock screen also appears when you resume your computer from Sleep mode (this behavior can be changed if desired; see Chapter 7, "Windows 10 Security" for more information). You can select from any of the sample images displayed here or click **Browse** to use one of your own images. Doing so takes you to the Pictures library, from which you can drill down through its subfolders to locate an image to be used. You can also choose to play a slide show from the chosen location on the Lock screen (disabled by default). You can also choose which apps (such as Mail, Calendar, Messaging, and so on) show quick messages on the Lock screen. For example, this can alert you to an incoming email even if you aren't logged on.

- **Themes:** Enables you to choose from a variety of Windows themes that control desktop appearance. You can select other links that connect to Control Panel applets that control the appearance of desktop icons, mouse pointers, as well as default sounds played by Windows.

- **Start:** Controls the appearance of the Start menu. This provides a series of toggles that enable you to see items such as most used apps, recently added apps, and recently opened items in jump lists on Start or the taskbar. By clicking the link labeled **Choose Which Folders Appear on Start**, you can select from the various library folders as well as several commonly used apps. Note that this includes a toggle for accessing Settings itself. This is normally set to **On**; if you set it to **Off**, you need to type **settings** into the Search bar to access the Settings app at a later time.

- **Taskbar:** Shown in Figure 1-13, this option enables you to configure taskbar properties similar to those found in the Taskbar tab of the Taskbar and Navigation Properties dialog box. You have the options described in the list that follows.

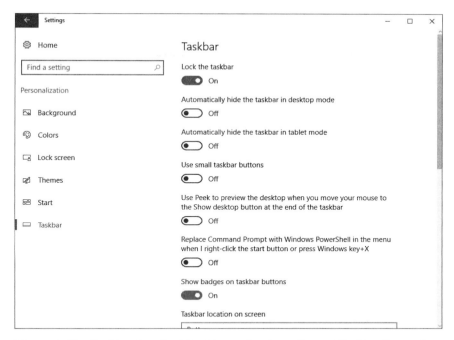

Figure 1-13   Taskbar App Enabling You to Configure Several Taskbar Properties

- **Lock the Taskbar:** Determines whether the taskbar is always visible at the bottom of the display.

- **Automatically Hide the Taskbar:** Determines whether the taskbar disappears automatically after a program is started; there are separate settings for desktop and tablet modes.

- **Use Small Taskbar Buttons:** Shrinks the size of icons on the taskbar buttons.

- **Use Peek to Preview the Desktop When You Move Your Mouse to the Show Desktop Button at the End of the Toolbar:** Enables the view of the desktop by hovering the mouse over a small area to the right of the clock at the end of the taskbar.

- **Replace Command Prompt with Windows PowerShell in the Menu When I Right-click the Start Button or Press Windows Key+X:** Enables you to open a Windows PowerShell session rapidly by performing the indicated actions.

- **Show Badges on Taskbar Buttons:** For Windows Store or UWP apps, allow notification badges to be shown on the app icon. For instance, the Mail app will show a badge on its icon when you have new email.

- **Taskbar Location on Screen:** Enables you to choose between top, bottom, left, or right.

- **Combine Taskbar Buttons:** Provides the following three options for display of taskbar buttons.

  - **Always Hide Labels:** Provides the default Windows 10 view already described.

  - **When Taskbar Is Full:** Displays icons in a similar fashion to that of Vista with descriptive labels that are combined only when a large number of applications are open.

  - **Never:** Offers a similar display but does not combine icons for open programs.

- **Notification Area:** The two options here enable you to choose what items are displayed in the Notification area on the bottom-right side of the taskbar. Some third-party programs add options to this applet when installed on your computer.

- **Multiple Displays:** Provides options for displaying taskbars and their buttons when more than one monitor is attached to the computer. You can choose which taskbar application buttons appear and whether to combine taskbar buttons on other taskbars.

Accounts

As shown in Figure 1-14, you can create and modify user accounts and account properties, including the tasks described in the list that follows.

Figure 1-14   Accounts Utility Enabling You to Modify User Account Properties or Create New User Accounts

- **Your Info:** This option enables you to view and configure options related to the account with which you are currently signed in. Click **Sign In with a Microsoft Account Instead** to use a Microsoft account, such as Hotmail, Messenger, or Xbox Live, as your user account. This enables you to perform actions such as downloading apps from the Windows Store, obtain online content in Microsoft apps, and sync settings online to make different computers act in the same fashion, including settings such as browser favorites and history. Follow the instructions presented in the wizard that displays. From this option, you can also select a picture to be associated with the account. If you have a camera attached to your computer, you can click **Camera** to photograph yourself and create a personalized account picture. Alternatively, click **Browse for One** to access the Pictures folder and locate an image on your computer.

- **Email & App Accounts:** Enables you to manage accounts used by your email program and other programs. This includes your Microsoft account, if you have one. Click **Manage** to modify account settings for any account; for a Microsoft account, this takes you to the home page on the account.microsoft.com website.

- **Sign-in Options:** Enables you to specify the following options related to your user account password:

  - **Windows Hello:** Enables you to use devices such as facial recognition or fingerprint readers to sign in to your computer, if so equipped. For more information, refer to "Windows Hello and Privacy" at https://privacy.microsoft.com/en-US/windows-10-windows-hello-and-privacy.

  - **Password:** Click **Change** to change the password on the account currently in use.

  - **PIN:** Enables you to create a PIN for logging on to your computer. This is a 4-digit code used in place of a password. This is most useful when using a tablet where a virtual keyboard will be displayed onscreen during the logon process. Confirm your password; then enter and confirm your PIN.

  - **Picture Password:** You can use a picture password for a more personal option when logging on to your user account. This involves tracing a series of up to three gestures on an image that you select. This type of password is more secure than a traditional password. Follow the instructions provided to select any picture from your Pictures folder and create your three desired gestures. You will be asked to confirm these gestures.

TIP   Use a fairly simple image and easily repeatable gestures when creating a picture password.

  - **Privacy:** Determines whether account details such as email address appear on the Sign-In screen.

  - **Related Settings:** Click **Lock Screen** to display the Lock Screen utility previously described under the Personalization section.

- **Access Work or School:** Provides a Connect option to connect to a work or school network and gain access to resources such as email, apps, and the corporate network. Options are also provided for adding or removing a provisioning package, exporting management log files, setting up an account for taking tests, and enrolling in device management.

- **Family & Other People:** Enables you to add additional user accounts. Click **Add Someone Else to This PC** and follow the instructions provided on the How Will This Person Sign In? page to add an additional user by means of an email address. If you want to add a user without an email address, select the **Sign In Without a Microsoft Account** option on the How Will This Person Sign in? page and then select **Local Account**. Click **Set Up Assigned Access** to create a standard user account that is restricted to a single Windows app.

You can also use the User accounts applet in Control Panel, described later in this chapter. Any user accounts added to the computer appear beneath the Add a user option. Note that the local user account cannot download apps from the Microsoft store and is not shared with other computers.

- **Sync Your Settings:** When using a Microsoft account or work account, this enables you to sync Windows settings such as theme, Internet Explorer settings, password, language preferences, ease of access, and other Windows settings to other computers on the network.

We discuss user accounts, picture password, PINs, password policies, and other account properties in more detail in Chapter 7, "Windows 10 Security."

Time and Language

As shown in Figure 1-15, the Time and Language utility enables you to specify options related to the display format of dates and times and the time zone in which your computer is located. Click **Region and Language** to specify the country or region used by Windows and apps to provide local content, or add an additional language if you need to work with documents written in different languages. Click **Speech** to choose default languages and voices spoken with your device. You can also set up a microphone for speech recognition from this location.

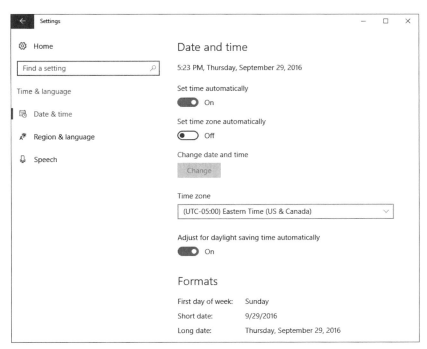

Figure 1-15   The Time & Language Utility Enables You to Modify Options Related to Display of Dates and Times and Languages Used on Your Computer

Ease of Access

As shown in Figure 1-16, Ease of Access enables you to configure accessibility options for vision- and hearing-challenged users.

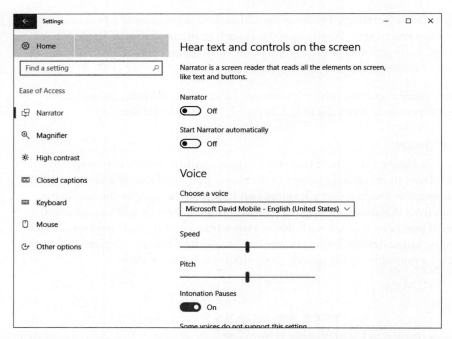

Figure 1-16 The Ease of Access Utility Enables You to Configure Several Accessibility Options

You have the following options:

- **Narrator:** Enables you to have a computerized voice read the options displayed on the screen for sight-impaired users. Set the Narrator option at the top to **On** to enable the other options, including the voice used and the type of information that is read back to you. You can also have the cursor highlighted and the insertion point follow the information read by the narrator.

- **Magnifier:** Magnifies information on the display to aid sight-impaired users. You can also have Windows track the keyboard focus and follow the mouse cursor.

- **High Contrast:** Enables you to select from one of several preconfigured high contrast themes. You can also customize the appearance of text, hyperlinks, disabled text, selected text, button text, and the background.

- **Closed Captions:** Enables you to configure several options related to captions that are provided for hearing-impaired users.

- **Keyboard:** Enables you to display an onscreen keyboard, which you can use by clicking with your mouse or tapping on a touchscreen. You can turn on the additional keyboard options:

  - **On-Screen Keyboard:** Enables you to turn on the onscreen keyboard. This enables you to use your mouse to type on your computer.

  - **Sticky Keys:** Enables you to press one key at a time for keyboard shortcuts.

  - **Toggle Keys:** Sounds a tone when you press the Caps Lock, Num Lock, and Scroll Lock keys.

  - **Filter Keys:** Ignores brief or repeated keystrokes.

  - **Other Settings:** Enable you to underline shortcuts and display warning messages or make sounds when using shortcuts.

- **Mouse:** Enables you to specify the size and color of the mouse pointer for improved visibility. You also have options to use the numeric keypad to move the mouse; use Ctrl to speed up the mouse pointer motion or Shift to slow it down, and determine whether mouse keys can be used when Num Lock is on.

- **Other Options:** You can specify whether animations are played or the Windows background is shown. You can also select a time interval (5 seconds by default) for which notifications are shown (it provides several durations of up to 5 minutes). The Cursor thickness option enables you to increase the visibility of the cursor by specifying the number of pixels (up to 20) used. The Visual notifications for sound option provide several choices for flashing portions of the display when a sound is played.

Privacy

This utility enables you to modify privacy settings associated with the following subtopics:

- **General:** As shown in Figure 1-17, this utility lets you modify your privacy settings associated with Internet browsing (all are set to On by default). Click **Manage My Microsoft Advertising and Other Personalization Info** to display a web page from Microsoft that provides several choices for receiving personalized advertising from Microsoft and other companies. Click **Privacy Statement** to display a web page that describes privacy information for users of Windows 10, including options for use of your personal information and contact options. Links provided in this document enable you to address additional privacy details.

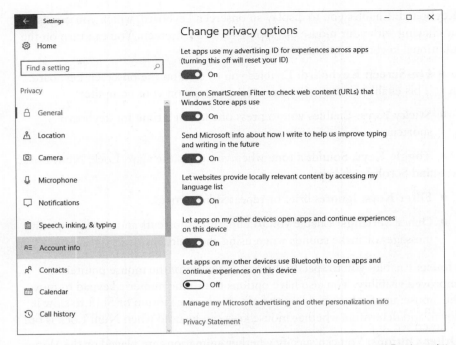

Figure 1-17   The Privacy Utility Enables You to Control How Apps and Devices Attached to Your Computer Use Your Personal Information

- **Location:** Enables you to determine whether Windows and installed apps can use your geographic location.
- **Camera:** Enables you to determine whether several installed apps can use your camera if one is installed on your computer.
- **Microphone:** Enables you to determine whether several installed apps can use your microphone if one is installed on your computer.
- **Notifications:** Enables you to choose which apps can access your notifications.
- **Speech, Inking, & Typing:** Enables Windows and Cortana to learn your voice and writing habits to improve their service. You can also manage personal information stored on the cloud.
- **Account Info:** Enables you to choose whether apps can access your name, picture, and other account information.
- **Contacts:** Enables you to determine whether several Windows apps can access your contacts.
- **Calendar:** Enables you to choose apps that can access your calendar.
- **Call History:** Enables you to choose apps that can access your call history.

- **Email:** Enables you to choose apps that can access and send email. Note that the built-in Mail and Calendar apps are always allowed this access.

- **Messaging:** Enables you to choose apps that are permitted to read or send messages.

- **Radios:** Enables you to choose apps that can use radios, such as Bluetooth, to send or receive data.

- **Other Devices:** If your computer is equipped with other devices that enable you to control app access, these devices would be displayed on this page.

- **Feedback & Diagnostics:** Enables you to select when Windows asks for feedback or sends device diagnostic and usage data to Microsoft.

- **Background Apps:** Enables you to choose which apps can perform tasks such as receiving info, sending notifications, and staying up-to-date, even when not in use. You can conserve power by turning background apps off.

Update and Security

As shown in Figure 1-18, this utility provides the update and security-related options described in the list that follows.

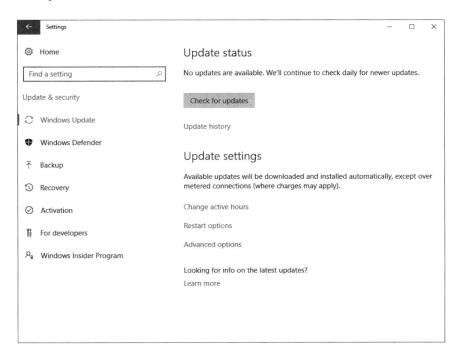

Figure 1-18   The Update & Security Utility Enables You to Configure Update Settings and Several Security-Related Options

This utility enables you to specify whether your computer will search for and install updates automatically. Click **Check Now** to connect to the Windows Update website and look for updates. Select **File History** to enable the automatic backup of copies of your personal files in libraries to an external drive. We discuss Windows Update in more detail later in this chapter and the recovery options in Chapter 20, "Configuring System Recovery Options." Select **Recovery** to access the following options:

- **Windows Update:** Specifies whether your computer will search for and install updates automatically. Click **Check for Updates** to connect to the Windows Update website and look for updates. Select **Update History** to view a history of your most recent updates. You have the other options shown in Figure 1-18 to configure update settings. More information is found later in this chapter.

- **Windows Defender:** This utility protects your computer against several types of malicious software, including viruses, spyware, and so on. Select the command button provided to run Windows Defender. It is disabled if you are using a third-party virus and malware scanner.

- **Backup:** Enables you to use File History or Windows Backup and Restore to back up your data. We discuss file backups in Chapter 21, "Configuring File Recovery."

- **Recovery:** Provides the following options for recovering your computer and data in the event that serious problems have occurred. We discuss these options in Chapter 20, "Configuring System Recovery Options."

  - **Reset This PC:** Enables you to either keep or remove your files, and then reinstall Windows.

  - **Go Back to an Earlier Build:** If you have upgraded to a newer build of Windows within the previous 10 days and have encountered problems, this option lets you go back to the previous build.

  - **Advanced Startup:** Enables you to restart your computer from one of several advanced startup settings.

  - **More Recovery Options:** Connects you to a web page that provides information and a download tool for installing a clean copy of the most recent version of Windows 10. Ensure that you read the information and warnings thoroughly before proceeding.

- **Activation:** Displays your Windows 10 edition and activation status and enables you to activate your Windows installation, change its product key, and troubleshoot problems with activation.

- **For Developers:** Provides several developer-related options, including advanced developer features, Device Portal, Windows Explorer settings, Remote Desktop, and PowerShell. Some of these features are discussed later in this Cert Guide.

- **Windows Insider Program:** Enables you to obtain future Windows updates and improvements early and provide feedback. You can link your Microsoft account as an Insider account from this page.

> **NOTE** For additional introductory information on Windows 10 apps, utilities, and settings, refer to any introductory text on Windows 10, such as *Windows 10 In Depth* (Que Publishing, 9780789754745).

Control Panel

The Windows 10 Control Panel includes the same eight categories as in Windows 8.1, and includes most of the same links that assist you in performing many common tasks. Click **Start,** then scroll the program list that appears to select **Windows Settings**, and choose **Control Panel** to display the window shown in Figure 1-19. You can also type **control** into the Search field, and then click **Control Panel** in the list that appears.

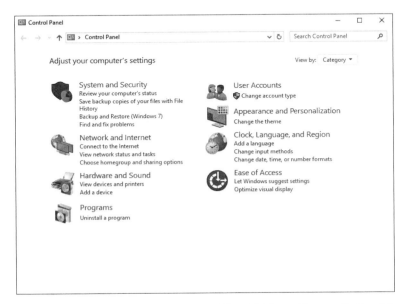

Figure 1-19 The Windows 10 Control Panel Links to Frequently Used Applets

This section provides a quick introduction to the Control Panel features. You learn about many of these features in detail in subsequent chapters of this book.

System and Security

Shown in Figure 1-20, the System and Security category includes several tasks that enable you to configure performance options and obtain information about your computer. Note that the left side of the window includes links to other Control Panel categories. This feature assists you in navigating among categories and is displayed for all Control Panel categories.

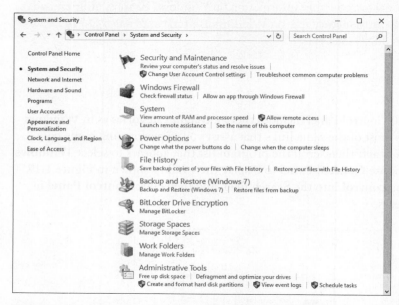

Figure 1-20   System and Security Category Including Basic System- and Security-Related Configuration Tasks

The task options available through the System and Security category include the following:

- **Security and Maintenance:** Provides information on the status of several security and maintenance settings, and enables you to configure changes in most of these settings. To enable or disable the display of messages regarding most of these settings, click the **Change Security and Maintenance Settings** link on the left side of the window. You can then select or clear the check boxes in the Change Security and Maintenance Settings dialog box as needed.

- **Windows Firewall:** Builds upon the firewall first introduced in Windows XP SP2 that protects your computer against both incoming and outgoing threats.

You can configure which programs are permitted to send or receive data through the firewall.

- **System:** Provides a summary of information related to your computer, including the hardware configuration, computer name, workgroup or domain information, and activation status.

- **Power Options:** Enables you to select a power plan to conserve energy by turning off items such as your display or hard disks after a period of inactivity or maximize performance of your computer. You can also customize a power plan to suit your needs.

- **File History:** Enables you to save copies of your files to a backup location in the event of loss or corruption or to restore files to a previous point in time.

- **Backup and Restore (Windows 7):** Enables you to perform automatic backup copies of files and folders on your computer, using an application first introduced in Windows 7 but removed in Windows 8.1. This program helps to protect data against system or disk failure. We discuss File History and Backup and Restore in detail in Chapter 21, "Configuring File Recovery."

- **BitLocker Drive Encryption:** Enables you to encrypt the contents of your hard drive so that intruders or thieves are unable to access your data. You can also enable BitLocker To Go, which protects the contents of removable drives from unauthorized access.

- **Storage Spaces:** Enables you to save files to additional drives to help protect you against a drive failure.

- **Work Folders:** First introduced in Windows 8.1, this applet enables you to set up Work Folders to keep your work files separate from your personal files and keep them in sync with data stored on a file server and on all your devices. You can use your work email address to retrieve corporate settings.

- **Administrative Tools:** Links to a large number of administrative tools, many of which we discuss in subsequent chapters of this book.

NOTE   For more information on the new Work Folders feature, refer to "Work Folders in Windows 10" at https://support.microsoft.com/en-us/help/12370/windows-10-work-folders.

Network and Internet

Shown in Figure 1-21, the Network and Internet category includes several tasks that enable you to configure connections to your local area network (LAN) or the

Internet, as well as several other network-related tasks. If you've installed connections to other Internet-based resources such as iCloud, these will appear.

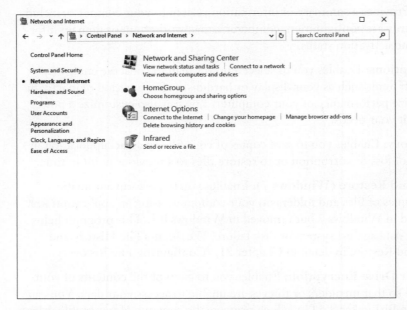

Figure 1-21   The Network and Internet Category Enables You to Perform Network-Related Tasks

The task options provided by the Network and Internet category include the following:

- **Network and Sharing Center:** Enables you to establish and configure options related to networks accessible to your computer. It provides a local view of the network to which your computer is attached and enables you to perform several tasks related to sharing of items such as files, folders, printers, and media. You can view the current status of your network connections, enable or disable network connections, and diagnose connectivity problems.

- **HomeGroup:** Enables you to modify sharing options for libraries and printers. You can also stream pictures, music, and videos to other networked devices, and modify HomeGroup security options.

- **Internet Options:** Enables you to configure the properties of the new Edge Internet browser. You can specify your home page, delete your browsing history, modify tabbed browsing, configure security and privacy options, and many more actions. Configuring Edge is discussed in Chapter 3, "Post-Installation Configuration."

- **Infrared:** Enables you to configure several options related to sending or receiving files over an infrared connection.

Hardware and Sound

Shown in Figure 1-22, the Hardware and Sound category includes applets that enable you to configure all your computer's hardware components. Note that the applets that appear in this category depend on the hardware present on your computer; third-party manufacturers might add additional applets to the category.

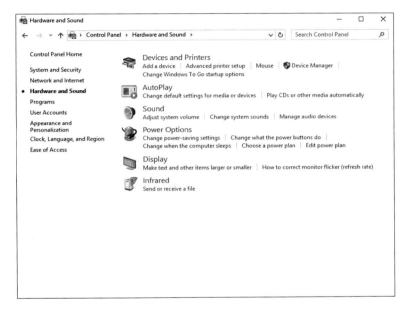

Figure 1-22   The Hardware and Sound Category Enables You to Manage a Diverse Range of Hardware Components

The Hardware and Sound category includes the following applets:

- **Devices and Printers:** Enables you to add printers and fax devices and configure properties of these devices. You can view and manage print queues, configure printer permissions, modify settings related to a specific printer type, and troubleshoot problems related to printers and faxes. You can configure mouse properties such as button settings, pointer appearance, scroll wheel actions, and so on. You can also access the Device Manager, which enables you to view information on hardware devices on your computer. Device Manager enables you to enable or disable devices; identify resources used by each device; identify, update, and roll back device drivers; and so on.

- **AutoPlay:** Enables you to configure default actions that take place when you insert media of a given type, such as audio CDs, DVDs, blank discs, and so on.

- **Sound:** Enables you to configure the settings associated with audio recording and playback devices. You can create and modify sound schemes that include the sounds that are associated with Windows and program events.

- **Power Options:** Enables you to choose and configure a power plan, the same as accessed through the System and Security category.

- **Display:** Enables you to specify the size of text and other items on the screen. Links from this applet enable you to adjust screen resolution and the use of Clear Type text and access the Magnifier tool, which can temporarily enlarge a portion of your screen.

- **Windows Mobility Center:** Available on laptops, tablets, and other mobile devices only, this applet enables you to adjust parameters such as display settings, presentation settings, connected devices, and so on. It also includes a display of battery charge status.

- **Infrared:** Same as with the Network and Internet category.

Programs

Shown in Figure 1-23, the Programs category includes applets that enable you to configure features related to applications installed on your computer, including programs that run by default at startup as well as locating, downloading, installing, and removing of applications.

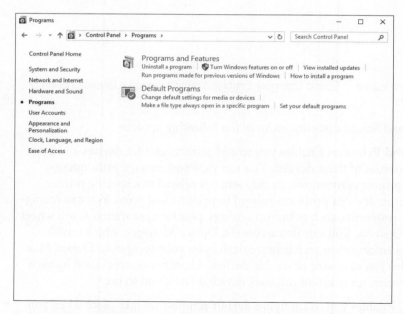

Figure 1-23 The Programs Category for Managing Applications on Your Computer

Applets provided by the Programs category include the following:

- **Programs and Features:** This is a complete reworking of the Add or Remove Programs applet in Windows versions prior to Vista; it enables you to uninstall, change, or repair applications installed on your computer. You can also view installed updates or run programs created for previous Windows versions.

- **Default Programs:** Enables you to configure which applications Windows uses by default for opening files of specific types. You can also control access to various types of applications and configure AutoPlay settings.

User Accounts

Shown in Figure 1-24, the User Accounts category enables you to configure several options related to user accounts and logon credentials.

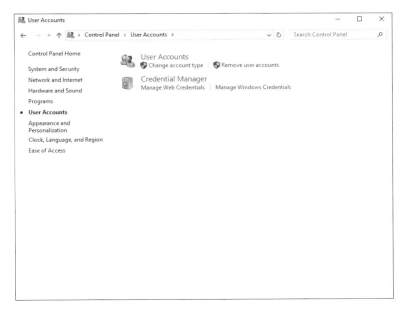

Figure 1-24   The User Accounts Category Enables You to Configure User Account Properties

Applets provided by the User Accounts and Family Safety category include the following:

- **User Accounts:** Enables you to create or remove user accounts and modify user account properties.

- **Credential Manager:** Enables you to configure the Windows Vault, which stores credentials used for logging on to other computers or websites.

Appearance and Personalization

As shown in Figure 1-25, the Appearance and Personalization category enables you to configure properties of your computer related to how items appear on the display.

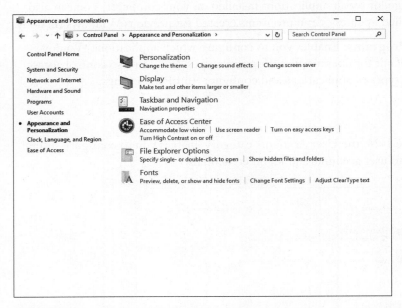

Figure 1-25 The Appearance and Personalization Category Enables You to Configure Appearance-Related Options

The Appearance and Personalization category includes the following:

- **Personalization:** Enables you to configure a large range of mostly display-related options, such as color and appearance of windows, desktop background, screen saver, Windows themes, display resolution and refresh, and so on. You can go online to get additional themes.

- **Display:** Enables you to configure display properties, the same as in the Hardware and Sound category.

- **Taskbar and Navigation:** The same as accessed by right-clicking the taskbar and choosing **Settings,** or from the Personalization option in Windows Settings as already discussed.

- **Ease of Access Center:** Contains several accessibility options that enable vision- and mobility-challenged users to use the computer. You can access a wizard that helps you select the appropriate options for individuals with different requirements.

- **File Explorer Options:** Enables you to modify how folder windows display their contents. You can configure whether files open with a single- or double-click, show hidden files and folders, and so on.

- **Fonts:** Enables you to manage fonts stored on your computer. You can add or remove fonts and display samples of fonts installed on your computer.

Clock, Language, and Region

The Clock, Language, and Region category contains three applets that enable you to configure the time and date displayed on your computers; configure your time zone; add additional display languages (so that you can view windows and dialog boxes in another language); and select how your computer displays items such as dates, times, numbers, and currency according to the country in which you live. You can also add or remove display languages, set which language is displayed by default, and adapt your keyboard for specific languages.

Ease of Access

The Ease of Access category provides access to the Ease of Access Center, which is also included in the Appearance and Personalization category. It also includes the Speech Recognition applet, which enables you to configure microphones and train your computer to understand your voice. You can view a tutorial that shows you how to use speech on your computer and view or print a list of speech-related commands.

The Computer Management Snap-in

First introduced in Windows 2000 and improved on with each successive Windows version, the Computer Management snap-in enables you to perform a series of management actions on Windows 10 computers. You can access this snap-in by right-clicking **Start** and choosing **Computer Management**. As shown in Figure 1-26, this snap-in includes the following management tools:

- **Task Scheduler:** Used for configuring programs and utilities to run at predetermined times and repeated schedules.

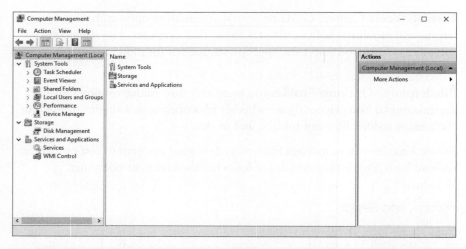

Figure 1-26 The Computer Management Snap-in Includes Several Important Windows 10 Management Utilities

- **Event Viewer:** Used for providing information that assists you in trouble-shooting errors.

- **Shared Folders:** Used for managing shares and connections to your computer.

- **Local Users and Groups:** Used for managing local users and groups on the computer.

- **Performance:** Used for troubleshooting errors as well as optimizing performance.

- **Device Manager:** Used for configuring devices, updating or uninstalling device drivers, rolling back device drivers, enabling and disabling devices, and troubleshooting.

- **Disk Management:** Used for viewing and managing volume and disk configuration.

- **Services:** Used for starting and stopping services related to a device.

- **WMI Control:** Used for turning error logging on or off or backing up the Windows Management Instrumentation (WMI) repository. (In most cases, you will not use this tool.)

Configuring Windows Updates

Windows Update is a Windows Settings utility that enables you to maintain your computer in an up-to-date condition by automatically downloading and installing critical updates as Microsoft publishes them. By default, your computer automatically checks for updates at the Windows Update website. Critical updates are automatically installed on a daily basis, and you are informed about optional updates that might be available. User input is needed only on the rare occasion for which you will receive an alert in the Notification area of the taskbar. The following are several key features of Windows Update:

- Windows Update scans your computer and determines which updates are applicable to your computer. These updates include the latest security patches and usability enhancements that ensure your computer is kept as secure and functional as possible.

- Windows Update delivers updates to all programs, including the default Windows apps.

- Updates classified by Microsoft as High Priority and Recommended can be downloaded and installed automatically in the background without interfering with your work.

- Windows Update informs you if a restart is required to apply an update. You can postpone the restart so that it does not interfere with activities in progress. Should an update apply to a software program with files in use, Windows 10 can save the files and close and restart the program.

In Windows 10, Windows Update supports the distribution and installation of the following types of updates:

- **Important Updates:** Updates that Microsoft has determined are critical for a computer's security. These are typically distributed on Patch Tuesday, as already mentioned. In general, they fix problems that intruders can exploit to perform actions such as adding administrative accounts, installing rogue software, copying or deleting data on your computer, and so on.

- **Optional Updates:** Potentially useful updates that are not security related. These might include software and driver updates, language packs, and so on.

- **Update Roll-ups:** Packaged sets of updates that fix problems with specific Windows components or software packages such as Microsoft Office.

- **Feature Updates:** Comprehensive operating system updates that package together all updates published since launch of the operating system or issuance of the previous feature update. We provide more information later in this chapter.

Configuring Windows Update Settings

The Update & Security app in Windows Settings includes the Windows Update utility, which enables you to configure and work with the various options that are offered. Use the following procedure to work with Windows Update:

Step 1. Click **Start**, access **Settings**, and click **Update & Security**. This opens the Update & Security app to Windows Update, as previously shown in Figure 1-18.

Step 2. To perform a manual check for updates, click **Check for Updates**. Windows Update checks on the Microsoft website. After a minute or two, it informs you of any available updates and offers to install them.

Step 3. To view your history of recent updates, click **Update History**. As shown in Figure 1-27, the Update History window displays a list of successfully installed updates.

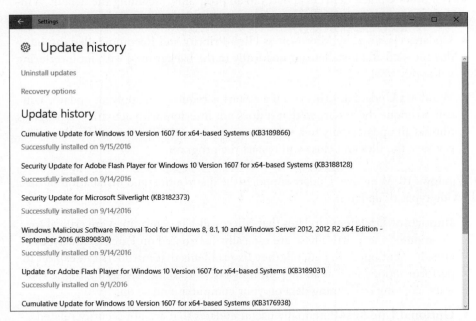

Figure 1-27 The Update History Page Displays a List of Recently Installed Updates and Provides Options for Uninstalling and Recovery

Step 4.   If an update has cause problems with your computer, click **Uninstall Updates** to display the Uninstall an update applet shown in Figure 1-28. Select the problematic update, click **Uninstall**, and then click **Yes** in the confirmation message box that appears. You can also click **Recovery Options** to access additional options that were introduced earlier in this chapter and discussed in detail in Chapter 20.

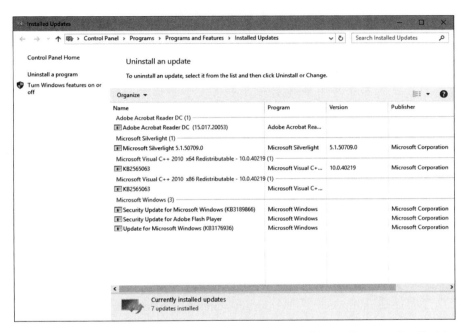

Figure 1-28   The Uninstalling an Update Applet Enables You to Remove Any Problematic Updates

Step 5.   To modify the active hours during which Windows will restart your computer if required by an update, click **Change Active Hours**. Specify an appropriate time in the Active Hours window shown in Figure 1-29, and then click **Save**.

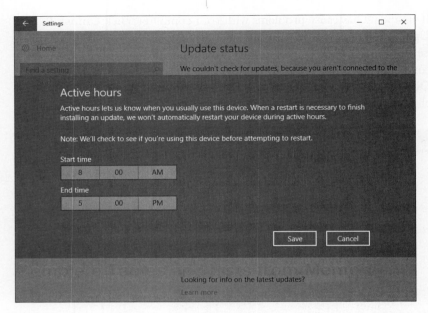

Figure 1-29   The Active Hours Page Displays the Default Active Hours During Which the Computer Will Not Automatically Restart, Enabling You to Modify These Hours

Step 6.   If you want to specify a custom restart time that overrides active hours, click **Restart Options**. In the Restart Options window that appears, move the toggle to **On** and specify the desired time and day.

Step 7.   To access additional update options, click **Advanced Options** to display the Advanced Options dialog box shown in Figure 1-30. The options are as follows.

- **Give Me Updates for Other Microsoft Products When I Update Windows:** Automatically provides updates for programs such as Microsoft Office.

- **Defer Feature Updates:** When selected, Windows doesn't download or install some new features and non-security-related updates for several months. You will not receive the latest Windows features as soon as they're available.

- **Use My Sign-In Info to Automatically Finish Setting Up My Device After an Update:** Enables Windows to use your sign-in info to create a special token that enables automatic logon after a restart, and then lock your computer to keep your account and personal info safe.

- **Privacy Statement:** Click this to open your browser to a Microsoft Privacy web page that informs you how Microsoft uses personal data it collects, how it uses this data, and reasons it shares personal data. Microsoft also informs you how you can access and control your personal data, use of cookies and similar technologies, and other important privacy information. Product-specific details are also provided for a large range of Microsoft products.

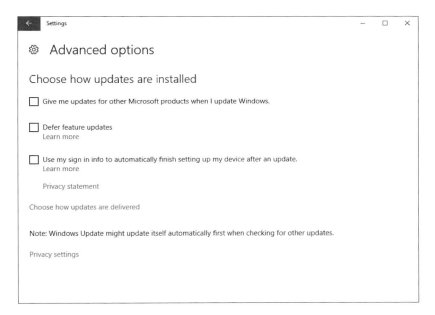

Figure 1-30   The Advanced Options Dialog Box Provides Several Additional Options for Installing Updates

- **Choose How Updates Are Delivered:** Enables you to download updates from other computers on your network, as well as from Microsoft. Set the toggle to **On** to enable this option that also enables your computer to send updates to other computers on your network. You can select from two options: PCs on My Local Network or PCs on My Local Network, and PCs on the Internet.

- **Privacy Settings:** Accesses the Privacy category of the Settings app previously shown in Figure 1-17, enabling you to configure all settings available there.

NOTE   Windows 10 no longer provides the options found on the Choose Your Windows Update settings page in Windows 7/8/8.1 that enabled you to select from Install Updates Automatically, Download Updates but Let Me Choose Whether to Install Them, Check for Updates but Let Me Choose Whether to Download and Install Them, or Never Check for Updates. An Internet search in September 2016 found several third-party websites describing fixes for this situation, including Registry modifications. However, third-party solutions are not tested on any Microsoft exam.

Using a WSUS Server with Windows 10

Windows Server Update Services (WSUS) is a server-based component that enables you to provide update services to computers on a corporate network without the need for individual computers to go online to the Microsoft Windows Update website to check for updates. It saves valuable bandwidth because only the WSUS server connects to the Windows Update website to receive updates, and all other computers on the network receive their updates from the WSUS server. Furthermore, WSUS provides network administrators with the ability to test updates for compatibility before enabling computers on the network to receive the updates, thereby reducing the chance of an update disrupting computer or application functionality across the network.

You can download WSUS 3.0 Service Pack 2 (SP2) from Microsoft and install it on a computer running Windows Server 2012/R2. You can also install WSUS as a server role on Windows Server 2016. The most recent release of WSUS supports new Windows Server 2016 and Windows 10 machines. Configuration of the WSUS server is beyond the scope of the 70-697 and 70-698 Windows 10 exams and is not discussed here.

Configuring Windows Update Policies

Group Policy in Windows 10 provides a series of policies that govern the actions performed by Windows Update. To view and configure these policies, open the Local Group Policy Editor by performing the following steps:

Step 1.   In the taskbar Search field, type **gpedit.msc** and then select **gpedit.msc** from the list displayed. You can also right-click **Start**, click **Run**, type **gpedit.msc**, and press Enter.

Step 2.   If you receive a User Account Control (UAC) prompt, click **Yes**.

Step 3.   Navigate to the Computer Configuration\Administrative Templates\ Windows Components\Windows Update node to obtain the policy settings shown in Figure 1-31.

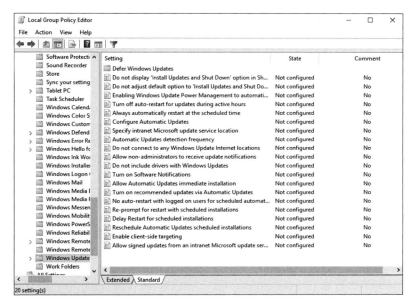

Figure 1-31   The Group Policy in Windows 10 Provides a Series of Settings Governing the Operation of Windows Update

Step 4.   To use Group Policy to specify the behavior of automatic updates, double-click the **Configure Automatic Updates** policy setting (shown in Figure 1-31) to receive the Configure Automatic Updates properties dialog box shown in Figure 1-32.

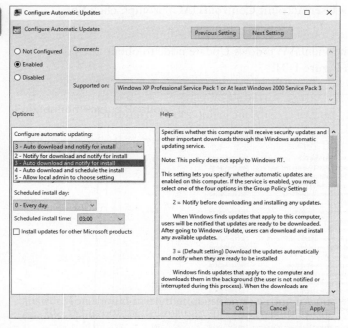

Figure 1-32   The Configure Automatic Updates Dialog Box Offers Four Choices for Configuring Automatic Updating of Windows 10 Computers

Step 5.   Select **Enabled**, and then choose one of the following settings from the Configure Automatic Updating drop-down list:

- **2–Notify for Download and Notify for Install:** Windows Update notifies you when updates are available by displaying an icon in the Notification area and a message stating that updates are available for download. The user can download the updates by clicking either the icon or the message. When the download is complete, the user is informed again with another icon and message; clicking one of them starts the installation.

- **3–Auto Download and Notify for Install:** Windows Update downloads updates in the background without informing the user. After the updates have been downloaded, the user is informed with an icon in the Notification area and a message stating that the updates are ready for installation. Clicking one of them starts the installation. This is the default option.

- **4–Auto Download and Schedule the Install:** Windows Update downloads updates automatically when the scheduled install day and time arrive. You can use the drop-down lists on the left side of the dialog box to specify the desired days and times, which, by default, are daily at 3:00 a.m.

- **5–Allow Local Admin to Choose Setting:** Enables local administrators to select a configuration option of their choice from the Automatic Updates control panel, such as their own scheduled time for installations.

Step 6.   Click **OK** to return to the Local Group Policy Editor.

The following describes several of the other important available policy settings shown in Figure 1-31:

- **Defer Windows Updates:** New to Windows 10 and Windows Server 2016, this folder contains policy settings that enable you to select when each of the two following update types are received:

  - **Feature Updates:** *Feature updates* (previously referred to as upgrades) are updates that contain significant feature additions and changes, as well as security and quality revisions. Enable this policy to specify which branch readiness level (see Figure 1-33) from which feature updates will be received. You can also specify the number of days from which the update is received that you want to defer receiving it.

  - **Quality Updates:** *Quality updates* are the traditional updates most often released on Patch Tuesday, though they can be released at any time. Enable this policy to specify the number of days to be deferred before a quality update is received (up to 30 days).

- **Do Not Display "Install Updates and Shut Down" Option in Shut Down Windows Dialog Box:** Prevents the appearance of this option in the Shut Down Windows dialog box, even if updates are available when the user shuts down his computer.

- **Do Not Adjust Default Option to "Install Updates and Shut Down" Option in Shut Down Windows Dialog Box:** When enabled, changes the default shut down option from Install Updates and Shut Down to the last shut down option selected by the user.

- **Enabling Windows Update Power Management to Automatically Wake Up the System to Install Scheduled Updates:** Uses features of Windows Power Management to wake computers up from Sleep mode to install available updates.

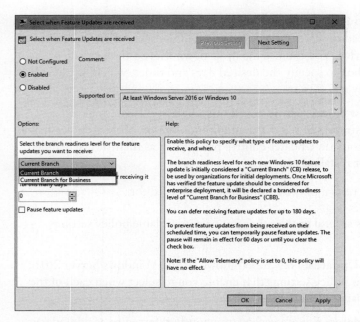

Figure 1-33 Specifying a Readiness Level and Deferral Interval for Receiving Feature Updates

- **Turn Off Auto-Restart for Updates During Active Hours:** Prevents the computer from automatically restarting after the installation of updates during the hours the user has specified as active (refer to Figure 1-29).

- **Always Automatically Restart at the Scheduled Time:** Enables you to specify a restart timer after which the computer will automatically restart after installing updates that require a restart. You can set this timer to between 15 and 180 minutes.

- **Specify Deadline Before Auto-Restart for Update Installation:** Enables you to specify a deadline between 2 and 14 days before automatically executing a scheduled restart outside of active hours.

- **Specify Intranet Microsoft Update Service Location:** Enables you to specify a WSUS server for hosting updates from the Microsoft Windows Update website (as described in the previous section).

- **Automatic Updates Detection Frequency:** Specifies the length of time in hours used to determine the waiting interval before checking for updates at an intranet update server. You need to enable the Specify Intranet Microsoft Update Service Location policy to have this policy work.

- **Allow Non-administrators to Receive Update Notifications:** Enables users who are not administrators to receive update notifications according to other Automatic Updates configuration settings.

- **Turn on Software Notifications:** Enables you to determine whether users see detailed notification messages that promote the value, installation, and usage of optional software from the Microsoft Update service.

- **Allow Automatic Updates Immediate Installation:** Enables Automatic Updates to immediately install updates that neither interrupt Windows services nor restart Windows.

- **Turn On Recommended Updates via Automatic Updates:** Enables Automatic Updates to include both important and recommended updates.

- **No Auto-Restart with Logged On Users for Scheduled Automatic Updates Installations:** Prevents Automatic Updates from restarting a client computer after updates have been installed. Otherwise, Automatic Updates notifies the logged-on user that the computer will automatically restart in five minutes to complete the installation.

- **Re-prompt for Restart with Scheduled Installations:** Specifies the number of minutes from the previous prompt to wait before displaying a second prompt for restarting the computer.

- **Delay Restart for Scheduled Installations:** Specifies the number of minutes to wait before a scheduled restart takes place.

- **Reschedule Automatic Updates Scheduled Installations:** Specifies the length of time in minutes that Automatic Updates waits after system startup before proceeding with a scheduled installation that was missed because a client computer was not turned on and connected to the network at the time of a scheduled installation, as previously specified by option 4 from the Configure Automatic Updating drop-down list.

- **Enable Client-Side Targeting:** Enables you to specify a target group name to be used for receiving updates from an intranet server such as a WSUS server. The group name you specify is used by the server to determine which updates are to be deployed.

- **Allow Signed Updates from an Intranet Microsoft Update Service Location:** Enables you to manage whether Automatic Updates accepts updates signed by entities other than Microsoft when the update is found on an intranet Microsoft Update location.

For more information on these policies, consult the Help information provided on the right side of each policy's Properties dialog box.

> **NOTE** For more information on deferring feature and quality updates, see "Manage Updates Using Windows Update for Business" at https://technet.microsoft.com/en-us/itpro/windows/manage/waas-manage-updates-wufb.

Managing Update History and Rolling Back Updates

The Windows Update applet enables you to review your update history and roll back problematic updates, as described in the following procedure:

Step 1.   Open the Update & Security Windows Settings app, as previously described.

Step 2.   From the list of options provided, select **Update History**. The Update history page previously shown in Figure 1-27 displays a list of the updates installed on your computer, including definition updates for Windows Defender. This page also indicates whether updates were successfully installed.

Step 3.   Click the installed line for any update to provide detailed information, as shown in Figure 1-34.

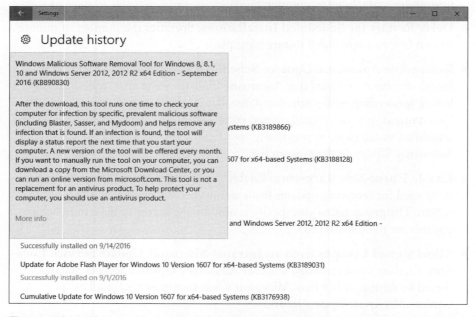

Figure 1-34 Windows Update Provides Information on All Updates It Has Installed and Links to Websites You Can Refer To

Step 4. If an update is causing problems and you want to remove it, click the **Uninstall Updates** link (found in the Update history page shown in Figure 1-27). On the Uninstall an Update page that appears, right-click the update you want to uninstall and select **Uninstall**. Confirm your intentions by clicking **Yes** in the message box that appears.

TIP In Windows 10, you can also specify policies for Windows Update Delivery Optimization, which enable you to download Windows updates and Windows Store apps from sources other than Microsoft. For more information, refer to "How to Use Group Policy to Configure Windows Update Delivery Optimization in Windows 10" at https://support.microsoft.com/en-us/kb/3088114.

Updating Windows Store Applications

Windows 10 gives you access to apps from the Windows Store. Thousands of apps are available from the Windows Store, and the latest version of Windows comes with several apps preloaded, such as the Contacts app (Microsoft People), Mail and Calendar, OneNote, Music, and others.

Windows apps are not updated automatically from Windows Update. Instead, app updates come from the Windows Store, and you can control when to perform updates and which apps you want updated when new versions are available. Use the following procedure to check for updates and install them.

Step 1. Click the **Start** button and select the **Store** tile.

Step 2. Click your account icon (next to the Search bar), and then select **Downloads and Updates** (see Figure 1-35).

NOTE You can also select the Settings option, where you can toggle Update Apps Automatically on or off. If this setting is turned on, apps will update automatically when you are connected to the Internet.

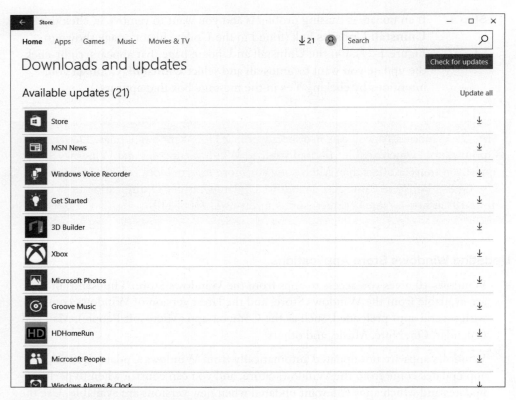

Figure 1-35   Windows Store Updates

Step 3.   Select the **Check for Updates** button to check all your installed apps for any updates.

Step 4.   On the App updates screen, the app updates are listed at the top. Click the download icon (on the far right) for the app or apps you want to update or the **Update All** link to update all the listed apps.

Step 5.   The app appears in the download queue at the bottom of the update screen indicating the download and update progress. When the update is finished, the app is removed from the Downloads and updates screen.

Windows 10 includes some command-line utilities and Group Policy options for managing Windows app updates. You can install and remove Store apps by using PowerShell cmdlets, and you also can check the logs for app installations and updates. For instance, if an app update fails, you can enter **Get-Appxlog** to display the error messages to help troubleshoot the issue.

These PowerShell commands generally apply to a single user profile. You can use elevated privileges, such as inside and administrative or command prompt, to display additional information or take action on other user profiles.

Table 1-3 lists the set of Appx cmdlets available along with a brief description of their use.

Table 1-3 PowerShell Cmdlets for Managing Windows Store Apps

Cmdlet Name	Description
Add-AppxPackage	Adds an app package to a user account
Get-AppxLastError	Gets the most recent error recorded from an app installation
Get-AppxLog	Displays the application log created during an app installation
Get-AppxPackage	Lists the app packages installed, or information about a specific app installed in a user profile
Get-AppxPackageManifest	Displays the manifest of an app package
Remove-AppxPackage	Removes an app package

Configure Updates in the Enterprise

With the release of Windows 10, Microsoft has implemented a new way of building, deploying, and updating Windows, called Windows as a service. This new model simplifies update tasks for IT professionals and eases the transition to new features for end users.

In the past, Microsoft has released a Preview version of new Windows operating systems for developers and implementers to use for testing, training, and planning deployments. In the new model, Windows feature upgrades are instead delivered to the Windows Insider community, so that customers and businesses can see what Microsoft is developing and begin testing as soon as possible.

Traditional Windows releases came in three types: major releases (Windows 8.1, Windows 7, etc.), service packs, and security updates. With Windows 10 there are now only two release types: feature updates that provide new functionality and quality updates for security and reliability. Managing updates to Windows devices requires the implementation of deployment rings, assigned to service branches. Enterprises can design their own rings based on the risk they can tolerate for each group and the groups with applications needing testing. Table 1-4 outlines a typical deployment ring design.

Table 1-4 Example Deployment Ring Planning

Deployment Ring	Servicing Branch	Schedule After Release	Target Group
Preview	Windows Insider	Pre-CB	Developers and Engineering
Ring 1	CB	Release + 0 days	IT Pilot
Ring 2	CB	Release + 5 days	Business Pilot
Ring 3	CB	Release + 15 days	IT Users
Ring 4	CBB	Release + 0 days	Power Business Users
Ring 5	CBB	Release + 10 days	General Business
Ring 6	CBB	Release + 20 days	Risk-averse Business Users

Note that the LTSB is not included in the table. That's because high-risk devices, such as medical equipment, ATMs, and other special-purpose devices, are not upgraded like general business devices are.

After you have planned out the deployment rings for your organization and identified the testers and pilot users for each group, you can begin to assign devices to each deployment ring and servicing branch. For servicing tools, you can use Windows Update, Windows Update for Business, Windows Server Update Services (WSUS), or System Center Configuration Manager. The CBB is not available for Windows Update standalone.

Implement Insider Preview

You can assign computers to the Insider Preview branch from the Windows settings screens. These will be the computers in the Preview ring depicted in Table 1-4.

Step 1. From the Start menu, select **Settings**, and then select **Update and Security**.

Step 2. Select **Windows Insider Program** from the menu on the left.

Step 3. Select **Get Started**. Information about the program and links to the privacy statement and program terms appear. After reading the information, click **Next**.

Step 4. Click **Confirm**, and then select a time to restart the computer.

NOTE   When you assign the computer to the Insider Preview program, it will be difficult to opt out in the future. Doing so may require that you remove everything from the computer and reinstall Windows. For more information see https://answers.microsoft.com/en-us/insider/forum/insider_wintp-insider_repair/how-to-stop-receiving-insider-builds/28b954d5-49bb-41f1-82bc-2046bec50b13.

After Windows restarts, repeat Steps 1 and 2 to return to the Windows Insider Program screen to select the Insider level. The computer will receive the most recent version of the Windows Insider build for the selected level. There are three levels of releases.

- **Release Preview:** This level is the latest to receive builds of Windows and will receive the update just before it is released to CB. This is the best level for users that need to perform early application compatibility testing before computers in the CB branch are updated.

- **Slow:** The Slow Windows Insider level is for users who want to see new builds of Windows but with minimal risk of disruption. It allows these users to provide feedback to Microsoft about their experience with the new build.

- **Fast:** This level is best for developers who want to take advantage of new features and users who want to participate in identifying and reporting issues to Microsoft and provide suggestions on new functionality.

After selecting the desired Insider level, the computer will be ready to get previews of new Windows builds from Windows Update when they become available.

Current Branch (CB)

The CB is the default servicing branch for Windows. Computers will receive Windows feature updates when Microsoft releases them for general availability.

You can ensure computers are assigned to the CB branch using the Group Policy setting Select When Feature Updates Are Received, which is found in Group Policy under Computer Configuration/Administrative Templates/Windows Components/Windows Update/Defer Windows Updates.

You can use this policy to select the servicing branch as well as the number of days after release the computer should be updated. For example, to assign a computer to Ring 3, as defined in Table 1-4, enable this policy, select **Current Branch**, and enter **15** in the number of days to defer box, as shown in Figure 1-36.

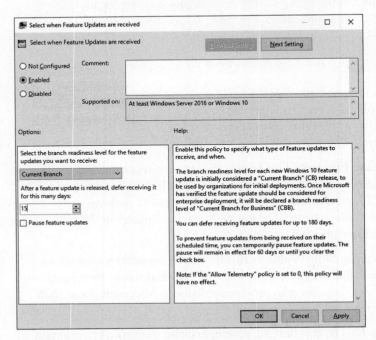

Figure 1-36   Setting the Group Policy Select When Feature Updates Are Received

Current Branch for Business (CBB)

Use the following procedure to assign a Windows computer to the CBB:

Step 1.   From the Start menu, select **Settings**, and then select **Update and Security**.

Step 2.   Select **Advanced Options** from the Update settings menu.

Step 3.   Check the Defer feature updates check box.

The computer will not download or install updates for several months after it is released.

You can also use Group Policy to assign computers to the CBB. The group policy setting is Select When Feature Updates Are Received and is found in the node Computer Configuration/Administrative Templates/Windows Components/ Windows Update/Defer Windows Updates. Enable the policy and set branch readiness level to CBB.

Long Term Servicing Branch (LTSB) Scenarios

The LTSB is designed for computers being run in high-risk environments or for special-purpose applications. Examples include devices used as ATMs, medical devices such as patient monitoring machines, manufacturing device controllers, and other specialized devices. As a general rule, if a computer is used for email and running Microsoft Office, it should not be using the LTSB.

This branch is available only for enterprises using volume licenses, and only the Enterprise Edition of LTSB is available. No feature updates will be available for these computers. They must be updated using the traditional Windows in-place upgrade process. Microsoft provides a 10-year support model for the LTSB editions, and it is expected that typical devices deployed with LTSB will be replaced before an upgrade is necessary.

Note that LTSB devices will receive security and quality updates on a regular basis, as do other Windows 10 computers. Servicing branches apply only to feature upgrades, not security patches.

Because the devices targeted for LTSB are mission-critical devices used for a special purpose, this edition does not include many of the end-user applications of other editions. LTSB does not include the Windows Store, for example, or any of the Windows Store apps included with other editions of Windows 10. Other features excluded are Microsoft Edge, Cortana (but limited search capabilities are available), Microsoft Mail, Calendar, OneNote, Weather, News, Sports, Money, Photos, Camera, Music, and Clock.

Exam Preparation Tasks

Review All the Key Topics

Review the most important topics in the chapter, noted with the Key Topics icon in the outer margin of the page. Table 1-5 lists a reference of these key topics and the page numbers on which each is found.

Table 1-5   Key Topics for Chapter 1

Key Topic Element	Description	Page Number
List	Describes available Windows 10 editions	10
Figure 1-1	Displays the Windows 10 Desktop as it appears after you install Windows 10 for the first time	18
Figure 1-3	Shows the actions you can perform in Windows 10 by right-clicking the Start button	20
Figure 1-8	The Windows settings screen enables you to configure a large number of settings that affect the behavior of your computer	26
List	Describes types of updates handled by Windows Update	53
Figure 1-32	Configuring Automatic Updates properties	60
List	Group Policy provides four settings that control the downloading and installation of updates	60
Step List	Shows you how to manage and roll back updates	64
Step List	Shows you how to assign computers to the Insider Preview branch	68

Definitions of Key Terms

Define the following key terms from this chapter, and check your answers in the glossary.

apps, feature updates, File Explorer, quality updates, Service Pack (SP), Windows Update, Windows Server Update Services (WSUS)

This chapter covers the following subjects:

- **Preparing for Installation Requirements:** This section discusses factors that you need to know prior to installing Windows 10, such as hardware requirements, screen resolution, upgrades versus clean installs, and so on.

- **Performing a Clean Installation:** This section describes the procedure for performing a basic installation of Windows 10 from DVD media.

- **Upgrading to Windows 10 from a Previous Version of Windows:** This section describes several upgrade paths Microsoft provides for users with older computers wanting to upgrade to Windows 10.

- **Using Alternate Installation Media:** You can host a complete copy of Windows 10 on a virtual hard disk (VHD) that can be copied and deployed to many computers in an enterprise situation. This section introduces VHDs and shows you how to install a completely functional version of Windows 10 together with applications and settings on a supported USB drive.

- **Installing Additional Windows Features:** After Windows 10 is installed, you may want to add additional features, depending on the type of device and the role of the computer.

- **Configuring Native Boot Scenarios:** VHDs with native boot are frequently used in several scenarios. This section shows you how to enable a computer to boot from the VHD.

This chapter covers the following objectives for the 70-698 exam:

Prepare for installation requirements: Determine hardware requirements and compatibility; choose between an upgrade and clean installations; determine appropriate editions according to device type; determine requirements for particular features, such as Hyper-V, Cortana, Miracast, virtual smart cards, and Secure Boot; determine and create appropriate installation media.

Install Windows: Perform clean installations, upgrade using Windows Update, upgrade using installation media, configure native boot scenarios, migrate from previous versions of Windows, install to virtual hard disk (VHD), boot from VHD, install on bootable USB, install additional Windows features, configure Windows for additional regional and language support.

Implementing Windows

The Microsoft 70-698 exam assesses your ability to install, configure, and administer Windows 10 and focuses on how to do so in a business environment. Basic to any installation type is the manual, clean installation of Windows 10 on a new computer.

As an adjunct to Murphy's Law, what can go wrong during an operating system installation does go wrong, and then the situation needs troubleshooting. Windows 10 is no exception. Knowing how to handle unexpected errors makes all the difference to a network support technician or administrator.

"Do I Know This Already?" Quiz

The "Do I Know This Already?" quiz allows you to assess whether you should read this entire chapter or simply jump to the "Exam Preparation Tasks" section for review. If you are in doubt, read the entire chapter. Table 2-1 outlines the major headings in this chapter and the corresponding "Do I Know This Already?" quiz questions. You can find the answers in Appendix A, "Answers to the 'Do I Know This Already?' Quizzes."

Table 2-1 "Do I Know This Already?" Foundation Topics Section-to-Question Mapping

Foundation Topics Section	Questions Covered in This Section
Preparing for Installation Requirements	1–3
Performing a Clean Installation	4–8
Upgrading to Windows 8.1 from a Previous Version of Windows	9–14
Using Alternate Installation Media	15–16
Installing Additional Windows Features	17–18
Configuring Native Boot Scenarios	19–20

CAUTION   The goal of self-assessment is to gauge your mastery of the topics in this chapter. If you do not know the answer to a question or are only partially sure of the answer, you should mark that question as wrong for purposes of the self-assessment. Giving yourself credit for an answer you correctly guess skews your self-assessment results and might provide you with a false sense of security.

1. What is the minimum processor speed required for a Windows 10 computer?

    a. 1 GHz

    b. 2 GHz

    c. 3 GHz

    d. 4 GHz

2. What is the minimum amount of hard drive space required for a 64-bit Windows 10 installation?

    a. 10 GB

    b. 15 GB

    c. 16 GB

    d. 20 GB

    e. 40 GB

3. Which of the following are true about the use of the 64-bit Windows operating system? (Choose all that apply.)

    a. Most 32-bit programs can run efficiently on a 64-bit machine, with the exception of some antivirus and other low-level system programs.

    b. 32-bit programs will not run on a 64-bit machine; you must upgrade all 32-bit programs to 64-bit.

    c. Programs specifically designed to run on a 64-bit machine won't work on 32-bit Windows.

    d. You need 64-bit device drivers to use all your hardware devices with 64-bit Windows. Drivers designed for 32-bit Windows won't work on a machine running 64-bit Windows.

    e. Any device driver written for 32-bit Windows will work perfectly well on a 64-bit Windows machine.

4. Which of the following are items you should have on hand before beginning a Windows 10 installation? (Choose all that apply.)

    a. Windows 10 drivers from the manufacturer for any hardware not appearing in the Windows Hardware Certification Program

    b. BIOS that meets the minimum requirements for Windows 10 compatibility

    c. Windows 10 product code

    d. Internet connection

    e. A CD-ROM drive

    f. Backup of all your existing data and the drivers for your backup device

5. Which of the following settings can you configure during an installation of Windows 10 from a DVD-ROM? (Choose all that apply.)

    a. Username and password

    b. Domain membership in a local Active Directory

    c. Computer name and background color

    d. Language, time, and currency format

    e. Domain membership in an Azure Active Directory

6. What tool would you use to create or edit answer files used for unattended installations of Windows 10?

    a. Windows SIM

    b. Windows AIK

    c. Windows ADK

    d. Sysprep

7. You want to set your computer up to triple-boot Windows 10, Windows 8.1, and Windows 7. What should you do first?

    a. Install Windows 7

    b. Install Windows 10

    c. Install Windows 8.1

    d. Install MS-DOS

8. Which Setup log records modifications performed on the system during Setup?

   a. netsetup.log

   b. setuperr.log

   c. setupapi.log

   d. setupact.log

9. Which of the following is true regarding the performing of an upgrade installation of Windows 10 versus a clean installation?

   a. A clean installation maintains all Windows settings, personal files, and applications from the previous Windows installation, whereas an upgrade installation of Windows 8.1 requires that you reinstall all programs and re-create all Windows settings.

   b. An upgrade installation maintains all Windows settings, personal files, and applications from the previous Windows installation, whereas a clean installation of Windows 10 requires that you reinstall all programs and re-create all Windows settings.

   c. An upgrade installation maintains Windows settings from the previous Windows installation but requires that you reinstall all programs. A clean installation maintains programs from the previous Windows installation but requires that you re-create all Windows settings.

   d. Both a clean installation and an upgrade installation require that you reinstall all programs and re-create all Windows settings.

10. You are preparing to upgrade your Windows 8.1 computer to Windows 10. Which of the following tasks should you perform before beginning the upgrade? (Choose all that apply.)

    a. Run the Windows Upgrade Assistant.

    b. Run the Windows Anytime Upgrade.

    c. Ensure that all hardware in use is listed in the Windows Certification Program.

    d. Check for any available upgrades for your computer's BIOS.

    e. Scan your computer for viruses.

    f. Remove or disable your antivirus program.

    g. Install the Windows updates for Windows 8.1.

11. Your computer is running Windows 7 Professional. You want to upgrade to Windows 10 Pro. Which of the following is the cheapest and simplest way to perform the upgrade?

    a. Insert the Windows 10 DVD and upgrade directly to Windows 10 Pro.

    b. Insert the Windows 8.1 DVD and upgrade to Windows 8.1 Pro. Then insert the Windows 10 DVD and upgrade to Windows 10 Pro.

    c. Insert the Windows 7 DVD and upgrade to Windows 7 Ultimate. Then insert the Windows 10 DVD and upgrade to Windows 10 Pro.

    d. Insert the Windows 10 DVD and install a clean copy of Windows 10 Pro.

12. Your computer is running Windows 7 Professional. You insert the Windows 10 DVD and choose the option to perform a clean installation of Windows 10. You then select the same partition on which the Windows 7 system files are located and proceed with the upgrade without formatting this partition. Which of the following best describes what happens to your Windows 7 system files?

    a. The Windows 7 system files are overwritten with the Windows 10 system files.

    b. The Windows 7 system files are placed in a new folder named Windows.old.

    c. The Windows 7 system files remain in the same location in an unaltered state, and you create a dual-boot system.

    d. The Windows 7 system files are moved to a new partition, and you create a dual-boot system.

13. Fred has saved a large number of Word documents on his computer running Windows 7 Home Edition. He installs Windows 10 on his computer, using the same partition on which Windows 7 was installed. He does not reformat this partition. What happens to these documents?

    a. They are placed in the Windows.old\Documents and Settings\Fred\My Documents folder.

    b. They remain in the Documents and Settings\Fred\My Documents folder.

    c. They are placed in the \Users\Fred\Documents folder.

    d. They are lost; Fred must restore them from backup.

14. Your computer runs Windows 10 Home and you want to upgrade to Windows 10 Pro. You have gone online and purchased a Windows 10 Pro upgrade license. What should you do?

    a. Click **Search**, type **add features** into the Search box, and then click **Settings**. Click **I Already Have a Product Key**, enter your product key, and then click **Next**. Select the check box to accept the license terms, and then click **Add Features**. Wait while Windows is upgraded and the computer is restarted.

    b. Click **Settings** and then click **Add Features**. Click **I Already Have a Product Key**, enter your product key, and then click **Next**. Select the check box to accept the license terms, and then click **Add Features**. Wait while Windows is upgraded and the computer is restarted.

    c. Insert the Windows 10 DVD, select the option to install Windows, enter the key code for the Pro edition, and run the upgrade.

    d. Insert the Windows 10 DVD, select the option to perform a clean install of Windows, and enter the key code for the Pro edition. Then wait while Windows is upgraded and the computer is restarted.

    e. From the Search bar, type **activation** and click the Activation shortcut; then click Change Product Key, enter the new product key, and follow the onscreen instructions.

15. Which of the following capabilities are enabled by using virtual hard disk (VHD)? (Select all that apply.)

    a. Standardize image formats and tool sets across an organization.

    b. Limit the number of images needed for supporting Windows installations in an organization.

    c. Test applications on multiple operating systems using the same device, and restore fresh images more quickly.

    d. Utilize devices with very little storage by using less disk space.

    e. Perform offline image management.

16. What are the types of VHDs that you can create?

    a. VHD, VHDX

    b. Limited, Expanding, Differencing

    c. Fixed, Dynamic, Differencing

    d. Fixed, Expandable, Differencing

    e. Dynamic, Fixed, Variable

17. Where would you go to install additional features in Windows 10?

    a. The Windows Store

    b. The Microsoft Downloads website

    c. The Control Panel Programs applet

    d. The App & Features menu of the modern settings page

    e. The Control Panel System applet

18. What command-line tool can you use to install Windows features?

    a. DiskPart

    b. DISM

    c. BCDedit

    d. Sysprep

    e. Windows PE

19. You are planning to use native boot VHDs to roll out some Windows 10 images for a business group in your organization. Which VHD type should you use?

    a. Fixed

    b. Dynamic

    c. Expandable

    d. Differencing

    e. VHDX

20. You are still in the planning stages for your deployment of Windows images using native-boot VHDs. What are some of the recommended best practices you should keep in mind as you develop your detailed deployment plan? (Choose all that apply.)

    a. Store mission-critical data outside the native-boot VHDs.

    b. Use VHD sizes larger than the minimum storage requirements for Windows.

    c. Use differencing VHDs for production environments and fixed VHDs for development and testing.

    d. Ensure sufficient space for host volume page files.

    e. Use Sysprep to generalize the image before using the VHD for native boot.

Foundation Topics

Preparing for Installation Requirements

Introducing Windows 10 into an enterprise environment requires careful consideration of many factors. Does the current hardware meet the requirements? Is the software used by the business compatible? Which edition of Windows 10 is appropriate for the environment? What type of testing will be needed?

You need to explore these questions and document the results before planning the roll-out and installations. This topic explores these questions and others.

Evaluating Hardware Readiness and Compatibility

As a network support technician, you will be faced with the task of deciding whether to upgrade existing computers to Windows 10, purchase new hardware to run Windows 10, or leave the current operating system on your company's computers. For the 70-698 exam, Microsoft expects you to know how to evaluate existing hardware for its capability to run Windows 10.

Windows 10 Hardware Requirements (Including Screen Resolution)

Microsoft has defined the minimum level of hardware requirements for computers running Windows 10. These represent the bare minimum required to run the core features of Windows 10 and provide a basic user experience.

Table 2-2 lists the base hardware requirements for Windows 10. Although these are the minimum hardware requirements for supporting the operating system, they are not necessarily adequate to support additional applications or for reasonable performance. When designing the hardware requirements for installation, you should allow for extra RAM and hard disk space and probably a faster processor for applications.

Table 2-2 Hardware Requirements for Windows 10

Device	Minimum Supported Hardware
Processor	1 GHz or faster processor or system on chip (SoC)
RAM	1 GB RAM (32-bit) or 2 GB RAM (64-bit)
Graphics processor	DirectX 9-capable with WDDM 1.0 or higher driver
Display	Capable of 800×600 resolution or higher
Hard disk	At least 16 GB (32-bit) or 20 GB (64-bit)

NOTE   Microsoft explicitly mentioned that Windows 8 required a processor that supports PAE, NX, and SSE2. Because processors without support for these features are so old, the requirement is no longer included as part of Windows 10 hardware requirements, but these features are still required. For more information on these processor characteristics, refer to the archived document "PAE/NX/SSE2 Support Requirement Guide for Windows 8" at https://technet.microsoft.com/en-us/library/dn482072.aspx. Microsoft also provides more detailed requirements for hardware device developers at https://msdn.microsoft.com/en-us/library/windows/hardware/dn915086.aspx.

If you want to access a network (including accessing the Windows Store to download and run apps), you should have a network adapter installed that is compatible with the network infrastructure. For Internet access, at a minimum you need a dial-up modem or broadband connection to connect to an Internet service provider (ISP). Video conferencing, voice, fax, and other multimedia applications generally require a high-speed connection, microphone, sound card, and speakers or headset. Video conferencing itself requires a video conferencing camera. Other required hardware depends on features you might use with Windows 10, such as the following:

- To use touch, you must have a tablet or monitor that is touch compatible.

- BitLocker requires the Trusted Platform Module TPM 1.2, TPM 2.0, or a USB flash drive.

- BitLocker To Go requires a USB flash drive.

- Windows Hello requires a specialized infrared camera for facial recognition or a fingerprint reader that supports Windows Biometric Framework.

- Secure boot requires firmware that supports UEFI v2.3.1 Errata B and has Microsoft Windows Certification Authority in the signature database.

Hardware Compatibility

Microsoft makes it easy to check your hardware's compatibility by providing a list of supported hardware. Microsoft designed the Windows Hardware Compatibility Program with the aim of assisting companies to deliver systems, software, and hardware components that are compatible with Windows 10 and Windows Server 2016. Microsoft states, "Windows Compatibility Program is designed to help your company deliver systems, software and hardware products that are compatible with Windows and run reliably on Windows 10 and Windows Server 2016." Microsoft's Windows Hardware Lab Kit (HLK) extends the functionality of the previous Logo and certification programs to provide benefits such as updated certification requirements and needs for products and drivers used with Windows 10, automation of much of the hardware test processes, improvement in diagnostics logged by the Event Viewer utility, and an enhanced test management console, among other improvements.

NOTE For more information on the Windows Hardware Compatibility program, refer to "Hardware Compatibility Specifications for Windows 10" at https://msdn.microsoft.com/windows/hardware/commercialize/design/compatibility/index and additional documents referenced in this article.

An issue that can interrupt the installation process is the use of incompatible critical device drivers. If a compatible driver is not available, Setup stops until updated drivers are found. Operating system upgrades will not migrate incompatible drivers based on older Windows operating systems. The only way to ensure a smooth installation is to make certain you have all the drivers available at the start of the installation process. Do not be concerned about unattended installations, because there is a folder in which you can place any additional or updated drivers for hardware that are not included in the base Windows 10 files.

Before you deploy Windows 10 on any system, you should ensure that the hardware and basic input/output system (BIOS) are compatible with the operating system. Older hardware may not have a compatible BIOS even though the devices within the PC itself are all listed in the Windows Hardware Certification Program. The original equipment manufacturer (OEM) should have an updated BIOS that can be downloaded from the OEM's website.

If you have an Internet connection, you can use the Windows Update feature to connect to the Windows Update website during setup. Windows 10 automatically downloads and installs updated drivers during the setup process from the Windows Update website. More information on Windows Update is provided in Chapter 1, "Introducing Windows 10."

Using 32-Bit or 64-Bit Windows

You can have either 32-bit or 64-bit Windows operating systems, but you cannot have both simultaneously. Consequently, you should know which bit level is most appropriate for your situation. In general, a 32-bit operating system runs on hardware equipped with a 32-bit processor, and a 64-bit operating system runs on hardware equipped with a 64-bit processor. Windows 10 and Windows Server 2016 support the Unified Extensible Firmware Interface (UEFI)-based hardware platforms. You need to match the architecture version of UEFI to that of the operating system. For example, a 32-bit UEFI platform can boot only 32-bit Windows, and a 64-bit UEFI platform can boot only 64-bit Windows.

The benefit of running 64-bit Windows is that it can handle large amounts of memory more efficiently than 32-bit Windows; this is most apparent for a computer equipped with 4 GB of RAM or more. Such a computer is more responsive when the user is running several programs at the same time and switching among them frequently.

Hardware platforms must meet one of the following requirements:

- A machine shipping with 32-bit Windows must be certified for 32-bit UEFI and Windows 10 x86.

- A machine shipping with 64-bit Windows must be certified for 64-bit UEFI and Windows 10 x64.

- A machine shipping with both 32-bit and 64-bit configurations must be certified for both configurations.

- A machine that is capable of both 32-bit and 64-bit support but shipping with one of these configurations must be certified for the configuration in which it ships.

- A machine that ships with Windows 7 installed must be certified for both Windows 7 with compatibility support module (CSM) and Windows 10 x64 with 64-bit UEFI.

NOTE For more information on UEFI, refer to "UEFI Firmware" at https://msdn. microsoft.com/en-us/windows/hardware/commercialize/manufacture/desktop/uefi-firmware.

You should also be aware of the following considerations when selecting 32-bit or 64-bit Windows 10:

- Most 32-bit programs can run efficiently on a 64-bit platform, with the exception of some antivirus programs.

- Programs specifically designed to run on a 64-bit platform won't work on 32-bit Windows. But some programs such as Microsoft Office 2010 and later are available in both 32-bit and 64-bit versions.

- You need 64-bit device drivers to use all your hardware devices with 64-bit Windows. Drivers designed for 32-bit Windows won't work on a machine running 64-bit Windows. Check the hardware device's website to locate and download 64-bit drivers.

Software Compatibility

Current software on your computer might not be compatible with the new operating system. This need to ensure software compatibility is frequently one of the more difficult parts of the development and testing phase of any operating system deployment project. The operating system that you deploy is important because it provides the basic functionality for the computer, but productivity usually depends on business applications that are installed, which makes applications more important to the organization. If an application is not compatible with the operating system, you have the following options:

- Upgrade the application to a compatible version.

- Replace the application with a similar type of application that is compatible with Windows 10.

- Retire the application.

Before you are faced with these decisions, your first task in determining software compatibility is to identify all the applications that are used *and* that will be installed in your deployment project. You should develop a matrix of applications that are organized according to priority of business productivity and by the number of users of the application. For example, if you determine that 100% of all your users use APP A, but that it does not directly contribute to business productivity (such as an antivirus application), you would place it in the high use, low productivity quadrant. If you determine that 10% of your users use APP B, and it contributes highly to business productivity, you would place it in the low use, high productivity quadrant. If 5% of users use APP C, and it has no impact on business productivity, you would place that in the low use, low productivity quadrant. The applications in that low use, low productivity quadrant are the ones that you should analyze for potentially retiring. If you find that 90% of all users use APP D and it is considered business critical, you would put APP D in the high use, high productivity quadrant. All applications in this quadrant should receive priority during the project. Figure 2-1 attempts to place these applications into this perspective.

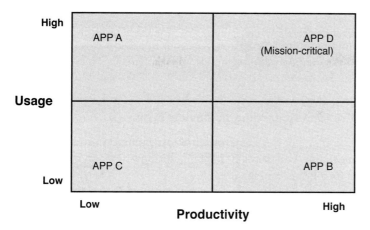

Figure 2-1 Prioritize All Applications Used in Your Company According to Their Usage and Productivity

You might decide to include additional criteria to your matrix to better pinpoint the applications that will require more of your time during the project. For example, you could identify which applications are developed for Windows 10, which are developed specifically for older Windows operating systems, and which have been developed in-house. Applications that have been developed for Windows XP, Windows Vista, or Windows 7 might not run properly on Windows 10. Antivirus applications are typically incompatible if they were developed for older Windows versions. In nearly all cases, applications that worked properly on Windows 8.1 will work with Windows 10; if problems occur, you should be able to run these applications in Compatibility mode.

After you have an inventory of your current software, you should then build a test lab and test the applications with Windows 10. With each application that has compatibility problems, you should decide whether the application is important enough to fix. If it is important, you should then determine the fixes you need to undertake to make it compatible. You can then package the fixes using the Windows Assessment and Deployment Kit. This toolkit assists software developers and corporate IT professionals in performing Windows servicing and deployment, including the Application Compatibility Toolkit (ACT). The ACT assists in evaluating and mitigating application compatibility issues. Finally, you should test the deployment and perform a quality assurance check on the test PCs to see whether the applications install and run properly.

NOTE For more information on the Windows Assessment and Deployment Kit, refer to "Windows 10 Deployment Tools" at https://technet.microsoft.com/en-us/itpro/windows/deploy/windows-deployment-scenarios-and-tools.

Determining Appropriate Editions According to Device Type

Windows 10 runs on a wide range of devices, from desktop computers and workstations to handheld phones. The Windows 10 Mobile editions—in standard and Enterprise—are designed for phones and small tablets.

Mobile Devices

Microsoft offers two editions of Windows 10 for mobile devices: Windows 10 Mobile and Windows 10 Mobile Enterprise. Most features are available on both editions, but there are a few features to keep in mind that are available only for the Enterprise edition:

- The Manage Updates capability allows mobile administrators to remotely manage the updates for Windows mobile devices from a central location.

- The Current Branch for Business (CBB) for Windows updates is available only on Windows 10 Mobile Enterprise.

- The Enterprise edition also allows administrators to control or turn off telemetry (diagnostic tracking services) for mobile devices.

Other Devices

You should review the list of features available for each edition of Windows 10, the type of devices used, and the type of work being performed by users. In some cases, it may be necessary to deploy different editions for different devices. In other enterprises, it may make sense to deploy the same Windows edition to all users, to simplify deployment and manageability.

Generally any device capable of running Windows 10 can run any edition. However, recall that running Windows 10 64-bit editions requires a 64-bit UEFI. Also, the 64-bit editions require slightly more disk space and the 32-bit editions can run more efficiently on very low memory devices. For heavier workloads, the 64-bit editions can make more use of devices with plenty of memory (over 4 GB). If you are selecting a single edition as a standard for an entire business, it may be necessary to evaluate the devices in use and replace any devices that are not a good fit for the chosen edition.

Specialized devices will require some additional consideration. If you have devices in the business used for things such as single-application kiosks, ATMs, or performing tasks such as medical monitoring or equipment control, deployment of these devices must be carefully managed. These are the types of devices that Windows Long Term Servicing Branch (LTSB) edition supports. It excludes many of the tools that would be inappropriate, such as Cortana and Windows Store, and receives security and quality updates, but all features are frozen for the life of the device.

Determining Requirements for Windows Features

Windows 10 introduces several new features that you can use according to the hardware configuration of your computer. These include the following:

- Client Hyper-V
- Windows Hello
- Miracast
- Cortana
- Virtual smart cards
- Secure Boot

Table 2-3 introduces the hardware requirements for each of these features.

Table 2-3 Hardware Requirements for New Windows Features

Feature	Minimum Supported Hardware
Client Hyper-V	A 64-bit computer with at least 4 GB RAM and running Windows 10 Pro or Enterprise, as well as a processor that supports virtualization. Additional RAM as needed to support the virtual machines being installed on your computer.
Windows Hello	A specialized illuminated infrared camera is required for face recognition to work for Windows Hello. Using fingerprint recognition requires a fingerprint reader that supports the Windows Biometric Framework.
Miracast	Miracast requires a display adapter that supports Windows Display Driver Model (WDDM) 1.3, and a Wi-Fi adapter that supports Wi-Fi Direct.
Cortana	To use Cortana with speech recognition, a microphone is required. Microsoft recommends a high-fidelity microphone array and a hardware driver with Microphone array geometry exposed.

Feature	Minimum Supported Hardware
Virtual smart cards	A Windows 10 Pro or Enterprise computer equipped with a TPM. You also need access to an Active Directory Domain Service (AD DS) domain with a domain server running a fully installed certificate authority (CA).
Secure Boot	A Windows 10.1 computer that meets the UEFI specifications version 2.3.1, Errata B, or higher, and that includes the Microsoft Windows certificate authority in the UEFI signature database. Note that a TPM is not required.

We take a look at installation and configuration of these features in Chapter 3.

Performing a Clean Installation

As an IT professional, you should run through at least one or two attended installations even if you are planning to deploy only unattended installations of Windows 10 throughout your organization. By going through the process, you can see each stage of installation and relate it to sections within the answer files and with the unattended process later on. If you need to troubleshoot an unattended installation, you will be better able to identify the point at which the installation failed if you have already become familiar with the attended installation process.

Performing an Attended Installation

You can run an attended installation process for either an upgrade or a clean installation of Windows 10. Upgrading to Windows 10 is covered later in this chapter, so we will be walking through a *clean* installation process in this section.

Before you begin, check to make certain that you have gathered all the information you need and are prepared to install. You should have the following:

- A computer that meets the minimum hardware requirements previously given in Table 2-2.

- Windows 10 drivers from the manufacturer for any hardware that does not appear in the Windows Hardware Certification Program. It's imperative that you have the hard disk drivers, especially if they are RAID or SCSI devices.

- Windows 10 DVD or installation files available across a network.

- BIOS that meets the minimum requirements for Windows 10 compatibility and the bitness of the edition you plan to install.

- Product code, which should be listed on the DVD package or provided to you from the network administrator.

- If across a network, a boot disk that can access network shares and appropriate network adapters.

- Internet connection for Automatic Updates and access to updated drivers and Windows Product Activation (WPA).

- A backup of all your existing data and the drivers for the backup device so that you can restore the data.

When you have all the preceding items in hand, you're ready to install Windows 10. Your first step in the installation is to boot the computer into the setup process. This process involves running Setup.exe, which is the application that installs Windows 10 on a new computer or updates an older Windows computer to Windows 10. Use the following procedure to install Windows 10 using a bootable DVD-ROM rather than a network installation:

Step 1. Insert the Windows 10 installation DVD and boot the computer. If you receive a message that the DVD has been autodetected and a prompt to Press Any Key to Boot from CD or DVD, press the spacebar or any other key within five seconds, or the computer will attempt to boot from the hard disk.

Step 2. The screen displays a Windows logo as initial files are loaded. After a minute or so, the Install Windows dialog box shown in Figure 2-2 appears. If you need to change the language, time, and currency format, or keyboard or input method settings, do so. Otherwise, click **Next** to proceed.

Figure 2-2   The Install Windows Dialog Box Options for Language, Time and Currency, and Keyboard or Input Method

Step 3.   Click **Install Now** to begin installation.

Step 4.   If you receive a dialog box prompting you to enter the product key to activate Windows, type the product key supplied (it should be on the box containing the DVD or provided with the download), and then click **Next**.

Step 5.   You are informed that Setup is starting, and then another Install Windows dialog box (see Figure 2-3) asks you to read the license terms. You must select the **I Accept the License Terms** check box to accept the licensing agreement as indicated at the bottom of the screen. Then click **Next**.

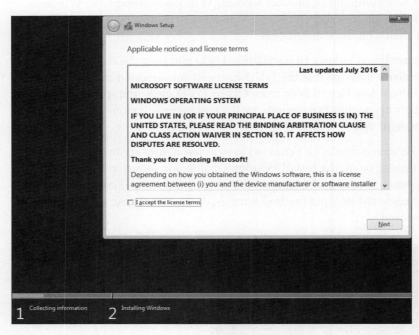

Figure 2-3   Accept the License Terms to Install Windows 10

Step 6.   The Which Type of Installation Do You Want? screen shown in Figure 2-4 offers you a choice of upgrade or custom installation. If you select the Upgrade option at this point, Windows setup will not allow you to proceed, because you booted the computer from the installation media. The Upgrade option is functional only if you are running the installation on a

computer running a compatible copy of Windows 7/8/8.1 with suffi-
cient free disk space to accommodate the upgrade, and you use the
Setup.exe program to start the installation from Windows. Select the
Custom: Install Windows Only (Advanced) option to continue.

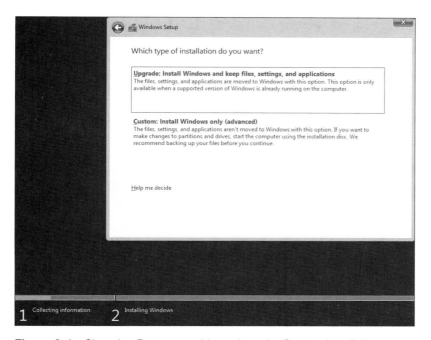

Figure 2-4   Choosing Between an Upgrade and a Custom Installation

Step 7.   The next screen shows the available partitions and unpartitioned disk
space where you can install Windows 10. Make certain you select a partition that has enough available disk space, preferably 40 GB, but at least
16 GB for an x86 installation or 20 GB for an x64 installation. If unpartitioned space is available, you can select the unpartitioned space and create a new partition for the operating system at this point. Click **Next**.

Step 8.   If the selected partition contains files from a previous Windows installation, you receive a message box informing you of this fact, and that these
files will be moved to a folder named Windows.old. Click **OK** to proceed
or **Cancel** to go back and select a different partition.

Step 9.   The next window tracks the progress of installing Windows 10 and
informs you that your computer will restart several times, as shown in
Figure 2-5. Take a coffee break.

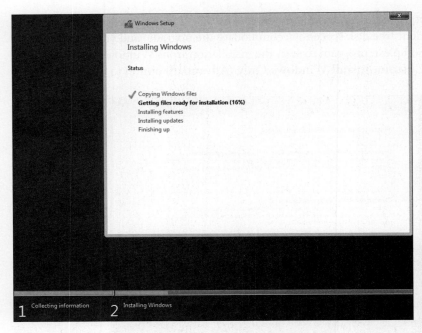

Figure 2-5   Tracking Progress of the Windows 10 Installation

Step 10.   After the final reboot, Setup displays the window shown in Figure 2-6. You can use the Customize Settings link to change the initial settings to your liking. Click **Use Express Settings**.

Step 11.   If you are installing Windows 10 Pro, you are asked if you own the computer or whether your work or school owns it. Selecting the My Work or School Owns It option allows you to join a local Active Directory or an Azure Active Directory for your organization. Select **I Own It**, and then click **Next**.

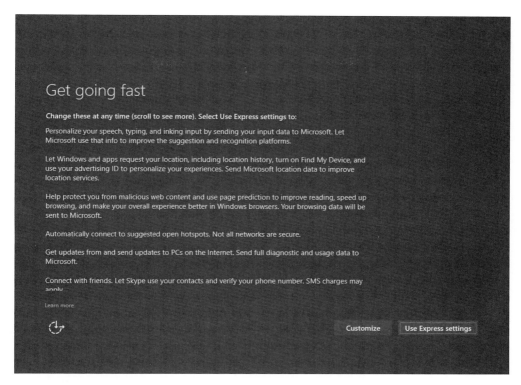

Figure 2-6   Setup Prompts You to Choose Express Settings or to Customize Settings

Step 12.   Setup asks you to sign in to your Microsoft account, as shown in Figure 2-7. This is an email account in the @hotmail.com or @outlook.com domain, which enables you to access the Windows Store as well as your email using the built-in Mail app. Type the email address and its associated password in the spaces provided, and then click **Next**. If you don't have a Microsoft account, click **Create a New Account** to create a Microsoft account or **Don't Have an Account** to proceed without creating a Microsoft account.

Figure 2-7   Setup Asks You to Sign In to Your Microsoft Account

NOTE   This screen is displayed only for Windows 10 Home or Windows 10 Pro editions. If you are installing an Enterprise edition, you will instead be prompted to join an Active Directory, either your local company domain or an Azure Active Directory. The Azure AD is for businesses using Microsoft cloud services, such as Office 365. For more about the Azure Active Directory, see https://docs.microsoft.com/en-us/azure/active-directory/active-directory-azureadjoin-user-frx.

Step 13.   Setup asks if you want to see what's most relevant to you by allowing Microsoft Advertising to use your account information, and if you want promotional offers. Check the boxes as appropriate and then click **Next**.

Step 14.   Setup offers the option of setting up a PIN. Skip this step by selecting the **Skip This Step** link.

Step 15.   Setup presents the Meet Cortana page. Click the **Use Cortana** button.

Step 16.   After a minute or two, the Windows 10 Start screen appears. You are now ready to work with Windows 10.

You have just completed a full, manual installation of Windows 10 from scratch. In a typical installation, you would next confirm the date, time, and time zone settings; specify networking settings; join a workgroup or domain; install additional applications; restore data from backup; and customize the desktop to meet your needs.

Performing an Unattended Installation of Windows 10

A typical installation of Windows 10, as explained in the previous section, is fine if you have only one or two computers to be installed. But what if you have a large number of computers on which you want to install Windows 10? Entering the same information repeatedly becomes tedious and error prone, so Microsoft has developed methods for automating the installation of Windows 10 on a series of computers. Unattended installations typically utilize an answer file that contains answers to questions asked by Setup.exe, so that an installation proceeds smoothly without operator intervention.

Understanding Answer Files

Typically called Unattend.xml or Autounattend.xml, the answer file was first used with Windows Vista and replaces the Unattend.txt file that was formerly used with older Windows operating systems. You can include setup options (such as partitioning and formatting of disks), which Windows image to install, and the product key that should be used. You can also include installation-specific items (such as usernames, display settings, and Internet Explorer favorites).

Windows System Image Manager (SIM) enables you to create answer files from information included in a Windows image (.wim) file and a catalog (.clg) file. You can also include component settings and software packages to be installed on the computers with Windows 10. The following are several actions you can accomplish using SIM:

- Create new answer files and edit existing ones.

- Validate the information in an answer file against a .wim file.

- View and modify the component configurations in a .wim file.

- Include additional drivers, applications, updates, or component packages in the answer file.

You can use SIM to create unattended answer files. You should have two computers, as follows:

- A computer from which you install SIM and create the answer files. Microsoft refers to this computer as the "technician computer."

- A computer without an operating system but equipped with a DVD-ROM drive and a network card (or USB support). Microsoft refers to this computer as the "reference computer."

Understanding Configuration Passes

When you use an unattended installation answer file for installing Windows, settings are applied at various stages of the setup process that Microsoft calls *configuration passes*. Table 2-4 describes the different configuration passes used in setting up Windows 10 and Windows Server 2016.

Table 2-4 Configuration Passes

Configuration Pass	Description
1 Windows PE	Configures Windows PE options and basic Windows Setup options. Use this configuration pass to add any drivers required for Windows PE to access the local or network hard drive. Also use this configuration pass to add any basic information such as a product key.
2 offlineServicing	Applies updates including packages, software fixes, language packs, and security updates to the Windows image.
3 generalize	Used only when running the Sysprep /generalize command, enables you to configure this command for removing system-specific settings such as the SID.
4 specialize	Creates and applies system-specific information such as network, domain, and international settings.
5 auditSystem	Used only when booting to Audit mode after running Sysprep; processes unattended Setup settings before a user logs on.
6 auditUser	Used only when booting to Audit mode after running Sysprep; processes unattended Setup settings after a user logs on.
7 oobeSystem	Applies Windows settings before Windows Welcome starts.

NOTE For more information on answer files and their usage, refer to "Answer Files Overview" at https://msdn.microsoft.com/en-us/library/windows/hardware/dn915072(v=vs.85).aspx. To find out about the latest features in the SIM and the Windows Assessment and Deployment Kit (ADK), see https://msdn.microsoft.com/windows/hardware/commercialize/what-s-new-in-kits-and-tools.

Creating an Answer File

Windows SIM is a component of the Windows Assessment and Deployment Kit (ADK) for Windows 10. To use SIM to create the files required for performing unattended installations, you first need to download and install the ADK from Microsoft and copy the appropriate files from the Windows 10 DVD-ROM. You should perform these steps on a computer running Windows 7, Windows 8.1, or Windows 10. Use the following steps to download and install the ADK.

Step 1.   Open Internet Explorer, navigate to https://developer.microsoft.com/
en-us/windows/hardware/windows-assessment-deployment-kit, and
follow the instructions provided to download the Windows ADK. Note
that there will be a different ADK for each Windows 10 build or update.
Select the correct one for the Windows 10 version you are working with.

Step 2.   You should receive a User Account Control dialog box. Click **Yes** to
display the Specify Location screen shown in Figure 2-8.

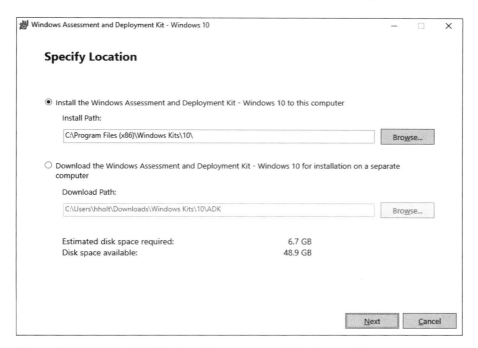

Figure 2-8   Installing the Windows Assessment and Deployment Kit

Step 3.   Accept the default installation path or click **Browse** to specify an
alternate location, and then click **Next**.

Step 4.   If you receive the Join the Customer Experience Improvement Program
screen, click **Next**.

Step 5.   Click **Accept** to accept the license agreement.

Step 6.   On the Select the Features You Want to Install page shown in Figure
2-9, accept the defaults, check the **Application Compatibility Tools**
check box, and then click **Install**.

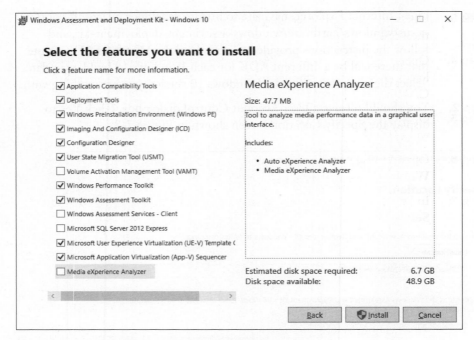

Figure 2-9   Selecting the ADK Features to Be Installed.

TIP   You might want to make sure you have selected the User State Migration Tool (USMT) when you study Chapter 9, "Managing User Data," and Application Compatibility Toolkit for use when you study Chapter 5, "Installing and Managing Software."

Step 7.   If you receive an additional UAC dialog box, click **Yes**.

Step 8.   An Installing Features page appears as the ADK tools are installed. This process can take up to an hour. When installation finishes, click **Close**.

After you have installed the ADK, a folder is present on the technician computer, from which you can create answer files. To create an answer file based on the default Windows image found on the Windows 10 DVD, use the following procedure:

Step 1.   Insert the Windows 10 DVD-ROM. If you receive an Install Windows screen, click **Cancel**.

Step 2.   If you receive an AutoPlay window, click the **Open Folder to View Files** option. If not, open a File Explorer (Computer on Windows 7 or Vista) window, navigate to the Windows 10 DVD-ROM, right-click, and select **Open**.

Step 3.   Open the Sources folder, navigate to the boot.wim file, right-click, and then choose **Copy**.

Step 4.   Open a File Explorer (or Computer) window, navigate to a suitable location, and create a folder to hold the installation files; for example, C:\Windows_Install.

Step 5.   Open this folder and use Ctrl+V to paste the boot.wim file into it. This will take several minutes.

Step 6.   Open Search and type **Windows System Image Manager**. Then select **Windows System Image Manager** from the list that appears.

Step 7.   In Windows System Image Manager shown in Figure 2-10, click **File > Select Windows Image**.

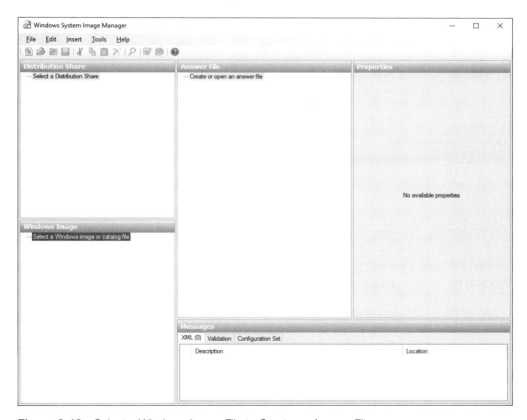

Figure 2-10   Select a Windows Image File to Create an Answer File

Step 8.   In the Select a Windows Image dialog box shown in Figure 2-11, navigate to the folder you copied the boot.wim file to, select this file, and then click **Open**.

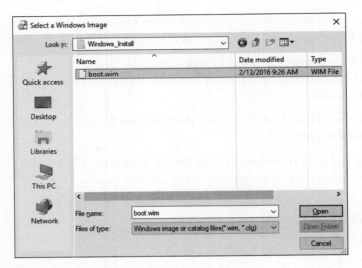

Figure 2-11   Selecting the boot.wim File

Step 9.   In the Select an Image dialog box shown in Figure 2-12, select **Microsoft Windows Setup (x64)**, and then click **OK**.

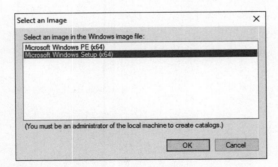

Figure 2-12   Selecting a Windows 10 Image

Step 10.   SIM displays the message shown in Figure 2-13, asking you to create a catalog file. Click **Yes**, and then click **Yes** in the User Account Control dialog box that appears.

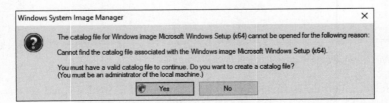

Figure 2-13   Create a Catalog File

Step 11. A Generating Catalog File message box appears as the files are processed and the catalog file is created. This takes several minutes. When the process of generating a catalog file is complete, click **OK**. You are returned to Windows SIM.

Step 12. In the Windows Image pane, expand the Components node to display the available components.

Step 13. To create a new answer file, click **File > New Answer File**. To use a sample answer file as a template for creating your answer file, click **File > Open Answer File**, and navigate to the C:\Program Files (x86)\ Windows Kits\10\Assessment and Deployment Kit\Deployment Tools\ Samples\Unattend folder. (These options are visible in Figure 2-10.) Either action displays a hierarchical tree of answer file components in the Answer File pane of Windows SIM, as shown in Figure 2-14, including the configuration passes previously described in Table 2-4 and placed in the Components node.

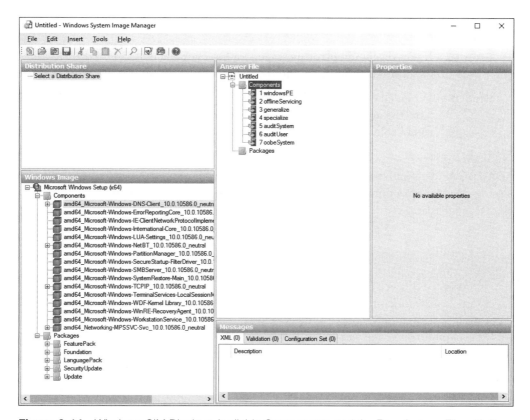

Figure 2-14   Windows SIM Displays Available Components and the Raw Answer File with Its Configuration Passes

Step 14. To add components to the answer file, right-click each desired component in turn and add to the configuration pass indicated in the pop-up menu that appears. Repeat this step as needed until you've added all needed components.

Step 15. To add packages to the answer file, expand the Packages node in the Windows Image section of Windows SIM, right-click each desired package in turn and choose **Add to Answer File**. Note that a package is used for adding software updates, service packs, language packs, security updates, and new Windows features to the Windows image.

Step 16. The Answer File pane should display all the settings you have added. To complete the creation of an answer file for a basic Windows 10 installation, select and configure any settings required for components you've added. To do this, expand the configuration path containing the component to be configured, select the required component, and then add or modify the desired setting displayed in the Properties pane of Windows SIM.

Step 17. Validate the settings you have configured by selecting **Validate Answer File** from the Tools menu.

Step 18. If you receive an error message, double-click the message in the Messages pane, correct the error, and then repeat Step 16.

Step 19. When all errors have been corrected, click **File > Save Answer File**. Save the answer file as Autounattend.xml, and then copy this file to removable media, such as a flash drive.

CAUTION Be aware that you cannot create catalog files for 32-bit computers when using the 64-bit version of Windows SIM. However, the 32-bit version is capable of creating catalog files for either 32- or 64-bit Windows installations.

NOTE For more information on answer files in Windows 10 and Windows Server 2016, refer to "Answer Files Overview" at https://msdn.microsoft.com/en-us/windows/hardware/commercialize/customize/desktop/wsim/answer-files-overview. For more information on using Windows SIM, refer to the topics listed in "Windows System Image Manager How-to Topics" at https://msdn.microsoft.com/en-us/windows/hardware/commercialize/customize/desktop/wsim/windows-system-image-manager-how-to-topics. Also refer to the Help files that come with Windows SIM. (From the Help menu, select **Windows System Image Manager Technical Reference**.) For more information on the Windows ADK, refer to "What's New in ADK

Kits and Tools" at https://msdn.microsoft.com/en-us/windows/hardware/
commercialize/what-s-new-in-kits-and-tools and the links to further documentation
and reference material.

CAUTION   It is possible to edit an answer file by using a text editor, such as Notepad. However, you must take care when editing answer files. When using Notepad
to edit the answer file or UDF file, you must ensure that you follow the rules of syntax exactly; otherwise, unattended installations will either fail or prompt the user for
additional information.

Using the Answer Files to Perform an Unattended Installation

Having created the answer files as described in the previous procedure, it is easy to
run the automated installation of Windows 10 on a new computer (often called the
target computer) without an operating system, as shown in the following steps:

Step 1.   Start the target computer and insert the Windows 10 DVD-ROM and
the flash drive you created in the previous procedure.

Step 2.   To run Setup.exe, press Ctrl+Alt+Delete. The computer restarts and
searches the flash drive for the Autounattend.xml file.

Step 3.   Setup should proceed automatically and install Windows 10 with all customizations you have previously configured.

Dual-Booting Windows 10

As in previous versions of Windows, you can install Windows 10 alongside a different version of Windows in a *dual-boot* configuration. This refers to installing two
operating systems (for example Windows 8.1 and Windows 10) side by side on the
same computer so that you can boot the computer to one operating system or the
other. By specifying a partition that does not have an operating system installed in
Step 7 of the procedure outlined in the section "Performing an Attended Installation," you can select a different partition on which to install Windows 10. This
retains all applications and settings you have configured in the previous version of
Windows and creates a clean installation of Windows 10 on the partition you have
specified. You can even create multiboot systems with more than two different operating systems, including different editions of Windows 10, on the same computer.
Dual-booting or multibooting has the following advantages:

- You can test various editions of Windows 10 without destroying your current operating system.

- If you are running applications that are not compatible with Windows 10, you can boot into an older operating system to run these applications.

- Developers can test their work on different Windows versions without needing more than one computer.

Boot Management Programs Used by Windows 10

Windows 10 includes several new boot management programs, which were first introduced in Windows Vista and Windows Server 2008, and replaced the older programs, such as BOOTMGR and bootcfg used with previous Windows versions. These include the following:

- **Bootcfg.exe:** Enables you to edit, modify, or delete boot entry settings in the boot.ini file used in older Windows operating systems.

- **Bcdedit.exe:** An editing application that enables you to edit boot configuration data on Windows Vista/7/8/8.1/10 or Windows Server 2008/2012/2016. This is the only program that offers boot management editing capabilities for Windows 8.1 and Windows 10.

- **Winload.exe:** The operating system loader, included with each instance of Windows Vista, Windows 7, Windows 8/8.1/10, Windows Server 2008, Windows Server 2012/R2, or Windows Server 2016 installed on any one computer. Winload.exe loads the operating system, its kernel, hardware abstraction layer (HAL), and drivers on startup.

- **Winresume.exe:** Included with each instance of Windows Vista, Windows 7, Windows 8/8.1/10, Windows Server 2008, Windows Server 2012/R2, or Windows Server 2016 installed on any one computer, this program resumes the operating system from hibernation.

NOTE   For more information on using Bootcfg.exe and Bcdedit.exe, refer to "Adding Boot Entries" at https://msdn.microsoft.com/en-us/windows/hardware/drivers/devtest/adding-boot-entries.

Setting Up a Dual-Boot System

The procedure for setting up a dual-boot operating system can vary, but you should generally proceed along the lines of the following:

Step 1.   If you haven't already installed the oldest operating system, install and configure it first. For example, you would install Windows 7, then Windows 8.1, and then Windows 10 in that order if you wanted a triple-boot configuration with these three operating systems.

Step 2.   While running the older operating system, insert the Windows 10 DVD-ROM.

Step 3.   When you receive the option with a choice of upgrade or clean installation (Step 6 of the procedure outlined in the section "Performing an Attended Installation"; refer to Figure 2-3), select the **Custom (Advanced)** option to continue.

Step 4.   The next screen displays the list of available partitions, which includes the partition or partitions on which you have installed the older operating system(s). Select a different partition or create a new partition from unpartitioned space, and then click **Next**.

Step 5.   Follow the remaining steps in the procedure for performing an attended installation to complete the installation of Windows 10.

Refreshing Windows 10

If you are encountering problems with an existing installation of Windows 10, you can reinstall Windows 10 on top of your current installation, also known as a reset and refresh. Refreshing your installation deletes all Windows settings and applications, but retains all data files and folders. Use the following procedure to refresh Windows 10:

Step 1.   From the Start menu, click the **Settings** icon.

Step 2.   From the Windows Settings screen, click **Update & Security**.

Step 3.   In the left column, click **Recovery**.

Step 4.   Under Reset This PC Without Affecting Your Files, click **Get Started**.

Step 5.   Choose from **Keep My Files** on the next dialog box.

Step 6.   Follow the instructions presented, which are similar to those described for a clean installation of Windows 10 earlier in this chapter.

You can also remove all applications, files, and settings, resetting Windows to its original installation settings. Ensure that you have backed up any data on the Windows partition that you want to retain before performing this action. Use the same steps as in the preceding procedure, except in Step 5, click **Remove Everything**.

Troubleshooting Failed Installations

A network administrator's best friend in a crisis is an error log file. This is also true for Windows 10 installation failures. While installing, Windows 10 Setup generates log files that point you in the right direction when you need to troubleshoot.

The Action log (Setupact.log) reports which actions Setup performed in chronological order. This log indicates which files were copied and which were deleted. It records whether any external programs are run and shows where errors have occurred.

Setup creates an Error log (Setuperr.log) to record only the errors. Given that the Action log is extremely large, this log makes it easier to review errors and their severity levels. Although you might see some errors in the Action log, you probably won't see them in the Error log unless they are fairly severe. For example, the Action log reports an error if Setup cannot delete a file because the file was already moved or deleted, but that error does not appear in the Error log.

Table 2-5 describes some of the more important logs created during installation:

Table 2-5 Windows 10 Setup Logs

Log File Name	Description
%systemroot%\panther\miglog.xml	Records information about the user directory structure, including security identifiers (SIDs).
%systemroot%\panther\setupact.log	Records modifications performed on the system during Setup.
%systemroot%\inf\setupapi.dev.log	Records data about Plug and Play devices and drivers. Check this file for device driver installation information.
%systemroot%\inf\setupapi.setup.log	Records data about Windows and application installation.
%systemroot%\setuperr.log	Records errors generated by hardware or driver issues during Windows installation.
%systemroot%\security\logs\scesetup.log	Logs the security settings for the computer.

Stop Errors or Blue Screen of Death (BSOD)

If you receive a Stop error that appears on the Microsoft blue screen (commonly known as the Blue Screen of Death), you have encountered a serious error with the installation. Stop errors have some instructions to follow on the screen. Not only should you follow the instructions, but you should also check the compatibility of the hardware before attempting to install again. Use the following steps to resolve a Stop error.

Step 1.   Shut down the computer.

Step 2.   Remove all new hardware devices.

Step 3.   Start up the computer and remove the associated drivers. Shut down.

Step 4.   Install one of the removed hardware devices. Boot the computer and install the appropriate driver. Reboot. If no BSOD occurs, continue adding devices, one at a time.

Step 5.   Open Device Manager and look for devices with a black exclamation point on a yellow background or a red X. Run hardware diagnostic software.

Step 6.   Check for hardware compatibility and BIOS compatibility. Check to see whether you have the latest available version of the BIOS.

Step 7.   Check the System log in Event Viewer for error messages. These may lead to a driver that is causing the Stop error.

Step 8.   Visit http://search.microsoft.com and perform a search on the Microsoft Knowledge Base for the Stop error number (for example, Stop: 0x0000000A). Follow the instructions given in the Knowledge Base article(s) for diagnosing and repairing the error.

Step 9.   Disable BIOS options such as caching or shadowing memory.

Step 10.   If the Stop error specifies a particular driver, disable the driver and then download and update the driver to the latest version available from the manufacturer.

Step 11.   Video drivers are commonly the cause of a BSOD. Therefore, switch to the Windows Low-resolution video (800×600) driver (available from the Advanced Startup Options menu) and then contact the manufacturer for updated video drivers.

Step 12.   If using a Small Computer System Interface (SCSI) adapter and device, ensure that the SCSI chain is properly terminated and that there are no conflicts with the SCSI IDs.

TIP   The code and text associated with a Stop error are a great help in troubleshooting. For example, an error could be STOP 0x00000001 (DRIVER IRQL NOT LESS OR EQUAL). You can search for this code number and text on Microsoft's website for an explanation of the cause and possible ways to fix the problem.

Stopped Installation

Windows 10 might stop in the middle of an installation. This can happen because of a hardware conflict, incompatibility, or unsuitable configuration. To resolve the conflict, you should follow the usual procedure of removing all unnecessary devices from the computer and attempting installation again. After Windows 10 is installed, you can add one device at a time back to the computer, load the latest manufacturer's drivers, and boot to see whether the computer functions properly. It is important that you add only one device at a time so that you can discover which device (or devices) might have been the cause of the problem.

> **NOTE**   For more information on various aspects of installing and deploying Windows 10, refer to links provided in the document "Deploy Windows 10" at https://technet.microsoft.com/itpro/windows/deploy/index. For information on enterprise-level Windows 10 deployment strategies, refer to "Windows 10 Deployment Considerations" at https://technet.microsoft.com/en-us/itpro/windows/plan/windows-10-deployment-considerations.

Upgrading to Windows 10

Many individuals who have purchased Windows 7 computers since its rollout in 2009 are attracted to the new Windows Start screen and its easy-to-use Windows Store apps and other features that we have already discussed in Chapter 1. Microsoft has provided paths for upgrading these computers to Windows 10. Microsoft offered free upgrades to Windows 10 for anyone using Windows 7, 8, or 8.1 until July 29, 2016. This section looks at which computers can be upgraded directly to Windows 10 and which computers require a complete reinstall of the operating system.

Other users might have purchased a computer running the Home edition of Windows 10, but later want to utilize features available only in a higher edition, such as Windows 10 Pro. Consequently, Microsoft has made upgrade paths available that enable these users to move to a higher version of Windows 10. As with the upgrade of an earlier version of Windows, these paths enable users to retain Registry settings and account information from the lower version of Windows 10.

Upgrade paths from previous Windows versions depend on the operating system version currently installed. Table 2-6 lists the available upgrade paths for older operating systems.

Table 2-6 Upgrading Older Operating Systems to Windows 10

Operating System	Upgrade Path
Windows 8.1 (any edition)	Can be upgraded to the same or higher version of Windows 10.
Windows 7 Starter, Home Basic, or Home Premium	Can be upgraded directly to Windows 10 or Windows 10 Pro.
Windows 7 Professional or Ultimate	Can be upgraded directly to Windows 10 Pro.
Windows 7 Professional (Volume license) or Enterprise (Volume license)	Can be upgraded directly to Windows 10 Enterprise.
Windows Vista (any edition)	Cannot be upgraded. You need to perform a clean installation of Windows 10.
Cross-architecture (32-bit to 64-bit) Windows Vista/7/8	Cannot be upgraded.
Non-Windows operating systems (UNIX, Linux, OS X)	Cannot be upgraded. You need to perform a clean installation of Windows 10.

NOTE For more information on Windows 10 upgrades and editions, see "Windows 10 Upgrade Paths" at https://technet.microsoft.com/en-us/itpro/windows/deploy/windows-10-upgrade-paths.

Furthermore, the type of data you can keep during upgrade depends on the installation path to Windows 10. It is possible that you can keep Windows data and system settings, personal files, applications, or nothing at all according to the upgrade path. Table 2-7 summarizes your options:

Table 2-7 Supported Upgrade Paths to Windows 10

Operating System	Keep Windows Settings, Personal Files, and Applications	Keep Windows Settings and Personal Files	Keep Personal Files Only	Keep Nothing
Windows 8.1 (any edition)	Yes	Yes	Yes	Yes
Windows 8 (any edition)	Yes	Yes	Yes	Yes
Windows 7 (any edition)	Yes	No	Yes	Yes
Windows Vista	N/A	N/A	N/A	N/A

Choosing Between an Upgrade and a Clean Installation

If you have a computer that is currently running Windows 7, 8, or 8.1 and meets the hardware requirements for running Windows 10, it might be possible to either upgrade the existing Windows installation to Windows 10 or perform a clean installation. The hardware requirements for Windows 10 have not changed from the requirements for Windows 8.1. Refer to the following considerations when deciding whether to upgrade your current installation:

- If you upgrade your current installation of Windows to Windows 10, all your applications, data, and settings, such as usernames and passwords, are retained and will work with Windows 10. However, if a program is not compatible with Windows 10, it will not work unless you are able to configure it in a Compatibility mode. Refer to the program manufacturer's website for further information; in many cases, it will be possible to purchase an upgrade for the program.

- You must ensure that all drivers used with hardware devices attached to your computer are compatible with Windows 10. Refer to the device's website for information on available drivers and to download updated drivers.

- If you perform a clean installation of Windows 10, you must reinstall all programs that you used with the previous version of Windows. Further, you must re-create all settings, such as usernames and passwords. If you use the same disk partition as the previous installation of Windows, all data stored on that partition will be lost; consequently, you must back up data to another location before starting your installation.

- If you perform a clean installation of Windows 10 to a different partition than your previous Windows installation, you will create a dual-boot system in which you can boot either Windows 10 or the previous installation of Windows. You can access any data stored on the previous Windows partition; however, you must reinstall all programs that you intend to use on Windows 10 (accessing programs on the previous Windows partition and double-clicking executable files will generally not work).

Preparing a Computer to Meet Upgrade Requirements

In addition to running one of the supported versions of Windows mentioned here, a computer to be upgraded to Windows 10 must meet the hardware requirements previously described in Chapter 1. Note that this should always be true because the hardware requirements for Windows 10 are the same as those for Windows 8. Furthermore, all hardware components should be found in the Windows Certification Program. Older software applications may not be compatible with Windows 10.

Such applications might need to be upgraded or replaced to work properly after you have upgraded your operating system.

Before you upgrade a Windows 7 or Windows 8.1 computer to Windows 10, you should perform several additional tasks, as follows:

- Check the BIOS manufacturer's website for any available BIOS upgrades, and upgrade the computer's BIOS to the latest available functional version if necessary. You should perform this step before a clean install or an upgrade to Windows 10.

- Scan and eliminate any viruses from the computer, using an antivirus program that has been updated with the latest antivirus signatures. You should then remove or disable the antivirus program because it may interfere with the upgrade process. In addition, you should use a third-party program to scan for and remove malicious software (malware).

- Install any upgrade packs that may be required to render older software applications compatible with Windows 10. Consult software manufacturers for details.

- Install the latest updates for Windows 8.1, or the latest service packs for Windows 7 (SP1 at the time of writing), plus any other updates that Microsoft has published. At the very minimum, Windows 7 must have SP1 installed.

Upgrading the Computer to Windows 10

After you have checked system compatibility and performed all tasks required to prepare your computer for upgrading, you are ready to proceed. The upgrade takes place in a similar fashion to a new installation, except that answers to some questions asked by the setup wizard are taken from the current installation. Perform the following procedure to upgrade a Windows 7, Windows 8, or Windows 8.1 computer to Windows 10:

Step 1. Insert the Windows 10 DVD-ROM.

Step 2. If you receive a UAC prompt, click **Yes**. (If running Windows 8/8.1, click **Continue**.)

Step 3. Setup copies temporary files, and then the Get the latest page appears. If you are connected to the Internet, select the **Go Online to Install Updates Now (Recommended)** option. Otherwise select the **No, Thanks** option. Then click **Next**.

Step 4. Type your product key and then click **Next**.

Step 5.   On the License terms page, select the check box labeled **I Accept the License Terms**, and then click **Accept**.

Step 6.   You receive the Choose What to Keep Page shown in Figure 2-15. Note that the options appearing in Figure 2-15 will depend on the upgrade path chosen, as described previously in Table 2-5. Select an option and then click **Next**.

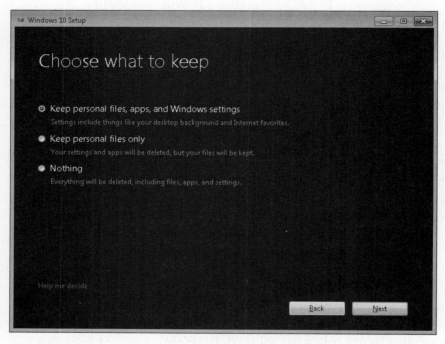

Figure 2-15   Choose Which Items Are to Be Kept from the Previous Windows Installation

Step 7.   Setup checks for anything that might need your attention and displays the Compatibility details page with information about any applications or drivers that are not supported in Windows 10. Note the information provided, and then click **Next**. If the compatibility check does not find any issues, this page does not appear.

Step 8.   Setup presents a Ready to Install page as shown in Figure 2-16, which summarizes the settings you've chosen. Click **Back** if you need to make any changes. When finished, click **Install**.

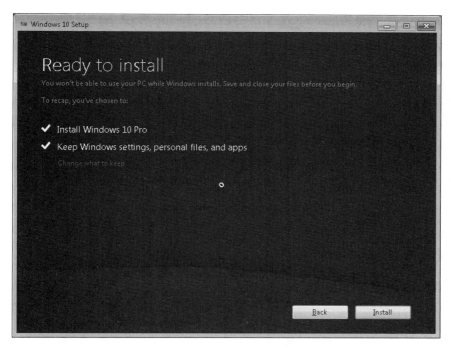

Figure 2-16   Ready to Install Page Provides a Summary of the Selections You've Made

Step 9.   Setup displays an Installing Windows 10 screen as it proceeds with the upgrade. This proceeds in a fashion similar to that of a clean installation. It only asks for any information it cannot retrieve from the previous Windows installation.

Step 10.   After installation has completed and the computer has rebooted, you receive the Sign-on screen, which displays the username obtained from the previous Windows version. Type the same password that you used in Windows 7 or Windows 8. Windows 10 should accept these and, after a minute or two, the Start screen will appear.

Upgrading from One Edition of Windows 10 to Another

Chapter 1 introduced you to the editions Microsoft has produced for Windows 10. Just as you can upgrade Windows 7 or 8 to Windows 10, you can also upgrade a lower edition of Windows 10 to a higher one. Table 2-8 summarizes the available upgrade paths.

Table 2-8   Upgrading One Edition of Windows 10 to a Higher One

Windows Edition You Are Upgrading	You Can Upgrade to This Edition
Windows 10 Home	Windows 10 Pro, Windows 10 Pro for Education, Windows 10 Education
Windows 10 Pro	Windows 10 Pro for Education, Windows 10 Education, Windows 10 Enterprise
Windows 10 Education	Cannot be upgraded further
Windows 10 Enterprise	Windows 10 Education
Windows 10 Mobile	Windows 10 Mobile Enterprise

Microsoft makes available the Windows 10 Pro Pack for upgrading the Home edition of Windows 10. Use the following procedure to upgrade from Windows 10 Home to Windows 10 Pro:

Step 1.   In the Search bar, type **add features**.

Step 2.   Click **Add Features to Windows 10** and then do one of the following:

- To purchase a product key, select **I Want to Buy a Product Key Online**. You will be guided through the required steps and, after purchase, the product key will be entered for you.

- If you already have a product key, click **I Already Have a Product Key**.

Step 3.   Enter your product key and then click **Next**.

Step 4.   You receive the license page. Select the check box to accept the license terms, and then click **Add Features**.

Step 5.   Wait while Windows is upgraded. The computer will restart automatically and Windows 10 Pro will be ready for use.

NOTE   After upgrading to Windows 10, it is possible to revert to the Windows 7 or Windows 8.1 operating system you were running before the upgrade. Refer to https://support.microsoft.com/en-us/instantanswers/1235b5b0-bf94-4b77-9cbd-1c1a8337070c/going-back-to-windows-7-or-windows-8.1 for the procedure and troubleshooting information.

Using Alternate Installation Media

There are various reasons why installing Windows 10 using a DVD would be diffi-cult or inappropriate. If you're installing Windows on a large number of computers, walking around to each computer with the physical disc would be very time consum-ing. You might have some devices that do not have DVD drives for various reasons; in fact, many small form-factor laptops and hybrid devices do not include optical drives at all.

Microsoft offers a media creation tool that you can use to create a bootable USB flash drive, DVD, or ISO file if you need physical media to upgrade a PC or install Windows 10. But for most enterprises, other methods are also available that will reduce the time and manual intervention needed to deploy Windows on a large number of devices. You learn about these methods in this section.

Installing to a Virtual Hard Disk (VHD)

A virtual hard disk (VHD) is a special type of image file that contains all the operat-ing system files, applications, and data that might be found on a typical hard disk partition, encapsulated in a single file. Using VHD technology, Microsoft has expanded the field of client virtualization (also known as desktop virtualization) to provide powerful new means of management for desktops in a corporate envi-ronment. It is even now possible to utilize servers with lots of RAM and several powerful processors with a series of virtual machines installed on these servers and accessed by users from their own desktop. Users can communicate with these virtual desktops by means of a client device that supports protocols such as Remote Desk-top Protocol (RDP).

Understanding VHDs

The virtual hard disk (VHD) specification consists of a single file that includes all the files and folders that would be found on a hard disk partition—hence the term *virtual hard disk*. This file is capable of hosting native file systems and supporting all regular disk operations. First supported in Windows 7 and Windows Server 2008 R2, Microsoft has continued the support of the use of VHDs in Windows 8.1, Win-dows 10, Windows Server 2012 (all editions except Foundation Edition), and Win-dows Server 2016, without the need for a hypervisor (an additional layer of software below the operating system for running virtual computers). These operating systems enable you to create, configure, and boot physical computers directly from VHD. They provide administrators and developers with the following capabilities:

- You can standardize image formats and toolsets used within the company.
- You can reduce the quantity of images that must be cataloged and supported.

- Developers can test applications on multiple operating systems; if applications break operating systems, developers can restore the operating system with minimum lost time and cost.

- You can have a common image format that runs on both physical and virtual machines.

- VHDs enable you to replace images for server redeployment or recovery.

- You can use disk-management tools to attach a VHD and perform offline image management.

Types of Virtual Hard Disks

Windows 10 and Windows Server 2016 offer three types of VHDs: fixed, dynamic, and differencing. Table 2-9 explains how these types differ.

Table 2-9   Types of VHDs

Tool	Description
Fixed	Describes a VHD with a fixed size. For example, if you create a fixed VHD of 30 GB, the file size will always be about 30 GB (some space is used for the internal VHD structure) regardless of how much data is contained in it.
Dynamic	The VHD is only as large as the data contained in it. You can specify the maximum size. For example, if you create a dynamic VHD of 30 GB, it starts out at around 8.10 MB but expands as you write data to it. It cannot exceed the specified maximum size. Fixed VHDs are recommended over dynamic, because they offer the highest I/O performance; also, as a dynamic disk expands, the host volume could run out of space, causing write operations to fail.
Differencing	Also known as a child VHD, this VHD contains only the modified disk blocks of the parent VHD with which it is associated. The parent VHD is read-only, and all modifications are written to the differencing VHD. The parent VHD can be any of these three VHD types, and multiple differencing VHDs are referred to as a differencing chain. A differencing VHD is useful in a test environment; when a developer performs tests, all updates are made on the differencing VHD. To revert to the clean state of the parent VHD, all you need to do is delete the differencing VHD and create a new one.

CAUTION   If you are using differencing VHDs, you should not modify the parent VHD. If you do so, the block structure between the parent and differencing VHD will no longer match, resulting in corruption of the differencing VHD. Furthermore, you must keep both the parent and differencing VHDs within the same folder on a local volume for native-boot scenarios. Otherwise, the differencing VHD will not boot. If the differencing VHD is not used for native-boot, the VHDs can be on different folders or volumes.

Tools Used with Virtual Hard Disks

Microsoft provides several tools that you can use for configuring and managing VHDs, available either as part of the Windows 10 operating system or included with the Windows Assessment and Deployment Kit (ADK). Table 2-10 introduces these VHD management tools. We discuss the use of these tools in Chapter 10, "Windows Hyper-V."

Table 2-10   Tools Used with VHDs

Tool	Description
Disk Management	A Microsoft Management Console (MMC) snap-in that enables you to manage VHDs, including creating, attaching, detaching, expanding, and merging VHDs.
DiskPart	A command-line tool that enables you to perform VHD management activities similar to those available with Disk Management. You can script these actions using DiskPart.
BCDedit	A command-line tool that enables you to manage boot configuration data (BCD) stores.
BCDboot	A command-line tool that enables you to manage and create new BCD stores and BCD boot entries. You can use this tool to create new boot entries when configuring a system to boot from a new VHD.
Deployment Image Servicing and Management (DISM)	A command-line tool that enables you to apply updates, applications, drivers, and language packs to a Windows image, including a VHD.
Sysprep	A utility that enables you to prepare an operating system for imaging and deployment by removing user and computer-specific data.
Windows PE	Windows Preinstallation Environment (Windows PE) is included with the ADK and is used to prepare a computer for installation and servicing of Windows.
Windows Deployment Services	Windows Deployment Services (WDS) is a server-based application that enables organizations to remotely administer and deploy operating systems using Windows PE and the WDS server. Device images are managed over the network, and it automates the deployment of VHD images for native boot.

All these tools are included with Windows 10 and Windows Server 2016, except Windows PE, which is included with the Windows ADK. Also included with Windows Server 2016 and Windows 10 Pro, but not with Windows 10 Home, is the Windows Hyper-V Manager, which is an MMC snap-in that enables you to create VHD images, including the ability to install Windows from installation media or an ISO image file.

Using Disk Management

The Disk Management snap-in contains all the utilities necessary to create and configure disks and partitions. We look at this snap-in in detail in Chapter 9, "Managing User Data." Use the following procedure to create a VHD:

Step 1. Open File Explorer, right-click **This PC**, and choose **Manage**. This opens the Computer Management snap-in, which contains Disk Management as a component snap-in.

Step 2. In the console tree, click **Disk Management** to make its contents visible in the details pane.

Step 3. Right-click **Disk Management**, and choose **Create VHD**. This displays the Create and Attach Virtual Hard Disk dialog box, as shown in Figure 2-17.

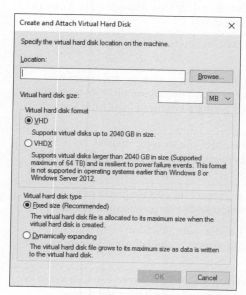

Figure 2-17 The Create and Attach Virtual Hard Disk Dialog Box Enables You to Create a New VHD

Step 4.   Type a path and filename for the VHD in the Location text box, or use the Browse button to browse to a suitable location.

Step 5.   Specify a size in the Virtual Hard Disk Size text box, and select from the choices available under Virtual Hard Disk Format.

- **Dynamically Expanding:** Creates a dynamic VHD, as described earlier in Table 2-9.

- **Fixed Size (Recommended):** Creates a fixed VHD.

Step 6.   For Virtual Hard Disk Format, choose **VHD**, and then click **OK**.

> **NOTE**   The VHDX format, first introduced in Windows 8.1 and Windows 2012, is used only for virtualization inside a hypervisor, and not for native boot. Chapter 10, "Windows Hyper-V," covers Virtualization and Hyper-V.

Step 7.   The disk is created and attached and appears as an unknown disk in Disk Management. This might take several minutes, particularly for a VHD large enough to hold a Windows 10 installation.

Step 8.   Right-click the unknown disk in Disk Management and choose **Initialize Disk**. In the dialog box shown in Figure 2-18, keep the default partition style and then click **OK**.

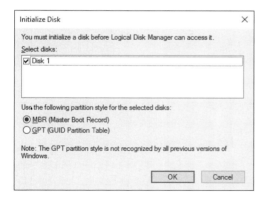

Figure 2-18   Initializing the VHD

Step 9.   It is not necessary to format the VHD; this will be done when we install Windows 10 to the disk.

Installing Windows 10 to a VHD

Now that we have a VHD prepared, we can use a number of techniques to apply an image to it and make it bootable. You can install Windows 10 or Windows Server 2016 directly from the installation DVD to a VHD file. This makes creating your initial image much simpler, and you can customize it within the VHD. When the image is ready, you only need to run Sysprep to generalize the image, and it is ready to deploy to multiple computers.

After you have created a VHD, write down the drive, folder, and filename of the VHD file; then insert the Windows 10 DVD and reboot the computer to the Windows 10 Setup program.

Step 1.   Start by following the initial Steps 1–6 in the "Performing an Attended Installation" section earlier in this chapter. At the end of Step 6 you should see the Which Type of Installation Do You Want? screen from Figure 2-4. We need a way to access the VHD on this computer so we can install Windows there instead of on the physical disks. In Windows 10 Setup, you can now invoke an administrative command prompt using Shift+F10.

Step 2.   Press Shift+F10 to open the administrative command prompt. As shown in Figure 2-19, Windows PE displays the prompt, defaulting to the X:\ drive (the Windows PE RAM disk).

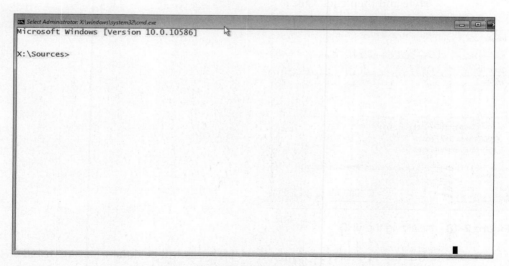

Figure 2-19   Press Shift+F10 During Setup to Display an Administrative Command Prompt

Step 3.   Type the **diskpart** command to open the DISKPART prompt; then select and attach the VHD using the following commands:

```
Select vdisk file=<letter>:\<filename>
Attach vdisk
```

where *<letter>* is the drive letter where the VHD file was created, and *<filename>* is the name of the VHD file.

> **NOTE**   The Windows PE environment might not have the same drive letters as the installed Windows 10 operating system. For instance, if you have a C: drive, a DVD drive, and an E: drive in Windows 10, Windows PE assigns a different letter to the DVD drive, and your E: drive will likely now be drive D:.

Step 4.   Type **exit** to close DiskPart; then type **exit** again to close the administrative command prompt.

Step 5.   Back at the Windows Setup screen, select **Custom: Install Windows Only (Advanced)**.

Step 6.   When the Where Do You Want to Install Windows? screen shown in Figure 2-20 is displayed, it will show all the available disks and partitions, including the VHD just attached using DiskPart. Select the VHD partition as the installation partition.

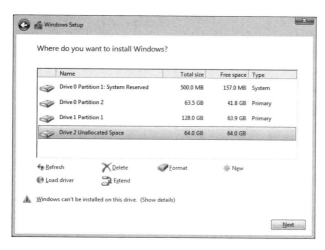

Figure 2-20   Selecting a VHD for Windows Setup

> **NOTE**   Windows will display a warning saying that Windows can't be installed on this drive when you select the VHD. The warning can be ignored.

Step 7.   Click **Next**, and Windows begins copying files and installing Windows 10. The installation will proceed, and the computer will reboot several times.

Step 8.   The last time that Windows boots, it presents two boot options, as shown in Figure 2-21. The volume numbers depend on the drives and partitions on the computer during setup. The default boot option is the VHD partition you just installed. You can change the description of the selections using BCDEDIT to make it less confusing.

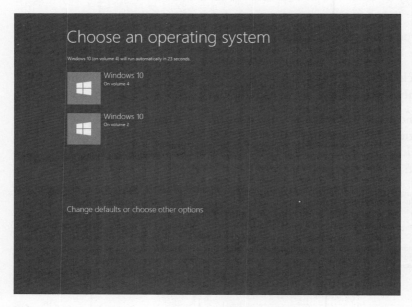

Choose an operating system

Windows 10 (on volume 4) will run automatically in 23 seconds.

Windows 10
On volume 4

Windows 10
On volume 2

Change defaults or choose other options

Figure 2-21   Windows Dual-Boot Options with VHD

You will need to run **Sysprep /generalize** on this VHD file before deploying it to multiple computers.

Installing Additional Windows Features

As introduced in Chapter 1, Windows 10 includes several additional Windows features, the installation and configuration for which we take a brief look at in this section. For the exam, you should familiarize yourself with the features that are not installed by default.

To view the Windows features available, open Control Panel, type **features** into the Search box, and click **Turn Windows Features On or Off**. The list of features is displayed. On a freshly installed Windows 10 device, you can tell which features are installed by default because they will be checked in the list. To install a feature, check the box next to the feature and click **OK**.

Figure 2-22 shows the features list for a newly installed Windows 10 Enterprise.

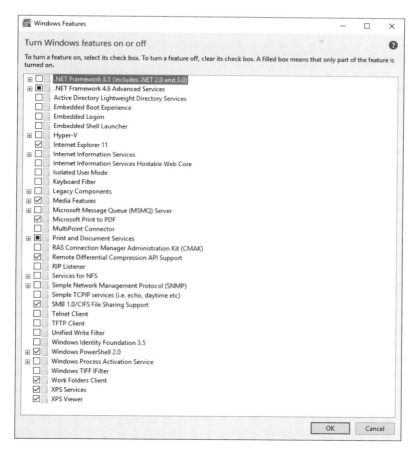

Figure 2-22   List of Optional Windows Features in Windows 10 Enterprise

You learn about some of these features in later chapters, and details on installing and configuring them. For now, understand where to install them in the graphical interface.

You also can install or remove optional features from the command line, using the Deployment Image Servicing and Management (DISM) tool. You can use the tool to check installed features, install and remove features, or use PowerShell scripts to automate the management of features.

For example, use the following procedure to check the installed features and install the Telnet client:

Step 1.   Open an administrative command prompt.

Step 2.   Type the following command:

```
DISM /Online /Get-Features
```

Step 3.   This displays a long list of Windows features similar to Figure 2-23. Note
that the *State* of each is either Enabled or Disabled. Scroll through the
list and find TelnetClient. Note that it is Disabled.

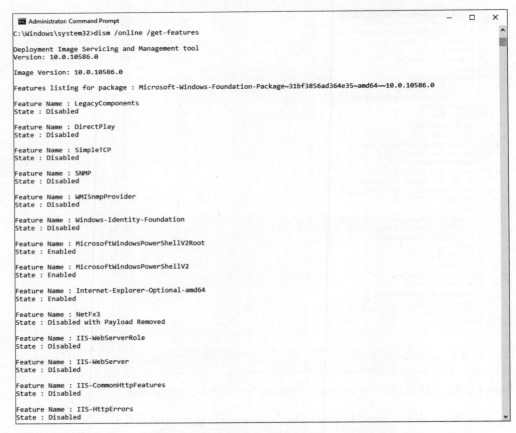

Figure 2-23   List of Optional Windows Features Listed by DISM Command-Line Utility

Step 4. To install the Telnet client, type the following command:

```
DISM /Online /Enable-Feature /FeatureName:TelnetClient
```

Step 5. The tool displays Enabling Feature(s) and a progress indicator.

Step 6. Type the **DISM /Online /Get-Features** command again to ensure that it is now listed as Enabled.

You can install or remove any of the features using the same technique. If you are working with an offline image, such as a VHD, use the **/Image** parameter instead of the **/Online** parameter to service the offline image. You learn more about using the DISM in Chapter 3, "Post-Installation Configuration."

NOTE For more information on the DISM tool and using it to service images, see "DISM Image Management Command-Line Options" at https://msdn.microsoft.com/en-us/windows/hardware/commercialize/manufacture/desktop/dism-image-management-command-line-options-s14.

Configuring Windows for Additional Regional and Language Support

Windows 10 includes support for hundreds of languages, including native letters and scripts. The Control Panel Language applet enables you to add or change available languages. Use the following procedure:

Step 1. Click **Start**, select **Settings**, and click **Time & Language**.

Step 2. Select **Region & Language** from the menu on the left.

Step 3. In the Languages section, click the **Add a Language** button.

Step 4. You see the screen shown in Figure 2-24. Scroll to select the desired language. If regional versions are available, a list is provided; select the desired version.

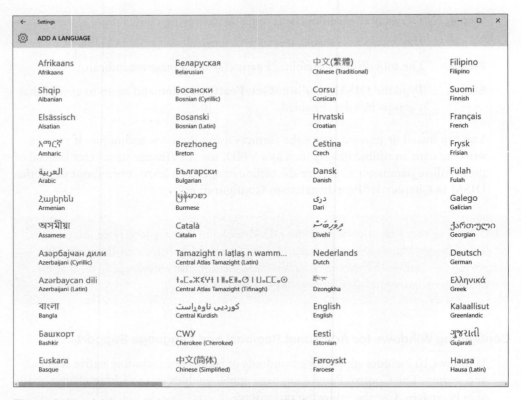

Figure 2-24   Adding an Additional Language from PC Settings

Step 5.   You are returned to the Time and Language page. To make the selected language your primary one, click it and then click the **Set as Default** button. To complete this procedure, log off and then log back on.

Step 6.   To configure additional language properties, click **Options**. This allows you to configure options such as freehand handwriting, speech, and available keyboards.

Step 7.   To remove a language, select it and click **Remove**.

You can also modify your language settings from the Control Panel Language applet, as follows:

Step 1.   Right-click **Start**, choose **Control Panel**, and select **Add a Language** under the Clock, Language, and Region category. The Language applet appears, showing the language or languages available on the computer.

Step 2.   Click **Add a Language**.

Step 3.   You receive the Add a language applet, as shown in Figure 2-25. Scroll this applet to locate the desired language, select it, and then click **Add**. If the selected language includes different regional versions, click **Open**, select the desired version, and then click **Add**. The language is added to the list of available languages in the Language applet.

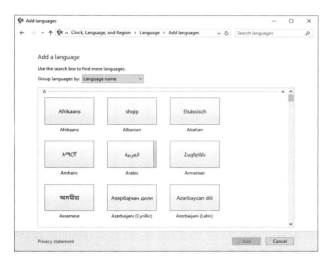

Figure 2-25   Adding an Additional Language from Control Panel

Step 4.   Languages on this applet are listed in order of preferences. To modify this list, select a language and click **Move Up** or **Move Down** as required.

Step 5.   To remove a language, select it and click **Remove**.

Configuring Native Boot Scenarios

For the 70-698 exam, you need to know how to work with VHDs, including how to install Windows 10 on the VHD, deploy a Windows 10 VHD to other machines, and methods for booting from the VHD. For installing Windows 10, you need to use a VHD with native-boot capabilities, which enables the VHD to run on a computer without a hypervisor such as Hyper-V.

Like Windows 8.1 and Windows Server 2012 R2, Windows 10 and Windows Server 2016 enable you to manage virtual disks directly in the disk management tools, without the need to install the Hyper-V Server role or the Hyper-V Manager console. You can use either the Disk Management MMC snap-in or the command line-based DiskPart tool to create and configure VHDs. We will use Disk Management here, and you learn about the DiskPart tool in Chapter 10, "Windows Hyper-V."

Native VHD boot requires at least two partitions—a system partition with the Windows 10 boot environment and boot configuration data (BCD) store, and a partition to store the VHD file. In addition, the partition containing the VHD must have enough free disk space for expanding a dynamic VHD and for the page file created when booting the VHD. When you use native boot VHDs, the page file is created outside the VHD.

There are also a few limitations to be aware of when working with native VHDs:

- Native VHD does not support hibernation (Sleep mode is supported, however).

- You cannot place a VHD inside a VHD (nesting).

- BitLocker encryption cannot be used on a host volume that contains a native boot VHD, nor on the volumes in the VHD.

- VHDs do not work with dynamic disks, so a VHD cannot be configured as a dynamic disk, and the parent volume of a VHD cannot be configured as a dynamic disk.

- You cannot use native boot VHDs over SMB shares.

Best Practices for Using Native-Boot VHDs

Microsoft recommends the following best practices for using native boot VHDs:

- **Store Mission-Critical Data Outside the Native Boot VHDs:** This facilitates recovery of the data should the VHD become corrupted.

- **Use Fixed VHDs in Production Environments:** It is possible to use any of the three VHD types; however, it is recommended to use fixed VHDs in production environments for reasons mentioned earlier. You can use dynamic or differencing VHDs in development and test scenarios.

- **Use a Maximum Size That Is Larger Than the Minimum Disk Requirements for Windows:** The VHD holds additional information about the virtual disk; furthermore, Windows updates take up disk space as they are added.

- **Ensure That Sufficient Space Is Available on the Host Volume for the Page File (pagefile.sys):** The page file is created on the host volume outside the VHD. You can use another physical volume for optimum performance.

- **Use Sysprep to Generalize the Image Before Using the VHD for Native Boot on a Different Computer:** Sysprep prepares the image for copying to additional computers. When you do so, Windows detects hardware devices and initializes properly for running on another computer.

TIP   You can use Windows Deployment Services (WDS) to deploy the VHD image to large numbers of computers. WDS in Windows Server 2016 includes the capability to add VHD image files to its image catalog, making them available to target computers using PXE boot. These computers copy the VHD file locally and configure booting from the VHD. On first boot, the computer configures Windows for the physical devices and performs the usual mini-setup. Using WDS in this manner facilitates rapid deployment of Windows to many computers. You can also script the use of WDS by using the command-line tool WDSUTIL.

TIP   Another way to create the VHD file is by using a PowerShell script Convert-WindowsImage.ps1, available from the TechNet Gallery at https://gallery.technet.microsoft.com/scriptcenter/Convert-WindowsImageps1-0fe23a8f. This command-line script converts the WIM file to a VHD that can be booted, and replaces the older Wim2VHD tool.

Booting VHDs

Windows 7 introduced the capability to boot from a VHD, and this capability exists in Windows 7 and later as well as Windows Server 2008 R2 and later. You must configure the boot loader from the default Windows installation, using the **bcdedit** command-line utility. This tool manages boot configuration data (BCD) stores, which replace the boot.ini file used in Windows versions prior to Vista. You can use **bcdedit** for several purposes, including creating new stores, modifying existing stores, adding or removing boot menu options, and so on. Use the following procedure:

Step 1.   Open an administrative command prompt.

Step 2.   Type **bcdedit**. This starts the Windows Boot Loader utility and displays the default Windows boot information, as shown in Figure 2-26.

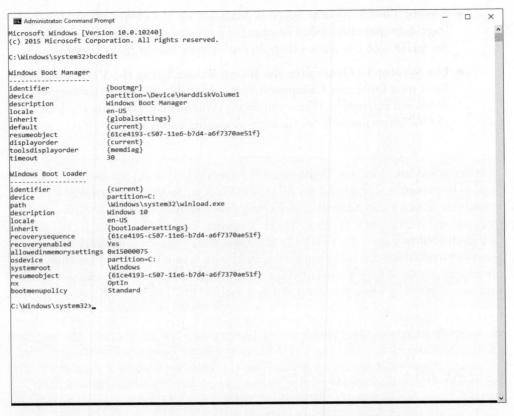

Figure 2-26 The Windows Boot Loader Program Provides Default Windows Boot Information

Step 3. Type **bcdedit /copy {current} /d "Boot from VHD"**. This command copies the current Windows boot loader information, creating a new entry that you can modify for booting from the VHD.

Step 4. Type **bcdedit** again. You will notice a duplicate entry, identified by the globally unique identifier (GUID) in the *identifier* line. Make careful note of this GUID.

Step 5. Type **bcdedit /set {*guid*} device vhd=[*drive*:]\<*path_to_vhd_file*>**, where *guid* is as noted in Step 4; *drive* is the drive on which the VHD file is located; and <*path_to_vhd_file*> is the location of the VHD file on its drive. For example:

```
bcdedit /set {35bbc226-7920-11de-b6f7-a0288f236347} device
VHD="[E:]\VHDImages\Win10Ent-1.vhd"
```

Step 6. Set the OS device by typing **bcdedit /set {***guid***} osdevice vhd=[***drive***:]\\<***path_to_vhd_file***>**. The syntax of this command is identical to the previous one, except that **device** is replaced by **osdevice**.

Step 7. Set the Detect Hal command by typing **bcdedit /set {***guid***} detecthal on**.

Step 8. Provide a description for this boot by typing **bcdedit /set {***guid***} description <***description***>**, where *description* is a description of the boot that will appear at startup. Enclose the description in double quotes if it contains spaces.

Step 9. Verify your output by typing **bcdedit** again. You should see something similar to Figure 2-22, allowing you to boot either into the full, previously configured operating system or to the VHD file.

If you want to delete the entry, take note of the GUID listed in **bcdedit** and use the following command:

```
bcdedit /delete {GUID} /cleanup
```

Exam Preparation Tasks

Review All the Key Topics

Review the most important topics in the chapter, noted with the Key Topics icon in the outer margin of the page. Table 2-11 lists a reference of these key topics and the page numbers on which each is found.

Table 2-11   Key Topics for Chapter 2

Key Topic Element	Description	Page Number
Table 2-2	Describes the minimum hardware requirements for running Windows 10	82
List	Lists considerations when selecting 32-bit or 64-bit Windows editions	85
Table 2-3	Hardware requirements for specific features of Windows 10	89
List	Lists the items you should have on hand prior to performing an attended install of Windows 10	90
Step List	Shows you how to install Windows 10 from an installation DVD	91
Step List	Using Windows ADK to create an answer file	100

Key Topic Element	Description	Page Number
Step List	Using an answer file to perform an unattended installation of Windows 10	105
List	Describes advantages of setting up a dual-boot system	106
Table 2-5	Describes important Windows 10 setup log files	108
Table 2-6	Describes available paths for upgrading older Windows operating systems to Windows 10	111
Table 2-7	Describes the types of information that can be kept when upgrading older Windows operating systems to Windows 10	111
List	Describes tasks you should perform before upgrading to Windows 10	113
Step List	Procedure for upgrading a computer to Windows 10	113
Table 2-8	Describes available paths for upgrading to a higher edition of Windows 10	116
Table 2-9	Lists types of VHDs	118
Table 2-10	Lists tools used for configuring VHDs	119
Step List	Shows how to create a VHD using Disk Management	120
List	Describes several limitations when installing Windows 10 to a VHD	130
Step List	Shows how to edit the boot loader for booting a VHD	131

Complete the Tables and Lists from Memory

Print a copy of Appendix B, "Memory Tables" (found on the book's website), or at least the section for this chapter, and complete the tables and lists from memory. Appendix C, "Memory Tables Answer Key," also on the website, includes completed tables and lists to check your work.

Definitions of Key Terms

Define the following key terms from this chapter, and check your answers in the glossary.

basic input/output system (BIOS), bcdboot, bcdedit, differencing VHD, DISM, dynamic VHD, fixed VHD, hypervisor, Setup.exe, virtual hard disk (VHD), Windows Hardware Certification Program, Windows To Go

This chapter covers the following subjects:

- **Configuring and Customizing the User Interface According to Device Type:** This section discusses the various options available for customizing the Windows 10 user interface (UI) and selecting the right options for the type of device, be it a small form factor such as a phone or small tablet, a hybrid laptop/table, or a full-function desktop computer.

- **Configuring Windows 10 Options:** This section introduces configuration for several features of Windows 10, including accessibility options, Cortana, Microsoft Edge, Internet Explorer, Hyper-V, and power settings.

- **Configuring Devices and Device Drivers:** This section teaches you how to install device drivers and use Device Manager for configuring and Windows Update for updating drivers. It introduces the concept of driver signing and checking for valid driver signatures. It also discusses permissions for installing drivers and settings that you can configure from a driver's Properties dialog box, and also covers managing driver packages.

This chapter covers the following objectives for the 70-698 exam:

Perform post-installation configuration: Configure and customize Start menu, desktop, taskbar, and notification settings according to device type; configure accessibility options; configure Cortana; configure Microsoft Edge.

Configure devices and device drivers: Install, update, disable, and roll back drivers; resolve driver issues; configure driver settings, including signed and unsigned drivers; manage driver packages; download and import driver packages; use the Deployment Image Service and Management (DISM) tool to add packages.

CHAPTER 3

Post-Installation Configuration

Windows 10 is designed to run on many different devices. To improve the experience on the various screens and form factors, it may be necessary to customize the Start menu, desktop, taskbar, and adjust the notification settings. Windows has always provided ways to customize the desktop, colors, and other user interface (UI) settings, but with Windows 10 comes a new level of customization. You should be familiar with the various options and how they can improve the Windows experience. For the 70-698 exam, you are expected to know the configuration settings and ways to configure and enforce those settings.

Beyond the basic UI, there are also options for customizing how some of the common applications are presented to the user. This includes the global search tool, Cortana, and the ways it can be used, as well as the new Internet browser Microsoft Edge, the Windows 10 version of Internet Explorer, the Hyper-V virtualization client, and the device power settings.

When you first install Windows 10, it performs an inventory of all devices it finds on the computer and records information about them in the Registry under HKEY_LOCAL_MACHINE\Hardware. Each device is associated with a software program called a *driver*. This is a program that enables the device to communicate properly with the operating system. Typically, a driver is in the form of an .inf file (for example, Mydevice.inf). These files are typically located in the subfolder, %systemroot%\inf. Device manufacturers frequently issue driver updates that improve device functionality or solve problems that users have reported. In addition, Microsoft issues updates at least once a month. For the 70-698 exam, Microsoft expects you to know how to use Device Manager to ensure that your devices are installed, updated, and working properly, and to be able to troubleshoot problems with drivers and ensure that drivers are configured with the proper settings.

"Do I Know This Already?" Quiz

The "Do I Know This Already?" quiz allows you to assess whether you should read this entire chapter or simply jump to the "Exam Preparation Tasks" section for review. If you are in doubt, read the entire chapter. Table 3-1 outlines the major headings in this chapter and the corresponding "Do I Know This Already?" quiz questions. You can find the answers in Appendix A, "Answers to the 'Do I Know This Already?' Quizzes."

Table 3-1 "Do I Know This Already?" Foundation Topics Section-to-Question Mapping

Foundation Topics Section	Questions Covered in This Section
Configuring and Customizing the User Interface, According to Device Type	1–3
Configuring Windows 10 Options	4–6
Configuring Devices and Device Drivers	7–16

CAUTION The goal of self-assessment is to gauge your mastery of the topics in this chapter. If you do not know the answer to a question or are only partially sure of the answer, you should mark that question as wrong for purposes of the self-assessment. Giving yourself credit for an answer you correctly guess skews your self-assessment results and might provide you with a false sense of security.

1. You are using Windows 10 on a desktop computer, and would like a larger Start menu to be able to find your many apps and desktop applications more quickly. What is the best way to size your Start menu to your liking?

   a. Switch the computer to Tablet mode.

   b. Drag the top and right edges of the Start menu.

   c. Expand by dragging the left and bottom edges of the Start menu.

   d. Use the modern Settings screen to customize the Start menu size.

2. The company where you are a Windows system administrator has decided that all users' Windows 10 workstations should use the same custom Start menu layout with the approved and in-house applications, because so many users roam offices. You are creating a Group Policy Object to enforce the approved Start menu layout on all computers in the domain OU. What else is needed to roll out the customizations?

    a. A policy that implements the specific layout customization parameters and settings

    b. An .XML file on an accessible file share generated from the custom layout

    c. A folder on an accessible file share with files describing the custom Start menu layout

    d. A domain object containing the Start menu customizations

    e. A PowerShell script called from the user profile to configure the Start menu at login

3. You will be using your laptop to display a presentation on a wide screen to a group of your company's business managers in the afternoon. You realize that your laptop has been sending notifications from a number of applications that need attention. You ignore them as you prepare, but want to make sure these notifications do not show up and interrupt your presentation. What is the best way to make sure notifications are not displayed during the afternoon meeting?

    a. From the modern Settings screen, select the Taskbar page, and select **Turn System Icons On or Off**.

    b. From the Notifications & Actions modern Settings page, turn the Show Notifications on the Lock Screen toggle to **Off**.

    c. From the Notifications & Actions modern Settings page, turn off the senders that are sending notifications.

    d. From the Notifications & Actions modern Settings page, toggle the Hide Notifications When I'm Duplicating My Screen to **On**.

    e. From the Action Center icon, turn on **Quiet Hours**.

4. Which of the following customization options for Cortana can be toggled on or off?

    a. Microphone, Hey Cortana, Lock Screen, Other Privacy Settings

    b. Hey Cortana, Lock Screen, My Device History, Send Notifications Between Devices

    c. Microphone, Lock Screen, Send Notifications Between Devices

    d. Lock Screen, Cortana Language, Bing SafeSearch

5. Which of the following are *not* included in the new Edge browser in Windows 10, but are included in Internet Explorer 11? (Choose all that apply.)

   a. Integration with Adobe Flash

   b. Really Simple Syndication (RSS) feeds

   c. Ability to pin websites to the taskbar

   d. Tabbed browsing

   e. Compatibility View

   f. The ability to directly access the Internet options dialog box (as opposed to accessing this dialog box from Control Panel)

6. Your organizations use a number of legacy web applications internally for accounting and HR functions, as well as other groups. These were mostly created by consultants and will not be updated anytime soon. You are deploying Windows 10, but the web applications were developed for Internet Explorer 7, and some features do not work with Edge or Internet Explorer 11. You want to implement a group policy to ensure the sites work for all your users. Which policy should you use?

   a. Turn on Internet Explorer 7 Standards Mode

   b. Turn on Internet Explorer Standards Mode for Local Intranet

   c. Turn off the Compatibility View button

   d. Include updated website lists from Microsoft

   e. Use Policy List of Quirks Mode sites

7. From which of the following locations can you access Device Manager in Windows 10? (Choose all that apply.)

   a. Right-click **Start** and choose **Computer Management**. Then select **Device Manager** from the console tree of the Computer Management console.

   b. Right-click **Start** and choose **Device Manager**.

   c. From a File Explorer window, right-click **This PC** and choose **Properties**. Then select **Device Manager** from the list of options in the left column.

   d. In the Search bar, type **device manager** into the Search box. Then click **Device Manager**.

   e. From the Action Center, select **All Settings**, select **Devices**, and then click the **Device Manager** link.

   f. From the Hardware tab of the System Properties dialog box, click **Device Manager**.

8. You are looking in Device Manager to determine whether any hardware devices are disabled. What icon should you look for?

    a. A black exclamation point icon on a yellow triangle background appearing next to the device icon indicates that a device is functioning but experiencing problems.

    b. A red "X" appearing over the device icon.

    c. A yellow question mark.

    d. A blue "i" on a white field.

9. You would like to review the actions taken by Windows in the past few months with regard to the drivers used by your computer's network adapter card, so you open Device Manager and select the Properties dialog box for the network adapter. Which tab provides you with this information?

    a. General

    b. Driver

    c. Details

    d. Events

10. You are removing an old device from your computer and are not planning to replace it in the immediate future. You want to ensure that its drivers are permanently removed. What should you do?

    a. Use Device Manager to disable the driver.

    b. Use Device Manager to uninstall the driver.

    c. Use Device Manager to roll back the driver.

    d. Use Windows Update to update all drivers on your computer.

11. What program would you use to determine whether any unsigned drivers are present on your computer?

    a. sfc.exe

    b. sigverif.exe

    c. msinfo32.exe

    d. gpedit.exe

12. You install an updated driver for your network adapter card and now the card does not work. What should you do to get the card working again?

    a. Update the driver

    b. Roll back the driver

    c. Uninstall the driver

    d. Disable the driver

13. You install a new network interface card (NIC) on your computer. When you restart your computer, you discover that not only does this device not work, but also you are unable to hear any sound. What should you be looking for?

    a. A resource conflict

    b. Insufficient power from your computer's power supply

    c. Outdated device drivers

    d. Unsigned device drivers

14. Which of the following tools enables you to view device-related problems but does not provide any tools to correct these problems?

    a. Device Manager

    b. sigverif.exe

    c. Action Center

    d. System Information

15. What task should you perform before installing or upgrading device drivers?

    a. Create a System Image

    b. Backup user files

    c. Run Driver Verifier

    d. Create a Restore Point

16. You need to change the speed of a network adapter. Which tab of the driver's Properties tab will allow you to change this setting?

    a. Details

    b. Properties

    c. Advanced

    d. Power Management

Foundation Topics

Configuring and Customizing the User Interface, According to Device Type

Customizing the Windows 10 user interface has changed significantly since Windows 7 and from Windows 8 and 8.1. In fact, the reception of the tiled Start screen and elimination of the Start menu from Windows 8 were not received well by the Windows user community, and Microsoft quickly moved to make changes. Windows apps and tiles still exist, but with Windows 10 the Desktop returned to front-and-center of the interface for most devices. Tiles are also easier to work with and are displayed more like the windowed interface similar to desktop applications.

The tiled screen, originally termed "Metro" before the release of Windows 8, was actually a functional paradigm for small devices like mobile phones. And with Windows 10 and Windows 10 Mobile, the Universal Windows Platform (UWP) apps menu can still be customized with a look very similar to the original modern UI that Microsoft presented with Windows 8. Windows 10 truly unified the platform, and small-screen mobile devices can be configured to work well with the menu and interface while large desktops present a more familiar desktop with all the productivity users demand.

In this topic you learn about the various customizations available for the Start menu and taskbar, the Windows 10 Desktop, and the notifications.

Configuring the Start Menu and Taskbar

As described in Chapter 1, "Introducing Windows 10," the Start menu in Windows 10 consist of a list on the left that includes recently used items, and, by default, icons for File Explorer, Settings, Power, and All Apps. At the top is the user icon that displays the username you can use to log out or access account settings. To the right of this list are blocks of tiles. By dragging the edge of the Start menu outline from the top, you can set the Start menu to be taller or shorter. Figure 3-1 depicts the short and narrow Start menu.

Figure 3-1 Start Menu Set to the Smallest Horizontal and Vertical Size

Similarly by dragging the right edge of the Start menu, you can make the Start menu fit more tile groups across the space or narrow down to a single tile group wide. Figure 3-2 depicts the wide and tall Start menu setting.

Figure 3-2 Start Menu Set to the Largest Horizontal and Vertical Size

Note that when you size the Start menu to a smaller size, a scroll bar is available so that you can scroll to the tile group that is hidden from the screen.

Tiles on the Start menu can be rearranged, unpinned, and resized. To move a tile, drag and drop the tile to locate it where you would like. Other tiles within the tile group adjust as you drag the tile. Tiles from one tile group can be moved to a different tile group in the same manner. Right-clicking any tile displays the context menu with the following options:

- Unpin from Start

- Resize (Small, Medium, Wide, and Large Options)

- More

  - Turn Live Tile Off (if applicable)

  - Rate and Review (if applicable)

  - Share (if applicable)

  - Pin to Taskbar (If the app is already pinned to the taskbar, this item becomes Unpin from Taskbar.)

Any app from the All Apps menu can be added to a tile group by dragging it from the All Apps menu to the tile group. You can also create a new tile group this way. When you drag an app to the top or bottom edge of the tile groups area, a blue bar appears. Dropping the app into this area creates a new tile group. The group name (at the top of the tile group) will initially be called Name Group. Click the name to change it to something appropriate. Figure 3-3 shows the result of adding a tile group, called Calculations, with the calculator app pinned inside.

Figure 3-3   The Start Menu Displays a New Customized Tile Group

For smaller devices, and for Windows 10 Mobile, it improves the user experience to have an even larger Start menu, similar to the Start screen from Windows 8 and 8.1. This setting is available in all editions of Windows 10. To make your Start menu full screen, use the following procedure:

Step 1.   Click the Notification icon to reveal the Action Center and select **All Settings**.

Step 2.   From the Settings menu, select **Personalization**.

Step 3.   From the menu on the left, select **Start**. This displays the options shown in Figure 3-4.

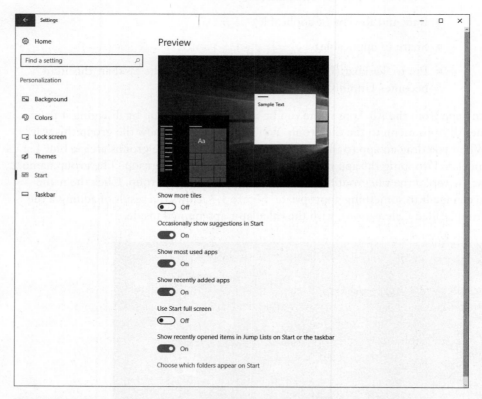

Figure 3-4   Start Settings on the Personalization Settings Screen

Step 4.   Click the toggle for **Use Start Full Screen** to **On**.

Step 5.   Close the Settings screen by clicking the X in the upper-right corner.

A few other customization toggles are available on the Start section of the Personalization screen. For instance, you can turn Jump Lists on or off. A Jump List extends items you can open with an application. For instance, the Jump List on the File Explorer displays common and recently opened folders; the Jump List for Microsoft Word displays recently opened documents, and so on.

- **Show More Tiles:** With this option on, the tile groups on the Start menu will have a wider width, providing room for more tiles.

- **Occasionally Show Suggestions in Start (On by Default):** Allows Windows to show you some suggestions for Windows store applications you might find useful.

- **Show Most Used Apps (On by Default):** You can show or hide the "most used apps" section of the Start menu with this toggle. The apps displayed are dynamically adjusted by Windows as you use various apps.

- **Show Recently Added Apps (On by Default):** You can show or hide any apps you have recently installed on the Start menu. These appear in a section just below the "most used" apps.

- **Use Start Full Screen:** Turning this toggle on causes the Start menu to take up the entire screen of the device.

- **Show Recently Opened Items in Jump Lists on Start or the Taskbar (On by Default):** Similar to recently added apps, this setting enables extended items on a Start menu option.

- **Choose Which Folders Appear on Start:** Clicking this link displays toggles for things that can appear directly on the left-side list on the Start menu. File Explorer and Settings are on by default. You can add several other items, such as Documents, Music, Pictures, and so on.

Another way to get a full-screen Start menu is to switch to Tablet mode. This is especially handy for small form-factor devices, such as tablets. Switch to Tablet mode by clicking the Notification icon on the taskbar and selecting Tablet mode. Notice in Tablet mode that the Desktop disappears, replaced by the Start menu. Also, all apps run only in full screen in Tablet mode.

By default, Tablet mode does not display app icons in the taskbar. You can change this behavior in Settings, by opening **All Settings** from the Action Center, selecting **System**, and then clicking the Tablet mode menu. From here you can toggle the **Hide App Icons on the Taskbar in Tablet Mode** setting. This screen has some other options. The **When I Sign In** setting allows you to configure which mode to use at sign in, and you can configure what option to take when the device automatically switches to Tablet mode. There are also two toggles on this screen that allow you to **Hide App Icons on the Taskbar in Tablet Mode**, and to **Automatically Hide the Taskbar in Tablet Mode**.

Tablet mode is designed for hybrid devices, such as Microsoft's Surface devices. These powerful computers with touchscreens act as both small laptops and tablets, and they can automatically switch modes depending on the orientation of the device and whether the keyboard is attached. Tablet mode settings allow you to control this behavior precisely for the way you want to work.

Group Policies for Start Menu and Taskbar

New Group Policy settings are available for customizing the Start menu and taskbar. You can use a different Group Policy Object (GPO) attached to specific device types, departments, or organizations to deploy the customizations needed.

NOTE The Group Policy for controlling Start menu and taskbar settings is available only for Windows 10 Enterprise and Windows 10 Education. Controlling Start menu and taskbar layout is not supported in Windows 10 Pro or Home.

The following components are needed to provide Start menu and taskbar customization control:

- The Start.xml layout file.
- The Export-StartLayout PowerShell cmdlet, which is used to create the Start.xml layout file from a customized Start menu.
- The Start Layout policy settings in Group Policy, found in \Computer Configuration\Administrative Templates\Start Menu and Taskbar section of the GPO.
- A network share that is available to users when they log in to Windows. Users will need read-only access to the Start.xml file on the share.

You can use the following procedure to apply Start menu and taskbar customizations through Group Policy:

Step 1. On a Windows 10 reference computer, apply the desired customizations to the Start menu and taskbar.

Step 2. From an administrative command prompt, export the layout to an .xml file, for example:

```
PowerShell Export-StartLayout -Path "C:\Layouts\Layout-1.xml"
```

Step 3. Copy the layout file to a network share.

Step 4. Start the Group Policy Management Console, and configure a GPO. Navigate to \Computer Configuration\Administrative Templates\Start Menu and Taskbar, and open the **Start Layout** setting.

Step 5.   Select **Enabled** to enable the policy.

Step 6.   Enter the UNC name for the layout file to use in the Start Layout File box, as shown in the example in Figure 3-5.

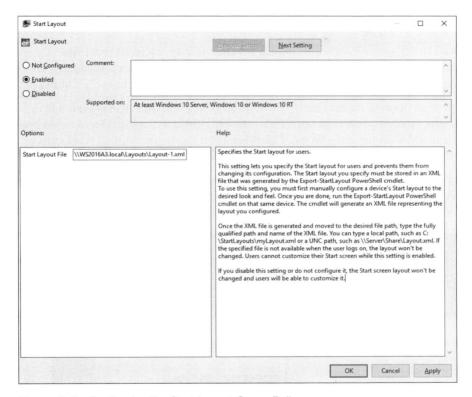

Figure 3-5   Configuring the Start Layout Group Policy

Step 7.   Click **OK** to save the Start Layout setting.

Step 8.   Apply the GPO to the appropriate container in the Active Directory.

After this Group Policy is configured, any computers with the GPO applied will use the Start menu and taskbar configuration specified by the .xml file. You can update the file at any time, and devices will update their Start menu configuration during the next login.

NOTE   For more information about the PowerShell cmdlets available for managing layout files, see "Start Layout Cmdlets" at https://technet.microsoft.com/en-us/library/mt188239.aspx. For details on Start menu and taskbar customization and managing configurations with Group Policy Objects, see "Manage Windows 10 Start and

Taskbar Layout," and the links to related topics, at https://technet.microsoft.com/en-us/itpro/windows/manage/windows-10-start-layout-options-and-policies.

Configuring the Desktop

Windows 10 offers several configurations for the desktop, accessed from the Personalization Settings screen shown in Figure 3-4. From this screen you can set background options and colors, configure the Lock screen, and choose a Theme.

Most of these options are similar to the desktop configuration settings available in Windows 8, 7, and even Windows XP. However, Windows 10 introduces a new feature that enables multiple desktops. This allows you to create multiple workspaces, each with its own set of running applications, open folders, documents, and so on.

When you click the Task view, Windows displays large icons for all the apps currently running. Also notice that there is a New Desktop button at the bottom right of the screen, as shown in Figure 3-6. Click the plus sign (+) to create a new desktop.

Figure 3-6 Click the Task View Icon to Create and View Multiple Desktops

Windows will create a new desktop and call it Desktop 2, as shown in Figure 3-7. Select the new desktop icon to switch to your new, clean desktop environment.

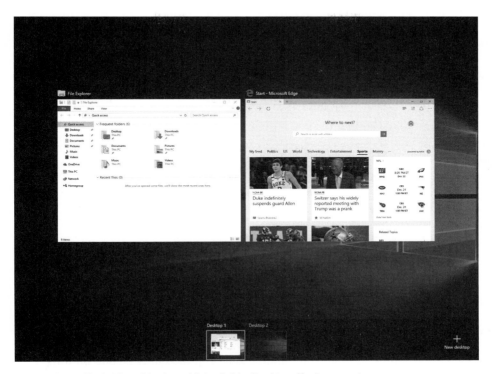

Figure 3-7   Task View Displays All Available Desktop Environments

You can also move applications between desktops. To do so, open the Task view and drag the application from the current desktop to the destination desktop at the bottom. The application then appears on the other virtual desktop.

When you are finished working with Desktop 2, click the Task view icon, roll the cursor over the desktop, and click the X in the corner to remove it. If any applications are still active in that desktop, they will automatically be moved to Desktop 1.

Configuring Notification Settings

Windows 10 offers many configuration options for notifications and the Action Center. To access the configuration options, select **All Settings** from the Notification icon, click **System**, and then select **Notifications & Actions** from the menu. This displays the options as shown in Figure 3-8. The section on the bottom, **Get Notifications from These Senders**, will have different options depending on the apps installed that are capable of sending notifications.

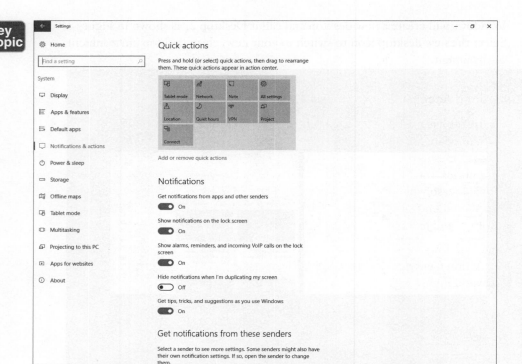

Figure 3-8   Configuration Options for Notifications & Actions

In the Quick Actions section, you can drag and drop the Quick Action buttons to arrange them according to your requirements. Clicking the **Add or Remove Quick Actions** link displays a screen with toggles to turn on or off each of the quick actions.

As shown in Figure 3-8, Windows provides several toggles for controlling the types of notifications that can appear in the notification center. You can also configure Quiet Hours to tell Windows when to turn off notifications during certain times of day. This is handy if you have a portable device and you don't want to hear notification sounds or Lock screen displays during certain hours or while you are sleeping. If you are using your device for a presentation for a room full of people, you can toggle the **Hide Notifications When I'm Duplicating My Screen** to **On** so that notifications don't pop up and interrupt your presentation.

Configuring Windows 10 Options

In this topic you learn about configuring some of the built-in options available with Windows 10. For the exam, and to provide support for Windows 10 in an

organization, you should understand the configuration options available for these features, as well as how to deploy and enforce customizations in a networked environment.

Configuring Accessibility Options

Microsoft has made considerable effort to make Windows easy to use, and to accommodate users with vision or hearing disabilities by implementing assistive technologies in the operating systems. In organizations, the Americans with Disabilities Act and similar rules in Europe and elsewhere require employers to provide reasonable accommodations for employees with disabilities of any kind. You should know the options available in Windows to provide greater accessibility for users and help employees be as productive as they can be.

The Windows 10 accessibility options are available by selecting **All Settings** from the Action Center, and then clicking **Ease of Access**. This displays the screen shown in Figure 3-9.

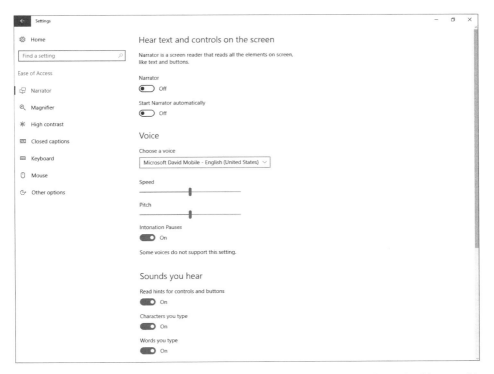

Figure 3-9   The Windows 10 Ease of Access Settings Screen Defaults to the Narrator Menu

You should be familiar with the options available for configuring accessibility and how they work. The menu options available for the Ease of Access settings include the following:

- **Narrator:** Enables a voice narrator for navigating Windows screens and applications; provides configuration settings for how the narrator will sound and the types of onscreen dialogs the narrator will describe for the user.

- **Magnifier:** Enables an onscreen magnifying glass users can use to zoom in on the screen and sections of the screen they are working with or need to read.

- **High contrast:** Allows you to turn on high contrast for onscreen elements, and select a high-contrast theme. This setting may make Windows screens easier to read for some people.

- **Closed captions:** Provides options for providing closed captions on screens with audio, similar to closed captioning in movies and television.

- **Keyboard:** Displays configurations to enable the onscreen keyboard, turn on audio cues for certain key presses, and enable sticky keys for single-handed users.

- **Mouse:** Options for pointer size and color, as well as options to use arrow keys to move the mouse cursor around the screen.

- **Other options:** This menu displays some improved visual options, such as the capability to play animations, visual notifications for sound, and adjust the cursor thickness, among others.

NOTE   To learn more about assistive technologies in Windows 10, refer to the links in "Accessibility in Windows 10" at https://www.microsoft.com/enable/products/windows10/default.aspx.

Cortana and the Windows 10 Search

You saw a quick overview of the Windows 10 search tool, Cortana, in Chapter 1, and how to use it for searching your computer for apps and documents, search the Web for information, and use the voice interface for Cortana. Cortana is positioned as a unified search tool and personal assistant. You can customize Cortana's behavior in Windows and enforce Cortana behaviors in an organization.

When you activate Cortana, you can click the Settings icon to display the configuration options available, as shown in Figure 3-10.

Figure 3-10 Cortana Settings

In the latest versions of Windows 10 Home and Pro, there is no option to turn off or disable Cortana, but you can control some aspects of Cortana's behavior.

- **Microphone:** Options to configure the microphone and speech system so that Cortana can recognize your voice and respond to queries.

- **Hey Cortana:** Turning on this option enables you to interact with Cortana with speech, without touching the device, by saying "Hey Cortana." If you turn this on, you will also have the option to turn off Sleep mode so that your device will always respond when it is plugged in. If you want to ensure that Cortana responds only to you, select the **Learn How I Say "Hey Cortana"** link to configure your voice, and then select **Try to Respond Only to Me**. Or you can select **Respond When Anyone Says "Hey Cortana"** so it can be activated by anyone.

- **Lock Screen:** Options to allow Cortana to function when the screen is locked.

- **Taskbar Tidbits:** Cortana can provide hints and tips in the Search box from time to time with this option turned on.

- **Send Notifications Between Devices:** Allow Cortana to provide notifications about other device statuses on this device.

- **Cortana Language:** Choose the language settings for Cortana.

- **History View:** Enable history in Cortana for apps, settings, web, search, and other items Cortana knows about.

- **My Device History:** With this turned on, Cortana will learn your search history and perform better searches on the PC or local device. This section also includes a button to clear the device history.

- **Bing SafeSearch Settings:** This link brings up the search settings in Bing.com, using your default browser. Cortana uses Bing for Web search.

- **Other Privacy Settings:** A link to the device's Change Privacy Options screen.

Cortana Group Policy Settings

Cortana configuration, and search settings in general, can be controlled in Group Policy for the Enterprise and Education editions of Windows 10. If you disable the Allow Cortana Group Policy, Cortana will not be enabled on the device, but users will still be able to search the device.

The following group policies can be used to manage Cortana on devices and are found in the GPO under \Computer Configuration\Administrative Templates\ Windows Components\Search.

- **Allow Cortana:** Enable or disable Cortana universal search and voice interface. Local search still works when this policy is disabled.

- **Allow Cortana Above Lock Screen:** Use this policy to disable the ability of Cortana's speech interface to work on the Lock screen.

- **Allow Search and Cortana to Use Location:** You can disable providing Cortana access to the device's location using this policy.

Configuring Microsoft Edge and Internet Explorer

Windows 10 includes Internet Explorer (IE) version 11, which provides new management and usability features that enhance the Internet browsing experience while providing the latest security enhancements that help to maintain a safe environment while accessing websites and other Internet resources.

Windows 10 also introduces a new browser, Edge, which is enabled as the default browser. Edge has a more minimalistic design than IE and is designed to work well with tablets, so it is easy to use with a touch interface and improves battery life over using IE. The simple interface, along with a new, faster rendering engine, means that Edge performs faster than IE.

Microsoft Edge

Edge includes a new Reading mode for certain web pages, such as news articles, which presents the core content of the page in a simplified and more readable screen, perfect for reading on a tablet or small form-factor device. You can configure how Reading mode works in the Edge Settings screen. Reveal Edge settings by clicking the ellipse menu and selecting **Settings**. This displays the Settings screen as shown in Figure 3-11.

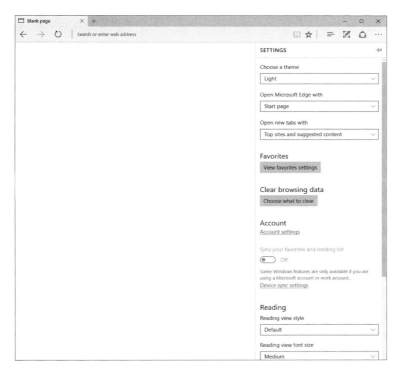

Figure 3-11   Edge Settings Screen

The Favorites button behaves similarly to Favorites in IE; however, Edge adds a new Reading List option that allows you to add pages as reading list items to read later. These links appear in the Edge Hub.

The Edge Hub is accessed from the three-line icon to the right of the Favorites star. From the Hub you have access to your favorites, reading list, history, and downloads. You can clear your downloads and history from the Hub as well.

The icon to the right of the Hub icon provides access to Web Notes. This feature ties into OneNote on your device. From this interface you can highlight portions of the page, draw with the pen, snip a portion of the page, and save snippets and notes to OneNote.

The latest version of Microsoft Edge also includes the capability to add extensions. Clicking Extensions in the ellipse menu will show the installed extensions and a link to Get Extension from the Store. Clicking the link displays some popular extensions, such as Office Online, Evernote Web Clipper, Translator for Microsoft Edge, and others.

Internet Explorer

Internet Explorer 11 includes an extensive series of new improvements; the most significant are the following:

- **Improved web browsing and navigation:** Users can access information more rapidly, with improved browsing efficiency even across slow networks. Smarter web page caching that includes prefetch and prerender help to enhance the rate of access to information.

- **Compatibility with many device types:** Supports orientation-based viewing on tablets and other portable devices. On touch-based screens, Internet Explorer 11 supports such actions as touch-based drag-and-drop, hover, and highlighting of active links. On large monitor systems, Internet Explorer supports multimonitor support and high-pixel scaling for optimal viewing experience. You can also sync your browsing history and favorites across multiple devices.

- **Phone capability:** Provides clickable links when used with phone-based apps such as Skype or Windows Phone devices.

- **Integration with Adobe Flash:** Included out-of-the box.

- **New Group Policy settings:** Additional settings enable you to control actions such as use of the swiping motion, automatic phone number detection, the provision of personalized search results, and many more.

- **Do Not Track (DNT) exceptions:** By default, websites are not allowed to track users. Websites can ask for exceptions from users based on DNT. If the user grants it, headers can be sent from the user to the website that enable tracking, allowing users to develop a trusted privacy relationship with desired websites.

- **Improved developer features:** Internet Explorer 11 supports an enhanced set of web standards, as well as new debugging utilities and APIs for actions such as animated scrolling effects and enhanced video capabilities.

Internet Explorer includes a wealth of configuration options for users and businesses. You should be familiar with the major options and how to control them and enforce policies for your business.

Compatibility View

To configure Internet Explorer to add or remove websites displayed in Compatibility View, press **Alt** to view the menu bar and then click **Tools > Compatibility View Settings**. This displays the Compatibility View Settings dialog box shown, with the current website displayed in the Add This Website text box. Click **Add** to specify that this website will be displayed in Compatibility View. This adds the website to the list under Websites You've Added to Compatibility View, thereby enabling the website to always be displayed in Compatibility View on future visits to the same website. To remove a website from this list, select it and click **Remove**. You can also modify Compatibility View settings by configuring the following two options at the bottom of the Compatibility View Settings dialog box:

- **Display Intranet Sites in Compatibility View:** Select this check box if your company's intranet websites were designed for older versions of Internet Explorer. This check box is selected by default.

- **Use Microsoft Compatibility Lists:** Microsoft provides lists of websites that function better in Compatibility View. These lists also include lists of hardware devices, such as graphics devices, that have known compatibility issues. Selecting this check box enables these lists to be downloaded and used. This check box is selected by default.

You can also use Group Policy to configure Compatibility View in an Active Directory Domain Services (AD DS) domain. From either the Computer Configuration or User Configuration section of the Group Policy Object Editor, access the **Administrative Templates\Windows Components\Internet Explorer\ Compatibility View** node. This provides the following policies:

- **Turn On Internet Explorer 7 Standards Mode:** Forces all websites to display in a mode compatible with Internet Explorer 7.

- **Turn Off Compatibility View:** Prevents users from using the Compatibility View feature or the Compatibility View Settings dialog box.

- **Turn On Internet Explorer Standards Mode for Local Intranet:** Controls the display of local intranet websites so that they appear in a mode compatible with Internet Explorer 7. Enable this setting if your company's intranet websites do not display properly in Internet Explorer 11.

- **Turn Off Compatibility View Button:** Prevents users from using the Compatibility View button on the toolbar.

- **Include Updated Website Lists from Microsoft:** Enables the browser to use the compatible website lists provided by Microsoft. These websites are automatically displayed in Compatibility View.

- **Use Policy List of Internet Explorer 7 Sites:** Enables users to add specific sites that are displayed in Compatibility View.

- **Use Policy List of Quirks Mode Sites:** Enables Internet Explorer to use an Internet Explorer 7 user agent string of websites, which are displayed in Quirks Mode. This mode enables Internet Explorer to match the behavior of other leading browsers while retaining the compatibility support generally expected by users.

SmartScreen Filter

The SmartScreen Filter first introduced in Internet Explorer 8 and continued in versions 9, 10, and 11 enhances the capabilities of the phishing filter first introduced with Internet Explorer 7. Besides checking websites against a list of reported phishing sites, this filter checks software downloads against a list of reported malware websites. The practice of *phishing* refers to the creation of a fake website that closely mimics a real website and contains a similar-looking URL, intending to scam users into sending confidential personal information, such as credit card or bank account numbers, birthdates, Social Security numbers, and so on. The attacker sends email messages that appear to originate from the company whose website was spoofed so that users connect to the fake website and provide this type of information. The attacker can use this information for identity theft and other nefarious purposes.

Microsoft built the SmartScreen Filter into Internet Explorer 11 to check websites for phishing activity using the following methods:

- Comparing website addresses visited by users with dynamically updated lists of reported legitimate sites saved on your computer.

- Comparing website addresses against lists of dynamically updated lists of sites reported as downloading malicious software to your computer.

- Analyzing website addresses against characteristics (such as misspelled words) used by phishing sites.

- Comparing website addresses with those in an online service that Microsoft operates for immediate checking against a list of reported phishing sites. This list is updated several times each hour using material gathered by Microsoft or other industries or reported by users. Other global databases of known phishing sites are also used.

If the SmartScreen Filter detects a known phishing or malware site, Internet Explorer displays the address bar in red and replaces the website with a message informing you of the risks. You receive options to close the website or continue to it. If the site is not a known phishing or malware site but behaves in a similar manner to such a site, the address bar appears in yellow and a warning message appears. The user can report the site to the Microsoft SmartScreen Filter list or gather further information to report a false positive if the site turns out to be legitimate.

Use the following procedure to configure the SmartScreen Filter:

Step 1.   Open Internet Explorer to a website that you suspect might be a phishing site, or access SmartScreen Filter from the Tools menu.

Step 2.   On the Safety menu, select one of the following options:

- **Check This Website:** Checks the current website. Click **OK** in the SmartScreen Filter message box that appears to receive a message informing you of the result.

- **Turn On SmartScreen Filter:** Displays a dialog box that enables you to turn the filter on or off as desired. This menu item appears as Turn Off SmartScreen Filter when the filter is already on.

- **Report Unsafe Website:** Enables you to report a phishing website or remove an authentic site that has been flagged as a phishing one.

Internet Explorer Group Policies

There is a wealth of other options also available for IE 11. Selecting Internet Options from the IE gear menu displays the tabbed dialog box with the following tabs:

- **General:** Includes the IE home page, startup options, tab control options, browsing history, and appearance settings.

- **Security:** Used to configure trust levels for websites and the security level to use.

- **Privacy:** Control handling of cookies, whether to provide location to websites, pop-up blocker, and InPrivate browsing.

- **Content:** Options for SSL encryption certificates, AutoComplete behavior, and feeds and Web Slices.

- **Connections:** This tab allows you to set up an Internet connection, VPN, and configure LAN settings.

- **Programs:** Set IE as the default browser in this tab, and manage add-ons, HTML editing, and configure default programs for email.

- **Advanced:** Configure advanced IE settings, or reset IE settings to their installation defaults.

You should be generally familiar with these options and how they work.

Organizations usually want to control how IE is configured in the enterprise, and this is done through Group Policy. Figure 3-12 shows the comprehensive list of Group Policies available under \Computer Configuration\Administrative Templates\Windows Components\Internet Explorer.

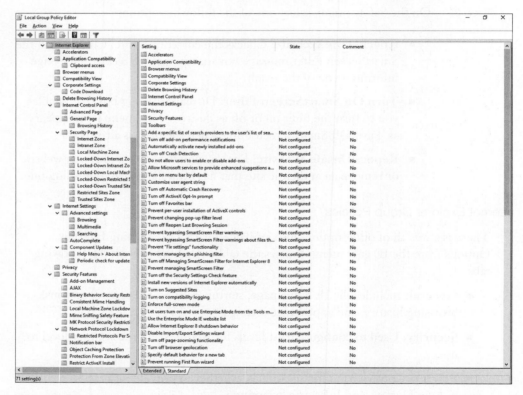

Figure 3-12   Group Policies for Internet Explorer

As you can see, there are Group Policies for controlling every aspect of Internet Explorer and users' web browsing experience in general. For instance, if you enable the **Prevent Bypassing SmartScreen Filter Warnings** policy, users will not be able to click through to websites that SmartScreen has detected as a security issue. This helps improve the security profile of the organization.

When controlled through Group Policies, generally users will be blocked from modifying those settings in the Internet Options dialogs.

NOTE   For more information on Group Policies for Internet Explorer, see the topics listed in "Group Policy and Internet Explorer 11" at https://technet.microsoft.com/en-us/itpro/internet-explorer/ie11-deploy-guide/group-policy-and-ie11.

Internet Explorer Compared to Edge

Internet Explorer is not shown on the taskbar or Start menu when Windows 10 is first installed. You can find it by searching for Internet Explorer or by switching your default browser in the Default Apps Settings screen. Edge also includes an option on the ellipse, Open with Internet Explorer, that will open the current page in IE. Each of these browsers presents a slightly different experience. The major differences in the two browsers are as follows:

- Edge is a streamlined mobile-friendly version that behaves in a manner similar to that of other Windows Universal apps, whereas IE behaves in a similar fashion to Internet Explorer in Windows 8.1 and Windows 7.

- Edge does not support ActiveX controls.

- Edge includes several features not available in IE:

  - Web Note

  - Reading List

  - Cortana

- IE includes nine document modes for emulation of older IE versions.

To improve the web browser experience in organizations with legacy applications, you can configure Windows to always open specific sites in IE 11 that require ActiveX controls or older IE version compatibility. To configure a list of sites to automatically use IE, enable the Group Policy **Allows You to Configure the Enterprise Mode Site List**, which is found in the GPO under \Computer Configuration\Administrative Templates\Windows Components\Microsoft Edge.

This policy requires an XML document stored on a Windows share. Windows 10 devices will access the XML document to determine which sites to automatically load in IE instead of Microsoft Edge. You create the document using a downloadable tool called the Enterprise Mode Site List Manager. Enter any site in the tool and select **Open in IE 11** for the sites and domains that require it. Save the file to a network share and configure the Group Policy to use the file.

> **NOTE**   For more information on using Enterprise Mode, see "Use Enterprise Mode to Improve Compatibility" at https://technet.microsoft.com/en-us/itpro/microsoft-edge/emie-to-improve-compatibility.

Configuring Hyper-V

You learn details about virtualization, managing Hyper-V virtual machines and devices, and other topics needed for Exam 70-697 in Chapter 10, "Windows Hyper-V." Even if you are only taking the 70-698 exam, you should study that chapter to ensure you have a thorough understanding of Hyper-V and how to configure it for Windows 10.

Recall from Table 2-3 in Chapter 2 that Hyper-V requires some additional requirements above the base requirements of Windows 10; namely, you must use a 64-bit edition of Windows 10 Pro, Enterprise, or Education. Your computer must also have a processor that supports virtualization. Virtualized machines will also take up disk space, parts of RAM, and slices of the processor cores for themselves, so you should plan for those additional resources, depending on the number of virtual machines that will be set up on the device.

Hyper-V is not installed by default. To install it, open Control Panel, select Programs and Features, and then choose Turn Windows Features On or Off. Check the box for Hyper-V and click OK to install all the Hyper-V features. If your computer cannot support Hyper-V, the **Hyper-V Platform** option will be grayed out, as shown in Figure 13-13.

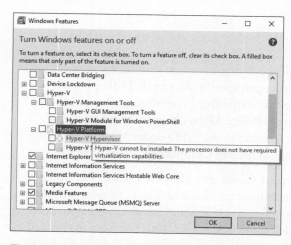

Figure 3-13   Hyper-V Installation Disabled on a Computer Without Required Processor Capabilities

After Hyper-V is installed, you can run the Hyper-V Manager and begin creating virtual machines, virtual switches, and other devices. For details on creating and managing virtual machines, see Chapter 10, "Windows Hyper-V."

Configuring Power Settings

Microsoft has dedicated a lot of resources to ensuring that Windows runs efficiently on many devices, especially to conserve power on portable devices and phones. Access the power configuration by clicking the **Action Center**, selecting **System** from the Settings screen, and then clicking on **Power & Sleep**. A link called Additional Power Settings displays the Power Options Control Center applet, where you can change your power plan or change power plan settings.

If you are using a mobile device, you will also see battery options, which allow you to adjust battery saver options for your device. Different settings are available for when the device is plugged in and when it is running on battery power.

Exam 70-697 also requires you to know about configuring power settings, and this topic is covered in more depth in Chapter 11, "Configuring and Securing Mobile Devices." Be sure to review the "Power Policies" section in that chapter.

Configuring Devices and Device Drivers

Device drivers are software utilities that enable hardware components to communicate with the operating system. All components that you see in Device Manager—including disk drives, display adapters, network interface cards, removable media (CD-ROM, DVD-ROM, and so on) drives, keyboards, mice, sound cards, USB controllers, and so on—utilize drivers for this purpose. External components such as printers, scanners, and so on also use drivers. With each new version of the operating system, it becomes necessary for hardware manufacturers to produce new drivers. Drivers written for older operating systems, such as Windows Vista or Windows 7, might work with Windows 10 but can result in reduced device functionality, or they might not work at all. Windows 10 shares the same driver model as Windows 8.1, so most drivers should work the same. You need to be able to install, configure, and troubleshoot drivers for various components for the 70-698 exam and for real-world computer support tasks.

When you first install or upgrade your computer to Windows 10, the operating system searches for hardware devices attached to your system and loads drivers required for these devices to function. In most cases, this process occurs automatically without the user even knowing that it's taking place. It is only when the operating system is unable to locate the proper drivers for a device that you become aware that a problem might exist.

Windows 8 and 8.1 brought about several improvements to hardware drivers for new hardware components and features. Windows 10 continues support for new hardware and features. Some of the recent improvements in Windows hardware support include the following:

- **Support for USB 3.0:** First introduced with Windows 8, Windows 10 includes a new driver stack in support of USB 3.0 devices. Included is support for new capabilities of USB 3.0, including static streams support and remote suspend and wake-up features according to the USB 3.0 specification.

- **Support for the USB Attached SCSI Protocol (UASP):** Windows 10 includes a USB storage driver that uses static streams for bulk endpoints, according to the implementation of UASP.

- **Support for Windows To Go:** Windows To Go enables booting Windows from a flash drive or external drive. Support for the required drivers is included.

- **New device driver interfaces:** New interfaces are included that support the new features and improvements in Windows 10 and USB 3.0.

- **Enhanced diagnostic and debugging capabilities:** Windows 10 provides utilities that facilitate the rapid diagnosis of USB 3.0 problems. Included are USB 3.0 kernel debugger extensions that examine USB 3.0 host controller and device statuses.

- **New diagnostic failure messages in Device Manager:** Provided are USB 3.0-specific error messages that describe the reason for failure to enumerate an attached USB device.

In addition to driver installation, Windows Update offers updates to software applications installed on your computer and the operating system itself. We discussed Windows Update in Chapter 2, "Implementing Windows."

Device Setup

When you connect a Plug and Play (PnP) device to a Windows 10 computer, Windows automatically makes the device ready to use by automatically locating and installing all required software so that the device will function as intended. Included in the setup process is the distribution of device drivers, metadata, and Windows Store apps. The device metadata contains information about the device. Windows Store device apps are provided by device manufacturers to enhance device functionality in Windows 10; such apps are automatically distributed to users from the Windows Store according to instructions contained in the device metadata.

You can initiate device setup either manually or automatically in several fashions, by performing such actions as plugging in a USB device, using the Add a Device Wizard to recognize a Bluetooth device or Windows phone, setting up a network printer, adding the device to the network to which the computer is connected, connecting the computer to a new network (thereby initiating the setup of network devices accessed by the computer), and so on. Installing hardware devices typically takes three steps:

Step 1. **Adding the device:** For internal devices such as hard drives or network adapters, you need to shut down your computer and, for some devices, open the case and insert it into the appropriate expansion slot or bay. For a USB or FireWire device, you plug it into a connector located somewhere on the computer. For network devices, you plug them into the network or plug the computer into a new network.

Step 2. **Locating appropriate device drivers for the device:** Windows detects the device at startup and displays a message on the taskbar that it is installing device driver software. In most cases, this message goes away within a few seconds and your device is ready for use.

Step 3. **Configuring device settings:** For PnP devices, this generally happens automatically. If Windows is unable to locate the driver, it requests any needed information, including any manufacturer-supplied media. You might also be able to locate hardware drivers from the Microsoft Windows Update website.

When device setup is complete, a sound is played. If a Windows Store device app is associated with the device, a tile for the device app appears on the Start screen.

Devices and Printers

Devices and Printers works like Device Stage in Windows 7, but is now part of the Control Panel in Windows 10. It acts as a home page for hardware devices, providing a single location from which you can manage all devices that have been properly installed on your computer, as shown in Figure 3-14. You can access Devices and Printers by selecting **Control Panel** from **Start > Windows Settings**, and then selecting **View Devices and Printers** under the Hardware and Sound category. You can also use Cortana to search for **devices**.

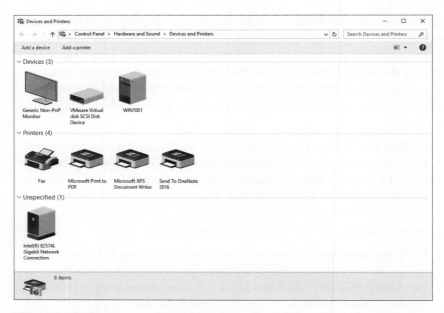

Figure 3-14   Devices and Printers Applet in Control Panel Displaying All Devices Connected to the Computer

When you connect a device, Devices and Printers attempts to add it automatically with the aid of an XML-based definition file provided by the manufacturer. If the device is not automatically detected, you can click **Add a Device** to start the Add a Device Wizard that searches for devices that might be attached to your computer. Ensure that your device is properly plugged in and turned on. The wizard should display a selection of device types from which you can select the appropriate device. Click **Next** and follow the remaining steps presented to install your device. When the process is complete, the device is added to the Devices list shown in Figure 3-14.

TIP   If you do not want Windows to automatically download drivers for new hardware devices, you can modify this behavior. Access the Hardware tab of the System Properties dialog box and click the **Device Installation Settings** command button. On the dialog box that appears, click **No (Your Device Might Not Work as Expected)**. Select the desired option from those displayed in Figure 3-15, and then click **Save Changes**.

Figure 3-15   Modifying the Default Driver Installation Behavior

> **NOTE**   For more information on setting up and configuring device drivers in Windows, refer to "Overview of Device and Driver Installation" and the topic links at https://msdn.microsoft.com/en-us/windows/hardware/drivers/install/overview-of-device-and-driver-installation.

Updating Drivers

Windows Update provides a seamless, automatic means of updating all the device drivers on your computer. Windows Update does not display driver updates individually. Windows now installs drivers for Windows 10 and many devices automatically through Windows Update.

Microsoft places drivers on the Update site only if they are digitally signed, meet certain Web publishing standards, and have passed the testing requirements for the Windows Certification Program. These procedures verify that drivers included on the site are certified to do what they are supposed to do.

Using Device Manager

The majority of the work involving device implementation, management, and troubleshooting for many types of hardware devices is found in the Device Manager utility. You can run Device Manager either as a standalone Microsoft Management Console (MMC) snap-in or as a component of the Computer Management snap-in.

You can access Device Manager in any of the following ways:

- Right-click **Start** and choose **Computer Management**. This opens the Computer Management console, from which you can open Device Manager by clicking its icon in the console tree.

- Right-click **Start** and choose **Device Manager**. This opens Device Manager in its own console.

- From a File Explorer window, right-click **This PC** and choose **Properties**. Then select **Device Manager** from the list of options in the left column.

- From Cortana or the Search bar, type **device manager** into the Search box. Then click **Device Manager**.

- From the Settings icon on the **Start** menu, select **Devices**, select the **Printers & Scanners** category, and then select **Device Manager** under Related Settings.

- From the Hardware tab of the System Properties dialog box, click **Device Manager**.

As shown in Figure 3-16, Device Manager displays a list of all types of hardware components that might be installed on your computer. Click the arrows (>) on the various device categories to expand them and display the actual devices that are present (as shown for monitors and network adapters).

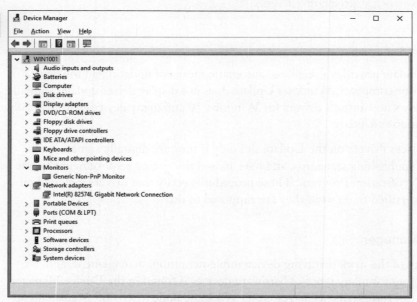

Figure 3-16 Device Manager Enables You to Configure and Troubleshoot All Hardware Devices on Your Computer

After you determine that a hardware device is installed correctly and is listed in the Windows Certification Program, you should check to see whether the device is detected by Windows 10 and is functioning by checking Device Manager for its listing. Devices shown in Device Manager might display icons that indicate their status. These include the following:

- If a device is disabled, an icon with a black downward-pointing arrow appears over the device icon. A disabled device is a device that is physically present in the computer and is consuming resources, but does not have a protected-mode driver loaded.

- A red X appearing over the device icon indicates that the device is disabled.

- A black exclamation point icon on a yellow triangle background appearing next to the device icon indicates that a device is functioning but experiencing problems.

- A yellow question mark icon in place of the device's icon indicates a hardware device that is not properly installed or is in conflict with another device in the system.

- A blue "i" (for Information) on a white field indicates that the device has been configured manually with resource configurations.

When you right-click a device, a shortcut menu similar to the one displayed in Figure 3-17 appears. You can select to update the driver, or uninstall or disable the device. You may also scan the device for hardware changes or access the device's properties. When you open the device's Properties dialog box, you can put a variety of configurations into effect, as well as disable or enable the device.

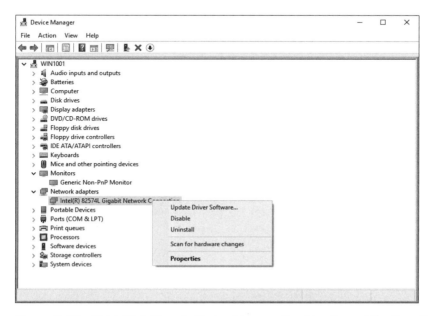

Figure 3-17 Right-Click Menu in Device Manager Provides Several Configuration Options

Every device has its own Properties dialog box (see Figure 3-18), specific to its device type and sometimes specific to the manufacturer and model (depending on the installed driver). Table 3-2 describes the standard tabs found in any device's Properties dialog box (not all these tabs are found for every device, and manufacturers might add additional tabs not included here).

 Table 3-2   Tabs Found in a Device's Properties Dialog Box

Tool	Description
General	Displays the device's description and status.
Advanced	Provides additional configurable properties.
Driver	Displays the current device driver's information, and enables you to perform several configuration options.
Details	Displays the device's specifications. You can choose from a long list of device properties.
Events	Displays a time-based list of actions that have occurred with regard to the device. Actions include such things as installing and configuring drivers, adding services, and so on.
Resources	Displays the system resources being consumed, including interrupt requests (IRQs), input/output (I/O) ports, and physical memory range. Displays whether these resources are in conflict with any others being used in the system.
Power Management	Provides options to allow the computer to turn off the device when not in use to save power, and allow the device to wake the computer from Sleep mode.

Figure 3-18   Configure Specific Device Properties Using the Properties Dialog Box for the Device

Using Device Manager to Uninstall Drivers

When you uninstall a device driver, the driver is completely removed from the computer. To uninstall a driver, right-click the device in Device Manager and choose **Uninstall**. In the Confirm Device Uninstall dialog box shown in Figure 3-19, select the **Delete the Driver Software for This Device** check box, if desired, and then click **OK**. Note that Windows will redetect the device at the next restart (if the device is still attached to the computer) and attempt to reinstall it.

Figure 3-19   Uninstalling a Driver

Using Device Manager to Disable Drivers

Rather than uninstalling the device completely, you can disable the driver. The hardware configuration is not changed. Right-click the device in Device Manager and choose **Disable**. You receive a confirmation message box. Click **Yes** to disable the driver. The device appears in Device Manager with a small black arrow indicating that it is disabled. To reenable the device, right-click it again and choose **Enable**. The device is reenabled without any further prompts.

Maintaining Device Drivers

Manufacturers often release updated drivers for their devices, which provide new features or improve the functionality of their device. Occasionally an updated driver will not function properly on a particular machine. At times, you might need to download an updated driver from Microsoft or the manufacturer's website to fix problems with device functionality caused by poorly written drivers or by changing technology. You need to know how to maintain device drivers to ensure that all the computers in your responsibility function properly, and individuals using these computers can get their work done.

Managing and Troubleshooting Drivers and Driver Signing

Driver signing is a process that Microsoft follows to validate files that a third-party manufacturer creates for use in a Windows 10 computer. A manufacturer submits its drivers to Microsoft, and after Microsoft completes a thorough quality assurance testing process, Microsoft signs the files digitally. This digital signature is an electronic security mark that indicates the publisher of the software and information that can determine whether a driver has been altered. Driver signing is an extra assurance of the quality of the software installed on the computer.

Device drivers that are included on the Windows 10 installation DVD or downloaded from the Microsoft Update website include a Microsoft digital signature. If you have problems installing a driver, or if a device is not working properly, you should access Windows Update as described earlier in this chapter to look for optional driver updates. You should also visit the device manufacturer's support website to obtain an up-to-date digitally signed driver for your device.

Driver Signing Requirements in Windows 10

The following driver signing requirements were initiated in Windows 7 and continued through to Windows 10:

- Standard (nonadministrative) users can install only drivers that have been signed by either a Windows publisher or trusted publisher. These drivers are placed in a protected location on the computer called the *driver store*. Microsoft implemented this requirement because drivers run as a part of the operating system with unrestricted access to the entire computer. Therefore, it is critical that only properly authorized drivers be permitted.

- Standard users cannot install unsigned drivers or drivers that have been signed by an untrusted publisher; you cannot modify this policy in Windows 10.

- Administrators can install drivers that have been signed by an untrusted publisher, and they can also add the publisher's certificate to the trusted certificates store, thereby enabling standard users to install drivers signed by this publisher. This is known as *staging* driver packages.

- If drivers are unsigned or have been altered, administrators are warned. They can proceed in a manner similar to how they would if the drivers were from an untrusted publisher.

- All new Windows 10 kernel mode drivers must be submitted to and digitally signed by the Windows Hardware Developer Center Dashboard portal, a Microsoft service for hardware developers.

NOTE   You cannot install a driver that lacks a valid digital signature, or one that was altered after it was signed, on x64-based versions of Windows.

If you install a device, Windows 10 looks for the driver signature as a part of System File Protection, which is a feature that prevents applications from replacing critical Windows files by creating and maintaining backups of many critical program files. When it fails to find one, Windows notifies you that the drivers are not signed and prompts you to continue or stop the installation, provided you have administrative privileges. Otherwise, the installation attempt fails. If you continue with the installation, Windows 10 automatically creates a restore point, which facilitates returning to the previous configuration. Restore points are discussed in more depth in Chapter 20, "Configuring System Recovery Options."

> **NOTE**   For more details on signing and staging device drivers, refer to the topic "Device and Driver Installation Fundamental Topics" at https:// msdn.microsoft.com/en-us/windows/hardware/drivers/install/device-and-driver-installation-fundamental-topics. Information in this guide should be applicable to Windows 10 and Windows Server 2016. Note that Microsoft has recently changed its driver signing requirements. See "Driver Signing Changes in Windows 10, Version 1607" at https://blogs.msdn.microsoft.com/windows_hardware_certification/ 2016/07/26/driver-signing-changes-in-windows-10-version-1607.

Checking Drivers for Digital Signatures

Dynamic-link libraries (DLLs) and other files are often shared by programs. Sometimes a program overwrites files that were originally installed by a digitally signed driver. If a device behaves oddly, you might want to verify that its driver still has the signature. You can check to validate the driver by looking in Device Manager. Double-click the device and click the **Driver** tab of its Properties dialog box. You should see this statement: **Digital Signer: Microsoft Windows** or **Digital Signer: Microsoft Windows Hardware Compatibility Publisher**.

You can check individual files further by clicking the **Driver Details** button. Files that are signed have an icon of a sealed certificate, which appears to the left of the name. Files that have not been digitally signed do not have a certificate icon next to the filename.

If you want to verify device drivers throughout the system, you can run the sigverif application. To do so, access Cortana or the Search bar and type **sigverif** into the Search field. Then click **Run Command**. The File Signature Verification program starts, as shown in Figure 3-20. Click the **Advanced** button and verify that **sigverif** will log the results and save them to a file. Click **OK** and then click **Start**. After the program has completed its check, the program displays any files that were not signed in a window, and you can see the results in the Sigverif.txt file. If the program does not detect any unsigned files, it displays a message box with the message,

Your Files Have Been Scanned and Verified as Digitally Signed. Otherwise, it displays a list of files that have not been digitally signed.

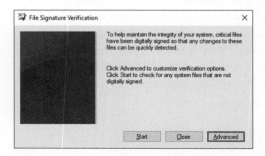

Figure 3-20   File Signature Verification Program Checking All Drivers for Digital Signatures

Unsigned drivers might not cause a problem. If you are having problems with a device that has an unsigned driver, you should disable the driver. If you are having unspecified problems, such as the computer does not go into Sleep mode, you should determine which devices have unsigned drivers, disable them one at a time, and then test to see whether the problem is resolved. To disable an unsigned driver that has already been installed, you should disable the device that uses the driver, uninstall the driver, or rename the driver files.

TIP   When in doubt, check the system files. The System File Checker, which you can execute from an administrative command line with sfc.exe, can check the digital signature of system protected files. With other uses, such as repopulating the DLLCACHE folder and replacing system files that are missing or incorrect, you can execute sfc.exe from a batch program or script. This program has several options; the /scannow option is one of the most useful, scanning the integrity of all protected system files and performing repairs where possible. This process takes several minutes. To view information on all available options, run **sfc.exe /?**. Note that in Windows 10, as was the case in Windows Vista and 7, you must run this command as an administrator; right-click the Command Prompt option, select **Run as Administrator** from the list of options displayed at the bottom of the screen, and then click **Yes** in the UAC dialog box.

Driver Installation Permissions in Windows 10

In versions of Windows prior to Windows 7, only users with administrative privileges could install drivers. Consequently, many enterprises provided their users with local administrative rights; this enables users to perform these tasks, but they also allowed users to undertake actions that could compromise security or configure the computer so that it would not run properly. These actions resulted in increased support costs and demands on the help desk.

In Windows 10, as was the case in Windows 7, an administrator can implement a policy that prevents the installation of a driver according to its device ID or device setup class. If such a policy is present, Windows will not install devices that are forbidden by these policies. An administrator can also permit standard users to install device drivers that are members of specified device setup classes.

Managing Driver Packages

A *driver package*, in essence, is the full set of files installed as part of a device driver. When you select the Driver Details button on the driver properties Driver tab, a list of the files associated with the driver is displayed. For many drivers, these files make up the entirety of the driver package. All files that make up the driver are considered critical to installation of the device.

Some manufacturers may deliver a driver package with a richer set of functionality than a simple interface to the operating system. Instead, some driver packages include a custom user interface (UI), utilities, administration tools and other software. These packages are usually deployed as installable files, such as executables or Microsoft Software Installer (MSI) files, and provide the user with additional features for controlling the device.

Examples of devices that will often include a richer driver package include the following:

- Printer drivers often include diagnostic software, custom color adjustments, or calibration tools.

- Digital cameras and camcorders often include customized UI screens to allow the user to copy pictures and videos to the computer or its own photo sharing software.

- Scanners nearly always include additional software and control packages for use in previewing scans, adjusting the scan image, conversion programs, or Optical Character Recognition (OCR) capability.

These are just a few examples. Other devices may also include rich driver packages, and not all printers, cameras, and scanners require custom user interfaces. But you should have an idea of the potential varied functionality that could be included in a driver package.

When you install a device driver in Windows 10, it adds the driver to the driver store for the system. Administrators can install signed and unsigned drivers to the store, which will make them available for any user who plugs in a matching device.

In this way, standard images can be deployed with drivers for all the devices typically used in a business, and they will be available for any user.

You can add drivers to the store using a setup program provided by Microsoft or the device manufacturer, by including the drivers in a Windows Setup answer file during an automated deployment, or using the PnPUtil program.

PnPUtil is a command-line utility for installing and staging device drivers using an .inf file. It requires an administrative command prompt and the name of the driver .inf file. You can use several parameters with the PnPUtil command to manage drivers:

- **/e** is used to enumerate (or list) all third-party driver packages.

- **/a** is used to add the driver to the driver store.

- **/i** is used to install the driver package.

- **/d** is used to delete the package associated with the .inf file.

> **NOTE**   For more details on PnPUtil, reference "PnPUtil Examples" at https://msdn.microsoft.com/en-us/windows/hardware/drivers/devtest/pnputil-examples?f=255&MSPPError=-2147217396.

Resolving Driver Issues

Even with all the improvements Microsoft has made in device and driver management in recent Windows versions, problems still occur. Drivers use system resources, including IRQ lines, I/O ports, and physical memory addresses. If two hardware components attempt to use the same location of any of these resources, a conflict results and these components will not work. For example, you install a new scanner and discover that your network adapter does not work. Such a situation happens more often when using a non-PnP device. In such a situation, you should check resource assignments for conflicts. It is frequently necessary to modify settings on the non-PnP device, for example, with the aid of jumpers or DIP switches. Some devices may have configuration settings available in the computer BIOS, such as built-in devices. Reconfigure the device with the aid of manufacturer instructions, which may be located on a label placed on the device or manufacturer's documentation.

In this section, we take a look at troubleshooting driver resource conflicts and resolving other driver issues.

Using Device Manager to Resolve Driver Conflicts

You can use Device Manager to determine whether a resource conflict exists by changing the view. Device Manager offers several view types that assist in monitoring, as described in Table 3-3.

Table 3-3   Device Manager Views

View	What It Displays
Devices by type	Displays devices by the type of installed device, such as monitor or mouse. This is the default view. If you have multiple monitors, for example, you see each of the monitors displayed below the Monitor node.
Devices by connection	Displays devices according to the type of connection, For example, all the disk drives and CD or DVD drives connected to the SATA controller are displayed under the SATA connection node.
Resources by type	Displays devices according to resource type, including I/O, IRQ, and memory. For example, Figure 3-21 shows devices listed in the order of the I/O resources it uses.
Resources by connection	Displays resources according to their type of connection. This also serves to indicate which resources are currently available.

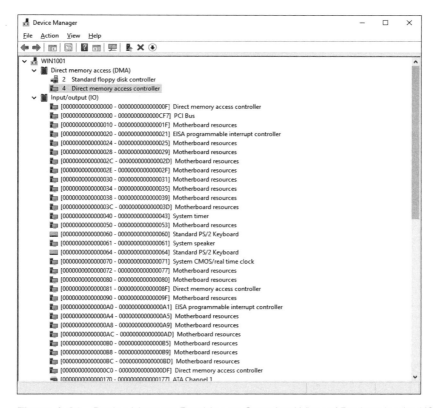

Figure 3-21   Device Manager Provides an Organized View of Devices by the I/O Resources They Consume

The View menu also offers two customization options that affect what you see. To expand the views to show non–PnP devices, select **Show Hidden Devices**. To modify what items Device Manager shows, select **Customize**. This displays the Customize View dialog box shown in Figure 3-22, which enables you to select what items are shown by Device Manager.

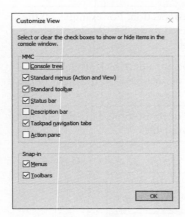

Figure 3-22   Select Which Items Are Displayed in the Device Manager Window

To view resources being used by a specific device, access the Resources tab of the device's Properties dialog box. As shown in Figure 3-23, this tab displays a list of all resources in use and reports conflicts that might be occurring. To change resource settings, clear the **Use Automatic Settings** check box and then click **Change Setting**. In the dialog box that appears, select a setting that does not conflict with other settings. Device Manager will inform you if these settings conflict with any other devices; if so, modify the settings so that no conflicts occur and then click **OK**.

Figure 3-23   Resources Tab of a Device's Properties Dialog Box Displaying All Resources in Use and Informing You of Any Conflicts

Use of the Action Center to View Device-Related Problems

The Windows 10 Action Center also offers information on device-related problems. Action Center is a central place for viewing alerts and taking actions that can help resolve issues and keep Windows running reliably. Action Center uses notifications to report problems that have occurred on your computer; you can click the problems displayed to obtain additional information.

When a problem occurs, you can allow Action Center to search for solutions on the Internet. The user is notified when a solution to a device-related problem is found. A web link is supplied, and notification is suppressed after the user has installed the application. Action Center can also display messages alerting you to problems and solutions related to devices that don't post drivers at Windows Update. The user is alerted to the need to download and install a driver update and a link is provided, specifying the device and providing links to the latest signed driver from the manufacturer's site.

Use of System Information to View Device-Related Problems

The System Information utility is another place you can check devices and locate potential problems. In the taskbar Search field, type **msinfo32**, and then click **msinfo32.exe**. Expand the Hardware Resources category to obtain information, as shown in Figure 3-24. Note that the information displayed in the Conflicts/Sharing subnode does not necessarily indicate problems, because some resources can be shared without creating a problem. Also note the Forced Hardware node, which displays information about devices whose default configuration has been modified by the user. Information in this node can be useful when troubleshooting resource conflicts.

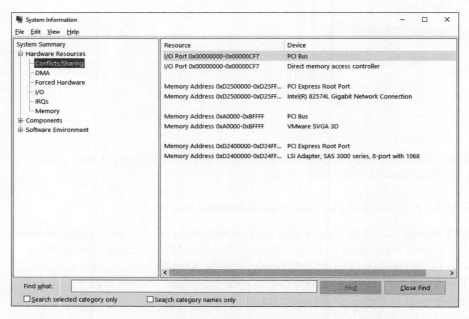

Figure 3-24   System Information Displaying Details About Hardware Resources, Including Resource Conflicts and Sharing

Using Windows 10 Rollback to Resolve a Problem Driver

If you update an existing driver to a new version and then you experience system problems, you should roll back the driver to the previous version. In versions of Windows prior to Windows XP, this was almost impossible to do. As was the case in previous versions of Windows, Windows 10 maintains a copy of the previous driver each time a new one is updated. If, at any time, you want to restore the previous version, simply roll back the driver (we cover rolling back a driver in the following section, "Configuring Driver Settings").

TIP   It is usually helpful to create a Restore point before installing the new driver. This enables you to restore your computer to its status before the driver installation, using the System Restore feature. Use of System Restore for performing these actions is covered in Chapter 20, "Configuring System Recovery Options."

You can roll back all device drivers except for printers. You might receive a UAC prompt before either updating a driver or rolling it back to a previous version.

In some cases, your computer might not even start after installing a problem driver and rebooting. You can try the following options:

- Reset This PC resets the device to a fresh install. This is especially helpful if you are unsure how the problem started.

- Automatic Repair looks for common issues, including recent device changes, and attempts to resolve the issue automatically.

- You can also use System Image Recovery if you have a recent image and Recovery Drive available.

- If you are unsure which driver is causing the issue, you can use your PC's Startup and Recovery dialog, as shown in Figure 3-25, to enable options like boot logging, Safe Mode, and disable automatic restart on system failure to gather more information about the problem.

We discuss these and other startup options in Chapter 20.

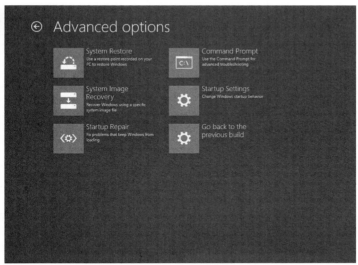

Figure 3-25   Advanced Options in Windows 10 Startup Provides Alternate Troubleshooting Tools for Resolving Driver Issues

Configuring Driver Settings

Like Windows 7 and Windows 8.1, Windows 10 provides access to a comprehensive list of device driver settings for each device. Ordinarily you would not need to change these settings from their installation defaults, but you should understand some of the more common settings and how to modify them if needed, for the 70-698 exam and when working as a Windows support professional.

In previous sections we covered some of the basic driver settings, such as resources, drivers, and how to modify those. This section covers some of the more advanced settings, when they might be needed, and how to adjust the settings when necessary.

Driver Verifier

Windows Driver Verifier is included in all versions of Windows since Windows 2000, and in versions of Windows Server 2003 and later. You can use this tool to troubleshoot issues with a driver or to help identify any driver or driver setting that may be causing an issue.

Use Driver Verifier by starting Verifier, selecting the options you want, and restarting the computer. Verifier checks the drivers based on your options and collects the information for you to review.

Step 1.   To start Driver Verifier, click in the **Search** bar, type **verifier** into the Search box, and select **Run Command** under *verifier* from the results that appear. The Driver Verifier dialog box shown in Figure 3-26 appears, allowing you to select from a list of settings for how to run the Verifier.

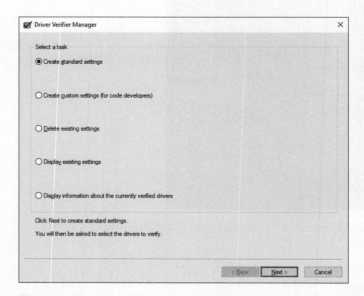

Figure 3-26   Driver Verifier Manager Provides Several Driver Verification Options

Step 2.   From the Select a Task screen of the Driver Verifier Manager, select **Create Standard Settings** and then click **Next**. This is the option to start with the first time you verify your drivers. After Verifier has run, you can choose from other Verifier Manager options:

    a. Create custom settings (for code developers).

    b. Delete existing settings.

    c. Display existing settings.

    d. Display information about the currently verified drivers.

Step 3.   The Select What Drivers to Verify screen appears. From here you can select a subset of drivers to verify based on the issue you are working to resolve. For instance, you may suspect a driver that was developed for an older Windows version, or that an unsigned driver may be causing the problem. Otherwise, select the **Automatically Select All Drivers** option and click **Next**.

Step 4.   Click the **Finish** button, and then restart Windows.

Step 5.   When Windows restarts, run Verifier again to see the results of the verifications you selected.

Driver Verifier Manager is an advanced tool for troubleshooting drivers and issues. Typically you would use this tool if you have a computer displaying bug checks or blue screens, and you need to identify which driver or device is behaving poorly.

NOTE   After you have finished working with Verifier, run the Verifier Manager again and select **Delete Existing Settings**. Verifier injects code into each driver and can affect the performance of Windows if it is left running.

NOTE   For more information on using Driver Verifier, refer to "Driver Verifier" at https://msdn.microsoft.com/en-us/windows/hardware/drivers/devtest/driver-verifier.

Advanced Driver Settings

Windows drivers will typically install with the best or most compatible settings available, based on the operating system and the underlying hardware. Situations may arise, however, when these settings need intervention for a specific use case or requirement. For instance, a network driver may fail to negotiate properly with a hub or switch and run at a slower speed than it is capable of, impacting overall performance.

Depending on the driver and manufacturer, advanced settings may be displayed on an **Advanced** tab in the driver Properties. Note the tabs available as described in Table 3-2 in the "Using Device Manager" section. Not all drivers will provide the Advanced tab. These drivers might not have options for modifying advanced settings, or they may come with additional software for managing them. For instance, many video driver settings will include an integrated application for setting options the manufacturer has made available.

As shown in Figure 3-27, there may be many advanced settings for a driver, and network adapters typically have the most. To modify a setting on this tab, select the setting you want to change from the Property box on the left, and select the setting you want from the Value selection on the right. You can modify several properties in this manner. Clicking the **OK** button applies the changes.

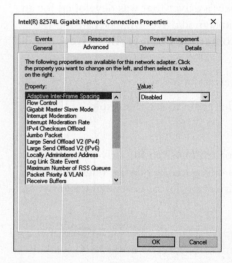

Figure 3-27 Driver Settings Available on the Advanced Tab of the Network Interface Card

You will occasionally need to modify driver settings. Table 3-4 lists some of the most common advanced driver settings that you will encounter.

Table 3-4 Common Advanced Driver settings.

Setting	Device Type	How It Is Used
Enable DMA	ATA bus or Optical Drive	Direct Memory Addressing or DMA allows disks and optical drives to perform faster. This setting may need to be adjusted if a device is malfunctioning or DMA capability was not detected properly.

Setting	Device Type	How It Is Used
Speed & Duplex	Network Adapter	The default Auto Negotiation may fail due to issues with the switch or hub, leaving the network running too slow or failing to connect. Ensure that the value for this setting matches the capabilities of the switch or hub, and select the value from the list.
Jumbo Packet	Network Adapter	This setting is typically disabled on network adapters to maintain compatibility with most Ethernet and WAN networks. However in a corporate setting with Gigabit Ethernet, enabling this setting can significantly improve network performance. Your network administrator will know if jumbo frames should be disabled or what size should be used.
Port Settings	Serial, LPT, or USB Serial Converter	Allows configuration of the device's communication characteristics, such as the speed, parity, and number of data bits. This is dependent on the requirements of the device connected to the communications port.

There are many other devices, device types, and settings that you may encounter managing Windows computers, far too many to cover here. Which ones need to be manually configured and the settings required will depend entirely on the device and operating characteristics. You will learn about them when necessary, but for the exam and as a starting point, you should know where to find these settings and the steps to modify them.

Using Deployment Image Servicing and Management (DISM) to Add Driver Packages

You were introduced to the tool capable of offline servicing, Deployment Image Servicing and Management (DISM), in Chapter 2, "Implementing Windows." The command-line tool is included in Windows 10. For previous installations of Windows, DISM can be installed with the Windows Automated Installation Kit (AIK), which can be downloaded from the Microsoft Download Center.

DISM takes the legwork out of the mix by allowing an administrator to mount the image file, similar to mounting a hard disk, and issue commands to update the image. After the updating is complete, changes are committed to the image and the file is unmounted, in which case the image is ready for the next deployment. Some key points and best practices to consider when using DISM are the following:

- Must be run as administrator.

- Service an image offline whenever possible.

- If Windows image files are split or spanned across multiple types of media, you must copy them centrally to a single folder to service. Without this, mounting the image is not possible.

- Keep architecture consistent, meaning don't inject x64 drivers into x86 images.

- Remote image updates are not currently supported. To make any changes, you must first copy the Windows image to the local machine, perform the necessary updates, and then copy the image back to the repository.

- After deployment, use the system file checker sfc.exe /verifyonly option.

TIP DISM is typically used for updating offline images, but it can also be used to update devices that are online, especially in cases when you need a fast method to standardize or update to a higher edition of Windows.

There are several parameters that you should understand when servicing images. Table 3-5 outlines some of the key parameters.

Table 3-5 Useful DISM Parameters

Command	Meaning
/Get-ImageInfo	Used to gather information from the image file, such as index number, image name, description, and image size.
/ImageFile	Used to identify the location of the source image file.
/Mount-Image	Parameter used to mount the image. When mounting the image, you must also specify an index number or the name associated with the image. This information can be extracted from the /Get-ImageInfo parameter.
/MountDir	Directory in which the image is mounted. For optimal performance, this should be on the local computer that is updating the image. **Dism /Mount-Image /ImageFile:C:\TestImages\TestImage.wim /Name:"Image Name" /Mountdir:C:\MountedImage**
/Cleanup-Mountpoints	In some cases images may become locked/orphaned and are unable to be remounted. Use this switch when experiencing trouble with mounting images that may have been previously mounted.
/Add-Package	Adds one or more install packages or cabinet files (.cab) to a mounted image. When applying multiple packages, packages are listed in the order in which they should be installed. **/Add-Package /PackagePath:[package path\package.cab] /PackagePath:[second package path\package2.cab]**

Command	Meaning
/Add-Driver	Adds a driver to the offline image. For third-party drivers, you may choose the /ForceUnsigned switch.
/Remove-Driver	Removes a driver from the offline image.
/Commit-Image	Applies changes made to a mounted image and leaves the image mounted for additional changes.
/Get-Packages	Produces a list of packages from the mounted image in the mount directory. This can also be piped > to a .txt file for easy reading.
/Get-Features	Produces a list of features by their case-sensitive name and their enabled/disabled status. This can also be piped > to a .txt file for easy reading. Used in conjunction with **/Get-FeatureInfo /FeatureName:**[*FeatureName*] to output additional details for the feature.
/Enable-Feature	Enables a specific feature.
/Disable-Feature	Disables a specific feature.
/Remove-Package	Removes an installed package.
/Unmount-Image	Unmounts the Image. Use the **/commit** or **/discard** switches to apply or cancel any changes made before the image is unmounted.
/Set-Edition	Used to change an offline windows image to a higher edition. This may also be done online with the **/AcceptEula** and **/ProductKey** switches.

NOTE   This list introduces only a few of the DISM parameters. For a full list of options, refer to "DISM Reference (Deployment Image Servicing and Management)" at https://msdn.microsoft.com/en-us/windows/hardware/commercialize/manufacture/desktop/dism-reference--deployment-image-servicing-and-management.

Now that you have an understanding of DISM and some of the key options, you'll see it in action by adding a driver package to an offline image. The first thing you need to do is obtain a copy of the source image. In this example, we use one of the default Windows image files found on the Windows 10 Enterprise installation media. To add a driver package to an offline image, perform the following steps:

Step 1.   Gather identifying information from the image using the /Get-ImageInfo option using the following command example:

```
Dism /Get-ImageInfo /ImageFile:E:\WinImages\Win10Ent-1.wim
```

Step 2.   Using either the index number or name of the image, mount the image to a temporary mount directory. This will extract the contents of the image to a directory structure in the temp mount directory specified. This process may take time depending on the speed of your computer. The following example will mount the image:

```
Dism /Mount-Image /ImageFile:E\WinImages\Win10Ent-1.wim
    /Name:"Windows 10 Enterprise" /MountDir:E:\test\offline
```

Step 3. Use the Add-Package command to add your driver or other package to the image, such as in the following command. Note that the /Image parameter points to the mount location from the /MountDir parameter in the previous command.

```
Dism /Image:E:\test\offline /Add-Package /PackagePath:E:
    \packages\MFD-Print.cab
```

Step 4. Commit changes to the image and unmount the .wim file using the command example that follows. This will repackage the image file with the package included. It may take some time depending on the speed of your computer.

```
Dism /Unmount-Image /MountDir:E:\test\offline /Commit
```

> **NOTE** When unmounting images, it is important to close all windows and applications, especially File Explorer windows. This will help prevent locks during the unmounting process.

Exam Preparation Tasks

Review All the Key Topics

Review the most important topics in the chapter, noted with the Key Topics icon in the outer margin of the page. Table 3-6 lists a reference of these key topics and the page numbers on which each is found.

Table 3-6 Key Topics for Chapter 3

Key Topic Element	Description	Page Number
Figure 3-1	Shows an example of the Start menu in the smallest configuration	144
Step List	How to make the Start menu full screen	146
Step List	Deploy Start menu and taskbar customizations using Group Policy	148
Figure 3-8	Configuring notification settings	152

Key Topic Element	Description	Page Number
List	Accessibility settings under Ease of Access	154
Figure 3-10	Cortana configuration settings	155
Step List	Configuring the SmartScreen Filter	161
Step List	Installing new hardware devices	167
Figure 3-16	Device Manager enabled you to configure and troubleshoot devices	170
Table 3-2	Tabs on a device's Properties dialog box	172
Figure 3-19	Uninstalling a driver	173
Table 3-3	Device manager views	179
Figure 3-25	Advanced options in Windows 10 Startup	183
Table 3-4	Common Advanced Driver settings	186
Step List	Adding a device driver to a Windows image	189

Complete the Tables and Lists from Memory

Print a copy of Appendix B, "Memory Tables" (found on the book's website), or at least the section for this chapter, and complete the tables and lists from memory. Appendix C, "Memory Tables Answer Key," also on the website, includes completed tables and lists to check your work.

Definitions of Key Terms

Define the following key terms from this chapter, and check your answers in the glossary.

Action Center, device driver, Device Stage, driver package, driver signing, sigverif.exe, Plug and Play (PnP), FireWire, Device Manager, interrupt request (IRQ), input/output (I/O) port address, Microsoft Edge, msinfo32

This chapter covers the following subjects:

- **Active Directory:** This section introduces Active Directory and describes the logical building blocks that Microsoft assembled in creating the structure of Active Directory. You learn about working with Active Directory Domain Service (AD DS), joining computers to a domain, and some basics of working within a domain environment.

- **Windows in an Enterprise Environment:** Larger organizations with many Windows computers to manage need tools for managing their network and the devices they support. In this topic you learn about the Image and Configuration Designer for creating standard configuration packages for Windows deployments and how to manage activation of domain-joined Windows devices using Active Directory services.

This chapter covers the following objectives for the 70-698 exam:

Implement Windows in an enterprise environment: Provision with the Windows Imaging and Configuration Designer (ICD) tool; implement Active Directory-based activation; implement volume activation using a Key Management Service (KMS); query and configure activation states using the command line; configure Active Directory, including Group Policies; configure and optimize user account control (UAC).

CHAPTER 4

Managing Windows in an Enterprise

Managing Windows computers and devices in a large organization can be challenging, but fortunately Microsoft provides many tools for administrators and technical professionals to manage a variety of devices in a large organization or an enterprise.

You will learn about a few tools in this chapter, most importantly Active Directory, as well as the Windows Imaging and Configuration Designer (ICD) and tools for managing Windows Activation on all your organization's devices.

"Do I Know This Already?" Quiz

The "Do I Know This Already?" quiz allows you to assess whether you should read this entire chapter or simply jump to the "Exam Preparation Tasks" section for review. If you are in doubt, read the entire chapter. Table 4-1 outlines the major headings in this chapter and the corresponding "Do I Know This Already?" quiz questions. You can find the answers in Appendix A, "Answers to the 'Do I Know This Already?' Quizzes."

Table 4-1 "Do I Know This Already?" Foundation Topics Section-to-Question Mapping

Foundation Topics Section	Questions Covered in This Section
Active Directory	1–6
Windows in an Enterprise Environment	7–9

CAUTION The goal of self-assessment is to gauge your mastery of the topics in this chapter. If you do not know the answer to a question or are only partially sure of the answer, you should mark that question as wrong for purposes of the self-assessment. Giving yourself credit for an answer you correctly guess skews your self-assessment results and might provide you with a false sense of security.

1. Which of the following are logical components of an Active Directory structure? (Choose all that apply.)

    a. Forests

    b. Trees

    c. Sites

    d. Domains

    e. Organizational units (OUs)

    f. Global catalogs

2. Active Directory Domain Service (AD DS) allows an ordinary user to join up to _____ computers to the Active Directory Domain.

    a. 5

    b. 10

    c. 20

    d. 100

3. After logging on to your Domain account, if you want to log on to the computer using your local account again, you need to use the domain syntax for your login name. For your local computer account, what is the domain name?

    a. Local

    b. The same as the domain name

    c. The computer name

    d. None of these answers are correct.

4. Remote Server Administration Tools (RSAT) includes which of the following? (Choose all that apply).

    a. Server Manager

    b. MMC snap-ins

    c. PowerShell cmdlets

    d. OU Manager

5. In Active Directory Users and Computers, which default folder uses a different icon?

    a. Computers

    b. Domain Controllers

    c. Users

    d. Groups

6. You can use Group Policy to control which of following configuration settings to objects in Active Directory?

    a. Setting of subnet masks

    b. Logon scripts

    c. Startup scripts

    d. Application deployment

7. Which Group Policy Object (GPO) tab enables you to view and modify GPO permissions?

    a. Scope

    b. Details

    c. Settings

    d. Delegation

8. The component of the Windows Assessment and Deployment Kit (ADK) that streamlines the customization and provisioning of Windows images and that can create Windows provisioning answer files, build a provisioning package, and create custom variants and specify the settings for each variant is called_____.

    a. The Windows Imaging and Configuration Designer (ICD)

    b. Active Directory Users and Computers

    c. Windows Management Instrumentation

    d. None of the above

9. For volume license customers with many computers to manage, Microsoft offers the capability to activate computers on the internal network through the implementation of which kind of license?

    a. Volume Azure

    b. Key Management Server (KMS)

    c. Active Directory Forest

    d. Site Services

Foundation Topics

Active Directory

At the turn of the 21st century, Microsoft introduced its hierarchical enterprise directory service known as Active Directory. Since that time, Active Directory has become entrenched as a widely used enterprise business directory service. Microsoft built the Active Directory domain structure on the concepts of X.500 and Lightweight Directory Access Protocol (LDAP). Since its beginnings with Windows 2000, Active Directory has matured and gained new features, improved security and functionality, and ease of configuration and management. This section presents a quick introduction to the structure and components of Active Directory Domain Service (AD DS); for detailed information, consult any Windows Server exam certification book, such as Benjamin Finkel's *MCSA 70-742 Cert Guide: Identity with Windows Server 2016* (ISBN: 9780789757036).

The Building Blocks of Active Directory

In creating the hierarchical database structure of Active Directory, Microsoft facilitated locating resources such as folders and printers by name rather than by physical location. These logical building blocks include domains, trees, forests, and organizational units (OUs). The physical location of objects within Active Directory is represented by including all objects in a specific location in its own site.

Active Directory includes the following basic logical components:

- **Domains:** A logical grouping of computers that shares a common directory database and security, the domain represents the core unit of the network structure. Further, a domain can be considered as a security boundary. In other words, the domain administrator can define access control lists (ACLs) that determine users' access rights and permissions to objects within the domain at the domain level.

- **Trees:** A group of domains that share a contiguous namespace. In other words, a tree consists of a parent domain plus one or more sets of child domains whose name reflects that of a parent. For example, a tree can include a parent domain named pearson.com with child domains named students.pearson.com and teachers.pearson.com, and others, as shown in Figure 4-1.

- **Forests:** A group of domain trees that do not share a contiguous namespace. For example, you can have two trees with parent domains named pearson.com and peachpit.com, as shown in Figure 4-1.

- **Organizational Units (OUs):** A logical subgroup within a domain. It is convenient for locating resources used by a single work group, section, or department in a company and applying policies that apply to only these resources.

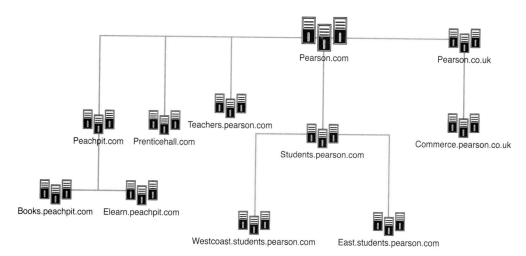

Figure 4-1   An Active Directory Tree Structure

Included in each of these components is a series of physical components:

- **Sites:** Used to group together resources within a forest according to their physical location and/or subnet. A site is a set of one or more IP subnets, which are connected by a high-speed, always available local area network (LAN) link.

- **Domain Controllers:** Any server on which you have installed Active Directory is a *domain controller (DC)*. These servers authenticate all users logging on to the domain in which they are located, and they also serve as centers from which you can administer Active Directory.

- **Global Catalogs:** The *global catalog* is a subset of domain information created for enabling domain controllers in other domains in the same forest to locate resources in any domain. By default, the first domain controller installed in a new domain becomes a global catalog server.

- **Operations Masters:** Domain controllers that are specifically designated to perform specific actions within a forest or domain. Active Directory defines two forest-wide operations masters, the schema master and domain naming master, and three domain-wide operations masters, the infrastructure master, primary domain controller (PDC) emulator, and the relative identifier (RID) master.

> **NOTE**   For more information on AD DS, refer to "Active Directory Domain Services Overview" at https://technet.microsoft.com/en-us/windows-server-docs/identity/ad-ds/get-started/virtual-dc/active-directory-domain-services-overview, plus the references cited therein.

Joining a Domain

You should be familiar with working with AD DS both as your support role in an organization, and for preparation for the 70-698 exam. Although there are a lot of topics and study needed to support Active Directory in a large enterprise, and most are out of scope of this book and the 70-697 and 70-698 exam, being able to work with AD DS at a basic level is necessary. We cover the basics of working with domain objects as well as how to join and work with domains from the client end.

When you set up Windows 10 Pro or Enterprise, Windows setup asks if you would like to join a local Active Directory domain or a Microsoft Azure domain. Selecting Join a Local Active Directory Domain during setup installs Windows with a local account, and you are told that you can join the domain later.

By default, AD DS allows a normal user account to join up to 10 computers to the domain without any additional privileges. Members of the Domain Administrators group and users with the Create Computer Objects in the Active Directory are not restricted to 10 computers and can add computers to the domain as needed. Follow this procedure in Windows 10 to join the domain.

Step 1.   Start by accessing the computer properties by right-clicking **This PC** in File Explorer and selecting **Properties** from the context menu. You can also access this dialog from the Control Panel or by right-clicking the **Start** button and selecting **System**.

Step 2.   On the System page, under Computer name, domain, and workgroup settings, click **Change Settings**. This displays the System Properties dialog shown in Figure 4-2. Currently, the computer named WIN1001 is joined to a workgroup.

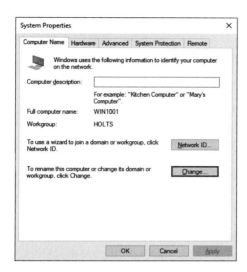

Figure 4-2 System Properties Dialog Box

Step 3.   Click the **Change** button to display the Computer Name/Domain Changes dialog box as shown in Figure 4-3.

Figure 4-3 Computer Name/Domain Changes Dialog Box

Step 4.   In the Member Of section, select the **Domain** radio button, and type in the name of the domain you want to join, and then click **OK**.

Step 5.   You are logged in to the computer using a local account, so Windows will prompt you for the credentials of a domain account, as shown in Figure 4-4. Enter your domain login and password and click **OK**.

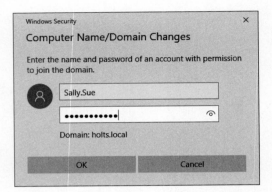

Figure 4-4   Prompts for Domain Account Credentials When Joining the Domain

Step 6.   The AD DS will check your credentials, create an account for your computer, and then display the welcome message shown in Figure 4-5. Click **OK**, and Windows will warn you that you must restart your computer.

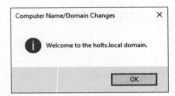

Figure 4-5   Welcome to the Domain

Step 7.   Click **OK**; then click **Close** on the System Properties page. When the restart prompt appears, click **Restart Now** to restart the computer.

After the computer is started, you can sign in with your domain account. The first time you use the domain account, you need to click the **Other User** button and type in your domain account name (we used Sally.Sue to join, as shown in Figure 4-4). The computer should default to the domain you just joined.

To use your local account again, you need to use domain syntax for your login name. This is in the form *domain\user*. You can also use your User Principal Name (UPN), which is *user@domain.name*. So, for instance, if Sally.Sue is a member of the test.local domain, she can use either TEST\Sally.Sue or Sally.Sue@test.local. For local computer accounts, the domain name is the name of the computer. To log in to the local computer, Sally would use WIN1001\Sally.Sue.

NOTE   For more information on UPN and username formats, see "User Name Formats" at https://msdn.microsoft.com/en-us/library/windows/desktop/aa380525(v=vs.85).aspx.

Remote Server Administration Tools

Remote Server Administration Tools (RSAT) is a collection of tools that are useful for managing Server Core as well as Full GUI installations. RSAT includes Server Manager, MMC snap-ins, PowerShell cmdlets, and additional command-line tools used to manage remote computers.

As a best practice, RSAT should be installed on a dedicated management server or client computer to limit the amount of access or load on production servers.

NOTE   RSAT tools are included as an installable feature under the Windows Server 2016 Full GUI installation, or they can also be downloaded from Microsoft and installed under Windows 10. They cannot be run from a Windows Server Core. Access https://www.microsoft.com/en-us/download/details.aspx?id=45520 in your web browser to download RSAT for Windows 10.

Installing RSAT on Client Workstations

Unlike previous versions of RSAT for Windows 7 and Windows 8.1, you no longer need to use Windows Features to enable the RSAT tools after installation. The Windows 10 client automatically enables all tools during setup. You can install RSAT by completing the following steps on a Windows 10 client management workstation:

Step 1. Download and install the Remote Server Administration Tools for Windows 10, which is available from the Microsoft Download Center.

Step 2. When prompted to install the update for Windows, click **Yes** to install the package.

Step 3. Read the license agreement and accept the terms by clicking **I Accept**.

Step 4. After the installation wizard completes, click **Close**.

Step 5. By default, all administration tools are installed, as shown in Figure 4-6.

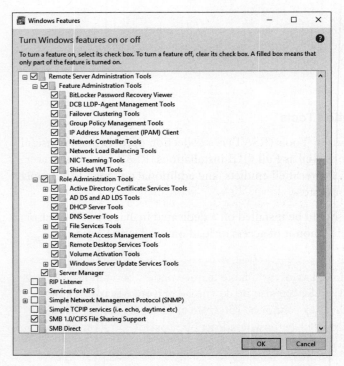

Figure 4-6   Windows Features: Remote Server Administration Tools for Windows 10

Step 6.   Select or deselect the appropriate tools and click **OK**.

After the Remote Server Administration Tools have been installed and enabled, you will be able to access Server Manager, Active Directory, PowerShell and other snap-ins for MMC, as shown in Figure 4-7.

Figure 4-7   Remote Server Administration Tools for Windows 10

Active Directory Users and Computers

With the RSAT tools installed, you can use your Windows 10 workstation to manage your AD domain. The most commonly used tool is going to be the Active Directory Users and Computers (ADUC). As the name implies, you can use this tool to manage users and computers in the domain, as well as user groups and the entire structure of the AD. A new domain will look similar to Figure 4-8, which shows the holts.local domain, which currently contains only the AD DS default containers.

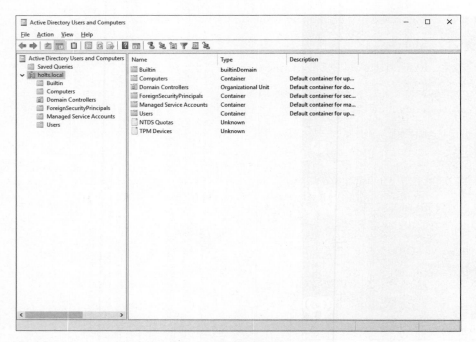

Figure 4-8 Active Directory Users and Computers

Take note of the icon for Domain Controllers, which is different than the blank folder icon for the other containers because it is a special container called an organizational unit (OU). When first created, an Active Directory domain will place all user accounts into the Users container. That is fine for a small organization, but most businesses will want to create OUs for specific groups of users, such as Accounting, Sales, IT, and so on, because these users will likely have different requirements and access to different resources. Active Directory (AD) is the central tool for enabling delegation of authority. AD, along with Group Policies, enables an organization to centralize and enforce policies for the entire organization while providing autonomy for departments or divisions within their realm of responsibility.

To create an OU, and any other object in the domain, you must have privileges to do so. Typically this means you must be a member of the Domain Admins group, but some authority to create objects can be delegated to other users. Joining a domain from a PC is one example, because this creates a computer account object. There are also other groups created by default when you create a new AD DS domain that can be used to provide privileges to users without granting full domain administrative authority. To create OUs in a domain, follow these steps:

Step 1. Log in using a domain account with Domain Admins privileges.

Step 2. Run ADUC.

Step 3. Expand the domain from the tree in the left menu.

Step 4. Select either the domain or an existing OU (you cannot create an OU in a default container).

Step 5. Right-click, and select **New > Organizational Unit** from the context menu, as shown in Figure 4-9.

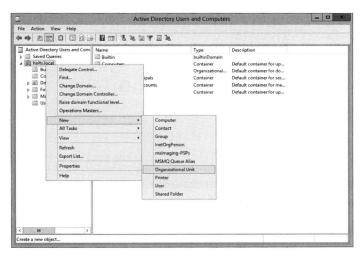

Figure 4-9 Creating a New Organizational Unit

Step 6. On the resulting dialog box, type a name into the **Name** box and then click **OK**.

Step 7. Repeat Steps 4–6 to create the OUs you need.

Figure 4-10 is an example of creating some OUs in a domain. The domain now has some OU containers for organizing user and computer accounts in the domain. We can put the user accounts for employees in accounting, IT, and sales in different containers. The Win10 Laptops, Servers, and the Mobile Devices OUs are intended for computer accounts that will be joined to the domain. In this example, only the sales employees use mobile devices, so we have nested that OU inside the Sales OU.

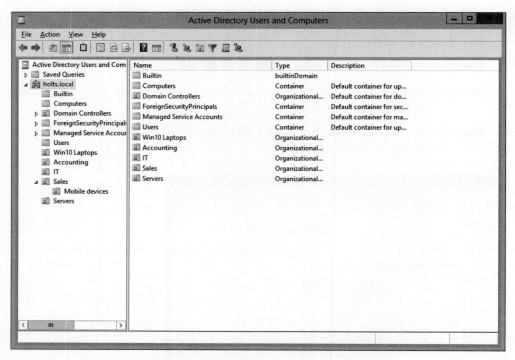

Figure 4-10   An Active Directory Domain with Some Configured OUs

This configuration is not intended to be a recommended or typical domain structure; it is just an example of how OUs can be created for a new domain. Organization of the domain requires careful planning and consideration. As you add users
and computers to the domain, they can be dragged from their default container into
the appropriate OU.

NOTE   For a discussion on how to plan and design an Active Directory structure
for an organization, start with "AD DS Design and Planning" at https://
technet.microsoft.com/en-us/windows-server-docs/identity/ad-ds/plan/ad-ds-
design-and-planning?f=255&MSPPError=-2147217396.

Group Policies

Group Policy lies at the heart of every Active Directory implementation. It does
far more than just define what users can and cannot do with their computers. It is a
series of configuration settings that you can apply to an object or series of objects in
Active Directory to control a user's environment in numerous contexts, including
the following:

- **Network access:** Enables you to control access to network devices including terminal servers, wireless access, and so on.

- **Folder redirection:** Enables you to use Group Policy settings to redirect users' local folders to network shares.

- **Logon/logoff/startup/shutdown scripts:** Enables you to assign scripts on a user or computer basis for such events as logon, logoff, startup, or shutdown.

- **Application deployment:** Enables you to administer applications on your network, including their assignment, publication, updating, repair, and removal.

- **Security options of all types:** Enables you to use Group Policy security settings to enforce restrictions and control access on user or computer properties.

You can apply Group Policy to server and client computers running all recent versions of Windows, and include both computer and user settings. As the names suggest, computer policies are computer-specific and are applied when the computer starts up; user policies are user-specific and are applied when the user logs on to the computer.

Creating and Applying GPOs

You perform all Group Policy administrative activities, including creating, editing, and applying GPOs from the Group Policy Management Console (GPMC). GPMC provides a simplified user interface for managing Group Policy in multisite, multidomain environments. It enables an administrator to back up, restore, copy, and import GPOs in these environments. You can create scripts to simplify the various management tasks. Key features of GPMC include the following:

- An advanced GUI that facilitates the use and management of Group Policy

- The ability to back up and restore GPOs

- The ability to copy, paste, import, and export GPOs and Windows Management Instrumentation (WMI) filters

- Enhanced management of security within Group Policy

- Enhanced reporting by means of HTML for policy settings as well as Resultant Set of Policy (RSoP) data

- The ability to script Group Policy-related tasks

Windows Server 2016 includes all the Group Policies needed to support Windows 10, but for existing Active Directory implementations, you will need to download and install the Administrative Templates (.admx) files for Windows 10 from Microsoft's website and add them to your domain controllers.

NOTE For information on managing .admx files and a central store for administrative templates, see "How to Create and Manage the Central Store for Group Policy Administrative Templates in Windows" at https://support.microsoft.com/en-us/kb/3087759.

Let's take a look at the GPMC and go through a sample procedure showing how you would create and link a new GPO:

Step 1. From the Start menu, click **Windows Administrative Tools** to expand the category, and then select **Group Policy Management** from the list of tools that appears. You can also open the GPMC by typing **Group Policy Management** into the Cortana search bar. Either method opens the GPMC, which shows a node for your forest in the console tree that you can expand to reveal subnodes for every domain with entries for each OU as well as a Group Policy Objects node.

Step 2. In the console tree, expand your forest to display your domain, and then expand your domain. You will notice several default folders, including one for Group Policy Objects.

Step 3. Expand the Group Policy Objects node. You will notice two default GPOs—the Default Domain Policy and the Default Domain Controllers Policy. These are installed automatically when you create your domain. Policy settings that you define here are automatically applied to the entire domain and to the domain controllers, respectively.

Step 4. Select one of these policies. As shown in Figure 4-11, the details pane displays GPO properties and configuration options. Included are the following tabs:

- **Scope:** Enables you to display GPO link information and configure security group filtering and WMI filtering.

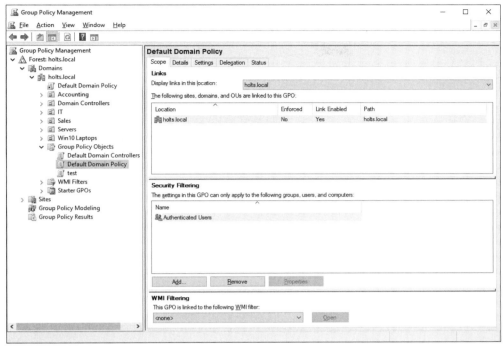

Figure 4-11   Performing All Group Policy Management Activities from the GPMC

- **Details:** Displays information on the owner, dates created and modified, version numbers, GUID value, and enabled status. The enabled status is the only configurable option on this tab.

- **Settings:** Enables you to display policy settings, as shown in Figure 4-12. You can expand and collapse nodes to locate information on any policy setting. Note that the account settings shown in this figure are configured for the Default Domain Policy GPO by default when you install AD DS.

- **Delegation:** Enables you to view and modify GPO permissions.

- **Status:** Displays the status of AD DS and SYSVOL replication for the domain as related to Group Policy.

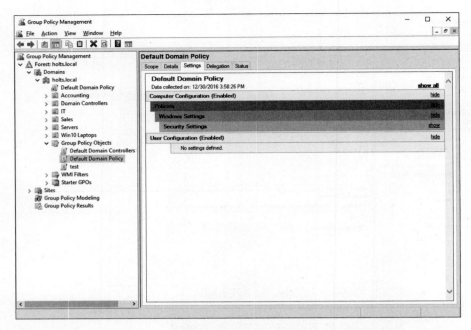

Figure 4-12   Settings Tab of a GPO Enabling You to View Configured Policy Settings

Step 5.   To create a GPO, right-click the **Group Policy Objects** folder desired domain or OU and select **New**. This displays the New GPO dialog box, as shown in Figure 4-13.

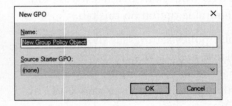

Figure 4-13   New GPO Dialog Box Enabling You to Create and Name a New GPO

Step 6.   Type a suitable name for the GPO. If you have a Starter GPO that includes settings you want to include in the new GPO, select it from the Source Starter GPO drop-down list and then click **OK**. The new GPO is added to the list in the console tree under the Group Policy Objects node.

Step 7.   To define policy settings for the new GPO, right-click it and choose **Edit**. This brings up the Group Policy Management Editor console, as shown in Figure 4-14. You have been introduced to some of the more significant policy settings you should be familiar with in previous chapters, and you will see more throughout this book.

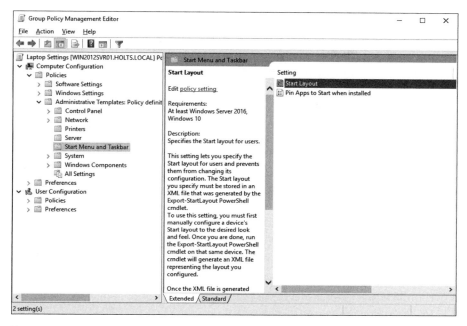

Figure 4-14   Configuring All Policy Settings Associated with a GPO from the Group Policy Management Editor Snap-in

After you have modified the GPO to apply the policy settings needed, you can drag the GPO to an OU and the policies will be applied to all users or computers in that OU. For instance, you can create separate Start menu layouts for your laptop users and for your desktop users, and link each to OUs such as Win10 Laptops and Win10 Desktops. The next time users log in to the computer with their domain account, the settings will be applied.

UAC

User Account Control (UAC) was first introduced in Windows Vista as an additional security measure to protect against things such as privilege escalation attacks. UAC is discussed in Chapter 7, "Windows 10 Security."

Windows in an Enterprise Environment

As well as managing Windows security policies from Active Directory and computer policies using GPOs, Microsoft provides a number of additional tools for administrators in large organizations to help in the configuration and deployment of Windows devices. In this topic you learn about the Windows Imaging and Configuration Designer, a component of the ADK. You learned about the ADK in Chapter 3,

"Post-Installation Configuration." You also learn about ways to manage Windows activation and tools for managing activation in an enterprise environment.

The Windows Imaging and Configuration Designer (ICD)

In Chapter 2, "Implementing Windows," you learned about virtual hard disks (VHDs) for deploying virtual images of Windows 10. In Chapter 3 you learned about servicing Windows images using the Deployment Image Servicing and Management (DISM) command-line tool.

Another component of the Windows Assessment and Deployment Kit (ADK) is the Windows Imaging and Configuration Designer (ICD). A new version of the ADK is released for each version of Windows, so to service Windows 10, version 1607, you need the ADK for Windows 10, version 1607. There is even a version of the ADK for Insider Preview members, to assess prerelease versions of Windows.

The ICD tool streamlines the customization and provisioning of Windows images. It is provided for OEMs, system integrators, and IT departments of organizations that provision bring-your-own-device (BYOD) and organizational devices. You can use ICD for the following tasks:

- Viewing the configurable settings and policies for a Windows 10 image or provisioning package.

- Creating Windows provisioning answer files.

- Adding drivers, apps, or other packages to an answer file.

- Creating custom variants and specifying the settings for each variant.

- Building and flashing a Windows image to a device.

- Building a provisioning package.

After you have the ADK installed, you can find the Windows Imaging and Configuration Designer on your Start menu programs, under Windows Kits. Starting the application requires UAC authorization for administrator privileges (the ICD must run under an administrator account). The initial startup screen will be similar to Figure 4-15.

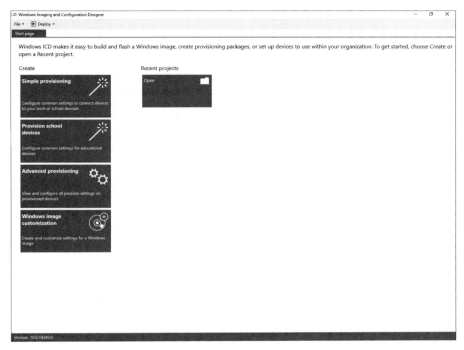

Figure 4-15 Windows Imaging and Configuration Designer (ICD) Startup Screen

The ICD provides wizards for some simple provisioning projects called Simple Provisioning or Provision School Devices for educational institutions. You can also choose Advanced Provisioning, which provides many more options for your provisioning package. Use the following procedure to provision packages with the ICD, using Advanced Provisioning.

Step 1. From the ICD start page, select **Advanced Provisioning**. This displays the dialog shown in Figure 4-16.

Figure 4-16 Windows ICD New Project Dialog Box

Step 2.   Enter a project name into the Name box, and select a location using the Project Folder box. You can optionally enter a description for your project. Click **Next** to proceed.

Step 3.   When the project page opens, the basic options allow you to set up the device and the network, enroll in Active Directory, and save your project.

   a. On the Set Up Device form, enter an expression that ICD can use to generate a unique device name. You can include either %SERIAL% to generate a hardware-based serial number, or %RAND:x%, to generate a random number with x characters, as shown in Figure 4-17. Optionally, enter a product key in the space provided.

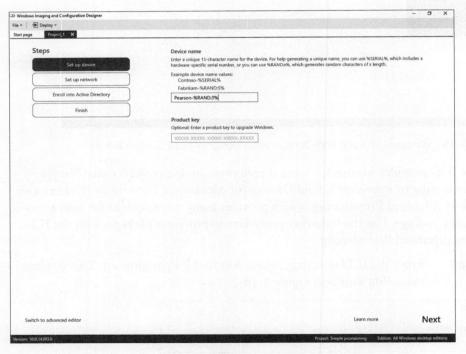

Figure 4-17   Device Settings Screen of the ICD Provisioning Tool

   b. On the Set Up Network page, you can optionally provide Wi-Fi parameters for the device to use. You must include the Wi-Fi SSID. The Network Type must be either Open or WPA2-Personal. You must include a password for WPA2-Personal. If you will be using a wired network, slide the Connect Devices to a Wi-Fi Network toggle to **Off**.

    c. The Enroll into Active Directory page allows you to optionally enroll in an Active Directory domain during provisioning. You must supply the domain name, the username, and the user password to use during the domain-join operation. If you choose not to enroll in Active Directory, you need to provide a username and password for a local administrator account.

    d. On the Finish page, you can review your options and create the package. You can also create a password to protect your package. Protecting your package is recommended, because you have included a password in the package itself.

Step 4.   Click **Create** to save your package. It is now ready for deployment.

Step 5.   To include other options in your package, click the **Switch to Advanced Editor** link. This displays the advanced customizations screen shown in Figure 4-18. You can create a log of various options, as shown in the Available Customizations menu. Clicking an option on the menu displays help from Microsoft's website. For instance, you may want to include a Start menu layout (see Chapter 3, "Post-Installation Configuration," for information on how to create the Start menu XML file).

Figure 4-18 ICD Advanced Customizations Screen

Step 6.   To save a package from the Advanced Editor, click the **Export** menu. This walks you through creating a password for your package and saving the package for use.

After your provisioning package is created, you can apply it to an existing Windows installation, or you can use it during setup of a new Windows 10 installation.

The next option on the ICD Start page is Windows Image Customization. You use this menu to create a custom Windows installation image, apply your provisioning package to it, and save it to media to install on a device. For example, you could use the install.wim image from a Windows 10 DVD media and build the image on a USB key. When you use the USB to boot and install Windows on a new device, your customized provisioning settings are applied.

NOTE   For more information on using the ICD for creating custom Windows images, see "Build and Deploy an Image for Windows 10 Desktop" at https://msdn.microsoft.com/en-us/library/windows/hardware/dn916105(v=vs.85).aspx.

Activation of Windows Computers in the Enterprise

Microsoft provides retail licenses for end users and small businesses, and provides a single product key for each of these licenses. However, most businesses, even with as few as five computers to license, can take advantage of Microsoft's volume licensing agreements. For volume license customers, Microsoft offers Multiple Activation Key (MAK) licenses or Key Management Server (KMS) licenses. As the names imply, the difference is how these licenses are activated. Small organizations will probably use MAKs, and each computer will activate with Microsoft's servers, where the licenses and counts will be tracked. Larger organizations can opt for KMS licenses, and implement internal KMS servers to activate clients.

KMS provides advantages for organizations with many devices to manage. Computers do not need to access the Internet for activation, saving bandwidth charges. Organizations may also have isolated devices that do not need Internet access, and these computers can be activated on the internal network instead.

Deploying Windows 10 throughout an organization, whether manually, over the network, or using custom images, also requires Windows activation for each of those devices. Microsoft provides ways to activate your organization's Active Directory, so if you're joining workstations to the organization's domain, you can configure Active Directory-based activation for those devices.

All currently supported versions of Windows Server running AD DS can activate clients, but you must have at least one domain controller on Windows Server 2012 or higher as part of the domain, and run adprep.exe on that domain controller to update the schema.

> **NOTE** You should be aware of the 2012 AD DS schema requirement for the 70-698 exam; however, performing this process is out of scope of this text. For details on running adprep.exe, see "Running Adprep.exe" at https://technet.microsoft.com/en-us/library/dd464018(v=ws.10).aspx.

Volume activation for older computers running Windows 7 or Windows Server 2008 R2 or earlier requires a Key Management Server (KMS), and any devices that are not joined to the domain will also use KMS for activation. For organizations without these requirements, KMS can be removed from the network and all devices can use AD DS activation.

Domain-joined computers will attempt to refresh their activation periodically by checking with an available domain controller. This reactivation occurs every 7 days by default. However, once activated, devices will maintain their activation state for up to 180 days. So if you have laptops that operate outside the network for extended periods, they will remain activated as long as they can contact a domain controller at least once every 6 months.

You can enable volume activation of your Windows 10 computers and earlier versions using a Key Management Service (KMS) host, which can run on Windows 10 or Windows Server 2012 R2 or later. If you have an existing KMS, you can use that host, but you must download and install an update from Microsoft to enable activation of Windows 10, as well as obtain a new KMS host key from Microsoft.

Implement Volume Activation Using a KMS

To implement KMS in your organization, first obtain a KMS host key from Microsoft. When you install the activation services, the KMS host attempts to activate the host key with Microsoft's servers and can start receiving activation requests from other clients. KMS is designed for activation of a large number of computers, so it includes a minimum threshold for activation. This means that until the KMS server receives at least 25 activation requests, it will not activate any clients. After the minimum has been reached, all clients will then be able to successfully activate through the server.

If you need KMS activation services (for instance, you want to activate Windows 7 computers or activate devices that are not joined to the domain), be sure to install KMS services prior to installing Active Directory-based activation.

To implement KMS activation using a Windows Server computer, use the following steps:

Step 1. Sign in to the server. You must use an account that is a member of the Enterprise Administrators group.

Step 2. From the Server Manager, select **Tools** and then **Add Roles and Features**.

Step 3. Click **Next** on the Add Roles and Features Wizard until the Server Roles screen is displayed, and then click the check box for **Volume Activation Services**.

Step 4. The dialog shown in Figure 4-19 is displayed. Make sure Include Management Tools (If Applicable) is checked, and then click **Add Features**.

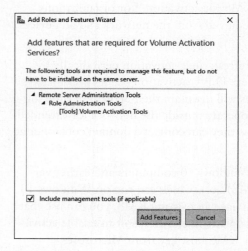

Figure 4-19 Confirm Features for the Volume Activation Service

Step 5. On the Add Roles and Features Wizard, click the **Next** button until the Confirmation screen is displayed, and then click **Install**.

Step 6. Installation of the Volume Activation Service will proceed. Click **Close** to close the Add Roles and Features Wizard. Wait for the installation to complete, and then click **Tools** and select **Volume Activation Tools**.

Step 7. The Volume Activation Tools dialog will display, as shown in Figure 4-20. Read the information on the Introduction page and then click **Next**.

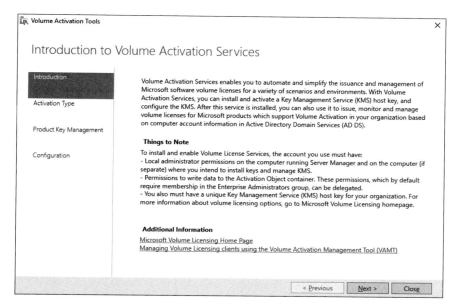

Figure 4-20   Configuring the Volume Activation Tool Services

Step 8.   On the next screen, select **Key Management Service (KMS)**, and then enter the computer name in the box provided (if you are installing the KMS on the current server, use the current server's name). Click **Next**.

Step 9.   In the Install Your KMS Host Key, enter the KMS host key provided by Microsoft, and then click **Commit**.

Step 10.   On the Configuration page, select whether to activate your KMS key online or by phone. After activation is complete, click **Commit**, and then click **Close**.

NOTE   For more information about KMS, how it works, and how to plan a KMS infrastructure, see "Understanding KMS" at https://technet.microsoft.com/en-us/library/ff793434.aspx.

Implement Active Directory-Based Activation

To implement Active Directory-based activation, you add the Volume Activation Service role to a Windows 2012 or Windows 2016 server. After this service is configured on the network, domain-joined clients will automatically contact the Active Directory for activation, without user intervention.

The steps to install Active Directory-based activation are the same as the steps previously listed for installing a KMS, except in Step 8 you select Active Directory-Based Activation instead of KMS, and you do not need to enter a hostname. You can configure the service on the same computer with the KMS service, but you must use Windows Server version 2012 or later.

Query and Configure Activation States

After your Volume Activation Service is installed and the KMS host key activated, clients can begin activating using Active Directory. You can test the activation service by starting a computer running Windows 10 with a KMS key, and checking the activation status. Activation status is found by clicking **All Settings** from the Action Center, selecting **System**, clicking **About** from the System menu, and then clicking the **Change Product Key or Upgrade Your Edition of Windows** link from the About page. If the computer is currently using a digital license or an MAK, you can use the Change Product Key link to enter a KMS key, and test the activation of the license.

Microsoft provides a command-line tool called the Software License Manager to check license activation. The tool is implemented as a script called *slmgr.vbs*, and it is installed on Windows 10 during setup. You can use this tool to get details about the client activation process. To force Windows to attempt activation, open an administrative command prompt and type the command

```
Slmgr /ato
```

Windows will attempt reactivation and display the license state and some detailed Windows version information. To display detailed licensing information, use the command

```
Slmgr /dlv
```

This displays information similar to Figure 4-21.

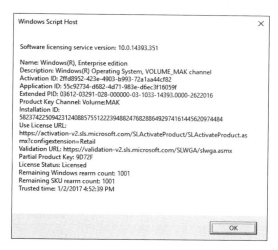

Figure 4-21   Displaying Detailed Licensing Information

If you have recently installed KMS and the server is below the 25 activation minimum, the command displays an error that states the KMS activation count is too low. This confirms the KMS is working, even if it is not ready to start activating clients. Review Table 4-2 for some of the most commonly used options for the **slmgr** command.

Table 4-2   Commonly Used **slmgr** Command-Line Options

Command Parameter	Description
/ipk product_key	Install or change the product key. The key is validated and installed if valid. This key is used in all subsequent validation attempts.
/ato	Attempt activation of Windows. If a volume license key (KMS key) is installed, KMS activation is attempted. If an MAK or retail key is installed, Windows attempts activation over the Internet with Microsoft's servers.
/dli	Display license information.
/dlv	Display detailed license information.
/xpr	Display the activation expiration date. Retail and MAK licenses are perpetual, so this parameter is useful only for KMS volume-licensed clients.

NOTE   For details about the **slmgr.vbs** command-line tool, and all options available, see "Slmgr.vbs Options" at https://technet.microsoft.com/library/ff793433.aspx.

Exam Preparation Tasks

Review All the Key Topics

Review the most important topics in the chapter, noted with the Key Topics icon in the outer margin of the page. Table 4-3 lists a reference of these key topics and the page numbers on which each is found.

Table 4-3   Key Topics for Chapter 4

Key Topic Element	Description	Page Number
List	The building blocks of Active Directory	196
Step List	Configure Active Directory	205
Step List	Creating Group Policy Objects	208
Figure 4-11	Group policy management using the GPMC	209
Step List	Using the ICD to create provisioning packages	213
Step List	Implement KMS activation	218
Table 4-2	Query activation states using the command line	221

Complete the Tables and Lists from Memory

Print a copy of Appendix B, "Memory Tables" (found on the book's website), or at least the section for this chapter, and complete the tables and lists from memory. Appendix C, "Memory Tables Answer Key," also on the website, includes completed tables and lists to check your work.

Definitions of Key Terms

Define the following key terms from this chapter, and check your answers in the glossary.

Active Directory (AD), domain, domain controller (DC), forest, Group Policy, Group Policy Management Console (GPMC), Group Policy Object (GPO), KMS, organizational unit (OU), site, SLMGR, tree

This chapter covers the following subjects:

- **Microsoft Account:** First introduced in Windows 8 and 8.1 and also available in Windows 10 is the ability to use a *cloud account*, specifically a Microsoft account for Windows, to log on to the PC and perform tasks. In this section you learn how to use a Microsoft account in Windows 10, how to manage Microsoft account access, and other details related to the use of a cloud account.

- **Windows Store and Cloud Apps:** Windows Store applications, or apps, were first introduced in Windows 8, and many apps and games are available for Windows 10 on desktops, laptops, mobile devices, and even Xbox. In this section you learn about the Windows Store, how to download and install new apps, and how to maintain control of Store apps in an Enterprise.

This chapter covers the following objectives for the 70-697 exam:

Support Windows Store and cloud apps: Install and manage software by using Microsoft Office 365 and Windows Store apps, sideload apps by using Microsoft Intune, Sideload apps into online and offline images, deep-link apps by using Microsoft Intune, integrate Microsoft account including personalization settings.

CHAPTER 5

Installing and Managing Software

All users on a Windows 10 computer must be known to the operating system—in other words, they must be authenticated to Windows and authorized to use resources on the local computer and located on the network. This chapter covers authorizations that you need to configure and delves into the many ways of authenticating users in Windows 10, including cloud-based Microsoft account authentication. Microsoft expects you to be knowledgeable about all these topics and the new features when taking the 70-697 exam.

In a modern Internet-connected workplace with a growing number of users joining the always-available networked world of devices, Windows 10 brings an entirely new suite of small-scale applications, simply called apps, which users can purchase and download from the new Windows Store. Although some of these apps can enhance productivity in a corporate environment, downloading and using many of them can become a major distraction for users during the workday. Further, such practices can consume bandwidth and create security risks. Consequently, administrators and desktop support specialists need to know how to limit or even prevent access to the Windows Store in the corporate environment. You also need to know how to place limits on traditional executable files, scripts, Windows Installer files, and other similar files. Microsoft provides AppLocker to deal with performing these tasks, as well as the older Software Restriction Policies.

"Do I Know This Already?" Quiz

The "Do I Know This Already?" quiz allows you to assess whether you should read this entire chapter or simply jump to the "Exam Preparation Tasks" section for review. If you are in doubt, read the entire chapter. Table 5-1 outlines the major headings in this chapter and the corresponding "Do I Know This Already?" quiz questions. You can find the answers in Appendix A, "Answers to the 'Do I Know This Already?' Quizzes."

Table 5-1 "Do I Know This Already?" Foundation Topics Section-to-Question Mapping

Foundation Topics Section	Questions Covered in This Section
Microsoft Account	1–3
Windows Store and Cloud Apps	4–10

CAUTION   The goal of self-assessment is to gauge your mastery of the topics in this chapter. If you do not know the answer to a question or are only partially sure of the answer, you should mark that question as wrong for purposes of the self-assessment. Giving yourself credit for an answer you correctly guess skews your self-assessment results and might provide you with a false sense of security.

1. What type of email account can you use for a Microsoft account for Windows?

    a. Exchange server

    b. Outlook.com

    c. Hotmail.com

    d. Any email account

2. What are the benefits to users when using a Microsoft account? (Select all that apply.)

    a. Integration of contacts with Internet accounts such as Facebook, Twitter, and Hotmail.

    b. Access and sharing of Internet-based storage such as SkyDrive, Facebook, and Flickr.

    c. Using and synchronizing Windows Store apps.

    d. Personal settings are kept in sync among all Windows devices.

3. Management at your organization has decided to set up corporate Microsoft accounts for all users, but does not want users to use their own Microsoft accounts on the company computers. How do you enforce this policy?

    a. Set the Group Policy Block Microsoft Accounts to Disabled.

    b. Set the Group Policy Disallow Microsoft Accounts to Enabled.

    c. Set the Group Policy Block Microsoft Accounts to Users Can't Add Microsoft Accounts.

    d. Set the Group Policy Block Microsoft Accounts to Users Can't Add or Log On with Microsoft Accounts.

4. Which of the following techniques can you use to install Windows Store Packaged apps? (Choose all that apply.)

    a. Downloading and installing from the Windows Store

    b. Using the Control Panel Programs and Features applet

    c. Apploading using Group Policies

    d. Sideloading using Group Policies

5. Which of the following is *not* a distinguishing characteristic of Windows Store apps?

    a. Can use live tiles that are dynamically updated

    b. Uses active icons to display content

    c. Enables touchscreen and pen input

    d. Shares content with other apps

6. How does Windows notify you that updates are available for your Windows Store apps currently installed?

    a. Notification icon in the system tray

    b. Pop-up balloon from the Notification area

    c. The number of available updates is displayed in Windows Store

    d. Notice in the Windows Action Center

7. Office 365 cloud apps are an example of what type of cloud service?

    a. PaaS

    b. SaaS

    c. NaaS

    d. IaaS

    e. Hybrid

8. What types of devices can you manage with Microsoft Intune? (Select all that apply.)

    a. Windows 10 mobile devices

    b. Apple iOS phones

    c. Domain-joined Windows 10 workstations

    d. Apple OSX laptops

    e. Android phones

9.   What methods can you use to deploy Office 365 to computers in your organization? (Select all that apply.)

   a.   Group Policy

   b.   Startup scripts

   c.   Manual install through the Office portal

   d.   Add packages to an image

   e.   Microsoft System Center Configuration Manager (SCCM)

10.   The developers in your organization have several UWP apps they have developed that you want to deploy to users' devices. What is required for Windows 10 devices before the apps can be installed? (Select all that apply.)

   a.   The apps must be certified and deployed to the Windows Store.

   b.   The apps must be signed and the digital certificates installed on the devices.

   c.   The devices must have sideloading enabled.

   d.   The devices must be joined to the domain and group policies applied to allow sideloading.

Foundation Topics

Microsoft Account

With Windows 10, Microsoft consolidated its latest operating system for PCs, tablets, smartphones, and major portability. Users may have a work computer, a home PC, a smartphone, and a tablet all running Windows 10, and they expect their settings, Windows apps, and services to work the same across all these devices. The way to enable the consistency across all these devices is by using a Microsoft account.

When the same Microsoft account is used on all of a user's devices, they have automatic access to many resources, apps, files stored on clouds and remote computers, and consistent settings, which roam from device to device.

Sign In Using a Microsoft Account

Recall from Chapter 2 that the default method for creating the first account at the end of the setup process of Windows 10 Home or Pro was to use a Microsoft account. You can use any email address for the Microsoft account. Users only need to provide their email address, create a password for the Microsoft account, and they can use the account on any Windows 10 computer.

Using a Microsoft account provides several advantages, especially for home users:

- Integration of contacts and friends status from Outlook.com, Facebook, Twitter, and LinkedIn.

- Access and sharing of photos, documents, and other files with OneDrive, Facebook, and Flickr.

- Using Windows Store apps and Microsoft Office 365 is easier and requires a Microsoft account. You can use purchased apps installed on one computer on up to 10 devices using Windows, and you can use your Office 365 applications on up to five devices.

- Personal settings are automatically kept in sync online and among all the devices using the same Microsoft account. It includes themes, browser favorites and history, and content and settings for Microsoft apps and services.

Creating a Microsoft account for use with Windows 10 is a simple process. Assuming you are already using a Local account, you can switch to using a Microsoft account using this procedure:

Step 1.   Click the **Action Center** icon and select **All Settings**.

Step 2.   Select **Accounts**, and then from the menu select **Email & App Accounts**.

Step 3.   Click the **Add a Microsoft** account link.

Step 4.   Enter the credentials for your Microsoft account. If you do not have an email address you want to use, or you want to create a new one, click the **Create One!** link. You can then use an email account of your own, or click the **Get a New Email Address** link to create a new email address @outlook.com.

Step 5.   Fill out the Create a Microsoft Account form, as shown in Figure 5-1. Note that passwords must have a minimum of eight characters and contain at least two out of this list: uppercase letters, lowercase letters, numbers, and symbols.

Figure 5-1   Setting Up a Microsoft Account

Step 6.   When the form is complete, click **Next**.

Step 7.   On the Add Security Info screen, you can enter some additional information in case you lose your password. Fill out the fields as desired and then click **Next**.

Step 8.   On the Finish Up screen, sign up for the advertising and promotional material you want to receive, and then click **Next**.

Step 9.   The next screen asks you to confirm you are a real person. Enter the scrambled letters that appear on the screen and click **Next** when done.

Step 10.   Windows will take a few moments creating your account. When it is done, click **Finish** to sign on to Windows with your new Microsoft account.

Like many online accounts that you create, you will be asked to confirm your email address for your Microsoft account by clicking a link in an email from Microsoft's servers. The Windows Action Center displays a warning in Windows until you have confirmed your account.

Like other methods of signing on to Windows 10, when you set up a Microsoft account the first time, it will become the default sign-on method. To sign on using a different method, select the **Your Info** link. If you are signed in with a Microsoft account, click the **Sign On with a Local Account Instead** link, as shown in Figure 5-2. If you are currently signed on with a local account, you will be presented with a Sign On with a Microsoft Account Instead link. This is the only way to switch the sign-on option. You cannot simply log out and log back in with a different account. Only one account type will be functional at a time.

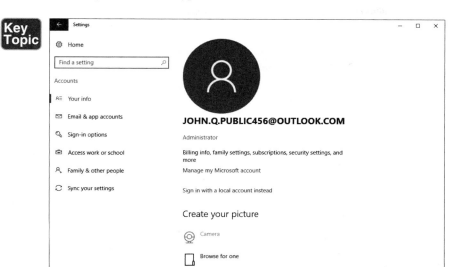

Figure 5-2   Your Info Page, with a Link to Switch to a Local Account

Domain Accounts

Users on domain-joined Windows 10 computers cannot connect their domain account to their Microsoft account. They can add a Microsoft account to the computer and use it for email and other apps. This provides the capability to sync their settings, favorites, and Microsoft apps from their home PC or tablet with their domain-joined computer, but they will not be able to sign in to the computer with the Microsoft account.

The process for creating the account is similar to that listed for a nondomain account, but domain users will not be presented with a Connect Your Microsoft Account option. Microsoft accounts can only be connected to local computer accounts.

Managing the Use of Microsoft Accounts

In many organizations it may be inappropriate to allow users to sign on to their PCs using a Microsoft account. As described in the previous section, using a Microsoft account on a business PC means that a lot of personal information is synched and made available on the local PC. This may cause disruption and possible security risks.

To block the use of Microsoft accounts, you can configure the Group Policy Accounts: Block Microsoft Accounts, which is found under Computer Configuration\Windows Settings\Security Settings\Local Policies\Security Options. There are three options:

- **This Policy Is Disabled:** Users can create and log on with Microsoft accounts and connect their domain-joined computer to their Microsoft account.

- **Users Can't Add Microsoft Accounts:** Users will not be able to create new Microsoft accounts, switch a local account to a Microsoft account, or connect a domain account to a Microsoft account.

- **Users Can't Add or Log On with Microsoft Accounts:** Existing Microsoft account users will not be able to log on to Windows.

> **NOTE**   The Block Microsoft Accounts setting applies only to using Microsoft accounts for local system logon and synching with a domain account. Users can still use their Microsoft account for things like accessing email over the Internet, using OneDrive to access cloud-based storage, and other purposes.

Integrating Microsoft Accounts Including Personalization Settings

Adding a Microsoft account to your Windows 10 computers allows you to access apps and other cloud settings using your Microsoft account and settings. As we have seen, you can link your Microsoft account to a local account on a nondomain computer and log in to a local account and use your Microsoft account automatically for email, calendar, OneDrive, and other apps.

Even if you are using a domain account for work or your organization, you can still use your Microsoft account for your personal settings without linking it to your work account. This allows you to keep your personalization settings, bookmarks, and other information in sync on your work computer, home computer, mobile device, and other Windows 10 devices.

The Accounts setting page menu called Sync Your Settings is used to customize the settings you want to keep in sync with your other devices, as shown in Figure 5-3. The Sync Settings toggle turns sync on or off completely. Toggles for turning on synchronization of specific settings are available in the Individual Sync Settings section.

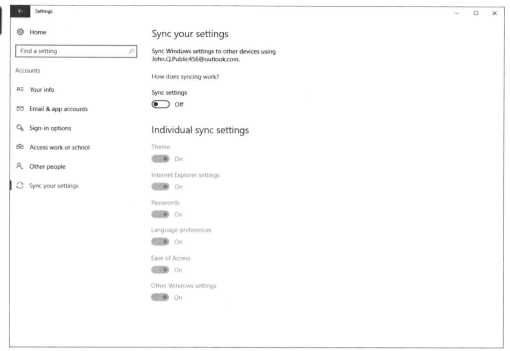

Figure 5-3   Customize Settings to Sync with Other Devices on the Sync Your Settings Page

Several settings are for personalization or look and feel of Windows that you may have modified. You can sync your language preferences and your accessibility customizations as well. Turning on Internet Explorer settings will synchronize all your Internet options, including favorites and your home page. If you turn on Other Windows settings, Windows syncs some device settings for things such as printers and mouse options, as well as File Explorer settings and notification preferences.

Windows Store and Cloud Apps

The Windows Store is an online app store integrated with Windows 10 that enables users to quickly and easily buy and download small applications (known simply as apps) that may be developed by Microsoft, software vendors, or even independent developers. After users create an account in the app store, they can easily shop and click to add functionality to their Windows computer.

This can be fun and convenient for users, but in a large organization with limited IT resources, it can quickly cause problems for management, network administrators, and support personnel. Windows provides some tools for assisting IT administrators in taking control of the use of Windows Store, the ability to download and run applications, and management of applications that are authorized by the organization.

Introduction to Windows Store Apps

Windows Store apps, now called Universal Windows Platform (UWP) apps, are not like typical Windows desktop applications. They are a new type of app designed for ease of use, new interfaces, and focusing on content. Apps can be designed for consumer use or for Line-of-Business (LOB) functionality. UWP apps are designed to function not just on Windows desktops, but to perform as well on tablets, smartphones and mobile devices, Xbox One, and Microsoft HoloLens.

Windows has revamped the interface for UWP apps considerably in Windows 10. They are now displayed in a mouse-friendly windowed interface with Close buttons and Minimize and Maximize controls. Typically, apps will have certain unique characteristics:

- Apps display in one window and enable multiple views, altering their interface to best fit the size of the user's device display.

- It must be a standalone app.

- Designed for touchscreens and pen input.

- Apps share and expose personalized content, allowing users to search for content across all their Windows Store apps.

- Apps implement new UI controls, including the apps bar and Start menu tile settings.

- Apps use tiles instead of icons, and content can be delivered through a tile even when the app is not running.

The main delivery channel for apps is the Windows Store, and apps are available only by downloading them through the Windows Store app. These apps meet certain Microsoft requirements and must be certified and signed by Microsoft before they are made available. However, Microsoft has provided enterprises a way to *sideload* unsigned apps on Windows 10 Enterprise edition computers that are joined to the organization's Active Directory domain. You can also enable sideloading on other computers by enabling developer features. See the section "Sideloading Apps" later in this chapter for details.

Installing and Managing Software by Using Microsoft Office 365 and Windows Store Apps

Microsoft Office 365 is Microsoft's cloud-based offering of Office applications, accessible through a user-based paid subscription. Users can access their licensed Microsoft Office products on up to five compatible devices.

Office 365 updates are applied automatically. There is no need for software maintenance tasks, such as installing updates or upgrading versions, so administrators don't need to worry about updating devices manually. However, the company is still in control of updates and can decide how and when these will be provided to users. Administrators can also decide where user data is stored: on the back office servers of the enterprise, in private cloud-based storage, in the public cloud, or a combination.

Office 365 is a type of Software as a Service (SaaS). With SaaS, end users have access to a managed software product that they can use and consume on demand over the Internet. An organization might choose a SaaS product like Office 365 to reduce maintenance and installation tasks, reduce licensing costs, or simplify the software portfolio and license management in an organization. SaaS products such as Office 365 also offer the benefit of access to apps and saved documents from any location or computer, provided an Internet connection is available.

Configuring and Managing Office 365

You will need an Office 365 Business account to begin configuring Office 365 on a Windows computer. Access the Office 365 Admin Center at https://portal.microsoftonline.com/admin/default.aspx.

You can configure several installation settings from Office 365 Admin Center. Locate the User Software page, located under Service Settings, in the Office 365 Admin Center. If you are using the new Admin Center, you can find this under Services & Add-ins on the Settings menu. From the page, you can select the applications that you will enable users to install, such as Office and Skype for Business. After you have enabled this option, users can install Office on their computers by completing the steps in the list that follows:

Step 1.   In a web browser, navigate to https://portal.microsoftonline.com.

Step 2.   Sign in to your Office 365 account.

Step 3.   From the Office 365 portal page, click **Install Office**.

Step 4.   Click **Run** to start the installation, click **Yes** to continue, and then click **Next** to start the wizard.

Step 5.   Select whether to send updates to Microsoft, and then click **Accept**.

Step 6.   Click **Next** on the Meet OneDrive page.

Step 7.   Click **Next** to accept defaults, select **No Thanks**, and then click **All Done**. The progress page shown in Figure 5-4 is displayed as Office is installed.

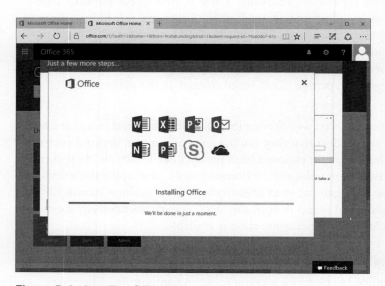

Figure 5-4   Installing Office 365

The preceding method describes a self-service method for installing Office on a single Windows computer, but you can also deploy Office in an enterprise using other methods. The Office Deployment tool enables you to configure information about the language(s) to download, select the architecture, configure a deployment network share, learn how to apply updates to existing Office installations, and determine which version to install. Deployment methods include Group Policy, startup scripts, or Microsoft System Center Configuration Manager (SCCM).

Working with apps from the Windows Store is designed to be easy and user friendly. Users need to sign up with a Microsoft account (or use an existing account), scroll through or search for the app they want, and click it to install. By default, users do not need any administrative or special privileges to install Windows Store apps. The following steps outline a typical process for an application example, Acrobat Reader Touch:

Step 1.   From the Start menu, click the **Store** tile.

Step 2.   Scroll through the categories to look for an app, or use the Search for Apps box in the upper right. This example shows how to install Acrobat Reader for Touch.

Step 3.   Click in the Search bar and type **Adobe Reader Touch**. We will install the Windows Store Adobe Reader Touch app in this example. Click the icon when you have located it.

Step 4.   The next screen displays user ratings, a description, and some screenshots of the app in use. You can scroll down to see things like details, system requirements, and user Reviews. Click the **Get** button to install the app.

Step 5.   If you are not logged in to a Microsoft account, you are prompted to enter your Microsoft account credentials. You can also sign up for a new one by clicking the link.

Step 6.   The Get button changes to show download and then installation progress, and eventually changes to display a Launch button.

Step 7.   Click the **Launch** button to start the new UWP app.

> **NOTE**   When you run Adobe Reader, you will notice how different it is from the Adobe Reader desktop application used in older versions of Windows. It implements all the app characteristics from the introduction section and is touchscreen enabled.

Managing Software Using Office 365

You can manage all aspects of the Office 365 environment from Office 365 Admin Center. The admin center contains configuration and management pages for all the different features that affect Office app installation:

- Dashboard provides a view of service health of Office-related components and includes shortcuts to administrative tasks and user management functions.

- The Users page includes functions for adding, removing, and editing users' accounts in Office 365. From here you can also configure Active Directory synchronization and configure authentication policies and requirements.

- The Domains page allows you to manage and add domains used by Office 365 in your enterprise.

- Service Settings includes several pages, including Updates, User Software, Passwords, Rights Management, and Mobile.

- Tools includes configuration, health, and readiness tools for Office, and includes Office 365 health, readiness, and connectivity checks; Office 365 Best Practices Analyzer; and Microsoft Connectivity Analyzer.

NOTE   You might want to learn about other features for managing Office 365, including click-to-run installation and managing Office 365 using PowerShell. For details, refer to the TechNet article at https://technet.microsoft.com/en-us/library/dn568031.aspx.

Updating Windows Store Apps

Updating Windows Store apps is a similar process, but it is even easier because you do not have to scroll or search through so large a list of options and apps; only installed apps with updates are available for selection:

Step 1.   Click the **Start** button and select the **Store** tile.

Step 2.   Click your account icon (next to the Search bar), and then select **Downloads and Updates**.

NOTE   You can also select the **Settings** option, where you can toggle **Update Apps Automatically** on or off. If this setting is turned on, apps update automatically when you are connected to the Internet.

Step 3.   Select the **Check for Updates** button to check all your installed apps for any updates.

Step 4.   On the App updates screen, the app updates are listed at the top. Click the **Update Available** button for the apps you want to update.

Step 5.   The Downloading progress bar is displayed. You can watch the installation progress or continue working on something else while they install. When the app is installed, the button text changes to Completed.

Windows Store makes installing apps easy and quick for end users. If you have browsed through the apps available, you may have noticed all the games and entertainment apps. Managers in many organizations would prefer their staff not to have access to these kinds of distractions during the workday and turn to IT for a solution.

Thankfully, Microsoft has considered this, and has provided Windows system administrators with a number of ways to control access to the Windows Store and the apps. The tools you use will depend on your environment.

As noted in Table 5-2, controlling access to specific apps using AppLocker policies is available only for domain-joined computers running Windows 10 Enterprise.

Table 5-2 Options for Controlling Access to Windows Store

Requirement	Tool to Use
Turn off Windows Store to all Windows computers.	Group policies
Control which apps can be installed on Windows 10 Enterprise computers.	AppLocker
Control which apps can be installed on Windows 10 Pro computers.	N/A
Control which users can access the Windows Store.	Group policies
Control which computers can access the Windows Store.	Group policies

Controlling Windows Store Access

If you need to block access to the Windows Store, you can use Local Policies or GPOs for domain-joined computers. You can lock these down either by disallowing users to modify Local Policies or by enforcing them with Group Policy objects, as shown in Figure 5-5. To turn off access to the Store, you can use the Turn Off the Store Application policy.

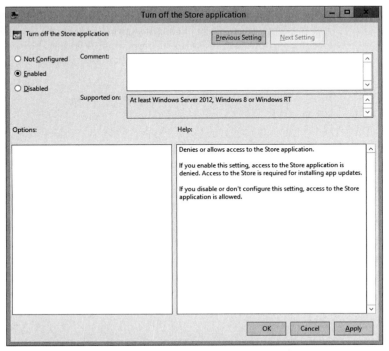

Figure 5-5 Disabling Access to Windows Store Using GPOs to Block the Store Application

Table 5-3 lists the Group Policies available for controlling access to the Windows Store.

Table 5-3 Group Policies for Windows Store

Policy Setting	Applies To	Help Text
Turn off the Store application	User or Machine	Denies or allows access to the Store application. If you enable this setting, access to the Store application is denied. Access to the Store is required for installing app updates. If you disable or do not configure this setting, access to the Store application is allowed.
Allow Store to install apps on Windows To Go workspaces	Machine	Allows or denies access to the Store application on Windows To Go workspaces. If you enable this setting, access to the Store application is allowed on the Windows To Go workspace. Only enable this policy when the Windows To Go workspace will be used only with a single PC. Using it with multiple PCs is not supported. If you disable or do not configure this setting, access to the Store application is denied on the Windows To Go workspace.
Turn off Automatic Download of updates	Machine	Enables or disables the automatic download of updates. If you enable this setting, automatic download of updates is turned off. If you disable or do not configure this setting, automatic download of updates is turned on.

Sideloading Apps

Microsoft has somewhat restricted the ability to sideload apps for security and other reasons. Apps can only be installed through the Windows Store by default; however, organizations and independent developers may find it useful to develop their own Line-of-Business (LOB) apps that they do not want to have certified and loaded on the Windows Store for others to use. Microsoft has relaxed restrictions on sideloading apps with the release of Windows 10 and no longer requires sideloading license keys.

If your organization has LOB apps to deploy, you can enable sideloading in your enterprise. You can also enable sideloading on any Windows 10 device in settings. The following is required for sideloading uncertified apps:

- Clients must be running Windows Server 2012/R2 and must be joined to a Windows Active Directory domain. Windows 10 computers must have sideloading unlocked in enterprise policy or through settings, as shown in Figure 5-6.

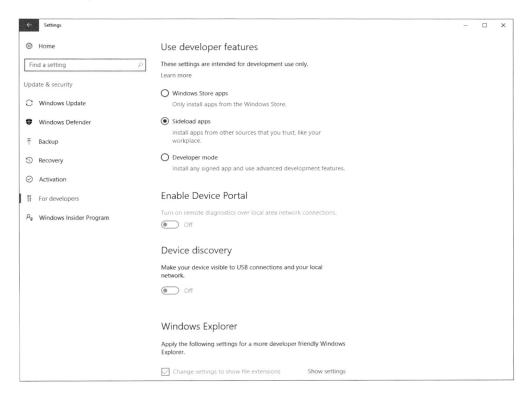

Figure 5-6   Enabling Sideloading in Windows 10 Settings

- You must enable the Group Policy Allow All Trusted Applications to Install, as shown in Figure 5-7.

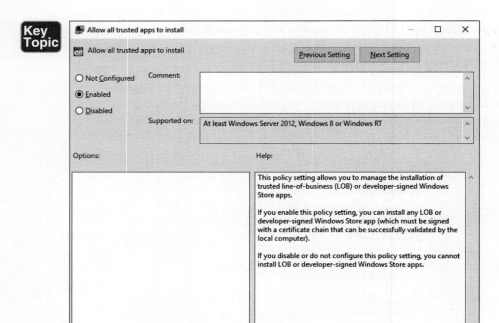

Figure 5-7 Enabling Sideloading Using Group Policies

- To sideload apps for a Windows 10 Pro computer, you must unlock the device for sideloading using Group Policy or through Settings.

- Windows 10 Enterprise computers that are not joined to a domain also require the device to be unlocked for sideloading.

- Apps need to be signed using a certificate from a public certificate authority (CA), an enterprise CA, or a self-signed certificate, and you must install the certificate on the device.

You cannot install an unsigned package to Windows 10. All apps must be crypto-graphically signed, and your Windows 10 device must trust the certificate used to sign the app. You can use an enterprise certificate or a self-signed certificate, but you must install the certificate to the Trusted Root Certificate Authorities folder of the local computer before you can install the signed app. You can use Group Policy to install apps on domain-joined devices. On Windows 10 mobile devices, you will need to use a provisioning package to install the certificate. Note that apps downloaded from the Windows Store cannot be sideloaded. To install apps signed by the Windows Store, you must use the Windows Store installation process.

> **NOTE** For information on installing and managing certificates on Windows Mobile, see "Install Digital Certificates on Windows 10 Mobile" at https://technet.microsoft.com/en-us/itpro/windows/keep-secure/installing-digital-certificates-on-windows-10-mobile.

Sideloading into Online and Offline Images

If you are deploying Windows images, you can use tools to sideload apps into images for deployment, or into the images of current deployments of Windows 10. You can use PowerShell or the DISM command-line tool to sideload apps into images. The process is similar to the process for installing driver packages using DISM, as you learned about in Chapter 3, "Post-Installation Configuration."

Apps can be added in two ways:

- The user can install the app, and it will be available only to that user.

- The app can be installed into the Windows image, and it will be available to every user.

Apps added to the Windows image are referred to as *provisioned* apps. You are limited to 24 provisioned apps in an image.

You can provision an app to an online image with a single **DISM** command. The online image is the current device image you are using and logged in to. To provision the app, run the following command from an administrative command prompt. Replace the C:\LOBApps\app1.appx with the path to the app you want to sideload.

```
DISM /Online /Add-ProvisionedAppxPackage /PackagePath:C:\LOBApps
  \app1.appx /SkipLicense
```

The **DISM /Add-ProvisionedAppxPackage** command is also used to provision the app to an offline image. You must first mount the image, and use the **/Image** switch instead of the **/Online** switch. For example, the following commands will mount an offline image, provision the package, then unmount the image.

```
DISM /Mount-Image /ImageFile:E:\WinImages\Win10Ent-1.wim /
  Name:"Windows 10 Enterprise" /MountDir:E:\test\offline
DISM /Image:E:\test\offline /Add-ProvisionedAppxPackage /
  PackagePath:C:\LOBApps\app1.appx /SkipLicense
DISM /Unmount-Image /MountDir:E:\test\offline /Commit
```

Provisioning an app using this process allows you to create an image for Windows 10 that can be used to deploy the operating system to a device, and the apps you provision will be available to all users. You can also use the **Add-ProvisionedAppxPackage** command to update an app on an offline or online image. To remove a provisioned app, use the **Remove-ProvisionedAppxPackage** command instead.

NOTE   For more information on the DISM /Add-ProvisionedAppxPackage command and syntax, see "DISM App Package Servicing Command-Line Options" at https://msdn.microsoft.com/windows/hardware/commercialize/manufacture/desktop/dism-app-package--appx-or-appxbundle--servicing-command-line-options.

Sideloading Apps Using Microsoft Intune

Microsoft Intune is a cloud-based service, part of the suite of cloud product offerings like Office 365. Intune is used to help you manage Windows mobile devices, and it can also be used to manage iOS and Android devices as well. We discuss more details about using Microsoft Intune to manage devices throughout this book and focus specifically on Intune in Chapter 13, "Microsoft Intune." You should revisit this topic after reviewing Chapter 13 and have learned more about managing devices with Intune.

One of the useful features of Intune is that it allows you to sideload apps into the Windows 10 mobile devices or Windows 10 desktops that you manage through the Intune portal. When you log in to the portal as an administrator, you click the **APPS** menu to obtain the screen shown in Figure 5-8. Adding apps for sideloading and deploying them to computers or groups of computers is a simple process outlined in the steps that follow:

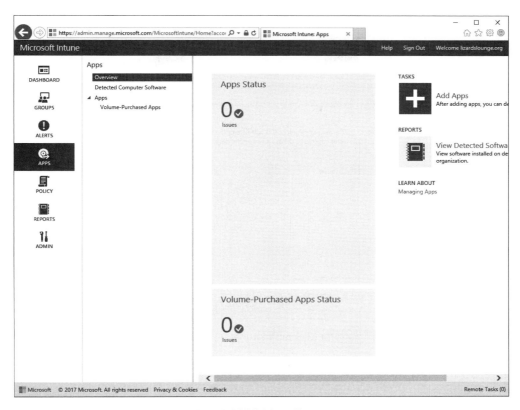

Figure 5-8 Intune Administration Portal APPS Menu Page

Step 1.   Click the **Add Apps** button. This displays the Add Software dialog shown in Figure 5-9. If you are prompted to log in, use your Intune administrator credentials. Click **Next**.

Figure 5-9   Add Software Dialog for Microsoft Intune

Step 2. From the Select the Software Installer File Type drop-down list, select **Windows App Package**.

Step 3. Click the **Browse** button to find the app or app package you would like to install. Windows will verify that your app is available and is a valid UWP app. Click **Next**.

Step 4. Fill out the information on the Describe the Software page. At a minimum, you need to include the Publisher, the app's Name, and the Description, as shown in Figure 5-10. It's a good idea to also include an icon or graphic for your app so it is recognizable to your users. Click **Next**.

Step 5. On the Summary screen, click **Upload**. When the upload completes, click the **Close** button. The app is uploaded to the Intune portal and is now ready for deployment to your users. From the Apps menu, select **Apps** to view the details of the apps you have uploaded, as shown in Figure 5-11.

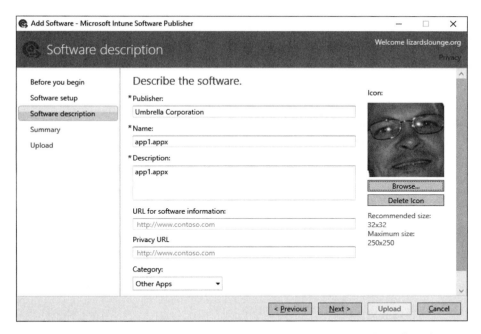

Figure 5-10   Describing the Software to Be Uploaded to the Intune Apps Portal

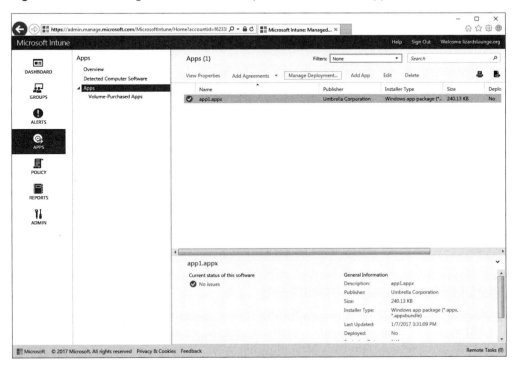

Figure 5-11   Intune Apps Menu Section Displaying the Apps for Deployment to Managed Devices

Step 6.   To deploy the app, select **Manage Deployment** from the menu. This displays the Select Groups page of the deployments manager.

Step 7.   From the Select Groups page, you can select users or devices for the deployment. Select the groups for the deployment and click **Add** to add them to the Selected groups. Click **Next**.

Step 8.   On the Deployment Action screen, shown in Figure 5-12, select an Approval type. To require this app, select **Required Install**. Click **Finish**.

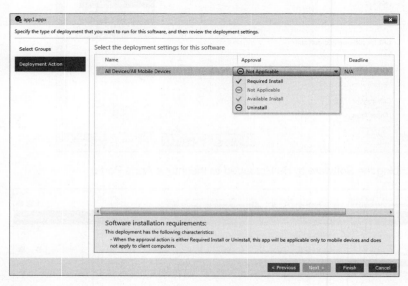

Figure 5-12   Deploying an App to Device Groups in Microsoft Intune

If you selected Required Install in Step 8, the app will be installed on all devices in the selected group the next time any user logs in to the devices.

NOTE   For more information on sideloading LOB apps, refer to "How to Add and Remove Apps" at https://technet.microsoft.com/en-us/itpro/windows/deploy/sideload-apps-in-windows-10.

Deep Link Apps by Using Microsoft Intune

In addition to any company apps (LOB) or custom-developed apps that your users will want access to, you can also deploy other apps, or make them available to users, by adding apps available from the online app store. You can deep link apps for iOS, Android, and any edition of Windows 10.

This process is very similar to the process for sideloading apps from Intune, as described earlier. However, store apps cannot be sideloaded in Windows 10, so instead of hosting the app on the Intune portal, you provide the link to the app store when you add the app to the portal.

When you start the Add Software dialog from the Intune portal, select **External Link** from the Select How This Software Is Made Available to Devices drop-down, as shown in Figure 5-13.

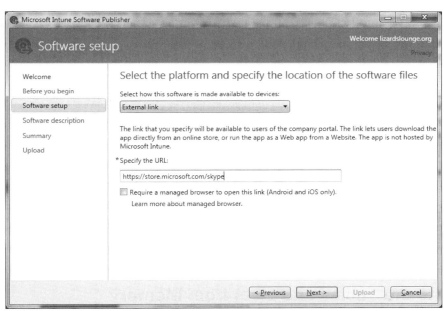

Figure 5-13   Deep Link Apps Using Intune by Adding a Link to the App Store for the Application

Apps that you deep link this way will automatically be available to all users of the devices that you specify for the app.

Exam Preparation Tasks

Review All the Key Topics

Review the most important topics in the chapter, noted with the Key Topics icon in the outer margin of the page. Table 5-4 lists a reference of these key topics and the page numbers on which each is found.

Table 5-4   Key Topics for Chapter 5

Key Topic Element	Description	Page Number
Step List	Adding a Microsoft account	229
Figure 5-2	Switch the Windows login to a local account or a Microsoft account	231
List	Group Policy to govern the use of Microsoft accounts	232
Figure 5-3	Sync settings with your Microsoft account	233
Step List	Installing Office 365	235
Step List	Installing an app from the Windows Store	237
Step List	Updating Windows Store apps	238
Table 5-2	Lists options for controlling access to Windows Store	239
Figure 5-5	Group Policy to disable access to the Windows Store	239
Table 5-3	Describes Group Policies for Windows Store	240
List	Requirements for sideloading LOB apps	241
Figure 5-7	Enabling sideloading in Windows 10 settings	242
Commands	Using DISM to sideload apps in a Windows 10 image	243
Step List	Sideloading apps using the Microsoft Intune portal	245
Figure 5-13	Deep linking apps using Microsoft Intune	249

Complete the Tables and Lists from Memory

Print a copy of Appendix B, "Memory Tables" (found on the book's website), or at least the section for this chapter, and complete the tables and lists from memory. Appendix C, "Memory Tables Answer Key," also on the website, includes completed tables and lists to check your work.

Definitions of Key Terms

Define the following key terms from this chapter, and check your answers in the glossary.

authentication, authorization, CA, certificate, cloud, credentials, deep link, LOB, Microsoft account, Microsoft Intune, provisioned apps, SaaS, sideloading

This chapter covers the following subjects:

- **Configuring TCP/IP Settings:** TCP/IP is the primary protocol suite used by computers connecting with each other and the Internet. This section introduces you to the important components of versions 4 and 6 of the TCP/IP protocol suite that you must be familiar with for the 70-697 and 70-698 exams. In this section you are introduced to the various types of IPv4 and IPv6 addresses that are used on Windows-based networks.

- **Configuring IP:** In this section you learn about the various settings in Windows that enable you to connect to wired or wireless networks, including the Internet. You are also introduced to the wireless networking protocols used by Windows 10 and the available security settings that help protect your connection.

- **Configuring Network Settings:** Network adapters available in Windows 10 include wired Ethernet connections, wireless adapters, Bluetooth PAN adapters, as well as virtual adapters used for tunneling, VPN, and dial-up connectivity. This section shows you how to configure your network adapter settings, networking configurations, and other options specific to adapters and adapter types. When connecting to wireless networks, manually and automatically, it is important to make sure that the network access points that Windows finds and accesses are the intended networks. This section discusses ways for managing preferred wireless networks and how each connection should be handled.

This chapter covers the following objectives for the 70-697 and 70-698 exam:

Configure IP settings: Configure and support IPv4 and IPv6 network settings; configure name resolution, connect to a network, configure network locations.

Configure networking settings: Connect to a wireless network, manage preferred wireless networks, configure network adapters, configure location-aware printing; troubleshoot network issues.

CHAPTER 6

Windows 10 Networking

Connectivity between Windows 10 computers and other networks (inclusive of the Internet and other computers) is provided in a variety of ways. Windows 10 computers utilize a variety of tools, applications, and protocols for connecting to networks. You learn about the Network and Sharing Center, which consolidates many of these applications and utilities into one convenient location from which you can create and manage different types of network connections as well as file and printer sharing. This chapter starts by introducing networking components, including how to install, configure, and manage them:

- Dial-up networking
- Wireless networking
- Configuring network adapters
- Location-aware printing

Not only do you explore each of these components in this chapter, you also look at their features and dependencies as they exist within the Windows 10 operating system.

"Do I Know This Already?" Quiz

The "Do I Know This Already?" quiz allows you to assess whether you should read this entire chapter or simply jump to the "Exam Preparation Tasks" section for review. If you are in doubt, read the entire chapter. Table 6-1 outlines the major headings in this chapter and the corresponding "Do I Know This Already?" quiz questions. You can find the answers in Appendix A, "Answers to the 'Do I Know This Already?' Quizzes."

Table 6-1   "Do I Know This Already?" Foundation Topics Section-to-Question Mapping

Foundation Topics Section	Questions Covered in This Section
Configuring TCP/IP Settings	1–7
Configuring IP	8–10
Configuring Network Settings	11–15

CAUTION   The goal of self-assessment is to gauge your mastery of the topics in this chapter. If you do not know the answer to a question or are only partially sure of the answer, you should mark that question as wrong for purposes of the self-assessment. Giving yourself credit for an answer you correctly guess skews your self-assessment results and might provide you with a false sense of security.

1. Which of the following are component protocols contained within TCP/IP? (Choose three.)

    a. User Datagram Protocol (UDP)

    b. Internet Control Message Protocol (ICMP)

    c. Dynamic Host Configuration Protocol (DHCP)

    d. Address Resolution Protocol (ARP)

2. You need to ensure that your IPv4-enabled computer can access other subnets on your company's network, as well as the Internet. Which addressing component should you ensure is specified properly?

    a. IP address

    b. Subnet mask

    c. Default gateway

    d. DNS server address

    e. WINS address

3. Your computer is configured with the IP address 131.107.24.5. To which class does this IP address belong?

    a. A

    b. B

    c. C

    d. D

    e. E

4. Your company is making use of the 192.168.21.0/24 network. This network address is an example of what type of address notation?

    a. Windows Internet Name Service (WINS)

    b. Unicast

    c. Multicast

    d. Classless interdomain routing (CIDR)

5. Your company has transitioned to using the IPv6 protocol, and you are responsible for configuring Internet servers that need direct access to the Internet. Which of the following types of IPv6 addresses should you use for this purpose?

    a. Global unicast

    b. Link-local unicast

    c. Site-local unicast

    d. Multicast

    e. Anycast

6. Your computer is using an IPv6 address on the fe80::/64 network. What type of IPv6 address is this?

    a. Global unicast

    b. Link-local unicast

    c. Site-local unicast

    d. Teredo

7. Your computer is using an IPv6 address that includes the 32-bit prefix of 2001::/32. What type of IPv6 address prefix is this?

    a. Global unicast

    b. Link-local unicast

    c. Site-local unicast

    d. Teredo

8. You need to configure a client computer running Windows 10 Pro to respond to three different DNS servers in order to resolve all names on the network. What should you do?

   a. From the General tab of the Internet Properties dialog box, select the **Use the Following DNS Server Addresses** option and type the IP addresses of the three DNS servers in the text boxes provided.

   b. From the General tab of the Internet Properties dialog box, select the **Use the Following DNS Server Addresses** option and type the IP addresses of the two most used DNS servers in the text boxes provided. Then select the **Alternate Configuration** tab and type the IP address of the third DNS server at this tab.

   c. From the General tab of the Internet Properties dialog box, select the **Use the Following DNS Server Addresses** option and click the **Advanced** button. On the Advanced TCP/IP Settings dialog box that appears, click **Add** and type the three DNS server IP addresses, one at a time. Then ensure that they are sequenced in the order they will most likely need to be accessed.

   d. You cannot specify more than two DNS servers at the client computer; you must configure the DHCP server to supply the required DNS server IP addresses.

9. Your network is configured to use DHCP for assignment of IP addresses and DNS servers. Which of the following options should you ensure are selected in the Internet Protocol Version 4 (TCP/IPv4) Properties dialog box? (Choose two.)

   a. Obtain an IP Address Automatically

   b. Use the Following IP Address

   c. Obtain DNS Server Address Automatically

   d. Use the Following DNS Server Addresses

10. Your computer is configured to use the IPv4 address 169.254.183.32. What system is being used by your computer?

    a. Dynamic Host Configuration Protocol (DHCP)

    b. Automatic Private Internet Protocol Addressing (APIPA)

    c. Private IPv4 network addressing

    d. Alternate IP configuration

11. Your network provider charges for all of your bandwidth based on the amount of data transferred over the connection. You want to set up a wireless connection to ensure that the amount of data transferred while connected is minimized. What setting should you use?

   a. Estimated data usage

   b. Turn sharing on or off

   c. Metered connection

   d. Dial-up connection speed

12. You currently have several wireless networks that you connect to frequently. Your home network uses WEP, the engineering department near your office uses WPA2-Personal, the coffee shop around the corner uses Open Wi-Fi, and the conference room near your office uses WEP. You hosted a demonstration in the conference room before you left the office yesterday, and then you used your home AP to VPN to the company network last night. When you arrive at the office in the morning and turn on your laptop, which network will your Windows 10 computer attempt to connect with first?

   a. Your home network AP

   b. The conference room

   c. The engineering department

   d. The coffee shop

13. You have been traveling a great deal with your Windows 10 laptop and want to clean up the leftover wireless network profiles that you will probably not use again in the near future. How can you delete the wireless profiles?

   a. Select each from the Network list, right-click, and select **Forget This Network**.

   b. Use the **netsh** command **netsh wlan delete** for each profile.

   c. Use the Network and Sharing center to delete the network connections.

   d. You cannot delete the profiles.

14. You need to make changes to the Advanced properties of a network adapter device. To access the properties, you open the Change Adapter settings from the Network and Sharing Center, access the adapter properties from the right-click menu, and then the NIC properties using the Configure button. This is similar to the properties from the Device Manager device properties, but some settings are unavailable. What can you not configure from this dialog that is available when using Device Manager?

   a. Advanced properties

   b. Driver details

   c. Power Management

   d. Resources

15. Which of the following Advanced properties of a network adapter are available for a wireless connection? (Choose all that apply.)

   a. 802.11n mode

   b. Speed and Duplex

   c. Transmit Buffers

   d. Preferred Band

   e. Receive Buffers

Foundation Topics

Configuring TCP/IP Settings

To favor seamless integration with the Internet, Microsoft has standardized on the use of TCP/IP and no longer uses older, proprietary network protocol suites that were once common. Since its introduction of Active Directory in Windows 2000, Microsoft has made TCP/IP the protocol suite required for Windows networks that use Active Directory. This is largely because of the Active Directory's dependence upon Domain Name System (DNS) to provide the name and address resolution for all Active Directory resources.

TCP/IP is a suite of protocols governing the transmission of data across computer networks and the Internet. The following is a brief description of the major protocols that you should be aware of:

- **Transmission Control Protocol (TCP):** Provides connection-oriented, reliable communication between two hosts, typically involving large amounts of data. Note that a *host* includes any device on the network (such as a computer or router) that is configured for TCP/IP. This kind of communication also involves acknowledgments that data has been correctly received.

- **User Datagram Protocol (UDP):** Used for fast, non-connection-oriented communications with no guarantee of delivery, typically small, short bursts of data. Applications using UDP data transmission are responsible for checking their data's integrity.

- **Internet Protocol (IP):** Handles, addresses, and routes packets between hosts on a network. It performs this service for all other protocols in the TCP/IP protocol suite.

- **Internet Control Message Protocol (ICMP):** Enables hosts on a TCP/IP network to share status and error information. It is specifically responsible for reporting errors and messages regarding the delivery of IP datagrams. It is not responsible for error correction. Higher layer protocols use information provided by ICMP to recover from transmission problems. The **ping** command uses ICMP to check connectivity to remote computers.

- **Address Resolution Protocol (ARP):** Used to resolve the IP address of the destination computer to the physical or Media Access Control (MAC) address, which is a unique 12-digit hexadecimal number that is burned into ROM on every network adapter card.

These are only a few of the many protocols that make up the TCP/IP protocol suite. If you need additional information on these protocols and details on the other protocols that make up TCP/IP, refer to any book that specializes in computer internetworking.

By default, the earliest versions of Windows used version 4 of the IP protocol, simply known as IPv4. With its 32-bit address space, this version has performed admirably well in the more than 30 years since its initial introduction. However, with the rapid growth of the Internet in recent years, its address space has approached exhaustion, and security concerns have increased. Consequently, the Internet Engineering Task Force (IETF) introduced version 6 of the IP protocol with Request for Comment (RFC) 1883 in 1995 and updated with RFCs 2460, 3513, and 4193 in more recent years. Simply known as IPv6, this protocol provides for 128-bit addressing, which allows for a practically infinite number of possible addresses, as well as the following benefits:

- **An efficient hierarchical addressing scheme:** IPv6 addresses are designed to enable an efficient, hierarchical, and summarizable routing scheme, making way for multiple levels of Internet service providers (ISPs), which is becoming more common nowadays.

- **Simpler routing tables:** Backbone routers on the Internet are more easily configured for routing packets to their destinations.

- **Stateful and stateless address configuration:** IPv6 simplifies host configuration with the use of stateful address configuration (configuring IP addresses in the presence of a Dynamic Host Configuration Protocol [DHCP] server) or the use of stateless address configuration (configuring IP addresses in the absence of a DHCP server). Stateless address configuration enables the automatic configuration of hosts on a subnetwork according to the addresses displayed by available routers.

- **Improved security:** IPv6 includes standards-based support for IP Security (IPsec). In fact, IPv6 requires IPsec support. You can configure IPsec connection security rules for IPv6 in the same fashion as with IPv4. IPsec is discussed further in Chapter 16, "Configuring and Maintaining Network Security."

- **Support for Link-Local Multicast Name Resolution (LLMNR):** This enables IPv6 and IPv4 clients on a single subnet to resolve each other's names without the need for a DNS server or using NetBIOS over TCP/IP.

- **Improved support for Quality of Service (QoS):** IPv6 header fields improve the identification and handling of network traffic from its source to destination, even when IPsec encryption is in use.

- **Extensibility:** You can add extension headers after the IPv6 packet header, which enable the inclusion of new features as they are developed in years to come.

By using a TCP/IP implementation known as the Next Generation TCP/IP stack (first included with Windows Vista), Windows 10 enables a dual IP layer architecture enabling the operation of both IPv4 and IPv6 at the same time. Unlike with Windows XP and older Windows versions, Windows 10 does not require you to install a separate IPv6 component; IPv6 is installed and enabled by default.

NOTE   For more introductory information on IPv6, refer to "Microsoft's Objectives for IP Version 6" at http://technet.microsoft.com/en-us/library/bb726949.aspx.

Configuring and Supporting TCP/IP Version 4 Settings

Much of TCP/IPv4 is transparent to users and to administrators. The administrator may need to configure the address information applied to the network interface. Table 6-2 describes this address information.

Table 6-2 IPv4 Addressing Components

Addressing Component	Description
IP address	The unique, logical 32-bit address, which identifies the computer (called a host or node) and the subnet on which it is located. The IP address is displayed in dotted decimal notation (each decimal represents an octet of binary ones and zeros). For example, the binary notation of an address may be 10000000.00000001.00000001.000 00011, which in dotted decimal notation is written as 128.1.1.3.
Subnet mask	The subnet mask is applied to an IP address to determine the subnetwork address and the host address on that subnet. All hosts on the same subnet must have the same subnet mask for them to be correctly identified. If a mask is incorrect, both the subnet and the host address will be wrong. (For example, if you have an IP address of 128.1.1.3, and an incorrect mask of 255.255.128.0, the subnet address would be 128.1.0 and the host address would be 1.3. If the correct subnet mask is 255.255.255.0, the subnet address would be 128.1.1 and the host address would be 3.)
Default gateway	The address listed as the default gateway is the location on the local subnet to which the local computer will send all data meant for other subnets. In other words, this is the IP address for a router that is capable of transmitting the data to other networks.
DNS server address	The place where names of IP hosts are sent so that the DNS server will respond with an IP address. This process is called *name resolution*. DNS is a distributed database of records that maps names to IP addresses, and vice versa. A HOSTS file that maps names to IP addresses can be placed on the local computer and used instead of DNS, which renders this an optional setting, although it is rare that a network is small enough to make a HOSTS file more efficient than a DNS server. When a user types in a DNS name, such as BlakePC.mydomain.local, the computer sends the name to the DNS server. If the name is one that the DNS server knows, it sends back the IP address. Otherwise, the DNS server sends the name request to a higher-level DNS server, and this recursive process continues until either the IP address is found and returned to the original requestor or until all avenues have been exhausted and the original requestor is notified that the name cannot be found.
Windows Internet Name Service (WINS) address	The WINS server address is the location where network computers send requests to resolve NetBIOS names to IP addresses. WINS is used on Microsoft Windows networks where older Windows computers or applications require NetBIOS naming. When a user types in a NetBIOS name, such as BLAKEPC, the computer sends the name to the WINS server. Because WINS is a flat-file database, it returns an IP address or a Name Not Found message. WINS server addresses, like DNS server addresses, are optional. A computer can use a local LMHOSTS file to map the NetBIOS names to IP addresses rather than use WINS.

Static IPv4 Addressing

IP addresses indicate the same type of location information as a street address. A building on a street has a number, and when you add that number to the street name, you can find it fairly easily because the number and the street will be unique within a city. This type of address scheme—an individual address plus a location address—allows every computer on the Internet to be uniquely identified.

A static IP address is one that is permanently assigned to a computer on the network. Certain computers (such as routers or servers) require static IP addresses because of their functions. Client computers are more often assigned dynamic addresses because they are more likely to be moved around the network or retired and replaced. DSL and cable modem users are usually given a dynamic IP address (but this doesn't change for a long time, generally until the cable company next reconfigures the network), whereas dial-up users are provided with dynamic addresses that change each time the user connects to the network.

As discussed earlier, IP addresses consist of two parts: one that specifies the network and one part that specifies the computer. These addresses are further categorized with classes, as described in Table 6-3.

Table 6-3 IPv4 Address Classes

Class	Dotted Decimal Hosts per Range	First Octet Binary	Usage	Number of Networks	Number of Hosts per Network
A	1.0.0.0– 126.255.255.255	0xxxxxxx	Large networks/ ISPs	126	16,777,214
B	128.0.0.0– 191.255.255.255	10xxxxxx	Large or mid-size ISPs	16,384	65,534
C	192.0.0.0– 223.255.255.255	110xxxxx	Small networks	2,097,152	254
D	224.0.0.0– 239.255.255.255	1110xxxx	Multicasting	N/A	N/A
E	240.0.0.0– 254.255.255.255	1111xxxx	Reserved for future use	N/A	N/A
Loopback	127.0.0.1– 127.255.255.255	01111111	Loopback testing	N/A	N/A

NOTE The concept of loopback testing is the usage of a predefined IP address that a computer can dial itself up to see whether the TCP/IP stack is properly set up. If TCP/IP is configured, you should be able to run the **ping 127.0.0.1** command when troubleshooting a connectivity problem.

The portion of the address that decides on which network the host resides varies based on the class, and, as you will see further on, the subnet mask. In the following list, the uppercase *N*s represent the part of the IP address that specifies the network, and the lowercase *C*s represent the part of the address that specifies the computer. This explains why there are differing numbers of networks per class and different numbers of hosts per network, as listed in Table 6-3.

- **Class A:** NNNNNNNN.cccccccc.cccccccc.cccccccc

- **Class B:** NNNNNNNN.NNNNNNNN.cccccccc.cccccccc

- **Class C:** NNNNNNNN.NNNNNNNN.NNNNNNNN.cccccccc

These address portions coincide with the default subnet masks for each address class. A Class A subnet mask is 255.0.0.0, a Class B subnet mask is 255.255.0.0, and a Class C subnet mask is 255.255.255.0.

Subnet masks enable you to reconfigure what constitutes the network portion and what constitutes the computer portion. When you apply the subnet mask to the IP address by using a bitwise logical AND operation, the result is a network number. A bitwise logical AND operation adds the bit, whether 1 or 0, to the corresponding bit in the subnet mask. If the subnet mask bit is a 1, the corresponding IP address bit is passed through as a result. If the subnet mask bit is a 0, a zero bit is passed through. For example, if the IP address is 141.25.240.201, you will have the following:

IP address: 10001101.00011001.11110000.11001001

Subnet mask: 11111111.11111111.00000000.00000000

Result from bitwise logical AND

Network: 10001101.00011001.00000000.00000000

This shows the network address as 141.25.0.0 and the host address to 0.0.240.201. If you add bits to the mask, you will be able to have additional subnetworks when you perform a bitwise logical AND, and each subnetwork will have fewer hosts because fewer bits are available for the host portion of the address. If you use the same address and add five bits to the subnet mask, you would receive the following:

IP address: 10001101.00011001.11110000.11001001

Subnet mask: 11111111.11111111.11111000.00000000

Result from bitwise logical AND

Network: 10001101.00011001.11110000.00000000

In this case, the subnet mask changes the network address to 141.25.240.0. The host address changes to 0.0.0.201. Other IP addresses that are under the default Class B subnet mask that would otherwise be part of the same network (such as 140.25.192.15 and 140.25.63.12) are now on different subnets.

For an organization with a large number of physical networks where each requires a different subnet address, you can use the subnet mask to segment a single address to fit the network. You can easily calculate how many subnets and hosts you will receive when you subnet a network. The formula is 2^n-2, where n is the number of bits. 2^n is the number 2 raised to the power of the number of bits, and that result minus 2 (the addresses represented by all 1s and all 0s) equals the available subnets or hosts. Therefore, if you have a subnet of 5 bits (as previously shown), you are able to achieve $2^5-2 = 32-2 = 30$ subnets. Because there are 11 bits left for host addresses, each subnet will have $2^{11}-2 = 2048-2 = 2,046$ hosts.

Classless Interdomain Routing

When you multiply 2046 by 30, you will see that you have 61,380 addresses available for network hosts and that you "lost" 4,154 addresses. This is the problem that classless interdomain routing (CIDR) solves.

When you consider that a Class A address has over 16 million host addresses and that no organization with a Class A address has managed to utilize each of those addresses, you realize the use of classful addressing (an IP addressing system that does not segment the network into smaller subnetworks) is extremely wasteful. CIDR was developed to prevent the Internet from running out of IP addresses by reusing some of the unused addresses and expanding the addresses available when subnetting.

With CIDR, a subnet mask is not considered separate from the network portion of the mask. Instead, whatever portion of the mask is used for the network determines how many networks there are. This means that a company can "supernet" two (or more) Class C addresses to put more than 254 hosts on a single physical network. Supernetting is the process of subtracting bits from the default subnet mask. This adds bits to the host portion, increasing the number of hosts available.

CIDR notation allows you to simply specify the number of bits that are used for a mask after the IP address. For example, 192.168.1.0 with a subnet mask of 255.255.255.0 is written as 192.168.1.0/24. If the address were supernetted, it could be 192.168.1.0/22.

Private IPv4 Networks

IPv4 specifications define sets of networks that are specified as *private IPv4 networks*. The private IP address classes are used on private networks that utilize Network Address Translation or proxy services to communicate on the Internet. Internet routers are preconfigured to not forward data that contains these IP addresses. Table 6-4 describes these networks.

Table 6-4   Private IPv4 Network Addresses

Class	Dotted Decimal Hosts per Range	First Octet Binary	Number of Networks	Number of Hosts per Network
A	10.0.0.0–10.255.255.254	00001010	1	16,777,214
B	172.16.0.0–172.31.255.254	10101100	1	65,534
C	192.168.0.0–192.168.255.254	11000000	254	254

NOTE   For more information on TCP/IP version 4, refer to "IPv4 Addressing" at https://technet.microsoft.com/en-us/library/dd379547(v=ws.10).aspx and "Fundamentals of Classful IPv4 addressing" at https://learningnetwork.cisco.com/docs/DOC-12872.

Configuring and Supporting TCP/IP Version 6 Settings

The 128-bit addressing scheme used by IPv6 enables an unimaginably high number of 3.4×10^{38} addresses, which equates to a total of 6.5×10^{23} addresses for every square meter of the Earth's surface. Consequently, this is a complicated addressing scheme, as described in the following sections.

IPv6 Address Syntax

Whereas IPv4 addresses use dotted-decimal format as explained earlier in this chapter, IPv6 addresses are subdivided into 16-bit blocks. Each 16-bit block is portrayed as a 4-digit hexadecimal number and is separated from other blocks by colons. This addressing scheme is referred to as *colon-hexadecimal*.

For example, a 128-bit IPv6 address written in binary could appear as follows:

0011111111111110 1111111111111111 0010000111000101
0000000000000000 0000001010101010 0000000011111111
1111111000100001 0011101000111110

The same address written in colon-hexadecimal becomes 3ffe:ffff:21a5:0000:00ff:fe21:5a3e.

You can remove any leading zeros, converting this address to 3ffe:ffff:21a5::ff:fe21:5a3e.

In this notation, note that the block that contained all zeros appears as "::", which is called *double-colon*.

IPv6 Prefixes

Corresponding to the network portion of an IPv4 address is the prefix, which is the part of the address containing the bits of the subnet prefix. IPv6 addresses do not employ subnet masks; they use the same CIDR notation used with IPv4. For example, an IPv6 address prefix could be 3ffe:ffff:21a5::/64, where 64 is the number of bits employed by the address prefix.

Types of IPv6 Addresses

IPv6 uses the following three types of addresses:

- **Unicast:** Represents a single interface within the typical scope of unicast addresses. In other words, packets addressed to this type of address are to be delivered to a single network interface. Unicast IPv6 addresses include global unicast, link-local, site-local, and unique local addresses. Two special addresses are also included: unspecified addresses (all zeros, equivalent to the IPv4 address of 0.0.0.0) and the loopback address, which is 0:0:0:0:0:0:0:1 or ::1, which is equivalent to the IPv4 address of 127.0.0.1.

- **Multicast:** Represents multiple interfaces to which packets are delivered to all network interfaces identified by the address. Multicast addresses have the first eight bits set to ones, so begin with "ff".

- **Anycast:** Also represents multiple interfaces. Anycast packets are delivered to a single network interface that represents the nearest (in terms of routing hops) interface identified by the address.

Table 6-5 provides additional details on the IPv6 classes and subclasses.

Table 6-5 IPv6 Address Classes and Subclasses

Class	Address Prefix	Additional Features	First Binary Bits	Usage
Global unicast	2000::/3	Use a global routing prefix of 45 bits (beyond the initial 001 bits), which identifies a specific organization's network, a 16-bit subnet ID, which identifies up to 54,536 subnets within an organization's network, and a 64-bit interface ID, which indicates a specific network interface within the subnet.	001	Globally routable Internet addresses that are equivalent to the public IPv4 addresses
Link-local unicast	fe80::/64	Equivalent to APIPA-configured IPv4 addresses in the 169.254.0.0/16 network prefix.	111111101000	Used for communication between neighboring nodes on the same link. These addresses are assigned automatically when you configure automatic addressing in the absence of a DHCP server.
Site-local unicast	fec0::/10	Equivalent to the private IPv4 address spaces mentioned previously in Table 6-4. Prefix followed by a 54-bit subnet ID field within which you can establish a hierarchical routing structure within your site.	111111101100	Used for communication between nodes located in the same site.
Unique local IPv6 unicast	fc00::/7	Prefix followed by a local (L) flag, a 40-bit global ID, a 16-bit subnet ID, and a 64-bit interface ID.	11111100	Provide addresses that are private to an organization but unique across all the organization's sites.

Class	Address Prefix	Additional Features	First Binary Bits	Usage
Multicast	ff	Use the next 4 bits for flags (Transient [T], Prefix [P], and Rendezvous Point Address [R]), the following 4 bits for scope (determines where multicast traffic is forwarded), and the remaining 112 bits for a group ID.	11111111	Multiple interfaces to which packets are delivered to all network interfaces identified by the address.
Anycast	(from unicast addresses)	Assigned from the unicast address space with the same scope as the type of unicast address within which the anycast address is assigned.	(varies)	Only utilized as destination addresses assigned to routers.

NOTE Site-local IPv6 addresses are equivalent to the private IPv4 addresses mentioned in Table 6-4. You can access site-local addresses only from the network in which they are located; they are not accessible from external networks such as the Internet.

NOTE For more information on IPv6 and its latest enhancements as it relates to Windows 10, refer to "Internet Protocol Version 6 (IPv6) Overview" at http://technet.microsoft.com/en-us/library/hh831730.

Compatibility Between IPv4 and IPv6 Addresses

To assist in the migration from IPv4 to IPv6 and their coexistence, several additional address types are used, as follows:

- **IPv4-compatible addresses:** Nodes communicating between IPv4 and IPv6 networks can use an address represented by 0:0:0:0:0:0:w.x.y.z, where w.x.y.z is the IPv4 address in dotted-decimal.

- **IPv4-mapped address:** An IPv4-only node is represented as ::ffff:.w.x.y.z to an IPv6 node. This address type is used only for internal representation and is never specified as a source or destination address of an IPv6 packet.

- **Teredo address:** Teredo is a tunneling communication protocol that enables IPv6 connectivity between IPv6/IPv4 nodes across Network Address Translation (NAT) interfaces, thereby improving connectivity for newer IPv6-enabled applications on IPv4 networks. Teredo is described in RFC 4380. Teredo makes use of a special IPv6 address that includes the following components in the sequence given:

    - A 32-bit Teredo prefix, which is 2001::/32 in Windows Vista/7/8/10 and Windows Server 2008/2012/2016.

    - The 32-bit IPv4 address of the Teredo server involved in creating this address.

    - A 16-bit Teredo flag field and an obscured 16-bit UDP port interface definition.

    - An obscured external IPv4 address corresponding to all Teredo traffic across the Teredo client interface.

- **6-to-4 address:** Two nodes running both IPv4 and IPv6 across an IPv4 routing infrastructure use this address type when communicating with each other. You can form the 6-to-4 address by combining the prefix 2002::/16 with the 32-bit public IPv4 address to form a 48-bit prefix. This tunneling technique is described in RFC 3056.

> **NOTE** More information on compatibility addresses and technologies used for transition to IPv6 is available in "Internet Protocol Version 6, Teredo, and Related Technologies in Windows 7 and Windows Server 2008 R2" at http://technet.microsoft.com/en-us/library/ee126159(WS.10).aspx. Although this paper was written for Windows 7 and Windows Server 2008 R2, the technologies involved are largely unchanged for Windows 10 and Windows Server 2016.

Configuring IP Settings

Now that you understand the workings of the TCP/IP protocol suite, we turn our attention to the following aspects of configuring IP settings on a Windows 10 computer:

- **Configuring Name Resolution:** Computers on the network are identified by their computer names that are assigned when Windows 10 is installed, or later when a user changes the initially assigned computer name. It is necessary to resolve this name to an IPv4 or IPv6 address so that the computer can be accessed from another one on the network.

- **Connect to Network:** Searches for the wireless router or access point you want to configure and then attempts to configure this device for you. Although the wizard states that it might take up to 90 seconds to display unconfigured devices, this process can take considerably longer.

- **Configure Network Locations:** Enables you to connect directly to another wireless-enabled computer without the need for a wireless access point. If you do set up a connection of this type, you are disconnected from other wireless networks.

Configuring Name Resolution

As previously noted, Windows 10 uses DNS as its primary name resolution service. DNS is the name resolution service used by all servers on the Internet; when you type a URL into the address box in Internet Explorer or any other browser, DNS resolves this URL into an IP address so that you can obtain the desired website.

> **NOTE**   If your network includes a DNS server, this server is used directly for any name resolution requirements within the network. When a client requests an Internet resource such as www.microsoft.com, an iterative name resolution process occurs in which the local DNS server accesses a series of Internet DNS servers to obtain the IP address of the requested resource. Each server that is accessed knows the locations of one level of servers within the hierarchical DNS namespace (in other words, is authoritative for this level by possessing in its database what is known as an A [address] resource record, which holds the hostname to IPv4 address mapping). For example, the following happens when you type http://www.Microsoft.com into your web browser:
>
> 1. The local DNS server checks with a root server on the Internet to locate the IP address of a server that is authoritative for .com addresses.
>
> 2. The .com server on the Internet locates the IP address of a server that is authoritative for Microsoft.com addresses.
>
> 3. The Microsoft.com server on the Internet locates the IP address of the www.Microsoft.com web server.
>
> 4. These servers return the required IP address to the client, whose browser then displays the home page of the requested website.

The Local Area Connection Properties dialog box enables you to configure your computer to access a DNS server, as outlined in the following procedure:

Step 1. Right-click the **Start** button and select **Network Connections**.

Step 2. Find the appropriate network adapter from the list, right-click, and then select **Properties** from the context menu.

Step 3. Locate Internet Protocol Version 4 (TCP/IPv4) from the list of items, select it, and then click the **Properties** button. The Properties box will look like the one in Figure 6-1.

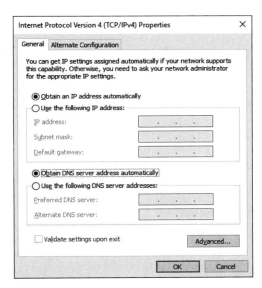

Figure 6-1 Internet Protocol Version 4 (TCP/IPv4) Properties Box

Step 4. If your network is configured to use DHCP to automatically configure client computers with the address of the DNS server, you need only ensure that the Obtain DNS Server Address Automatically option is selected.

Step 5. If your network is not configured with DHCP, click the **Use the Following DNS Server Addresses** option and type the IP address for at least one DNS server.

Step 6. Click **Advanced** to bring up the Advanced TCP/IP Settings dialog box shown in Figure 6-2.

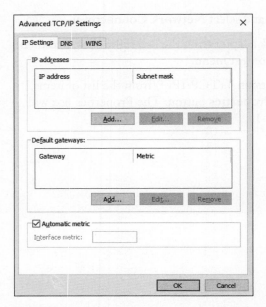

Figure 6-2   Advanced TCP/IP Settings Enabling You to Configure Custom Network Settings

Step 7.   Click the **DNS** tab to display the settings shown in Figure 6-3.

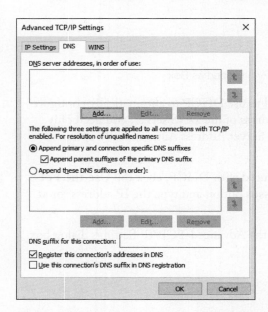

Figure 6-3   DNS Tab of Advanced TCP/IP Settings Enabling You to Configure Additional DNS Settings to Be Used by Your Network Connection

Step 8. To specify additional DNS servers, click the **Add** button under the DNS server addresses section, type the IP address to the additional DNS server, and then click **Add**.

Step 9. The lower section of the DNS tab applies to the fully qualified domain name (FQDN) of resources. Users sometimes use a simple name for a computer or printer. This section enables you to configure the last portion of the domain name that will be appended to the simple name to create an FQDN. For example, if you have configured mydomain.local and jubilee.local in this box, and the user typed in **server**, the computer automatically attempts to contact server.mydomain.local. If that fails, the computer then attempts to contact server.jubilee.local. Click the **Append These DNS Suffixes (in Order)** option. Then click the **Add** button to configure the DNS suffixes.

Step 10. For a DNS server that provides Dynamic DNS, and when you want to share files or printers from your computer, you should register your computer's DNS name and IP address in the DNS database. To do so, select the **Register This Connection's Addresses in DNS** check box.

Step 11. Click the **WINS** tab. WINS provides resolution for NetBIOS names to IP addresses on Windows networks. If you use legacy networks, or have applications that require NetBIOS names, you should configure the address for a WINS server on the network.

> **TIP** You can also use the **netsh.exe** tool to configure IPv4 from the command line. This tool enables you to perform almost any network configuration action from the command prompt. For example, the command **netsh interface ip set address "Local Area connection" static 192.168.0.2 255.255.255.0 192.168.0.1** configures the computer's local area connection with the static IP address 192.168.0.2, subnet mask 255.255.255.0, and default gateway 192.168.0.1. For more information, refer to "Netsh Overview" at http://technet.microsoft.com/en-us/library/cc732279(WS.10).aspx.

Configuring TCP/IPv6 Name Resolution

You can configure name resolution with IPv6 in much the same way as done with IPv4, as the following steps demonstrate:

Step 1. Use the procedure outlined in the previous section to access the Internet Protocol Version 6 (TCP/IPv6) Properties dialog box.

Step 2. If your network is configured to use DHCP to automatically configure client computers with the address of the DNS server, you need only ensure that the Obtain DNS Server Address Automatically option is selected.

Step 3. If your network is not configured with DHCP, click the **Use the Following DNS Server Addresses** option and type the IPv6 address for at least one DNS server.

Step 4. Click **Advanced** to bring up the Advanced TCP/IP Settings dialog box previously shown in Figure 6-2 (settings for IPv6 will not have a WINS tab).

Step 5. Click the **DNS** tab to display the available DNS settings, which are identical to those found in the DNS tab for IPv4 described previously and shown in Figure 6-3. Click **Add** under the DNS Server Addresses section to add the IPv6 addresses of additional DNS servers, as required.

Step 6. To specify additional DNS servers, click the **Add** button under the DNS server addresses section, type the IPv6 address to the additional DNS server, and then click **Add**.

Step 7. As was the case with IPv4, if you need additional DNS suffixes to specify the FQDN of resources, click the **Append These DNS Suffixes (in Order)** option. Then click the **Add** button to configure the DNS suffixes.

Step 8. For a DNS server that provides Dynamic DNS, and when you want to share files or printers from your computer, you should register your computer's DNS name and IP address in the DNS database. To do so, select the **Register This Connection's Addresses in DNS** check box.

Step 9. Click **OK** until you're returned to the Local Area Connection Properties dialog box.

NOTE DNS name resolution in IPv6 operates in a manner similar to that previously mentioned for IPv4, except that DNS servers use AAAA resource records to hold the hostname to IPv6 address mapping, as opposed to A records used for IPv4 mapping.

Disabling IPv6

You cannot remove IPv6 from a Windows 10 computer. However, you can disable IPv6 on a specific connection. From the Ethernet Properties dialog box, clear the check box beside **Internet Protocol Version 6 (TCP/IPv6)** and then click **OK**. You can do this selectively for each network connection on your computer.

> **NOTE**   You can also selectively disable IPv6 components. This is a more complex procedure that involves editing the Registry and is beyond the scope of this book. For more details, refer to "How to Disable IPv6 or Its Components in Windows" at http://support.microsoft.com/kb/929852.

Connecting to a Wired Network

Windows 10 simplifies the process of connecting to diverse types of networks, including wired and wireless networks. In this section, you learn about connecting your computer to wired networks. Chapter 8, "Windows 10 Data Security," extends this discussion to include methods used for connecting to and securing wireless networks. In Windows 10, you can quickly obtain a view of available network devices by opening File Explorer Network. The Network Explorer applet displays this information, as shown in Figure 6-4.

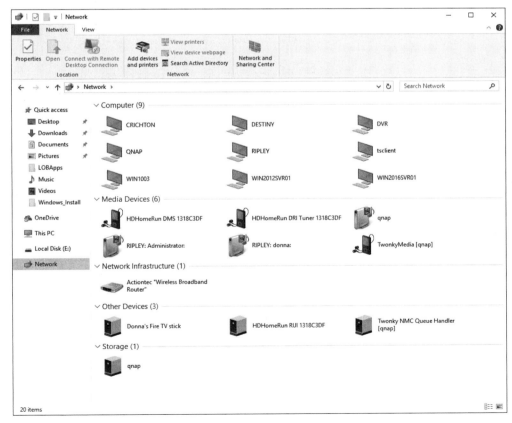

Figure 6-4   Network App in Windows 10 Displaying Several Types of Networked Devices

The Network and Sharing Center

First introduced in Windows Vista and continued in Windows 7, Windows 8.1, and Windows 10, the Network and Sharing Center, shown in Figure 6-5, brings all networking tasks together in a single convenient location. You can configure connections to other computers and networks; share folders, printers, and media; view devices on your network; set up and manage network connections; and troubleshoot problems from this location.

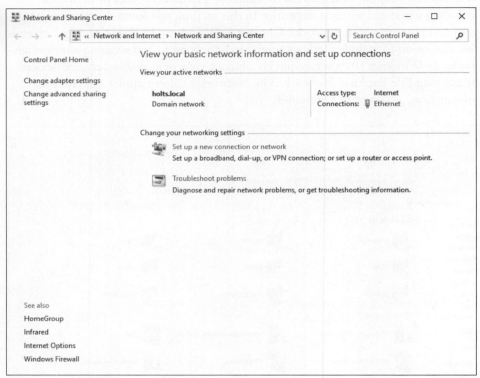

Figure 6-5 Network and Sharing Center Providing a Centralized Location for Configuring Network Properties

You can open the Network and Sharing Center by using any of the following methods:

- If you have the Network window open as previously shown in Figure 6-4, click the icon for the Network and Sharing Center on the menu bar.

- Access the Search box or Cortana and type **network**. From the icons displayed, click **Network and Sharing Center**.

- Open the Network icon from Action Center and click **Network Settings**. On the Settings page, click the **Network and Sharing Center** link.

The Network and Sharing Center enables you to configure connections to other computers and networks; share folders, printers, and media; view devices on your network; set up and manage network connections; and troubleshoot connectivity problems.

Using the Network and Sharing Center to Set Up a TCP/IPv4 Connection

You can configure TCP/IP version 4 on a Windows 10 computer either manually or dynamically. The default method is to dynamically configure TCP/IP. If the infrastructure includes DHCP services that deliver IP addresses to network computers, a Windows 10 computer can connect upon logon with the default configuration of the network adapter. However, if you need to apply a static IPv4 address and other parameters, your only option is to manually configure the network adapter. Manually configuring a single computer is time-consuming and error-prone. Multiply that by hundreds of computers and you can see why dynamic configuration has become so popular. Use the following procedure to configure a network adapter with a static IPv4 address:

Step 1.   Open the Network and Sharing Center by any of the methods described in the previous section.

Step 2.   From the Tasks list on the left side of the Network and Sharing Center, click **Change Adapter Settings**. This opens the Network Connections dialog box, as shown in Figure 6-6.

Figure 6-6 Network Connections Displaying the Network Connections Configured for Your Computer

Step 3. Right-click the connection that represents the adapter you are going to configure and select **Properties**. If you receive a User Account Control (UAC) prompt, click **Yes**. The Ethernet Properties dialog box opens, as shown in Figure 6-7.

Step 4. Click to select **Internet Protocol Version 4 (TCP/IPv4)**. (You might need to scroll through other services to reach this item.) Click **Properties**. The Internet Protocol Version 4 (TCP/IPv4) Properties dialog opens, as shown previously in Figure 6-1.

Step 5. To use DHCP services, you should make certain that Obtain an IP Address Automatically is selected, and if the DHCP server provides extended information—including the DNS server information—you would also select Obtain DNS Server Address Automatically. To manually configure the IP address, you should click **Use the Following IP Address**.

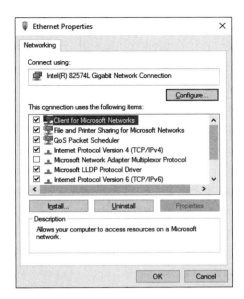

Figure 6-7   Network Adapter Is Considered a Network Connection

Step 6.   In the IP address box, type the address that will function on the current network segment. For example, if the network segment uses a Class C address 192.168.1.0 with a subnet mask of 255.255.255.0, and you've already used 192.168.1.1 and 192.168.1.2, you could select any node address from 3 through 254 (255 is used for broadcasts), in which case you would type **192.168.1.3**.

Step 7.   In the Subnet Mask box, type the subnet mask. In this case, it would be **255.255.255.0**.

Step 8.   In the Default gateway box, type the IP address that is assigned to the router interface on your current segment that leads to the main network or the public network. In this case, the IP address of the router on your segment is 192.168.1.1, and the IP address of the router's other interface is 12.88.54.179. In the Default Gateway box, you would type **192.168.1.1**.

Step 9.   To configure an alternate IP address on a computer configured to use DHCP, click the **Alternate Configuration** tab to display the dialog box shown in Figure 6-8. Click **User Configured** and then enter the required IP address, subnet mask, default gateway, and DNS and WINS server information. Then click **OK**. This is useful if your computer must connect to different networks, such as work and home.

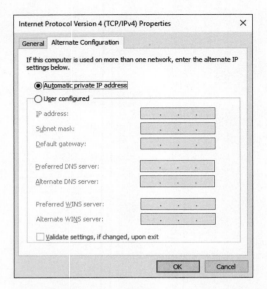

Figure 6-8   TCP/IPv4 Alternate Configuration Tab

Step 10.   Click the **Advanced** button. The Advanced TCP/IP Settings dialog box opens, as shown previously in Figure 6-2.

Step 11.   If you require more than one IP address for a computer, such as for hosting two different websites, you can configure the additional IP addresses in this dialog box by clicking the **Add** button under IP addresses. You cannot configure any additional IP addresses if you are using DHCP.

Step 12.   If your network segment is connected to more than one router leading to the main or outside networks, you can configure these gateway addresses in the Default Gateways section by clicking the **Add** button.

Step 13.   When finished, click **OK** until you're returned to the Network Connections dialog box.

> **TIP**   Many hardware routers, including those used when connecting home networks to high-speed Internet connections, include DHCP functionality. If you are using one of these, leave the defaults selected in step 5 of the preceding procedure.

Implementing APIPA

The Automatic Private Internet Protocol Addressing (APIPA) system provides an alternate configuration to DHCP for automatic IP addressing in small networks. When a computer uses APIPA, Windows 10 assigns itself an IP address and then verifies that it is unique on the local network. To work effectively, APIPA is useful only on a small local area network (LAN) or as a backup to DHCP.

When a Windows 10 computer begins its network configuration, it performs the following procedures:

Step 1. It checks to see whether there is a manually configured (or static) IP address.

Step 2. If there is none, it contacts a DHCP server with a query for configuration settings. A response from a DHCP server leases—or validates the lease of—an IP address, subnet mask, and extended IP information, such as DNS server, default gateway, and so on.

Step 3. If there is no DHCP server response within 6 seconds, Windows 10 looks to see whether an alternate configuration has been applied by the administrator.

Step 4. If there is no alternate configuration, Windows 10 uses APIPA to define an IP address unique on the LAN.

APIPA defines its IP addresses in the range of 169.254.0.1 to 169.254.255.254. The subnet mask on these addresses is configured as 255.255.0.0. You do have administrative control over APIPA. When Windows 10 selects an address from this range, it performs a duplicate address detection process to ensure that the IP address it has selected is not already being used, while continuing to query for a DHCP server in the background. If the address is found to be in use, Windows 10 selects another address. The random IP selection occurs recursively until an unused IP address is selected, a DHCP server is discovered, or the process has taken place 10 times.

Connecting to a TCP/IP Version 6 Network

You can let IPv6 configure itself automatically with a link-local address described previously in Table 6-5. You can also configure IPv6 to use an existing DHCP server or manually configure an IPv6 address as required. Configuration of IPv6 addresses is similar to the procedure used with configuration of IPv4 addresses, as the following procedure shows:

Step 1. Open the Network and Sharing Center by any of the methods previously described.

Step 2. From the Tasks list on the left side of the Network and Sharing Center, click **Change Adapter Settings**. This opens the Network Connections dialog box, as previously shown in Figure 6-6.

Step 3. Right-click the connection that represents the adapter you are going to configure and select **Properties**. If you receive a UAC prompt, click **Yes**.

Step 4.   Click to select **Internet Protocol Version 6 (TCP/IPv6)**. (You might need to scroll through other services to reach this item.) Click **Properties**. The Internet Protocol Version 6 (TCP/IPv6) Properties dialog opens, as shown in Figure 6-9.

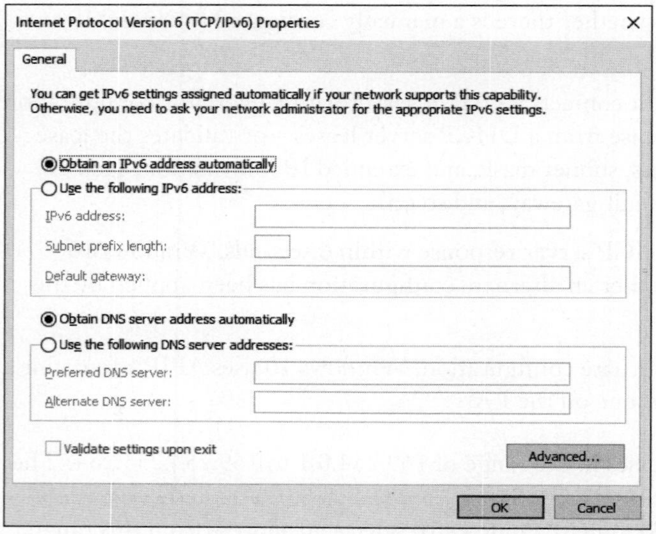

Figure 6-9   Internet Protocol Version 6 (TCP/IPv6) Properties Lets You Define Manual or Dynamic IPv6 Address Information

Step 5.   To use DHCP, ensure that the Obtain an IPv6 Address Automatically radio button is selected. If the DHCP server provides DNS server information, ensure that the Obtain DNS Server Address Automatically radio button is also selected. You can also select these options to configure IPv6 automatically with a link-local address using the address prefix fe80::/64 previously described in Table 6-5.

Step 6.   To manually configure an IPv6 address, select **Use the Following IPv6 Address**. Then type the IPv6 address, subnet prefix length, and default gateway in the text boxes provided. For unicast IPv6 addresses, you should set the prefix length to its default value of 64.

Step 7.   To manually configure DNS server addresses, select **Use the Following DNS Server Addresses**. Then type the IPv6 addresses of the preferred and alternate DNS server in the text boxes provided.

Step 8.   Click **Advanced** to display the Advanced TCP/IP Settings dialog box shown in Figure 6-10.

Figure 6-10   Advanced TCP/IP Settings Allowing You to Control Granular IPv6 Addressing Options

Step 9. As with IPv4, you can configure additional IP addresses if you are not using DHCP. Click **Add** and type the required IP address into the dialog box that appears.

Step 10. As with IPv4, if your network segment is connected to more than one router, configure additional gateway addresses in the Default Gateways section by clicking the **Add** button.

Step 11. When finished, click **OK** until you're returned to the Network Connections dialog box.

TIP   You can also use the **netsh.exe** tool with the **interface IPv6** subcommand to configure IPv6 from the command line. For example, **netsh interface IPv6 set address "local area connection 2" fec0:0:0:ffee::3** sets the IPv6 address of the second local area connection to the specified address. For more information, refer to "IPv6 Configuration Information with the **Netsh.exe** Tool" at http://technet.microsoft.com/en-us/library/bb726952.aspx#EBAA.

Configuring Network Locations

A network location defines a set of conditions contained within a network profile that govern whether computers on the network can view your computer and resources such as files, folders, and printers to which it is connected. Microsoft makes available network profiles corresponding to private and public network locations that are configured by default to enhance the security of your computer when connected to a public network such as a Wi-Fi hotspot.

Setting Up New Network Connections

The Network and Sharing Center enables you to set up new networking connections. Click **Set Up a New Connection or Network** (refer to Figure 6-5) to display the Set Up a Connection or Network Wizard shown in Figure 6-11. (Note that this dialog box may not display all these options; the options vary according to the networking hardware attached to your computer.)

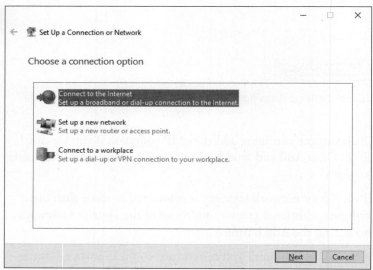

Figure 6-11   Set Up a Connection or Network Wizard Offering Several Options for Connecting Your Computer to Networks

Select from the following options, and then click **Next**:

- **Connect to the Internet:** Detects any type of device (such as a cable or DSL broadband connection) and enables you to enter the username and password provided by your ISP, as shown in Figure 6-12. You can also enter a connection name that helps you to identify this connection later. If you want to enable other users on the computer to connect, select **Allow Other People to Use This Connection**.

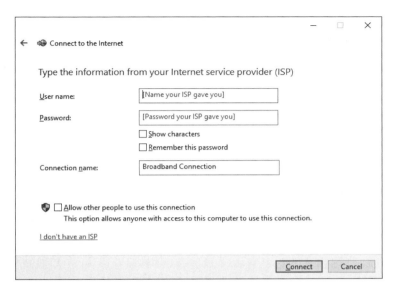

Figure 6-12   Entering Username and Password to Connect to the Internet

- **Set Up a New Network:** Searches for the wireless router or access point you want to configure and then attempts to configure this device for you. Although the wizard states that it might take up to 90 seconds to display unconfigured devices, this process can take considerably longer.

- **Manually Connect to a Wireless Network:** Enables you to enter the wireless network information required for connecting to the network. We discuss wireless networking in Chapter 11, "Configuring and Securing Mobile Devices."

- **Connect to a Workplace:** Enables you to connect by means of a virtual private network (VPN) connection across the Internet or to dial directly to the workplace network using a phone line without using the Internet. We discuss VPN connections in Chapter 15, "Configuring Remote Access."

- **Set Up a Wireless Ad Hoc (Computer-to-Computer) Network:** Enables you to connect directly to another wireless-enabled computer without the need for a wireless access point. If you do set up a connection of this type, you are disconnected from other wireless networks.

Connecting to Existing Networks

You can manage your network connections using the Network & Internet settings page. From the Action Center, select the **Network** icon and then click **Network Settings**. This displays the settings for your current connections, as shown in Figure 6-13.

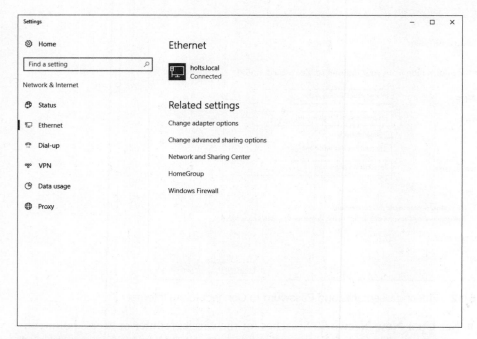

Figure 6-13   Network & Internet Settings Page to Manage Your Connections

When you open this settings page, or click the **Network** icon in Action Center, you are informed which network you are connected to and which networks are available. Select a desired network and then click **Connect**. To disconnect from a network, select it and then click **Disconnect**.

These operations apply only to dial-up and Wi-Fi connections. To disconnect from a wired or Ethernet connection, access the Network Connections screen, select the device, and then select **Disable This Network Device**.

Setting Up Network Sharing and Discovery

You can access additional sharing and network discovery options from the Network & Internet Settings page. Click the **Change Advanced Sharing Settings**, found in the Related Settings section of the device you are connected to. As shown in Figure 6-14, the Advanced Sharing Settings dialog box enables you to configure the additional networking options provided in the list that follows. (Available options depend on the profile you're using, either Private, Guest or Public, Domain, or All Networks.)

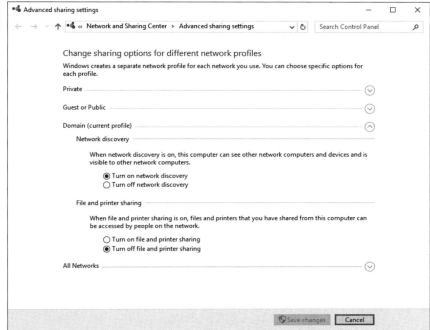

Figure 6-14 Advanced Sharing Settings Enabling You to Configure Sharing Options for Different Network Profiles

- **Network Discovery:** Enables your computers to see other network computers and devices and enables these machines to access your computer. To ensure that all network devices are detected and configured, ensure that the Turn On Automatic Setup of Network Connected Devices option is selected. (This option is selected by default.)

- **File and Printer Sharing and Public Folder Sharing:** These options enable you to share files and printers on your computer that will be visible to other computers on the network. We discuss these options in Chapter 14, "Configuring File and Folder Access."

- **Media Streaming:** Enables machines on the network to access shared photos, videos, and music stored on your computer. Enables your computer to locate these types of shared information on other network computers.

- **File Sharing Connections:** Enables you to select the strength of encryption used for protecting file sharing connections with other machines on the network. By default, file sharing is enabled for machines that use 40- or 56-bit encryption, but you can choose to increase security by selecting 128-bit encryption. However, devices that do not support 128-bit encryption will be unable to access resources on your computer.

- **Password Protected Sharing:** Requires users attempting to access shared resources on your computer to have a user account with a password. Turn this option off if you want to enable users without a password to have access.

- **HomeGroup Connections:** Enables you to determine whether Windows will utilize simple homegroup-based sharing or use the classic type of file sharing model employed by Windows versions prior to Windows 7. More information is provided in Chapter 14.

> **TIP**   You can configure sharing options for up to four network profiles:
>
> 1. Private
> 2. Guest or Public
> 3. Domain (on a domain-joined computer)
> 4. All Networks
>
> This enables you to maintain these network profiles when switching between different network types, so that when you connect to a public network, you can select the **All Networks** option to apply more restrictive sharing options automatically.

Using Internet Connection Sharing to Share Your Internet Connection

Quite often, it is not feasible for a small office or a home user to install a high-speed dedicated link to the Internet (such as a T1 line) or have each computer dial up to an ISP. Nowadays, home users can utilize a dedicated broadband link, such as a reasonably priced cable or DSL link.

One of the growing trends for small office or home networks is to share an Internet connection with all the members of the network. Windows 10 contains a feature called Internet Connection Sharing (ICS), which enables a small office or home network to use one computer on the network as the router to the Internet.

Windows 10's ICS components consist of the following:

- **Auto-dial:** A method of establishing the Internet connection when attempting to access Internet resources on a computer that does not host the Internet connection.

- **DHCP Allocator:** A simplified DHCP service that assigns IP addresses from the address range of 192.168.0.2–192.168.0.254, with a mask of 255.255.255.0 and default gateway of 192.168.0.1.

- **DNS Proxy:** Forwards DNS requests to the DNS server and forwards the DNS replies back to the clients.

- **Network Address Translation (NAT):** Maps the range of private Class C IPv4 addresses (192.168.0.1–192.168.0.254) to the public IP address, which is assigned by the ISP. NAT is a specification in TCP/IP that tracks the source private IP addresses and outbound public IP address(es), reformatting the IP address data in the header dynamically so that the source requests reach the public resources, and the public servers can reply to the correct source-requesting clients.

> **NOTE**   NAT runs on a server or router and is capable of translating multiple external IP addresses to internal private IP addresses used on client computers. The NAT server/router can also be configured to provide DHCP services to the client computers. For more information on NAT, refer to the "Network Address Translation (NAT) FAQ" at www.cisco.com/c/en/us/support/docs/ip/network-address-translation-nat/26704-nat-faq-00.html.

You can use ICS to share any type of Internet connection, although it must be a connection that is enabled for all users on the PC dial-up for sharing to be effective. To enable ICS, you need to make sure that the Internet-connected computer has been configured with connections for a modem and a network adapter. If you are using broadband, you need two network adapters: one to connect to the broadband device for the Internet and the other to connect to the network. Use the following procedure at the computer that is connected to the Internet to set up ICS:

Step 1.   From the Network and Sharing Center, click **Change Adapter Settings**, found on the left side. This opens the Network Connections dialog box previously shown in Figure 6-6.

Step 2.   Right-click the connection you want to share and choose **Properties**. If you receive a UAC prompt, click **Yes**.

Step 3.   Select the **Sharing** tab to receive the dialog box shown in Figure 6-15.

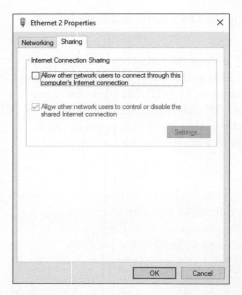

Figure 6-15   Sharing Tab of the Ethernet Properties Dialog Box Enabling You to Share Your Computer's Internet Connection with Other Computers on the Network

Step 4.   Select the check box labeled **Allow Other Network Users to Connect Through This Computer's Internet Connection**.

Step 5.   If desired, select the check box labeled **Allow Other Network Users to Control or Disable the Shared Internet Connection**.

CAUTION   Before you configure ICS, you should ensure that no computers are currently assigned an IP address of 192.168.0.1, because the network adapter on the ICS computer is automatically assigned that address when ICS is configured.

After you have shared your connection, you need to configure the other computers to use this connection, as follows:

Step 1.   In the bottom-left corner of the Network and Sharing Center, click **Internet Options** to display the Internet Properties dialog box.

Step 2.   Select the Connections tab.

Step 3.   Click the **LAN Settings** command button.

Step 4.   On the Local Area Network (LAN) Settings dialog box shown in Figure 6-16, clear the check boxes for **Automatically Detect Settings**, **Use Automatic Configuration Script**, and **Use a Proxy Server for Your LAN**. Then click **OK**.

Figure 6-16   Local Area Network (LAN) Settings Dialog Box with All Check Boxes Cleared

Step 5.   From the Network Connections dialog box previously shown in Figure 6-6, right-click the shared connection and choose **Properties**.

Step 6.   Click **Internet Protocol Version 4 (TCP/IPv4)** or **Internet Protocol Version 6 (TCP/IPv6)** and then click **Properties**.

Step 7.   On the Properties dialog box, select **Obtain an IP Address Automatically or Obtain an IPv6 Address Automatically**.

If you have problems with ICS, you should open Event Viewer and check out the System log for any errors related to ICS. In addition, you can view the NSW.LOG file to look for errors. The following are several additional suggestions in case users are unable to access the Internet from the client computers:

- Check the configuration of the client Internet browser. We mentioned client configuration earlier in this section.

- Ensure that the client can connect to the host computer. Check the connection by typing **ping 192.168.0.1**. If this ping is unsuccessful, check the physical network connections.

- Use **ipconfig** to check the client computer's IP configuration. Ensure that the client has an IP address on the proper subnet and that the default gateway is set to 192.168.0.1.

NOTE   For more information on ICS, including its use with IPv6, refer to "Using Wireless Hosted Network and Internet Connection Sharing" at https://msdn.microsoft.com/en-us/library/windows/desktop/dd815252(v=vs.85).aspx. The article discusses Windows 7 and Windows 8, but the functionality is the same for Windows 10 and Windows Server 2016.

Configuring Network Settings

In the previous section, you learned about TCP/IP network connections, working with network adapters, configuring protocols, and connection-level settings for Windows networks. In this section, you move on to learning about connecting to wireless networks, configuring your wireless network preferences, and about group policies for managing network configuration settings.

You should also know some techniques for troubleshooting network connections and dealing with network issues, and you will learn about some tools and techniques for doing that in this section.

Connecting to Wireless Networks

The recent advances in wireless networking technology have enabled individuals to connect to networks from virtually any place a wireless access point is available. Many offices are taking advantage of the ease of setup of wireless local area networks (WLANs), which allow for mobility and portability of computers and other devices located within the office. Public access points in locations such as restaurants and airports permit users to send and receive data from many places that would have been unthought of not too many years ago. Along with this convenience comes an increased chance of unauthorized access to the networks and the data they contain.

Wireless networks are easy to install and use, and they have gained tremendous popularity for small home and office networks. Security is still not perfected for wireless networks, so large corporations have been slower to implement large wireless networks. Windows 10 supports the 802.11 protocols for wireless LANs and is capable of transparently moving between multiple wireless access points (WAPs), changing to a new IP subnet, and remaining connected to the network. Each time the IP subnet changes, the user is reauthenticated. In Windows 10, you can configure wireless networking in the Network and Sharing Center. This enables you to connect to wireless networks, configure an ad hoc connection or the use of a WAP, and manage your wireless networks.

Windows 10 provides similar wireless technologies to those of Windows 7 and 8.1, improving upon wireless support for Windows so that wireless networking is as well integrated with the operating system as normal networking. Consequently, wireless network reliability, stability, and security are considerably enhanced over older versions of the Windows operating system. The following are some of the more important security improvements in wireless networking available in recent Windows versions:

- Windows 10 minimizes the amount of private information, such as the service set identifier (SSID) that is broadcast before connecting to a wireless network.

- When users connect to an unencrypted public network (such as an airport or restaurant Wi-Fi hotspot), users are warned of the risks so that they can limit their activities accordingly.

- Windows 10 supports a complete range of wireless security protocols, from Wired Equivalent Privacy (WEP) to Wi-Fi Protected Access (WPA and WPA2), Protected Extensible Authentication Protocol (PEAP), and its combination with Microsoft Challenge Handshake Authentication Protocol version 2 (MS-CHAPv2) and Extensible Authentication Protocol Transport Layer Security (EAP-TLS).

- Windows 10 uses WPA2-Personal for maximum security when communicating by means of an ad hoc wireless network (direct communication with another wireless computer without use of an access point). This helps to protect against common vulnerabilities associated with such unprotected networks.

- On an Active Directory Domain Services (AD DS) network, administrators can use Group Policy settings to configure Single Sign On (SSO) profiles that facilitate wireless domain logon. The 802.1x authentication precedes the domain logon, and users are prompted for wireless credentials only if absolutely necessary. The wireless connection is therefore in place before the domain logon proceeds.

Wireless Networking Protocols

Table 6-6 describes four wireless networking protocols available to Windows 10.

Table 6-6   Characteristics of Wireless Networking Protocols

Protocol	Transmission Speed	Frequency Used	Comments
802.11b	11 Mbps	2.4 GHz	The 2.4 GHz frequency is the same as that which is used by many appliances such as cordless phones and microwave ovens; this can cause interference. This technology also is limited in that it supports fewer simultaneous users than the other protocols.
802.11a	54 Mbps	5 GHz	While reducing interference from other appliances, this technology has a shorter signal range and is not compatible with network adapters, routers, and WAPs using the 802.11b protocol. However, some devices are equipped to support either 802.11a or 802.11b.

Protocol	Transmission Speed	Frequency Used	Comments
802.11g	54 Mbps	2.4 GHz	You can have 802.11b and 802.11g devices operating together on the same network. This standard was created specifically for backward compatibility with the 802.11b standard. The signal range is better than that of 802.11a, but this technology suffers from the same interference problems as 802.11a.
802.11n	Up to 150–600 Mbps depending on the number of data streams	2.4 or 5 GHz	This technology is compatible with devices using the older protocols at the same frequency. It also has the best signal range and is most resistant to interference, though it can have the same problems as 802.11b if using the 2.4 GHz frequency.
802.11ac	Up to 1.3 Gbps	5 GHz	New technology that improves upon 802.11n by offering faster speeds and improved scalability. Computer and device manufacturers are beginning to produce compatible units, with devices expected to be available by 2015.

NOTE For more information on 802.11ac and the improvements it offers, refer to "802.11ac: The Fifth Generation of Wi-Fi Technical White Paper" at www.cisco.com/en/US/prod/collateral/wireless/ps5678/ps11983/white_paper_c11-713103.html.

Setting Up a Wireless Network Connection

Windows 10 provides a wizard that simplifies the process of setting up various types of network connections and connecting to wireless and other networks. Use the following procedure to set up a wireless network connection:

Step 1.   Use one of the methods outlined earlier in this chapter to access the Network and Sharing Center.

Step 2.   Click **Set Up a New Connection or Network** (refer to Figure 6-5) to start the wizard.

Step 3.   Click **Set Up a New Network** and then click **Next**. You are informed that it might take up to 90 seconds for unconfigured network devices to be detected.

Step 4.   When the wizard detects the required wireless router or WAP, select it and click **Next**.

Step 5.   On the Give Your Network a Name page, type the network name and security key used by the required router or WAP. Choose the required security level and encryption type (more about these later in this chapter) and then click **Next**.

Step 6.   The wizard configures your network. When done, click **Finish**.

You can connect to a network that you have not previously set up by following these steps:

Step 1.   From the Network and Sharing Center, click **Set Up a New Connection or Network**.

Step 2.   Click **Manually Connect to a Wireless Network**, and then click **Next**.

Step 3.   The wizard displays the Manually Connect to a Wireless Network page shown in Figure 6-17. Enter the following information and then click **Next**.

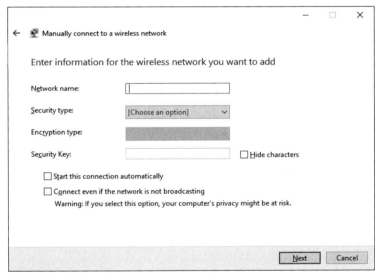

Figure 6-17   Manually Connect to a Wireless Network Page Enabling You to Enter Information Required for Connecting to a Wireless Network

- **Network Name:** The name (SSID) of the wireless network you are connecting to.

- **Security Type:** Authentication method to be used in connecting to the wireless network. Table 6-7 lists the available security types.

- **Encryption Type:** The encryption type will be selected for you depending on the Security type. The options are None (for No authentication), WEP (for WEP connections or 802.1x), or AES for WPA2-Personal or WPA2-Enterprise (see Table 6-7).

- **Security Key:** Enter the security key required by the security type selected (the WEP key for the WEP security type), or the WPA2 preshared key (for the WPA2-Personal security type). Clear the Hide Characters check box to view the information typed here.

- **Start This Connection Automatically:** When selected, Windows 10 automatically connects to the network when you log on. When cleared, you must use the Connect to a Network option from the Network and Sharing Center to connect to the network.

- **Connect Even if the Network Is Not Broadcasting:** Specifies whether Windows will attempt to connect even if the network is not broadcasting its name. This can be a security risk because Windows 10 sends Probe Request frames to locate the network, which unauthorized users can use to determine the network name. Consequently, this check box is not selected by default.

Step 4. The wizard informs you that it has successfully added the network you specified. Click the link specified to connect to the network, or click the **Close** button to finish the wizard without connecting.

Table 6-7 Available Wireless Security Types

Security Type	Description	Available Encryption Types
No authentication (open)	Open system authentication with no encryption	None
WEP	Open system authentication using WEP	WEP
WPA2-Personal	Version 2 of WPA using a preshared passphrase or key	AES (default)
WPA2-Enterprise	Version 2 of WPA using IEEE 802.1x authentication	AES (default)
802.1x	IEEE 802.1x authentication using WEP (also known as dynamic WEP)	WEP

NOTE WPA2-Enterprise security provides the highest level of wireless networking authentication security. It requires authentication in two phases: first, an open system authentication; second, authentication using EAP. It is suitable for domain-based authentication and on networks using a Remote Authentication Dial-In User Service (RADIUS) authentication server. In environments without the RADIUS server, you should use WPA2-Personal security.

The wireless network you configured is visible in the Network and Sharing Center, from which you can connect later if you have not chosen the Start This Connection Automatically option. You can also connect by selecting the **Network** icon from the Action Center.

> **TIP**   On the 70-697 or 70-698 exams, you may be asked if you are required to type a security key or passphrase; you should select the **WPA2-Personal** option. If you are not required to type a security key or passphrase, you should select the **WPA2-Enterprise** option.

Managing Wireless Network Connections

After you have configured one or more wireless network connections, you can manage them from Settings. From the main Settings screen, select **Network & Internet**, select **Wi-Fi** from the menu, and then click the **Manage Known Networks** link. This displays the Settings screen as shown in Figure 6-18, with the networks you have configured in the list.

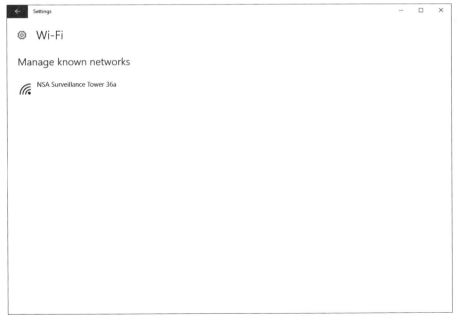

Figure 6-18   Connecting to Wireless Networks and Context Menu Options for Connected Network

To access the properties of a network connection, you can use the Network icon from Action Center. From there, click the wireless network icon and name. Click a network to connect to it, and to select or deselect the **Connect Automatically** option, as shown in Figure 6-19. This dialog is also displayed if you click the Show Available Networks link from the Wi-Fi settings page.

Figure 6-19   Wireless Networks and Connection Options

Several options are available for any network in range that you have connected to from the Manage Known Networks Settings page. If you select one of the networks from the Manage Known Networks page, Windows will display Properties and Forget buttons. Selecting Forget will clear out your settings for that Wi-Fi connection and automatically disconnect. When you select the Properties button of any wireless network, the following selections are available:

- **Connect Automatically When in Range:** This toggle tells Windows you want to connect to this Wi-Fi access point whenever it is available.

- **Make This PC Discoverable:** For private or work networks, this option will turn sharing and discoverability on for the network. You should not use this option when connecting to open or public Wi-Fi access points.

- **Metered Connection:** Turning this toggle on tells Windows that you have to pay for all the bandwidth you use on this connection. Windows will attempt to limit data usage on metered connections.

- **Copy:** A list of detailed properties of the network connection is displayed on this screen, as shown in Figure 6-20. Clicking the **Copy** button places those details as text into the Clipboard, in case you need to save the Wi-Fi Properties to a file or email.

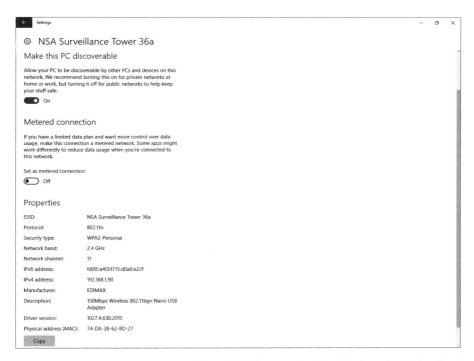

Figure 6-20   Detailed Properties of the Wi-Fi Connection Are Displayed and Can Be Copied to the Clipboard

Managing Preferred Wireless Networks

For Windows 10, Microsoft has simplified the user experience for working with wireless connections. Normally, Windows detects the type of wireless network, sets the security option, and manages profiles behind the scenes. Untrusted networks are set as public, and sharing is disabled. Private networks with security available are preferred, and Windows uses these networks before unsecured networks when available.

When you view available network connections, a small shield icon will appear on some network connections. This indicates to the user that the network is not secured, and Windows will treat the network as public. As described earlier, users can override the automated sharing selected and turn sharing on or off when connected to the network.

Whenever you connect to a new network and enable the **Connect Automatically** option, Windows places that network at the top of the priority list of preferred wireless networks.

Windows adjusts the priority of your list of preferred wireless networks based on the following criteria:

1. On connection to a new (undefined) wireless network, with Connect Automatically enabled, that network is added to the list, and Windows will connect to that network while it's in range.

2. If you connect to another wireless network while in range of the first network, also setting the Connect Automatically option, Windows will prefer the second network over the first one.

3. For mobile broadband networks, manually connecting to a mobile broadband network when there is a Wi-Fi network in range will set the mobile broadband network as preferred only for that session. The next time the computer is in range of both networks, the wireless network will be preferred. Mobile broadband networks are typically metered, but this behavior persists even if the mobile broadband network is not specifically marked as metered.

4. To force Windows to prefer a mobile broadband network over Wi-Fi, click the Wi-Fi network in the list of networks, and then click **Disconnect**. Windows will not automatically connect to that Wi-Fi network.

Wireless Network Profiles

When you need to delete or make changes to the settings, you can usually do so from the Wi-Fi settings page of the connection as described in the previous section. However, some tasks require the use of the command prompt. For instance, managing the automatically created wireless profiles Windows 10 maintains for your wireless connections requires the use of the **netsh** command-line utility.

A wireless network profile is a set of wireless networks available to a given user on a Windows 10 computer. The profile contains information such as the SSID, the security settings as configured earlier in this chapter, and whether the network is an infrastructure or ad hoc network. There are two types of wireless network profiles:

- **Per-User Profiles:** These profiles apply to specific users of the computer and are connected when that user logs on to the computer. Note that these profiles can cause a loss of network connectivity when logging off or switching between users.

- **All-User Profiles:** These profiles apply to all users of the computer and are connected regardless of which user is logged on to the computer.

To view the list of wireless profiles for the current user, open a command prompt, and type **netsh wlan show profiles**. To view the All-User profiles, run the same command from an administrative command prompt. The result will be similar to Figure 6-21.

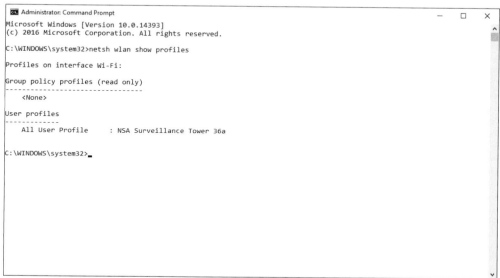

Figure 6-21   netsh wlan Commands Used to Manage Wireless Profiles

The **netsh** command lists all wireless network profiles, even if not in range, while the network list, as shown previously in Figure 6-19, includes only networks that are currently in range. You can delete a network profile using **netsh** commands, which is the same function as the Forget This Network option accessible from the Options menu.

Other important **netsh** commands for managing wireless networks and profiles are listed in Table 6-8. You should be aware that these commands will return profiles based on the user context. To manage all user profiles, use an administrative command prompt.

Table 6-8   Important **netsh** Wireless Networking Commands

Command	Description
netsh wlan show profiles	Displays all wireless profiles on the computer
netsh wlan show profile name="*<profilename>***" key=clear**	Displays security key information for a profile named *< profilename>* that's out of range
netsh wlan delete profile name="*<profilename>***"**	Deletes a profile that's out of range

Command	Description
netsh wlan set profileparametername= "*<profilename>*" connectionmode=manual	Stops automatically connecting to a network that's out of range

NOTE   Many other **netsh** commands are available for managing networks. For more information, download the Network Shell (Netsh) Technical Reference from http://technet.microsoft.com/en-us/library/jj129394.aspx.

In addition to using the **netsh** command to manage wireless network profiles, you can also use Group Policy to deploy or maintain wireless network profiles. Whenever you connect to a wireless network, Windows creates a wireless profile entry in the Group Policies for the local computer. You will find the profiles under Computer Configuration\Policies\Windows Settings\Security Settings\Network List Manager Policies. You can set various policies for each network, as shown in Figure 6-22. Note that both wired and wireless networks are included.

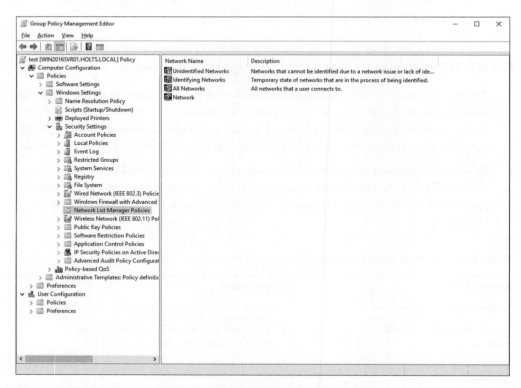

Figure 6-22   Local Group Policy Settings for Configured Networks

Deploying wireless network profiles can also be performed from Windows Server using domain-based group policies.

Configuring Network Adapters

In Chapter 3, "Post-Installation Configuration," you learned how to use Device Manager to install, configure, and troubleshoot various types of hardware devices. In this section, we take a further look at the use of Device Manager and the network adapter dialogs and the options that can be used for configuring wired and wireless network adapters.

The majority of the work involving device implementation, management, and troubleshooting for many types of hardware devices is found in the Device Manager utility. From the utility, you can access many of the hardware properties of network adapters. We covered the network properties of the adapter earlier in the section "Configuring IP Settings," but there are more NIC-level properties you can set for the device. The available properties will depend on the specific device, the type of network it enables, and the capabilities of the hardware and device driver.

When you open a network device's Properties dialog box from the Device Manager, you have access to a variety of configuration options from the Advanced tab, as shown in Figure 6-23. As you select an item in the Properties list, the current value is displayed in the section on the right, which may be a drop-down, a spinner, a text box, or other control type based on the type of value required for the property.

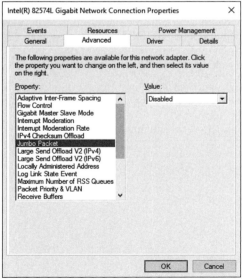

Figure 6-23 Advanced Tab of a Network Adapter Device with Several Configuration Options

The configuration settings available for the network adapter can vary widely. Wireless adapters will have different options than wired connections, and different devices from manufacturers expose different options through the driver interface. Typically you would not need to adjust any of these settings, but there are a few you should be aware of, and that may need to be changed for specific environments or application and network requirements.

Table 6-9 lists many of the more common options you may encounter and need to adjust.

Table 6-9   Important Network Adapter Advanced Properties

Property	Adapter Type	Description
Preferred Band	Wireless	Some wireless networks can use 2.4 GHz or 5.2 GHz to communicate with the AP. You can adjust the preferred band to use.
Wireless Mode	Wireless	Specify whether to use 802.11a, 802.11b, 802.11g, or some combination.
802.11n Mode	Wireless	Specify whether to enable the ability to use 802.11n mode.
Jumbo Packet/ Jumbo Frames	Wired	For fast networks (gigabit or faster), enabling Jumbo Frames (also known as Jumbo Packet) can improve performance when all devices on a network path can transmit larger packets.
Speed and Duplex	Wired	Typically the network adapter will negotiate with the switch to determine the speed and full- or half-duplex operation. If the autonegotiation is not working correctly, you can manually tell the adapter the speed and duplex mode to use.
Transmit Buffers/ Receive Buffers	Wired	These properties allow you to set the number of buffers used when moving data between memory and the network. Increasing the number of buffers consumes more system memory.

Troubleshooting Network Issues

If there is an issue at the computer's hardware layer, it can often be resolved by resetting the network adapter. You can perform this task from the device's Properties dialog box. You can also do this from the Network and Sharing Center, by selecting the Change Adapter Settings link and right-clicking the connection, as shown in Figure 6-24. The adapter is reset by selecting **Disable** from the pop-up box, waiting for the adapter to shut down, and then selecting **Enable** from the right-click menu.

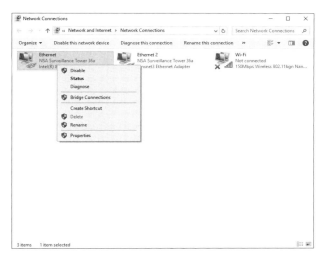

Figure 6-24   Enabling and Disabling a Network Adapter from the Network Connections Dialog Box

You can troubleshoot problems specific to the network adapter using the Windows 10 troubleshooting tool. To troubleshoot problems with the network adapter, follow these steps:

Step 1.   Click **Start**, then scroll the program list that appears to select **Windows System**, and choose **Control Panel**.

Step 2.   In the Search box, type **troubleshooting**, and then click the **Troubleshooting** link.

Step 3.   From the Troubleshooting screen, click the **Network and Internet** link. This opens the dialog displayed in Figure 6-25.

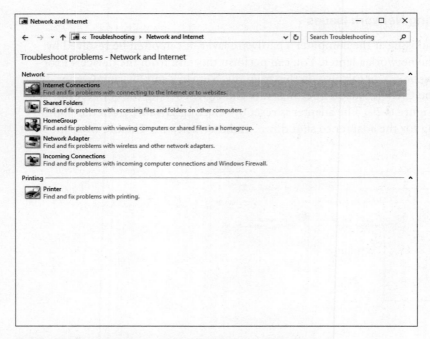

Figure 6-25   Network and Internet Troubleshooting Options

> **Step 4.**   Select the **Network Adapter** option to start the adapter troubleshooting
> wizard shown in Figure 6-26.

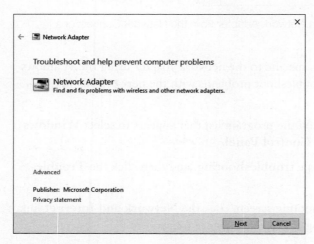

Figure 6-26   Network Adapter Troubleshooting Wizard

Step 5.   To be most effective, the wizard can be run in Administrator mode. To do so, click the **Advanced** link, and then click **Run as Administrator**. Click the **Next** button to proceed.

Step 6.   The wizard will run, starting diagnostics. If you have more than one network adapter, the wizard will then prompt you to select the adapter to troubleshoot, as shown in Figure 6-27. You can select a specific adapter or All Network Adapters. Click the **Next** button.

Figure 6-27   Selecting the Adapter to Use with the Network Adapter Troubleshooting Wizard

Step 7.   The wizard diagnoses the adapter or adapters and attempts to fix any issues that are found.

When the wizard completes, it indicates whether any issues were found and whether the troubleshooter was able to fix them. You can click the **View Detailed Information** link to access a set of reports on the network adapter issues and the detection details. The report contains a lot of detailed information, and if the issue was not fixed, you can print the report for a hardware technician or vendor to help determine where the problem lies.

Exam Preparation Tasks

Review All the Key Topics

Review the most important topics in the chapter, noted with the Key Topics icon in the outer margin of the page. Table 6-10 lists a reference of these key topics and the page numbers on which each is found.

Table 6-10   Key Topics for Chapter 6

Key Topic Element	Description	Page Number
Table 6-2	IPv4 addressing components	261
Table 6-3	IPv4 address classes	262
List	IPv4 address bitwise calculations and masking	263
Table 6-4	Private IPv4 network addresses and ranges	265
Table 6-5	IPv6 address classes and subclasses	267
List	IPv4 to IPv6 intercommunication address types	268
Step List	Procedure to manually configure IPv4 addresses and DNS services	271
Step List	Procedure to manually configure IPv6 addresses and services	273
Figure 6-5	Network and Sharing Center	276
Step List	Configuring a network adapter for IPv4	277
Step List	Configuring a network adapter for IPv6	281
Figure 6-11	Using Set Up a Connection or Network Wizard to configure a network connection	284
Figure 6-14	Advanced Sharing settings	287
Step List	Setting up Internet Connection Sharing (ICS)	289
Table 6-6	Characteristics of wireless networking protocols	293
Step List	Manually configuring a wireless network connection	294
Figure 6-17	Setting up a manually configured wireless network connection	295
Table 6-7	Available wireless security types	296
List	How Windows determines which wireless network connection to prefer	300
Figure 6-21	Using the **netsh** command to list network profiles	301
Figure 6-23	Advanced tab of a network adapter and possible configuration options	303
Table 6-9	Important network adapter properties	304

Complete the Tables and Lists from Memory

Print a copy of Appendix B, "Memory Tables" (found on the book website), or at least the section for this chapter, and complete the tables and lists from memory. Appendix C, "Memory Tables Answer Key," also on the website, includes completed tables and lists to check your work.

Definitions of Key Terms

Define the following key terms from this chapter, and check your answers in the glossary.

802.11, AES, Address Resolution Protocol (ARP), Anycast IPv6 address, Automatic Private IP Addressing (APIPA), classless interdomain routing (CIDR), default gateway, Domain Name System (DNS), duplex, Dynamic Host Configuration Protocol (DHCP), global unicast IPv6 address, host, Internet Connection Sharing, Internet Control Message Protocol (ICMP), ipconfig, IP version 4 (IPv4), IP version 6 (IPv6), IP address, jumbo frames, link-local IPv6 address, Link-Local Multicast Name Resolution (LLMNR), metered connection, multicast IPv6 address, Network Address Translation (NAT), Network and Sharing Center, NIC, Service Set Identifier (SSID), site-local IPv6 address, subnet mask, Teredo, WAP, WEP, WPA, wireless network profile, WLAN

This chapter covers the following subjects:

- **Configuring Authentication and Authorization:** In this section you learn about the processes for verifying the identity of objects, services, and users in Windows 10, and the techniques available for ensuring only proven identities are recognized and allowed access to resources. You then learn how to configure and manage users' and administrators' credentials on Windows 10. Finally, you learn how to modify UAC settings that determine when a user is presented with prompts that require him to provide administrative credentials.

- **Supporting Authentication and Authorization:** For the 70-697 exam, you must understand how to support authentication and authorization for users and devices, and how to resolve issues with various types of authentication problems. You also learn about configuring Windows Hello, managing account policies, and network authentication methods such as HomeGroup and workgroups.

- **Configuring NTFS Permissions:** Windows 10 enables you to secure files and folders on your computer so that you can determine who can access them and what level of access they are granted or denied. This section shows you how to configure these permissions and how they interact with shared folder permissions.

This chapter covers the following objectives for the 70-697 and 70-698 exams:

**MCSA
70-697**

Support authentication and authorization: Identifying and resolving issues related to the following: multifactor authentication including certificates, Microsoft Passport, virtual smart cards, picture passwords and biometrics; workgroup versus domain, Homegroup, computer and user authentication including secure channel, account policies, credential caching, and Credential Manager; local account versus Microsoft account; Workplace Join; configuring Windows Hello.

**MCSA
70-698**

Configure authorization and authentication: Configure Microsoft Passport, configure picture passwords and biometrics, configure workgroups, configure domain settings, configure HomeGroup settings, configure Credential Manager, configure local accounts, configure Microsoft accounts, configure Device Registration, configure Windows Hello, configure Device Guard, configure Credential Guard, configure Device Health Attestation, configure UAC behavior.

CHAPTER 7

Windows 10 Security

All users on a Windows 10 computer must be known to the operating system—in other words, they must be authenticated to Windows and authorized to use resources on the local computer and located on the network. In Chapter 14, "Configuring File and Folder Access," you learn how to configure and provide access to files, folders, shared printers, and other local and network resources. This chapter covers other authorizations that you need to configure and delves into the many ways of authenticating users in Windows 10, including cloud-based Microsoft account authentication. Microsoft expects you to be knowledgeable about all these topics and the new features when taking the 70-697 or 70-698 exam.

In a modern Internet-connected workplace with a growing number of users joining the always-available mobile workforce, it becomes increasingly important that users of our systems can positively identify themselves when accessing systems from anywhere in the world. Being able to trust that users are who they say they are when accessing sensitive data and using expensive networked resources is a matter of ensuring that system authentication methods are robust, easy to use, and hardened against impersonation. Lots of confidential information is out there, and it must be protected from access by those who are not entitled to view it.

At home, family members need to share things like photos, videos, and music. But parents have sensitive information, such as family finances, that must be protected as well.

"Do I Know This Already?" Quiz

The "Do I Know This Already?" quiz allows you to assess whether you should read this entire chapter or simply jump to the "Exam Preparation Tasks" section for review. If you are in doubt, read the entire chapter. Table 7-1 outlines the major headings in this chapter and the corresponding "Do I Know This Already?" quiz questions. You can find the answers in Appendix A, "Answers to the 'Do I Know This Already?' Quizzes."

Table 7-1   "Do I Know This Already?" Foundation Topics Section-to-Question Mapping

Foundation Topics Section	Questions Covered in This Section
Configuring Authentication and Authorization	1–12
Supporting Authentication and Authorization	13–18
Configuring NTFS Permissions	19–22

CAUTION   The goal of self-assessment is to gauge your mastery of the topics in this chapter. If you do not know the answer to a question or are only partially sure of the answer, you should mark that question as wrong for purposes of the self-assessment. Giving yourself credit for an answer you correctly guess skews your self-assessment results and might provide you with a false sense of security.

1. Which of the following is an example of authentication?

   a. User access to a shared folder

   b. Membership in the Administrator account

   c. User signing in with a password

   d. User rights assignment

2. Configuring a picture password requires how many gestures over the picture?

   a. One

   b. Two

   c. Three

   d. Six

   e. Eight

3. Which of the following are true about the Windows 10 Logon screen? (Choose three.)

   a. When a Windows 10 computer is joined to a domain, users must press Ctrl+Alt+Delete to log on by default.

   b. To sign in with a domain account for the first time, select the **Other User** option on the logon screen and enter the domain and username.

   c. By default, a domain-joined Windows 10 computer allows users the options to sign on using a Microsoft account, a local account, or a domain account.

   d. Users cannot use a PIN to log on to a domain-joined computer.

   e. You change any user's password using the Users section of PC settings.

4. Your administrator at work installed Windows 10 and provided a domain account for you to use. You would now like to log in to the computer using your Microsoft account, which you created for your Windows Mobile phone. You have already added your Microsoft account to your computer for One-Drive and Mail. How do you log in to your Windows 10 computer with your Microsoft account?

   a. Sign out from your local account, and enter your Microsoft credentials at the Sign-in screen.

   b. Use the Accounts settings Sign-in Options menu to switch to your Microsoft account.

   c. Use the Accounts settings Your Info menu to switch to your Microsoft account.

   d. You cannot sign in to a domain-joined computer using a Microsoft account.

   e. Access your Microsoft account using a web browser and add your domain account.

5. Which of the following are required for using Windows Hello? (Select all that apply.)

   a. A Microsoft account

   b. A PIN

   c. A high-resolution camera or fingerprint reader

   d. A fingerprint reader or IR camera

   e. A strong password for a local or domain account

6. You attempt to join your Windows 10 Pro computer to a homegroup, but the option for joining the homegroup is not available. Which of the following is a valid reason for the inability to join a homegroup?

   a. Your computer is joined to an Active Directory Domain Services (AD DS) domain.

   b. Your computer should be running the basic (home) version of Windows 10.

   c. The homegroup you want to join has no password configured.

   d. Your network location is set to Public.

7. You are evaluating Device Guard for use in your organization to improve security and are determining whether all of your organization's devices are compatible. Which of the following hardware requirements are needed for Device Guard? (Select all that apply.)

   a. A 64-bit CPU

   b. UEFI with Secure Boot

   c. At least 8 GB of RAM

   d. CPU virtualization extensions

   e. Support for SLAT or extended code pages

8. Device Health Attestation confirms the integrity of which of the following components on a Windows 10 device? (Select all that apply.)

   a. BitLocker

   b. Secure Boot

   c. EFS

   d. Windows Firewall

   e. Early Launch Anti-Malware (ELAM)

9. You right-click **This PC** and choose **Properties** to obtain system settings and perform some basic configuration activities on your Windows 10 computer. You notice a shield icon against several actions that you can access from here. What does this mean for a default configuration?

   a. When you select one of these actions, you will always receive a UAC prompt regardless of your user credentials.

   b. When you select one of these actions while running as a standard (non-administrative) user, you will receive a UAC prompt.

   c. When you select one of these actions while running as a standard (nonadministrative) user, you will have to log off and log back on as an administrator.

   d. These icons merely warn you to be careful with the actions you're intending to perform, but you will be able to do them regardless of your user credentials.

10. You have downloaded an executable file from the Internet. When you attempt to run this program, you receive a UAC message box with a red title bar and red shield informing you that the program has been blocked. What does this mean, and what should you do to run this program?

   a. This program is an unsigned program from a verified publisher. Simply click **Yes** to run it.

   b. This program is an unsigned program from a nonverified publisher. Click **Yes** and reenter your password to run it.

   c. This program is a high-risk program from a nonverified publisher. Click **Yes** and reenter your password to run it.

   d. This program is a high-risk program that Windows has blocked completely. You cannot run it in its present form, and you should check the program's publisher on the Internet and locate a certified version that will run.

11. You sometimes use the built-in Administrator account on your Windows 10 computer, so you have configured this account with a strong username and password. You want to have this account display UAC prompts in the same fashion as other administrative accounts. What should you do?

   a. From the User Account Settings Control Panel applet, select the **Always Notify** option.

   b. From the User Account Settings Control Panel applet, select the **Notify Me Only When Programs Try to Make Changes to My Computer** option.

   c. In Group Policy, you should enable the **Admin Approval Mode for the Built-In Administrator Account** policy.

   d. Do nothing. By default, this account works just like any other user account that belongs to the Administrators group.

12. You have had problems with users installing unapproved software on the Windows 10 computers in your small office. These users all have standard user accounts. You would like to configure UAC to block any programs that require elevated privileges to run the programs. So you access the Group Policy editor. What policy should you enable?

   a. You should enable the **Behavior of the Elevation Prompt for Standard Users** policy and then select the **Prompt for Credentials** option.

   b. You should enable the **Behavior of the Elevation Prompt for Standard Users** policy and then select the **Prompt for Credentials on the Secure Desktop** option.

   c. You should enable the **Behavior of the Elevation Prompt for Standard Users** policy and then select the **Automatically Deny Elevation Requests** option.

   d. You should enable the **Only Elevate Executables That Are Signed and Validated** policy.

13. Which of the following types of credentials can be backed up to a remote location using Credential Manager? (Choose three.)

   a. Web Credentials

   b. Windows Credentials

   c. Certificate-based Credentials

   d. Generic Credentials

   e. Windows app Credentials

14. You use a Microsoft account for your home computer and a Windows Mobile tablet, and your Web Credentials are available on these computers when you are browsing the web. You have a domain-joined Windows 10 computer at work, and you have added your Microsoft account, but your credentials are not working. What could be wrong?

   a. You used the wrong Microsoft account.

   b. You must restore your Web Credentials to the work computer.

   c. Credential roaming is disabled on domain-joined computers.

   d. Your administrator has deleted the credentials.

15. Which Windows 10 tool do you use to manage certificates?

    a. The Certificates Control Panel applet

    b. The Certificates MMC snap-in

    c. The Certificates Windows app

    d. The Certificates Manager on the PC settings screen

16. Your network administrator has provided a certificate for you to use when signing in to the secure server. You would like to add the credential to the Credential Manager so it is available when you try to access the server. Which certificate store should you use when installing the certificate?

    a. Trusted Publishers

    b. Enterprise Trust

    c. Personal

    d. Trusted People

17. What password policy actually weakens password security and is therefore not recommended for use by Microsoft?

    a. Enforce Password History

    b. Minimum Password Age

    c. Maximum Password Age

    d. Complexity Requirements

    e. Store Passwords Using Reversible Encryption

18. You want to ensure that users cannot cycle rapidly through a series of passwords and then reuse their old password immediately. Which password policy should you enable to prevent this action from occurring?

    a. Enforce Password History

    b. Minimum Password Age

    c. Maximum Password Age

    d. Password Must Meet Complexity Requirements

    e. Store Passwords Using Reversible Encryption

19. You have granted a user named Bob the Read NTFS permission on a folder named Documents. Bob is also a member of the Managers group, which has Full Control NTFS permission on the Documents folder. What is Bob's effective permission on this folder?

    a. Full Control

    b. Modify

    c. Read

    d. Bob does not have access to the folder.

20. You have granted a user named Jim the Read NTFS permission on a folder named Documents. Jim is also a member of the Interns group, which has been explicitly denied the Full Control NTFS permission on the Documents folder. What is Jim's effective permission on this folder?

    a. Full Control

    b. Modify

    c. Read

    d. Jim does not have access to the folder.

21. You have granted a user named Sharon the Full Control NTFS permission on a shared folder named Documents on your Windows computer's C: drive, which also has the Read Shared Folder permission granted to Everyone. Sharon will be accessing this C: drive folder on your computer. What is Sharon's effective permission on this folder?

    a. Full Control

    b. Modify

    c. Read

    d. Sharon does not have access to the folder.

22. You have granted the Managers group Full Control NTFS permission on a folder named Accounts, which is located within the C:\Documents folder, which has the Modify NTFS permission applied to it. You copy the Accounts folder into the D:\Confidential folder, to which the Managers group has been granted the Read permission. A user named Ryan, who is a member of the Managers group, accesses the D:\Confidential\Accounts folder. What effective permission does Ryan have to this folder?

    a. Full Control

    b. Modify

    c. Read

    d. Ryan does not have access to the folder.

Foundation Topics

Configuring Authentication and Authorization

To use a Windows 10 computer, whether the computer belongs to a workgroup or HomeGroup or to an Active Directory Domain Services (AD DS) domain, a user must prove that she is who she says she is. This is what authentication is all about. Simply put, authentication is the process of a user or computer proving its identity to the operating system. Ensuring that credentials are authentic is an important factor in any computer system, but becomes even more important when applied to remote access communications through telephone lines or through the Internet. You learn about remote access authentication in Chapter 15, "Configuring Remote Access." Here we discuss authentication on the local network and Windows 10 local logon.

After authentication, users must be authorized to use a network or system resource, and resources are secured from access or modification by unauthorized users. Authorization is the process of determining the available access allowed for a specific user. In contrast to authentication, a user who has been authenticated is trusted to be who they say they are; authorization is the process of determining what that user can do.

Authentication

For years, most companies have generally employed the simple means of usernames and passwords for authenticating users to their networks. In recent years, with increased prevalence of password-guessing schemes and hacking software, companies have moved to multifactor authentication systems employing technology such as smart cards and biometric devices to improve the reliability of authentication. Microsoft has provided support for many types of authentication in Windows 10 to improve the integrity of user credentials and create more reliable authentication measures. You should be aware of these technologies and how to configure them.

This section focuses on the knowledge and skills required for the 70-698 exam, but some of the topics are also required for 70-697. The following section, "Support Authentication and Authorization," includes references to this section rather than duplicating the material.

Microsoft Passport

> **NOTE**   When Windows 10 first shipped, it included Microsoft Passport and Windows Hello. In subsequent Windows 10 feature releases, Microsoft combined the technologies under the Windows Hello name to improve supportability and to simplify deployment. The functionality included in Microsoft Passport has not changed, so organizations using Microsoft Passport will not experience any changes.

Microsoft Passport is a technology for implementing strong two-factor authentication (2FA). It can verify user credentials by creating a device-specific credential protected by a biometric device or a PIN. It is similar to smart card systems, but does not require the extra components needed for smart cards. Microsoft passport provides some significant advantages over traditional Windows authentication.

- **Flexibility:** Passport can be implemented using existing hardware, using biometrics where available or PINs instead. It can be enhanced by implementing policies using Active Directory and is even supported in Azure AD. It can supplement or replace smart cards or tokens.

- **Standardization:** Microsoft is working with an industry alliance called the Fast IDentity Online Alliance (FIDO) to develop standards for strong authentication and devices. Windows 10 is now a reference implementation of the concepts in the FIDO 1.0 specifications—the User Authentication Framework (UAF) and Universal 2nd Factor (U2F). These concepts will be used to define the next generation of FIDO standards, 2.0, and will form the basis of an implementation standard that any company can implement to provide authentication across device types and in mixed computing environments.

- **Effectiveness:** Microsoft Passport, by design, helps to mitigate two common vulnerabilities: the risk of stolen credentials and the risk that a compromised device can be used to gain access to other devices in the network or organization. By using strong encryption, leveraging Trusted Platform Module (TPM) standards and device-specific authentication requirements, the risk of both of these vulnerabilities is significantly reduced.

- **Enterprise-ready:** Microsoft Passport is implemented in all editions of Windows 10, and enterprises can leverage Active Directory and Group Policies with Windows 10 Professional and Enterprise using Microsoft Passport for Work.

> **NOTE**   For more information about the FIDO alliance and the U2F and UAF specifications, refer to the "Specifications Overview" at http://fidoalliance.org/specifications/overview/.

Microsoft Passport registration can be used with any type of Windows 10 account, including Microsoft accounts, local accounts, or Active Directory accounts. Using a Microsoft account automatically sets up Passport on the device, and no further configuration is required to use it. In this case, the Microsoft servers act as the Identity Provider (IDP) for the device. The user can then enable PIN authentication, which will be associated with the credential. Setting up a PIN is a simple process.

The options available for 2nd Factor authentication will depend on the capabilities of the device, and, for domain-joined computers, the policies implemented in Active Directory. For instance, using Windows Hello facial recognition requires a compatible illuminated IR camera; using biometrics requires a fingerprint or other reader, and so on.

Step 1. From Action Center, select the **All Settings** icon.

Step 2. In Settings, select **Accounts**.

Step 3. Click the **Sign-in Options** menu on the Account settings page. This displays the page shown in Figure 7-1.

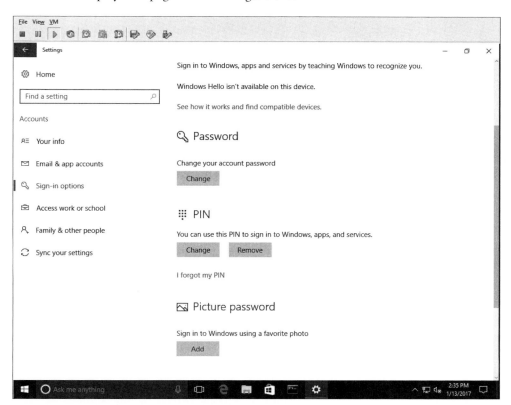

Figure 7-1 Account Settings Sign-in Options

Step 4.   In the PIN area, click the **Add** button. This displays the Set Up a PIN dialog.

Step 5.   Enter your PIN in the New PIN box and again in the Confirm PIN box, and then click **OK**.

After setting up your PIN, you can use it to sign on to your device. From the Windows 10 sign-in screen, you can switch between the PIN sign in or your password using the **Sign-in Options** link, which will reveal the icons to switch between PIN and password, as shown in Figure 7-2.

Figure 7-2   Sign-in Options on the Windows 10 Sign-in Screen Enable You to Switch Between PIN and Password Login

NOTE   For more information on Microsoft Passport and how it implements authentication systems, see the "Microsoft Passport Guide" at https://technet.microsoft.com/en-us/itpro/windows/keep-secure/microsoft-passport-guide.

NOTE   When Microsoft released Windows 10 version 1511, it included Windows Passport and Windows Hello working together for 2FA. With the release of version 1607, the "Anniversary Update," it combined the branding under Windows Hello. Windows Hello has the same functionality as Microsoft Passport for Business.

Picture Password and Biometrics

The traditional logon previously described will work on any Windows 10 computer. But a new feature first introduced for Windows 8 is the picture password. You can enable this security feature if your computer has a touch-enabled device or screen. On a tablet or touch device that you often use without a keyboard at all, this can provide a more convenient and secure password than using a touch-based soft keyboard.

A picture password is probably better termed a *gesture password*. You select a picture as the basis; then your gestures across the picture become the basis of your logon authentication.

Before enabling a picture password, make sure you have a picture saved to the local Windows 10 machine that you want to use. Then follow this procedure to set it up:

Step 1.   From Action Center, select **All Settings**; then select **Accounts**.

Step 2.   From the Sign-in Options section, shown previously in Figure 7-1, select **Add** under Picture Password.

Step 3.   Windows prompts you for your current password. Enter the password and click **OK**.

Step 4.   The next screen is the Welcome to Picture Password screen. Click the **Choose Picture** button to browse for the picture you want to use.

Step 5.   On the How's This Look? screen, shown in Figure 7-3, you have the opportunity to reposition the picture or use Choose New Picture. When you are satisfied, select the **Use This Picture** option.

Figure 7-3   Selecting a Picture for Picture Password

Step 6.   Start drawing your gestures. You will draw three gestures as the wizard walks you through the steps. There are three types of gestures:

- Circles
- Straight lines
- Taps

Your three gestures can be any combination of these types. Remember when you enter your picture password, you must repeat the gestures in the same place on the picture and in the same order. See Figure 7-4 for an example of a straight-line gesture.

Figure 7-4   Using Gesture Replay to Confirm Picture Password

Step 7.   Enter your three gestures a second time to confirm your password. When you have entered the gestures the same way twice, click the **Finish** button to confirm your new password.

Step 8.   If you forget your picture password, but remember your plain-text password, you can return to the Picture Password screen and use Replay to practice your original gestures again.

After a picture password has been set up, the system will prompt for the password using the picture selected. You also have the option of using the text password; just select **Switch to Text Password** at the Picture Password screen. When you do so, the text password prompt is used until you switch back to picture passwords. By default, if you perform the wrong gesture five times in a row, Windows automatically switches back to text passwords.

In a business or corporate environment, you may want to disable the use of picture passwords by users. You can accomplish this using Local Group Policies, or GPOs, in a domain. Navigate to Computer Configuration\Administrative Templates\ System\Logon and select **Turn Off Picture Password Sign-in**. Enabling this policy, as shown in Figure 7-5, disables the use of the picture password, and users will be unable to use or configure them for their account.

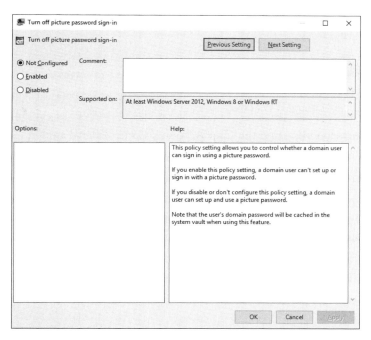

Figure 7-5   Disabling the Use of Picture Password Sign-in Using Local Group Policy Editor

Configuring Local Accounts

To create new local accounts in Windows 10, you use the Account Settings screen. Click the **Family and Other People** menu option, and then select **Add Someone Else to This PC**. To add a local account, click the **I Don't Have This Person's Sign-in Information** link, and then select **Add a User Without a Microsoft Account**. This reveals the screen to add a local account, as shown in Figure 7-6.

Figure 7-6   Adding a New Local Account in Windows 10

You can manage existing accounts using the User Accounts Control Panel applet, or the Local Users and Groups section of the Computer Management snap-in. The snap-in provides greater control of local accounts and allows you to use specific groups to provide authorization for each account. You can add users to groups from the Local Users and Groups node of the Computer Management snap-in. Right-click the desired group in the Groups folder shown in Figure 7-7 and choose **Properties**. In the Properties dialog box that appears, click Add, type the desired username, and then click **OK**. Click **OK** again in the group's Properties dialog box to close it and add the user to the group.

Figure 7-7   Windows 10 Built-in Groups in Local Users and Groups Snap-in

When you change the Account Type using the Control Panel User Accounts applet, you can select either a Standard account or an Administrator account. This simply adds or removes the user from the local Administrators group. There are several additional built-in groups you can use for better control of authorization. Table 7-2 summarizes the available built-in local groups.

Table 7-2   Built-in Local Groups in Windows 10

Group Name	Default Rights	Default Local Membership
Access Control Assistance Operators	Access to remotely query authorization attributes and permissions for resources.	N/A
Administrators	Unrestricted access and all privileges.	Administrator

Group Name	Default Rights	Default Local Membership
Backup Operators	Access to run Windows Backup and sufficient access rights that override other rights when performing a backup or restore.	N/A
Cryptographic Operators	Authorized to perform cryptographic operations.	N/A
Distributed COM users	Launch, activate, and use Distributed COM objects on the local computer.	N/A
Event Log Readers	Read access to event logs.	N/A
Guests	Limited to explicitly granted rights and restricted usage of the computer.	Guest (disabled by default)
Hyper-V Administrators	Members of this group have complete and unrestricted access to all features of Hyper-V.	N/A
Network Configuration Operators	Some administrative privileges to manage network configuration and features.	N/A
Performance Log Users	Schedule logging of performance counters, enable trace providers, and collect event traces both locally and remotely.	N/A
Performance Monitor Users	Access to performance counter data locally and remotely.	N/A
Power Users	Used only for backward compatibility with Windows XP and earlier; limited administrative privileges.	N/A
Remote Desktop Users	Provides access to the computer using Remote Desktop.	N/A
Remote Management Users	Can access WMI resources over management protocols such as the Windows Remote Management service. Limited by WMI namespace access granted to the user.	N/A
Replicator	Supports file replication in a domain.	N/A
System Managed Accounts Group	Users in this group, new for Windows 10, are managed by the system, as implied by the name, and should not be manually modified.	DefaultAccount
Users	Users are prevented from making accidental or intentional systemwide changes and can run most applications.	All local accounts and Authenticated Users in a domain-joined environment

By default, a Windows 10 computer that is not part of a domain displays the Lock screen at startup, and after a user has logged off. Touching or clicking the Lock screen displays the Windows 10 logon screen, which is also displayed when a user selects the Switch User option from the Ctrl+Alt+Del menu. The logon screen displays all currently enabled user accounts, allowing a user to select the appropriate account and enter the password if one has been specified.

In Chapter 2, "Implementing Windows," we covered how to create an account for a newly installed Windows 10 computer using either a Microsoft account or a local account. When you create new accounts for Windows 10, they can either use a local logon or a Microsoft account.

Although the default logon screen is convenient, especially in a home environment, it does pose a security risk in a corporate environment, even in a small office. In an AD DS environment, the classic logon screen is no longer enabled by default in Windows 10. Instead, an option called Other User is made available to allow the user to enter domain credentials previously unknown by the local machine.

You can change the way that a domain-joined Windows 10 displays the logon screen using the User Accounts applet. From the Search bar or Cortana, search for **netplwiz** and click the **Run Command** link that is displayed. Select the **Advanced** tab in the applet, and then click the check box in the Secure Sign-in section labeled **Require Users to Press Crtl+Alt+Delete**, as shown in Figure 7-8.

Figure 7-8 Enabling Secure Sign-in Using the User Accounts Control Panel Applet

You can use Group Policy to require the use of the logon screen on domain-joined as well as non-domain-joined Windows 10 computers.

For a workgroup or non-domain-joined computer, open the Local Group Policy Editor, which you can find by searching for Group Policy from the Search bar or Cortana. Navigate to the Computer Configuration\Windows Settings\ Security Settings\Local Policies\Security Options node and then disable **Interactive Logon: Do Not Require CTRL+ALT+DEL** (see Figure 7-9).

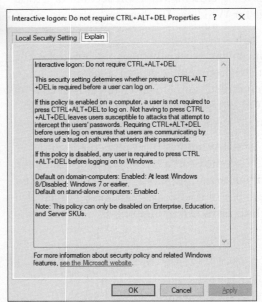

Figure 7-9   Requiring Users to Use Ctrl+Alt+Del Using Group Policy Editor

Note that the Interactive Logon: Do Not Require CTRL+ALT+DEL security policy setting works when the computer is not in a domain, or it can be defined in a GPO linked to an OU in the domain.

To remove the display of the last username, navigate to the Computer Configuration\Windows Settings\Security Settings\Local Policies\Security Options node and enable the Interactive Logon: Do Not Display Last Username policy.

Configuring Microsoft Accounts

With Windows 10, Microsoft consolidated its latest operating system for PCs, tablets, and smartphones for maximum portability. Users may have a work computer, a home PC, a smartphone, and a tablet all running Windows 10 or Windows 10 Mobile, and they expect their settings, Windows apps, and services to work the same across all these devices. The way to enable the consistency across all these devices is using a Microsoft account.

When the same Microsoft account is used on all of a user's devices, the user has automatic access to many resources, apps, files stored on clouds and remote computers, and consistent settings that roam from device to device.

Sign In Using a Microsoft Account

Recall from Chapter 2, "Implementing Windows," that the default method for creating the first account at the end of the setup process was to use a Microsoft account. You can use any email address for the Microsoft account; users only need to provide their email address, create a password for the Microsoft account, and they can use the account on any Windows 10 Windows Mobile computer.

Using a Microsoft account provides several advantages, especially for home users:

- Integration of contacts and friends status from Outlook.com, Google, iCloud, and LinkedIn service using Cortana.

- Access and sharing of photos, documents, and other files with OneDrive, Facebook, and Flickr.

- Using Windows Store apps is easier using a Microsoft account. You can use purchased apps installed on one computer on up to 10 devices using Windows 10 or Windows Mobile.

- Personal settings are automatically kept in sync online and among all the devices using the same Microsoft account. It includes themes, browser favorites and history, and content and settings for Microsoft apps and services.

Creating a Microsoft account for use with Windows 10 is a simple process. Assuming you are already using a local account, you can switch to using a Microsoft account using this procedure:

Step 1.   From the Action Center, click the **All Settings** icon, and then select **Accounts**.

Step 2.   From the Accounts settings page, select the **Your Info** menu, and then click the **Sign In with a Microsoft Account Instead** link.

Step 3.   When prompted, enter your email, phone, or type the username and current password, and then click **Sign In**. If you do not have an email address you want to use, or you want to create a new one, click the **Create One!** link. You then have the option of creating a Microsoft account with an email address you have. You can also select the **Get a New Email Address** link to set up a new email address on outlook.com.

Step 4.   On the next page, enter your current Windows password at the prompt, and then click **Next**.

Step 5.   After your Microsoft account has been authenticated, you can sign out of the computer and log back in with your Microsoft account credentials.

After you switch your logon to a Microsoft account, you cannot log in using your local account again; you must use the Microsoft account. If you want to switch back to the local account, first log in with your Microsoft account, access the Accounts Settings **Your Info** menu again, and select the **Sign In with a Local Account Instead** link.

Managing the Use of Microsoft Account

In many organizations it may be inappropriate to allow users to sign on to their PCs using a Microsoft account. As described in the previous section, using a Microsoft account on a business PC means that a lot of personal information is synched and made available on the local PC. This may cause disruption and possible security risks.

To block the use of Microsoft accounts, you can configure the Group Policy Accounts: Block Microsoft Accounts, which is found under Computer Configuration\Windows Settings\Security Settings\Local Policies\Security Options. There are three options:

- **This Policy Is Disabled:** Users can create and log on with Microsoft accounts and connect their domain account to their Microsoft account.

- **Users Can't Add Microsoft Accounts:** Users will not be able to create new Microsoft accounts, switch a local account to a Microsoft account, or connect a domain account to a Microsoft account.

- **Users Can't Add or Log On with Microsoft Accounts:** Existing Microsoft account users will not be able to log on to Windows.

NOTE   The Block Microsoft Accounts setting applies only to using Microsoft accounts for local system logon. Users can still use their Microsoft account for things like accessing email over the Internet, using OneDrive to access cloud-based storage, and other purposes.

Configuring Windows Hello

Windows Hello is a new authentication system introduced with Windows 10. Windows Hello and Windows Hello for Business, which now includes the technologies first introduced as Microsoft Passport, provide many advantages over traditional password-based authentication and mitigate many of the vulnerabilities associated with passwords.

You can use Windows Hello with either a compatible infrared (IR) camera or a fingerprint reader. Devices are becoming available now that meet the FIDO alliance specifications and can work with Windows Hello. The specifications ensure that devices meet certain standards for False Acceptance rate (FAR), True Positive rate, and False Negative rate. IR cameras are required instead of typical optical cameras in order to prevent spoofing, or fooling the device into thinking the real person is present. Optical cameras can often be spoofed using a photograph of the user, a technique that is not possible with an IR camera.

To use Windows Hello, you first enroll your device using your fingerprint or facial recognition. To enroll your device for Windows Hello, follow these steps:

Step 1.   Select the **Start** button and click the **Settings** icon.

Step 2.   Select **Accounts**, and then click the **Sign-in Options** menu.

Step 3.   Under Windows Hello, you see options for your fingerprint or IR camera device. If no device is available, Windows displays Windows Hello Isn't Available on This Device, as shown in Figure 7-10.

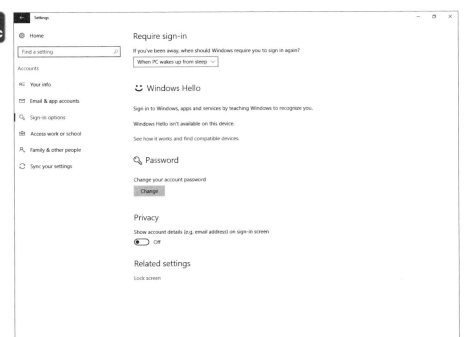

Figure 7-10   Sign-in Options Disable Windows Hello on a Computer Without a Fingerprint Reader or IR Camera

Step 4. If you have not set up a PIN for your device, you will be required to con-figure a PIN before setting up Windows Hello. Add a PIN to your device if prompted.

Step 5. Click the **Set Up** button for your device, and follow the instructions. If you are configuring facial recognition, Windows will capture an image of your face. You can select the **Improve Recognition** button to perform more captures.

When Windows has finished recognizing you through your camera or fingerprint device, it displays **All Set!**

After enrolling your device with Windows Hello, you no longer need a password. Windows will log you in by recognizing your face or fingerprint. From the Sign-in Options menu, you can also toggle the Automatically Unlock the Screen If We Rec-ognize Your Face option. If the toggle is on, Windows automatically logs you in to Windows when it recognizes you.

Windows Hello for Business

Windows Hello for Business is available on Windows 10 Pro and Enterprise edi-tions. You can configure Windows Hello for Business using Group Policy, or MDM policy through Microsoft Intune. It provides an additional layer of protection and uses key-based or certificate-based authentication. The Hello gesture (face recogni-tion or fingerprint) does not roam the network and never leaves the device; how-ever, a public key is generated during registration, and the authenticating server uses this to validate the user's identity.

With recent updates to Windows 10 since its first release, Microsoft has combined Microsoft Passport with Windows Hello. Windows Hello for Business includes all the functionality discussed in the previous section on Microsoft Passport, and orga-nizations that deployed Microsoft Passport will see no change in functionality.

Table 7-3 lists the important group policies available for managing Windows Hello for Business using AD DS.

Table 7-3 Group Policies for Managing Windows Hello for Business in a Domain

Policy	Options
Use Windows Hello for Business	**Not configured:** Users can provision Windows Hello, which encrypts their domain password.
	Enabled: Devices are provisioned for Windows Hello using keys or certificates for all users.
	Disabled: Device does not provision Windows Hello for Business for any user.
Use a hardware security device	**Not configured:** Windows Hello for Business will be provisioned using TPM if available, and will be provisioned using software if TPM is not available.
	Enabled: Windows Hello for Business will only be provisioned using TPM.
	Disabled: Windows Hello for Business will be provisioned using TPM if available, and will be provisioned using software if TPM is not available.
Use biometrics	**Not configured:** Biometrics can be used as a gesture in place of a PIN.
	Enabled: Biometrics can be used as a gesture in place of a PIN.
	Disabled: Only a PIN can be used as a gesture.
PIN Complexity: Minimum PIN length	**Not configured:** PIN length must be greater than or equal to 4.
	Enabled: PIN length must be greater than or equal to the number you specify.
	Disabled: PIN length must be greater than or equal to 4.
PIN Complexity: Expiration	**Not configured:** PIN does not expire.
	Enabled: PIN can be set to expire after any number of days between 1 and 730, or PIN can be set to never expire by setting policy to 0.
	Disabled: PIN does not expire.
PIN Complexity: Require uppercase letters	**Not configured:** Users cannot include an uppercase letter in their PIN.
	Enabled: Users must include at least one uppercase letter in their PIN.
	Disabled: Users cannot include an uppercase letter in their PIN.

NOTE For more information about Windows Hello for Business, refer to the article "Manage Identity Verification Using Windows Hello for Business" at https://technet.microsoft.com/en-us/itpro/windows/keep-secure/manage-identity-verification-using-microsoft-passport.

Authorization

Users of Windows 10 computers and in a network or domain are authorized based on the access rights configured by network or domain administrators, or the owner of a remote resource the user is attempting to use. A number of technologies are used in Windows to secure resources and allow or deny users based on their role or the authorization level required by the resource.

Workgroups

Ever since Windows for Workgroups version 3.11 was introduced in 1993, Windows has supported network access to printers, remote files, and other resources using Workgroups. At the most basic level, a workgroup is a named collection of computers that operate together and are discoverable to each other. This discoverability first worked only on a single network segment, not across routers, and used a proprietary NETBIOS protocol instead of TCP/IP.

Windows networking has changed considerably since that time, but the workgroup is still available and often used in homes and small businesses. When Windows 10 is first installed, the default setup is to join the computer to a workgroup called *WORKGROUP*. This can be modified to use a domain, or a different workgroup name, as you saw in Chapter 2, "Implementing Windows." Follow these steps to join a workgroup in Windows 10:

Step 1.   From File Explorer, right-click **This PC** and select **Properties**.

Step 2.   From the System control panel applet, look for Computer Name, Domain, and Workgroup Settings and click the **Change Settings** link.

Step 3.   From the resulting System Properties dialog box, click the **Change** button. This displays the form shown in Figure 7-11.

Step 4.   Select the **Workgroup** radio button and type the name of the workgroup in the box provided. This should match the workgroup name of the other computers in your workgroup.

Step 5.   Optionally change the Computer name, and then click **OK**.

Step 6.   Windows displays the Welcome to the Workgroup message box. Click **OK**.

Step 7.   Windows will inform you that you must restart the computer. Click **OK**.

Step 8.   Click Close on the System Properties dialog box. When prompted, click the **Restart Now** button to restart the computer.

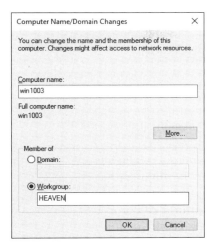

Figure 7-11   Using Computer Name/Domain Changes to Change the Computer's Name and to Join a Workgroup, or Domain.

After Windows restarts, the computer will be a member of the workgroup you specified. Click the **Network** icon from the **Start** menu to see your network and the computers that you can access.

Domain Account Settings

Users on domain-joined Windows 10 computers can connect their domain account to their Microsoft account. This will provide the capability to sync their settings, favorites, and Microsoft apps from their home PC or tablet with their domain-joined computer without signing into services separately.

The process is similar to that listed for a nondomain account, but domain users will be presented with an Add a Microsoft Account option on the Accounts screen. When that option is selected, users can choose what settings to synchronize, as shown in Figure 7-12. Choose the desired sync settings and click **Next**, and the rest of the process is the same.

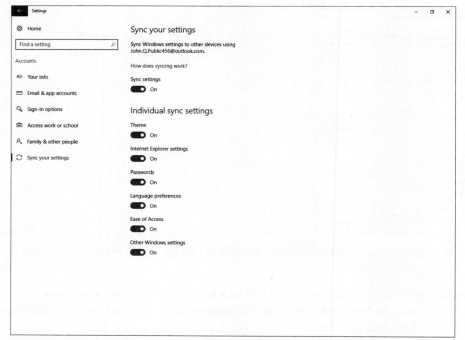

Figure 7-12   Selecting the PC Settings to Sync with Your Domain Account

HomeGroup

First introduced in Windows 7 and improved in Windows 10 is the concept of a HomeGroup, which is a small group of Windows 7, 8.1, or 10 computers connected together in a home or small office network that you have designated in the Network and Sharing Center as a home network. Computers running any edition of Windows 7, 8.1, or 10 can join a HomeGroup, but you cannot create a HomeGroup using Windows RT or Windows 7 Starter or Home Basic editions. Computers running Windows Vista or earlier cannot join a HomeGroup. To create or join a HomeGroup, your computer's network location profile setting (discussed in Chapter 14) must be set to Private.

You can create a HomeGroup from the HomeGroup applet, which is accessed from the Network and Internet category of Control Panel by clicking **HomeGroup**. You can also access this applet by using the Search bar or Cortana, or by clicking **Home-Group** from the Network and Sharing Center. From the Share with Other Home Computers dialog box shown in Figure 7-13, click **Create a Homegroup** and then click **Next**. As shown in Figure 7-14, the Create a Homegroup Wizard enables you to select the type of resources you want to share with other computers. For each resource listed here, select **Shared** or **Not Shared** as required. After making your selections and clicking **Next**, the wizard provides you with a unique password that you can use to add other computers to the HomeGroup (see Figure 7-15). Make note of this password so that you can join other computers to the HomeGroup, and then click **Finish**.

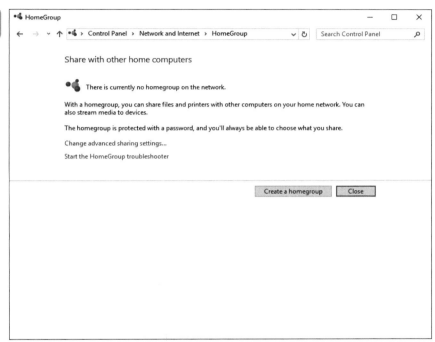

Figure 7-13   The HomeGroup Control Panel Applet

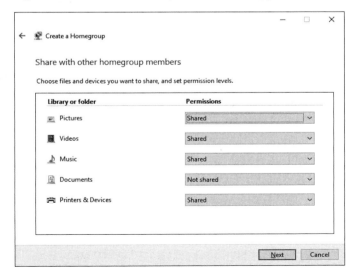

Figure 7-14   Determining the Type of Resources You Want to Share on the HomeGroup

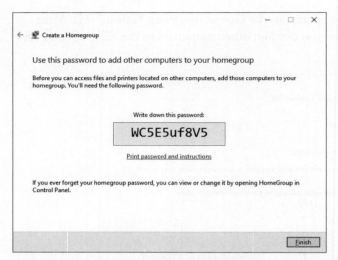

Figure 7-15   The Create HomeGroup Wizard Displaying the HomeGroup Shared Password

Joining a HomeGroup

After you have created a HomeGroup, when you move to another computer on the network, the computer recognizes the HomeGroup, and the Share with Other Home Computers dialog box informs you of this (see Figure 7-16). Click **Join Now** to join the HomeGroup, select the libraries you want to share, and then type the HomeGroup password when requested.

Figure 7-16   The HomeGroup Control Panel Applet Detecting an Existing HomeGroup on the Network

NOTE   If your computer is joined to a domain, you can still join a HomeGroup. However, you cannot share libraries or printers to the HomeGroup. This feature enables you to bring a portable computer home from work and access shared resources on your home network. Furthermore, it is possible to use Group Policy to prevent domain computers from being joined to a HomeGroup.

Modifying HomeGroup Settings

After you've joined a HomeGroup, you receive the Change HomeGroup settings dialog box shown in Figure 7-17 when you access the HomeGroup option in the Control Panel Network and Internet category. From here you can change the types of libraries and printers that are shared with other HomeGroup computers. You can also perform any of the other self-explanatory actions shown in Figure 7-17 under Other HomeGroup actions. Selecting the Change Advanced Sharing Settings option takes you to the Advanced Sharing Settings dialog box shown in Figure 7-18.

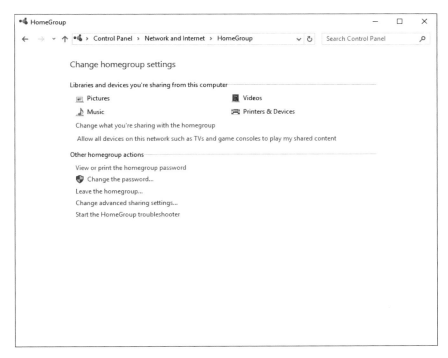

Figure 7-17   The Change HomeGroup Settings Dialog Box

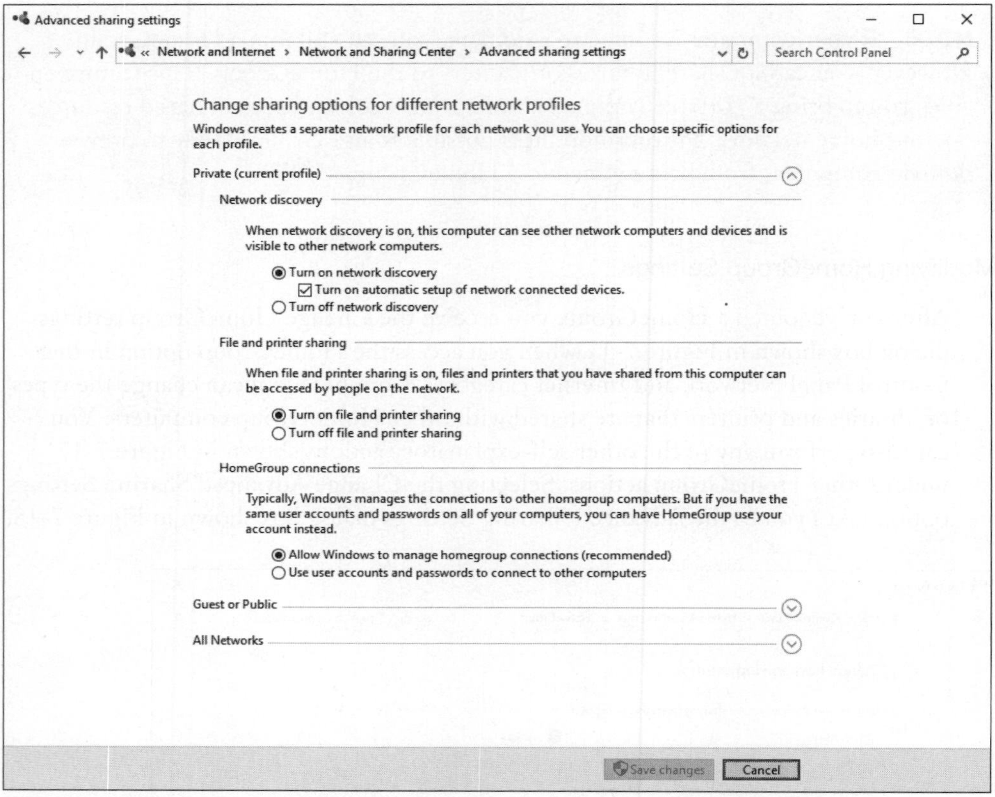

Figure 7-18   Advanced Sharing Setting Dialog Box

From the dialog box shown in Figure 7-17, selecting the **Allow All Devices on This Network Such as TVs and Game Consoles to Play My Shared Content** option displays the dialog box shown in Figure 7-19. The list includes all computers and other media devices found on the network including media players, electronic picture frames, and others. You can allow or block media access to each device individually by selecting the drop-down lists provided, or you can allow or block all devices by choosing from the appropriate command buttons provided.

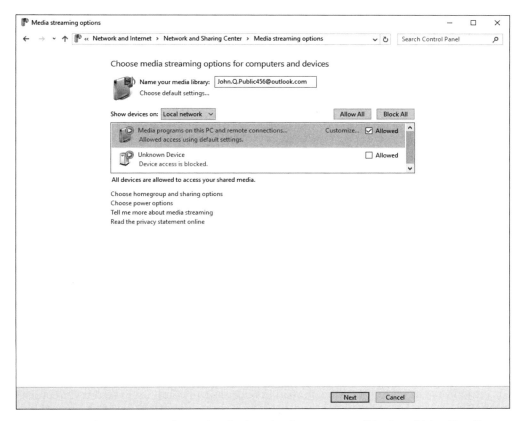

Figure 7-19   Choose Media Streaming Options for Computers and Devices Dialog Box Enabling You to Choose Which Devices Are Allowed to Access Shared Media

You can also modify the file-sharing options for subfolders located within any of your shared libraries. To do this, navigate to the desired library in File Explorer and select the folder. From the Share With section on the Share tab, choose one of the following:

- **Homegroup (View):** Shares the file or folder with Read permission to all users in the homegroup.

- **Homegroup (View and Edit):** Shares the file or folder with Full Control permission to all users in the homegroup.

- **Specific People:** Displays the Choose People to Share With dialog box shown in Figure 7-20. Type the name of the user with whom you want to share the folder and then click **Add**.

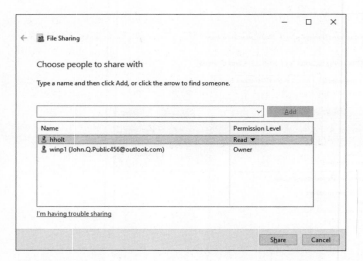

Figure 7-20   File Sharing Dialog Allowing You to Manage the Share Permissions for Your Libraries

Configuring Device Registration

Large organizations and enterprises have lots of options from Microsoft for keeping the workforce connected, managing devices, providing access to resources and applications, and managing and securing the network. Implementing a PKI infrastructure, a private and public domain in a forest, and configuring Active Directory Federation Services (AD FS) allows companies to provide their employees with secure and trusted access to workplace resources. Technologies like Workplace Join allows users to connect their devices to secured applications the organization has created over the Internet using their Windows 10 devices, mobile phones, and even Android and iOS devices.

Recent innovations from Microsoft in cloud-based services and technologies such as Microsoft Intune and Azure AD allow companies to leverage existing infrastructure by integrating with the cloud. This provides a way to evaluate technologies without investing in new infrastructure hardware and simplifies the deployment of new capabilities with integration between cloud services and internal company resources.

These cloud services can also help much smaller companies use technologies that would take a lot of resources and expertise to deploy from scratch. In Chapter 5, "Installing and Managing Software," you learned about Windows Store apps and Office 365, and in Chapter 13, "Microsoft Intune," you learn more about using Intune to manage devices, and you learn more about Microsoft Azure in Chapter 17, "Managing Mobile Apps." Device registration provides a way for users to securely authenticate to your organization and use a single, trusted credential from anywhere they have an Internet connection. Implementation and configuration of the entire infrastructure required to enable this functionality is beyond the scope of this text; however, for the 70-697 and 70-698 exams you should understand how device registration works with Windows 10 and Azure AD.

When a device is registered, Azure Active Directory Device Registration provides it with a trusted identity that is used to authenticate the device when a user signs in. The device attributes can then be used to enforce access policies for applications in the organizations or the cloud. Combined with Microsoft Intune, administrations can create conditional access rules for devices that meet organization policies and security requirements.

To enable device registration, first enable devices in Azure AD, as shown in Figure 7-21. In your directory's devices configuration, make sure that All is selected under Users May Join Devices to Azure AD, and select the maximum devices that you want to allow per user. As shown in Figure 7-21, two-factor authentication is not enabled by default. To require two-factor authentication, you need to configure a two-factor authentication provider in Azure AD and configure your user accounts.

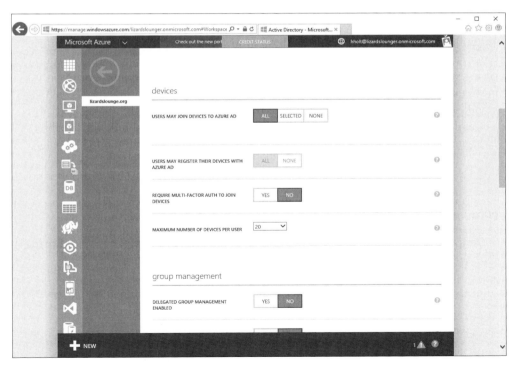

Figure 7-21   Enabling Device Registration in Azure AD

After you have configured the Azure AD, registering the device in Windows 10 is automatic when you join the device to the Azure AD. You will need to create user accounts in Azure AD for your users. Use the following steps to join Azure AD and register the device.

Step 1.   Click **Start** and then select the **Settings** icon.

Step 2.   Select the **Accounts** menu and then click **Access Work or School**.

Step 3.   Click the **Connect** button. On the Set Up a Work or School Account page, shown in Figure 7-22, click the link **Join This Device to Azure Active Directory**.

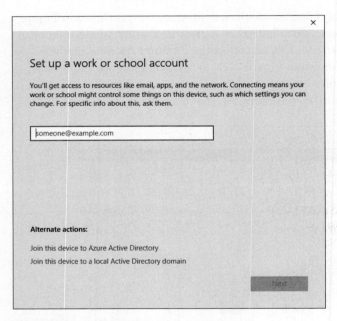

Figure 7-22   Connecting to School or Work

Step 4.   Enter your Azure AD credentials and then click **Sign In**. The confirmation box shown in Figure 7-23 is displayed. Click **Join** to continue.

Figure 7-23   Confirming That You Want to Join an Organization's Azure AD

> **Step 5.**   After a few minutes, the confirmation page shown in Figure 7-24 is displayed. Click **Done**.

Figure 7-24   Confirming Successful Connection to Azure AD

After registration, users can log in to their devices using the credentials for your organization's Azure AD. You can manage devices from the Azure directory or from Intune. From the Azure AD administration console, you can view the devices that users have registered, as shown in Figure 7-25.

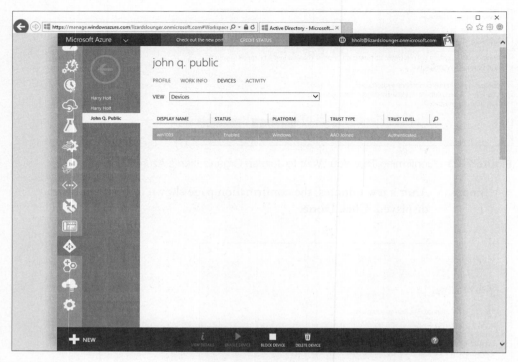

Figure 7-25   Viewing Devices That Users Have Registered in the Azure AD Administration Portal

Configuring Device Guard

Device Guard is a new security technology for Windows 10 and Windows Server 2016 that helps protect computers from malicious software or rogue applications. On devices that support virtualization, Device Guard leverages the virtualization capabilities of the processor to create a protected system using virtualization-based security (VBS). With Device Guard, you create a "whitelist" of programs and applications that are allowed to run on the device, known as a Device Guard *profile*. The profile contains the digital signatures of approved applications, called *code integrity policies*, that Device Guard will enforce. Any application that attempts to load but does not match the profile will not be allowed to run.

Device Guard and Credential Guard (discussed later in the section "Configuring Credential Guard") are a set of features that protect the system by using Virtual

Secure Mode (VSM). VSM leverages the processor-based virtualization extensions to sequester critical processes and their memory against tampering from malicious entities or software. In this way, a separate operating system is created on top of the hypervisor where security-sensitive operations can occur, independent of the host OS. Code integrity consists of both Kernel Mode Code Integrity (KMCI), which controls kernel and kernel-level device drivers, and Hypervisor Code Integrity (HVCI), which controls the security of user mode software.

Deploying Device Guard requires some specific hardware on the computers where it will be implemented, as described in the list that follows:

- A 64-bit CPU.

- CPU virtualization extensions, such as VT-x for Intel processors or AMD-V for AMD.

- Extended page tables, also called Second Level Address Translation (SLAT).

- UEFI firmware version 2.3.1.c or higher, with UEFI Secure Boot. The firmware must also support secure firmware update.

Also note that Device Guard is supported only in Windows 10 Enterprise, Windows 10 Education, Windows 10 Mobile, or Windows Server 2016.

Applications that you want to configure for Device Guard must be digitally signed, either through an embedded signature or using a catalog. Windows has required drivers to be signed since Windows 8, and most applications have digital signatures. Custom or LOB applications that your organization creates must also be signed or referenced in a catalog of digital certificates. If you use a catalog, it must be updated along with any updates to the applications.

Implementation of Device Guard in an organization requires careful planning and consideration. You must ensure the devices you want to protect meet the hardware requirements. You will need reference computers that you can use to collect information on the allowed applications to create your code integrity policies. You can run Device Guard in Audit mode, which will not block applications but will create event log entries when an application outside the policy is loaded. When you are satisfied with your code integrity policy, you should pilot the profile with a few users to ensure that critical processes and applications are working as expected.

One of the first steps to deploying Device Guard is to use a reference computer, or *golden computer*, a device with the same hardware and software as the target devices in your organization, and begin creating your code integrity policy. Use the following steps to create the code integrity policy:

Step 1. From an elevated PowerShell prompt, use the following example commands to create the XML files and binary policy file. In this example, the files will be called DGScan.xml and DGPolicy.bin, respectively. The files will be written to the C:\DGPolicy directory.

```
$CIPolicyPath="C:\DGPolicy\"
$InitialCIPolicy="$CIPolicyPath+"DGScan.xml"
$CIPolicyBin=$CIPolicyPath+"DGPolicy.bin"
```

Step 2. Use the **New-CIPolicy** cmdlets to create the new code integrity policy. This will scan the system for installed applications.

```
New-CIPolicy -Level PcaCertificate -FilePath $InitialCIPolicy
-UserPEs 3 > C:\DGPolicy\CIPolicyLog.txt
```

Step 3. Use the **ConvertFrom-CIPolicy** cmdlets to convert the code integrity policy to a binary format that Device Guard can use.

```
ConvertFrom-CIPolicy $InitialCIPolicy $CIPolicyBin
```

The original .xml file and the Device Guard binary file will be available in C:\DGPolicy. You can use these files when enabling Device Guard.

Microsoft provides a hardware readiness tool you can use to ensure your device can support Device Guard, and it enables the Device Guard features for you. The tool is distributed as a .zip file with a PowerShell script, default audit and enforcement policies, and instructions for using the tool. You need to run the DG_Readiness_Tool_v2.1.ps1 script using an elevated (administrator) PowerShell prompt. Running the script with no parameters will produce the syntax instructions as shown in Figure 7-26.

Figure 7-26 Running the DG_Readiness_Tool Script with No Parameters Displays the Available Command Syntax

The first thing to do is to ensure your device is capable of running Device Guard by running the script with the **-Capable** command. When the script is first run, it runs Driver Verifier to check the code integrity of your drivers, which will require a reboot. You can add the **-AutoReboot** switch to let the script reboot the computer whenever it needs to do so. After validating your drivers, the script will check other software and hardware requirements, and then present a summary, as shown in

Figure 7-27. The summary in the image tells us that we cannot use Device Guard or Credential Guard on this machine because Secure Boot Validate Failed. Several warnings are also included. Warnings mean you can use VBS features, but it will be less secure and reliable because of the missing features. The script will also create a log file in C:\DGLogs, which you can use to review the tool's output.

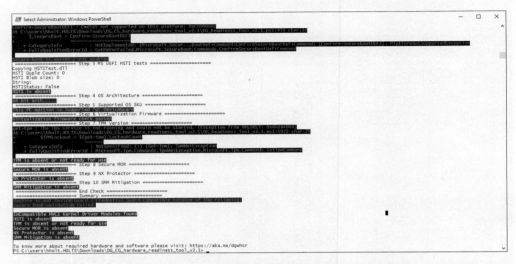

Figure 7-27   DG_Readiness_Tool Running with the **-Capable** Switch to Check Hardware and Software Compatibility

After you have confirmed that your computer meets the hardware and software requirements, you can enable Device Guard. To use the tool, run it with the **-Enable** command-line switch. To use the specific policy you created, use the **-Path** switch and provide the path to your policy file. For example:

```
DG_CG_ReadinessTool_2.1.psi -Enable -Path C:\DGPolicy\DGPolicy.bin
```

This turns on the Hyper-V hypervisor and IOMMU memory settings, and creates the Registry keys to set up Device Guard and Credential Guard.

You can also enable VBS and Device Guard using Group Policy Objects. The policies are located under Computer Configuration\Administrative Templates\System\Device Guard. To install your custom policy, use the Deploy Code Integrity Policy, as shown in Figure 7-28. You will need to copy your binary policy file to a server file share accessible to all the devices you are configuring.

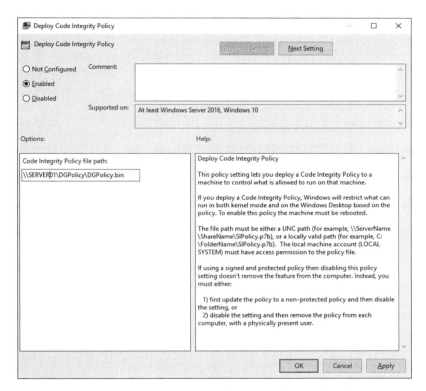

Figure 7-28   Setting the Code Integrity Policy for Device Guard

To enable the policy on Windows devices, use Turn On Virtualization Based Security. You can enable both Device Guard and Credential Guard using this policy, as shown in Figure 7-29. You can select whether to use UEFI lock for each (Device Guard is called *Virtualization Based Protection of Code Integrity* in the policy). If you select Enabled with UEFI Lock, you will not be able to disable the settings using Group Policy; the VBS protection will be locked down on the device.

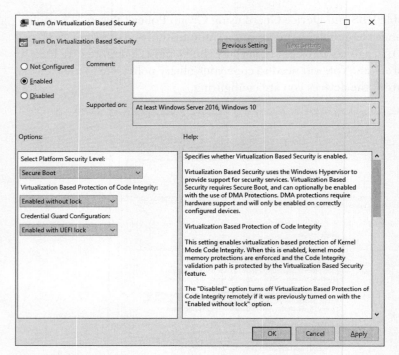

Figure 7-29   Enabling Device Guard and Credential Guard Using Group Policy Objects

NOTE   To learn more about Device Guard and Credential Guard and details of how they work and how to deploy these technologies, see the "Device Guard Deployment Guide" at https://technet.microsoft.com/en-us/itpro/windows/keep-secure/device-guard-deployment-guide.

Configuring Credential Guard

Credential Guard works the same as Device Guard in a VBS environment, but instead of protecting against malicious software, it works to protect secrets in a similar way. To prevent credential theft attacks, Credential Guard stores NTLM password hashes and Kerberos tickets and passwords stored in Credential Manager in a secure virtualized location inaccessible to most credential theft attacks.

The hardware and software requirements for Credential Guard are the same as those for Device Guard. You can also use the same tools to validate your devices and enable Credential Guard, as you learned in the previous discussion of Device Guard. When Credential Guard is enabled, it works automatically to protect your credentials from vulnerabilities.

Configuring Device Health Attestation

New to Windows 10 and Windows Server 2016 is Device Health Attestation (DHA). DHA helps enterprises improve security by monitoring devices and hardware and ensuring they are guarded against security threats. DHA is a service that monitors Windows devices and reports the status of the devices' Secure Boot, BitLocker integrity, and the Early Launch Anti-Malware Driver (ELAM), which is loaded first after Secure Boot to protect against bootloader malware. DHA is implemented using hardware components of each device, and validating the health of these components is performed using the Windows Health Attestation Service, which is available in several flavors:

- DHA Cloud Service is a Microsoft-managed service accessible from anywhere in the world.

- DHA On-Premises Service is enabled through a new server role in Windows Server 2016, available to any customers licensed for Windows Server 2016.

- DHA Azure Cloud Service is enabled using a virtual host in Microsoft Azure. The Azure cloud service requires a virtual host and licenses for DHA on-premises service.

DHA is a useful service especially for organizations with BYOD (bring-your-own-device) policies. You can check the hardware health status of employees' personal devices to ensure they meet your security standards and have not been compromised by malware or bootloader viruses.

To enable DHA within an organization, you can configure the Windows Server 2016 server role, as shown in Figure 7-30. The role requires IIS, as the reports you receive on device health will be accessed through the DHA website on the role server. You can configure DHA to check the security of a Windows 10 device before it is granted access to your network. This helps protect your entire organization from rogue, untrusted, or infected devices.

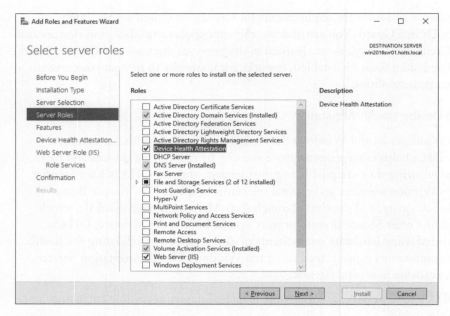

Figure 7-30   Installing the DHA Role in Windows Server 2016

You can also configure your cloud services, such as Office 365 or Azure AD, to check with the DHA service and deny access to any devices that do not meet the security policies, by configuring conditional access for those services.

> **NOTE**   For more information about DHA services, see "Control the Health of Windows 10-Based Devices" at https://technet.microsoft.com/en-us/itpro/windows/keep-secure/protect-high-value-assets-by-controlling-the-health-of-windows-10-based-devices.

Configuring UAC Behavior

In versions of Windows prior to Vista, many users became frustrated with the inability to perform many common tasks and therefore ran their computers with an administrative user account, often the default Administrator account created when Windows was installed. These users received total system privileges as required for installing and configuring applications, modifying system configuration, running background system tasks, installing device drivers, and performing other system configuration actions. Such a practice left the computers open to many types of attacks by malware programs, such as viruses, worms, rootkits, and others.

Administrators and technical support personnel in a corporate environment were often left in a dilemma. They could grant users administrative privileges, which can result in users changing settings, either accidentally or deliberately, that disrupted computer or network performance or compromised security. Or they could limit user privileges, which often limited productivity because users were unable to perform basic tasks, such as connecting to a wireless network or installing a printer driver.

Beginning with Windows Vista, Microsoft addressed this problem by introducing a new feature called User Account Control (UAC). Simply put, UAC requires users performing high-level tasks to confirm that they initiated the task. Members of the Administrators group are logged on with only normal user privileges and must approve administrative actions before such actions will run. Nonadministrative users must provide an administrative password. Providing administrative approval to run such tasks places the computer into Admin Approval mode.

However, the implementation of UAC in Windows Vista generated large numbers of system prompts, even for such tasks as moving, renaming, or deleting files created or modified by a different user. One of the authors of this book frequently experienced this problem in working with his extensive collection of photographic images, many of which had been originally copied onto an older computer running Windows XP. These annoying prompts contributed to the overall low consumer satisfaction of Vista and led many people to disable UAC completely, thereby negating its advantages. Microsoft improved UAC when Windows 7 was introduced, making it more user friendly and less annoying while still providing protection against undesirable activities (such as installing unwanted software, unwittingly installing malware, and so on). UAC in Windows 10 behaves much the same as it did in Windows 7 and 8.1. You can now configure UAC to manage the extent of prompts provided, as discussed in later sections.

NOTE   For additional introductory information on UAC in Windows 10 and Windows Server 2016, refer to "User Account Control Overview" at https://technet.microsoft.com/en-us/itpro/windows/keep-secure/user-account-control-overview.

Features of User Account Control

UAC requests approval before running administrative tasks on the computer. UAC redefines what a standard user is permitted to do. Such a user can perform many basic functions that pose no security risk; these functions previously required a user to have administrative privileges. In addition, UAC facilitates the act of providing administrative credentials when users need to perform higher-level tasks, such as installing an application or configuring system settings. Furthermore, UAC makes administrative accounts safer by limiting the types of tasks that can be performed without users providing additional consent. UAC still requests consent before allowing users to perform tasks that require higher privileges, such as system tasks.

Under UAC, all users (administrative or not) can perform the following tasks without supplying administrative credentials:

- Viewing the system clock and calendar and configuring the time zone (but users cannot change the system time)

- Modifying power management settings

- Installing printers and hardware devices that an administrator has allowed using Group Policy

- Interfacing portable devices (such as Bluetooth) with the computer

- Using Wired Equivalent Privacy (WEP) to connect to approved wireless networks

- Creating and configuring approved virtual private network (VPN) connections

- Installing ActiveX controls from sites that an administrator has approved

- Installing critical updates from Windows Update

> **TIP**   The tasks summarized here are similar to those granted to members of the Power Users group in Windows versions prior to Vista. Windows 10 includes the Power Users group solely for backward compatibility purposes. You do not need to add users to this group to perform these functions. Only add users to this group if required for running noncertified or legacy applications.

When authenticating a member of the Administrators group, Windows 10 issues two access tokens:

- **A full administrator token:** The administrator token is used only when administrative privileges are required.

- **A standard user token:** The standard token is used for all actions that do not require administrative privileges.

Windows 10 also marks tasks and programs as belonging to one of two integrity levels, which are implied levels of trust in these actions:

- **Low integrity:** A task or application (such as a web browser, email, or word processing program) that is less likely to compromise the operating system.

- **High integrity:** An action that performs tasks (such as installing applications) that have a higher potential for compromising the system. Applications running at low integrity levels cannot modify data in applications using a higher integrity level.

Windows 10 informs you when a task requires elevated (administrative) privileges by displaying shield icons, such as those that appear in the left column of the System applet shown in Figure 7-31. On selecting one of these tasks, you receive a UAC prompt as shown in Figure 7-32. Click **Yes** to proceed with the task or **No** to cancel it. When you selected one of these tasks on a Windows Vista computer, the screen dimmed and a UAC prompt (also known as an *elevation prompt)* displayed. When you accepted the prompt, the administrative access token granted you elevated privileges, enabling you to perform the task you selected. In Windows 10, as was the case with Windows 7 and 8.1, this behavior depends on the UAC setting you've specified (as you learn later in this section). The default setting enables administrators to perform most of the actions marked with shield icons without receiving UAC prompts; they receive prompts for performing tasks such as installing programs or running the Registry Editor or other programs that have a high potential for producing damaging effects.

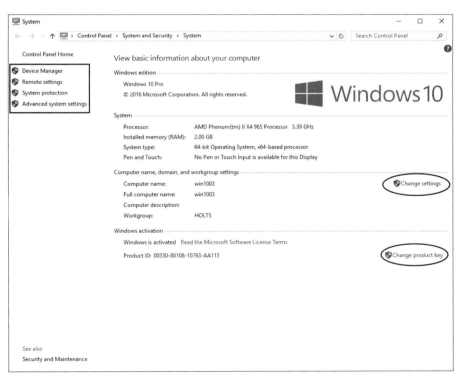

Figure 7-31   A Shield Icon Informing You When a Task Requires Administrative Privileges

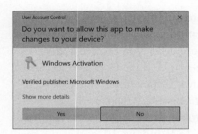

Figure 7-32 User Account Control Displaying This Prompt to Ask for Approval of an Administrative Task

The blanked screen indicates that the UAC prompt is running in Secure Desktop mode (such as when the Ctrl+Alt+Delete prompt appears when logging on to a domain-based computer). This means that you must either approve or cancel the UAC prompt before you can continue performing any other task on the computer.

A user who is not a member of the Administrators group receives only the standard user token when access is authenticated. Such a user receives the UAC prompt, which requires that a password for an Administrator user account be entered. By default in Windows 10, a nonadministrative user receives this prompt for any action marked by a shield icon.

CAUTION   When you receive a UAC prompt, always ensure that the action that launches the prompt is the one you want to perform. This is especially true if a UAC prompt appears unexpectedly, which could indicate a malware program attempting to run. Should this happen, click **No** and the program cannot run. You should then scan your computer with one or more malware-detection programs.

If a background application that is minimized to the taskbar requires elevated privileges, the UAC prompt appears on the taskbar and blinks to draw attention. An example of where this would happen is in the downloading of an application from the Internet. When the download completes and approval for installation is required, the user can click the prompt to approve it. This enables the user to continue performing other tasks, such as reading email, while the download is underway; the user can continue with these tasks without being interrupted by the dimming of her screen and a UAC prompt displaying onscreen.

Application Prompts

UAC causes some third-party applications to display prompts when you attempt to run them. This helps to secure your computer because the prompt informs you of the program that is attempting to run so that you can verify that this is a program you really want to run. Click **Yes** to run the program or **No** to exit. The type of shield icon depends on the security risk involved in running the program:

- **High-Risk Blocked Program:** Windows displays a message box with a red title bar and red shield stating This Program Has Been Blocked for Your Protection. Such a program comes from a blocked publisher and cannot be run under any circumstances.

- **Program Signed by Windows:** The UAC prompt includes a blue title bar and name of the publisher. Click **Yes** to run the program. For a nonadministrative user, provide an administrative username and password to run the program.

- **Unsigned Program from a Verified Publisher:** When running with an administrative account, a program with a legitimate digital signature that includes its name and publisher will display the publisher name and a Show More Details link. Clicking the Details link displays the program location and a link to Show Information About the Publisher's Certificate. Click **Yes** to run the program. A nonadministrative user will receive a prompt that asks for an administrative password.

- **Unsigned Program from a Nonverified Publisher:** If the third-party program does not have a digital signature that includes its name and publisher, the prompt that appears is a stronger caution. It uses a yellow shield. Click **Yes** to run the program. Again, a nonadministrative user will receive a prompt that asks for an administrative password.

NOTE   For additional information on UAC in Windows and Windows Server 2016, including the various prompts that UAC can issue, refer to "How User Account Control Works" at https://technet.microsoft.com/en-us/itpro/windows/keep-secure/how-user-account-control-works.

Running Programs with Elevated Privileges

Microsoft has provided several means of configuring applications and tasks to run with elevated privileges. Use the following procedure to perform a task with elevated privileges:

Step 1.   Start the program or task that is displayed with a shield icon. The display background blanks out and the UAC prompt appears.

Step 2.   Verify that the UAC prompt is requesting privileges for the task you're attempting to run. (Remember, some malware can deceive you here, so make certain the correct program or task is described in this prompt.) If desired, click **Show Details** for more information on the task.

Step 3.   If this is indeed the correct program or task, click **Yes** to start the task or application.

You can also mark an application to always run with elevated privileges. This situation may occur if the application developer has coded the program to access protected folders such as the %ProgramFiles% or %Systemroot% folders, or requires access to the Registry. You can also configure a program to request administrative privileges from its shortcut properties. When you do this, the program always displays a UAC prompt when started from its shortcut. Use the following procedure to mark an application to always run with elevated privileges:

Step 1.   Ensure that you are logged on to the computer as a member of the local Administrators group.

Step 2.   If necessary, drag a shortcut to the desktop.

Step 3.   Right-click the shortcut and choose **Properties**.

Step 4.   On the Shortcut tab, click the **Advanced** button.

Step 5.   On the Advanced Properties dialog box, select the **Run as Administrator** check box.

Step 6.   Click **OK** to close the shortcut Properties dialog box.

CAUTION   If you are logged on using the default Administrator account created when you installed Windows 10, you do not receive any UAC prompts. Do not use this account except under emergency conditions. Best practices recommend that this account remain disabled; it is disabled by default in Windows 10.

Configuring User Account Control

In Windows 10, as already mentioned, you can configure several levels of UAC that determine whether prompts are displayed and how they appear on the screen. Open Control Panel, select **System and Security**, and then select **Change User Account Control Settings** under Security and Maintenance. Alternatively, you can type **User Account Control** into the taskbar Search field and then select this option from the Search list. Select from the following options, click **OK**, and then accept the UAC prompt that appears:

- **Always Notify Me When:** Windows displays a UAC prompt whenever you make changes to Windows settings or programs try to install software or make changes to your computer. This behavior is similar to that of Vista.

- **Notify Me Only When Apps Try to Make Changes to My Computer (Default):** The default setting in Windows 8.1, this setting does not prompt you when you make changes to Windows settings. You are prompted on the secure desktop (that is, the desktop dims) when you perform higher-level actions, such as installing programs or accessing the Registry Editor.

- **Notify Me Only When Programs Try to Make Changes to My Computer (Do Not Dim My Desktop):** Similar to the default setting, except that the desktop does not dim when a UAC prompt appears. With this setting, you can ignore the UAC prompt and continue performing tasks other than the task that is requesting approval.

- **Never Notify Me When:** Disables UAC completely. You are not notified if apps try to install software or make changes to your computer, or when you make changes to Windows settings. This setting is not recommended; you should use it only when absolutely necessary to run a program that displays the red shield icon mentioned earlier in this section.

CAUTION   If you select the Never Notify Me When option, Windows 10 will not let you run any Windows Store apps.

User Account Control Policies

Microsoft has provided a series of policies in Windows 10 Group Policy that govern the behavior of UAC. These policies are available from the Group Policy Management Editor snap-in (gpedit.msc) or from the Local Security Policy snap-in.

You can use this procedure to configure the following UAC policies:

- **Admin Approval Mode for the Built-in Administrator:** Governs the behavior of the built-in Administrator account. When enabled, this account displays the UAC prompt for all actions requiring elevated privileges. When disabled, this account runs all actions with full administrative privileges. This policy is disabled by default.

- **Allow UIAccess Applications to Prompt for Elevation Without Using the Secure Desktop:** Determines whether User Interface Accessibility (UIAccess) programs can automatically disable the secure desktop with a standard user. When enabled, these programs (such as Remote Assistance) automatically disable the secure desktop for elevation prompts. When disabled, the application runs with UIAccess integrity regardless of its location in the file system. Note that UI (User Interface) Access-application programs and accessibility tools are used by developers to push input to higher desktop windows that require the uiAccess flag to be equal to true (i.e., uiAccess=true). Also, the application program that wishes to receive the UIAccess privilege must reside on the hard drive in a trusted location and be digitally signed. This policy is disabled by default.

- **Behavior of the Elevation Prompt for Administrators in Admin Approval Mode:** Determines the behavior of the UAC prompt for administrative users. This policy has the following options:

  - **Prompt for Consent for Non-Windows Binaries:** Prompts a user on the secure desktop to select either Permit or Deny when a non-Microsoft program needs elevated privileges. Select **Permit** to run the action with the highest possible privileges. This option is the default setting.

  - **Prompt for Consent:** Prompts a user to select either Permit or Deny when an action runs that requires elevated privileges. Select **Permit** to run the action with the highest possible privileges.

  - **Prompt for Credentials:** Prompts for an administrative username and password when an action requires administrative privileges, but does not display the secure desktop. When selected, administrative users receive a prompt similar to Figure 7-32, requiring administrator credentials.

  - **Prompt for Consent on the Secure Desktop:** Prompts a user to select either Permit or Deny on the secure desktop when an action runs that requires elevated privileges. Select **Permit** to run the action with the highest possible privileges.

  - **Prompt for Credentials on the Secure Desktop:** Prompts for an administrative username and password on the secure desktop when an action requires administrative privileges. When selected, administrative users will receive a UAC prompt requiring username and password for the administrator account.

  - **Elevate Without Prompting:** Enables the administrator to perform the action without consent or credentials. In other words, the administrator receives Admin Approval mode automatically. This setting is *not* recommended for normal environments.

- **Behavior of the Elevation Prompt for Standard Users:** Determines the behavior of the UAC prompt for nonadministrative users. This policy has the following options:

  - **Prompt for Credentials:** Displays a prompt to enter an administrative username and password when a standard user attempts to run an action that requires elevated privileges. This option is the default setting.

- **Prompt for Credentials on the Secure Desktop:** Displays a prompt on the secure desktop to enter an administrative username and password when a standard user attempts to run an action that requires elevated privileges.

- **Automatically Deny Elevation Requests:** Displays an Access is Denied message when a standard user attempts to run an action that requires elevated privileges.

- **Detect Application Installations and Prompt for Elevation:** When enabled, displays a UAC prompt when a user installs an application package that requires elevated privileges. When disabled, domain-based Group Policy or other enterprise-level technologies govern application installation behavior. This option is enabled by default in an enterprise setting and disabled by default in a home setting.

- **Only Elevate Executables That Are Signed and Validated:** When enabled, performs public key infrastructure (PKI) signature checks on executable programs that require elevated privileges before they are permitted to run. When disabled, no PKI checks are performed. This option is disabled by default.

- **Only Elevate UIAccess Applications That Are Installed in Secure Locations:** When enabled, runs applications only with UIAccess integrity if situated in a secure location within the file system, such as %ProgramFiles% or %Windir%. When disabled, the application runs with UIAccess integrity regardless of its location in the file system. This option is disabled by default.

- **Run All Administrators in Admin Approval Mode:** When enabled, enforces Admin Approval Mode and other UAC policies. When disabled, all UAC policies are disabled and no UAC prompts are displayed. In addition, the Windows Security Center notifies the user when disabled and offers the option to enable UAC. This option is enabled by default.

- **Switch to the Secure Desktop When Prompting for Elevation:** When enabled, displays the secure desktop when a UAC prompt appears. When disabled, the UAC prompt remains on the interactive user's desktop. This option is enabled by default.

- **Virtualize File and Registry Write Failures to Per User Locations:** When enabled, redirects application write failures for pre-Windows 10 applications to defined locations in the Registry and the file system, such as %ProgramFiles%, %Windir%, or %Systemroot%. When disabled, applications that write to protected locations fail, as was the case in previous Windows versions. This option is enabled by default.

CAUTION   If you disable the Run All Administrators in Admin Approval Mode policy setting, you disable UAC completely and no prompts will appear for actions requiring elevated privileges. This leaves your computer wide open for attack by malicious software. Do *not* disable this setting at any time!

NOTE   For more details on Group Policy Object settings for UAC, see "User Account Control Group Policy and Registry Key Settings" at https://technet.microsoft.com/en-us/itpro/windows/keep-secure/user-account-control-group-policy-and-registry-key-settings.

Supporting Authentication and Authorization

For the 70-697 exam, you will need to understand Windows authentication methods and authorization technologies and be able to support them and resolve issues for users.

Windows 10 Lock Screen and Logon Prompts

By default, a Windows 10 computer that is not part of a domain displays the Lock screen at startup and after a user has logged off. Touching or clicking the Lock screen displays the Windows 10 logon screen, which is also displayed when a user selects the Sign Out option from the user icon menu. The logon screen displays all enabled user accounts, allowing a user to select the appropriate account and enter the password if one has been specified.

First introduced in Windows 8.1 and enhanced with Windows 10 is the capability to use a Microsoft account to log on to the local computer. In Chapter 2, "Implementing Windows," we covered how to create an account for a newly installed Windows 10 computer using either a Microsoft account or a local account. When you create new accounts for Windows 10, they can either use a local logon or a Microsoft account. The process is covered later in this section.

Although the default logon screen is convenient, especially in a home environment, it does pose a security risk in a corporate environment, even in a small office. In an AD DS environment, the classic logon screen is no longer enabled by default in Windows 10. Instead, an option called Other User is made available to allow the user to enter domain credentials previously unknown by the local machine.

You can change the way that a domain-joined Windows 10 displays the logon screen using the User Accounts applet, which you can find by typing **netplwiz** into the Search bar or Cortana and selecting **Run Command**. From the Advanced tab, click the check box in the Secure Sign-in section labeled **Require Users to Press Crtl+Alt+Delete**, as shown in Figure 7-33.

Figure 7-33   Enabling Secure Sign-in Using the User Accounts Applet

You can use Group Policy to require the use of the logon screen on domain-joined as well as non-domain-joined Windows 10 computers.

For a workgroup or non-domain-joined computer, open the Local Group Policy Editor, which you can find by searching for Group Policy from the Search bar or Cortana. Navigate to the Computer Configuration\Windows Settings\Security Settings\Local Policies\Security Options node and then disable Interactive Login: Do Not Require CTRL+ALT+DEL (see Figure 7-34).

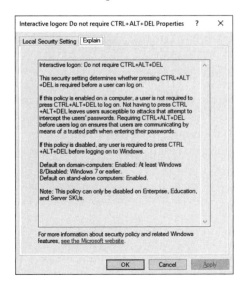

Figure 7-34   Disabling Interactive Logon: Do Not Require CTRL+ALT+DEL Using Local Group Policy Editor

This policy also works for domain-joined Windows 10 computers, and is enabled by default.

NOTE   The behavior of this setting changed beginning with Windows 8. On Windows 7 and earlier editions, a domain-joined computer disabled this policy by default (disabled means users were required to press Ctrl+Alt+Del). For Windows 8, 8.1, and Windows 10 computers, the policy is enabled by default, so users are not required to press Ctrl+Alt+Del.

To remove the display of the last username, navigate to the Computer Configuration\Windows Settings\Security Settings\Local Policies\Security Options node and enable the Interactive Logon: Do Not Display Last User Name policy.

Picture Password

You should be familiar with how users set up their picture passwords and how to manage the capability for users to use them, as covered in the previous section. Users should have an easier time managing their picture password than traditional passwords, which will typically require some complexity and frequent changes. Picture passwords can be not only more secure but also more reliable than plain-text passwords. Picture passwords can have a much larger range of possible combinations, making them much harder to guess or even crack using brute-force attacks.

If you want to allow your users to use picture passwords, be careful about the group policies that you implement in your domain. Enabling the Group Policy Do Not Display Last User Name (found under Computer Policy\Windows Settings\Security Settings\Local Policies\Security Options) seems like a good security practice; however, it will disallow users from using picture passwords to log in to their devices.

If a user forgets his picture password gesture, he can use the Sign-in Options link to switch to either a PIN (if he enabled one) or the text-based password. If he is unable to recover using a PIN or password, and the device is not joined to the domain, he may need to reset the device and start over if an organizational administrator does not have an account on the device.

Managing Credentials

Users will also need access to other network resources not controlled by Windows or the local Active Directory domain. This can include websites, terminal servers, applications, and other resources that require credentials to use.

Windows 10 provides the Credential Manager for storing credentials in an electronic Windows vault, facilitating logon to these other resources. You can use Credential Manager to created stored credentials for each resource a user needs to work with.

You can start Credential Manager from the Control Panel under User Accounts, or by searching for **credential** using the Search bar or Cortana. Credential Manager organizes credentials as either Web Credentials or Windows Credentials, presenting these options:

- Windows Credentials are used to store authorization accounts for other Windows servers and computers.

- Certificate-based Credentials are used to associate Internet or network addresses with user-based certificates. The certificates used for these credentials must be stored in the user's Personal store in Certificate Manager. Managing certificates is covered in the next section.

- Generic Credentials include things like OneDrive and other cloud accounts, Microsoft accounts, and other integrated services credentials.

Adding, Editing, and Removing Credentials in Credential Manager

To add a credential, start by opening Credential Manager as previously described, and then select the desired type of credential. For a Windows or generic credential, you see a screen similar to that shown in Figure 7-35. Enter the required server or network name, username, and password, and then click **OK**. You are returned to the Credential Manager, where the added credential appears under the appropriate category. You can now add additional credentials if needed.

Add a Windows Credential	— □ ×

← → ∨ ↑ ▣ > Control Panel > User Accounts > Credential Manager > Add a Windows Credential   ∨ ↻ | Search Control Panel   ₽ |

Type the address of the website or network location and your credentials

Make sure that the user name and password that you type can be used to access the location.

Internet or network address
(e.g. myserver, server.company.com):   [_____]

User name: [_____]

Password: [_____]

[OK   ] [Cancel]

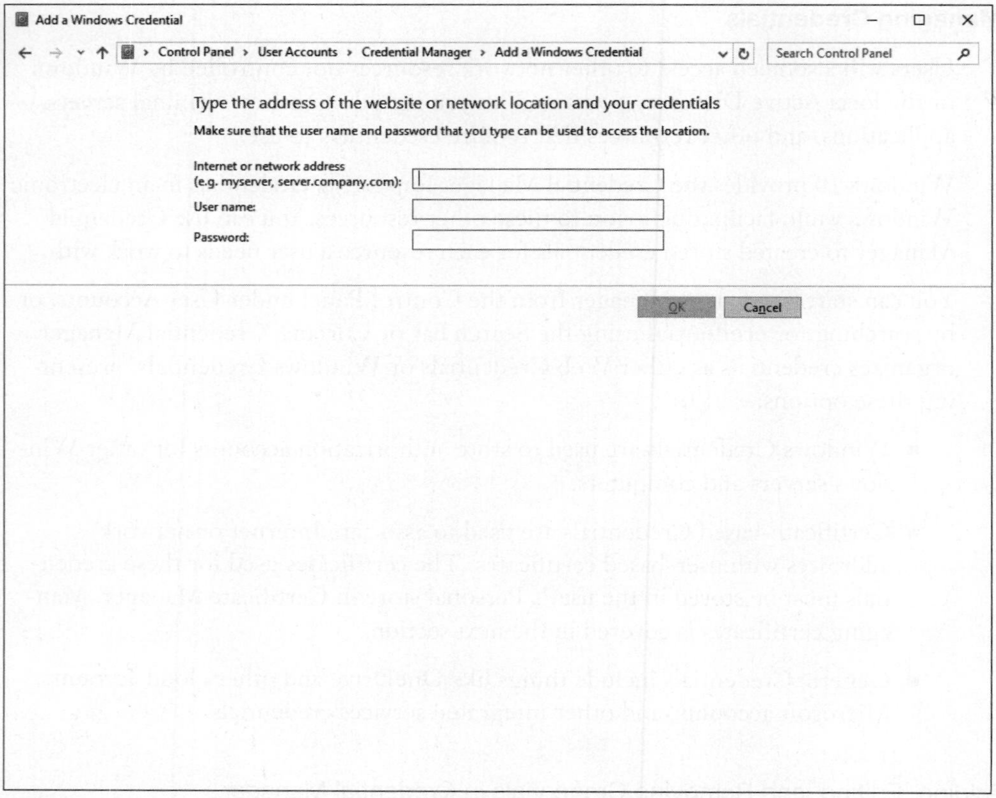

Figure 7-35   Entering a New Windows Credential into Credential Manager

Entering a certificate-based credential is slightly different. Enter the required server or network name, and then click **Select Certificate** to locate a certificate that should be stored in the Personal store of Certificate Manager, or on a smart card. When done, click **OK**.

Credential Manager also enables you to modify or remove existing credentials. Click the arrow next to the stored credential to expand its entry. Clicking **Edit** takes you to the Edit Windows Credential screen, on which you can change the username and password or certificate. To delete a credential, click **Remove** and then click **Yes** to confirm your intentions.

Credential Manager can also be leveraged by Windows 10 apps, so if you have an online identity associated with a Windows app, it can place your credentials into the Credential Manager. If you use a Microsoft account for your PC, your credentials will follow you to each device you use with your Microsoft account. This type of credential roaming is enabled by default on non-domain-joined computers and disabled on domain-joined computers.

TIP Windows automatically adds credentials to Credential Manager for you when you are working and saves a logon that you have entered. For instance selecting the Remember My Credentials check box when logging in to a Remote Desktop Connection, or checking the box when connecting to a remove file share, will tell Windows to save the credential in Credential Manager.

Windows Credentials Backup and Restore

You can back up your Windows Credentials using Credential Manager, store them in a separate location, and restore your credentials if your computer or hard drive is replaced. Use the following procedure:

Step 1.   In Credential Manager, select Windows Credentials and then click **Back Up Credentials**.

Step 2.   Type the path to the desired location or click **Browse** to locate the appropriate folder. It is recommended that you use removable media or a trusted network location. Click **Next**.

Step 3.   On the next screen, press Ctrl+Alt+Delete to continue the backup on the Secure Desktop.

Step 4.   The next screen asks you to secure the backup with a password. Enter and confirm your password in the text boxes provided, and then click **Next**. Be sure to use a good password that you will remember. You will need this password if you need to restore your credentials.

Step 5.   The next screen indicates that the backup was successful. Click the **Finish** button to exit the wizard.

Restoring your credentials follows a similar process. You can use this if your computer or hard drive is replaced, or you want to transfer your credentials from one computer to another. Use the following procedure to restore credentials:

Step 1.   In Credential Manager, select **Windows Credentials**, and then click **Restore Credentials**.

Step 2.   On the resulting dialog box, type the path to the backup file, or click the **Browse** button to navigate to it. Click the **Next** button.

Step 3.   On the next screen, press Ctrl+Alt+Delete to continue the restore on the Secure Desktop.

Step 4.   Enter the password you used when backing up the credentials.

Step 5.   The credentials are restored. If you used removable media for the backup location, you can remove it, and then click **Finish**.

Web Credentials

The Web Credentials store was a new feature in Windows 8 and is included in Windows 10. This credentials store is integrated with Internet Explorer and Edge and is used to store any saved passwords for websites, FTP sites, and other Internet services accessed through the web browser.

The alternate way to access Web Credentials is using the Internet Explorer Options:

Step 1. From the Internet Explorer settings menu, select **Internet Options**.

Step 2. Click the **Content** tab from the Internet Options dialog.

Step 3. Under the AutoComplete section, click the **Settings** button.

Step 4. From the resulting AutoComplete Settings dialog box, click the **Manage Passwords** button.

The Credential Manager will be displayed with the Web Credentials section selected. From here you can display the credential details, remove credentials, and display the password by clicking the **Show** link.

Note that unlike Windows Credentials, there is no interface for adding credentials, or for backing up and restoring Web Credentials. Because Web Credentials can display the original plain-text password used, backing up these credentials to another location can cause a security risk.

Managing Multifactor Authentication

When you use Credential Manager to store a certificate-based credential as discussed in the previous section, it looks for the certificate in the Personal store of Certificate Manager. When you log on using a smart card, the smart card contains a certificate with information that verifies your identity. When you use Encrypting File System (EFS) to encrypt a file you will learn about in Chapter 14, "Configuring File and Folder Access," you create a certificate that is stored in the same certificate store. Windows 10 provides the Certificate Manager Microsoft Management Console (MMC) snap-in to manage stored certificates.

Certificates are managed in several stores, and Windows 10 maintains three separate sets of stores: one set for your user account, another for the computer Service accounts, and one for the Computer account itself. That means there can be a large number of separate sets, depending on the number of users on the computer and the number of service accounts for installed services. There is always only one set of stores for the local computer itself.

You can open Certificate Manager from the page in Credential Manager that enables you to add a certificate-based credential. You can also load Certificate

Manager by typing **certificates** into the Search box or Cortana and selecting the mode of certificates to manage. You can choose from Manage File Encryption Certificates, Manage Computer Certificates, or Manage User Certificates. Certificate Manager opens and displays a series of certificate stores, as shown in Figure 7-36. Expand any of these certificate stores and click the **Certificates** subnode to display any available certificates. Double-click a certificate to display its details. You can see the purposes for which the certificate is intended and the validity period. The Details tab includes information such as the serial number, signature hash algorithm, issuer, public key value, and so on.

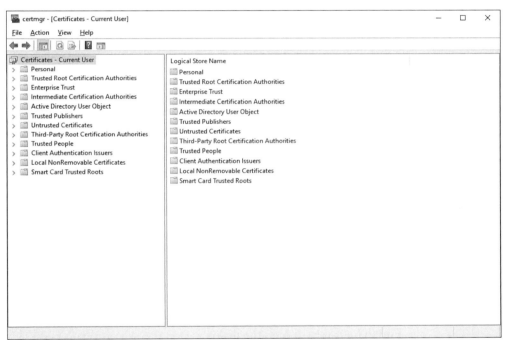

Figure 7-36   Using Certificate Manager to View and Manage Different Types of Certificates in Different Certificate Stores

You can also view additional information and configure certificate properties by selecting the Details tab and clicking the **Edit Properties** button. From the Certificate Properties dialog box, you can modify the certificate purposes, specify cross-certificate download URLs, specify Online Certificate Status Protocol (OCSP) download URLs, and extend validation parameters.

Using the Friendly Name field and the Description field in the General tab can help to differentiate among similar certificates. Cross-certificates are used to establish trust between separate certificate authority (CA) hierarchies, such as those used on diverse networks. OCSP responders are used to verify certificate validity and check against certificate revocation lists issued by CAs.

Requesting Certificates

There are a number of ways to request a personal or computer certificate for use in encryption and authentication. You may be provided a certificate by your company, loaded on a smart card or installed on your workstation. Companies often implement their own public key infrastructure (PKI), with an internal CA to issue certificates.

A common way to implement certificate distribution in a large company is to provide users the ability to request certificates from the domain on any domain-joined computer using their Active Directory account. Using this technique, users only need to request a personal certificate. They can then use it for VPN, email, and other purposes. The procedure is as follows:

Step 1. Open Certificate Manager, either from Credential Manager or using the Search bar or Cortana.

Step 2. Right-click the **Personal** folder, select **All Tasks**, and then **Request New Certificate** from the context menu.

Step 3. The next page gives you information about the request you are about to make. Click **Next**.

Step 4. On the next page, select the **Active Directory Enrollment Policy** and then click **Next**.

Step 5. The next page displays the types of certificates you can request from the domain's PKI. Check the box next to **User** and then click **Enroll**.

Step 6. The last screen will confirm the status of the enrollment request. Click the **Finish** button to dismiss the dialog.

Step 7. You can expand the Personal and Certificates folder to confirm that the certificate is installed. Double-click the certificate to view the details.

NOTE   Enterprise Certificate Services is beyond the scope of the 70-697 exam and this text. If you would like to learn more about implementing and managing a PKI in a Windows environment, refer to "Active Directory Certificate Services Overview" at http://technet.microsoft.com/library/hh831740. Although the information refers to Windows Server 2012, no functionality has changed for Windows Server 2016.

Configuring Computer and User Authentication

You should understand some of the ways Windows helps secure authentication in Windows 10 computers to prevent sniffing, dictionary attacks, brute-force password hacking, and other threats to user credential security. This section covers Secure Channel, which implements private, cryptographic security for data in motion, including passing credential information. You also learn about account policies that you can enforce to help ensure that user credentials are more difficult to guess.

Secure Channel

Secure Channel is a security support provider (SSP), commonly known as *Schannel*, which provides security using a set of security protocols for authentication and encrypted communications. Schannel on Windows systems is used to implement HTTPS (secure HTTP), among other things. Confidentiality of network communication is implemented using Secure Sockets Layer (SSL) and Transport Layer Security (TLS) protocols, and Schannel handles the implementation of these protocols in Windows. Note that TLS is simply an updated version of the SSL protocol; however, due to recent revelations about vulnerabilities in the encryption of SSL communications, SSL 2.0 and SSL 3.0 are considered insecure, and the recommendation is to restrict the use of these protocols in favor of TLS 1.0, 1.1, or 1.2. All these network layer encryption protocol versions are still typically referred to as SSL.

SSL encryption is a form of public-key cryptography, using certificates which can be generated from a commercial CA or using an organization's PKI and private CA such as the Active Directory Certificate Services (AD CS) on Windows Server. The certificate consists of both a public key and a private key. When secure communications are set up between two computers, they first exchange keys, and each computer then has the public key of the other. When the first computer encrypts a message, it uses the destination's public key.

Authentication also uses public-key cryptography, but it works in reverse. If you want someone to be confident that a message is coming only from you, you can use your private key to encrypt it. Anyone can decrypt the message using your public key, so the decryption process authenticates that the message was encrypted by you, the only person with the private key.

SSL communication uses both techniques. You want to be sure that when your web browser connects to your bank, you are really communicating with your bank's website and not someone that wants to steal your credentials. Your browser knows the CA that issued your bank's certificate and can successfully decrypt the message and confirm that it really is the bank. This trust chain is the first step, using authentication to establish a trust. At that point, you can exchange public keys and set up a secure channel for communication using each other's public key, which can only be decrypted by the other party.

Secure Channel is also used to establish the trust relationship between AD domain controllers in a domain and the computers that are joined to the domain. When you join a computer to a domain, a computer account is created with an authentication and a password. You never see this password, but it's needed by your computer to communicate with the domain and access resource. By default, domain-joined computers will contact a domain controller and change its password every 30 days. When the password does not match, Windows displays the error message The Trust Relationship Between This Workstation and the Primary Domain Failed. When this happens, it may be necessary to rejoin the workstation to the domain. You can also use a PowerShell command to reset the machine password. Using the cmdlet **Reset-ComputerMachinePassword** from an administrative PowerShell prompt will fix this broken secure channel issue. You will need to run this command using a Domain Administrator account, or an account with privileges to reset computer accounts on the domain. To specify a credential, use the **-Credential** command-line switch and specify your domain username. You will be prompted for your password.

Account Policies

One of the most important security measures you can take is to ensure that users' passwords are complex, changed regularly, and kept secure. By default, Windows will allow fairly weak passwords and does not force users to change them at any regular interval. You should know how to enforce good password practices in Windows.

In a secure environment, you may want to modify some account policies used by your organization. For domain-joined computers you can use Group Policy Objects to set account policies and enforce them for the entire domain or specific groups. These policies are found in GPOs under Computer Configuration\Windows Settings\Security Settings\Account Policies. You can also set the policies on nondomain devices using the Local Security Policy applet.

The most important set of policies is found under the Password Policy heading. Review Table 7-4 for the password policies you can configure.

Table 7-4 Account Policies for Passwords

Policy Name	Description	Settings
Enforce Password History	This security setting determines the number of unique new passwords that have to be associated with a user account before an old password can be reused. The value must be between 0 and 24 passwords.	Enable this setting and specify the number of passwords to remember. The value must be between 0 and 24 passwords.

Policy Name	Description	Settings
Maximum Password Age	This security setting determines the period of time (in days) that a password can be used before the system requires the user to change it.	You can set passwords to expire after a number of days between 1 and 999, or you can specify that passwords never expire by setting the number of days to 0.
Minimum Password Age	The minimum password age must be less than the maximum password age, unless the maximum password age is set to 0, indicating that passwords will never expire. Configure the minimum password age to be more than 0 if you want Enforce Password History to be effective. Without a minimum password age, users can cycle through passwords repeatedly until they get to an old favorite.	If the maximum password age is set to 0, the minimum password age can be set to any value between 0 and 998. Otherwise, it must be less than the maximum password age.
Minimum Password Length	This security setting determines the least number of characters that a password for a user account may contain.	You can set a value of between 1 and 14 characters, or you can establish that no password is required by setting the number of characters to 0.
Password Must Meet Complexity Requirements	This security setting determines whether passwords must meet complexity requirements. If this policy is enabled, passwords must meet the following minimum requirements: ■ Not contain the user's account name or parts of the user's full name that exceed two consecutive characters ■ Be at least six characters in length ■ Contain characters from three of the following four categories: 　■ English uppercase characters (A through Z) 　■ English lowercase characters (a through z) 　■ Base 10 digits (0 through 9) 　■ Nonalphabetic characters (for example, !, $, #, %)	Enabled (enforce complexity) or Disabled (do not require complex passwords).

Policy Name	Description	Settings
Store Passwords Using Reversible Encryption	This security setting determines whether the operating system stores passwords using reversible encryption. This policy provides support for applications that use protocols that require knowledge of the user's password for authentication purposes. Storing passwords using reversible encryption is essentially the same as storing plain-text versions of the passwords. For this reason, this policy should never be enabled unless application requirements outweigh the need to protect password information.	Enabled (use reversible encryption) or Disabled (use nonreversible encryption).

Configuring NTFS Permissions

The New Technology File System (NTFS) that has existed since the early days of Windows NT enables you to secure and manage access to resources on both a network level and on a local level. These NTFS file and folder permissions are also known as *security permissions*; they can apply to both files and folders, and they apply on your computer to files and folders whether a folder is shared or not shared at all. Keep in mind, however, that although Windows 10 supports FAT and FAT32 partitions, NTFS permissions apply only on partitions that are formatted using NTFS. Because you are already familiar with shared folder permissions, we will use that as a jumping-off point to describe NTFS permissions.

NTFS File and Folder Permissions

Like the shared permissions, which you learn about in detail in Chapter 14, NTFS permissions for a folder control how users access a folder. Windows stores an access control list (ACL) with every file and folder on an NTFS partition. The ACL is a list of users and groups that have been granted access for a particular file or folder, as well as the types of access that the users and groups have been granted. Collectively, these kinds of entries in the ACL are called access control entries (ACEs). If you think of the ACL as a list, it isn't hard to conceive that a list contains entries of various kinds. Windows uses the ACL to determine the level of access a user should be granted when he attempts to access a file or folder.

NTFS file permissions control what users can do with files within a folder. More specifically, the permissions control how users can alter or access the data that files contain. Table 7-5 describes the standard NTFS file permissions in detail.

Table 7-5   NTFS File and Folder Permissions

Permission	What a User Can Do on a Folder	What a User Can Do on a File
Full Control	Change permissions, take ownership, and delete subfolders and files. All other actions allowed by the permissions listed in this table are also possible.	Change permissions, take ownership, and perform all other actions allowed by the permissions listed in this table.
Modify	Delete the folder as well as grant that user the Read permission and the List Folder Contents permission.	Modify a file's contents and delete the file as well as perform all actions allowed by the Write permission and the Read and Execute permission.
Read & Execute	Run files and display file attributes, owner, and permissions.	Run application files and display file attributes, owner, and permissions.
List Folder Contents	List a folder's contents; that is, its files and subfolders.	(n/a)
Read	Display filenames, subfolder names, owner, permissions, and file attributes (Read Only, Hidden, Archive, and System).	Display data, file attributes, owner, and permissions.
Write	Create new folders and files, change a folder's attributes, and display owner and permissions.	Write changes to the file, change its attributes, and display owner and permissions.

Applying NTFS Permissions

It is simple to apply NTFS permissions, as the following procedure shows:

Step 1.   From File Explorer, right-click a folder or file and choose **Properties**.

Step 2.   Select the **Security** tab of the Properties dialog box. Also known as the ACL Editor, the Security tab enables you to edit the NTFS permissions for a folder or file.

Step 3.   Click **Edit** to display the dialog box shown in Figure 7-37. You can configure the options described in Table 7-6 and either allow or deny the permissions already described in Table 7-5.

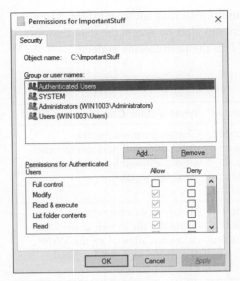

Figure 7-37   Permissions for (File/Folder Name) Dialog Box Enabling You to Configure Security Permissions

Table 7-6   Security Tab Options

Option	Description
Group or usernames	Start by selecting the user account or group for which you want to change permissions or that you want to remove from the permissions list.
Permissions for (user or group name as specified)	Select the **Allow** check box to allow a permission. Select the **Deny** check box to deny a permission.
Add	Click **Add** to open the Select User or Group dialog box to select user accounts and groups to add to the Name list.
Remove	Click **Remove** to remove the selected user account or group and the associated permissions for the file or folder.

Step 4.   When finished, click **OK** to return to the Security tab shown in Figure 7-37.

Step 5.   If you need to configure special permissions or access advanced settings, click **Advanced**. The next section discusses these permissions.

NOTE   You can also configure NTFS permissions from the command line by using the icacls.exe utility. This utility is useful for scripting permissions configuration. For more information on this utility, refer to "Icacls" at http://technet.microsoft.com/en-us/library/cc753525.aspx.

Specifying Advanced Permissions

For the most part, the standard NTFS permissions are suitable for managing user access to resources. There are occasions where a more specialized application of security and permissions is appropriate. To configure a more specific level of access, you can use NTFS special access permissions. It isn't a secret, but it is not obvious in the Windows 8.1 interface that the NTFS standard permissions are actually combinations of the special access permissions. For example, the standard Read permission is composed of the List Folder/Read Data, Read Attributes, Read Extended Attributes, and Read Permissions special access permissions.

In general, you will use only the standard NTFS permissions already described. In exceptional cases, you might need to fine-tune the permissions further, and this is where the special access NTFS permissions come in. To configure special access permissions, use the following steps:

Step 1.   From the Security tab of the appropriate file or folder, click **Advanced** to access the Advanced Security Settings dialog box.

Step 2.   To add a user with special access permissions, click **Add** to display the Permission Entry for (folder name) dialog box.

Step 3.   Click **Select a Principal** to display the Select User or Group dialog box.

Step 4.   Type the required user or group name and click **OK**. The user or group is added to the Permission Entry dialog box.

Step 5.   Click **Show Advanced Permissions**. The dialog box displays the advanced permissions, as shown in Figure 7-38.

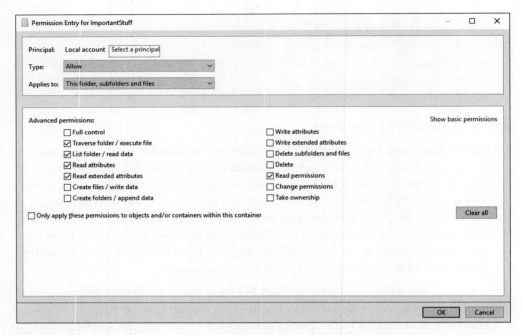

Figure 7-38   Permission Entry Dialog Box Enabling You to Configure Advanced Permissions

Step 6.   Configure the following options as required:

- **Principal:** The user account or group name appears on this line, but you can select a different one by clicking the **Select a Principal** link.

- **Type:** Select **Allow** or **Deny** as required.

- **Applies To:** You can adjust the level in the folder hierarchy at which the special permissions apply and are inherited. When permissions are not being inherited from a parent folder, you can choose between This Folder, Subfolders and Files, or any one or two of these components.

- **Advanced Permissions:** You can configure any one or more of the special access permissions by selecting their corresponding check boxes.

- **Only Apply These Permissions to Objects and/or Containers Within This Container:** Here you can adjust a particular folder's properties so that files and subfolders inherit their permissions from the folder you are working on. Selecting this option propagates the special access permissions to files within and folders below your current location in a folder hierarchy.

- **Clear All:** You can clear all selected permissions.

Step 7.   When finished, click **OK**.

Table 7-7 describes the special access file and folder permissions that you can configure from this location:

Table 7-7   NTFS Special Access Permissions

Folder Permission	What a User Is Allowed to Do	File Permission	What a User Is Allowed to Do
Full control	Includes all special access permissions.	Full control	Includes all special access permissions.
Traverse folder	Navigate through folders that a user normally can't access in order to reach files or folders that the user does have permission to access.	Execute file	Run executable files.
List folder	View files or subfolders.	Read data	View data in a particular file.
Read attributes	View folder attributes. These attributes are defined by NTFS.	Read attributes	View file attributes. These attributes are defined by NTFS.
Read extended attributes	View extended folder attributes. Extended attributes are defined by software and may vary.	Read extended attributes	View extended file attributes. Extended attributes are defined by software and may vary.
Create files	Create files within a folder.	Write data	Write changes to or overwrite a file.
Create folders	Create subfolders.	Append data	Make changes to the end of a file by appending data. Does not allow changing, deleting, or overwriting existing data.
Write attributes	Change the attributes of a folder, such as read-only or hidden. Attributes are defined by NTFS.	Write attributes	Change the attributes of a file, such as read-only or hidden. Attributes are defined by NTFS.
Write extended attributes	Change the extended attributes of a folder. Extended attributes are defined by programs and may vary.	Write extended attributes	Change the extended attributes of a file. Extended attributes are defined by programs and may vary.

Folder Permission	What a User Is Allowed to Do	File Permission	What a User Is Allowed to Do
Delete subfolders and files	Delete subfolders, even if the Delete permission has not been granted on the subfolder.	Delete subfolders and files	Delete files, even if the Delete permission has not been granted on the file.
Delete	Delete a folder or subfolder.	Delete	Delete a file.
Read permissions	Read permissions for a folder, such as Full Control, Read, and Write.	Read permissions	Read permissions for a file, such as Full Control, Read, and Write.
Change permissions	Change permissions for a folder, such as Full Control, Read, and Write.	Change permissions	Change permissions for a file, such as Full Control, Read, and Write.
Take ownership	Take ownership of a folder.	Take ownership	Take ownership of a file.

Taking ownership is a very special type of access permission. In Windows 10, each NTFS folder and file has an owner. Whoever creates a file or folder automatically becomes the owner and, by default, has Full Control permissions on that file or folder. If that person is a member of the Administrators group, then the Administrators group becomes the owner. The owner possesses the ability to apply and change permissions on a folder or file that he or she owns, even if the ACL does not explicitly grant that ability. This does make it possible for the owner of a particular file or folder to deny Administrators access to a resource. But an administrator can exercise the optional right to take ownership of any resource to gain access to it, if this becomes necessary.

In Table 7-5, which describes the standard access permissions, you might have noticed that a standard permission like Modify enables a user to do more than one thing to a file or folder. A special-access permission typically enables a user to do one thing only. All special permissions are encompassed within the standard permissions.

NTFS Permissions Inheritance

All NTFS permissions are inherited—that is, they pass down through the folder hierarchy from parent to child. Permissions assigned to a parent folder are inherited by all the files in that folder, and by the subfolders contained in the parent folder as well. Unless you specifically stop the process of files and folders inheriting permissions from their parent folder, any existing files and subfolders, and any new files and subfolders created within this tree of folders will inherit their permissions from the original parent folder. To use the fancy term, permissions are *propagated* all the way down the tree.

Windows 10 lets you modify this permissions inheritance sequence if necessary. To check whether permissions are being inherited and to remove permissions inheritance, use the following procedure:

Step 1. From the Advanced Security Settings dialog box previously shown in Figure 7-36, click the **Disable Inheritance** command button.

Step 2. You receive the Block Inheritance dialog box, which prompts you to specify one of the following permissions inheritance options:

- **Convert Inherited Permissions into Explicit Permissions on This Object:** Select this option to add existing inherited permissions assigned for the parent folder to the subfolder or file. This action also prevents subsequent permissions inheritance from the parent folder.

- **Remove All Inherited Permissions from This Object:** Select this option to remove existing inherited permissions assigned for the parent folder to the subfolder or file. Only permissions that you explicitly assign to the file or folder will apply.

- **Cancel:** Select **Cancel** to abort the operation and retain the default permissions inheritance.

Step 3. You are returned to the Advanced Security Settings dialog box. Click **OK** or **Apply** to apply your changes.

Taking Ownership of Files and Folders

In certain cases, you might need to grant the special Take Ownership permission to a user account. This can be valuable if a user is taking over responsibilities and resources from another individual. A user with the Full Control NTFS permission or the Take Ownership special permission can take ownership of a file or folder from the folder's Properties dialog box, as follows:

Step 1. From the Advanced Security Settings dialog box, click the **Change** link under Owner near the top of the dialog box.

Step 2. In the Select User or Group dialog box that appears, type the name of the desired user or group, and then click **OK**.

Step 3. You are returned to the Advanced Security Settings dialog box, and the Owner line reflects the new owner. Click **OK**.

Exam Preparation Tasks

Review All the Key Topics

Review the most important topics in the chapter, noted with the Key Topics icon in the outer margin of the page. Table 7-8 lists a reference of these key topics and the page numbers on which each is found.

Table 7-8 Key Topics for Chapter 7

Key Topic Element	Description	Page Number
Step List	Setting up PIN logins	321
Step List	Configuring Picture Password	323
Table 7-2	Built-in Local Groups in Windows	327
Figure 7-9	Group policies to require Ctrl+Alt+Del to log in	330
Step List	Sign in with Microsoft account	331
List	Group Policy to control the use of Microsoft accounts	332
Figure 7-10	Configuring Windows Hello	333
Table 7-3	Group policies for managing Windows Hello for Business	335
Step List	Joining a workgroup	336
Figure 7-13	Creating a HomeGroup	339
Step List	Joining Azure AD	346
Figure 7-31	UAC prompt	359
List	Types of UAC prompts	361
Step List	Configure a program to start with administrative privileges	362
List	Configuring UAC behavior	362
Figure 7-33	Enabling secure sign-in using the User Accounts applet	367
Figure 7-35	Adding a new Windows credential to Credential Manager	370
Figure 7-36	Using Certificate Manager to manage certificates	373
Table 7-5	NTFS file and folder permissions	379

Complete the Tables and Lists from Memory

Print a copy of Appendix B, "Memory Tables" (found on the book's website), or at least the section for this chapter, and complete the tables and lists from memory. Appendix C, "Memory Tables Answer Key," also on the website, includes completed tables and lists to check your work.

Definitions of Key Terms

Define the following key terms from this chapter, and check your answers in the glossary.

access control list (ACL), authentication, authorization, biometrics, CA, certificate, cloud, credentials, Credential Guard, Device Guard, Device Health Attestation, encryption, Microsoft account, MMC, OCSP, PIN, PIV, PKI, NTFS permissions, Special Access permissions, User Account Control (UAC)

This chapter covers the following subjects:

- **Support Data Security:** In Chapter 7 you learned about security in Windows for authentication and authorization. For the Windows 70-697 exam, you also need to know how to support data security, how to identify issues when they are encountered, and how to resolve them. In this topic you learn how to resolve issues related to NTFS permissions and Dynamic Access Control (DAC).

- **Encrypting File System:** Windows 10 provides the Encrypting File System (EFS), which provides an additional layer of protection for sensitive data. This section shows you how to use EFS and explains the need for backing up encryption keys and using data recovery agents to ensure that encrypted data can always be decrypted if users move or lose their encryption certificates and keys.

- **Configuring Local Security Policy:** To ensure that devices are secure, that user accounts follow best practices, and that Windows maintains security needs for each user, Microsoft provides local security policies for implementing some security best practices. You learn some of the important security policies you can implement using the local security policy editor.

- **Security for Mobile Devices:** Microsoft has enhanced the BitLocker whole drive encryption scheme, first introduced in Windows Vista, by allowing you to encrypt data partitions. BitLocker To Go extends the BitLocker drive encryption to USB drives and portable hard drives. This section also covers the use of removable disks and devices for storing startup keys for BitLocker and other purposes, and how to enable and manage BitLocker without a built-in TPM.

This chapter covers the following objectives for the 70-697 exam:

Support data security: Identifying and resolving issues related to the following: Permissions including share, NTFS, and Dynamic Access Control (DAC); Encrypting File System (EFS) including data recovery agent; access to removable media; BitLocker and BitLocker To Go, including data recovery agent and Microsoft BitLocker Administration and Monitoring (MBAM).

Configure security for mobile devices: Configure BitLocker, configure startup key storage.

CHAPTER 8

Windows 10 Data Security

In Chapter 7, "Windows 10 Security," we covered authentication and authorization in Windows, the various ways of authenticating users and computers, and authorization protocols used in Windows networking.

Now we take these steps further by showing you how to configure Local Security Policy, User Account Control (UAC), Secure Boot, SmartScreen Filters, and other technologies that protect your critical data. Local Security Policy is a subset of Group Policy settings available on Windows Servers that enables you to specify what users are allowed to do on the local computer and across the network. UAC provides additional security by requesting administrative permission before performing tasks such as installing applications or modifying the Registry. Secure Boot helps to prevent access to the computer by unauthorized firmware, operating systems, or drivers during system startup. SmartScreen Filter is a Windows security layer filter that protects browsing sessions and Internet access by detecting phishing websites and preventing the download or installation of malicious software.

"Do I Know This Already?" Quiz

The "Do I Know This Already?" quiz allows you to assess whether you should read this entire chapter or simply jump to the "Exam Preparation Tasks" section for review. If you are in doubt, read the entire chapter. Table 8-1 outlines the major headings in this chapter and the corresponding "Do I Know This Already?" quiz questions. You can find the answers in Appendix A, "Answers to the 'Do I Know This Already?' Quizzes."

Table 8-1 "Do I Know This Already?" Foundation Topics Section-to-Question Mapping

Foundation Topics Section	Questions Covered in This Section
Support Data Security	1–4
Encrypting File System	5–6
Configuring Local Security Policy	7
Security for Mobile Devices	8–12

> **CAUTION**   The goal of self-assessment is to gauge your mastery of the topics in this chapter. If you do not know the answer to a question or are only partially sure of the answer, you should mark that question as wrong for purposes of the self-assessment. Giving yourself credit for an answer you correctly guess skews your self-assessment results and might provide you with a false sense of security.

1. You have been notified by a user that she is not able to update a file on the Accounting server share that she should have access to. The user is in many groups and the share is available. What should you look at to troubleshoot the issue?

   a. NTFS Permissions

   b. Share Permissions

   c. Effective Access

   d. Group Policies

2. You have granted the Managers group Full Control NTFS permission on the C:\Documents\Projects.doc file. You move this file to the C:\Confidential folder, to which the Managers group has been granted the Read permission. A user named Jennifer, who is a member of the Managers group, accesses the C:\Confidential\Projects.doc file. What effective permission does Jennifer have to this file?

   a. Full Control

   b. Modify

   c. Read

   d. Jennifer does not have access to the folder.

3. You are using your Administrator account to move a folder from the D: partition on the file share server to a new E: partition added to increase storage. What happens to the NTFS permissions on the folder?

   a. The folder will have permissions only for the Administrator account.

   b. The folder will have the permissions for the E: drive.

   c. The folder will retain its permissions.

   d. The folder will have the permissions of the folder it is copied to.

4. Your organization is implementing new policies to prevent sensitive documents containing company secrets and personally identifying information (PII) from being accessed by employees. The security team will work with business users to identify all sensitive documents and label them appropriately. You will need to implement controls to ensure only authorized users can access the documents. What is the most appropriate technology you should look at to implement the new policies?

   a. NTFS permissions on file shares

   b. Share permissions on file shares

   c. Dynamic Access Control

   d. EFS Encryption

5. You want to encrypt the Confidential folder. This folder is located on the D:\ volume, which is formatted with the FAT32 file system. You access the folder's Properties dialog box and click the Advanced button. But the option to encrypt the folder is not available. What do you need to do to encrypt this folder? (Each correct answer presents a complete solution to the problem. Choose two.)

   a. Format the D:\ volume with the NTFS file system.

   b. Use the Convert.exe utility to convert the D:\ volume to the NTFS file system.

   c. Move the Confidential folder to the D:\ volume, which is formatted with the NTFS file system.

   d. Decompress the Confidential folder.

6. You are the desktop support specialist for your company. A user named Peter has left the company, and you have deleted his user account. Later you realize that he had encrypted his Work folder on his Windows 10 computer, and you must regain access to this folder. What should you do?

   a. Log on to Peter's computer with your user account and decrypt the file.

   b. Log on to Peter's computer with the default administrator account and decrypt the file.

   c. Re-create Peter's user account, log on with this account, and decrypt the file.

   d. You cannot access this folder; it is permanently lost.

7. One day after logging on to your Windows 10 computer, which you have shared with several others in your department, you notice that the time zone has been changed to an improper setting. You would like to discover who is making improper modifications to your computer's settings. Which of the following audit policies should you enable?

    a. Account management

    b. Policy change

    c. Privilege use

    d. System events

8. You are sure your Windows 10 Enterprise computer is equipped with a Trusted Platform Module (TPM), but when you go to enable BitLocker from the System and Security category of Control Panel, the BitLocker Drive Encryption option is not available. What do you need to do first?

    a. Enable TPM in the BIOS.

    b. Configure TPM to use a startup key.

    c. Use Group Policy to enable TPM.

    d. Contact your hardware manufacturer for a firmware update.

9. Which of the following is something you should *not* do when enabling BitLocker and BitLocker To Go on your Windows 10 computer?

    a. Use BitLocker To Go to encrypt your USB flash drive containing the BitLocker recovery key.

    b. Use AD DS to save backup copies of your recovery keys.

    c. Use BitLocker without additional keys on a computer that is equipped with a TPM.

    d. Use Group Policy to enable BitLocker on a computer that is not equipped with a TPM.

10. Which of the following are possible ways you can use to back up BitLocker recovery keys and passwords? (Choose all that apply.)

    a. Save the key to a USB flash drive.

    b. Save the key to a file on a portable drive.

    c. Save the key to Active Directory Domain Services (AD DS).

    d. Save the key to a Microsoft account.

    e. Print the key.

11. You would like to use BitLocker on a computer without TPM, but when you try to enable it, an error is displayed indicating you must contact an administrator to enable it. What must you do to use BitLocker on this computer?

    a. Enable BitLocker from the Control Panel.

    b. Enable the Require Additional Authentication at Startup group policy.

    c. Disable the BitLocker TPM group policy.

    d. Update the signature of the operating system drive in Disk Management.

12. You are configuring BitLocker on a computer without a built-in TPM. Which of the following is not an option for saving your recovery key?

    a. Writable DVD or CD

    b. Microsoft account

    c. To the domain (on a domain-joined computer)

    d. From a printed hard-copy of the recovery password

Foundation Topics

Support Data Security

As an IT professional, or even as a user of Windows 10, you need to know how to protect your data from access by nefarious individuals or other unauthorized users. Windows has many tools and technologies to help secure your data, and you should understand how to use these tools to ensure that authorization to view and update data according to your organization policies is enforced by the system tools.

When designing your data security profile, you should keep in mind that you need to make sure that only authorized users can access the data, and that users obtain the least amount of privilege that allows them to do their job. If a user is having trouble accessing a drive with data that they need, you can easily resolve the issue by providing the user with administrative access to the entire storage location. That may solve the immediate issue, but will create many more, because now the user may have access to information that the data owner does not want her to have. It may be that the user needs only to view the data and should not be allowed to modify it. Make sure you are granting the minimum level of access that is required, based on organizational policies.

Issues Related to Shared Folder and NTFS Permissions

In Chapter 7, "Windows 10 Security," we introduced the shared folder permissions that control a user's ability to access data in folders that are shared across the network. We then introduced the concept of NTFS security permissions, which you can apply to files and folders stored on the local computer, and which apply whether you access these items locally or across the network. In this chapter, we take these concepts a step further, and show you how these file share permissions interact with NTFS ACLs, and how to resolve some problems that might prevent users from accessing their data.

Viewing a User's Effective Permissions

Windows 10 enables you to view a user's or group's effective permissions. This is most useful in untangling a complicated web of permissions received by a user who is a member of several groups. Use the following procedure:

Step 1.   From the Security tab of the folder's Properties dialog box, click **Advanced** to display the Advanced Security Settings dialog box shown in Figure 8-1, and then click the **Effective Access** tab.

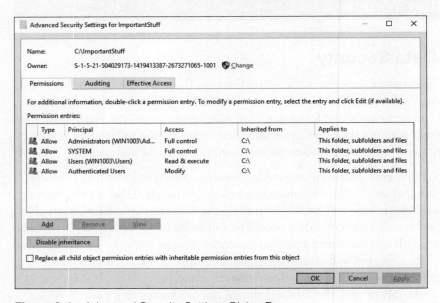

Figure 8-1   Advanced Security Settings Dialog Box

Step 2.   To view effective permissions for a user or group, click **Select a User** to display the Select User or Group dialog box.

Step 3.   Type the name of the desired user or group, click **OK**, and then click the **View Effective Access** command button.

Step 4.   You are returned to the Effective Access tab, which now displays the effective permissions for the user or group, as shown in Figure 8-2. In the case illustrated here, the user's access was limited by a denial of access specified in a group to which the user belonged; this limitation is indicated by the red "X" entries and the File Permissions entry appearing in the Access Limited By column of the dialog box.

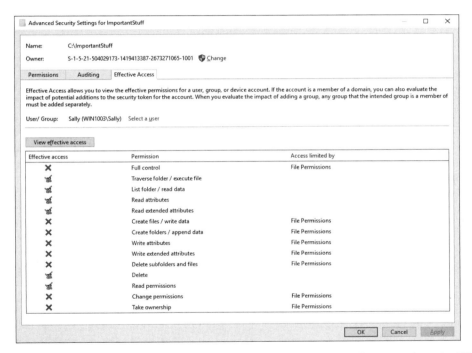

Figure 8-2   Viewing a User or Group's Effective Permissions to a Resource from the Effective Access Tab of the Advanced Security Settings Dialog Box

Copying and Moving Files and Folders

When you copy or move a file or folder that is configured with NTFS permissions, those NTFS permissions can change. The action that occurs depends on whether you are copying the file or folder or whether you are moving the file or folder.

Copying Files and Folders with NTFS Permissions

When you copy a file or folder that is configured with NTFS permissions, those NTFS permissions can change. If you are copying files and folders to a place where the NTFS permissions match exactly, the permissions will stay the same. The potential for change is always there, however, when you copy files and folders with NTFS permissions. There are no exceptions to this rule. To ensure that NTFS permissions are applied effectively on your computer, you will need to keep in mind how copying can change NTFS permissions. There are essentially three possible outcomes, as outlined in Table 8-2.

Table 8-2   The Effect of Copying Files or Folders on Their NTFS Permissions

Action	Result
Copy a file or folder within the same partition	The copy inherits the NTFS permissions of the destination folder.
Copy a file or folder from one NTFS partition to another NTFS partition	The copy inherits the NTFS permissions of the destination folder.
Copy a file or folder from an NTFS partition to a FAT or FAT32 partition	The copy of a file or folder loses its NTFS permissions completely. NTFS permissions cannot apply anywhere else but on an NTFS partition.

To copy files from an NTFS partition, you need to have at least the Read permission for the originating folder. To complete the copy operation so that the copied versions are written to disk, you need to have at least the Write permission for the destination folder.

CAUTION   A close look at Table 8-2 should alert you to the fact that copying a file or folder from an NTFS partition to a FAT or FAT32 partition will strip the file or folder of its NTFS permissions and make it fully available to all users at the local computer.

Moving Files and Folders with NTFS Permissions

Moving files with NTFS permissions may change those permissions. Depending on the circumstances, especially the destination of the move, the permissions may change or they may stay the same. As outlined in Table 8-3, there are also three possible outcomes.

Table 8-3   The Effect of Moving Files or Folders on Their NTFS Permissions

Action	Result
Move a file or folder within the same partition	The file or folder retains its NTFS permissions, regardless of the permissions that exist for the destination folder.
Move a file or folder from one NTFS partition to another NTFS partition	The file or folder inherits the NTFS permissions of the destination folder.
Move a file or folder from an NTFS partition to a FAT or FAT32 partition	The file or folder loses its NTFS permissions completely. NTFS permissions cannot apply anywhere else but on an NTFS partition.

To move files within an NTFS partition or between two NTFS partitions, you need to have at least the Modify permission for the originating folder. To complete the move operation so that the moved versions are written to disk, you need to have at least the Write permission for the destination folder. The Modify permission is required at the source so that source files and folders can be deleted after the files or folders are safely relocated to their new home.

NOTE   After you have had time to think about how copying and moving files and folders affects NTFS permissions, there is an easy way to remember how all these possible outcomes will work. One simple sentence can serve to summarize what is going on: "Moving within retains." The only sure way to retain existing NTFS permissions during a copy or move operation is to move files within a single NTFS partition. All the other options hold a very real potential for altering NTFS permissions.

Using the Mouse to Copy or Move Objects from One Location to Another

Keep in mind the following facts about dragging objects between locations:

- When you use the mouse to drag an object from one folder to another on the *same* partition, you are *moving* that object.

- If you drag the object to a folder on *another* partition, you are *copying* that object.

- If you hold down the Ctrl key while dragging, you are *copying* the object, whether it is to the same or another partition.

- You can also right-drag the object. In this case, when you release the mouse button, you receive choices of copying the object, moving it, or creating a shortcut to the object in its original location.

Dynamic Access Control

Introduced in Windows Server 2012 and available in Windows Server 2016 is Dynamic Access Control (DAC), which is a new feature that helps to enhance data security and maintain compliance by factoring in user identity and device security access factors in granting access to data. You can enable users' roaming profiles and redirected folders to be immediately available when they log on from any device and remove sensitive data availability when they log off. Security auditing has also been enhanced with new expression-based audit policies and the capability to audit new types of securable objects, as well as data located on removable storage devices. Although there is nothing to configure in Windows 10 specifically, Microsoft requires you to know about DAC and how it works for the 70-697 exam.

DAC helps to implement security policies on document and folder access that NTFS cannot do, or cannot do well. You have learned how NTFS uses groups, nested groups, and user permissions to secure data, and how complicated it can be to determine exactly what permission a user may have. What if you have a folder with some specific access requirements that require membership in two separate groups? NTFS has no easy way to implement that rule, without creating a third group, further complicating permissions. When users can access resources from multiple devices and multiple locations, security becomes increasingly important, but what if you want to restrict access to certain documents only from certain locations? NTFS permissions cannot help with that, either.

These are the access requirement problems that DAC is designed to solve. You can impose multigroup requirements and impose requirements on user locations or devices, and other controls. You can tag data in file servers and classify the data based on how sensitive or secret it is. You can create audit files if you need to record which users accessed sensitive data and when it was accessed. These features can go a long way to help organizations with strict requirements such as HIPAA or Sarbanes-Oxley to ensure their systems are enforcing policy requirements.

Implementing DAC in an Active Directory environment has several requirements:

- The server role File Server Resource Manager (FSRM) on at least one Domain Controller.
- The server role Active Directory Rights Management Services (AD RMS) on any server that will host sensitive files.
- Domain Functional Level Windows Server 2012 or higher.
- The Microsoft Office Filter Packs installed on any server that will host sensitive files.
- A Group Policy Object to enable DAC on the domain.
- An Access Policy or set of Access Policies for the organization.

The details for planning and configuring each of these requirements are out of the scope of this text. You should understand that DAC is implemented using Active Directory, a set of Group Policies, and the server roles to enforce the policies, specifically the FSRM and AD RMS.

> **NOTE** For more information about Dynamic Access Control and the various scenarios for using DAC to secure sensitive data, see "Dynamic Access Control: Scenario Overview" at https://technet.microsoft.com/en-us/windows-server-docs/ identity/solution-guides/dynamic-access-control--scenario-overview.

With DAC configured and in place in your organization, you have new options for securing and classifying your files. For instance, you may want to create rules to allow only certain people to access documents that contain personally identifying information (PII), or audit any access of those files.

The first step is to use the FSRM to create Classification Properties you can use to classify documents. Figure 8-3 illustrates a Classification Property named Contains PII. This property can then be used on documents in the server's file shares.

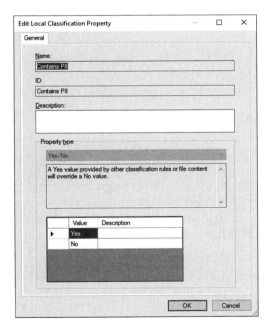

Figure 8-3   Using the FSRM to Create Classification Properties

Documents stored on the server can then use these properties, enforcing your organization's policies for classification of sensitive data. You can access the classification properties for any document by right-clicking a document and selecting **Properties** from the context menu. A new Classification tab is now available, as shown in Figure 8-4. As shown, the Contains PII property can be set for the document. This is a Yes/No property. You can leave the property as None, which will cause DAC to ignore it, or set it to Yes or No. The "HR-Secrets" document does contain PII, so we set the property as Yes. DAC will use this property, along with any audit or access rules you define, whenever users access the file.

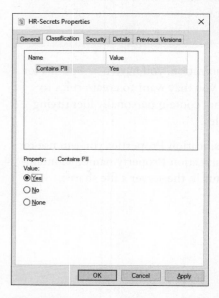

Figure 8-4   Setting Classification Properties on Organization Documents

Access to Removable Media

Many organizations in government or private industry maintain sensitive data that must be carefully controlled and kept secret. To maintain a controlled environment, it's necessary to ensure that people are not walking out of the organization with classified documents on a removable disk or USB thumb drive. These devices are easily hidden and easily lost, leading to unknown disclosures of secrets.

We will talk about encryption later in this chapter, which is useful to avoid issues of unsecured data getting lost. Your organization may have policies requiring encryption for any removable media or USB drives, or policies may simply state that these devices are not allowed to be used at all. In the latter case, you can enforce these policies using Group Policy Objects (GPOs).

The section in Group Policy called Removable Storage Access, found under Computer Configuration\Administrative Templates\System, contains many policies for fine-grained control over removable media on any domain-joined computer in the organization, as shown in Figure 8-5.

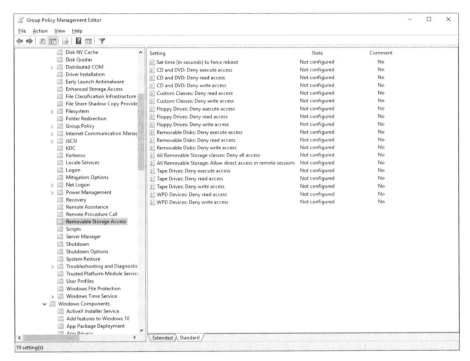

Figure 8-5   Group Policies for Removable Storage Access

For instance, you might want to prevent anyone from writing data to a DVD or CD drive, but should be allowed to read them or install applications from DVD. You can enable the CD and DVD: Deny Write Access policy and leave the execute and read access policies as Not Configured.

There are several categories of devices that you can set policies for, including what is called Windows Portable Devices (WPD). As shown in the description in Figure 8-6, these include things like cell phones, media players, and other consumer electronics (CE devices).

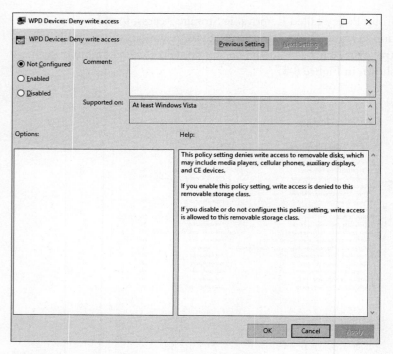

Figure 8-6   WPD Devices: Deny Write Access Group Policy

If needed, you can set a global policy for any removable storage by configuring the All Removable Storage Classes policy, denying any access to removable storage of any kind.

Encrypting File System

You often hear news reports that mention thefts of laptop computers containing valuable data. In one such case, a computer stolen from a doctor's car in Toronto contained the records of thousands of patients, exposing them to misuse and potential identity theft. The computer was protected with a password but the data was not encrypted. Windows 10 includes the following two systems of data encryption, designed to protect data not only on your laptop when you are in a place such as an airport or hotel where a thief can grab it when you're momentarily distracted, but also at any other place where an unauthorized individual might attempt to either connect to it across the network or physically access it.

- First introduced with Windows Vista, BitLocker Drive Encryption encrypts a computer's entire system partition. We cover BitLocker later in this chapter.

- First introduced with Windows 2000 and refined with each successive iteration of Windows, the Encrypting File System (EFS) can be used to encrypt files and folders on any partition that is formatted with the NTFS file system. We discuss EFS in this section.

EFS enables users to encrypt files and folders on any partition that is formatted with the NTFS file system. The encryption attribute on a file or folder can be toggled the same as any other file attribute. When you set the encryption attribute on a folder, all its contents—whether subfolders or files—are also encrypted.

The encryption attribute, when assigned to a folder, affects files the same way that the compression attribute does when a file is moved or copied. Files that are copied into the encrypted folder become encrypted. Files that are moved into the encrypted folder retain their former encryption attribute, whether or not they were encrypted. When you move or copy a file to a file system that does not support EFS, such as FAT16 or FAT32, the file is automatically decrypted.

TIP   Remember that the file system must be set to NTFS if you want to use EFS, and no file can be both encrypted and compressed at the same time. On the exam, you may be presented with a scenario where a user is unable to use EFS or file compression on a FAT32 volume; the correct answer to such a problem is to convert the file system to NTFS, as described in the section "Preparing a Disk for EFS."

Encrypting File System Basics

EFS uses a form of public key cryptography, which utilizes a public and private key pair. The public key or digital certificate is freely available to anyone, and the private key is retained and guarded by the user to which the key pair is issued. The public key is used to encrypt data, and the private key decrypts the data that was encrypted with the corresponding public key. The key pair is created the first time a user encrypts a file or folder using EFS. When another user attempts to open the file, that user is unable to do so. Therefore, EFS is suitable for data that a user wants to maintain as private, but not for files that are shared.

Windows 10 has the capability to encrypt files directly on any NTFS volume. This ensures that no other user can use the encrypted data. Encryption and decryption of a file or folder are performed in the object's Properties dialog box. Administrators should be aware of the rules to put into practice to manage EFS on a network:

- Only use NTFS as the file system for all workstation and server volumes.

- Keep a copy of each user's certificate and private key on a USB flash drive or other removable media.

- Remove the user's private key from the computer except when the user is actually using it.

- When users routinely save documents only to their Documents folder, make certain their documents are encrypted by having each user encrypt his own Documents folder.

- Use two recovery agent user accounts that are reserved solely for that purpose for each Active Directory Domain Services (AD DS) organizational unit (OU) if computers participate in a domain. Assign the recovery agent certificates to these accounts.

- Archive all recovery agent user account information, recovery certificates, and private keys, even if obsolete.

- When planning a network installation, keep in mind that EFS does take up additional processing overhead; plan to incorporate additional CPU processing power in your plans.

A unique encryption key is assigned to each encrypted file. You can share an encrypted file with other users in Windows 10, but you are restricted from sharing an entire encrypted folder with multiple users or sharing a single file with a security group. This is related to the way that EFS uses certificates, which are applicable individually to users, and how EFS uses encryption keys, which are applicable individually to files. Windows 8.1 continues the capability introduced with Windows Vista to store keys on smart cards. If you are using smart cards for user logon, EFS automatically locates the encryption key without issuing further prompts. EFS also provides wizards that assist users in creating and selecting smart card keys.

You can use different types of certificates with EFS: third-party–issued certificates, certificates issued by certificate authorities (CAs)—including those on your own network—and self-signed certificates. If you have developed a security system on your network that utilizes mutual authentication based on certificates issued by your own CA, you can extend the system to EFS to further secure encrypted files. For more information on using certificates with EFS, refer to the Windows 10 Help and Support Center.

NOTE   For more information on the technology behind EFS, refer to "How EFS Works" at http://technet.microsoft.com/en-us/library/cc962103.aspx.

Preparing a Disk for EFS

Unlike versions of Windows prior to Vista, the system and boot partition in Windows 10 must be formatted with NTFS before you can install Windows 10, as you learned in Chapter 2, "Implementing Windows." However, a data partition can be formatted with the FAT or FAT32 file systems. But you must ensure that such a partition is formatted with NTFS before you can encrypt data using EFS. If it is not, you can convert the hard disk format from FAT to NTFS or format the partition as NTFS. There are two ways to go about this:

- Use the command-line Convert.exe utility to change an existing FAT16 or FAT32 partition that contains data to NTFS without losing the data.

- Use the graphical Disk Management utility to format a new partition, or an empty FAT partition, to NTFS. If the volume contains data, you will lose it. (You can also use the command-line Format.exe utility to format a partition as NTFS.)

The Convert.exe utility is simple to use and typically problem-free, although you should make certain to back up the data on the partition before you convert it as a precaution. Perform the following steps to use this utility:

Step 1.   Log on to the computer as an administrator. Know which drive letter represents the partition that you plan to convert because only the partition that contains the encrypted files needs to be formatted with NTFS. For example, if users store all their data on drive D: and want to encrypt those files, you will convert drive D: to NTFS.

Step 2.   From the Search bar or Cortana, type **cmd** into the Search box, and press **Enter**.

Step 3.   The command prompt window opens. At the prompt, type **convert d: /fs:ntfs**.

Step 4.   The conversion process begins. If you are running the Convert.exe utility from the same drive letter prompt as the partition you are converting, or a file is open on the partition, you are prompted with a message that states Convert Cannot Gain Exclusive Access to D:, So It Cannot Convert It Now. Would You Like To Schedule It to Be Converted the Next Time the System Restarts (Y/N)? Press **Y** at the message.

Step 5.   Restart the computer. The disk converts its format to NTFS. This process takes considerable time to complete, but at completion, you can access the Properties dialog box for the disk you've converted and note that it is formatted with the NTFS file system.

Encrypting Files

You can use either the **cipher** command-line utility or the advanced attributes of the file or folder to encrypt a file. To use the cipher utility for encrypting a file named Myfile.txt located in the C:\mydir folder, the full command to use is as follows:

```
cipher /e /a c:\mydir\myfile.txt
```

To change the Advanced encryption attribute of a file, open File Explorer and navigate to the file. Right-click the file and select **Properties**. On the General tab, click the **Advanced** button in the Attributes section. The Advanced Attributes dialog box opens, as shown in Figure 8-7.

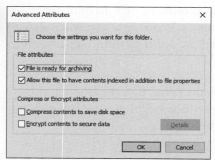

Figure 8-7 Advanced Attributes Dialog Box Enabling You to Either Compress or Encrypt a File

Select the **Encrypt Contents to Secure Data** check box and click **OK**. Then click **OK** again to close the file's Properties dialog box. You are given a warning dialog that lets you choose between encrypting just the file that you had selected or both the file and its parent folder. Select one of the options and click **OK**.

> **NOTE**   Note that the compression and encryption attributes are mutually exclusive. In the Advanced Attributes dialog box, if you select the Compress Contents to Save Disk Space check box, the check mark disappears from the Encrypt Contents to Secure Data check box. These two attributes are mutually exclusive—you can select only one.

After a file has been encrypted, you can view its encryption attribute details by again right-clicking the file, selecting **Properties**, and then clicking the **Advanced** button on the General tab. In the Advanced Attributes dialog box, click the **Details** button. The User Access To (file) dialog box opens, as shown in Figure 8-8.

Figure 8-8 User Access Dialog Box Enables Adding User Permissions

You can see who is able to open the encrypted file and you can add other user accounts to share the encrypted file and view the designated data recovery agent, if any. Click the **Add** button to share the encrypted file. A dialog box listing all the EFS-capable certificates for users opens. If a user has never been issued a certificate, the user's account does not appear in this dialog box.

TIP If the desired user has not been issued an EFS certificate, she needs only to log on to the computer and encrypt a different file. This automatically creates a certificate that will be visible the next time you attempt to share an encrypted file.

After a file is encrypted, an unauthorized user attempting to open the file is given an error message that says the user does not have access privileges. If an unauthorized user tries to move or copy an encrypted file, the user receives an Access Is Denied error message.

Backing Up EFS Keys

What if a user were to encrypt a file using EFS, and then the user's account were to become corrupted or be deleted for any reason? Or what if the user's private key were to become corrupted or lost? On a domain-joined computer, you may be able to use an administrator recovery certificate to recover the file. However, on a workgroup or standalone device without some kind of recovery agent configured, you would be unable to decrypt the file, and it would be permanently inaccessible. Recovery agents are discussed next, but Windows 10 offers the capability for backing up EFS certificates and keys to reduce the likelihood of losing access to information without a recovery agent. Use the following procedure to back up EFS keys:

Step 1.   From the User Access dialog box previously shown in Figure 8-8, select the username and then click **Back Up Keys**.

Step 2.   The Certificate Export Wizard starts. Click **Next**.

Step 3.   On the Export File Format page, the Personal Information Exchange-PKCS #12 (.PFX) format is selected by default. If desired, select the **Include All Certificates in the Certification Path if Possible** and **Export All Extended Properties** options, and then click **Next**.

Step 4.   On the Password page, type and confirm a password. This is mandatory, and you should choose a hard-to-guess password that follows the usual complexity guidelines. Then click **Next**.

Step 5.   On the File to Export page, type the name of the file to be exported and then click **Next**. By default, this file is created in the user's Documents library with the .pfx extension.

Step 6.   Review the information on the completion page and then click **Finish**.

Step 7.   You are informed the export was successful. Click **OK**.

Step 8.   You should move this file to a location separate from the computer, such as a USB key that you store securely (such as in a locked cabinet).

Decrypting Files

The process of decryption is the opposite of encryption. You can either use the **cipher** command or change the Advanced attribute for encryption on the file.

To use the **cipher** command to decrypt the file, access the Search bar or Cortana, type **cmd** into the Search box, and then press Enter. At the command prompt, type **cipher /d /a c:\myfolder\myfile.txt** and press Enter. The file will be decrypted.

To use the Advanced Attributes method, open File Explorer and navigate to the file. Right-click the file and select **Properties**. On the General tab, click the **Advanced** button. In the ensuing Advanced Attributes dialog box, clear the **Encrypt Contents to Secure Data** check box. Click **OK** and then click **OK** again.

If you are not the person who originally encrypted the file, or if you are not the designated recovery agent, you will receive an error for applying attributes that says the access is denied.

EFS Recovery Agents

What if the user's keys, even though backed up, were to become lost or corrupted? Without some type of recovery capability, such a file would become permanently inaccessible. EFS in Windows 10 uses the concept of *recovery agents* as a means to recover encrypted data in such a situation.

Designated recovery agents are user accounts authorized to decrypt encrypted files. When a user account is designated as a recovery agent, you essentially are granting it a copy of the key pair. If you lose the key pair, or if they become damaged, and if there is no designated recovery agent, there is no way to decrypt the file and the data is permanently lost. By designating a recovery agent before a user first uses EFS, you can ensure that encrypted files and folders remain accessible by someone responsible for their maintenance.

Windows 10 can include two levels of EFS recovery agents:

- **Local computer:** By default, the local administrator account created when you first install Windows 10 is the recovery agent. Note that this account is not the account whose name you specify during Windows 10 installation; it is a built-in account that can be accessed from the Local Users and Groups node of the Computer Management snap-in. The account is disabled by default, but you can enable it from its Properties dialog box by clearing the **Account Is Disabled** check box.

- **Domain:** When you create an AD DS domain, the first domain administrator account is the designated recovery agent. You can use Group Policy to designate additional recovery agents, and you can delegate the responsibility of EFS recovery to other users if desired.

You can use Group Policy to designate additional recovery agents. A user must have an appropriate certificate before he can be designated as a recovery agent. Use the following procedure:

Step 1. Open Group Policy and navigate to the Computer Configuration\ Windows Settings\Security Settings\Public Key Policies\Encrypting File System node.

Step 2. Right-click this node and choose **Add Data Recovery Agent**.

Step 3. The Add Recovery Agent Wizard starts with a Welcome page. Click **Next**.

Step 4. On the Select Recovery Agents page shown in Figure 8-9, select a user from the Recovery Agents list and then click **Next**. (If necessary, click **Browse Folders** to locate a certificate for the desired user.)

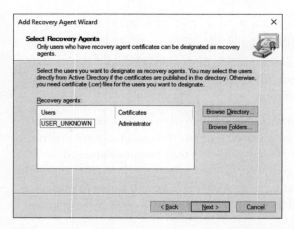

Figure 8-9   Add Recovery Agent Wizard Enabling You to Designate Additional Users as EFS Recovery Agents

Step 5.   You are informed that you have successfully completed the wizard. Review the information about the designated recovery agents, and then click **Finish**.

> **NOTE** For more information on backing up keys and designating recovery agents in EFS, refer to "How to Back Up the Recovery Agent Encrypting File System (EFS) Private Key in Windows" at http://support.microsoft.com/kb/241201 and "Encrypting File System" at https://technet.microsoft.com/en-us/library/cc749610(v=ws.10).aspx. Although written for older versions of Windows, the information in these references is for the most part applicable for Windows 10.

Configuring Local Security Policy

You can access the Local Security Policy snap-in through Administrative Tools under Control Panel's System and Security category or by accessing the Search bar or Cortana, typing **local security**, and then clicking **Local Security Policy**. The policies defined in this utility affect all users on the computer, unless the policies allow you to configure them on a per-user or per-group basis. This snap-in is shown in Figure 8-10.

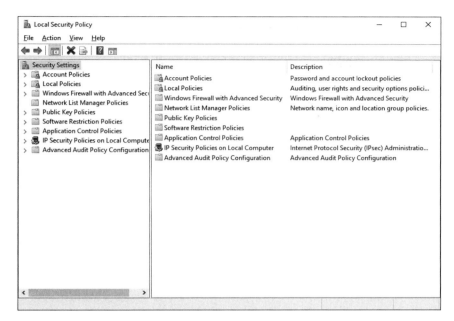

Figure 8-10 Configuring Numerous Local Security Policy Settings Using the Local Security Policy Snap-in in Windows 10

The Local Security Policy snap-in enables you to configure a large range of security-related policy settings. These settings are summarized next:

- **Account Policies:** Includes password policies and account lockout policies. We discuss account policies later in this section.

- **Local Policies:** Includes audit policies, user rights assignment, and security options. We discuss these policies later in this chapter.

- **Windows Firewall with Advanced Security:** Enables you to configure properties of Windows Firewall for domain, private, and public profiles. You can specify inbound and outbound connection rules as well as monitor settings.

- **Network List Manager Policies:** Enables you to control the networks that computers can access and their location types such as public and private (which automatically specifies the appropriate firewall settings according to location type). You can also specify which networks a user is allowed to connect to.

- **Public Key Policies:** Enables you to configure public key infrastructure (PKI) settings. Included are policies governing the use of Encrypting File System (EFS), Data Protection, and BitLocker Drive Encryption.

- **Software Restriction Policies:** Enables you to specify which software programs users can run on network computers, which programs users on multiuser computers can run, and the execution of email attachments. You can also specify whether software restriction policies apply to certain groups, such as administrators.

- **Application Control Policies:** These are a set of software control policies first introduced with Windows 7 that include the AppLocker feature. AppLocker provides new enhancements that enable you to specify exactly what users are permitted to run on their desktops according to unique file identities. We covered software restriction policies and application control policies in Chapter 5, "Installing and Managing Software"

- **IP Security Policies on Local Computer:** Controls the implementation of IP Security (IPsec) as used by the computer for encrypting communications over the network.

- **Advanced Audit Policy Configuration:** First introduced in Windows 7, this node contains many policy settings that enable you to select explicitly the actions that you want to monitor and exclude actions that are of less concern.

NOTE   Be aware that in an Active Directory Domain Services (AD DS) domain environment, all these policies can be configured at the site, domain, or organizational unit (OU) level, and that any policies configured at these levels override conflicting local policies. If a local policy does not apply as configured, consult your domain administrator for assistance.

Configuring Local Policies

The Local Policies subnode of Security Settings enables you to configure audit policies, user rights assignment, and security options.

Audit Policies

You have the ability to audit user access to files, folders, and printers by configuring the Audit policy for the local computer. If you need to audit computers that are members of a domain, you can configure the Group Policy in the OU that contains these computers. Otherwise, you can configure the Audit Policy node, which is under Local Policies, as shown in Figure 8-11.

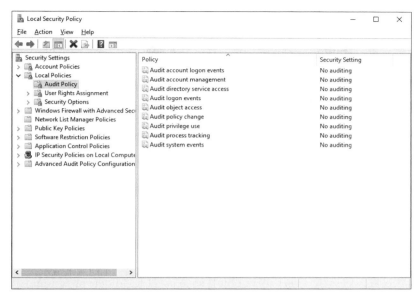

Figure 8-11   Enabling Auditing in the Local Policies Section of the Local Security Policy Console

Using the audit policy settings, you can identify undesirable activities on the computer. For example, if you had a computer whose local user and group configuration was inexplicably changed, you can enable the Audit Account Management policy and select **Success** to determine who has made these changes. Figure 8-12 depicts this policy configuration.

Figure 8-12   Enabling Auditing to Trigger an Event Log Entry When an Action Has Completed Successfully, or Has Failed, or Both

Windows 10 enables you to audit the following types of events:

- **Account logon:** Logon or logoff by a domain user account at a domain controller or using a local account. You should track both success and failure.

- **Account management:** Creation, modification, or deletion of computer, user, or group accounts. Also included are enabling and disabling of accounts and changing or resetting passwords. You should track both success and failure.

- **Directory service access:** Access to an AD DS object as specified by the object's SACL. This category includes the four subcategories mentioned earlier in this section; enabling directory service access from the Group Policy Management Editor enables all four subcategories. Enable this category for failures (if you record success, a large number of events will be logged).

- **Logon events:** Logon or logoff by a user at a member server or client computer. You should track both success and failure (success logging can record an unauthorized access that succeeded).

- **Object access:** Access by a user to an object such as a file, folder, or printer. You need to configure auditing in each object's SACL to track access to that object. Track success and failure to access important resources on your network.

- **Policy change:** Modification of policies including user rights assignment, trust, and audit policies. This category is not normally needed unless unusual events are occurring.

- **Privilege use:** Use of a user right, such as changing the system time. Track failure events for this category.

- **Process tracking:** Actions performed by an application. This category is primarily for application developers and does not need to be enabled in most cases.

- **System events:** Events taking place on a computer, such as an improper shutdown or a disk with very little free space remaining. Track success and failure events.

Group Policy or Local Security Policy enables you to configure success or failure for these types of actions. In other words, you can choose to record successful actions, failed attempts at performing these actions, or both. For example, if you are concerned about intruders that might be attempting to access your network, you can log failed logon events. You can also track successful logon events, which is useful in case the intruders succeed in accessing your network. For purposes of auditing files, folders, or printers, you need to enable object access auditing.

There is an additional policy that is more applicable to domain controllers than it is for Windows 10 client computers; that is, the Audit Account Logon Events. This, although similar to Audit Logon Events, will only trigger an event log entry when a user logs on to a computer but has been authenticated by another computer. You might want to use this and the Audit Logon Event policies together on your domain controllers to get an idea of how your AD DS site configuration is affecting your logon traffic, but it will not give you much to go on for a Windows 10 computer that is not part of a domain.

NOTE   For more information on auditing and new features in Windows 10 and Windows Server 2016, refer to "Security Auditing" at https://technet.microsoft.com/en-us/itpro/windows/keep-secure/security-auditing-overview.

Security Options

The Security Options subnode within this node includes a large set of policy options, as shown in Figure 8-13, that are important in controlling security aspects of the local computer. The list that follows describes several of the more important options you should be familiar with.

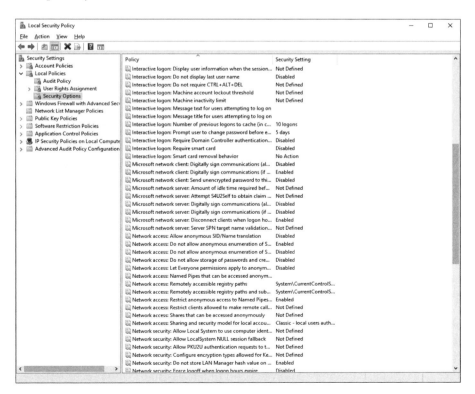

Figure 8-13   Security Options Subnode Containing a Comprehensive Set of Policy Settings That Help Enhance the Security of a Windows 10 Computer

- **Accounts: Block Microsoft Accounts:** First introduced in Windows 8, this policy allows you to prevent users from adding Microsoft accounts. By selecting Users Can't Add Microsoft Accounts, you can prevent users from adding Microsoft accounts, switching local accounts to a Microsoft account, or connecting a domain account to a Microsoft account. By selecting Users Can't Add or Log On with Microsoft Accounts, you can prevent existing Microsoft account users from logging on. Be aware that this option might make it impossible for an existing administrator to log on if the administrator is using a Microsoft account. Microsoft recommends that you keep this policy disabled or not configured.

- **Accounts: Rename Administrator Account:** This option renames the default administrator account to a value you specify. Intruders cannot simply look for "Administrator" when attempting to crack your network.

- **Interactive Logon: Do Not Display Last User Name:** Enable this option to prevent the username of the last logged-on user from appearing in the logon dialog box, thus preventing another individual from seeing a username. This can also help to reduce lockouts.

- **Interactive Logon: Require Smart Card:** When enabled, users must employ a smart card to log on to the computer.

- **User Account Control:** Several policy settings determine the behavior of the UAC prompt for administrative and nonadministrative users, including behavior by applications that are located in secure locations on the computer, such as %ProgramFiles% or %Windir%. We discuss UAC in the next section.

> **NOTE**   For more information on the policy settings in the Security Options subnode, refer to "Security Options" at https://technet.microsoft.com/en-us/library/cc749096(v=ws.10).aspx.

You can obtain additional information on many of these policy settings in the Windows 10 Help and Support Center.

Security for Mobile Devices

With the new focus on mobility, tablets, laptops and Windows Mobile devices, cloud services, and other innovations, the workforce in companies and organizations is more mobile than ever. This presents both opportunities and challenges for workers and organizations. As Edward Snowden and Julian Assange's WikiLeaks website have so forcefully demonstrated, information leaks happen at every level of government and private organizations.

Although avoiding intentional leaks presents its own challenges, it is just as important to ensure that unintentional leaks do not occur. Making sure that those travelling mobile devices are protected when they are lost or stolen is vitally important. Laptops and mobile devices are left at the airport, in taxi cabs and Uber cars, in hotels, and at other places at increasing frequency. When someone picks up one of these devices, accessing the data stored on it can be trivially easy.

BitLocker and BitLocker To Go are encryption technologies available on Windows that can prevent unauthorized access of mobile devices by protecting the entire hard drive or storage device. Protecting the device boot process with passwords also helps prevent unauthorized access. You will learn about these technologies and how to use them to protect data in this section.

Configuring BitLocker and BitLocker To Go

First introduced with Windows Vista, BitLocker is a hardware-enabled data encryption feature that serves to protect data on a computer that is exposed to unauthorized physical access. Available on the Pro and Enterprise editions of Windows 10, BitLocker encrypts the entire Windows volume, thereby preventing unauthorized users from circumventing file and system permissions in Windows or attempting to access information on the protected partition from another computer or operating system. BitLocker even protects the data should an unauthorized user physically remove the hard drive from the computer and use other means to attempt access to the data.

BitLocker uses startup keys to allow users to access the encrypted drive when the boot drive is encrypted. Typically the startup keys are stored on the hardware-based TPM module, as discussed in previous chapters. BitLocker can also be used on computers without TPM using removable media such as a USB drive. Storing startup keys is discussed in the next subsection.

Introduced with Windows 7 and available for Windows 10 Pro, Education, and Enterprise editions is BitLocker To Go, which offers similar data encryption features to USB portable drives and external hard drives. BitLocker To Go creates a virtual volume on the USB drive, which is encrypted by means of an encryption key stored on the flash drive. BitLocker To Go also includes a Data Recovery Agent feature, which is modeled on the Encrypting File System (EFS) recovery agent that you learned about earlier in this chapter.

BitLocker Drive Encryption

Available on selected editions of Windows 10 and all editions of Windows Server 2016, BitLocker utilizes the Trusted Platform Module (TPM) version 1.2 to provide secure protection of encryption keys and checking of key components when

Windows is booting. A TPM is a microchip that is built in to a computer that is used to store cryptographic information such as encryption keys. Information stored on the TPM is more secure from external software attacks and physical theft. You can store keys and passwords on a USB flash drive that the user must insert to boot his computer. You can also employ an option that requires the user to supply a PIN code, thereby requiring multifactor authentication before the data becomes available for use. If an unauthorized individual has tampered with or modified system files or data in any way, the computer will not boot up.

On a computer that is equipped with a compatible TPM, BitLocker uses this TPM to lock the encryption keys that protect the contents of the protected drive; this includes the operating system and Registry files when you have used BitLocker to protect the system drive. When starting up the computer, TPM must verify the state of the computer before the keys are accessed. Consequently, an attacker cannot access the data by mounting the hard drive in a different computer.

At startup, TPM compares a hash of the operating system configuration with an earlier snapshot, thereby verifying the integrity of the startup process and releasing the keys. If BitLocker detects any security problem (such as a disk error, change to the BIOS, or changes to startup files), it locks the drive and enters Recovery mode. You can store encryption keys and restoration passwords on a USB flash drive or a separate file for additional data security and recovery capability. Should a user need to recover data using BitLocker's recovery mode, she merely needs to enter a recovery password to access data and the Windows operating system.

The following are several enhancements to BitLocker in Windows 10:

- Nonadministrative users are able to reset the BitLocker PIN and password on protected drives.

- When you enable BitLocker, you can choose to encrypt just the used space on a drive. Additional space is encrypted as required.

- BitLocker supports pre-encrypted hard drives that meet the Windows Logo requirements.

- Administrators can unlock BitLocker-protected drives without the PIN entry when using a special network key on a trusted wired network. This enables you to perform remote maintenance on BitLocker-protected computers without physical presence at the computer.

- On an AD DS network, you can tie a BitLocker key protector to a user, computer, or group account. You can use this key protector to unlock BitLocker-protected data volumes when logged on with proper AD DS credentials.

- In Windows 10, BitLocker has support for encryption on computers equipped with a TPM that supports connected standby.

A user's computer does not need to be equipped with the TPM to use BitLocker. If your computer is equipped with TPM, you can use BitLocker in any of the following modes:

- **TPM Only:** TPM alone validates the boot files, the operating system files, and encrypted drive volumes during system startup. This mode provides a normal startup and logon experience to the user. However, if the TPM is missing or the integrity of the system has changed, BitLocker enters Recovery mode, in which you will be required to provide a recovery key to access the computer.

- **TPM and PIN:** Uses both TPM and a user-supplied PIN for validation. You must enter this PIN correctly or BitLocker enters Recovery mode.

- **TPM and Startup Key:** Uses both TPM and a startup key for validation. The user must provide a USB flash drive containing the startup key. If the user does not have this USB flash drive, BitLocker enters Recovery mode.

- **TPM and Smart Card Certificate:** Uses both TPM and a smart card certificate for validation. The user must provide a smart card containing a valid certificate to log on. If the smart card is not available or the certificate is not valid, BitLocker enters Recovery mode.

> **NOTE**   For additional introductory information on BitLocker in Windows 10 and Windows Server 2016, refer to "BitLocker" at https://technet.microsoft.com/en-us/itpro/windows/keep-secure/bitlocker-overview.

> **NOTE**   Many newer computers are equipped with TPM, but TPM is not always activated. You might need to enter your BIOS setup system to enable TPM. The location of this setting depends on the BIOS in use, but is typically in the Advanced or Security section.

Enabling BitLocker

If your computer is equipped with a TPM, you can use the following procedure to enable BitLocker on your operating system drive:

Step 1.   Access the Control Panel and click **System and Security > BitLocker Drive Encryption**. You receive the BitLocker Drive Encryption dialog box, as shown in Figure 8-14. You can also access this utility by typing **bitlocker** into the Search field and then selecting **Manage BitLocker** from the Programs list.

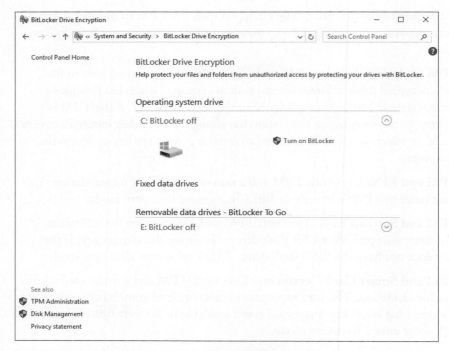

Figure 8-14   Using BitLocker to Protect All Available Drives

Step 2.   Opposite the drive you want to encrypt, click the **Turn on BitLocker** link. You can also right-click the desired drive in an Explorer window and choose **Turn on BitLocker**.

Step 3.   If you receive a UAC prompt, click **Yes** to proceed.

> **NOTE**   If you receive a dialog box indicating This Device Can't Use a Trusted Platform Module, as shown later in Figure 8-24, it means that the computer does not have a compatible TPM module. You will need to perform the procedure given in the "Configuring Startup Key Storage" section before you can enable BitLocker.

Step 4.   Windows checks your computer's configuration, and after a few seconds, the BitLocker Drive Encryption setup window appears, informing you that the computer will prepare your drive for BitLocker and then encrypt the drive.

Step 5.   Click **Next**. Windows prepares your drive for BitLocker and informs you that an existing drive or unallocated free space will be used to enable BitLocker.

Step 6. Click **Next**. You are informed that you will no longer be able to use Windows Recovery Environment unless it is manually enabled and moved to the system drive.

NOTE If you have previously configured BitLocker drive encryption, you might not see all of Steps 3 to 6 when you next perform this procedure.

Step 7. Click **Next**. The Choose How to Unlock Your Drive at Startup page provides options for inserting a USB flash drive or entering a password. Choose the desired option. If you choose the Insert a USB Flash Drive option, insert the drive and select it from the Save Your Startup Key page that appears. Then click **Save**. If you choose the Enter a Password option, type and confirm the password on the page that appears.

Step 8. Click **Next**. The How Do You Want to Back Up Your Recovery Key? page provides the four options shown in Figure 8-15. Use one or more of these options to save the recovery password. If you print it, ensure that you save the printed document in a secure location. Click **Next** when finished.

Figure 8-15 *Four Options for Storing Your Recovery Key*

Step 9. You receive the Choose How Much of Your Drive to Encrypt page shown in Figure 8-16. Choose the appropriate option and then click **Next**.

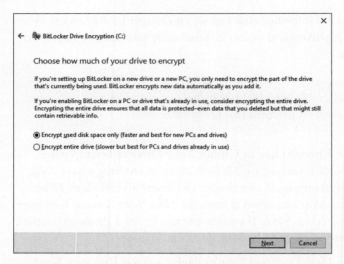

Figure 8-16   Choosing to Encrypt Used Disk Space Only (the Default) or Encrypt the Entire Drive

Step 10.   You may be asked whether to use New Encryption Mode or Compatible Mode. If you are encrypting a drive that you may want to later remove and use in a different device, use the Compatible mode. The New Encryption mode is recommended. Click **Next**.

Step 11.   You receive the Are You Ready to Encrypt This Drive? dialog box shown in Figure 8-17. Ensure that the check box labeled Run BitLocker System Check is selected, and then click **Continue** to proceed.

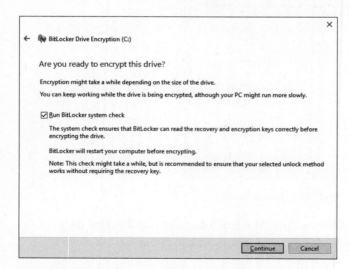

Figure 8-17   Selecting Continue to Encrypt Your Partition

Step 12.   You will need to restart your computer to proceed. Click **Restart Now**.

Step 13.   Encryption takes place and Windows 8.1 displays an icon in the Notification area. This process can take an hour or longer, but you can use your computer while it is occurring. You can track the progress of encryption by hovering your mouse pointer over this icon. You are informed when encryption is complete. Click **Close**.

CAUTION   Ensure that you do not lose the recovery password. If you lose the recovery password, your Windows installation and all data stored on its partition will be permanently lost. You will need to repartition your hard drive and reinstall Windows. Consequently, you should create at least two copies of the password as described in the previous procedure, and store these in a secure location.

Managing BitLocker

After you've encrypted your drive using BitLocker, the BitLocker applet shows additional options for the protected drive, as shown in Figure 8-18. The Suspend Protection option enables you to temporarily disable BitLocker. Select this option and then click **Yes**. After doing so, this option changes to Resume Protection; click it to reenable BitLocker. The Back Up Your Recovery Key option enables you to create an additional backup; selecting this option brings up the dialog box previously shown in Figure 8-15. You can also back up this information into Active Directory if your computer belongs to an Active Directory Domain Services (AD DS) domain.

The change password option brings up a Change Startup Password dialog box that is similar to the dialog box presented when you change a user account password. The Remove Password option enables you to remove a password; it is available only if you have configured another unlocking mechanism, such as a USB key.

The Turn Off BitLocker option enables you to remove BitLocker protection. To do so, select **Turn Off BitLocker**. On the BitLocker Drive Encryption dialog box that appears, select **Turn Off BitLocker**. This procedure decrypts your volume and discards all encryption keys; it begins immediately without further prompts. You will be able to monitor the decryption action from an icon in the Notification area.

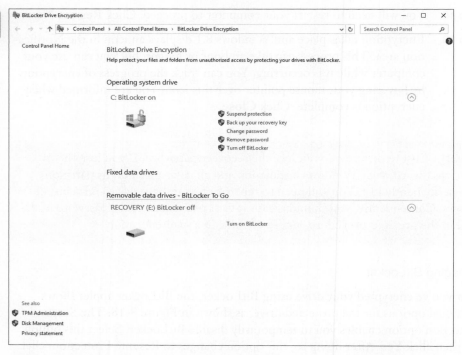

Figure 8-18   BitLocker Applet Displaying a Distinctive Icon for the Protected Drive and Providing Several Options for Its Management

BitLocker To Go

As already mentioned, BitLocker To Go extends the full volume encryption capabilities of BitLocker to USB flash drives and portable hard drives. You can protect all portable drives regardless of whether they are formatted with the FAT, FAT32, or NTFS file systems. Microsoft engineers modified BitLocker to overlay what they called a "discovery volume" on top of the original physical volume on the portable drive. This volume includes a BitLocker To Go Reader that also enables use of the BitLocker To Go volume on computers running older versions of Windows, such as Vista. Users of these computers can download a reader from the Microsoft Download Center.

Use the following procedure to enable BitLocker To Go:

Step 1.   Access the Control Panel and click **System and Security > BitLocker Drive Encryption** to display the screen previously shown in Figure 8-14.

Step 2.   Insert the USB drive and click **Turn On BitLocker** beside the drive icon.

Step 3.   You receive the Choose How You Want to Unlock This Drive dialog box shown in Figure 8-19. If using a password, select this option and then type and confirm a strong password. If using a smart card, insert the smart card in your reader. Then click **Next**.

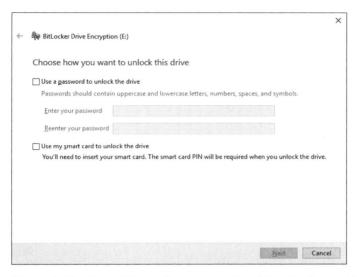

Figure 8-19   Using Either a Password or Smart Card to Secure Your USB Drive with BitLocker To Go

Step 4.   Select an option to save the recovery password to your Microsoft account, save it to a file, or print it. Then click **Next**.

Step 5.   You receive the Choose How Much of Your Drive to Encrypt page. Choose the appropriate option and then click **Next**.

Step 6.   You receive the Choose Which Encryption Mode To Use page. For a removable USB drive, you should select the **Compatible Mode** option (recommended for drives that can be moved from this device). Select the option you want and then click **Next**.

Step 7.   From the Are You Ready to Encrypt the Drive page, select **Start Encrypting**.

Step 8.   You are returned to the BitLocker Drive Encryption applet, which tracks the progress of encrypting your drive and informs you when the drive is encrypted. Do not disconnect your drive until encryption is completed.

CAUTION   Do not enable BitLocker To Go on the USB drive containing your Bit-Locker startup key. Windows 10 currently does not permit this, although a future update or service pack might add this capability.

BitLocker Policies

Besides the policy already mentioned to enable BitLocker on a computer that is not equipped with a TPM, Group Policy has a series of settings that help you to manage BitLocker. You can access these policies from the Computer Configuration\Administrative Templates\Windows Components\BitLocker Drive Encryption node. This node has three subnodes: Fixed Data Drives, Operating System Drives, and Removable Data Drives, as well as several policies that affect all types of drives. Microsoft provides recommendations for many of these settings at "BitLocker Group Policy Settings" at http://technet.microsoft.com/en-us/library/jj679890.aspx. Although it references Windows 8.1 and Windows Server 2012, the Group Policy settings have not changed for Windows 10.

Operating System Drives

As shown in Figure 8-20, you can configure a large number of policies that govern BitLocker as used on operating system drives, including the following:

- **Allow Network Unlock at Startup:** Introduced for Windows 8 and Windows Server 2012, this policy controls a portion of the behavior of the Network Unlock feature. When enabled, clients using BitLocker are enabled to create the necessary network key protector during encryption.

- **Allow Secure Boot for Integrity Validation:** This policy controls how BitLocker-enabled system volumes behave in conjunction with Secure Boot. When enabled, Secure Boot validation takes place during the boot process, verifying boot configuration data (BCD) settings for platform integrity.

- **Require Additional Authentication at Startup:** As mentioned in the "Configuring Startup Key Storage" section later in this chapter, this setting enables you to use BitLocker on a computer without a TPM. By enabling this policy, you can also specify whether BitLocker requires additional authentication including a startup key and/or PIN.

- **Require Additional Authentication at Startup (Windows Server 2008 and Windows Vista):** Enables similar settings for Windows Vista and Windows Server 2008 computers, except that you cannot utilize both a startup key and PIN.

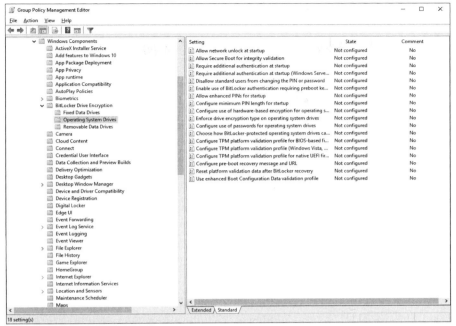

Figure 8-20   Group Policy Providing Settings for BitLocker Used on Operating System Drives

- **Allow Enhanced PINs for Startup:** Enables the use of a PIN that contains additional characters, including uppercase and lowercase letters, symbols, numerals, and spaces.

- **Configure Minimum PIN Length for Startup:** Specifies a minimum length for the startup PIN. You can choose a minimum length of anywhere from 4 to 20 digits.

- **Configure Use of Hardware-Based Encryption for Operating System Drives:** Enables you to manage use of hardware-based encryption on fixed data drives and specify permitted encryption algorithms.

- **Enforce Drive Encryption Type on Operating System Drives:** Enables you to specify the encryption type used by BitLocker. You can choose either Full Encryption to require that the entire drive be encrypted, or Used Space Only Encryption to require only the portion of the drive in use to be encrypted.

- **Choose How Users Can Recover BitLocker-Protected Drives:** Enables the use of a data recovery agent. We discuss this policy later in this section.

- **Configure TPM Platform Validation Profile for BIOS-Based Firmware Configurations:** Enables you to specify how the TPM security hardware secures the BitLocker encryption key on computers running Windows Server 2012 R2 or Windows 8.1. The validation profile includes a set of Platform Configuration Register (PCR) indices, each of which is associated with components that run at startup. You can select from a series of indices provided in the policy's options.

- **Configure TPM Platform Validation Profile (Windows Vista, Windows Server 2008, Windows 7, Windows Server 2008 R2):** Provides a validation profile with a similar set of PCR indices for computers running Windows Vista, Windows Server 2008, Windows 7, or Windows Server 2008 R2.

- **Configure TPM Platform Validation Profile for Native UEFI Firmware Configurations:** Provides a validation profile and PCR indices for Windows 8.1 or Windows Server 2012 R2 computers equipped with UEFI firmware (as opposed to BIOS-based firmware).

Fixed Data Drive Policies

As shown in Figure 8-21, you can configure the following policies that govern Bit-Locker used on fixed data drives (in other words, internal hard drive partitions containing data but not operating system files):

- **Configure Use of Smart Cards on Fixed Data Drives:** Enables you to specify whether smart cards can be used to authenticate user access to drives protected by BitLocker. You can optionally require the use of smart cards.

- **Deny Write Access to Fixed Drives Not Protected by BitLocker:** Enables you to require BitLocker protection on writable drives. If enabled, any drives not protected by BitLocker are read-only.

- **Configure Use of Hardware-Based Encryption for Fixed Data Drives:** Enables you to manage use of hardware-based encryption on fixed data drives and specify permitted encryption algorithms.

- **Enforce Drive Encryption Type on Fixed Data Drives:** Enables you to specify the encryption type used by BitLocker. You can choose either Full Encryption to require that the entire drive be encrypted, or Used Space Only encryption to require only the portion of the drive in use to be encrypted.

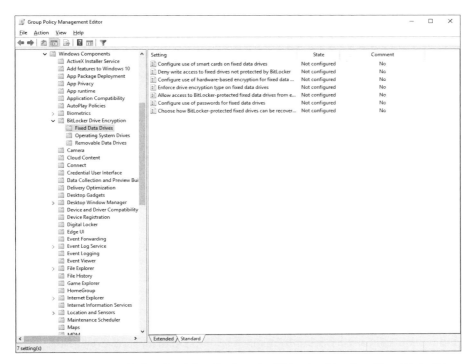

Figure 8-21   Group Policy Providing Settings for BitLocker Used on Fixed Data Drives

- **Allow Access to BitLocker-Protected Fixed Data Drives from Earlier Versions of Windows:** Specifies whether drives formatted with the FAT or FAT32 file system can be unlocked and viewed on computers running earlier Windows versions (back to Windows XP SP2).

- **Configure Use of Passwords for Fixed Data Drives:** Enables you to specify whether a password is required for unlocking BitLocker-protected fixed data drives. You can optionally specify that a password is required, and you can choose to allow or require password complexity and specify the minimum password length.

- **Choose How BitLocker-Protected Fixed Drives Can Be Recovered:** Similar to the corresponding operating system drives policy.

More information on all these policies is available from the Help field in each policy's Properties dialog box. These policies are also available for removable drives (BitLocker To Go) in the Removable Data Drives subnode of Group Policy.

Use of Data Recovery Agents

A data recovery agent (DRA) is a user account that is configured for recovering data encrypted with BitLocker in a manner analogous to the EFS recovery agent described previously in this chapter. The DRA uses his smart card certificates and public keys to accomplish this action.

To specify a DRA for a BitLocker-protected drive, you must first designate the recovery agent by opening the Local Group Policy Editor and navigating to the Computer Configuration\Windows Settings\Security Settings\Public Key Policies\BitLocker Drive Encryption node. Right-click this node and choose **Add Data Recovery Agent**. This starts a wizard that is similar to that used for creating EFS data recovery agents. You can browse for the required certificates or select them from AD DS in a domain environment.

After you've specified your data recovery agent, you need to access the Computer Configuration\Administrative Templates\Windows Components\BitLocker Drive Encryption node of Group Policy and enable the **Provide the Unique Identifiers for Your Organization** policy (see Figure 8-22). In the text boxes provided, specify a unique identifier that will be associated with drives that are enabled with BitLocker. This identifier uniquely associates the drives with your company or department and is required for BitLocker to manage and update data recovery agents. After doing so, this identifier will be automatically associated with any drives on which you enable BitLocker.

You can add this identifier to drives previously protected with BitLocker by opening an administrative command prompt and typing the following command:

```
manage-bde -SetIdentifier drive_letter
```

where *drive_letter* is the drive letter for the BitLocker-protected drive. This utility sets the identifier to the value you've specified in Group Policy and displays a message informing you that this identifier has been set.

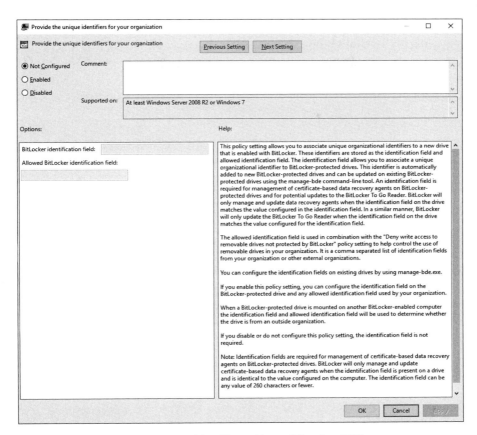

Figure 8-22   Providing a Unique Identifier to Use a BitLocker DRA

After you have specified a DRA and the unique identifiers, you can configure policies in each subnode of the Computer Configuration\Administrative Templates\
Windows Components\BitLocker Drive Encryption node of Group Policy that
choose how BitLocker-protected drives can be recovered. Each of the three subnodes contains a similar policy setting that is shown for operating system drives in
Figure 8-23. Enable each of these policies as required and select the **Allow Data
Recovery Agent** check box. Then configure the following options as required:

- **Allow 48-Digit Recovery Password:** This drop-down list provides choices
  to allow, require, or not allow a 48-digit recovery password. Use of a 48-digit
  recovery password improves DRA security.

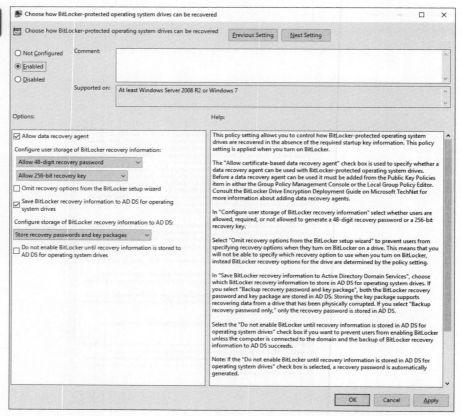

Figure 8-23   Group Policy Providing These Data Recovery Options for Operating System Drives

- **Allow 256-Bit Recovery Key:** This drop-down list provides choices to allow, require, or not allow a 256-bit recovery key. Use of a 256-bit recovery key improves DRA security.

- **Omit Recovery Options from the BitLocker Setup Wizard:** Blocks the appearance of the recovery options previously shown in Figure 8-15; when enabled, these recovery options are determined by policy settings.

- **Save BitLocker Recovery Information to AD DS for Operating System Drives:** Enables you to choose the BitLocker recovery information that will be stored in AD DS.

- **Configure Storage of BitLocker Recovery Information to AD DS:** Determines how much recovery information is stored in AD DS when you have selected the preceding option. You can choose to store recovery passwords and key packages or to store recovery passwords only.

- **Do Not Enable BitLocker Until Recovery Information Is Stored to AD DS for Operating System Drives:** When enabled, prevents users from enabling BitLocker unless the computer is attached to the domain and Bit-Locker recovery information can be backed up to AD DS.

Similar options are provided for fixed and removable data drives; the wording of the last policy setting changes to reflect the type of drive being configured.

> **NOTE** BitLocker provides several additional DRA management options, including verification of the identification field and listing of configured DRAs. For more information, refer to "Using Data Recovery Agents with BitLocker" at http://technet.microsoft.com/en-us/library/dd875560(WS.10).aspx. For additional information on BitLocker as a whole, refer to "BitLocker Frequently Asked Questions (FAQ)" at https://technet.microsoft.com/en-us/itpro/windows/keep-secure/bitlocker-frequently-asked-questions.

Microsoft BitLocker Administration and Monitoring (MBAM)

For large enterprises that need to manage BitLocker encryption across a large number of client devices and workstations in an Active Directory forest, the Microsoft BitLocker Administration and Monitoring (MBAM) tool provides a simplified interface. MBAM is configured through custom Group Policy Templates, allowing organizations to set BitLocker Drive Encryption policies as needed, as well as providing monitoring of the encryption status of computers and the entire enterprise.

MBAM can be implemented as a component of the System Center Configuration Manager (SCCM), or as a standalone tool. Deploying MBAM requires a set of server features configured on one or more server computers, based on the size and requirements of the organization. Typically in a large enterprise, the features will be distributed across multiple servers:

- Recovery Database
- Compliance and Audit Database
- Reports Database, including the SQL Server Reporting Services role
- Administration and Monitoring Server, which runs the Web Server Role for hosting the Administration and Monitoring interface
- Self-Service Portal, which also runs a Web Server Role and hosts the self-service interface for end-user support
- Management Workstation running the MBAM client used to configure and manage the MBAM infrastructure components

With the MBAM infrastructure in place, you can manage BitLocker and the Bit-Locker enabled computers in your organization. For instance if a user enters the incorrect PIN too many times, he may get locked out of the TPM, and the computer. Using the Administration and Monitoring website, you can retrieve the TPM password file and reset the TPM lockout.

You can also use MBAM to recover a drive in the event of a hardware failure, change in personnel, or if the encryption keys for the drive are lost for any reason.

NOTE   Details of the deployment and operation of MBAM are beyond the scope of this text and the 70-697 and 70-698 exams, but you should know about the concepts and how MBAM can be used to manage BitLocker across enterprise computers. For details of MBAM operations and management, start with "Operations for MBAM 2.5" at https://technet.microsoft.com/en-us/itpro/mdop/mbam-v25/operations-for-mbam-25.

Configuring Startup Key Storage

In the previous section, we learned about BitLocker drive encryption and using startup keys to unlock the drive for access. TPM is typically used for storing the startup key, but, as mentioned, you can use a USB flash drive or other removable disk instead. In this section we discuss using USB drives for the storage of startup keys for BitLocker, as well as other methods for securing Windows on a mobile device, and how to protect your data from unauthorized access even when it is lost or stolen.

If the computer does not have a TPM, BitLocker uses either a USB flash drive or smart card containing a startup key. In this case, BitLocker provides encryption, but not the added security of locking keys with the TPM. When you use a USB drive to store your startup key, it is vital that you keep it secure, which means maintaining a backup. If your USB drive becomes corrupt, nonfunctional, or lost, you will permanently lose access to your Windows system.

Preparing a Computer Without a TPM to Use BitLocker

You can use a computer that does not have a TPM module if you have a USB flash drive to store the encryption keys and password. By default, Windows blocks an attempt to enable BitLocker on such a computer and displays the message shown in Figure 8-24.

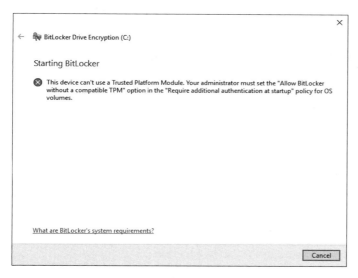

Figure 8-24 Windows Displaying TPM Error for BitLocker

As mentioned in the error, you need to enable BitLocker without a TPM from Group Policy, as the following procedure describes:

Step 1. Access the Search field and type **gpedit.msc** into the Search text box. Then select **gpedit.msc** from the list that is displayed.

Step 2. In the Local Group Policy Editor, navigate to Computer Configuration\ Administrative Templates\Windows Components\BitLocker Drive Encryption\Operating System Drives.

Step 3. Double-click **Require Additional Authentication at Startup**, enable this policy, select the **Allow BitLocker Without a Compatible TPM** option, and then click **OK**.

Step 4. Close the Local Group Policy Editor.

Step 5. In the Search box or Cortana, type **Gpupdate /force**, and then press **Enter**. This forces Group Policy to apply immediately.

After you've completed this procedure, you are ready to enable BitLocker as described next. The procedure is similar to the procedure in the previous section, but without a TPM available, Windows presents a few different options. Begin the procedure as described in "Enabling BitLocker" in the "BitLocker Drive Encryption" subsection. Select **BitLocker Drive Encryption** from the Control Panel, and select **Turn on BitLocker** for the drive.

Step 1. Windows checks your computer's configuration, and after a few seconds, the BitLocker Drive Encryption setup window appears, informing you that the computer will prepare your drive for BitLocker and then encrypt the drive.

Step 2. Click **Next**. Windows prepares your drive for BitLocker and informs you that an existing drive or unallocated free space will be used to enable BitLocker.

Step 3. Click **Next**. You are informed that you will no longer be able to use Windows Recovery Environment unless it is manually enabled and moved to the system drive.

Step 4. Click **Next**. You receive the Choose How to Unlock Your Drive at Startup window shown in Figure 8-25. Choose to either insert a USB flash drive or enter a password as desired.

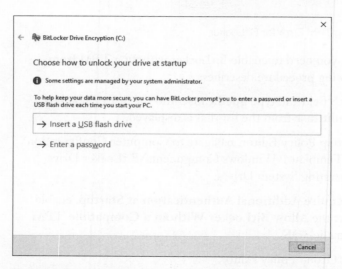

Figure 8-25 BitLocker Drive Encryption Applet in Control Panel Offering Two Choices for Unlocking Your Drive at Startup

Step 5. The next step depends on the choice made in Figure 8-25. If you choose to insert a USB flash drive, insert the drive and click **Save**. If you choose to use a password, type and confirm a strong password when prompted. Then click **Next**.

Step 6. If you save it to a USB flash drive, you see the dialog box shown in Figure 8-26. Click **Save**, and then click **Next**.

Figure 8-26   Selecting the Appropriate USB Drive for Saving Your Password

Step 7.   The How Do You Want to Back Up Your Recovery Key? page provides the three options shown previously in Figure 8-25, as well as the additional option to use a USB drive. Use one or more of these options to save the recovery password. If you print it, ensure that you save the printed document in a secure location.

The remainder of the process is the same as using a TPM (see Steps 8–11 in the "Enabling BitLocker" section), including restarting and encrypting the drive.

After you have completed this procedure, you must have the USB drive to start your computer if you have chosen this option in Step 5 of the previous procedure. Alternately, you can use the Recovery mode and type the recovery password that was automatically created while enabling BitLocker. BitLocker provides the BitLocker Drive Encryption Recovery Console to enable you to insert the USB drive that contains the recovery password. Or press Enter, type the recovery password, and press Enter again.

CAUTION   Ensure that you do not lose the recovery password. If you lose the recovery password, your Windows installation and all data stored on its partition will be permanently lost. You will need to repartition your hard drive and reinstall Windows. Consequently, you should create at least two copies of the password as described in the previous procedure and store these in a secure location. Do not leave the startup USB flash drive in your laptop bag; attach it to your key chain, or store it elsewhere on your person. Note that you may end up with two USB drives—one with the startup key and the other with the recovery password.

Syskey Startup Keys

Another method used to protect Windows computers, included in Windows since NT 4.0 SP3, is Syskey. The Syskey utility encrypts the SAM database, which contains all the login credentials and passwords on the local system. Note that Syskey does *not* protect your data from access if your computer is stolen or lost, because it encrypts only the SAM database, not your files or the hard drive. Syskey is useful for protecting against casual intrusion, however, by providing a layer of security to your login accounts.

If you have used EFS to encrypt files, or you have saved or cached credentials, Syskey will also protect that information because your account login is used to unlock EFS files, your credentials stored in Credential Manager, and personal certificates. Syskey will also protect the master key that Windows uses to unlock IPsec keys, computer keys, and SSL certificate keys.

Syskey can be used with a simple password, but the best level of security is to use a floppy disk or removable drive to store the startup key. The removable disk is then required to sign on to the computer and access any protected information. As with a BitLocker startup drive, you should take care to keep the removable drive or floppy disk with your startup key secured, stored separately from the computer, and be sure to maintain a backup in case the primary one is lost or damaged. Use the following procedure to enable Syskey:

Step 1.   Access the Search bar or Cortana and type **syskey** into the Search box. When you select it, Windows displays a UAC confirmation dialog. Select **Yes** to start the Syskey wizard shown in Figure 8-27.

Figure 8-27   Securing the Windows Account Database

Step 2.   Select the Update button.

Step 3.   On the Startup Key page, you have the option of setting a Password Startup or using a System Generated Password , which can be stored locally or on a floppy disk. We want to use the most secure option, so select **Store Startup Key on Floppy Disk**, and then click **OK**.

Step 4.   The computer will prompt you to enter the disk. Make sure the disk is in the drive, and then click **OK**.

Step 5.   After Windows writes the startup key to the floppy disk, you will receive a message that the disk will now be required to start up the computer.

Step 6.   Finally, the Success dialog box is displayed, indicating that the Account Database Startup Key was changed.

The next time Windows starts, Syskey will prompt you to enter the startup disk. You will need to insert the disk with the startup key and click **OK** before Windows will load.

> **NOTE**   Although Syskey will only store your startup key on the A: drive, you can use a USB flash drive if you do not have a floppy disk drive. Simply run the Disk Management tool, right-click on your USB drive, and select Change Drive Letter and Paths. On a computer with no floppy disk drive, you can assign the USB drive the letter A:, and then run the Syskey utility to write your startup key there.

Exam Preparation Tasks

Review All the Key Topics

Review the most important topics in the chapter, noted with the Key Topics icon in the outer margin of the page. Table 8-4 lists a reference of these key topics and the page numbers on which each is found.

Table 8-4   Key Topics for Chapter 8

Key Topic Element	Description	Page Number
List	Requirements for deploying Dynamic Access Control	398
Figure 8-7	The Advanced Attributes dialog box enables you to compress or encrypt a file	406
Step List	Backing up EFS keys	408
List	Security-related policy settings	411
List	Event types that can be audited in Windows 10	414
Paragraph	Describes how BitLocker functions	417

Key Topic Element	Description	Page Number
Step List	Shows how to enable BitLocker	419
Figure 8-18	Shows management options for BitLocker-encrypted drives	424
Figure 8-20	Shows BitLocker Policy settings for providing a unique identifier to use a BitLocker DRA	427
Figure 8-23	Group Policy options providing data recovery for operating system drives	432
List	Server features required for implementation of MBAM	433
Figure 8-26	Shows how to select the appropriate USB drive for saving your password	437

Complete Tables and Lists from Memory

Print a copy of Appendix B, "Memory Tables" (found on the book's website), or at least the section for this chapter, and complete the tables and lists from memory. Appendix C, "Memory Tables Answer Key," also on the website, includes completed tables and lists to check your work.

Definitions of Key Terms

Define the following key terms from this chapter and check your answers in the glossary.

account lockout policy, Admin Approval mode, BitLocker, BitLocker To Go, data recovery agent, Local Security Policy, Microsoft BitLocker Administration and Monitoring (MBAM), password policy, Secure Boot, SmartScreen, UEFI

This chapter covers the following subjects:

- **Configuring Data Storage:** Windows 10 enables you to create several types of disk volumes on your computer. This section introduces you to these volume types and shows you how to create, manage, and troubleshoot problems with disks. It also shows you how to defragment your disks so that performance is kept optimum.

- **Supporting Data Storage:** This section provides an overview of Distributed File System (DFS), which places shared folders located on different servers into a single folder tree, to simply access by users. Storage Spaces is a recent technology innovation in Windows that lets you consolidate multiple disks into a single logical drive. This section introduces Storage Spaces in Windows and how it is used and configured. It also covers OneDrive cloud storage for Windows systems.

- **User Data Migration and Configuration:** You can redirect library folders, such as documents, music, pictures, and videos, to common locations such as shared folders on a server. This enables you to keep track of users' documents and ensure that they are properly and regularly backed up.

- **Configuring Local, Roaming, and Mandatory Profiles:** Windows provides user profiles that are composed of desktop settings, files, application data, and the specific environment established by the user. You can configure roaming user profiles that are stored on a server so that they are available to a user regardless of the computer being used.

This chapter covers the following objectives for the 70-697 and 70-698 exams:

Support data storage: Identifying and resolving issues related to the following: DFS client including caching settings, storage spaces including capacity and fault tolerance, OneDrive.

Migrate and configure user data: Migrate user profiles; configure folder location; configure profiles including profile version, local, roaming, and mandatory.

Configure data storage: Configure disks, volumes, and files system options using Disk Management and Windows PowerShell; create and configure VHDs; configure removable devices; create and configure storage spaces; troubleshoot storage and removable device issues.

CHAPTER 9

Managing User Data

Now we take these file sharing concepts further and look into a Microsoft technology that assists users in locating these resources as their organizations grow in size and add additional file servers—the Distributed File System (DFS). DFS places all the shared resources into a single folder tree that encompasses all these servers and their shares, wherever they might be located on a large, sprawling network.

As the amount of information stored on hard disks and accessed across various types of networks has grown, information storage technology has kept pace. The Storage Spaces technology, which was first introduced for Windows 8 and Windows Server 2012, enables you to create cost-effective, highly available, scalable, and flexible storage systems by using virtualization technology to create pools of storage on groups of physical disks. Microsoft expects you to be up-to-date on this latest in information-storage technologies.

The OneDrive feature has become a staple of Microsoft's cloud offerings for Windows 10 and enables you to share images, documents, and so on among computers, smartphones, and other devices in different physical locations. Microsoft expects you to be knowledgeable about all these new features when taking the 70-697 exam.

Many companies can purchase new computers with Windows 10 already loaded or upgrade certain computers from Windows Vista, 7, or 8.1. Users who will be working with these computers may have been using older Windows computers for several years, and these computers will have applications with user- or company-specific settings as well as important data on them. Microsoft provides tools to assist you in migrating users and applications to new Windows 10 computers, and you are expected to know how to perform these migrations in an efficient manner as part of the 70-697 exam.

"Do I Know This Already?" Quiz

The "Do I Know This Already?" quiz allows you to assess whether you should read this entire chapter or simply jump to the "Exam Preparation Tasks" section for review. If you are in doubt, read the entire chapter. Table 9-1 outlines the major headings in this chapter and the corresponding "Do I Know This Already?" quiz questions. You can find the answers in Appendix A, "Answers to the 'Do I Know This Already?' Quizzes."

Table 9-1   "Do I Know This Already?" Foundation Topics Section-to-Question Mapping

Foundation Topics Section	Questions Covered in This Section
Configuring Data Storage	1–9
Supporting Data Storage	10–16
User Data Migration and Configuration	17–18
Configuring Local, Roaming, and Mandatory Profiles	19–20

CAUTION   The goal of self-assessment is to gauge your mastery of the topics in this chapter. If you do not know the answer to a question or are only partially sure of the answer, you should mark that question as wrong for purposes of the self-assessment. Giving yourself credit for an answer you correctly guess skews your self-assessment results and might provide you with a false sense of security.

1. Your hard disk is configured as a basic disk, and you do not want to convert it to dynamic storage because you want to enable dual-booting. Which of the following partition types can you configure on the disk? (Choose all that apply.)

    a. Simple volume

    b. Primary partition

    c. Extended partition

    d. Spanned volume

    e. Mirrored volume

    f. Striped volume

    g. Logical drive

    h. RAID-5 volume

2. You have added a new 5 TB hard disk to your Windows 10 computer and ini-
    tialized it. You now want to create a single volume that uses the entire space
    on the disk, so you start the DiskPart tool from an administrative command
    prompt. On attempting to create the volume, you receive an error. Which of
    the following commands should you execute first?

    a. **convert basic**

    b. **convert dynamic**

    c. **convert gpt**

    d. **convert mbr**

3. Which tab of a volume's Properties dialog box enables you to check the vol-
    ume for errors?

    a. General

    b. Tools

    c. Hardware

    d. Quota

    e. Customize

4. You want to add additional space to your D: partition so that you can store
    a large number of digital images. You do not want to add an additional drive
    letter, so you run the Extend Volume Wizard. What type of volume are you
    creating?

    a. Simple volume

    b. Spanned volume

    c. Mirrored volume

    d. RAID-5 volume

5. Which of the following RAID technologies are fault-tolerant? (Choose all that
    apply.)

    a. Spanning

    b. Striping

    c. Mirroring

    d. Striping with parity

6.   You have four hard disks in your computer and want to create a RAID-5 volume. The amount of free space on the disks is as follows: Disk 0, 2 TB; disk 1, 1.5 TB; disk 2, 800 GB; disk 3, 1 TB. What is the maximum size of RAID-5 volume that you can create?

  a.   2.4 TB

  b.   3.2 TB

  c.   4.5 TB

  d.   5.3 TB

7.   You want to ensure that your Windows 10 computer will always boot, so you decide that you want to implement fault tolerance on your system and boot volumes. Your computer has two hard disks. You start the DiskPart command and select the system/boot volume. What command should you use?

  a.   **create volume stripe disk=0,1**

  b.   **create volume mirror disk=0,1**

  c.   **create volume raid disk=0,1**

  d.   **add disk = 1**

8.   One morning, you start the Optimize Drives utility to optimize your C: drive. This drive is 250 GB in size with a free space of 22 GB. After lunch, this utility is still running, and you start to wonder what else you should do to optimize disk usage. Which of the following can you do to improve the rate of disk response? (Choose all that apply.)

  a.   Run the Disk Cleanup utility.

  b.   Back up old data and then delete this data from the drive.

  c.   Uninstall several applications whose files are on this drive.

  d.   Just let the Optimize Drives utility run overnight.

9.   Your computer has three volumes, C:, D:, and E:. You want to optimize the C: and D: volumes only from the command line. What command will do this? (Choose two; each is a complete solution.)

  a.   **defrag c: d:**

  b.   **defrag /e:**

  c.   **defrag /E e:**

  d.   **defrag /E c: d:**

10. What enables you to create logical groupings of shared folders on different servers that facilitate the access to data by users on the network?

   a. DFS Namespaces

   b. DFS Replication

   c. Disk Cleanup

   d. Storage Pools

11. You can use DFS Replication and DFS Namespaces either separately or together; each does not require the presence of the other. You can also use DFS Replication to replicate _____.

   a. standalone DFS namespaces

   b. Active Directory

   c. a server image

   d. the Registry

12. You have created a storage pool on a Windows 10 computer from two physical drives, each with 2 TB capacity. What is the maximum size you can specify for a storage space created from this pool?

   a. 4 TB

   b. 2 TB

   c. 1 TB

   d. No limit

13. You are planning to use Storage Spaces in Windows, and would like to use parity resiliency because it makes the most efficient use of disk capacity. How many drives must exist (minimum) in the storage pool?

   a. 2

   b. 3

   c. 5

   d. 1

14. You have two storage spaces, called "movies" and "music," created from a single storage pool. The total pool capacity is 500 GB, so you have created each storage space to use 250 GB size (maximum). You have used only 10% of the pool space, but you now need to copy a 300 GB file to the "movies" storage space. What is the easiest way to configure Storage Spaces to be able to copy the file?

   a. Delete the "music" storage space and expand the "movies" storage space.

   b. Add an additional drive to the storage pool.

   c. Just copy the file, because there is room in the storage pool.

   d. Increase the size of the "movies" storage space.

15. You have a folder connected to your OneDrive storage on your Windows 10 PC, but would like to use a new corporate OneDrive account with more storage. How can you change your OneDrive folder?

   a. Go to OneDrive.com and configure the account to use a different computer and folder name.

   b. Open Control Panel, find the OneDrive applet, and change the credentials in OneDrive settings.

   c. Add the corporate account to the computer, and log on to the system with the new corporate account.

   d. Open PC Settings, access the OneDrive settings, and change the OneDrive account credentials under Sync settings.

16. You are using a Windows 10 PC and have a number of files on your OneDrive storage that you want to keep in sync on your local computer automatically. What would you use to enable this feature?

   a. Configure the OneDrive Windows app to copy the files.

   b. Open the OneDrive app, select the folders and files you want to keep in sync, and select the **Make Offline** app command to make the files available offline.

   c. Log in to OneDrive.com and select the computer and synchronization settings you want to use.

   d. Use the OneDrive mobile app to copy your files.

17. Which of the following folders can you redirect to a shared folder on a server so that they can be easily backed up? (Choose all that apply.)

    a. Documents

    b. Music

    c. Pictures

    d. Videos

18. Which of the following are components of a domain-based folder redirection implementation? (Choose all that apply.)

    a. A Windows Server 2012 R2 or higher computer configured as a router

    b. A Windows Server 2012 R2 or higher computer configured as a domain controller

    c A Group Policy Object (GPO) that specifies folder redirection settings

    d. A Windows Server 2012 R2 or higher computer configured as a global catalog server

    e. A Windows Server 2012 R2 or higher computer configured with a shared folder accessible to network users.

19. You want to ensure that all users on your company's network are provided with common settings that appear on any computer on the network, regardless of the computer they log on to. Further, you want to ensure that these settings cannot be modified by users and kept after logging off. What profile type do you configure?

    a. Roaming profile

    b. Mandatory profile

    c. Local profile

    d. Permanent profile

20. You want to copy a user profile so that another user of the same computer can use the same settings specified in the first profile. What do you do?

   a. From the System dialog box, click **Advanced System Settings**. In the System Properties dialog box that appears, select the **Profiles** tab, select the default profile, and then click **Copy To**. Then type or browse to the desired location and click **OK**.

   b. From the System dialog box, click **Advanced System Settings**. In the System Properties dialog box that appears, select the **Profiles** tab and then click **Settings**. Select the default profile and click **Copy To**. Then type or browse to the desired location and click **OK**.

   c. From the System dialog box, click **Advanced System Settings**. In the System Properties dialog box that appears, select the **Advanced** tab and then click **Settings** under User Profiles. Then, in the User Profiles dialog box, select the default profile and click **Copy To**. Then type or browse to the desired location and click **OK**.

   d. In File Explorer, browse to %systemdrive%\Users\Default User\ Profiles. Right-click this folder, choose **Copy**, browse to the desired user in the Users subfolder, access the \Profiles subfolder of this user, right-click it, and choose **Paste**.

Foundation Topics

Configuring Data Storage

Storage needs for computers have changed significantly over time. You could feed the data of hundreds of computers from just 10 years ago into a single computer today and still not fill its hard disk. Part of the reason is that today's data is much different than that of 10 years ago. It includes multimedia files, 20-plus megapixel images, extended attributes, complex formulas, and WYSIWYG (What You See Is What You Get) formatting. The result is that the size of a single file can be hundreds of megabytes (MB) or even several gigabytes (GB). So, although storage space has grown, the demand for storage space has increased along with it.

As the amount of information stored on hard disks and accessed across various types of networks has grown, information storage technology has kept pace. Microsoft introduced Storage Spaces technology in 2012, which enables you to create cost-effective, highly available, scalable, and flexible storage systems by using virtualization technology to create pools of storage on groups of physical disks. New for Windows Server 2016 is Storage Spaces Direct, which brings new features to this software-defined storage technology, enabling multiple servers to participate in a shared virtual storage cluster. This topic focuses on Storage Spaces for Windows 10.

Configuring Storage Using Disk Management and Windows PowerShell

Windows 10 offers several tools and utilities that assist you in working with disks and volumes, including removable disks. We discussed configuring policies with removable disks in Chapter 8, "Windows 10 Data Security." You can use the Computer Management Microsoft Management Console (MMC) snap-in or the DiskPart command-line utility to manage disks. We introduced the DiskPart utility in Chapter 2, "Implementing Windows," with regard to creating virtual hard disks (VHDs); here we discuss them in detail.

We introduced the Computer Management tool in Chapter 1, "Introducing Windows 10," and have mentioned its use in several other chapters of this book. This tool includes the Disk Management snap-in, which enables you to manage disks and other storage devices in Windows 10. To open Computer Management, right-click **Start** and choose **Computer Management** from the menu that appears.

Windows also enables you to open the Disk Management snap-in from its own console by right-clicking **Start** and choosing **Disk Management** from the menu that appears. Disk Management opens in its own console, as shown in Figure 9-1.

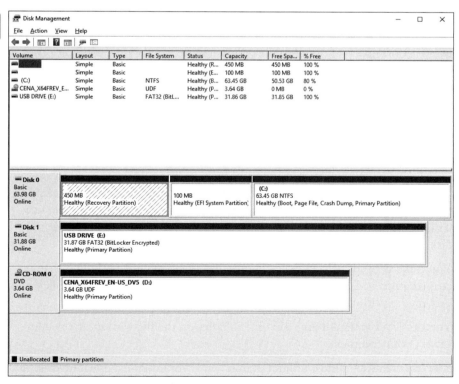

Figure 9-1 The Disk Management Tool Containing the Main Administration Utilities for Disk Devices

The following list summarizes the major actions you can perform from the Disk Management snap-in:

- **Create dynamic disks:** Disks can be either basic (the default) or dynamic. You can convert a basic disk to a dynamic disk but you cannot change back. Your only avenue to reverting to a basic disk is by deleting all volumes on the dynamic disk, losing the data, creating a new basic volume, and restoring the data from a backup.

- **Create volumes:** You can create several types of volumes on a dynamic disk and on a basic disk. Microsoft provides a wizard to assist you in creating these volumes.

- **Extend volumes:** You can add additional unallocated space on a disk to an existing volume. Windows 10 provides the Extend Volume Wizard to assist you in this action.

- **Shrink volumes:** You can reduce the size of a volume to generate unallocated space for creating or extending a different volume.

- **Display properties of disks and volumes:** For disks, you can obtain the same information as provided by Device Manager. For volumes, you can obtain information about free space and device properties. This feature also lets you optimize (defragment) the volume, share the volume, configure an access control list (ACL), back up all files on the volume, and create shadow copies of files and folders within the volume.

Basic and Dynamic Disks

When you first install Windows 10, the hard disk on which you install Windows is set up as a *basic disk*. When you add a brand new hard disk to your computer, this disk is also recognized as a basic disk. This disk type is the one that has existed ever since the days of MS-DOS. Starting with Windows 2000, Microsoft offered a new type of disk called a *dynamic disk*. This disk type offers several advantages over the basic disk, including the following:

- You can create specialized disk volumes on a dynamic disk, including spanned, striped, mirrored, and RAID-5 volumes. Basic disks are limited to primary and extended partitions, and logical drives.

- You can work with and upgrade disk volumes on the fly, without the need to reboot your computer.

- You can create an almost unlimited number of volumes on a dynamic disk. A basic disk can only hold a total of four primary partitions, or three primary plus one extended partition.

Dynamic disks have their disadvantages, however:

- The disk does not contain partitions or logical drives and therefore can't be read by another operating system.

- On a multiboot computer, the disk will not be readable by operating systems other than the one from which the disk was upgraded.

- Laptop computers do not support dynamic disks.

Besides a disk type, all disks have one of two partition styles:

- **Master Boot Record (MBR):** Uses a partition table that describes the location of the partitions on the disk. The first sector of an MBR disk contains the master boot record plus a hidden binary code file that is used for booting the system. This disk style supports volumes of up to 2 terabytes (TB) with up to four primary partitions or three primary partitions plus one extended partition that is subdivided into any number of logical drives.

- **GUID Partition Table (GPT):** Uses extensible firmware interface (EFI) to store partition information within each partition and includes redundant primary and backup partition tables to ensure structural integrity. This style is recommended for disks larger than 2 TB, and for disks used on Itanium-based computers. Not all previous Windows versions can recognize this disk style, however.

When you add a new disk of less than 2 TB, it is added as an MBR disk. You can convert an MBR disk to a GPT one using either Disk Management or the DiskPart tool, provided there are no partitions or volumes on the disk. To use Disk Management, right-click it and choose **Convert to GPT Disk**. To use DiskPart, proceed as follows:

Step 1.   Open an administrative command prompt, type **DiskPart**, and accept the User Account Control (UAC) prompt. You see the DiskPart command window.

Step 2.   Type **list disk** to get the disk number of the disks on your system.

Step 3.   Type **select disk** *n* where *n* is the number of the disk you want to convert.

Step 4.   Type **convert gpt**. DiskPart informs you that it has successfully converted the selected disk to GPT format.

If you want to convert a GPT disk back to MBR, the procedures are the same. You must back up all data and delete all volumes on the disk before performing the conversion. In Disk Management, right-click the disk and choose **Convert to MBR Disk**. In DiskPart, use the same steps and type **convert mbr** in the last one.

> **NOTE**   For more information on using GPT disks, refer to "Using GPT Drives" at https://msdn.microsoft.com/en-us/library/windows/hardware/dn653580(v=vs.85).aspx.

Working with Basic Disks

When you first install Windows 10 on a new computer or add a new disk to an existing Windows 10 computer, the disk appears in Disk Management as a basic disk. Windows 10 enables you to create a new partition (aka a simple volume) from the free space on a new or existing disk. This partition can be primary or extended or a logical volume. Keep in mind that a single basic disk can contain up to four primary partitions or three primary partitions plus an extended partition; the extended partition can contain any number of logical drives. Use the following procedure to create a partition:

Step 1.   Right-click **Start > Disk Management** to open the Disk Management snap-in. Alternatively, you can open Computer Management as already discussed and then select **Disk Management** in the left pane.

Step 2.   Locate the disk in the right pane that contains the unallocated space where the new volume will reside.

Step 3.   Right-click the unallocated space of the disk, and select **New Simple Volume** from the shortcut menu.

Step 4.   The New Simple Volume Wizard starts. Click **Next**.

Step 5.   On the Specify Volume Size page, type the size of the partition in megabytes and then click **Next**.

Step 6.   On the Assign Drive Letter or Path page shown in Figure 9-2, accept the drive letter provided or use the drop-down list to select a different letter. Then click **Next**.

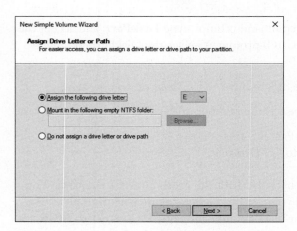

Figure 9-2   Assigning a Drive Letter to Your Partition or Mount It in an Empty NTFS Folder

Step 7.   On the Format Partition page shown in Figure 9-3, choose the file system (FAT, FAT32, or NTFS) to format the partition. Provide a volume label name or accept the default of New Volume (this name will appear in the Computer window). If formatting with NTFS, you can modify the allocation unit size and/or enable file and folder compression. When done, click **Next**.

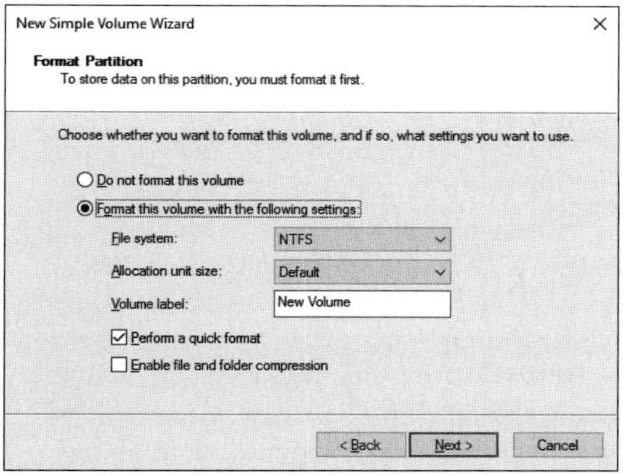

Figure 9-3   Choices for Formatting a New Partition

Step 8.   Review the information provided on the completion page and then click **Finish**. Windows creates and formats the partition and displays its information in the Disk Management snap-in.

On a basic disk, Disk Management also enables you to perform several other management activities. You can extend, shrink, or delete volumes as necessary. Extending a volume enables you to add unallocated space to the volume. Right-click the volume and choose **Extend Volume**. The Extend Volume Wizard informs you what space is available and enables you to add additional space or select a smaller amount of space, as shown in Figure 9-4. Modify the amounts in MB as required, click **Next**, and then click **Finish** to extend the volume.

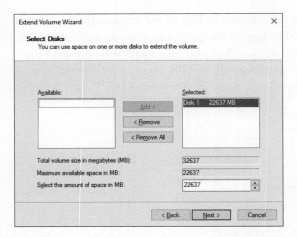

Figure 9-4   Extend Volume Wizard Helping Extend a Volume on a Basic or Dynamic Disk

NOTE   If you add additional space on another disk from the Available column in the Extend Volume Wizard, you will be creating a spanned volume. The wizard will ask you to convert the disks to dynamic storage. You learn more about this later in this chapter.

Shrinking a partition enables you to free up space to be used on a different partition. To do so, right-click the desired partition and choose **Shrink Volume**. In the Shrink Volume dialog box shown in Figure 9-5, type the amount of space you want to shrink the volume by. (Note the size after shrink to avoid overshrinking the volume.) Then click **Shrink**.

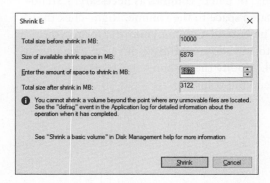

Figure 9-5   Shrink Volume Dialog Box for Shrinking a Partition or Volume

To view how a partition is configured, you can look at its properties in the Disk Management utility. Right-click the partition and select **Properties** from the shortcut menu. The Properties dialog box that appears has the following tabs (not all tabs will appear if the disk is not formatted with the NTFS file system):

- **General:** As shown in Figure 9-6, this tab provides an immediate view of the space allocation on the disk in a pie chart. The General tab also allows you to type a volume name and to click a button that executes the Disk Cleanup graphical utility. This utility enables you to remove unnecessary files from your disk, such as the Temporary Internet Files folder, downloaded program install files, and the Recycle Bin.

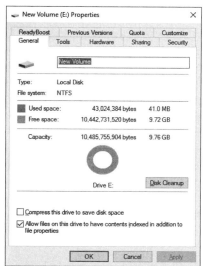

Figure 9-6   Volume's Properties Displaying Its Space Allocation

- **Tools:** This tab has the following two buttons:
  - **Check:** Displays an Error Checking dialog box that enables you to click **Scan Drive**, which executes the GUI version of Chkdsk.
  - **Optimize:** Executes the GUI version of Defrag.

- **Hardware:** Displays the storage device hardware for the computer. You can obtain properties for any device, similar to that obtained from Device Manager, by selecting it and clicking **Properties**.

- **Sharing:** Enables you to share the disk so that others can access information on it. Doing this for the entire drive is not considered a good practice. It is generally unnecessary because the computer automatically generates an administrative share for each partition when Windows starts.

- **Security:** Enables you to assign access permissions to files and folders on the disk, similar to those discussed in Chapter 8, "Windows 10 Data Security."

- **Quota:** Enables you to assign disk quotas to users on the disk. This lets you limit the amount of space used on the disk by an individual user, who will receive a Disk Full message if he attempts to use more space than assigned to his quota.

- **Customize:** Enables you to optimize folders on the disk for purposes such as general items, documents, pictures, music, or videos. You can also choose to display a different icon that will appear in the Computer window or restore default settings.

You can delete a logical drive or partition easily from within the Disk Management utility. Simply right-click the logical drive and select **Delete Volume** from the shortcut menu, as depicted in Figure 9-7. A prompt appears to verify that you want to delete the logical drive or partition. When you click **Yes**, Windows deletes the drive or partition. Windows prevents you from deleting the system partition, the boot partition, or any partition that contains an active paging file. Extended partitions can be deleted only if they are empty of data and logical drives.

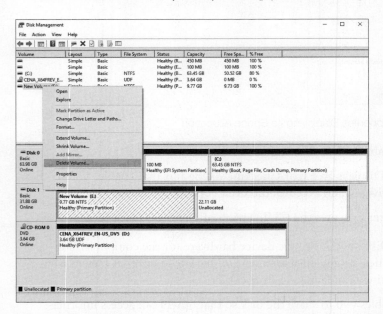

Figure 9-7 Disk Management Utility Enabling You to Delete a Partition or Logical Drive

Converting Basic Disks to Dynamic

The process to convert a basic disk to a dynamic disk requires that you have a minimum of 1 MB of available space on the disk. Best practices state that when you make changes to a disk configuration, you should back up the data before starting, just in case you need to restore it after you are finished. Even so, converting a basic disk to a dynamic disk should not have any effect on your data.

You can convert a basic disk to dynamic at any time. Any partitions that are on the disk are converted to simple volumes in this process. To perform a conversion, you must be logged on as an administrator of the computer.

Step 1.   In Disk Management, right-click the disk to be converted to dynamic and choose **Convert to Dynamic Disk**.

Step 2.   If more than one hard disk is present, you receive the dialog box shown in Figure 9-8. Select any additional disks that you want to convert to dynamic, and then click **OK**.

Figure 9-8   Converting Any of Your Disks to Dynamic Storage at the Same Time

Step 3.   The Disks to Convert dialog box shows you the disks that will be converted. Click **Convert** to proceed.

Step 4.   Disk Management warns you (see Figure 9-9) that you will be unable to start installed operating systems except the current boot volume. Click **Yes** to proceed.

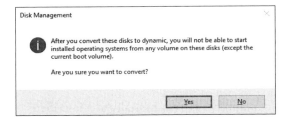

Figure 9-9   Warning That You Will Be Unable to Start Other Operating Systems if You Convert to Dynamic Storage

Step 5.   The disk is converted to dynamic, and the display in Disk Management is updated accordingly.

To convert a dynamic disk back to basic, you must first back up all data on the disk and delete all volumes. Then right-click the disk in Disk Management and choose **Convert to MBR Disk**. The conversion proceeds, and the display in Disk Management is updated within a few seconds.

Working with Dynamic Disks

When you convert a basic disk to a dynamic disk, the existing partitions are converted to simple volumes, and fault-tolerant volumes are converted into dynamic volumes. Dynamic volumes can be changed on the fly, as the name "dynamic" implies. A dynamic volume is a unit of storage initially created from the free space on one or more disks. Table 9-2 lists the volume types available on a dynamic disk.

Table 9-2   Dynamic Volume Types

Volume Type	Number of Disks	Configuration	Fault Tolerance
Simple	1	A single region or multiple concatenated regions of free space on a single disk.	None
Spanned	2 to 32	Two or more regions of free space on 2 to 32 disks linked into a single volume. Can be extended. Cannot be mirrored.	None
Striped	2 to 32	Multiple regions of free space from two or more disks. Data is evenly interleaved across the disks, in stripes. Known as RAID Level 0.	None
Mirrored	2	Data on one disk is replicated on the second disk. Cannot be extended. Known as RAID Level 1.	Yes, with maximum capacity of the smallest disk
RAID-5	3 to 32	Data is interleaved equally across all disks, with a parity stripe of data also interleaved across the disks. Also known as striping with parity.	Yes, with maximum capacity of the number of disks minus one (if you have five 200 GB disks, your volume would be 800 GB)

Creating a simple volume on a dynamic disk proceeds exactly as already described for creating a partition on a basic disk. As with basic disks, you can also extend, shrink, or delete a volume. We look at the methods of creating and working with striped, mirrored, and RAID-5 volumes later in this chapter.

Dynamic volumes allow you to change their properties on an as-needed basis. If you have a computer, for example, that is running short of space, you can install an extra hard drive and extend an existing simple or spanned volume so that the new space is immediately available without directing the user to use drive J for this data, drive C for that data, drive Y for the network, and so on. Users find multiple drive letters confusing, so being able to keep it all under one letter is highly preferable. Unfortunately, you cannot extend a system volume or a boot volume. Because most computers are installed with a single volume, C:, which includes boot and system files, any volumes created on a new disk added to the computer must have a separate drive letter from the C: drive.

To increase the size of a simple volume, in Disk Management, right-click the existing volume and select **Extend Volume** from the shortcut menu. The Extend Volume Wizard starts, and you are prompted to select the disk or disks that contain the free space you will be adding. After you specify the size of free space to add, you need to confirm your options and click **Finish**. The volume is extended and appears in the Disk Management window with new space allocated to it.

The Disk Management utility is fairly comprehensive, but it is not the only tool available in Windows 10 to configure or manage disks. Some of these tools harken back to the days of DOS and Windows 3.x, yet they are still very useful, especially if there is a problem accessing the graphical user interface (GUI):

- **Chkdsk.exe:** A command-line utility that verifies and repairs FAT- or NTFS-formatted volumes. (For NTFS drives, use the **CHKDSK C: /R** command to automatically check and repair disk problems.)

- **Cleanmgr.exe:** Also known as Disk Cleanup, a GUI utility that deletes unused files.

- **Defrag.exe:** Also known as Disk Defragmenter, a command-line utility that rearranges files contiguously, recapturing and reorganizing free space in the volume. Optimizes performance.

- **DiskPart.exe:** A command-line utility that can run a script to perform disk-related functions. DiskPart's nearest GUI counterpart is the Disk Management utility.

- **Fsutil.exe:** A command-line utility that displays information about the file system and can perform disk-related functions.

RAID Volumes

The acronym "RAID" refers to Redundant Array of Independent (or Inexpensive) Disks—it is a series of separate disks configured to work together as a single drive with a single drive letter. You have already seen three of the most common types of RAID arrays in Table 9-2: RAID-0 (disk striping), RAID-1 (mirroring), and RAID-5 (disk striping with parity). Other versions of RAID also exist but are generally unused; you are unlikely to see these referenced on the 70-698 exam.

When you use fault-tolerant volumes, a disk can fail and the operating system will continue to function. The failure can be repaired with no loss of data. Most Windows 10 computers do not have fault-tolerant volumes. An administrator should understand how to handle the errors that can plague a hard disk. Refer to Table 9-2 for common problems that can also plague fault-tolerant volumes.

CAUTION   Don't confuse the RAID-5 or mirrored volumes that you can create within the Windows 10 operating system with RAID-5 or mirrored drives that are configured in a hardware storage array. A disk array produces a highly performing, fault-tolerant volume that appears in Windows 10 Disk Management as a simple volume. When you create mirrored or RAID-5 volumes in Windows 10, you achieve fault tolerance but lose some performance to disk management processes, especially if a disk fails.

Creating a RAID-0 Volume

A RAID-0 (striped) volume contains space on 2 to 32 separate hard disks. Data is written in 64 KB blocks (*stripes*) to each disk in the volume, in turn. A striped volume offers considerable improvement in read/write efficiency because the read/write heads on each disk are working together during each I/O operation. A striped volume offers a maximum amount of space equal to the size of the smallest disk multiplied by the number of disks in the volume. However, the striped volume does not offer fault tolerance; if any one disk is lost, the entire volume is lost. Note that the system or boot volume cannot be housed on a striped volume.

You can create a striped volume by using 2 to 32 separate hard disks in Disk Management. Use the following procedure:

Step 1.   In Disk Management, right-click any one disk to be made part of the striped volume, and choose **New Striped Volume**.

Step 2.   The New Striped Volume Wizard starts and displays the Select Disks page shown in Figure 9-10. The disk you initially selected appears under Selected. Select the disks you want to use from the Available column and then click **Add**.

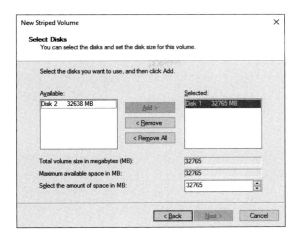

Figure 9-10   Select at Least Two Disks to Create a Striped Volume

Step 3.   Disks you add appear in the Selected column. If you want to change the amount of space to be allocated, modify the value under Select the Amount of Space in MB. When done, click **Next**.

Step 4.   From the Assign Drive Letter or Path page shown in Figure 9-11, accept the default or choose another drive letter or select the option to mount the volume in an empty NTFS folder, if desired. Then click **Next**.

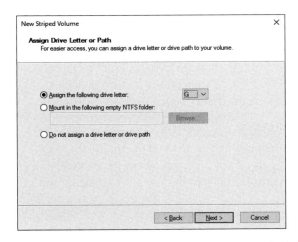

Figure 9-11   Assigning a Drive Letter or Mount Path for a Striped Volume

Step 5.   Choose the desired options in the Format Volume page shown in Figure 9-12 and then click **Next**.

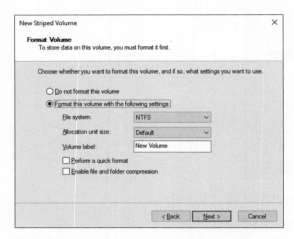

Figure 9-12   Options for Formatting Your Volume

Step 6.   Review the information on the completion page and then click **Finish**.

Step 7.   If any of the disks to be used in the volume are configured as basic disks, you receive the same message previously shown in Figure 9-9, warning you that you will be unable to boot other operating systems. To create your volume, you must click **Yes** and convert these disks to dynamic storage, as discussed earlier in this chapter.

Step 8.   The volume is created and formatted, and appears in the Disk Management snap-in display.

> **CAUTION**   Remember that RAID-0 is *not* fault-tolerant, as mentioned in Table 9-2. RAID-0 writes data in 64 KB blocks to each disk in the array sequentially, thereby improving read/write performance. However, if you lose any one of the disks in the array, all data is lost, and you must restore the data from backup after replacing the lost disk and re-creating the array.

Creating a Spanned Volume

You can extend storage space on an existing volume to a new disk by creating a spanned volume. This is essentially a volume that spans two or more disks and enables you to add space without the need to specify a new drive letter. Note that the spanned volume is even less fault-tolerant than a simple volume; if any one disk fails, all data is lost from all disks and must be restored from backup.

To create a spanned volume, right-click the desired volume and choose **Extend Volume**. From the Extend Volume Wizard, select the available disk(s) and complete the steps in this wizard, as previously described and shown in Figure 9-4. If you have multiple unallocated disks, you can alternatively select **New Spanned Volume**, and create your spanned volume using the New Spanned Volume Wizard. The process is the same.

Creating a Mirrored Volume

A mirrored volume contains two disks, each of which is an identical copy of the other, thereby providing fault tolerance at the expense of requiring twice the amount of disk space. You can use a mirrored volume to provide fault tolerance for the system and boot volumes, as well as any data volumes.

Creating a mirrored volume is similar to that of creating a striped volume. Use the following procedure:

Step 1.   In Disk Management, right-click any one disk to be made part of the striped volume and choose **New Mirrored Volume**.

Step 2.   Steps displayed by the New Mirrored Volume Wizard are similar to those of the New Striped Volume Wizard and outlined in the previous procedure. When you have completed the procedure, the mirrored volume appears in the Disk Management display.

Creating a RAID-5 Volume

A RAID-5 volume is similar to a striped volume in that data is written in 64 KB stripes across all disks in the volume; however, this volume adds a parity stripe to one of the disks in the array, thereby providing fault tolerance. The parity stripe rotates from one disk to the next as each set of stripes is written. The RAID-5 volume offers improved read performance because data is read from each disk at the same time; however, write performance is lower because processor time is required to calculate the parity stripes. You cannot house the system or boot volumes on a RAID-5 volume.

Creating a RAID-5 volume is also similar; remember that you must have at least three disks to create this type of volume. Select **New RAID-5 Volume** from the right-click options and follow the steps presented by the New RAID-5 Volume Wizard.

NOTE   For more information on how RAID-5 volumes function, refer to "RAID-5 Volumes" at http://technet.microsoft.com/en-us/library/cc938485.aspx.

Using DiskPart to Create Striped, Mirrored, and RAID-5 Volumes

You can use the DiskPart command-line utility to create striped, mirrored, and RAID-5 volumes. To perform any of these tasks, first execute the following commands from an administrative command prompt:

```
Diskpart
List disk
Select disk=n
Convert dynamic
```

The **List disk** command returns the disk numbers on your computer that you use when entering the commands to create the desired volume. The **Select disk** command selects a disk you want to work with and the **Convert dynamic** command converts the disk to a dynamic disk; repeat these two commands for each disk that needs to be converted to dynamic storage before beginning to create your volumes.

To create a mirror, you actually add a mirror to an existing simple volume. Use the **Select volume** command to select the volume to be mirrored, and then use the following command:

```
Add disk=n [noerr]
```

In this command, *n* is the disk number of the disk to be added to the current simple volume and **noerr** enables a script containing this command to continue processing even if an error has occurred. To obtain disk numbers used in this command, use the **List disk** command.

Use the following command to create a striped volume:

```
Create volume stripe [size=size] disk=n[,n[,…]] [noerr]
```

In this command, *size* is the number of MB used in each disk for the striped volume and *n* is the disk number (repeat from 2 to 32 times for each disk in the striped volume). If you do not specify a size, the size is assumed to be that of the smallest disk in the array. For example, if you specify three disks with unallocated space of 300, 400, and 500 GB and do not specify a size, DiskPart uses 300 GB per disk for a total striped volume size of 900 GB.

Creating a RAID-5 volume is similar to that of creating a striped volume. Use the following command:

```
Create volume raid [size=size] disk=n[,n[,…]] [noerr]
```

The parameters have the same meaning; in this case, repeat the disk number from 3 to 32 times. For the same example with three disks with unallocated space of 300, 400, and 500 GB, and which do not specify the size parameter, DiskPart uses 300 GB per disk for a total RAID-5 volume size of 600 GB.

Managing and Troubleshooting RAID Volumes

Several things can go wrong with RAID volumes. Spanned and striped volumes are particularly vulnerable; as has already been mentioned, failure of any one disk in the volume renders the entire volume useless, and data must be restored from backup. If one disk in a mirrored volume fails, you can break the mirror and use the data on the other disk as a simple volume. If one disk in a RAID-5 volume fails, the system reconstructs the missing data from the parity information and the volume is still usable, but without fault tolerance and with reduced performance until the failed disk is replaced. If more than one disk in a RAID-5 volume fails, the volume has failed and must be restored from backup after the disks have been replaced.

Besides the volume statuses already described for partitions on basic disks and simple volumes, Disk Management can display the following messages with RAID volumes:

- **Resynching:** Indicates that a mirrored volume is being reinitialized. This status is temporary and should change to Healthy within a few seconds.

- **Data Not Redundant or Failed Redundancy:** For a mirrored or RAID-5 volume, this status usually means that half of a mirrored volume was imported, or that half is unavailable, or that only part of the underlying disks of a RAID-5 volume were imported. You should import the missing disk(s) to re-create the volume. You can also break the mirror and retain the half that is functioning as a simple volume. If you have all but one of the underlying disks of a RAID-5 volume, you can re-create the RAID-5 volume by adding unallocated space of a different disk.

- **Stale Data:** This status is shown when you import a disk that contains a mirrored volume half, or a portion of a RAID-5 volume, with a status other than Healthy before it was moved. You can return the disk to the original PC and rescan the disk to fix the error.

Creating and Configuring VHDs

For the 70-698 exam, Microsoft expects you to know how to create and configure virtual hard disks (VHDs). VHDs can be used for creating and managing Windows images, and used for native boot scenarios as well as virtualized operating systems using Microsoft Hyper-V.

Review the material in Chapter 2, "Implementing Windows." VHDs are covered in the "Alternate Installation Media" section. VHDs used for virtualization are covered in Chapter 10, "Windows Hyper-V." The material in Chapter 10 is written for the 70-697 exam, but the section on "Virtual Disks" will also be needed for the 70-698 exam for a thorough understanding of how to create and configure VHDs.

Removable Devices

Windows Disk Management can be used to manage removable devices such as USB hard drives, thumb drives, SD cards, and other removable storage. The same tools are available for managing these storage devices that you use for internal drives.

There are a few things you should be aware of when working with removable storage. Review the section "Access to Removable Media" in Chapter 8, "Windows 10 Data Security." The section provides details on using Local Security Policy or GPOs to control user access to removable media. Issues related to the use of removable media may be identified or resolved using these policies.

Users may want to use their removable storage devices in more than one device, and they should know how to unplug or remove the device without corrupting or losing data. By default, Windows attempts to provide the best performance for the disk, but if users unplug the drive without telling Windows to eject the drive first, it can cause data errors. You can configure this setting in the Properties of the drive using the following procedure:

Step 1. In Disk Management, right-click the disk and select **Properties** from the context menu.

Step 2. Select the **Policies** tab to view the removal policy options, as shown in Figure 9-13.

Step 3. Select either **Quick Removal** or **Better Performance**.

Figure 9-13   Performance and Removal Policies of a Removable Storage Device

Storage Spaces

Windows 10 Storage Spaces, a technology first introduced for Windows 8, provides a more convenient method for adding additional storage to a computer when it is needed. Traditionally, when a Windows system becomes short on storage, adding an additional hard disk only partially solves the issue; it requires some careful management of storage, requiring movement of files over multiple disks or even reinstalling software to move the installation files to the new drive, freeing space on the original drive.

Storage Spaces solves this problem by allowing you to add the disk to a virtual storage space and managing the additional space for you, presenting two or more disks as a single drive. To the user, it appears as though the original drive has been replaced with a larger one.

With Storage Spaces, you organize physical disks together into a *storage pool* and use the pool capacity to create storage spaces. After a disk drive is part of a storage pool, you can add new drives to it to increase the size of the virtual drive. Note the following characteristics of Storage Spaces:

- Storage Spaces are presented as virtual drives in File Explorer. They are used like any other drive, making it easy to work with files on them.

- You can create Storage Spaces with lots of storage, adding more drives to them when you run low capacity in the pool. Drives can be attached through USB, SATA, or Serial Attached SCSI (SAS).

- Storage Spaces can provide some protection to your files. With two or more drives in the storage pool, you can create Storage Spaces with redundancy in case of a drive failure—or even failure of two drives by creating a three-way mirror Storage Space.

- Storage Spaces use *thin provisioning*, which means that physical space is allocated only when it is actually used to store files. Thin provisioning allows you to create Storage Spaces with more virtual capacity than actually exists on the physical drives in the storage pool.

Creating a Storage Space

You can create Storage Spaces after you have more than one drive connected to the Windows computer. When you have connected all the drives you want to use, use the following procedure to create a Storage Space:

Step 1.   Access the Search bar or Cortana, and enter **Storage Spaces** into the Search box.

Step 2.　Select the **Storage Spaces** item from the search results. The Storage Spaces Control Panel applet will be displayed, as shown in Figure 9-14.

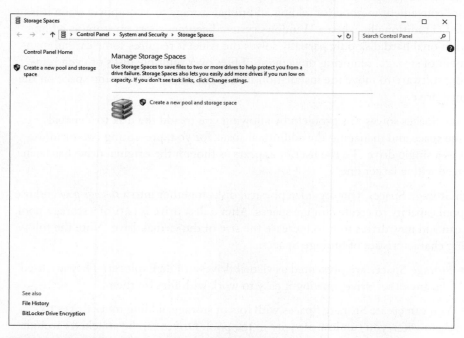

Figure 9-14　Storage Spaces Control Panel Applet

Step 3.　Click the **Create a New Pool and Storage Space** link. If the UAC confirmation dialog box is displayed, click **Yes** to proceed.

Step 4.　Select the drives you want to use for the new pool, and then click **Create Pool**.

Step 5.　Select a drive letter and name, the Resiliency type, and the maximum size for the storage space, from the screen as shown in Figure 9-15.

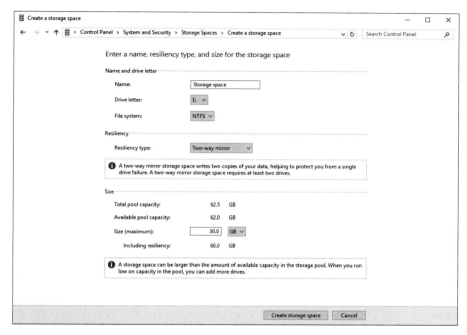

Figure 9-15   Entering a Name, Resiliency Type, and Size for a New Storage Space

Step 6.   Select the **Create Storage Space** button to complete the configuration and create the new Storage Space.

> **CAUTION**   When adding drives for use with Storage Spaces, there is no need to format or assign letters to the new drive. If any of the drives are formatted, Windows warns you that the drive will be reformatted, and any files on the drive will be permanently lost. Make sure you do not have any data that you want to keep on any of the drives you add to a storage pool, because the files will be destroyed and cannot be recovered.

After the Storage Space is created, you can now use it just as you would any other drive, with the drive letter you specified in Step 6.

The Resiliency Type can be used to provide protection from physical disk failure in your Storage Space, if you use more than one drive to create it. Table 9-3 lists the resiliency options, type of hardware failure protection, and the required number of drives for each.

Note that resiliency will require more disk space, similar to using a RAID volume discussed earlier in the chapter. Configuring a Storage Space using two-way mirror resiliency, for instance, will allow you to use only half of the storage capacity of the two drives.

Table 9-3 Storage Space Resiliency Options

Resiliency Type	Protection	Minimum Number of Drives
Simple (no resiliency)	None	1
Two-way mirror	Protects data from failure of a single drive	2
Three-way mirror	Protects data from failure of up to two physical drives	5
Parity	Protects data from failure of a single drive	3

Troubleshooting Storage and Device Issues

An administrator should understand how to handle the errors that can plague a hard disk. Common problems are listed in Table 9-4. We look at the Windows 10 Startup Repair Tool in Chapter 20, "Configuring System Recovery Options."

Table 9-4 Troubleshooting Disk Errors

Error	Problem or Process	Possible Repairs
Non-System Disk or Disk Error	Basic input/output system (BIOS) generates this error when the master boot record (MBR) or boot sector is damaged or when a different device is configured as the boot device in the BIOS.	Check the BIOS and reconfigure, if necessary. Remove any nonsystem media from the floppy, USB, or optical drives. Repair the boot volume with Windows 10 Startup Repair Tool. Reinstall Windows 10. Replace the hard disk.
There is not enough memory or disk space to complete the operation	Disk is full.	Free up space on the hard disk by deleting files, removing applications, or compressing files. Add another disk and extend the volume to span both disks.
Missing Operating System	No active partition is defined.	Check the BIOS settings and configure if they incorrectly identify the boot disk. Boot up with a floppy or other bootable media. Use Diskpart.exe to mark the boot volume as active. Use Windows 10 Startup Repair Tool. Reinstall Windows 10.

Error	Problem or Process	Possible Repairs
Invalid Media Type	Boot sector is damaged.	Repair the boot volume with Windows Startup Repair Tool.
		Reinstall Windows 10.
		Replace the hard disk.
Hard disk controller failure	BIOS's disk controller configuration is invalid, or the hard disk controller has failed.	Check the BIOS and reconfigure controller.
		Replace the hard disk controller.

The volume properties of a disk as displayed in the graphical display in the Disk Management snap-in (refer to Figure 9-1) provide you with a status display, which can help you in troubleshooting disk problems. The following volume statuses can appear:

- **Healthy:** This status is normal and means that the volume is accessible and operating properly.

- **Active:** This status is also normal. An *active partition* is a partition or volume on a hard disk that has been identified as the primary partition from which the operating system is booted.

- **Failed:** This status means that the operating system could not start the volume normally. Failed usually means that the data is lost because the disk is damaged or the file system is corrupted. To repair a failed volume, physically inspect the computer to see whether the physical disk is operating. Ensure that the underlying disk(s) has an Online status in Disk Management.

- **Formatting:** This status is temporary, appearing only while the volume is being formatted.

- **Unknown:** This status means that you've installed a new disk and have not created a disk signature, or that the boot sector for the volume is corrupt, possibly because of a virus. You can attempt to repair this error by initializing the underlying disk by right-clicking the disk and selecting **Initialize** from the shortcut menu.

- **Data Incomplete:** This status appears when a disk has been moved into or out of a multidisk volume. Data is destroyed unless all the disks are moved and imported on the new computer.

- **Healthy (At Risk):** This status indicates I/O errors have been detected on an underlying disk of the volume, but that data can still be accessed. The underlying disk probably shows a status of Online (Errors) and must be brought back online for the volume to be corrected.

When you see a status other than Healthy for your volumes, or other than Online for your disks, you can attempt to repair by selecting the **Rescan Disks** option from the Action menu in Disk Management.

Managing File System Fragmentation

All disks, regardless of the file system in use (FAT16, FAT32, or NTFS), divide disk space into clusters, which are groups of disk sectors that are the smallest units of space available for holding files. The size of clusters depends on the file system in use and the size of the partition; for example, for NTFS-formatted volumes of more than 2 GB but less than 16 TB in size, the default cluster size is 4 KB.

A file is stored in the first available clusters on a volume or partition, and not necessarily in contiguous space. Thus, if empty space has been left on the volume as a result of moving, editing, or deleting files, these small noncontiguous clusters will be used. Access to files that are fragmented in this way takes a longer time because extra read operations are required to locate and access all the pieces of the file. You can defragment your disks with either the Optimize Drives GUI tool or the command-line defrag.exe tool.

Optimizing Drives

Windows 10 provides a tool called the Optimize Drives utility (formerly called the Disk Defragmenter) to locate and consolidate these fragmented files into contiguous blocks of space. Consequently, access time is improved. You can access the Optimize Drives utility by clicking **Optimize** from the Tools tab of any partition's Properties dialog box or by accessing the Search charm and typing **defrag** into the Search field and clicking **Defragment and Optimize Drives** in the Programs list.

Any of these methods opens the newly redesigned Optimize Drives utility, as shown in Figure 9-16. This tool enables you to configure scheduled optimization or to analyze or optimize any disk volume immediately.

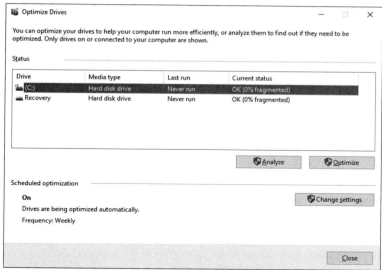

Figure 9-16   Optimize Drives Utility Enabling You to Perform On-Demand and Scheduled Optimization

You can perform the following actions from the Optimize Drives GUI utility:

- **Schedule Optimization:** Click **Change Settings** to set up a schedule. By default, Windows schedules optimization to take place on all disks weekly, as shown in Figure 9-17. You can choose to optimize disks on a daily or monthly basis if desired by selecting these options from the drop-down list shown, or select disks to be optimized by clicking the **Choose** command button.

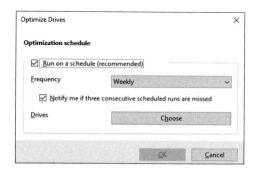

Figure 9-17   Optimize Drives: Optimization Schedule Dialog Box Enabling You to Specify the Schedule for Optimization

- **Analyze disk:** Select a disk and click **Analyze** to have the Optimize Drives utility check the current level of fragmentation. Although the dialog box says you need to first analyze your disks, they are first analyzed when you click **Optimize**.

- **Perform an On-Demand Optimization:** Select a disk and click **Optimize**. Disk optimization first analyzes the disk and then performs a multipass optimization, displaying its progress as shown in Figure 9-18. If you need to stop an optimization in progress, click **Stop**.

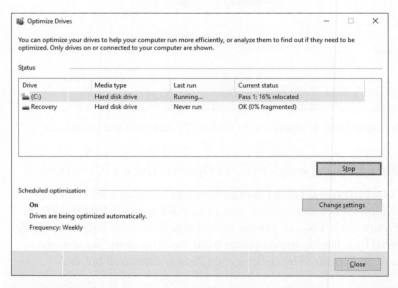

Figure 9-18   Optimize Drives Utility Displaying the Progress of Disk Optimization

NOTE   It is recommended that you have at least 15 percent of free space on a disk volume before running the Optimize Drives utility. Otherwise, the optimization process will take much longer and may be incomplete. Use the Disk Cleanup tool first, if necessary, to optimize the amount of available free space.

TIP   Disks can become quite fragmented after you've uninstalled applications or deleted large files. Further, when installing large applications, the installation runs much better when plenty of contiguous space is available, and the application will also run better later. It is a good idea to analyze your disk after deleting large files or before installing applications and then run the optimization if necessary.

The Defrag.exe Command-Line Tool

You can use Defrag.exe to optimize a volume from the command line. As with other command-line utilities, you can include it as part of a script to be executed when the disk is not in use. To do so, perform the following steps:

Step 1.   Right-click **Start** and choose **Command Prompt (Admin)**.

Step 2.   Click **Yes** to accept the UAC prompt, and then type the following command:

```
Defrag <volume> | /C | /E <volume> [/A | /X | /T] [/H] [/M] [/U]
[/V]
```

Table 9-5 describes the parameters of the **Defrag** command:

Table 9-5   Parameters Available with the **Defrag** Command

Parameter	Meaning
volume	The drive letter of the volume to be optimized. You can specify more than one drive letter if needed.
/B	Optimize boot files and applications but do not optimize the rest of the volume.
/C	Optimize all local volumes.
/E	Optimize all local volumes except those specified.
/A	Analyze the volume and display a report, but do not optimize.
/X	Perform free space consolidation.
/T	Track an optimization already in progress.
/H	Run the optimization at normal priority (by default, runs at low priority).
/M	Optimize multiple volumes simultaneously in parallel.
/U	Print the optimization process on the screen.
/V	Use verbose mode, which provides additional detailed information.

For example, the command **defrag C: /X /V** would optimize the C: volume, perform free space consolidation, and provide verbose output.

Error Checking

Occasionally, a volume might not appear in the Optimize Drives dialog box. This might happen because the disk contains errors such as bad sectors. You can check a disk for errors and repair problems by accessing the Tools tab of the disk's Properties dialog box and clicking **Check**. You receive the Error Checking dialog box shown in Figure 9-19. This dialog box shows any errors it finds on the drive; if none are found, it displays the You Don't Need to Scan This Drive message. In any case, you can perform a more thorough error-checking procedure by clicking **Scan Drive**. This displays an Error Checking message box and then reports any errors it happens to find.

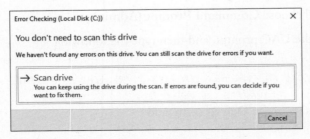

Figure 9-19   Checking a Disk for Errors

Supporting Data Storage

Windows 10 supports many data storage technologies that users can utilize to store their documents and files. In the previous section you learned how to configure Storage Spaces in Windows 10, and in this topic you learn more about Storage Spaces support and maintenance. You will also learn about support for Dynamic File System (DFS) caching used in Windows 10, and supporting OneDrive storage.

DFS Client Configuration Including Caching Settings

The typical large organization has many file servers that users require access to as they perform their assigned tasks. Imagine the difficulty that the average user could have in locating the appropriate server from dozens of possibilities when attempting to access that one vital piece of information when putting together a budget forecast for the upcoming fiscal year. Multiply that by the myriads of possibilities when marketing analysts are formulating trends for corporate products and deciding what should be emphasized in both manufacturing and advertising efforts in the months to come. Then you can see how much simpler such tasks become if the users need to access only a single tree of shared folders that includes all the servers that hold the required files. This is what Distributed File System (DFS) does—a user can type a single Universal Naming Convention (UNC) path such as \\servername\ sharename, or select a single root within the Network folder, and obtain access to shares located on multiple servers across the network. Users located in branch offices receive optimized access across the wide area network (WAN) to the most easily accessed file source; further, replication of files and folders can be optimized to facilitate access to everyone regardless of where they might be located within a multisite enterprise network.

First introduced with Windows Server 2003, DFS Replication provides WAN-friendly replication and simplified access to files wherever they are located. DFS includes the two technologies described in Table 9-6.

Table 9-6 Components of DFS

Component	Description
DFS Namespaces	Enables you to create logical groupings of shared folders on different servers that facilitate the access to data by users on the network. Such groupings are presented to users as a virtual folder tree or namespace. DFS Namespaces is optimized to connect users to data within the same Active Directory Domain Services (AD DS) site wherever possible, thereby minimizing the need for use of WAN links.
DFS Replication	An efficient multimaster replication component that synchronizes data between servers with limited bandwidth network links. DFS Replication replaces the older, problematic File Replication Service (FRS) used in older Windows server operating systems for replicating data across the network. DFS utilizes a new compression algorithm called Remote Differential Compression, which optimizes file replication by sending only the updated portions of changed files rather than the complete files. On AD DS networks operating at the Windows Server 2008 or higher domain functional level, DFS Replication is used for replicating AD DS partitions and the SYSVOL shared folder.

NOTE   You can use DFS Replication and DFS Namespaces either separately or together; each does not require the presence of the other. You can also use DFS Replication to replicate standalone DFS namespaces.

Understanding how DFS works is important for supporting client caching on Windows 10. The same pool of files can exist on multiple file servers throughout an organization's network. Users access the share using a common UNC filename. Typically this works automatically, but if a Windows computer is connected to a remote server over a slower link, it can cause performance issues for the network and for the user.

The DFS Namespace includes a referral list of actual shares (targets) the client can use to access the files. The referral list is ordered by network location, with the closest server at the top. The client will start connection attempts using the list, and when it cannot connect, it checks the next target in the referral list, and so on. If the current target becomes unavailable, the client will immediately switch to the next target location. Clients will use the referral list received from the domain for up to 30 minutes by default. This referral cache can become stale during that window, and clients will continue to attempt connecting to removed targets. You can modify these properties for a DFS namespace by using the Referrals tab on the Properties dialog for the namespace, as shown in Figure 9-20.

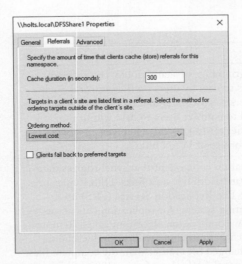

Figure 9-20 Using the Referrals Tab of the DFS Namespace Properties Dialog to Modify the Cache Duration and Fail Back

The Cache Duration setting determines how long clients will cache the referral list before requesting a new list of targets. Typically, if a client fails to connect to the first target in the referral list, it will connect to another target and continue to use that target during the session, even if the closer target becomes available. By checking the Clients Fail Back to Preferred Targets check box, you can force clients to disconnect from the more remote target and connect to the first target in the referral list as soon as it refreshes the list.

Managing Storage Spaces

In the previous section, "Configuring Data Storage," you learned about setting up Storage Spaces and how to troubleshoot them. It is important to note the distinction between storage pools and Storage Spaces. A storage pool consists of one or more physical hard drives grouped together to provide some amount of storage capacity. After you have added physical drives to a storage pool, they are no longer directly usable by Windows. You can add drives to a storage pool at any time, but note that after you have created storage space that makes use of the pool, drives cannot be removed from the pool without first deleting the storage space, which will destroy all the files it contains.

You can create multiple storage spaces for each storage pool. As shown previously in Figure 9-15, you can specify the maximum size for a storage space when you create it. You are not limited to the amount of capacity in the storage pool—this allows you to create storage spaces with more space than is actually available. As the storage space fills up, you can add more drives to the storage pool. You can change the storage space size at any time, as long as it is large enough to contain the files that have been written to it.

You can manage your storage spaces and pools from the screen shown in Figure 9-21. From the links at the top, click **Create a Storage Space**, **Add Drives**, or **Rename Pool** to perform these functions. The default name of the first pool will be Storage Pool, but as you add new storage pools to the system, you will want to give them meaningful names based on their use or the drives used to make up the pool. You can also add drives when you need to expand the capacity of a storage pool.

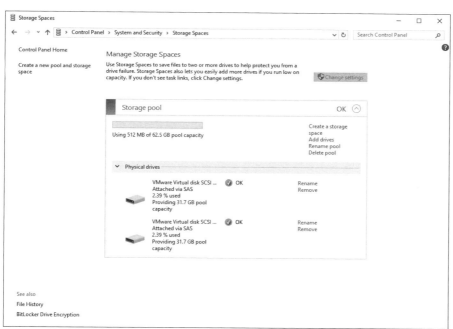

Figure 9-21   Managing Storage Spaces

The physical drives are listed in the bottom section of the screen. You can use the Rename link for each drive to provide a friendlier name. In the figure, there is no Remove link available for the drives. That is because the pool is already being used by storage spaces. If no storage spaces exist for the pool, the Remove option will also be available for each physical drive.

Configuring Fault Tolerance of Storage Spaces

If a physical drive in a storage pool fails, you can replace the physical drive, add it to the storage pool, and Windows will rebuild any resiliency for you. If a Simple (no resiliency) storage space was using the drive, the files on that storage space will be lost. Action Center will notify you when it detects a problem with the storage pool drive, and the Manage Storage Spaces will display Errors or Warnings, as shown in Figure 9-22.

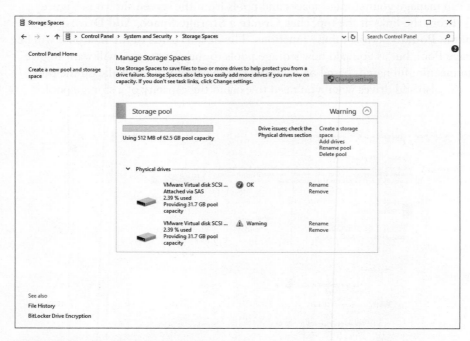

Figure 9-22   Storage Pool Drive Failure

After the drive has been replaced, access the Manage Storage Spaces screen and select the **Add Drives** link to add the replacement drive to the storage pool. Unlike RAID, the replacement drive need not match the failed drive in any way. Windows will begin repairing the resiliency on any existing storage spaces configured for resiliency in that storage pool. Figure 9-23 shows the pool with a new physical drive attached and ready to be added to the Main Pool. You can then use it to replace the failed drive to restore the resiliency to the storage space.

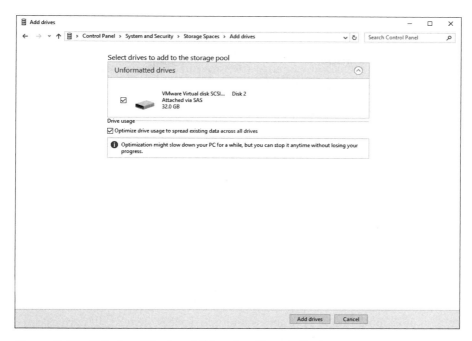

Figure 9-23 Failed and Replaced Drives in a Storage Pool

After the new drive has been added and resiliency on the storage space rebuilt, you can then remove the failed drive from the storage pool.

Managing Storage Spaces with PowerShell

Microsoft provides several PowerShell cmdlets for managing storage pools and storage spaces. Some of the useful cmdlets available are listed here:

- **Get-SpacesPhysicalDisk:** Gets all Physical Disks that can be used to create a storage pool.

- **New-SpacesPool:** Creates a new storage pool. Use the **-PhysicalDisks** parameter to specify the disks to use.

- **New-SpacesVolume:** Creates a new storage space. This command accepts parameters including **-DriveLetterToUse**, **-ResiliencyType**, and **-Size**.

- **Repair-SpacesConfiguration:** Use this command to force the rebuild of resiliency when replacing a failed drive or adding a new one.

NOTE   For more information on PowerShell cmdlets used for managing Storage Spaces and how to use them, refer to "Storage Spaces Cmdlets in Windows Power-Shell" at https://technet.microsoft.com/en-us/library/hh848705.aspx. Although the article references Windows Server 2012 R2 and Windows 8.1, the functionality of the cmdlets is the same in Windows 10.

Configuring OneDrive

As a companion to Windows 10 integration with cloud computing using cloud apps, cloud communication, and cloud accounts, Microsoft has integrated Windows 10 with its cloud storage solution called *OneDrive*. Like Windows Store Apps, use of OneDrive requires a Microsoft account. Each account has access to a limited amount of space for free, and Microsoft offers upgraded storage for an annual fee.

OneDrive enables a single cloud for every Windows user. A person's important files are centrally available, instantly accessible, and ready to share, enabled by single sign-on with a Windows account. OneDrive is the Windows 8.1 user's solution to the problem of keeping files in sync across multiple devices; instead, all devices connect to the OneDrive, and users can easily share files by providing permission for other Windows account users to access their files.

Windows account holders can access their OneDrive storage in four ways:

- The Windows 8.1 OneDrive app, available only on Windows 8.1 and Windows 10 computers.

- The OneDrive desktop application, which is available for Windows 7, Windows Vista, and Mac OS X. The features of the desktop application are built in to Windows 10.

- Using OneDrive.com from a web browser. From OneDrive.com, users can also share files with others by enabling permissions and access to their files from any computer.

- Using the OneDrive mobile app for tablets, Windows 10 Mobile, and other mobile devices.

Reference the following sections for information about the OneDrive app, the OneDrive desktop application, and the configuration options for OneDrive.

OneDrive App

Open the OneDrive app by clicking the **OneDrive** app on the Start menu, or the OneDrive link in File Explorer. If you are not logged in to your Windows account, you are prompted to log in or sign up for an account when you click the tile. The first time you sign in, the OneDrive app tells you where on your computer the One-Drive folder is located, which is in your local user directory by default (such as C:\ Users\Jane\OneDrive).

Initially, OneDrive will be blank except for the "Getting Started with OneDrive" PDF file, which you can open to view a tutorial for OneDrive. Use your OneDrive folder just like any other folder in File Explorer. You can drag and drop files from other locations, delete and rename files, and so on. You can also use the right-click menu option View Online, which will open your default browser so that you can log in to OneDrive and manage your files from the web interface.

Moving or copying files from your local PC to the OneDrive is accomplished using a copy-and-paste or cut-and-paste operation:

Step 1.   Browse the folders in This PC to the file you want to move or copy.

Step 2.   Right-click the file or files to select them.

Step 3.   Click **Cut** from the app commands to move the files, or **Copy** to copy them.

Step 4.   From the left-side menu, select **OneDrive**.

Step 5.   Right-click and then select **Paste**.

By default, all the files and folders in the OneDrive will be fully synched with your online OneDrive storage area. These files can always be browsed, but if you try to open or edit them, they will open in Read-Only mode. To edit the file, you can switch to Read-Write mode, and the file will be synched with your online storage the next time you are connected to the Internet.

You can choose which folders you want to sync locally. To do so, right-click **OneDrive** and then select **Choose OneDrive folders** to sync. You can uncheck any folders you do not want stored locally. They will disappear from your OneDrive folder but will still be available in the online storage.

If you have plenty of space on your PC, you may want to make the entire OneDrive available offline.

OneDrive Desktop

When you are logged in to a Windows account on your PC, OneDrive storage is integrated with File Explorer and desktop applications. You can use the OneDrive and the files and folders in it just like any other drive. Remember, however, that if you have shared any folders publicly, any new files in those folders are also shared publicly on the Internet.

You can save files directly from many desktop applications to the OneDrive folders just as you would to any other location. Notice that for many desktop applications, such as Microsoft Office, OneDrive will be the recommended location that appears when you save documents.

> **NOTE**   For computers running older versions of Windows, or other Mac OS X versions, the OneDrive desktop app must be downloaded from the Microsoft website before integration with the File Explorer will work. See https://onedrive.live.com/about/en-us/download/ for the download location. The download link will not appear on computers running Windows 8.1 or later.

OneDrive Settings

Some OneDrive settings in Windows 10 are now configured in the OneDrive web interface. You can use the right-click option View Online to open your default browser and log in to your OneDrive account. Click the gear icon, and then select **Options** to view the settings as shown in Figure 9-24. From this page you can access the OneDrive configuration settings, described further in the list that follows.

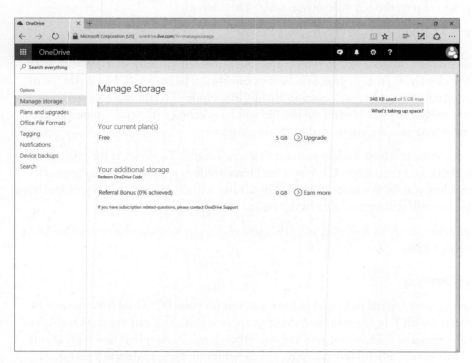

Figure 9-24   OneDrive Settings Available on the Web Interface

- **Storage:** By default, all Windows account users are provided 5 GB of storage at no charge. Additional storage can be purchased from Microsoft. From this screen you can buy additional storage.

- **Office File Formats:** The site also allows you to select the default file format for Office documents. You can choose between Microsoft Office Open XML format and OpenDocument Format. If you use the OneDrive app for iOS or Android devices, OpenDocument format may be more compatible for your use.

- **Tagging:** If your PC or other device has a camera, you can choose to automatically add tags to your photos. Tagging helps you organize your photos by date, location, and by the device you were using to capture the photo.

- **Notifications:** You can enable notifications that OneDrive sends you by email. Select whether you want OneDrive to notify you when someone makes changes to files you have shared. You can also get a notification when OneDrive recaps your photos. Turning off this notification will also stop OneDrive from creating photo albums for you, which it does when you have been taking photos of an event or a trip.

- **Device Backups:** If you are storing settings for any of your devices on OneDrive, you can view the backups by clicking the **Device Backups** link.

- The Sync Your Settings page of Windows 10 modern settings allows you to configure your PC to synchronize a number of local settings to your OneDrive storage. To access the page, select **All Settings** from the Action Center, select **Accounts**, and then click **Sync Your Settings**. Refer to Figure 5-3 in Chapter 5, "Installing and Managing Software," for more details on sync settings. By default, all your local settings will be uploaded to the OneDrive. This feature provides a convenient way to move from device to device and take your settings along, as long as you log in with your Microsoft account and have access to the Internet.

  You can toggle the following settings on or off for OneDrive sync:

    - Sync Settings automatically syncs your PC settings across all your devices when it is toggled on.
    - Theme
    - Internet Explorer Settings
    - Passwords
    - Language Preferences
    - Ease of Access
    - Other Windows Settings

The Other Windows Settings syncs items such as settings for some devices (printer and mouse options), File Explorer Settings, and notification preferences.

User Data Migration and Configuration

Users of Windows computers in an organization have lots of data that they keep track of and work with on a constant basis. They may have many Word documents, Excel spreadsheets, notes, databases, and all kinds of information. This is one of the pain points in migrating to a new version of Windows, such as Windows 10. Although performing an in-place upgrade is an option that will preserve users' settings and files and keep everything in the same place, it might not be a practical way of upgrading computers in a large enterprise. Users also need a way of restoring their files and settings if they need a new or updated device.

In this section, you learn some tools to help users migrate to a new computer without losing their settings by migrating their Windows profiles to their new device. You will also learn about folder redirection, which can help ensure that those important files and documents are stored in a safe location where they will be backed up and secured.

Migrating User Profiles

Windows 10 provides the User State Migration Tool (USMT) to assist you in migrating users from old computers to new ones. The tool is part of the Windows Assessment and Deployment Kit (ADK), which you learned about in previous chapters, including Chapter 2, "Implementing Windows." If you have a large number of users to migrate in a corporate environment, you can customize USMT to suit the needs of your migration requirements.

User State Migration Tool

Intuitively, you might first think that migrating a large number of users to new Windows 10 computers could be as simple as using the **xcopy** command or a tool such as Robocopy to move files from their old computers to a network share, and then moving them back to the new computers at a later time. However, users like to store data on various locations on their local hard drives; they have customized application settings and specific files (such as Microsoft Outlook PST files) that might be hard to locate after such a move is finished. Users also like to set up individual desktop preferences, such as wallpapers and screen savers. Using USMT enables you to move all these items and more in a seamless manner to their appropriate locations on the new computer so that the users can resume working on this computer with minimal delay.

You can use USMT to quickly and easily transfer any number of user files and settings as a part of operating system deployment or computer replacement. It includes migration of the following items:

- Local user accounts.

- Personalized settings from these accounts, such as desktop backgrounds, sounds, screen savers, mouse pointer settings, Internet Explorer settings, and email settings including signature files and contact lists.

- Personal files belonging to these accounts including user profiles, the Desktop folder, the My Documents folder, and any other folder locations users might have utilized. USMT includes the capability to capture files even when they are in use, by means of Volume Shadow Copy technology.

- Operating system and application settings, including the user profile folders, or storage folders on the local disk defined within specific application settings.

- Information contained in previous Windows installations and included in Windows.old folders.

This tool reduces the costs of operating system deployment by addressing the following items:

- Technician time associated with migration

- Employee learning and familiarization time on the new operating system

- Employee downtime and help desk calls related to repersonalizing the desktop

- Employee downtime locating missing files

- Employee satisfaction with the migration experience

USMT consists of three executable files: ScanState.exe, LoadState.exe, and UsmtUtils.exe, and three migration rule files: MigApp.xml, MigUser.xml, and MigDocs.xml. You can modify these migration rules files as necessary. They contain the following settings:

- **MigApp.xml:** Rules for migrating application settings

- **MigDocs.xml:** Rules that locate user documents automatically without the need to create custom migration files

- **MigUser.xml:** Rules for migrating user profiles and user data

NOTE   You should not use MigDocs.xml and MigUser.xml together in the same migration. Otherwise, some migrated files might be duplicated if these files include conflicting instructions regarding target locations.

You can also create customized .xml files according to your migration requirements, as well as a Config.xml file that specifies files and settings to be excluded from migration (such as a user's large folder full of images and music). ScanState.exe collects user information from the old (source) computer based on settings contained in the various .xml files, and LoadState.exe places this information on a newly installed Windows 10 (destination) computer. The source computer can be running Windows Vista, 7, 8, 8.1, or 10.

> **CAUTION**   USMT is designed specifically for large-scale, automated transfers. If your migrations require end-user interaction or customization on a computer-by-computer basis, USMT is not recommended. In these cases, use PC Mover Express (a third-party tool), File History (if migrating from Windows 8 or 8.1), or manually copy your User folder instead.

Using the USMT involves running ScanState.exe at the source computer to collect the user state data to be migrated and transferring it to a shared folder on a server. Then you must run LoadState.exe on the destination computer to load the user state data there, as shown in Figure 9-25. Microsoft refers to the server used for this purpose as the *technician computer*. When migrating multiple users, you can create a script to automate this process.

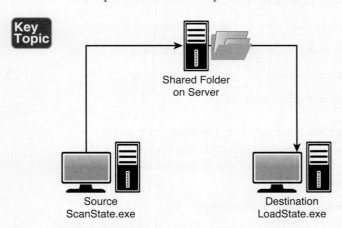

Key Topic

Figure 9-25   Components Involved in Performing a User State Migration Process

Preparing the Server to Run USMT

You need to create and share the appropriate folders on the technician computer before running USMT. This procedure requires the Windows Assessment and Deployment Kit (ADK) for Windows 10 1607, which you can download from https://developer.microsoft.com/en-us/windows/hardware/windows-assessment-deployment-kit and install. Use the following procedure:

Step 1. Create and share a folder named USMT on the technician computer. The migrating user should have Read permission to this folder, and the local administrator on the destination computer should have at least Modify permission to this folder. Ensure that this folder has enough storage space available to meet the needs of all computers to be migrated.

Step 2. Create and share a folder named MigStore on the technician computer. Both the migrating user and the local administrator on the destination computer should have at least Modify permission to this folder.

Step 3. In the USMT folder, create two subfolders named Scan and Load.

Step 4. Insert the Windows ADK disc and follow the instructions in the Setup program that automatically starts to install Windows ADK.

Step 5. Copy all files from the C:\Program Files(x86)\Windows Kits\10\ Assessment and Deployment Kit\User State Migration Tool structure using the correct architecture folder created during the Windows ADK installation to the USMT shared folder. You will have amd64, arm64, and x86. For example, use the following syntax:

```
xcopy " C:\Program Files (x86)\Windows Kits\10\Assessment and
    Deployment Kit\User State Migration Tool\x86" \\server\share\
    USMT
```

Step 6. Make any required modifications to the .xml files included in this folder, or create any additional .xml files as needed.

Collecting Files from the Source Computer

After you have created and shared the appropriate files on the technician computer, including the USMT folder and its contents, you are ready to scan the source computer and collect information to be exported to the new computer. Use the following procedure:

Step 1. Log on to the source computer with an account that has administrative privileges. This user should have permissions to the shares on the server as described in the previous procedure.

Step 2. Map a drive to the USMT share on the server.

Step 3. Open a command prompt and set its path to the Scan folder on the mapped USMT share.

Step 4.   To run ScanState, type the following command:

```
scanstate \\servername\migration\mystore /config:config.xml
    /i:miguser.xml /i:migapp.xml /v:13 /l:scan.log
```

In this command:

- **/i:** is the include parameter, which specifies an XML file that defines the user, application, or system state being migrated.

- **/config:** specifies the config.xml file used by scanstate.exe to create the store.

- *servername* is the name of the server on which you installed the Windows ADK tools.

- **l:** is a parameter that specifies the location of Scan.log, which is the name of a log file that will be created in the USMT share and will hold any error information from problems that might arise during the migration. If any problems occur, check the contents of this file.

- The **v:13** parameter specifies verbose, status, and debugger output to the log file.

NOTE   Both **ScanState** and **LoadState** support a large range of command-line options. Refer to the links in "User State Migration Tool (USMT) Command-Line Syntax" at https://technet.microsoft.com/en-us/itpro/windows/deploy/usmt-command-line-syntax.

Loading Collected Files on the Destination Computer

Before loading files to the destination computer, you should install Windows 10 and all required applications on this computer. However, do not create a local user account for the migrating user (this account is created automatically when you run **LoadState**). Join the computer to the domain if in a domain environment. Then perform the following procedure:

Step 1.   Log on to the destination computer as the local administrator (not the migrating account).

Step 2.   Map a drive to the USMT share on the server.

Step 3.   Open an administrative command prompt and set its path to the Load folder on the mapped USMT share.

Step 4.   To run **LoadState**, type the following command: (The set of .xml files should be the same as used when running ScanState.)

```
loadstate \\servername\migration\mystore /config:config.xml
    /i:miguser.xml /i:migapp.xml /lac /lae /v:13 /l:load.log
```

Step 5.   Log off and log on as the migrating user and verify that all required files and settings have been transferred.

In this command, **/lac** and **/lae** specify that local accounts from the source computer will be created and enabled on the destination computer. The other parameters are the same as defined previously for the ScanState tool. You can specify the password by using **/lac:ThePassword**.

> **NOTE**   For more information on LoadState, refer to "LoadState Syntax" at https://technet.microsoft.com/en-us/itpro/windows/deploy/usmt-loadstate-syntax.

Using the USMT in Offline Mode

As already discussed, USMT is designed for use when large numbers of users must be migrated from older computers to new computers running Windows 10. You can also use this tool when you have had to perform a full system reset due to an issue or for other reasons (system reset is covered in Chapter 20, "Configuring System Recovery Options"). After performing the restore, you can use a USB drive to hold the required commands for migrating user data from the Windows.old folder. Use the following procedure:

Step 1.   Download and install the Windows ADK as discussed earlier in this chapter.

Step 2.   Prepare an external USB drive by creating a USMT folder in the root directory. This folder should have x86 and amd64 subfolders for migrating 32-bit and 64-bit installations, respectively.

Step 3.   Copy the Program Files\Windows ADK\Tools\USMT folder from the computer on which you installed Windows ADK to the USMT folder in the USB drive.

Step 4.   Use Notepad to create a batch file for x86 file migrations. Microsoft suggests the following batch file:

```
@ECHO OFF
If exist D:\USMT\*.* xcopy D:\USMT\*.* /e /v /y C:\Windows\USMT\
If exist E:\USMT\*.* xcopy E:\USMT\*.* /e /v /y C:\Windows\USMT\
If exist F:\USMT\*.* xcopy F:\USMT\*.* /e /v /y C:\Windows\USMT\
If exist G:\USMT\*.* xcopy G:\USMT\*.* /e /v /y C:\Windows\USMT\
If exist H:\USMT\*.* xcopy H:\USMT\*.* /e /v /y C:\Windows\USMT\
If exist I:\USMT\*.* xcopy I:\USMT\*.* /e /v /y C:\Windows\USMT\
If exist J:\USMT\*.* xcopy J:\USMT\*.* /e /v /y C:\Windows\USMT\
If exist K:\USMT\*.* xcopy K:\USMT\*.* /e /v /y C:\Windows\USMT\
```

```
Cd c:\windows\usmt\x86
ScanState.exe c:\store /v:5 /o /c /hardlink /nocompress /
  efs:hardlink /i:MigApp.xml /i:MigDocs.xml /offlineWinOld:c:\
  windows.old\windows
LoadState.exe c:\store /v:5 /c /lac /lae /i:migapp.xml
  /i:migdocs.xml /sf /hardlink /nocompress
:EOF
```

Step 5.   Save this file to the USB drive as Migrate.bat.

Step 6.   Log on to the computer that has been upgraded using an administrative account.

Step 7.   Insert the USB drive and copy the Migrate.bat file to the desktop.

Step 8.   Right-click this file and choose **Run as Administrator**. If you receive a UAC prompt, click **Yes**.

Step 9.   When the batch file finishes, access the C:\ Users folder and confirm that all user files have been migrated to the appropriate file libraries.

This batch file locates USMT files and copies them to the C:\Windows folder so that the ScanState.exe command can create a hard-link migration store at C:\Store from the Windows\old folder. This hard-link migration process creates a catalog of hard links to files that are to be migrated. The **LoadState.exe** command then remaps the catalog of hard links to their appropriate locations in the Windows 10 installation. For AMD 64-bit machines, modify the batch file by changing the x86 subfolder references to amd64.

Configuring Folder Location

Microsoft includes the technologies of folder redirection and offline files for redirection of the paths of local folders to a network location while caching their contents locally for increased speed and availability. In this section, we take a look at folder redirection. Chapter 12, "Managing Mobile Devices," covers offline files in more detail. Using folder redirection, you can redirect the path of a known folder to a local or network location either manually or by using Group Policy. The process is transparent to the user, who works with data in the folder as if it were located in its default place.

> **NOTE**   For more information on folder redirection, see the links found at "Folder Redirection, Offline Files, and Roaming User Profiles Overview" at https://technet.microsoft.com/en-us/library/hh848267(v=ws.11).aspx.

Benefits of Folder Redirection

Users and administrators benefit from using folder redirection in the following ways:

- Users' documents are always accessible to them, regardless of which computer they log on to.

- When roaming user profiles are used, only the network path to a folder such as the Documents folder is part of the profile. This eliminates the need for copying the contents of this folder back and forth at each logon and logoff, thereby speeding up the logon/logoff process.

- You can configure the Offline File technology so that users' files are always available to them, even when they are not connected to the network. Their files are automatically cached and are in the same logical location (for example, the U: drive) on the laptop as they are when they are connected to the network, facilitating their working on the files when they are away from the office.

- It is easy to back up all users' files from a central server without interaction by the user. The administrator or backup operator can accomplish this task as part of the routine backup task.

- Administrators can use Group Policy to configure disk quotas, thereby controlling and monitoring the amount of disk space taken up by users' folders.

- You can standardize users' working environments by redirecting the Desktop folder to a common shared location. This standardization can help with remote support problems because the support staff will know the desktop layout of the users' computers.

Redirecting Library Folders

Libraries are sets of virtual folders (Documents, Pictures, Music, and Videos), which you can access by clicking the folder icon in the Windows 10 taskbar. You can also access libraries from any File Explorer window, where they are visible among the items listed in the left pane. Also recall that you can create a new library by right-clicking the **Libraries** node, choosing **New > Library** in the context menu, and providing a name for your new library.

First introduced with Windows 7 and continued in Windows 10 is the concept of virtualized folders. In Windows 10, a *library* is a set of virtual folders that are shared by default with other users of the computer. By default, Windows 10 includes six libraries (Documents, Pictures, Music, Saved Pictures, Camera Roll, and Videos). Documents, Pictures, Music, and Videos libraries are shown in File Explorer by default. To view all libraries categorized, select **Show Libraries** from the File Explorer's Navigation Pane drop-down. This will show the Libraries folder as shown in Figure 9-26. You can also see them when you open a File Explorer window and navigate to C:\Users\Public. The subfolders you see here are actually pointers to the folder locations on the computer. You can also think of them as the results of search queries. From the Libraries folder, you can create a new library by clicking **New Item** and selecting **Library** in the toolbar and providing a name for your new library.

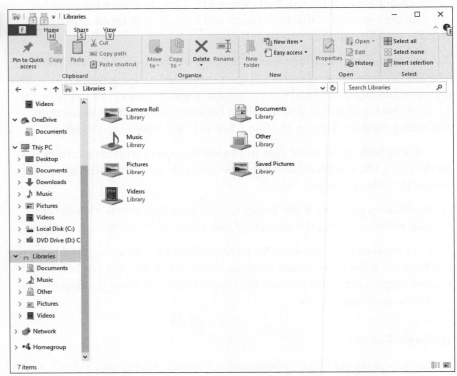

Figure 9-26 Windows 10 Four Default Libraries; You Can Create New Ones

Right-click any library and choose **Properties** to view its contents. Notice that each library contains a user-based subfolder, located by default at C:\Users\%username%. You can add additional folders by clicking the **Add** button shown in Figure 9-27 and navigating to the desired folder in the Include Folder dialog box, as shown in Figure 9-28; this can even include shared folders located on other computers on the network. You can also add folders to a library from any File Explorer window by selecting the folder and clicking the **Add to Library** option in the Explorer toolbar.

Figure 9-27 Each Library by Default Contains a User Subfolder

Figure 9-28 Adding a Folder to the Documents Library

The library's Properties dialog box also enables you to add folders and configure several additional properties. The check mark shown in Figure 9-27 indicates the default save location used by programs such as Microsoft Office. To change this location, select the desired location and click the **Set Save Location** command button. To change the location of public saved documents, select the appropriate folder and click the **Set Public Save Location** button. To remove a folder from the library, select it and click **Remove**. To remove all added folders from the library and reset it to its default settings, click the **Restore Defaults** button.

Implementing Domain-Based Folder Redirection

Implementation of folder redirection requires an Active Directory Domain Services (AD DS) domain and a server running Windows Server 2012/R2 or higher. You can also use a server running an older version of Windows Server, but some functionality might not be available. Use the following procedure to implement a Group Policy Object (GPO) that enables folder redirection in an AD DS domain or organizational unit (OU):

Step 1. Open Server Manager on a computer with the Group Policy Management console installed.

Step 2. Click **Tools > Group Policy Management** to display the Group Policy Management Console.

Step 3. Right-click the domain or OU where you want to configure Folder Redirection and choose **Create a GPO in This Domain, and Link It Here**.

Step 4. In the New GPO dialog box, type a name for the GPO and then click **OK**.

Step 5. Right-click this GPO and choose **Edit** to open the Group Policy Management Editor console.

Step 6. Navigate to User Configuration\Policies\Windows Settings\Folder Redirection. You receive the options shown in Figure 9-29.

Step 7. Right-click the folder to be redirected from the Details pane in Figure 9-29 and choose **Properties**. This action displays the Properties dialog box for the selected folder, as shown in Figure 9-30.

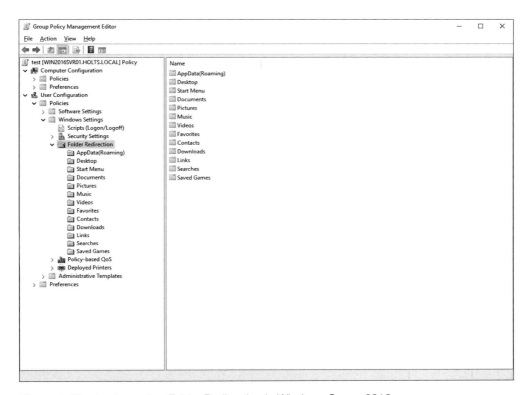

Figure 9-29 Implementing Folder Redirection in Windows Server 2016

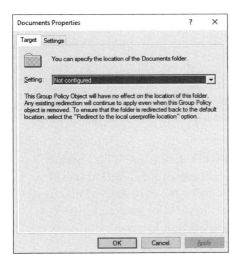

Figure 9-30 Choices for Implementing Folder Redirection in Windows Server 2016

Step 8. Under Setting, select from the following choices:

- **Basic–Redirect Everyone's Folder to the Same Location:** This option redirects all folders to this location.

- **Advanced–Specify Locations for Various User Groups:** This option redirects folders to different locations depending on the users' security group memberships. The bottom part of the dialog box changes so that you can specify a Universal Naming Convention (UNC) path for each security group.

- **Not Configured:** Folder redirection is not applied.

Step 9. Choose an option from those shown and described in the list that follows. To create a folder for each user, choose **Create a Folder for Each User Under the Root Path**. Type or browse to the desired path (in general, you will want to use a UNC path such as \\server1\documents), and then click **OK** or **Apply**.

- **Redirect to the User's Home Directory:** This option redirects users' folders to the home directory as specified in the user account's Properties dialog box in the Active Directory Administrative Center. This option works only for client computers running Windows 7 Professional, Windows Server 2008, or later, and is available only for the Documents folder.

- **Create a Folder for Each User Under the Root Path:** This option enables you to specify a root path in the form of a UNC path to a shared location. A subfolder is automatically created for each user in this location, and the folder path appears at the bottom of the dialog box.

- **Redirect to the Following Location:** This option enables you to specify a UNC path to the specific folder for each user. The username is automatically appended to the path you provided to create a unique folder name.

- **Redirect to the Local User Profile Location:** This option redirects users' folders to the local user profile location specified in the user account's Properties dialog boxes in Active Directory Administrative Center. This option is useful for returning redirected folders to their original default location.

Step 10. You receive a message box regarding Group Policy settings in Windows Server 2003 or older operating systems. Click **Yes** to accept this message and implement folder redirection.

Step 11.   You are returned to the Group Policy Management Console. Ensure that the GPO you created displays a GPO status of Enabled and that the Link Enabled column reads Yes.

NOTE   For more information on implementing folder redirection in a domain environment, including a complete procedure for deploying domain-based folder redirection, refer to "Deploy Folder Redirection with Offline Files" at https://technet.microsoft.com/en-us/library/jj649078(v=ws.11).aspx.

NOTE   Applying these policies requires security filtering, and a recent update may affect the capability of older computers to apply group policy updates. To correct this issue, make sure that the domain computers group has Read permissions on your GPO. For details, refer to "MS16-072: Security Update for Group Policy: June 14, 2016" at https://support.microsoft.com/en-us/help/3163622/ms16-072-security-update-for-group-policy-june-14,-2016.

Configuring Local, Roaming, and Mandatory Profiles

When a user logs on to a Windows 10 computer, the operating system generates a *user profile*. This profile is composed of desktop settings, files, application data, and the specific environment established by the user. For example, a user named Peter logs on to Windows 10, changes his desktop wallpaper to a picture of his dog, edits the user information in Microsoft Word, configures a dial-up connection to his Internet service provider (ISP), and adjusts the mouse so that it is easier to double-click. When Sharon logs on to the same computer using her own account, she sees the default settings for Windows 10, not Peter's settings. When Peter logs on next, Windows finds Peter's existing profile and loads his settings—the wallpaper, the Word data, the dial-up connection, and the mouse click settings.

Windows 10 provides the following profile versions:

- **Local:** A profile that is available only on the computer and for the user for whom it is configured.

- **Roaming:** A profile that has been placed on a server so that it is available to a given user no matter which computer she is logged on to. A user is free to make changes to this profile version at any time.

- **Mandatory:** A profile that has been placed on a server but is configured as read-only; the user is unable to make any changes to it.

In addition to these profile types, it is possible to set up a temporary profile, which is loaded by default if the user is unable to load her normal profile.

When Windows 10 is connected to a Windows network, you can configure a user profile to roam the network with the user. Because the profile is stored in a sub-folder in the Users folder on the %systemdrive% volume, you can configure the profile to be placed on a network drive rather than a local hard disk, thereby making it accessible to the user regardless of which computer she is using.

User profiles allow users to customize their own settings without impairing another user's configuration. User profiles were developed in response to organizations that routinely provided shared desktop computers. In cases where a user absolutely requires certain settings to use the computer comfortably, having to share a computer with another person who then removes the needed configuration can be frustrating, and it causes a loss of productivity. Another advantage to user profiles is that, when used in conjunction with network storage of data, the desktop computer is easily replaceable—users can use any computer on the network without having to perform extra tasks to customize the computer to suit their needs.

To use profiles, each user must have a separate user account. The user account can be a domain account or a local account. There are four types of profiles, which are detailed in Table 9-7.

Table 9-7 Profile Types

Profile	Created For	How It Works
Local	Every user at first logon	When the user logs on to a computer, whether it is connected to a network or not, a local profile is created and saved in the local Users folder for that user. All changes are saved when the user logs off.
Roaming	Users who log on to different computers on the network	The profile is stored on a server. When a user logs on to a network computer, the profile is copied locally to the computer. When the user logs off the network, changes to the profile are copied back to the server.
Mandatory	Administrative enforcement of settings (This is applied to user accounts that are shared by two or more users.)	The profile is stored on a server. When a user logs on to a network computer, the profile is copied locally to the computer. No changes are saved when the user logs off the server. Only an administrator can make changes to the profile.
Temporary	Users that were unable to load their profile	When an error condition exists that prevents a user from loading her normal profile, a temporary profile is loaded. When the user logs off, all changes are deleted.

User profiles consist of a Registry hive that incorporates the data typically found in NTuser.dat, saved as a file that is mapped to the HKEY_CURRENT_USER Registry node, and a set of profile folders.

You can change the location where Windows looks for a user's profile. When you do so, you must be logged on to the computer as a member of the Administrators group. Use the following procedure:

Step 1. Right-click **Start** and choose **Computer Management**.

Step 2. Expand the Local Users and Groups folder and select **Users**. Information about all users configured on the computer appears in the Details pane.

Step 3. Right-click a user account and select **Properties** from the shortcut menu.

Step 4. Click the **Profile** tab.

Step 5. Type the location of the profile in the Profile Path text box. For example, type the UNC path as shown in Figure 9-31. Then click **OK**.

Figure 9-31   Configuring a User's Profile Path

Step 6. From this dialog box, you can perform the following actions:

- Click **Default Profile** and then click **Copy To** in order to copy an existing profile to another computer. This is useful in a nondomain situation where you want to standardize profiles between computers.

- Click **Delete** to delete a profile for a user. This is useful when you are moving a computer to a different user.

- Click **Change Type** to change the profile from a local profile to a roaming profile, or vice versa.

Step 7.   When finished, click **OK**.

Using Roaming and Mandatory Profiles with Active Directory

Roaming and mandatory profiles require a network server for implementation. Although it is recommended that you have an AD DS network for this, you can implement these profiles on other network servers. An AD DS network is recommended for use with roaming and mandatory profiles because of the additional management features that are provided by Group Policy. For example, you can specify additional folders to include in the profile, as well as mark certain folders to exclude from the profile.

An additional advantage to using Group Policy in conjunction with roaming profiles is that you can prevent users from running applications that you deem to be unacceptable, or allow a user to run only a short list of applications. Even if a user has installed the application and incorporated its data into the user's profile prior to the restriction policy, the GPO will prevent the user from running it.

When you use Group Policy together with roaming profiles, you can ensure that a user's Windows 10 settings are exactly what you want the user to have. You can create a default user profile that includes the desktop icons, startup applications, documents, Start menu items, and other settings. Then, you can use Group Policy to manage the way that the user interacts with the network, such as preventing access to Control Panel. You can even use Group Policy to publish certain applications that the user can install, and you can redirect users' Documents and Desktop folders to a network location. When a user logs on to the network the first time, the desktop will be configured with the settings that are appropriate for your organization. If the user makes changes to the profile, those changes will be saved. The user can then log on to an entirely different computer the next day and automatically see the environment he configured for himself, plus have immediate access to his personal files, folders, and applications.

For more information on using roaming profiles in AD DS, including a detailed procedure for setting up a sample implementation, refer to "Deploy Roaming User Profiles" at https://technet.microsoft.com/en-us/library/jj649079(v=ws.11).aspx.

Implementing Roaming Profiles

Local profiles cause an administrative headache when users roam around the network, and when computers are routinely exchanged throughout the network. For example, if Joe logs on at PC1 and saves a file that holds key information for his job on his desktop, and later on Joe logs on at PC2 because PC1 was replaced with new hardware, he is likely to have a panic attack to discover that his file is missing. Roaming profiles overcome this problem.

When a user with a roaming profile logs on for the first time, the following process takes place:

1. Windows checks for the path to the user's roaming profile.

2. Windows accesses the path and looks for the profile. If no profile exists, Windows generates a folder for the profile.

3. Windows checks for a cached copy of the profile listed in HKLM\ SOFTWARE\Microsoft\Windows NT\Current Version\ProfileList. If a local profile is found, and the computer is a member of a domain, Windows looks in the domain controller's NETLOGON share for a default profile for the domain. The default domain profile is copied to the local computer folder %systemdrive%\Users\%username%. If there is no domain default, Windows copies the default local profile to the same location.

4. The NTuser.dat file is mapped to the Registry's HKEY_CURRENT_USER key.

5. Windows updates the user's %userprofile% environment variable with the new location of the profile.

6. When the user logs off, the local profile is copied to the network path configured in Windows.

7. The next time the user logs on to the same computer, Windows opens the locally cached copy of the user's profile and compares it with the copy on the domain server. Windows merges the contents of the two profiles.

You can make changes to whether a computer uses local or roaming profiles in Control Panel. Use the following procedure:

Step 1. From the System and Security category of Control Panel, click **System**. You can also right-click **Start** and choose **System** from the programs list that appears.

Step 2. From the System dialog box that appears, click **Advanced System Settings**.

Step 3. Click the **Advanced** tab and then click the **Settings** button under **User Profiles** to display the dialog box shown in Figure 9-32.

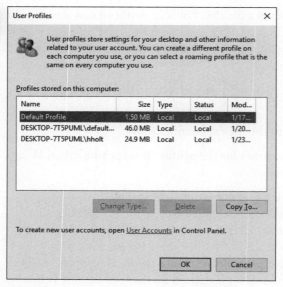

Figure 9-32   Profile Management Options

Step 4.   From this dialog box, you can perform the following actions:

- **Change Profile Type:** Select a profile and click **Change Type** to change the profile from a local profile to a roaming profile, or vice versa.

- **Delete a Profile:** Select a profile and click **Delete** to delete an existing profile. This is useful when you are moving the computer to a different user.

- **Copy a Profile:** Select a profile and click **Copy To** in order to use the same settings for another user on the same computer.

Step 5.   When finished, click **OK**.

Establishing Mandatory Profiles

A mandatory profile is a roaming profile that can't be changed by the user. You configure the profile identically to the roaming profile. After the profile has been configured and saved as the NTuser.dat file in the user's profile path on the network, you need to rename the file to NTuser.man.

When the NTuser.dat file is renamed with the .man extension, it is treated as though it is a read-only file. At user logon, the file is read the same way as a roaming profile. However, if a user makes any changes to the environment, the changes are discarded when the user logs off. A mandatory profile is helpful in managing the desktop environment for users who unpredictably and accidentally delete items from their desktop and Start menu, or make other unintended changes. A mandatory profile is not useful for users who need a dynamic environment for running a variety of applications.

Starting with Windows 8.1 and Windows Server 2012 R2, mandatory profiles become *super-mandatory* profiles when stored in a profile path ending in .man; for example, \\server\share\mandatoryprofile.man\. When a super-mandatory profile is in use, users who use these profiles cannot log on if the server on which the profile is stored becomes unavailable. With ordinary mandatory profiles, a user can log on with the locally cached copy of the mandatory profile.

When you configure a mandatory profile to be used in an organization to be shared by a variety of users or computers, and when a single user moves around a network to use different computers, the profile's graphical presentation should be made to run at a level that all the computers can support. For example, if you have some computers that support a maximum 1680 × 1050 resolution, you should not create a profile with a 1920 × 1080 resolution setting because it will not display correctly on some of the computers.

If you need to make changes to a mandatory profile, rename the profile back to NTuser.dat, log on as the user, and configure the computer. When you have completed the changes, you should log off so that the changes are saved to the profile. Then, after logging on as an administrator, you can rename the file as NTuser.man. If this is a profile that should be used by multiple people, you can replace the other users' NTuser.man files with the new version.

NOTE   For more information on mandatory user profiles, refer to "Create Mandatory User Profiles" at https://technet.microsoft.com/en-us/itpro/windows/manage/mandatory-user-profile.

User Profiles and Operating System Versions

Most networks include computers running different Windows versions, such as Windows 7, Windows 8.1, and Windows 10, as well as servers running either the original or R2 versions of Windows Server 2008 or 2012 along with Windows Server 2016. Each newer operating system version has introduced modifications to roaming and mandatory user profiles. Consequently, if a user moves between computers running different Windows versions, the user profiles are not compatible with each other. Profile versions include the following:

- Version 1 profiles used by Windows Vista, Windows Server 2008, and older Windows versions

- Version 2 profiles used by Windows 7 and Windows Server 2008 R2

- Version 3 profiles used by Windows 8 and Windows Server 2012

- Version 4 profiles used by Windows 8.1 and Windows Server 2012 R2

- Version 5 profiles used by Windows 10 and Windows Server 2016

- Version 6 profiles used by Windows 10, 1607 and Windows Server 2016, 1607.

When a user logs on to a Windows 10 computer for the first time after using an older computer, Windows 10 automatically updates the profile to version 5. If the user then logs on to an older computer, the available profile is incompatible and is not loaded; further, the profile might become corrupted.

Microsoft recommends that you keep roaming, mandatory, super-mandatory, and domain default profiles created in one Windows version separate from those that were created in a different Windows version. For more information, including the Registry entry that must be created, refer to "Deploy Roaming User Profiles" at https://technet.microsoft.com/en-us/library/jj649079.aspx.

Exam Preparation Tasks

Review All the Key Topics

Review the most important topics in the chapter, noted with the Key Topics icon in the outer margin of the page. Table 9-8 lists a reference of these key topics and the page numbers on which each is found.

Table 9-8   Key Topics for Chapter 9

Key Topic Element	Description	Page Number
Figure 9-1	Disk Management tool used for managing storage	451
Step List	Creating a new storage volume	454
Figure 9-6	Volume properties and space allocation	457
Table 9-2	Dynamic volume types	460
Step List	Creating a striped volume	462
Figure 9-13	Configuring removable storage	468
Step List	Creating a Storage Space	469
Table 9-4	Troubleshooting disk errors	472

Key Topic Element	Description	Page Number
Figure 9-16	Using the Optimize Drives utility	475
Table 9-5	Parameters available with the Defrag command	477
Figure 9-21	Managing Storage Spaces	481
Figure 9-25	Using the User State Migration Tool	490
List	Benefits of folder redirection	495
Figure 9-26	Creating and working with Windows Libraries	496
Step List	Implementing folder redirection	498
Figure 9-31	Configuring a user profile path for roaming profiles	503
Figure 9-32	Managing user profiles	506

Definitions of Key Terms

Define the following key terms from this chapter, and check your answers in the glossary.

active partition, basic disk, Disk Management snap-in, DiskPart, distributed file system (DFS), DFS folder, DFS Namespace, DFS Replication, dynamic disk, extended partition, folder redirection, local user profile, logical drive, mandatory profile, mirroring, partition, primary partition, RAID-5, roaming profile, storage pool, storage space, striping, user profile, volume

This chapter covers the following subjects:

- **Introduction to Virtualization:** In Chapter 2, "Implementing Windows," you learned about virtual hard disks (VHDs) and native boot VHDs and how to install Windows 10 on them. In this section, VHDs are covered in more detail; you learn about the new VHDX format optimized for Hyper-V and how to create, configure, and use VHDs in the virtual environment.

- **Creating and Configuring Virtual Machines:** Hyper-V is Microsoft's virtualization technology used in Windows Server 2008 and later and is now available for Windows 10. This section introduces Client Hyper-V, the virtualization technology used in Windows 10, how to deploy VHDs and virtual machines in Client Hyper-V, and how to configure virtual machines.

- **Creating and Managing Virtual Machine Checkpoints:** One of the benefits of working with virtual machines is the capability to run experiments with them using a safety net to fully restore the previous state. In Hyper-V, you can create checkpoints for your virtual machine for any point in time that you want to preserve. If something goes wrong, or if you just want to start over, you can return virtual machines to any checkpoint and resume working from there.

- **Creating and Configuring Virtual Switches:** When using Hyper-V, you work not only with virtual machines and hard disks, but also virtual networks. Virtual networks utilize software representations of network switches, and this section discusses the types of virtual switches used with Hyper-V, how to create and configure them, and how the virtual networks interact with the host computer and the outside world.

This chapter covers the following objectives for the 70-697 exam:

Configure Hyper-V: Create and configure virtual machines, including integration services; create and manage checkpoints; create and configure virtual switches; create and configure virtual disks; move a virtual machine's storage.

CHAPTER 10

Windows Hyper-V

Virtualization is a technique for carving up physical computer resources into multiple pseudo machines, allowing multiple operating systems to run on a single hardware platform. The virtual machine appears to be a complete physical computer to the operating system running inside it. A special underlying operating system known as a *hypervisor* is responsible for controlling access to the physical hardware and presenting the virtualized resources to the operating system guests.

This is not new technology. IBM came out with the first system capable of virtualization in 1972 with the release of VM/CMS for its mainframe systems. Microcomputers, using smaller, cheaper commodity hardware, slowly started replacing mainframes in the datacenter, and as the Intel and AMD platforms became more powerful, eventually virtualization was introduced in these platforms as well. Initially, virtualization for large servers and datacenters was a way to make use of all of the idle cycles on the servers, which became even more efficient when manufacturers began producing microprocessors with multiple cores on a single chip. For companies with requirements for lots of servers to run their businesses, virtualization was a way to save money on hardware, power, and rack space by running more servers on fewer machines.

Microsoft introduced the final production version of its virtualization product, now called Hyper-V, in June of 2008. Hyper-V is now available without additional license fees for all versions of Windows Server 2008 and later.

Client Hyper-V is now built in to Windows 10 and is the same virtualization technology as previously used in Windows Server 2008 and later. This allows you to run more than one operating system at the same time on the same workstation computer. Guest operating systems run in a virtual machine (VM), and you can quickly switch between the Windows 10 host operating system and any VM.

For the 70-697 exam, you are expected to understand some basics of how virtualization works, know the hardware and operating system requirements for running Client Hyper-V, and have the skills to install the Hyper-V hypervisor in Windows 10. You should also know how to create and manage virtual hard disks (VHDs), deploy virtual machines using VHDs, and how to configure and manage *virtual switches*, which are virtual representations of physical hardware that run right inside the host machine's virtualized environment.

"Do I Know This Already?" Quiz

The "Do I Know This Already?" quiz allows you to assess whether you should read this entire chapter or simply jump to the "Exam Preparation Tasks" section for review. If you are in doubt, read the entire chapter. Table 10-1 outlines the major headings in this chapter and the corresponding "Do I Know This Already?" quiz questions. You can find the answers in Appendix A, "Answers to the 'Do I Know This Already?' Quizzes."

Table 10-1   "Do I Know This Already?" Foundation Topics Section-to-Question Mapping

Foundation Topics Section	Questions Covered in This Section
Introduction to Virtualization	1–3
Creating and Configuring Virtual Machines	4–8
Creating and Managing Virtual Machine Checkpoints	9
Creating and Configuring Virtual Switches	10–11

CAUTION   The goal of self-assessment is to gauge your mastery of the topics in this chapter. If you do not know the answer to a question or are only partially sure of the answer, you should mark that question as wrong for purposes of the self-assessment. Giving yourself credit for an answer you correctly guess skews your self-assessment results and might provide you with a false sense of security.

1.   Virtual hard disks are used for deploying Windows operating systems in a number of ways, including in a Hyper-V virtual environment. What type of VHD is optimized for use in Hyper-V?

   a. Native-boot VHDs

   b. VHDX-formatted VHDs

   c. Hyper-VHDs

   d. VHDs in .AVHD format

2. The new VHD format optimized for Hyper-V supports which of the following features? (Select all that apply.)

    a. Storage capacity up to 2 TB

    b. Metadata logging to prevent file system corruption

    c. Larger block sizes for dynamic and differencing disks

    d. User-defined custom metadata

3. Which of the following tools can be used to create a virtual hard disk? (Select all that apply.)

    a. DiskPart

    b. Hyper-V Manager

    c. BCDEdit

    d. Disk Management

4. You are a desktop support technician for a large corporation, and one of the developers in your organization has asked you to install Hyper-V on a corporate workstation for use in testing some new application software. You have obtained the detailed order slip for that computer and realize that you will not be able to install Hyper-V on it. Which item did you discover on the order specifications that led to that conclusion?

    a. Dell computer with Intel Core i-7 processor

    b. Windows 10 Enterprise 32-bit

    c. 6 GB system RAM

    d. 250 GB internal IDE hard drive

    e. BIOS version 2012.23a with VT and XD enabled

5. You are a desktop support technician for a large corporation, and one of the developers in your organization has asked you to install Hyper-V on a corporate workstation for use in testing some new application software. The developer ordered a new workstation that meets all the necessary requirements and now you need to install the Hyper-V software. How do you obtain the necessary installation files?

    a. The software is already available on the computer.

    b. Download from the Microsoft website.

    c. Obtain a disk from your Enterprise License administrator.

    d. Order it from your software reseller.

6. You are modifying the configuration of a virtual machine in Client Hyper-V from the Hyper-V Manager. The computer has 12 GB of system RAM. What is the maximum amount of RAM you can select in the virtual machine's configuration settings?

   a. 12 GB

   b. 10 GB

   c. 120 GB

   d. 1 TB

7. You have a test computer with several Hyper-V virtual machines configured. One of the VMs is hosting an application that you want to test in various operating systems and configurations, so you have several VMs to use for testing access to the application. You have now run into problems when several of the VMs are running, and the host processors are running high utilization, that cause the application host to perform too slowly to test properly. What should you do to ensure that the VM hosting the application can respond properly?

   a. Enable Dynamic Memory.

   b. Increase the Memory weight of the application VM.

   c. Assign a higher relative weight to the application VM's processor.

   d. Add more processors to the test VMs.

8. You are running Client Hyper-V on a large workstation equipped with 16 GB of system RAM and two processors with four cores each. If you are running four virtual machines on this computer, what is the maximum number of virtual processors you can assign to each one?

   a. 2 virtual processors

   b. 4 virtual processors

   c. 8 virtual processors

   d. 16 virtual processors

9. You are performing testing on a Client Hyper-V virtual machine and have created checkpoints every day for the past 5 days. You select the first checkpoint from the list in the Hyper-V Manager and delete the first checkpoint. What happens to the virtual machine?

   a. All changes since the first checkpoint are lost.

   b. The VM is reverted to before the first checkpoint.

   c. Changes made since the checkpoint are merged into the running state.

   d. The virtual machine is restarted and the checkpoint changes are lost.

10. You are creating virtual switches for use with your virtual machines and would like to ensure that they can access the Internet and Windows Update. What type of virtual switch would you create for these VMs?

   a. Internal virtual switch

   b. External virtual switch

   c. Public virtual switch

   d. Private virtual switch

11. You have used the Hyper-V Manager to create a new internal virtual switch, and have connected all of your VMs to the new switch, but the VMs' network configurations are still using private autoconfiguration addresses, and you cannot ping any of the VMs from the host. What should you do to allow the host to communicate with the VMs?

   a. Manually configure the IP settings of the host and VMs.

   b. Use connection sharing on the Hyper-V host.

   c. Use an external virtual switch instead.

   d. Turn off the firewall.

Foundation Topics

Introduction to Virtualization

In Chapter 2, "Implementing Windows," we covered how to use a virtual hard disk (VHD) in Windows 10 and how to install Windows 10 on an existing VHD. Some of this material will be a review of the "Using a VHD" section of Chapter 2 and will then go further in depth into the types of VHDs, and how they are created, managed, and deployed in Hyper-V.

Recall from Chapter 2 that the VHD was used to create a new bootable Windows 10 installation, which was then added to the computer's boot menu. The technique was a convenient way to create a Windows 10 image that could then be copied to other computers and booted from the boot menu. It makes deploying Windows 10 to multiple machines very convenient, but VHDs are useful in many other ways, especially when combined with Hyper-V.

A VHD can be used not just for Windows 10 or Windows 7; it could alternatively contain Windows XP, a Linux or UNIX distribution, or a custom, bootable appliance. With Hyper-V, it is not necessary to add this image to the boot menu and restart the computer. Instead, the alternative OS can run in a virtual machine as a guest while the Windows 10 operating system is running as a host. Hyper-V is the same technology Microsoft uses to host virtual machines in the Azure cloud. You can even migrate virtual machines from your on-premises data center to Azure.

NOTE   You can explore virtual machine hosting on Azure at https://azure.microsoft.com/en-us/services/virtual-machines.

Creating and Configuring VHDs

Before creating and running operating system guests under Client Hyper-V, it is necessary to create a virtual disk for the guest OS to use. Client Hyper-V can run guests installed on VHD files, or the new VHDX format, designed specifically for virtual machines running under Hyper-V.

The new VHDX format provides several advantages over the VHD format, but note that VHDX formatted disks cannot be used as native-boot VHDs—only guests running in Hyper-V or Client Hyper-V can make use of VHDX files. The VHDX format supports the following features:

- Support for storage capacity up to 64 TB (compared to 2 TB for VHD format).

- Support for VHDX metadata logging, to protect against file system corruption during power failures and improper shutdown.

- Improved alignment for greater efficiency on large sector disks.

- Large block sizes for dynamic and differencing disks.

- Support for 4 KB logical sector VHDs.

- Support for user-editable custom metadata for the VHDX file.

- Support for smaller file sizes using trim, when using trim-compatible hardware.

In Chapter 2, we created a VHD using the Disk Management snap-in. We also used BCDEdit to manage the boot configuration for a native boot VHD. This is probably the most common method of creating a VHD in Windows 10, but there are other tools and procedures you should understand and know how to use. You should review Table 2-10 and be familiar with the available tools.

You can also create a VHD using the Hyper-V Manager in Windows 10. This utility can be run on any Windows 10 machine, even if the computer cannot support the Hyper-V platform. Installing and using the Hyper-V Manager are covered in the next section.

In this section we cover the process for creating a VHD using the DiskPart command-line tool. It is included with Windows as part of the default installation, and no further installation is needed to start using it.

Using DiskPart to Create a VHD

The DiskPart utility enables you to create a VHD from the command line. You can script this action to create multiple VHDs if necessary. The DiskPart command-line tool is also available in Windows 8, 7, Vista, and Windows Server editions 2008 and later. It is used to manage storage objects, including disks, partitions, and volumes by using scripts or directly from the command prompt.

Using DiskPart requires that you use commands to focus on an object using Disk-Part commands to list and select a particular storage object, then use commands that act on that object. In the list that follows, the **create** commands act to focus on the objects created, and subsequent **DiskPart** commands will act on that object.

> **NOTE**   For more information on the DiskPart utility, syntax, and commands, see the topic "DiskPart Commands" at https://technet.microsoft.com/en-us/library/cc770877(v=ws.11).aspx.

Step 1.   Open a command prompt by clicking the Search bar or Cortana, typing **cmd** into the Search box, right-clicking the **Command Prompt** link, and then selecting the **Run as Administrator** option from the pop-up menu. You can also right-click **Start** and choose **Command Prompt (Admin)** from the menu that appears. Click **Yes** in the User Account Control prompt that appears.

Step 2.   Type **diskpart** into the administrator command prompt window. You receive the **DISKPART>** command prompt.

Step 3.   To create a dynamic VHD of 20 GB using the VHDX format and named win01.vhdx, type **create vdisk file="c:\win01.vhdx" maximum=20000 type=expandable**. The format is taken from the extension used (VHD or VHDX).

Step 4.   When you are informed that DiskPart has successfully created the file, type **attach vdisk**.

Step 5.   When DiskPart informs you that the disk was attached, type **list disk** to show that the disk is present and online. This command also provides the disk number that you must enter in the next step of the procedure.

Step 6.   To create a partition on the VHD, type **select disk** *n*, press Enter, type **create partition primary**, and then press Enter again. In this command, *n* is the disk number you obtained from the previous step.

Step 7.   To perform a quick format on the partition using the NTFS file system, type **format fs=ntfs quick**.

Step 8.   To assign the drive letter F: to the new partition, type **assign letter=F**.

Step 9.   To mark the partition as active, type **active**.

These steps complete the creation of a VHD on drive F: that is suitable for installing a virtual copy of Windows. Figure 10-1 shows how these steps appear at the console. Table 10-2 outlines the parameters of the **vdisk** command that are most useful for creating and working with VHDs.

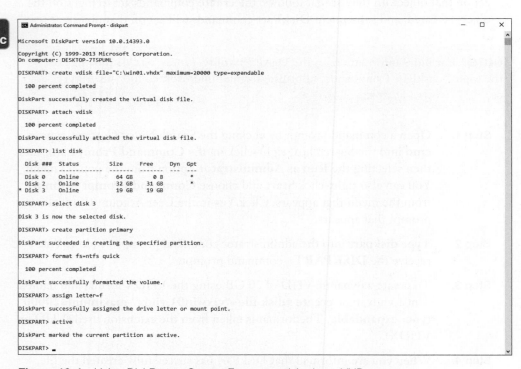

Figure 10-1   Using DiskPart to Create, Format, and Assign a VHD

Refer to Table 10-2 for some common DiskPart command parameters and how they are used.

Table 10-2   DiskPart Commands Used in Creating VHDs

Command	Purpose
create vdisk file="*filename*" **maximum= type=**	Creates a VHD with name of *filename*, maximum *size* stated in MB, and *type* = **fixed**, **expandable**, or **differencing**. The extension used for the filename determines whether the format used is VHD or VHDX.
attach	Attaches (mounts) the VHD.
list disk	Shows all disks (physical and virtual) attached to the system, together with their size and identifying number.
Select disk=	Selects the VHD so that it can be partitioned and formatted, where *n* is the number of the disk as shown by the **list disk** command.
create partition primary	Creates a primary partition on the VHD, using the maximum available space. If you want to use only a portion of the VHD, include the keyword **size=***nnnn*, where *nnnn* is the partition size in MB.
format fs=filesystem	Formats the partition using the file system *filesystem* (which can be **fat**, **fat32**, exFAT, ReFS, UDF, or **ntfs**). Add the keyword **quick** to perform a quick format.
assign letter=	Assigns a drive letter to the partition.
active	Marks the selected partition as active.

Mounting VHDs

The act of creating a VHD in the previous section also mounts the VHD automatically, so that it is accessible to the physical machine as a distinct drive with its own drive letter. It is also possible to create a VHD on one computer, make copies of it, and use these copies on other computers. To do so, you must *mount* the VHD on each new computer. Simply put, this is the virtual analogy of opening the computer, installing and connecting a new hard disk, closing the computer back up, and rebooting it. You can perform these tasks using Disk Management. Figure 10-2 shows the results of the preceding DiskPart commands in the Disk Management console.

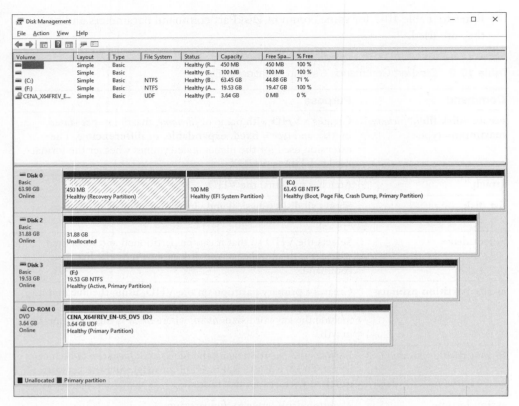

Figure 10-2 View of a VHD from Disk Management, Mounted and Assigned to Drive F

You can also dismount a VHD from either of these two utilities. In Disk Management, right-click the VHD in the Details pane and choose **Detach VHD**. In DiskPart, select the VHD and then type **detach vdisk**.

> **TIP** You can even mount a VHD located on another computer across the network, provided you have proper access permissions to its location. In Disk Management, click **Browse**, click **Network**, and browse to the proper network location. In Disk-Part, type the Universal Naming Convention (UNC) path to the shared location for "*path*" in Step 3 of the preceding procedure.

> **TIP** You can use Windows Deployment Services (WDS) to deploy the VHD image to large numbers of computers. WDS in Windows Server 2012 and later versions include the capability to add VHD image files to its image catalog, making them available to target computers using PXE boot.

Creating and Configuring Virtual Machines

After you create a VHD in Windows 10, you can create a VM guest using the VHD as the VM's drive. You can then load and run the VM in Client Hyper-V on your Windows 10 Pro or Windows 10 Enterprise workstation.

This is the easiest method for supporting a VM, but note that a VHD is not strictly a requirement. Virtual machines can also be run using actual disks, passed directly to the virtual machine. It is also possible to run a VM from a VHD on a remote file server.

To support Client Hyper-V, you need to be aware of the following requirements:

- A 64-bit version of Windows 10 Pro, Enterprise, or Education. Client Hyper-V will not run on Windows 10 Home or any 32-bit edition.

- A CPU that supports Second Level Address Translation (SLAT). All current versions of AMD 64-bit processors support SLAT, as do many 64-bit processors from Intel. Some budget and mobile editions of Intel processors do not support SLAT.

- A BIOS with virtualization support, either VT for Intel platforms or AMD-V for AMD-based systems.

- Hardware Data Execution Prevention (DEP). This is called Execute Disable, or XD, on Intel processors and No Execute, or NX, on AMD processors. The option must be enabled in the BIOS.

- At least 4 GB of system RAM.

The number of VMs you can run and the performance of each will depend on the amount of RAM you have available. You can create VMs that use up to 1 TB of RAM, and each VM will require some overhead memory, in addition to the memory required by the host operating system and the hypervisor.

> **NOTE**   For more details on hardware and software requirements for Client Hyper-V, see the Microsoft TechNet article "Windows 10 Hyper-V System Requirements" at https://docs.microsoft.com/en-us/virtualization/hyper-v-on-windows/reference/hyper-v-requirements.

Enabling Client Hyper-V in Windows 10

Windows 10 Pro and higher editions come with Client Hyper-V available out of the box, but it must be installed using the Windows Features installer from the Control Panel's Programs snap-in. The feature installer provides a convenient way to make sure that your Windows 10 computer can support the Hyper-V hypervisor, because it can detect many of the requirements and disable the option if any requirements are missing.

Use the following steps to enable Hyper-V:

Step 1.   Right-click the **Start** button and select **Control Panel** from the menu.

Step 2.   In the Control Panel window, select **Programs**.

Step 3.   From the list of Programs and Features functions, click **Turn Windows Features On or Off**.

Step 4.   Expand the Hyper-V folder, displaying the selections Hyper-V Management Tools and Hyper-V Platform.

NOTE   If Client Hyper-V is not supported due to any missing requirements, the Hyper-V Platform option will be disabled. Hover your pointer over the disabled option and Windows will display a tool tip to explain why you cannot install the Hyper-V Platform. In Figure 10-3, Hyper-V Platform is disabled because the processor does not have the required virtualization capabilities.

Figure 10-3   Hyper-V Cannot Be Installed Because the Processor Does Not Support the Necessary Virtualization Features

Step 1.   Select all Hyper-V options to include Management Tools and the Hyper-V Platform.

Step 2.   Click **OK** to install the Hyper-V features. Windows will take a few minutes to perform the installation and then request a reboot to complete the changes.

Step 3.   Click **Reboot Now** to complete the installation.

After Windows has restarted, Hyper-V will be installed and ready to use.

Creating a Hyper-V Virtual Machine

There are many scenarios that make the use of virtual machines in a client environment a compelling solution for efficient use of resources and time. Server virtualization provides many advantages for making the best use of costly hardware resources. Client Hyper-V offers some of the same efficiencies, but that is less of a consideration than other use cases. The following are several advantages of using Client Hyper-V:

- Maintaining multiple test environments for developers and system engineers.

- Running older versions of Windows for applications that will not run on current versions.

- Building a test lab infrastructure on a computer or laptop. Workstations or server VMs tested in the virtual lab can be migrated to a virtualized production environment.

- Developers or QA professionals can test applications or changes on multiple operating systems, using a single Client Hyper-V computer.

- Export a VM from the production environment to a Client Hyper-V test machine. From there troubleshooting can be performed, fixes applied and tested, and the system restarted multiple times without impacting the current production systems.

- Use VM checkpoints while a machine is running to test invasive changes. You can test changes and revert to the point-in-time before the checkpoint if things go wrong, or apply the checkpoint back to the running VM if the testing is successful.

- With a workstation with a fast processor and enough RAM, an entire working environment can be deployed as VMs on Client Hyper-V, to include all networking configurations and virtual switches. It can be used for testing, software development, or even demonstration of a proof-of-concept.

Designing a virtual environment for some of these scenarios may require some planning. Or it can serve as a proof-of-concept environment as a preliminary step to planning an environment. Because you are not deploying expensive hardware, all your changes can be easily reversed, changed, or simply deleted. A virtual environment provides the freedom to experiment with options without much risk. The changes you make and systems you design can be documented as you go, and planning can be performed when technical challenges are overcome. Deciding when to take a checkpoint of a VM or a set of VMs may be the most difficult planning decision to make during the testing. The only disruption any of your changes cause will be to a single workstation.

Note that one of the scenarios in the preceding list was based on a use case for running older applications that do not work in current versions of Windows. This may be a rare scenario, but it does happen. Applications can become obsolete and unsupported but are still required for business needs that cannot easily be replaced. In Windows Vista and Windows 7, this type of issue was addressed with Windows XP Mode, which allowed users to run a virtualized version of Windows XP on top of their Windows Vista or Windows 7 computer. In Windows 10, this trimmed-down virtualization feature has been replaced with Hyper-V.

Using the Hyper-V Manager

After you install Hyper-V and the Hyper-V management tools, the Hyper-V Manager is ready to run. You can start the Hyper-V Manager from the Start menu, or click the **Search** bar or Cortana and type **hyper** into the Search box. The link for the Hyper-V Manager will appear in the list. Click it to start the management interface. When you click the host computer name, it will look similar to Figure 10-4.

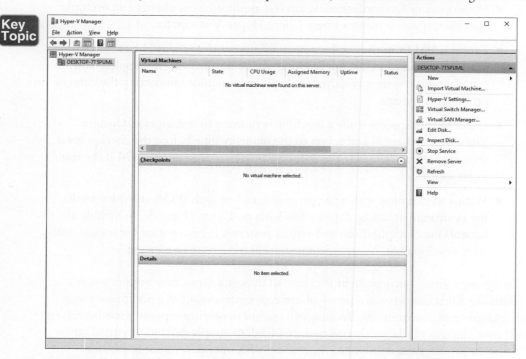

Figure 10-4   The Hyper-V Manager Screen Before Any Virtual Machines Are Added

The Hyper-V Manager is a central location for managing your Hyper-V virtual hosts and the VMs running on those hosts. Similar to other Microsoft Management Console snap-ins, you can connect to other computers and servers running the Hyper-V Platform and perform the same tasks on those hosts and VMs.

The manager interface is composed of three sections. The left navigation pane shows the Hyper-V host machines and allows you to focus on a specific host and add new ones to the inventory.

The central pane displays the VMs for the current host, an area to display Checkpoints for a selected VM, and finally a Details list for displaying configuration specifics of the VM you are working with. When a running VM is selected, the Details section displays a miniature image of the virtual console and tabs for checking the current Memory and Networking usage.

The right pane is the Actions section, where you can perform activities, such as creating new virtual machines, manage the host configuration settings, manage VHDs and SAN storage locations, and other functions. Each of these actions is also available from the right-click context menu of each hostname in the Navigation pane.

Creating Virtual Machines

You can create a new VM in Hyper-V Manager by following a simple wizard-like interface. The following steps create a basic virtual machine ready to run:

Step 1.   In Hyper-V Manager's Actions pane, click **New** and select **Virtual Machine** from the pop-up menu. The New Virtual Machine Wizard screen is displayed.

Step 2.   Read the information on the Before You Begin page and then click the **Next** button.

Step 3.   When the Specify Name and Location screen is displayed (see Figure 10-5), enter a descriptive name for the new VM in the box provided. Optionally, you can change the folder location for the VM. This location only refers to the configuration files for the VM itself, not the virtual disk that the VM guest will use for storage. Click the **Next** button to proceed.

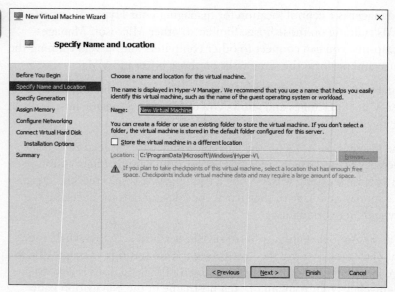

Figure 10-5   Creating a New Virtual Machine

Step 4.   On the Specify Generation page shown in Figure 10-6, you can select whether to create a Generation 1 or Generation 2 virtual machine. Generation 1 is selected by default, and this format will be the most compatible version of VM to use, in case you want to run the machine on a Windows 8.1 or Windows Server 2012 Hyper-V host. Note that if you are creating a 32-bit guest, you must use Generation 1. Select **Generation 1**, and then click the **Next** button.

Step 5.   On the Assign Memory screen shown in Figure 10-7, decide how much memory the VM will use. The minimum is 32 MB and the maximum depends on the amount of RAM available on the physical host. The default is 1024 MB of RAM. When you have assigned the memory you want the VM to use, click the **Next** button.

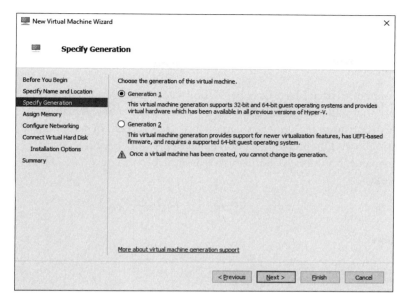

Figure 10-6 Creating a Generation 1 or Generation 2 Virtual Machine

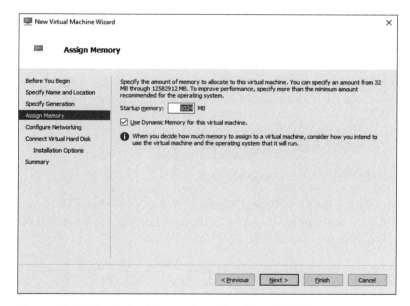

Figure 10-7 Assigning Memory for a New Virtual Machine

Step 6.   On the Configure Networking screen, you assign the VM to use a specific Virtual Switch. If none has been configured on the Hyper-V host, the only available selection will be Not Connected. Click the **Next** button to proceed.

Step 7.   The Connect Virtual Hard Disk page allows you to configure the virtual hard disk that will be used by the VM. You can create a new dynamic VHDX disk from the Connect Virtual Hard Disk screen, or you can use an existing one. The previous section covered creating a VHDX using DiskPart, and in Figure 10-8 this disk is assigned to the new VM. Then click **Next**.

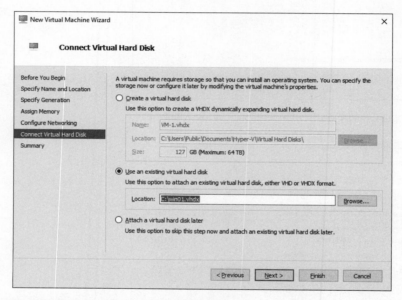

Figure 10-8   Assigning an Existing VHD to a New Virtual Machine

Step 8.   The Completing the New Virtual Machine Wizard page shown in Figure 10-9 displays a description of your selections. When you click the **Finish** button, the wizard will create the new VM.

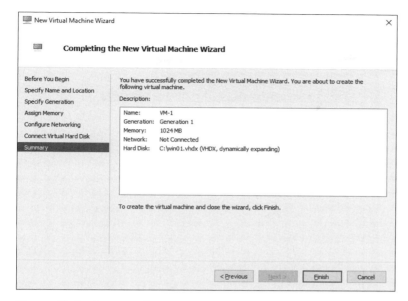

Figure 10-9   Ready to Create a New Virtual Machine with 1024 MB RAM and No Networking

The VM created with this method is a pretty basic machine. Unless you use a VHD with an existing Windows image, there will be no operating system. If the VM is not connected to a virtual switch, it has no networking. There are many ways to make the VM useful, which we cover in the following sections; however, first we should look at the many VM configuration options that were not available from the wizard.

Configuring Virtual Machines

When you first create a VM, it is added to the Hyper-V Manager turned off. Some settings can be changed only while the VM is powered off. To configure the settings for a powered-off VM, select it from the list, and then click the **Settings** action for the machine. The Settings page shown in Figure 10-10 is displayed.

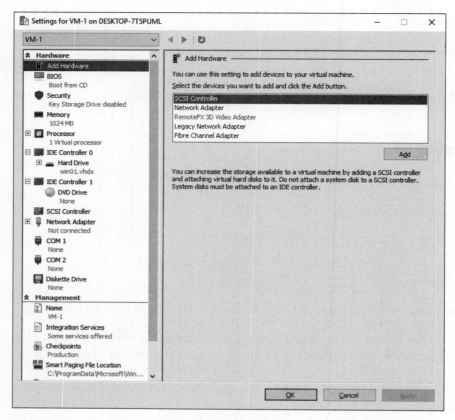

Figure 10-10 Configuring Virtual Machine Settings

The virtual machine settings include many of the same items you would consider when purchasing a physical computer, but in a virtual machine they either make use of existing hardware on the host machine or are simply carved out of thin air using software emulation. For instance, if you want to increase the amount of memory or disk space, the resources used by the VM would consume some memory or disk space on the host or storage attached to the host. On the other hand, you can also simulate items such as SCSI controllers, network adapters, COM ports, and other hardware inside the hypervisor, even if these items do not exist on the host computer.

The VM settings include the following configurable items, which are grouped as VM Hardware settings and Management settings:

- **Add Hardware:** Add new hardware to the virtual machine. The items available include the following:

- **SCSI Controller:** One controller is created for the virtual machine by default, but you can add additional controllers here. This allows you to simulate complex RAID configurations using VHDs that could all reside on a single disk drive.

- **Network Adapter:** Add a virtual network interface card to the VM. To enable a connection for the network adapter, a virtual switch must be available in the Hyper-V host environment.

- **RemoteFX 3D Video Adapter:** Add a graphics adapter for rich 3D graphical experience for the guest. This requires a DirectX 10-compatible graphics adapter on the host.

- **Legacy Network Adapter:** The legacy adapter is available for performing network-based installation of the guest operating system, or when integration services are not available on the guest. Guest VM integration services are covered later in this section. They are not available on Generation 2 guests.

- **Fibre Channel Adapter:** This adapter is used for connecting the guest to an existing physical Fibre Channel storage. It acts as a pass-through adapter so that a VM can access physical storage over Fibre Channel.

- **BIOS or Firmware:** Some basic BIOS settings are available; most important is the capability to select the startup order for boot devices. This is convenient for installation of operating systems on the VM. Generation 2 guests will have Firmware, Generation 1 will have BIOS.

- **Memory:** The amount of memory available to a VM will affect performance more than any other setting. The latest version of Hyper-V (included with Windows 10) includes support for Dynamic Memory. You should understand how these settings are used. Dynamic Memory is examined in detail in Table 10-3.

- **Processor:** Specify the number of virtual processors assigned to the VM. From this page you can also reserve or limit a percentage of resources the VM should use. Refer to Table 10-4 for details on the Processor configuration settings and how they are used.

- **IDE Controller:** By default, the New Virtual Machine Wizard will add two IDE Controllers (0 and 1) to a Generation 1 VM, and assign the first VHD to IDE Controller 0. Generation 2 VMs will not have IDE controllers, so the first hard drive will be assigned to a SCSI controller.

- **New Hard Drive:** When you add a new hard drive to the VM's IDE Controller, it can be either VHDs or attached to a physical hard disk available on the host computer. If you want to add a physical hard disk, it must be offline in the host before you can add it. That drive will be unavailable to the host operating system.

- **New DVD Drive:** If you want to add a DVD drive to the VM, it must be added to the IDE Controller. The guest SCSI controller does not support DVD drives. Similar to adding an IDE hard disk, the DVD drive can be either a physical drive from the host or a DVD image file in ISO format (an .ISO file).

- **SCSI Controller:** This is a virtual SCSI controller that the VM operating system will treat as an actual SCSI controller. You can add VHDs and physical disks to the VM's SCSI controller. Physical disks that you add to this simulated controller do not need to be attached to a physical SCSI device—they can be IDE disks or even USB disk drives.

- **Network Adapter:** You can modify a number of settings for the VM's network adapter, including changing the virtual switch it is using. This is analogous to moving the network cable from one switch to another on a physical computer. The section "Creating and Configuring Virtual Switches" covers more details about the network adapter configuration.

- **COM 1 and COM 2 (Generation 1 only):** You can attach the virtual COM ports to named pipes on the local host or a remote computer to simulate serial communications on the VM.

- **Diskette Drive (Generation 1 only):** Allows you to attach a simulated floppy disk drive to the VM. You cannot use a physical device for the VM; it must be a virtual floppy disk (.vfd) file.

- **Name:** Set the descriptive name for this VM used by Hyper-V. This section also allows you to add descriptions and notes for the VM, which is convenient for keeping track of how you are using the VM.

- **Integration Services:** Configure which hypervisor services will be available for the VM.

- **Checkpoints File Location:** Specify where on the host Hyper-V should store checkpoint images for the VM, and whether you want to use Production checkpoints or Standard checkpoints.

- **Smart Paging File Location:** Smart Paging allows the hypervisor to deal with excessive demands of memory from virtual machines, typically during startup. In this setting you can specify the folder Hyper-V should use to store the Smart Paging files for this VM.

- **Automatic Start Action:** Tell Hyper-V whether to automatically start this VM when the hypervisor is started. If you enable automatic start, you can also specify a number of seconds to delay the startup.

- **Automatic Stop Action:** Configure how Hyper-V will manage the VM state when the host is shut down. By default, Hyper-V will save the current state of the VM.

> **CAUTION**   If you select Turn Off the Virtual Machine for the VM's Automatic Stop Action, be aware that this is like immediately pulling the power on a physical machine. If the operating system is loaded and running when this happens, it can cause file system corruption, loss of data, and, potentially, disk errors that prevent the operating system from loading the next time the VM is started.

When configuring your Hyper-V virtual environment, you should be aware of the memory and processor settings available for the VMs. This will help manage the physical resources, and balance the requirements for the virtual machines between each other and the resources needed by the host operating system itself.

Table 10-3   Virtual Machine Dynamic Memory

Option	Description
Startup RAM	Startup RAM tells the hypervisor how much memory to assign the VM when it first loads. If Dynamic Memory is not enabled, this setting will specify the total amount of memory the VM will use at all times.
Enable Dynamic Memory	When Dynamic Memory is enabled, Hyper-V will adjust the amount of RAM assigned to the VM based on the demand from the guest operating system.
Minimum RAM	The minimum amount of memory to assign to the VM. If there is not enough physical memory on the host to satisfy this requirement, the VM will not load.
Maximum RAM	The maximum amount of memory that can be assigned to the VM by the hypervisor. The actual amount assigned will not exceed the amount of physical memory available on the host, regardless of this setting. In Windows 10 Hyper-V, a VM can be assigned as much as 1 TB of RAM, but the amount is also limited by the amount of physical memory in the host and the amount of RAM the guest operating system is capable of addressing.

Option	Description
Memory buffer	Hyper-V will use this setting to provide an amount of memory above the demands of the VM's operating system. Performance counters are used to determine the memory the VM is requesting for use. The buffer percentage will be used to add some amount to that demand when allocating memory. For instance if the operating system is requesting 1000 MB for its use, and the buffer is 20%, the hypervisor will assign 1200 MB of RAM to the VM.
Memory weight	The weighting set here, from Low to High, is used when there are multiple VMs running under the hypervisor requesting memory. Adjust this setting so that VMs that have a higher priority for performance are provided a higher weight. VMs with a lower rating will perform slower when there is a high demand for memory resources on the hypervisor as a whole.

The processor options that can be specified or used for a VM depend heavily on the physical processor characteristics available on the host machine. You should understand the basics of how these settings are used by Hyper-V.

Table 10-4 Virtual Machine Processor Configuration Options

Option	Description
Number of virtual processors	Set the number of processors the guest OS will see when it starts. You can assign as many processors as the number of cores in the host computer.
Resource control	Resource control is important when there are a number of VMs running at the same time on a single host. Note that these settings are specific to the number of virtual processors assigned. Reserve a percentage of the resources available to the VM to ensure that the VM always has that amount of processor available to use. Set a limit to ensure the VM never uses more resources on the processor(s) than that percentage amount. Finally, you can assign a relative weight for this VM. The weight is an arbitrary number, and is relevant only when compared to the weight of other VMs running on the host.
Processor compatibility	Generally, Hyper-V will maximize performance by using all the features and instruction sets available on the physical processor. If you are planning a VM architecture that may be deployed to a server environment or other hosts, you can select the compatibility setting to ensure that the virtual machines can be migrated to hosts with different types of processors. Hyper-V will use a basic set of features and instructions available on all supported processor architectures.

Option	Description
NUMA configuration	Nonuniform memory architecture, or NUMA, is a memory allocation technology that groups memory locations and processors into nodes, to avoid performance issues caused by multiple processors attempting to access the same memory location, or accessing memory in a location slower to access for the processor that requests it. The physical NUMA configuration can have an effect on VM performance, and in some high-performance applications it may be useful to simulate a NUMA topology different than the physical host. For best performance on the VMs, use the physical topology.

Deploying Virtual Machines

The Hyper-V virtual machine created using the steps in the previous section can be configured, started, and run, but if you used a new VHDX, or the one created using DiskPart in the first section, it does not have an operating system.

From the Hyper-V Manager, you can access a virtual console for any VM either by right-clicking the VM and selecting **Connect,** or by double-clicking the icon in the Summary tab at the bottom of the central pane. Click the **Start** icon or select **Start** from the Action menu, and the result will be similar to the illustration in Figure 10-11.

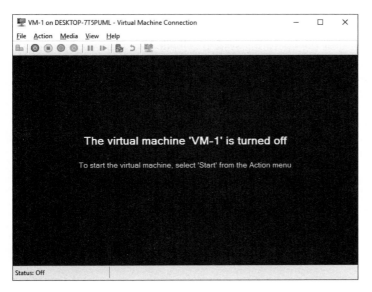

Figure 10-11   New Virtual Machine Started Up with an Empty Virtual Hard Disk

The obvious fix for this is to insert a boot DVD and install a new operating system. You cannot add a DVD drive to the VM while it is running, so you need to turn it off to add it. Recall that you can use an .ISO file as a DVD drive, and you can change the BIOS setting to boot from the DVD drive first. You can attach an image or DVD by using the **DVD Drive** option from the **Media** menu, as shown in Figure 10-12. Use the **Capture** option to use the host's DVD drive or use **Insert Disk** to use an .ISO file.

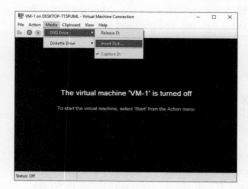

Figure 10-12   Adding a DVD Drive from an .ISO Image File

From there, you can connect to the console, start the VM by clicking the **Start** button on the console window's toolbar, and install Windows using the procedures described in Chapter 2. After the operating system is loaded, you can use it as you would a physical machine, either through the Hyper-V console connection or if the networking is configured using Remote Desktop Services.

Recall from Chapter 2 that you can streamline deploying Windows 10 to multiple computers by creating a VHD with an existing, configured Windows 10 image, which can be used on many machines. You can use the same technique to deploy multiple virtual machines using preconfigured VHD images.

The procedure for this is the same as the steps laid out earlier; the only change is copying the VHD with the image to a location accessible to the Hyper-V service on the host you want to use, then pointing to that file. Refer to Step 6 and Figure 10-8 presented previously in the "Creating Virtual Machines" procedure.

Integration Services

To take full advantage of Hyper-V enhancements for your virtual machines, you should use the Integration Services, available in the Settings menu for the guest VM, in the Management section. You can selectively turn these services on or off, as shown in Figure 10-13. The following options are available for most hosts:

- Operating system shutdown allows you to shut down the guest from the Hyper-V Manager

- Time synchronization with the Host's time

- Data Exchange

- Heartbeat

- Backup (volume shadow copy)

- Guest services

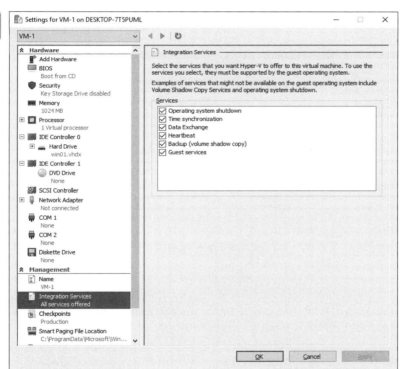

Figure 10-13 Windows Hyper-V Integration Services for Each Guest VM

You can check the version of Integration Services available on the guest by using the following command:

```
REG QUERY "HKLM\Software\Microsoft\Virtual Machine\Auto" /v
  IntegrationServicesVersion
```

You need to open an administrative command prompt in the guest operating system to run this command.

Each of the Integration Services runs as a Windows service on the guest. You can check to see which Integration Services are running using the Services MMC on the guest machine, as shown in Figure 10-14. You can stop and start the Integration Services from the console by selecting the service and clicking the **Start** or **Stop** icons on the menu bar.

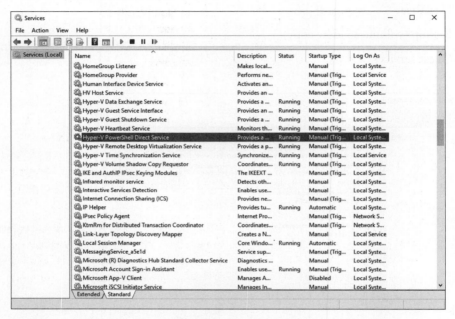

Figure 10-14   Windows Hyper-V Integration Services Running on the Guest OS

NOTE   The Integration Services for Windows guests are updated through Windows Update. If you have guests that are not connected to the Internet or cannot connect to Windows Update, you can download the updates from Microsoft's download center at https://support.microsoft.com/en-us/help/3071740/hyper-v-integration-components-update-for-windows-virtual-machines-that-are-running-on-a-windows-10-based-host.

Converting a Physical Machine

In some cases, you may need to convert a physical machine to a Hyper-V virtual machine. This may be needed in several scenarios, such as the following:

- To test some invasive changes on a production computer—for instance, an operating system upgrade, major application change, or other risky modification. You can reduce the risk by first testing the changes in a virtual copy of the system.

- To support an older PC with unsupported applications when rolling out a hardware or operating system upgrade. For instance, a business requirement may necessitate the use of an out-of-date application that will not run under Windows 10. Rather than leaving the users of this application on old hardware running unsupported Windows XP, the system can be converted to a VM and run under Hyper-V when the users need to use the application.

- To convert a set of physical computers to a virtual environment. This scenario takes a lot of careful planning, but because of the savings available using virtual hosts, it may be worth exploring this option when planning for hardware upgrades or replacements.

NOTE Techniques and procedures for converting physical machines to VMs is beyond the scope of this text and the 70-697 exam. There are several methods for converting physical machines, including Microsoft's Virtual Machine Manager and the Sysinternal's Disk2VHD tool. For more information, see "Virtual Machine Manager" at https://technet.microsoft.com/en-us/library/gg610610(v=sc.12).aspx and "Disk2vhd" at https://technet.microsoft.com/en-nz/sysinternals/ee656415 (en-us).aspx .

Creating and Managing Virtual Machine Checkpoints

A virtual machine checkpoint works exactly as it sounds. It saves a point-in-time state of the virtual machine. Checkpoints save not only the state of the hard disk files, but the state of the running machine and hardware configuration as well, by creating a copy of the machine's memory at the time the checkpoint is taken.

Using Virtual Machine Checkpoints

With Windows 10 and Windows Server 2016, you have the choice of using either Production checkpoints, which is the default, or the standard checkpoints. Production checkpoints utilize backup technology in the guest, instead saving state in the hypervisor. For Windows virtual machines, the Volume Shadow Copy Service (VSS) is used. For Linux virtual machines, the file system buffers are flushed to create a checkpoint that's consistent with the file system. This prevents issues with applications inside the guest when you revert the guest to a saved checkpoint.

NOTE   For more details on the differences between standard and production checkpoints, see "Choose Between Standard or Production Checkpoints in Hyper-V" at https://technet.microsoft.com/windows-server-docs/compute/hyper-v/manage/choose-between-standard-or-production-checkpoints-in-hyper-v.

Checkpoints work well for testing various software changes or applications that can significantly modify the computer. If things go wrong, you can quickly and easily return the machine to its previous state. It is handy in a production environment as well, if virtual machines are being used. Potentially risky operations like applying software updates or service packs can be rolled out after taking a snapshot of the machine. If testing shows issues with the update, you can quickly restore the machine to its previous state until the issue can be resolved.

A VM checkpoint is stored as an .AVHD or .AVHDX file, in the location specified in the virtual machine's settings. It is important not to keep snapshots around for an extended period of time, because they can grow large very quickly. Perform the changes that you planned, and apply or revert the snapshot when you are satisfied.

CAUTION   Do not expand a virtual hard disk used by a virtual machine while the VM has snapshots associated with it. It will make the snapshots unusable, the hard disk will be reverted to the previous state, and you will be unable to apply the snapshot changes.

There are several ways to create a checkpoint from the Hyper-V Manager interface:

- Right-click the VM and select **Checkpoint** from the pop-up menu.

- With the VM selected in the Virtual Machines list box, select **Checkpoint** from the Actions menu in the right pane.

- When connected to the virtual machine connection, click the **Checkpoint** button from the toolbar.

- Select **Checkpoint** from the Action menu of the Virtual Machine Connection screen.

When you create a checkpoint, it will be listed in the Checkpoints section of the Hyper-V Manager whenever the VM is selected in the list, as shown in Figure 10-15. Each checkpoint will appear in a hierarchy from the original state to the currently running state, and the VM can be reverted to any version in the list. Each checkpoint lists the date and time it was taken, and the current state of the VM is simply listed as Now.

Figure 10-15 Virtual Machine Checkpoints Are Displayed in a Hierarchy with the Oldest Version at the Top

The hypervisor will take a few seconds to a few minutes to create the checkpoint, depending on the state of the computer, amount of memory in use, size of the disk drives, and so on. While the checkpoint is created, the status column will display the current progress.

Working with checkpoints is a little counterintuitive. That is because when you select Delete Checkpoint from the context or Actions menu, the checkpoint is actually merged into the VM's current state. In other words, to delete the checkpoint means that you want to keep all the changes made to the VM and abandon the old, saved state. When you delete a checkpoint, the VM's status changes to Merge in Progress and displays the percentage complete as the changes are merged.

Alternatively, if you select a checkpoint and choose the Apply action, your changes since the checkpoint was created are removed, and the state of the running VM is reverted to the state of the checkpoint. Subsequent checkpoints, if any, remain available, so it is possible to return the state of the machine to the point-in-time of any of those checkpoints.

To illustrate, note in Figure 10-16 that the VM's current state (indicated by the Now icon in the list) is after the second checkpoint, but all the changes made in the last two checkpoints are not included. You can roll the VM state forward to one of the other checkpoints taken. Note that if you do this, any changes you make to the VM since applying the current checkpoint will be lost.

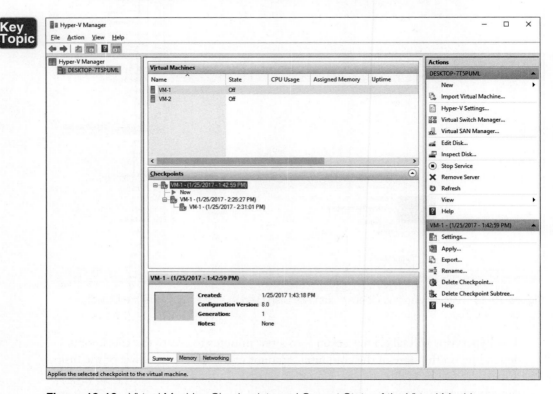

Figure 10-16 Virtual Machine Checkpoints and Current State of the Virtual Machine

Another way to abandon the changes made since the checkpoint was created is to right-click the virtual machine and select the **Revert** option. You are prompted to confirm that you want to revert the virtual machine to the previous state. Again, in this case you are deleting all the changes made to the VM since the checkpoint was created.

If you have created several checkpoints and want to merge all your changes, you can select the first checkpoint and apply the Delete Checkpoint Subtree action. This will merge all the changes at and below the checkpoint you select, and merge all the changes into the current state of the VM.

Creating and Configuring Virtual Switches

In the previous sections you learned about virtual hard disks and virtual machines. These are both very useful for testing, experimenting, running legacy applications, and other tasks. This section introduces virtual switches, which are needed if any of the Hyper-V virtual machines need to communicate with each other, your host machine, or the outside world.

Client Hyper-V's virtual machine connection is useful for interacting directly with the virtual machines, similar to using a physical monitor. This is the only way to utilize the VMs unless they are connected to a virtual switch. There are three basic types of virtual switches that you can create in the Client Hyper-V environment:

- **External:** Create a virtual switch merged with the host network adapter. The VMs will have full access to the host computer network.

- **Internal:** Create a virtual switch with connectivity for the VMs and the host computer. The VMs will be unable to access the host computer network, but the host and VMs can communicate with each other.

- **Private:** A virtual switch created using a private network will be completely isolated from the physical network and the host computer. Only the VMs can connect to the private virtual switch.

To enable basic networking for your Client Hyper-V guests and allow them to use the network just like the Windows 10 host, you would typically add an external virtual switch and connect the VMs to it. Note that this process will modify the host's network configuration. This allows the guests to connect through the existing physical NIC in the host, although in a roundabout way.

We discuss the mechanics of how the different virtual switches work later in this section. First we cover the basic steps for creating a virtual switch:

Step 1. From the Hyper-V Manager's Actions menu, select **Virtual Switch Manager**. The Virtual Switch Manager screen is displayed.

Step 2. From the left pane, select **New Virtual Network Switch**.

Step 3. In the right pane, a list box is displayed. Select the type of virtual switch you want, and then click the **Create Virtual Switch** button.

Step 4. On the next screen, as shown in Figure 10-17, you enter the properties for the new switch. The following properties are available:

- **Name:** Choose a descriptive name for your virtual switch. You may want to include the type of switch (External, Internal, or Private) as part of the name to quickly identify your switches.

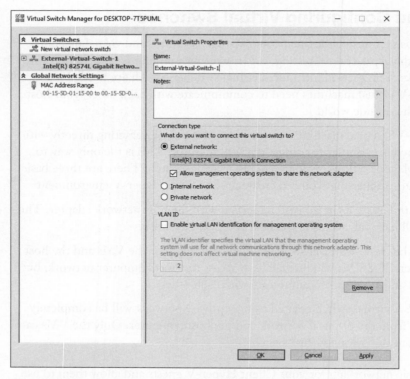

Figure 10-17   Creating a New Virtual Switch Using the Hyper-V Virtual Switch Manager

- **Notes (Optional):** A free text description of the switch.

- **Connection Type:** Choose the type of connection you want, as described previously. The type you selected on the previous screen is filled in for you, but you can change your selection here. Note that if you select External network, you also need to select the host computer's physical connection. That physical network will be connected to your external virtual switch.

- **VLAN ID:** If you want to use VLAN identification numbers, check the box here and choose a unique ID to associate with the VLAN. Typically you will not use this in a Client Hyper-V environment; it is used to create separate virtual LANs within a large virtual environment and "tag" all packets with the ID for more efficient routing and network filtering.

NOTE   For more information on VLAN IDs and tagging, refer to the "Understanding Hyper-V VLANs" in the "Virtual Networking Survival Guide" at https://blogs.msdn.microsoft.com/adamfazio/2008/11/14/understanding-hyper-v-vlans/.

Step 5.   Click **OK** to create the new virtual switch. Hyper-V will display a dialog box while it applies your changes.

Using an External Virtual Switch

Before adding switches to Hyper-V, examine the network configuration for the host. When Hyper-V services are installed, Windows adds the Hyper-V Extensible Virtual Switch protocol adapter to the network. As shown in Figure 10-18, the adapter is initially not bound to any of the host's NIC connections when there are no Hyper-V external virtual switches.

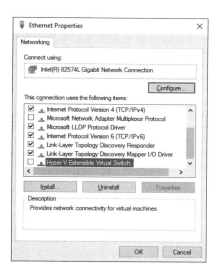

Figure 10-18   Ethernet Properties and the Hyper-V Extensible Virtual Switch

Note that there is one physical NIC in the computer connected to the physical switch using an Ethernet cable. When you create an external virtual switch, Hyper-V will create a virtual switch, but it will also create a new virtual NIC for your host.

Note the network depicted in Figure 10-19. This is how Hyper-V configures your host computer when it creates an external virtual switch. The physical NIC no longer communicates directly with the applications on your host. Instead, all traffic from the external network that flows through the host's network adapter is routed first to the virtual switch. From there it is routed either to one of the guest computers or to the new virtual NIC used by all network applications on the host.

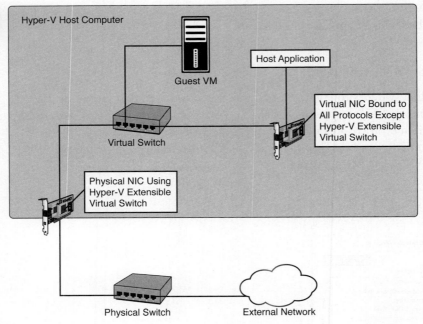

Figure 10-19   Network Routing in a Hyper-V Host Using an External Virtual Switch

Using Internal Virtual Switches

As described earlier, the Hyper-V internal virtual switch is a connection for your guest VMs that cannot access the host's physical network, but can communicate with the host OS. This provides better security for your VMs and avoids the routing modifications to the host network depicted in Figure 10-19. However, because the VMs cannot access the external network, they will not have access to the same network services that the host enjoys, such as DHCP automatic network addressing and DNS for hostname lookup.

We discussed configuring network settings in detail in Chapter 6, "Windows 10 Networking," and Chapter 7, "Windows 10 Security." Refer to those chapters for specifics on configuring your virtual network. Virtual networking uses the same concepts.

For your host to communicate with your VMs, Hyper-V creates a new Ethernet adapter connected to the new internal virtual switch, as shown in Figure 10-20. You can modify the settings for this adapter based on the network configuration of your VMs. By default, the new adapter, and the VM networks that you attach to it, will use Autoconfiguration IPv4 addresses and will be able to communicate over the network.

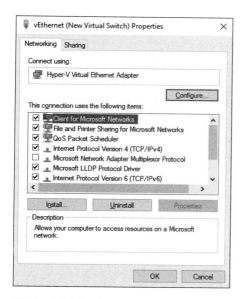

Figure 10-20   Creating a Virtual Ethernet Adapter for the Hyper-V Host to Use When Communicating with Hosted VMs

Using Private Virtual Switches

A private virtual switch works exactly like an internal virtual switch, but without the connection to the host computer. When Hyper-V creates a private virtual switch, it does not create the virtual Ethernet adapter illustrated in Figure 10-20.

Private virtual networks are useful for test environments, especially if you want to simulate an existing environment including the network configurations. You can copy the hosts as they are, and create multiple private virtual switches to match the physical switches in the environment you are simulating.

Connecting Virtual Machines

After you have created at least one virtual switch, you can connect your virtual machines to them. This is similar to connecting a network cable from a physical computer to a physical hub or switch. The VM operating system will detect the connection and attempt to set up the network configuration.

We covered modifying virtual machine settings in the previous section. To connect a VM to a switch, select the VM from the list in Hyper-V Manager, invoke the Settings function, and select the Network Adapter, as shown in Figure 10-21.

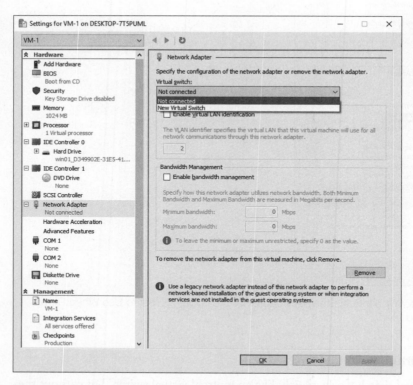

Figure 10-21   Virtual Machine Network Adapter Configuration

The following Network Adapter configuration settings are available:

- **Virtual Switch:** Select the previously created virtual switch you want to connect. If you have named your switches according to type, they will be easier to identify from the list.

- **VLAN ID:** If VLAN identifiers are needed for your network, you can enable VLAN IDs and enter the IDs here.

- **Bandwidth Management:** If you want to limit or reserve the amount of total network resources the VM can use, select the **Enable Bandwidth Management** check box. To limit the bandwidth for the VM, enter the Megabits per second (Mbps) in the Maximum Bandwidth box. Alternatively, you may want to ensure that the VM always has some amount of network bandwidth available. If so, enter an amount in the Minimum Bandwidth box, and Hyper-V will reserve that much bandwidth to the VM, regardless of the network demands from other VMs.

Exam Preparation Tasks

Review All the Key Topics

Review the most important topics in the chapter, noted with the Key Topics icon in the outer margin of the page. Table 10-5 lists a reference of these key topics and the page numbers on which each is found.

Table 10-5 Key Topics for Chapter 10

Key Topic Element	Description	Page Number
Step List	Using DiskPart to create a VHD	517
Figure 10-1	Using DiskPart to create, format, and assign a VHD	518
List	Client Hyper-V hardware and software requirements	521
Figure 10-4	The Hyper-V Manager	524
Figure 10-5	Creating a new virtual machine	526
List	Virtual machine hardware and management settings	530
Table 10-3	Virtual Machine Dynamic Memory	533
Table 10-4	Virtual Machine Processor configuration options	534
Figure 10-13	Hyper-V Integration Services	537
Figure 10-15	Managing virtual machine checkpoints	541
Figure 10-16	Virtual machine checkpoints and current state of the virtual machine	542
List	Types of virtual switches in Client Hyper-V	543
Step List	Creating a virtual switch using Hyper-V Manager	543
Figure 10-19	Network routing in a Hyper-V host using an external virtual switch	546

Complete the Tables and Lists from Memory

Print a copy of Appendix B, "Memory Tables," (found on the book's website), or at least the section for this chapter, and complete the tables and lists from memory. Appendix C, "Memory Tables Answer Key," also on the website, includes completed tables and lists to check your work.

Definitions of Key Terms

Define the following key terms from this chapter, and check your answers in the glossary.

Client Hyper-V, DEP, DiskPart, Fibre Channel, guest, hypervisor, integration services, ISO, NIC, NUMA, SLAT, Smart Paging, checkpoint, VFD, VHD, VHDX, virtual switch, virtual machine, virtualization, VLAN, VT, WDS, Windows XP Mode

This chapter covers the following subjects:

- **Configuring Offline Files and Sync Center:** The Offline Files feature enables users to work with files stored on a network share when they are disconnected from that share. You can specify how files are synchronized with the copies on the offline computer and how to deal with synchronization conflicts.

- **Configuring Power Policies:** Microsoft provides several options for configuring power management on Windows 10 computers. This section introduces you to these options as well as configuring Group Policy for power management settings.

- **Configuring Windows To Go:** Microsoft provides the capability to install a completely functional version of Windows 10 together with applications and settings on a supported USB drive. You can use this drive to boot a computer with supported hardware into the USB copy of Windows 10, bypassing the operating system installed on the computer you're using.

- **Configuring Wi-Fi Direct:** Wi-Fi Direct is a new technology that enables users on portable computers to create ad hoc wireless connections with devices such as smartphones and TVs and share data with these devices without the need for an access point.

This chapter covers the following objectives for the 70-697 exam:

Configure mobility options: Configure offline file policies, configure power policies, configure Windows To Go, configure sync options, configure Wi-Fi settings, configure Wi-Fi Direct, files, powercfg, Sync Center.

CHAPTER 11

Configuring and Securing Mobile Devices

Mobile computing has entered the mainstream of everyday business activity, with portable devices of all kinds, including laptops, tablets, and smartphones presenting an unprecedented level of computing power. You can do almost as much on a notebook or laptop computer or tablet as on a desktop, with the added convenience of portability to any workplace, client, hotel, or home situation as the demand requires. People are buying ultra-portable Surface devices and other hybrid computers that not only act as tablets but can be a fully functional replacement for laptops, with the capability to switch between those roles seamlessly.

Along with the convenience of portability comes the risk of exposing valuable data to unauthorized access as a result of loss or theft of the computer. Microsoft has enhanced the BitLocker full drive encryption feature and added the new BitLocker To Go portable drive encryption feature.

Windows 10 includes many useful mobile computing features, such as the capability to obtain a geographic location based on data collected by a GPS sensor, storage of startup keys, and the capability to remotely wipe information stored on a lost or stolen computer. Microsoft has continued and enhanced features introduced with older Windows versions, including the Windows Mobility Center, offline file access, improved power management, and presentation settings. This chapter introduces you to these portable computer features.

"Do I Know This Already?" Quiz

The "Do I Know This Already?" quiz allows you to assess whether you should read this entire chapter or simply jump to the "Exam Preparation Tasks" section for review. If you are in doubt, read the entire chapter. Table 11-1 outlines the major headings in this chapter and the corresponding "Do I Know This Already?" quiz questions. You can find the answers in Appendix A, "Answers to the 'Do I Know This Already?' Quizzes."

Table 11-1   "Do I Know This Already?" Foundation Topics Section-to-Question Mapping

Foundation Topics Section	Questions Covered in This Section
Configuring Offline Files and Sync Center	1–5
Configuring Power Policies	6–9
Configuring Windows To Go	10–11
Configuring Wi-Fi Direct	12

CAUTION   The goal of self-assessment is to gauge your mastery of the topics in this chapter. If you do not know the answer to a question or are only partially sure of the answer, you should mark that question as wrong for purposes of the self-assessment. Giving yourself credit for an answer you correctly guess skews your self-assessment results and might provide you with a false sense of security.

1. You have configured the Offline Files option on your Windows 10 computer and want to ensure that all available files on a network share are automatically cached to your computer. Which option should you enable?

   a. Open Sync Center

   b. Disk Usage

   c. Sync Selected Offline Files

   d. Always Available Offline

2. You are configuring server options for offline files and want to ensure that users can always run cached files locally, so that performance as experienced by the users is always optimized. Which settings should you configure? (Each answer represents part of the solution. Choose two.)

   a. Only the files and programs that users specify will be available offline.

   b. No files or programs from the shared folder are available offline.

   c. All files and programs that users open from the shared folder are automatically available offline.

   d. Optimize for performance.

3. You want to enable client computers to temporarily cache all files obtained across a slow WAN link. What Group Policy setting should you enable?

   a. Configure Background Sync

   b. Enable Transparent Caching

   c. Administratively Assigned Offline Files

   d. Configure Slow-Link Mode

4. Which offline file policy determines whether offline files are synchronized in the background when extra charges on cell phone or broadband networks could be incurred?

   a. Enable Transparent Caching

   b. Configure Slow-Link Mode

   c. Enable File Synchronization on Costed Networks

   d. Remove Work Offline Command

5. Which offline file policy controls caching of offline files across slow links so you can specify a network latency value above which network files are temporarily cached?

   a. Enable Transparent Caching

   b. Configure Slow-Link Mode

   c. Enable File Synchronization on Costed Networks

   d. Remove Work Offline Command

6. Windows 10 uses which mode, which automatically saves your work and configuration information in RAM and turns off the computer's monitor, hard disk, and other system components?

   a. Sleep

   b. Standby

   c. Hibernate

   d. Suspended

7. Which Windows 10 power plan turns off the display after 2 minutes and sleeps after 10 minutes when on battery power?

   a. Balanced

   b. Power Saver

   c. High performance

   d. Energy Star Qualified

8. You want to reduce the processor power being used so that you can watch a movie on your laptop computer while on a long flight without running out of battery power. What setting should you configure? (Choose two; each is a complete solution to this problem.)

   a. Balanced power plan

   b. Power Saver power plan

   c. Processor power management advanced setting

   d. Sleep advanced setting

   e. Multimedia advanced setting

9. Which of the following tasks can you configure directly from the battery meter on a Windows 10 portable computer? (Choose all that apply.)

   a. Choose a power plan.

   b. Use presentation mode.

   c. Adjust screen brightness.

   d. Specify hard disk settings.

   e. Open the Power Settings page.

10. Which of the following best describes Windows To Go?

   a. A portable computer on which Windows 10 is installed and booted with user credentials obtained from a USB device.

   b. A copy of Windows 10 located on a network drive that you access from any computer using a USB device that contains user credentials and a path to the network drive.

   c. A copy of Windows Mobile imaged onto a USB device that enables a user to boot any computer with compatible hardware into the operating system on the USB device.

   d. A copy of Windows 10 imaged onto a USB device that enables a user to boot any computer with compatible hardware into the operating system on the USB device.

11. Windows To Go works on which editions of Windows 10?

   a. Windows 10 Pro and Enterprise

   b. Windows 10 Enterprise and Education

   c. All except Windows Mobile

   d. Windows To Go can run any edition

12. You are planning to implement Wi-Fi Direct on your wireless network. Which of the following are advantages that you will gain from the Wi-Fi implementation? (Choose all that apply.)

  a. Computers will be able to connect seamlessly with any wireless devices without the need for additional hardware.

  b. You can create an ad hoc connection among five computers running any version of Windows 10.

  c. Computers can connect concurrently to the Internet and to devices such as smartphones.

  d. You can stream media between devices over a high bandwidth connection.

  e. Windows 10 UWP apps can communicate over Wi-Fi Direct without the need for additional setup and configuration.

  f. Devices requiring IP address assignment can automatically receive an IP address from a DHCP server or from a built-in DHCP allocator in Windows 10.

Foundation Topics

Configuring Offline Files and Sync Center

The Offline Files feature in Windows 10 enables a user to access and work with files and folders stored on a network share when the user is disconnected from that share. For example, such a situation could occur when the user is working from a laptop, tablet, or smartphone on the road or at home. This feature ensures that users are always working with the most recent version of their files.

When you enable Offline Files, the feature makes anything you have cached from the network available to you. It also preserves the normal view of network drives, and so on, as well as shared folder and NTFS permissions. When you reconnect to the network, the feature automatically synchronizes any changes with the versions on the network. Also, changes made to your files while online are saved to both the network share and your local cache. Windows 10 includes the Always Offline feature, which keeps the computer operating in Offline mode even when the server is available. This mode can enhance the performance of the computer because it always retrieves data from the local hard disk rather than going across the network to the server (which can limit performance if the network or server happens to be slow).

Offline files are stored on the local computer in a special area of the hard drive called a *cache*. More specifically, this is located at %systemroot%\CSC, where CSC stands for client-side caching. By default, this cache takes up 10 percent of the disk volume space.

You need to configure both the client computer and the server to use the Offline Files feature. Keep in mind that, in this sense, the "server" refers to any computer that holds a shared folder available to users of other computers. This may be a computer running Windows 7 Professional, Enterprise, or Ultimate, Windows 8.1 Pro or higher, or Windows 10 Pro or higher, as well as a server running Windows Server 2008 R2, Windows Server 2012/R2, or Windows Server 2016. It could even be a computer running an older version of Windows, although these versions are no longer supported.

> **NOTE**   For more information on new features of Offline Files in Windows 10 and Windows Server 2016, refer to "Folder Redirection, Offline Files, and Roaming User Profiles Overview" at https://technet.microsoft.com/en-us/library/hh848267(v=ws.11).aspx.

Client Computer Configuration

By default, the Offline Files feature is not enabled on the client computer. The following procedure shows you how to enable offline files and configure the available client options:

Step 1.   Click **Start**, then scroll the program list that appears and select **Windows System**, and choose **Control Panel**.

Step 2.   In the Control Panel search box, type **sync**, and then click the **Sync Center** link.

Step 3.   From the Sync Center applet, click the **Manage Offline Files** link.

Step 4.   The Offline Files dialog box appears. By default, Offline Files are disabled, and the dialog informs you that Offline Files is currently disabled. You will see an Enable Offline Files command button. Click this button to enable Offline Files. You may be asked to restart your computer. If so, after restarting, you will be able to access the available options shown in Figure 11-1.

Figure 11-1   Configuring Offline Files at the Client Computer from the Offline Files Dialog Box

Step 5.   From the General tab, select the following options as required:

- **Disable Offline Files:** Select this command button if you do not want to use Offline Files. You must restart your computer to disable Offline Files. If Offline Files is disabled, this command button enables you to enable Offline Files.

- **Open Sync Center:** Opens the Sync Center.

- **View Your Offline Files:** Opens a File Explorer window displaying the contents of the Offline Files folder.

Step 6.   Select the **Disk Usage** tab to configure the amount of disk space currently used for storing offline files. Click **Change Limits** to modify this setting. Click **Delete Temporary Files** to delete locally stored files.

Step 7.   Select the **Encryption** tab, and then click **Encrypt** to encrypt offline files. This feature uses the Encrypting File System (EFS) to encrypt offline files, keeping them secure from unauthorized users. By default, offline files are not encrypted.

Step 8.   Select the **Network** tab to check for slow network connections. You can specify the number of minutes (5 by default) at which Windows 8.1 checks for a slow connection.

Step 9.   When finished, click **OK** or **Apply**.

Sync Center

When you have enabled your computer for Offline Files, copies of files and folders you access across the network are stored automatically in your cache area according to the server configuration parameters in effect. These parameters are discussed in the next section.

You can also automatically cache all available files from a network share to which you have connected. Right-click the shared folder icon and choose **Always Available Offline**, as shown in Figure 11-2. This automatically caches all available files without your having to open them first. You can also synchronize your cached files manually when you are connected to the network share. To do so, right-click the shared folder icon and choose **Sync > Sync Selected Offline Files**.

Figure 11-2   Caching Files from a Network Share

The Sync Center was first included in Windows Vista; it enables you to manage cached offline files and folders after you have configured them as described in the previous sections. The Sync Center enables you to perform the following actions:

- **View sync partnerships:** View the devices and places you are syncing with.

- **View sync conflicts:** If different users have performed conflicting edits on a file (such as a Word document), the Sync Center informs you and enables you to save multiple copies of the edited file for later analysis.

- **View sync results:** You can check the status of sync with any of your offline files or partnerships.

- **Set up new sync partnerships:** Sync Center establishes sync partnerships for all shared folders that you have cached locally. You can configure these partnerships to specify how and when the folders are synced.

- **Manage offline files:** Displays the Offline Files dialog box, shown previously in Figure 11-1.

Use the following procedure to view sync partnerships and synchronize files:

Step 1.   Use one of the following methods to open the Sync Center:

- From the Search bar or Cortana text box, type **sync center** and click **Sync Center** in the list.

- From the Offline Files dialog box previously shown in Figure 11-1, click **Open Sync Center**.

Step 2.   In the task list on the left side of the Sync Center, click **View Sync Partnerships** to display configured partnerships.

Step 3.   To set up a new sync partnership, click **Set Up New Sync Partnerships**.

Step 4.   To synchronize a specific network share, right-click its partnership and then click **Sync Offline Files**.

Sync Center also enables you to schedule synchronization activities to take place at any of the following actions:

- At a specified time and synchronization interval

- When you log on to your computer

- When your computer has been idle for a specified number of minutes (15 minutes by default)

- When you lock or unlock Windows

Use the following steps to create a schedule:

Step 1.   In Sync Center, select **View Sync Partnerships**, double-click the **Offline Files** folder, and then select the required synchronization partnership. From the menu, select **Schedule**.

Step 2.   In the Offline Files Sync Schedule dialog box that appears, select the items to be synced on this schedule and then click **Next**.

Step 3.   To specify a time for the sync to begin, select **At a Scheduled Time**. To initiate synchronization when an event occurs, select **When an Event Occurs** and then select the desired action or actions. Available events include When I Log On to My Computer, My Computer Is Idle for a Specified Number of Minutes, I Lock Windows, and I Unlock Windows.

Step 4.   If you select At a Scheduled Time, Sync Center automatically provides the current date and time as a start time and a one-day repeat interval (see Figure 11-3). Accept these or specify a different date, time, and interval as required, and then click **Next**.

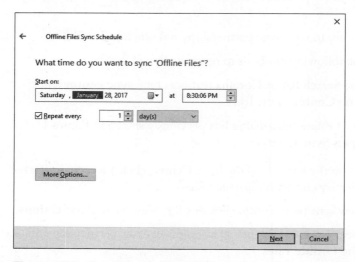

Figure 11-3   Specifying the Date, Time, and Synchronization Interval for Your Sync Schedule

Step 5.   Specify a descriptive name for the scheduled synchronization and then click **Save Schedule**.

After you have created a synchronization schedule, the Offline Files Sync Schedule dialog box provides additional options for viewing or editing an existing sync schedule or deleting the schedule.

If different users modify a synchronized file while working on different computers, a synchronization conflict occurs. Sync Center informs you when conflicts have occurred. To view information about sync conflicts, click **View Sync Conflicts** in the Tasks pane. Sync Center informs you about the file or files that are in conflict.

To resolve a conflict, select it and click **Resolve**. Sync Center enables you to keep either or both versions by using an altered filename, thereby allowing you to compare them and resolve differences at a later time.

Server Configuration

To enable the caching of files stored on a shared folder, you need to configure the shared folder on the server and specify the type of caching available. The following procedure shows you how to perform these tasks on a Windows 10 computer.

Step 1.   Right-click the shared folder and choose **Properties**.

Step 2.   On the Sharing tab of the folder's Properties dialog box, click **Advanced Sharing**. If you receive a UAC prompt, click **Yes**.

Step 3.   On the Advanced Sharing dialog box, click **Caching** to open the Offline Settings dialog box shown in Figure 11-4.

Figure 11-4   Offline Settings Dialog Box Providing Several Options for Enabling Offline Caching in Windows 10

Step 4.   Select from the following options and then click **OK**:

- **Only the Files and Programs That Users Specify Are Available Offline:** Requires that a user connecting to the share specifically indicate the files to be made available for caching. This is the default setting.

- **No Files or Programs from the Shared Folder Are Available Offline:** Effectively disables the Offline Files feature.

- **All Files and Programs That Users Open from the Shared Folder Are Automatically Available Offline:** Makes every file in the share available for caching by a remote user. When a user opens a file from the share, the file is downloaded to the client's cache and replaces any older versions of the file.

- **Optimize for Performance:** Enables expanded caching of shared programs so that users can run them locally, thereby improving performance. Available only if you have selected the All Files and Programs That Users Open from the Shared Folder Are Automatically Available Offline option.

Step 5.   Click **OK** to close the Advanced Sharing dialog box and then click **Close** to close the Properties dialog box for the shared folder.

Offline File Policies

Group Policy makes available a series of policy settings. In Local Group Policy Editor or Group Policy Management Editor, navigate to Computer Configuration\Administrative Templates\Network\Offline Files to display the policy settings shown in Figure 11-5. Note that some of the policy settings available here are applicable to computers running older Windows versions only and are provided for backward-compatibility purposes. Table 11-2 describes the more important policy settings relevant to Windows 10 and Windows Server 2016 computers that you should be aware of.

Table 11-2   Offline File Policies

Policy	Description
Specify Administratively Assigned Offline Files	Specifies network files and folders that are always available offline. Type the Universal Naming Convention (UNC) path to the required files.
Configure Background Sync	Enables you to control synchronization of files across slow links. You can configure sync interval and variance parameters, as well as blackout periods when sync should not occur.
Limit Disk Space Used by Offline Files	When enabled, limits the amount of disk space in MB used to store offline files.
Allow or Disallow Use of the Offline Files Feature	Determines whether users can enable Offline Files. When enabled, Offline Files is enabled and users cannot disable it; when disabled, Offline Files is disabled and users cannot enable it.
Encrypt the Offline Files Cache	When enabled, all files in the Offline Files cache are encrypted.
Enable File Screens	Enables you to block file types according to extension from being created in folders that are available offline. Specify the extensions to be excluded, separated by semicolons—for example, *.jpg; *.mp3.
Enable Transparent Caching	Controls caching of offline files across slow links. You can specify a network latency value above which network files are temporarily cached. More about this policy in the next section.
Configure Slow-Link Mode	Controls background synchronization across slow links and determines how network file requests are handled across slow links.

Policy	Description
Enable File Synchronization on Costed Networks	Determines whether offline files are synchronized in the background when extra charges on cell phone or broadband networks could be incurred.
Remove Work Offline Command	Prevents users from manually changing whether Offline Files is in online mode or offline mode, by removing the Work Offline command from File Explorer.

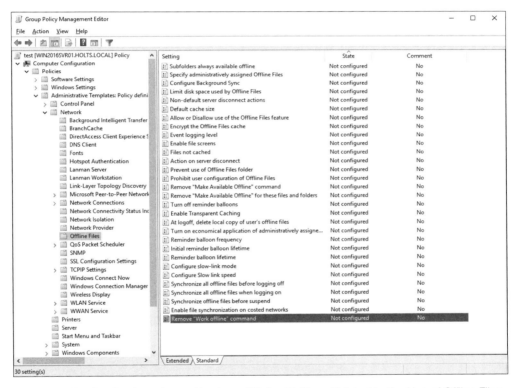

Figure 11-5   Configuring a Large Number of Policy Settings Related to the Use of Offline Files

Using the Always Offline Mode

The Always Offline mode enables faster access to cached files and redirected folders in an Active Directory Domain Services (AD DS) environment. Enabling this mode reduces bandwidth usage because users are always working offline, even when connected to the network.

Use the following steps to enable the Always Offline mode:

Step 1. At a server running Windows Server 2016 (or Windows Server 2012), or a computer running the Remote Server Administration Tools, access the Group Policy Management Editor and open a Group Policy Object (GPO) focused on the desired domain, site, or organizational unit (OU).

Step 2. Navigate to the Computer Configuration\Policies\Administrative Templates\Network\Offline Files node.

Step 3. Right-click the **Configure Slow-Link Mode** policy and choose **Edit** to display the Configure Slow-Link Mode dialog box shown in Figure 11-6.

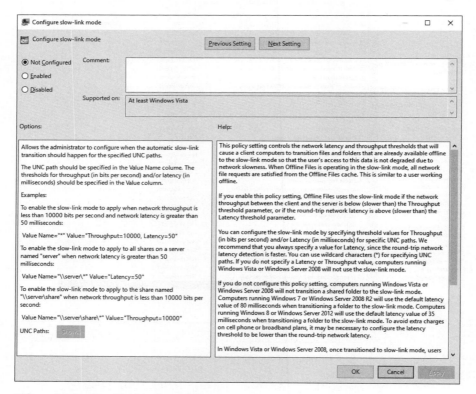

Figure 11-6   Configuring Slow-Link Mode

Step 4. Select **Enabled**.

Step 5. Scroll the Options section of this dialog box to click **Show** at the bottom of this section.

Step 6.   From the Show Contents dialog box, specify the file share for which the Always Offline mode should be enabled, as shown for \\win2016svr01\ HRPolicies in Figure 11-7.

Figure 11-7   Specifying a Shared Folder That Should Always Be Available Offline

Step 7.   In the Value column, specify a latency value in milliseconds (as shown for 1 millisecond in Figure 11-7) and then click **OK**.

Step 8.   Click **OK** to close the Configure Slow-Link Mode dialog box.

> **NOTE**   For more information on the Always Offline mode, refer to "Enable the Always Offline Mode to Provide Faster Access to Files" at https://technet.microsoft.com/en-us/library/hh968298(v=ws.11).aspx.

Configuring Transparent Caching of Offline Files

Introduced with Windows 7 and available in Windows 10 is the concept of *transparent file caching*, which enables client computers to temporarily cache files obtained across a slow WAN link more aggressively, thereby reducing the number of times the client might have to retrieve the file across the slow link. Use of transparent caching also serves to reduce bandwidth consumption across the WAN link. Prior to Windows 7, client computers always retrieved such a file across the slow link.

The first time a user accesses a file across the WAN, Windows retrieves it from the remote computer; this file is then cached to the local computer. Subsequently, the local computer checks with the remote server to ensure that the file has not changed and then accesses it from the local cache if its copy is up-to-date. Note that this type of file caching is temporary; clients cannot access these files when they go offline.

You can configure the Enable Transparent Caching policy shown in Figure 11-8 so that clients can perform transparent caching. Enable this policy and set the network latency value, which is the number of milliseconds beyond which the client will temporarily cache files obtained across the WAN.

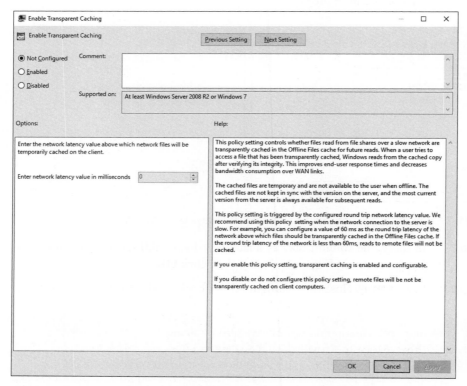

Figure 11-8   Enabling the Enable Transparent Caching Policy Setting So That Clients Can Temporarily Cache Files Obtained Across a Slow WAN Link

Configuring Power Policies

The Hardware and Sound category of Control Panel contains two applets of particular interest to mobile users. Open the Control Panel and select **Hardware and Sound** to display these options, which include the Power Options applet that enables you to configure power use for specific conditions, including connecting your computer to an AC outlet or running it on battery power.

Configuring Power Options

The chief issue with system performance for mobile users is that of managing power consumption on mobile computers when running on battery power. Microsoft provides the Control Panel Power Options applet for configuring several power management options that enable you to configure energy-saving schemes appropriate to your hardware.

> **NOTE** Although designed with mobile users in mind, the power options discussed in this section are available to all users of Windows 10. Users of desktop computers can utilize these options to decrease electricity consumption in these days of ever-increasing electric utility bills.

Windows 10 uses Sleep mode, which replaces the Standby mode used in Windows versions prior to Vista, and offers the following advantages compared to shutting down your computer:

- Windows automatically saves your work and configuration information in RAM and turns off the computer's monitor, hard disk, and other system components. Should your battery run low, Windows saves your work to the hard disk and turns off your mobile computer.

- Entering the sleep state is rapid: it takes only a few seconds.

- When you wake your computer, Windows restores your work session rapidly. You don't need to wait for your computer to boot and restore your desktop after logging on.

You can access the Power Options applet from the Hardware and Sound section or the System and Security section of Control Panel. You can also access this applet by accessing the Search bar or Cortana and typing **power options**. This opens the dialog box shown in Figure 11-9, from which you can configure the options described in the following section.

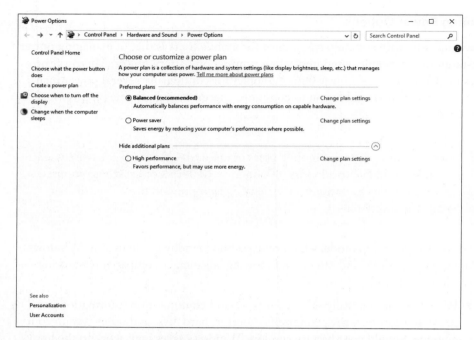

Figure 11-9   Power Options Applet Providing Several Options for Configuring Power Management

Power Plans

Microsoft has supplied three preconfigured power plans that help to strike a balance between usability and power conservation:

- The High-Performance power plan optimizes the computer for performance at the expense of battery life and is suitable for individuals who run graphics-intensive or multimedia applications frequently.

- The Power Saver plan optimizes battery life by slowing the processor down and is suitable for those who use the computer primarily for purposes such as email, Web browsing, and word processing.

- The Balanced plan strikes a balance between these extremes.

You can edit one of these power schemes or create a new one if the preconfigured power schemes do not fulfill your needs. Table 11-3 compares the three preconfigured power plans.

Table 11-3 Windows 10 Power Plans

Power Plan	When on Battery Power	When Plugged into AC Outlet
Balanced	Turns off display after 5 minutes Sleeps after 10 minutes	Turns off display after 10 minutes Sleeps after 20 minutes
Power Saver	Turns off display after 2 minutes Sleeps after 10 minutes	Turns off display after 5 minutes Sleeps after 15 minutes
High Performance	Turns off display after 10 minutes Does not sleep	Turns off display after 15 minutes Does not sleep

NOTE Some computers might label the Balanced power plan as Energy Star Qualified.

CAUTION Do not use Sleep mode when on a commercial airplane. Airline regulations forbid the use of electronic devices during takeoff and landing. Because a computer can wake to perform a scheduled task or other action, you should turn off your computer completely at these times.

Additional Power Plan Options

Windows 10 enables you to perform additional power management actions that you can use to tailor your computer's power scheme to your needs. When you first access these pages, settings will be read-only. Click the **Change Settings That Are Currently Unavailable** link, and respond to any UAC prompts displayed, to change the options.

Selecting the Change Plan Settings link next to any of the top three options on the task list in the Power Options applet previously shown in Figure 11-9 brings up the System Settings screen for that power plan, shown in Figure 11-10. This enables you to perform the following actions:

- **Turn Off the Display:** You can choose how much idle time to allow before turning off the computer's display.

Figure 11-10 Define Power Buttons and Turn On Password Protection Dialog Box Enabling You to Define Power Lid Actions, Configure Password Protection, and Enable Several Shutdown Settings

- **Put the Computer to Sleep:** Decide how long you want the computer to remain idle before going into Sleep mode.

- **Change Advanced Power Settings:** Clicking this link displays all the discrete power options for devices and subsystems shown in Figure 11-11. The Advanced power settings are discussed next.

Figure 11-11 Advanced Settings of Power Options Allowing You to Set Discrete Options for Your Power Plan

Advanced settings allow you to modify any of the existing power plans or create your own custom power plan.

Advanced Power Settings

Click **Change Advanced Power Settings** to bring up the dialog box shown in Figure 11-11 for the following additional options, each of which you can define separately for operation on battery power or when plugged in:

- **Hard Disk:** You can specify the number of minutes of inactivity after which the hard disk is turned off.

- **Internet Explorer:** You can configure the JavaScript Timer frequency for either maximum performance (the default when plugged in) or maximum power savings (the default when operating on battery power).

- **Desktop Background Settings:** You can choose whether to make the background slide show available, or to pause it.

- **Wireless Adapter Settings:** You can specify a maximum performance, or low, medium, or maximum power saving for the adapter. The more power saving you specify, the poorer the signal throughput might become.

- **Sleep:** You can specify the number of minutes after which your computer enters Sleep mode. You can also enable wake timers, enabling the PC to be brought out of sleep at a specific time, usually for running backups or other scheduled tasks. You enable all wake timers or Important Wake Timers Only, which includes things like reboots after a Windows update that requires one.

- **USB Settings:** You can enable USB Selective Suspend Setting, which enables Windows to turn off the USB root hub when not in use.

- **Power Buttons and Lid:** You can define the action that occurs when you close the lid or press the Power or Sleep buttons. You can also define the action (sleep, shut down, or turn off the display) that occurs when you select the Power Off button from the Start menu.

- **PCI Express:** You can define the level of power savings for *link state power management*, which controls the power management state for devices connected to the PCI Express bus if present in the computer.

- **Processor Power Management:** You can control the minimum and maximum power status of the processor, also known as throttling the processor. Reducing the processor power levels saves battery power at the expense of lengthening the time required to respond to keyboard and mouse actions. Also available is the System Cooling Policy, which covers the amount of power the fan requires. Active state increases the fan speed before slowing the processor, whereas setting the state to Passive slows the processor before increasing the fan speed.

- **Display:** You can control the display brightness and the length of time before it is turned off. You can also enable *adaptive display*, which increases the waiting time before turning off the display if you wake the computer frequently.

- **Multimedia Settings:** You can control whether the computer enters Sleep mode when sharing multimedia with other users. When you set this option to Prevent Idling to Sleep, the computer will not go to sleep if media is being shared with other computers or devices. You can also define what to do when playing video. The options are to Optimize Video Quality, Optimize Power Savings, or to use a Balanced setting.

- **Battery:** You can specify actions to take place when the battery power reaches a low or critical level, as well as the battery level at which these events occur. By default, low battery level is at 10 percent and produces a notification but takes no action. The critical level is at 5 percent; it notifies you and puts the computer into hibernation when running on battery power.

TIP   Configure power plans to turn off components after a period of inactivity. If you set up a power plan to turn off components separately after an interval of non-use, the computer progressively moves toward Sleep mode. This should happen if a user is away from his laptop for 20 or 30 minutes. At the same time, a user doing presentations should not have her computer go into Sleep mode. Remember that the user can enable presentation settings so that this and other actions do not occur.

You can customize a power plan to suit your needs if required. Use these steps to create a custom power plan:

Step 1.   From the left pane of the Power Options window previously shown in Figure 11-9, click **Create a Power Plan**.

Step 2.   On the Create a Power Plan dialog box that appears, select the default plan (Balanced, Power Saver, or High Performance) that is closest to your desired plan.

Step 3.   Provide a descriptive name for the plan and then click **Next**.

Step 4.   On the Change settings window, select the time interval after which the display is turned off and put to sleep, select the display brightness, and then click **Create**.

Step 5.   You are returned to the main Power Options window. If you want to configure additional settings for the plan you just created, click **Change Advanced Power Settings** to display the dialog box previously shown in Figure 11-11.

Battery Meter

Windows 10 uses the battery meter to help you keep track of remaining battery life. This is represented by a battery icon in the Notification area, which also contains a Plug icon when the mobile device is plugged into AC power. Hover your mouse over this icon to view the percentage of battery power left. To view the battery meter in full, as shown in Figure 11-12, click the Battery icon.

Figure 11-12   Battery Meter Informing You of the Current Battery Charge Level

From the battery meter, you can also change these settings:

- **Battery Saver:** Turns on Battery Saver mode (can be activated when on battery power).

- **Adjust Screen Brightness:** Lowers the screen brightness to save power.

- **Power and Sleep Settings:** Opens the Battery Settings page shown in Figure 11-13. This page changes the settings for the current power plan settings from the applet shown previously in Figure 11-10. You can click the **Additional Power Settings** link to display the Power Options applet from Figure 11-9.

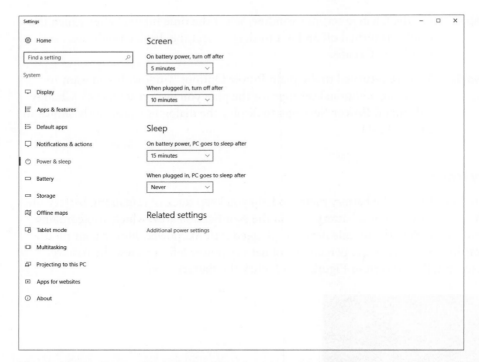

Figure 11-13 Battery Settings Page Enabling You to Modify the Default Screen and Sleep Settings.

Battery Saver is a new feature in Windows 10 designed to improve how long Windows can run on battery power. When Battery Saver is turned on, several background processes are suspended, such as noncritical Windows updates, Mail, and Offline Folder synching. Certain apps are stopped from running in the background (this is configurable; see the following list), some notifications are turned off, and by default the screen is dimmed.

You can adjust some of the behavior for Battery Saver in Settings by accessing the Action Center, selecting **All Settings**, clicking on **System**, and then selecting the **Battery** menu. This brings up the Battery Settings page shown in Figure 11-14. At the top of the page, the Overview displays the current charging status of your battery. The list that follows describes the available options from this page.

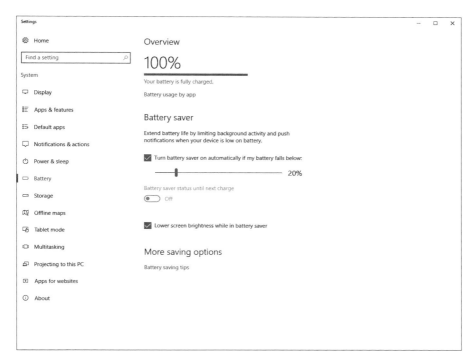

Figure 11-14   Battery Settings Page Allowing You to Adjust the Behavior of Battery Saver

- **Battery Usage by App:** Clicking this link displays a list of apps on your computer that have been consuming battery power and the percentage of battery power used by each. This can help you identify which apps are using the most power. You can select an app and click the **Details** button to get more information. For apps designed for Windows 10, you can limit the app's background activity, as shown in Figure 11-15.

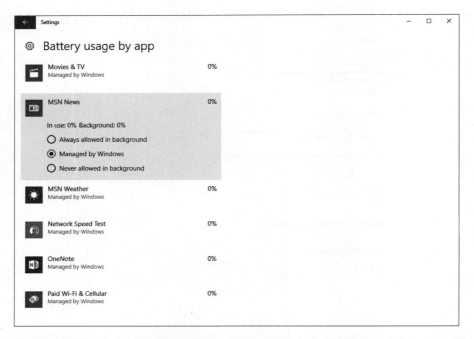

Figure 11-15 Customizing How Battery Saver Controls the Background Behavior of Each Windows App

- **Always Allowed in Background:** The app will always run in the background even when Battery Saver is turned on.

- **Managed by Windows:** The app will stop running in the background when Battery Saver mode is on, and will be temporarily turned off if there is a high battery drain and the app has not been used recently.

- **Never Allowed in Background:** The app will stop running in the background when Battery Saver is activated.

- **Battery Saver:** With the check box selected, Battery Saver will automatically turn on when the battery drains to a specific level; 20% is the default. You can use the slider to adjust the battery level at which you want Battery Saver to be activated.

- **Battery Saver Status Until Next Charge:** This toggle turns on Battery Saver until the next time you plug in your device.

- **Lowering the Screen Brightness While in Battery Saver:** Lowering the screen brightness will significantly save battery power, but if you do not want the screen dimmed while Battery Saver is on, you can uncheck this box.

- **Battery Saving Tips:** Opens the default browser to display the Microsoft Support page for tips on saving battery charge.

When the power drops below 10 percent, you receive a warning message informing you to either plug in your computer or shut it down and change the battery; the battery meter and icon display a red X icon. Some computers can sound an audible notification. You should plug your computer into a power outlet when this message appears.

NOTE For more details on Battery Saver and how it works, see "Battery Saver" at https://msdn.microsoft.com/en-us/windows/hardware/commercialize/design/component-guidelines/battery-saver.

Power Management and Group Policy

Windows 10 includes the capability for configuring power management settings in Group Policy. When you configure policies for power management, a nonadministrative user cannot modify the power settings.

Use the following procedure to use Group Policy to configure power management settings:

Step 1.   Open Group Policy Management Console (GPMC) either through the **Start** menu or by searching for **gpedit.msc**. You can edit a GPO for the domain or use the GPMC on the local computer.

Step 2.   Navigate to the Computer Configuration\Administrative Templates\System\Power Management node. You receive the policy settings shown in Figure 11-16.

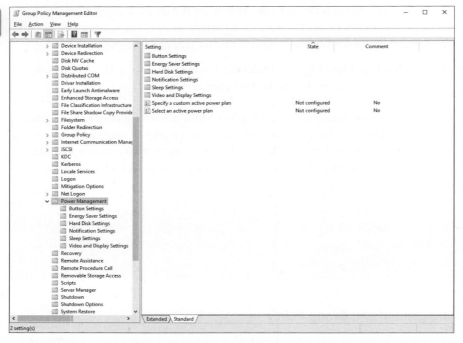

Figure 11-16   Group Policy Enabling You to Configure a Large Range of Power Management Settings

Step 3.   Configure the following groups of settings as required:

- **Button Settings:** Enables you to define the actions that occur when the Power button, Sleep button, or Start menu power button is pressed or the lid closed. You can define these separately for battery and AC power conditions.

- **Hard Disk Settings:** Enables you to specify when the hard disk will be turned off when the computer is plugged in and when the computer is running on battery.

- **Notification Settings:** Enables you to define the battery levels at which low and critical alarm notifications take place and the actions that will occur.

- **Sleep Settings:** Includes settings for controlling when and how the computer enters Sleep mode and when and how it reawakens.

- **Video and Display Settings:** Enables you to specify how long the computer must be inactive before the display is turned off and whether the time interval is adjusted according to the user's keyboard and mouse usage.

- **Energy Saver Settings:** Enables you to select either an active power plan or specify a custom power plan to be active on all computers controlled by the Group Policy Object.

Step 4. When finished, close the GPMC.

Configuring Windows To Go

Windows To Go enables you to create a workspace on a USB device that you can boot on any computer that meets the Windows 7 or later hardware certification requirements. Using Windows To Go, technicians can prepare standardized corporate Windows 10 images from which users can access their desktop on any machine in alternative work locations, such as home, hotel, or client computer location. All necessary files, applications, and the Windows 10 operating system are hosted on a portable USB drive, such as a thumb drive or portable hard drive.

Windows To Go can also be useful for staff or consultants that use their own non-domain-joined computers or laptops, tablets, or similar devices. You can provide them with a Windows To Go workspace to use in your environment. In this way you can enforce organizational network and domain policies without needing to provision a separate physical computer.

When you first insert a Windows To Go drive to a given host computer, Windows To Go detects all hardware on the computer and installs any required drivers. On subsequent boots of Windows To Go on the same computer, Windows To Go identifies the host computer and automatically enables all required drivers.

Windows To Go operates in much the same manner as any other Windows 10 installations, with the following exceptions:

- **Internal disks are offline:** Internal hard disks on the host computer are offline by default when the computer is booted into a Windows To Go workspace. This is to ensure that data security on the host computer is not compromised in any way.

- **Trusted Platform Module (TPM) is not used:** If BitLocker Drive Encryption is used, a preboot password is used for security rather than the TPM, because the TPM is linked to a specific computer and Windows To Go drives can move among different computers. You learned about BitLocker in Chapter 8, "Windows 10 Data Security."

- **Hibernation is disabled by default:** This is to ensure complete portability of Windows To Go workspaces between computers. However, you can reenable hibernation using Group Policy.

- **Windows Recovery Environment isn't available:** If you need to recover your Windows To Go workspace, simply re-image it with a new Windows image.

- **Refreshing or resetting:** Refreshing or resetting Windows is not supported for a Windows To Go workspace.

- **Windows Store is disabled by default:** This is because apps licensed from Windows Store are linked to specific hardware. It is possible to enable the store if Windows To Go workspaces won't be roaming among multiple host machines.

Preparing USB Drives for Windows To Go

Windows To Go requires specific types of USB drives. Most commodity flash drives cannot support Windows To Go; however, Microsoft has provided a Windows 10 certification program for hardware manufacturers that want to support the Windows To Go workspace functionality. These devices have been specially optimized for Windows To Go and meet several specific requirements for running a full version of Windows 10.

Drives certified for Windows To Go have certain specific characteristics:

- The drive must be a USB 3.0 drive and have read/write performance specifications that will support the demands of the Windows 10 operating system, including the thousands of random access I/O operations per second required.

- The drive is tuned to ensure it will boot and run on any computer that has been certified for use with Windows 7 and later.

- The drive has been manufactured to quality standards that ensure endurance under the typical demand for Windows To Go. This includes a manufacturer warranty for operation and reliability under normal use with a Windows To Go workspace.

> **NOTE**   You can find information about the USB drives Microsoft has certified for use with Windows To Go at https://technet.microsoft.com/en-us/itpro/windows/plan/windows-to-go-overview#wtg-hardware.

Provisioning a Windows To Go Workspace

To create the Windows To Go workspace, you will need an installation image file for your environment (a .WIM file) or a Windows 10 Enterprise or Education installation image file (.ISO) in DVD format. Typically, the .WIM file will be stored on a network share that you can access from your Windows 10 Enterprise or Education computer. The .ISO file with the Windows 10 installation needs to be downloaded to your local computer. You learned about creating and managing Windows images in Chapter 2, "Implementing Windows."

If you are using an .ISO file for the Windows 10 installation image, copy the .ISO file to your computer's Downloads folder, and then open the **Downloads** folder, right-click the Windows 10 installation image .ISO file, and then select **Mount**. Windows will mount the ISO file as a new drive letter and open the drive in Explorer.

You are then ready to create a Windows To Go workspace:

Step 1.   Open Control Panel by right-clicking the **Start** button and selecting **Control Panel**, or by any other method.

Step 2.   In the Control Panel Search box, type **windows to go** and then click the **Windows To Go** Control Panel link to open the Windows To Go provisioning tool, as shown in Figure 11-17.

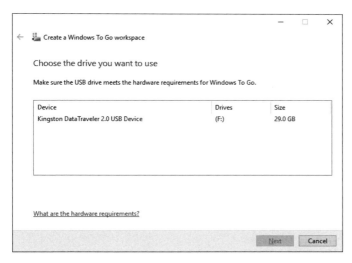

Figure 11-17   Windows To Go Provisioning Tool Will Search the Computer for Compatible USB Drives to Install the Windows To Go Workspace

Step 3.   Select your USB drive from the list. If your drive is not compatible with Windows To Go, Windows will not allow you to install Windows To Go on it. Also, if the drive is a slower device, Windows may present a warning. After selecting the USB device to use, click **Next** to proceed.

Step 4.   Windows searches for installation images to use. If the image file you want is not listed, click the **Search Options** button and select the folder where your .WIM file is located. If you mounted an .ISO image, select the drive where the image was mounted. When you have found the image you want to use, select it from the list and click **Next**.

Step 5.   Windows To Go provides an option to encrypt the workspace using Bit-Locker. Encrypting your portable drive is recommended because they are small and can be easily lost. Encrypting the drive will ensure that no one will be able to load your workspace or open your files if the drive is lost or stolen.

To encrypt the drive with BitLocker, select the check box Use BitLocker with My Windows To Go Workspace, type your password into the boxes supplied, and click **Next**.

If you do not want to use BitLocker, click the **Skip** button.

Step 6.   The last dialog box is displayed, describing the drive that will be used to create the Windows To Go workspace. When you are ready, click **Create**.

Step 7.   The provisioning tool will take some time to create your Windows To Go workspace on your USB drive.

Step 8.   After the workspace is installed, Windows asks you to Choose a Boot Option. This will change the computer's firmware to automatically boot from any plugged-in USB device. If you will be using this computer to boot Windows To Go, select Yes to allow Windows to change this setting. You can then either select **Save and Restart** to boot Windows To Go or select **Save and Close** if you want to continue working.

CAUTION   When Windows creates the Windows To Go workspace on your USB drive, it completely reformats and deletes all contents on the drive. Be sure that you select the correct drive and that any files on the drive are removed or backed up.

NOTE   For more information on using Windows To Go, refer to "Windows To Go: Feature Overview" at https://technet.microsoft.com/en-us/itpro/windows/plan/windows-to-go-overview and "Deploy Windows To Go in Your Organization" at https://technet.microsoft.com/en-us/itpro/windows/deploy/deploy-windows-to-go.

Using Windows To Go on a Host Computer

The Windows To Go USB drive will work on any desktop computer or laptop or tablet that is certified to run Windows 7 or later. It might be necessary to access the computer's BIOS or firmware settings to enable the computer to boot from a removable device.

For instance, on many Dell computers you can press the F12 button when the computer first posts to access the boot menu, and then select the boot drive or device. This technique provides a one-time option for booting the computer from an alternative device. If you will be using the computer frequently, it will be more convenient to change the BIOS settings so that the computer will attempt to boot from a USB device whenever one is available. Typically, the BIOS will allow you to set a boot order, so the computer checks each device in turn until it finds a bootable partition. If the first hard disk is set as the first boot device, it will never find the USB device to run the Windows To Go workspace.

The first time you load the Windows To Go workspace by booting a computer from the USB drive, Windows will take some time finding and loading device drivers and display Getting Devices Ready as it loads. If you used the Windows installation .ISO to create the workspace, Windows then walks you through a few setup tasks, just like it would for a new computer.

Step 1.   Windows displays a dialog box displaying the EULA ID. You must check the **I Accept the License Terms** check box and click **Next** to proceed.

Step 2.   The next screen asks you to pick a color and a PC name to personalize your Windows To Go workspace. You must enter a name in the box provided. Click **Next** to continue.

Step 3.   At this point, Windows displays the Settings dialog, where you have an opportunity to customize a number of settings, such as for security, location, updates, and more. This is the same Settings customization screen displayed during the Attended Installation in the first section of this chapter. You may want to adjust some of these settings for your Windows To Go workspace, which you can do by selecting the **Customize** option. If not, select **Use Express Settings** to proceed.

Step 4.   Windows To Go then asks you to Sign In to Your PC. You have the same options as you normally do for a Windows 10 workstation, using a Microsoft account or a Local account.

Step 5.   After a few minutes, your new Windows To Go workspace is ready to use.

Like all Windows operating systems starting with Windows XP, Your Windows To Go workspace requires activation, so it needs to be connected to a corporate network that supports volume activation. This can be implemented using either Key Management Service or Active Directory–based volume activation. KMS activation is good for 180 days, so mobile workers using Windows To Go can stay offline for an extended period of time. They will need to renew the activation within the 180-day period (by connecting to the corporate network), or the workspace activation will lose validity.

You can carry your Windows To Go USB drive from computer to computer and boot to a familiar environment everywhere you go. This is very convenient for workers who travel from place to place, where equipment is already available, and it can save costs over supplying each mobile worker with a separate laptop or tablet computer.

Configuring Wi-Fi Direct

Wi-Fi Direct is a new industry standard connectivity technology in Windows 10 that enables data and content sharing between devices and PCs on a peer-to-peer network without the need for separate Wi-Fi access points. It supplants the older ad hoc mode of wireless networking between two portable computers. In Windows 10, for example, you can sync data between a smartphone and a portable computer while sitting at the airport waiting for your flight to be called. Wi-Fi Direct supports the latest security technologies, including Wi-Fi Protected Access 2 (WPA2) security, which is enabled by default, minimizing the risk of data being intercepted by unauthorized users or devices. No infrastructure devices such as wireless routers are needed for the connection.

The following are several properties of Wi-Fi Direct in Windows 10:

- Wi-Fi Direct is integrated into the Wi-Fi stack and is enabled by default. You can connect to any device that supports Wi-Fi Direct.

- Wi-Fi Direct builds on existing Wi-Fi hardware. You can enable Wi-Fi Direct without the need for added hardware components, such as chipsets or antennas. Microsoft has worked with hardware manufacturers to ensure compatibility and support.

- Wi-Fi Direct permits concurrent connection to the Internet and to devices such as smartphones. The chipset can be used for multiple simultaneous connections.

- Wi-Fi Direct is optimized for power savings. It is turned on by demand and turns off when not in use.

- It is simple to set up devices for direct streaming of media between devices over a high-bandwidth connection—for example, sharing of high-definition video between computers and TVs, including video as you download it from the Internet.

- Windows UWP apps can communicate over Wi-Fi Direct without the need for additional setup. The apps can talk to each other by leveraging proximity application programming interface (API).

Windows automatically detects and installs devices after Wi-Fi Direct pairing occurs; consequently, installation and configuration of Wi-Fi Direct devices is simple, as the following procedure shows:

Step 1. From the Control Panel Devices and Printers applet, select **Add a Device**.

Step 2. Select the Wi-Fi Direct device from the list, and then click **Next**.

Step 3. If the device comes with a PIN, enter the PIN when requested.

Step 4. Windows installs any required drivers, and the device is ready for use.

Windows UWP apps can communicate between devices using Wi-Fi Direct. Proximity sensors on newer PCs and devices can detect each other when the devices are placed near to each other, and the computers can communicate with each other and share information when both computers are running the same app; users need only open the app on each computer with a simple tap on touch-sensitive screens or a click of the mouse. Developers can create additional apps that automatically connect with each other when in close proximity; such a connection is managed by Windows, and the developer does not need to manage Wi-Fi Direct semantics.

Wi-Fi Direct works in Windows by means of a simple three-step sequence:

1. **Finding the device:** This happens automatically when you click Add a Device as already explained. Extended attributes included with devices (known as the container ID) help identify the device.

2. **Pairing with the device:** In other words, Windows is creating a relationship to the device. This takes place after the user has selected the device. Extended attributes help to provide an improved experience during the pairing process and enable the user to remain in control. These attributes include a container ID, which represents the physical device, and a vertical device ID, which represents logical devices within the physical device.

3. **Connecting to the device:** The device remains connected only when actually in use. When the user resumes use of the device, an on-demand reconnection is initiated by Windows. This provides advantages, such as optimizing battery life on the device. Further, Wi-Fi Direct enables multiple devices to connect to Windows concurrently; however, only two computers can participate in a single Wi-Fi Direct session. Devices requiring IP address assignment can automatically receive an IP address from a DHCP server. A built-in lightweight DHCP allocator in Windows 10 can assign IP addresses in the range 192.168.173.0/24 to devices needing them.

NOTE   Wi-Fi Direct is an industry standard supported by many venders as well as Microsoft. For more information about Wi-Fi Direct, start with the Wi-Fi alliance documentation at https://www.wi-fi.org/discover-wi-fi/wi-fi-direct.

Exam Preparation Tasks

Review All the Key Topics

Review the most important topics in the chapter, noted with the Key Topics icon in the outer margin of the page. Table 11-4 lists a reference of these key topics and the page numbers on which each is found.

Table 11-4   Key Topics for Chapter 11

Key Topic Element	Description	Page Number
Step List	Enabling offline files and configuring the available client options	558
Table 11-2	Offline File Policies	564
Table 11-3	Windows 10 Power Plans	571
Figure 11-11	The Advanced settings of Power Options allows you to set discrete options for your power plan	572
Figure 11-16	Group Policy enables you to configure a large range of power management settings	580
List	Exceptions to Windows To Go operation	581
List	Characteristics of drives certified for Windows To Go	582
Step List	Creating a Windows To Go workspace	583

Complete Tables and Lists from Memory

Print a copy of Appendix B, "Memory Tables" (found on the book's website), or at least the section for this chapter, and complete the tables and lists from memory. Appendix C, "Memory Tables Answer Key," also on the website, includes completed tables and lists to check your work.

Definitions of Key Terms

Define the following key terms from this chapter and check your answers in the glossary.

battery meter, cache, hibernation, offline files, power plans, remote wipe, Sleep mode, Sync Center, synchronization conflicts, synchronizing files, Wi-Fi Direct, Wi-Fi triangulation, Windows To Go

This chapter covers the following subjects:

- **Mobile Device Policies:** Local Security Policy presents a subset of Group Policy with settings designed to enhance the security of a local Windows 10 computer. This section shows you how to configure policies affecting users logging on to the computer, as well as auditing of actions that users might perform on the computer and several other security-related settings. Remote Wipe is an important security tool for ensuring that when mobile devices are lost or stolen, the device can be reset and personal information cleared. In this section you learn about the state of Remote Wipe for Windows devices.

- **Managing Data Synchronization:** When your users need to work from anywhere, it can present challenges, especially in organizations where work product is typically managed on server file shares for sharing, security, and backup. Working with these documents offline and on the road is easier with Work Folders, which allows users to keep a local copy of shared folders on their laptop or mobile device and sync them back to the share when they reconnect. In this section you learn about Work Folders and how to manage synchronization across occasionally connected devices.

- **Managing Broadband Connectivity:** Road warriors need connectivity wherever they go, without relying on insecure coffee shop Wi-Fi or unreliable hotel connections, so they often rely on broadband devices for their mobile device network. In this section you learn about how to maximize your investment in metered broadband connections and the Windows features that can help you manage broadband connectivity.

This chapter covers the following objectives for the 70-697 exam:

Support mobile devices: Support mobile device policies including security policies, remote access, and remote wipe; support mobile access and data synchronization including Work Folders and Sync Center; support broadband connectivity including broadband tethering and metered networks; support Mobile Device Management by using Microsoft Intune, including Windows Phone, iOS, and Android.

CHAPTER 12

Managing Mobile Devices

New to Windows 10 are several useful mobile computing features, such as the capability to obtain a geographic location based on data collected by a GPS sensor and the capability to remotely wipe information stored on a lost or stolen computer. Microsoft has continued and enhanced features introduced with older Windows versions, such as offline file access, improved power management, and presentation settings. This chapter introduces you to these portable computer features.

"Do I Know This Already?" Quiz

The "Do I Know This Already?" quiz allows you to assess whether you should read this entire chapter or simply jump to the "Exam Preparation Tasks" section for review. If you are in doubt, read the entire chapter. Table 12-1 outlines the major headings in this chapter and the corresponding "Do I Know This Already?" quiz questions. You can find the answers in Appendix A, "Answers to the 'Do I Know This Already?' Quizzes."

Table 12-1 "Do I Know This Already?" Foundation Topics Section-to-Question Mapping

Foundation Topics Section	Questions Covered in This Section
Mobile Device Policies	1–5
Managing Data Synchronization	6–7
Managing Broadband Connectivity	8–9

CAUTION The goal of self-assessment is to gauge your mastery of the topics in this chapter. If you do not know the answer to a question or are only partially sure of the answer, you should mark that question as wrong for purposes of the self-assessment. Giving yourself credit for an answer you correctly guess skews your self-assessment results and might provide you with a false sense of security.

1. What password policy actually weakens password security and is therefore not recommended for use by Microsoft?

   a. Enforce Password History

   b. Minimum Password Age

   c. Maximum Password Age

   d. Complexity Requirements

   e. Store Passwords Using Reversible Encryption

2. You want to ensure that users cannot cycle rapidly through a series of passwords and then reuse their old password immediately. Which password policy should you enable to prevent this action from occurring?

   a. Enforce Password History

   b. Minimum Password Age

   c. Maximum Password Age

   d. Password Must Meet Complexity Requirements

   e. Store Passwords Using Reversible Encryption

3. You want to ensure that if someone tries to guess a password on a Windows device that the account will be locked out. Which security policy would you use? (Each correct answer presents part of the solution. Choose two.)

   a. Enforce Password History

   b. Minimum Password Age

   c. Account Lockout Duration

   d. Complexity Requirements

   e. Account Lockout Threshold

4. One day after logging on to your Windows 10 computer, which you have shared with several others in your department, you notice that the time zone has been changed to an improper setting. You would like to discover who is making improper modifications to your computer's settings. Which of the following audit policies should you enable?

   a. Account Management

   b. Policy Change

   c. Privilege Use

   d. System Events

5. A user has returned from a trip and has let you know that his Windows mobile device was lost during the trip, and he is now convinced he won't find it. You need to disable the device and assign a new one to the user. Your organization has a comprehensive set of management tools for mobile devices. What can you use to wipe corporate data from the device? (Each correct answer presents an entire solution. Choose two.)

   a. Offline File Sync

   b. Broadband Tethering Remote Wipe

   c. Microsoft Intune Remote Wipe

   d. Exchange ActiveSync

   e. A clean cloth

6. You have decided to implement Work Folders to allow your company's road warriors to work offline and on the road. They will need devices that can sync with the server, which you will be making accessible from the Internet. What kind of device will the users need?

   a. Windows 10 laptops

   b. Windows 10 Mobile phones

   c. iOS tablets

   d. Android devices

   e. Any of these

7. Which of the following is true of Work Folders? (Select all that apply.)

   a. Users can sync files using Window, iOS, or Android devices.

   b. Users can share files with other members of their workgroup.

   c. It is supported using any Windows Server 2008 or later.

   d. It keeps Work Folders in sync over the Internet or local network whenever the device is connected.

   e. It requires IIS, File and Storage Services, a valid CA certificate, and a DNS entry on the server side.

8. How is a broadband connection defined when discussing Windows network connections?

   a. Any high-speed Internet connection

   b. Any wired connection

   c. Any wireless connection

   d. Any metered connection

   e. LTE networks

9. You will be tethering your Windows 10 laptop to your mobile phone while you are on a trip to a remote Alabama location where Wi-Fi is not available. You are nearing your monthly limit of data on your phone, however, and would like to ensure that Windows does not use too much bandwidth while you are connecting. What can you do to limit Windows use of your data plan?

    a. Disable your device's security policies.

    b. Set your connection as a metered connection.

    c. Turn off File Synchronization.

    d. Turn off your email.

Foundation Topics

Mobile Device Policies

The proliferation of mobile devices and their use in an enterprise requires careful planning and consideration. Proprietary and sensitive data must be kept secure even as employees travel with their devices, accessing and modifying data from diverse locations and frequent public spaces where devices can be lost or stolen.

In previous chapters, you learned about some technologies available for protecting data on workstations and mobile devices, such as encryption and techniques for securing the network. In this section you learn about policies you can apply to your organization's mobile devices to help keep data secure and to enforce organizational requirements. Group policies can help secure domain-joined devices, and many of these policies can be set locally on Windows 10 devices.

Security Policies

You can access the Local Security Policy snap-in through Administrative Tools under Control Panel's System and Security category or by typing **local security** into the Search bar or Cortana and then clicking **Local Security Policy**. The policies defined in this utility affect all users on the computer, unless the policies allow you to configure them on a per-user or per-group basis. Figure 12-1 shows this snap-in.

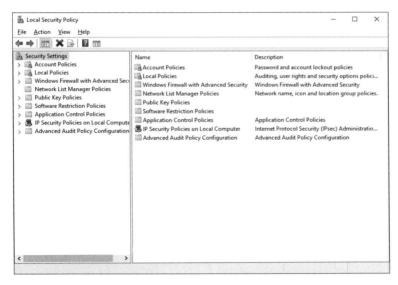

Figure 12-1 Configuring Numerous Local Security Policy Settings with the Local Security Policy Snap-in in Windows 10

The Local Security Policy snap-in enables you to configure a large range of security-related policy settings, as summarized in the following list:

- **Account Policies:** Includes password policies and account lockout policies. We discuss account policies later in this section.

- **Local Policies:** Includes audit policies, user rights assignment, and security options. We discuss these policies later in this chapter.

- **Windows Firewall with Advanced Security:** Enables you to configure properties of Windows Firewall for domain, private, and public profiles. You can specify inbound and outbound connection rules as well as monitoring settings.

- **Network List Manager Policies:** Enables you to control the networks that computers can access and their location types, such as public and private (which automatically specifies the appropriate firewall settings according to location type). You can also specify which networks a user is allowed to connect to.

- **Public Key Policies:** Enables you to configure public key infrastructure (PKI) settings. Included are policies governing the use of Encrypting File System (EFS), Data Protection, and BitLocker Drive Encryption.

- **Software Restriction Policies:** Enables you to specify which software programs users can run on network computers, which programs users on multiuser computers can run, and the execution of email attachments. You can also specify whether software restriction policies apply to certain groups such as administrators.

- **Application Control Policies:** These are a set of software control policies first introduced with Windows 7 that include the AppLocker feature. AppLocker provides new enhancements that enable you to specify exactly what users are permitted to run on their desktops according to unique file identities.

- **IP Security Policies on Local Computer:** Controls the implementation of IP Security (IPsec) as used by the computer for encrypting communications over the network.

- **Advanced Audit Policy Configuration:** First introduced in Windows 7, this node contains 62 new policy settings that enable you to select explicitly the actions that you want to monitor and exclude actions that are of less concern.

> **NOTE**   Be aware that in an Active Directory Domain Services (AD DS) domain environment, all these policies can be configured at the site, domain, or organizational unit (OU) level, and that any policies configured at these levels override conflicting local policies. If a local policy does not apply as configured, consult your domain administrator for assistance.

Configuring Account Policies

The Windows 10 Local Security Policy tool includes the Account Policies node, which contains settings related to user accounts, including the password policy and account lockout policy.

Password Policies

You can configure password policy settings that help to protect users of Windows 10 client computers. The options available in Windows 10 are similar to those found in previous Windows versions. Password policies are generally intended to make passwords more difficult for intruders to discover. Figure 12-2 shows the available password policies and their default settings.

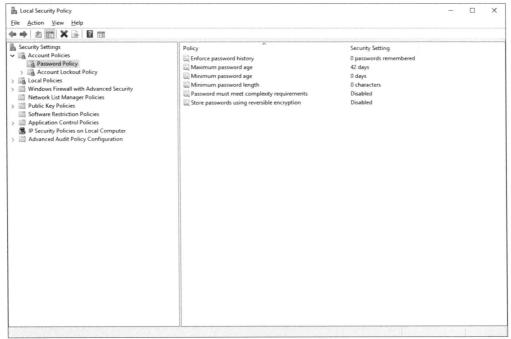

Figure 12-2   Windows 10 Providing Default Values for the Available Password Policies

The following password policy settings are available:

- **Enforce Password History:** Determines the number of passwords remembered by Windows for each user. Values range from 0 to 24. A user cannot reuse a password retained in the history list. A value of 0 means that no password history is retained, and a user can reuse passwords at will.

- **Maximum Password Age:** Determines the number of days that a user can use a password before being required to specify a new one. Values range from 0 to 999. A value of 0 means that a user is never required to change his password. The default is 42 days.

- **Minimum Password Age:** Determines the minimum number of days a password must be used before it can be changed. Values range from 0 to 998 days and must be less than the maximum password age. The default value of 0 allows the user to immediately change a new password. This value allows a user to cycle through an entire history list of passwords in a short time; in other words, a user can repeatedly change a password in order to reuse his old password. This obviously defeats the purpose of enforcing password history, so you should configure this value to be at least one day.

- **Minimum Password Length:** Determines the minimum number of characters that can make up a password. Values range from 0 to 14. A value of 0 permits a blank password. Use a setting of 10 or higher for increased security.

- **Password Must Meet Complexity Requirements:** Stipulates that a password must meet complexity criteria, as follows: The password cannot contain the user account name or full name or parts of the name that exceed two consecutive characters. It must contain at least three of the following four items:

  - English lowercase letters

  - English uppercase letters

  - Numerals

  - Nonalphanumeric characters such as $; [ ] { } ! .

- **Store Passwords Using Reversible Encryption:** Determines the level of encryption used by Windows 10 for storing passwords. Enabling this option reduces security because it stores passwords in a format that is essentially the same as plain text. This option is disabled by default. You should enable this policy only if needed for clients who cannot use normal encryption, such as those using Challenge Handshake Authentication Protocol (CHAP) authentication or Internet Information Services (IIS) Digest Authentication.

To configure these policies, expand the Account Policies\Password Policy node of the Security Settings tool as shown in Figure 12-2. Right-click the desired policy and choose **Properties**. Then configure the appropriate value and click **OK**. Each policy setting also has an Explain tab that provides additional information on the policy setting and its purpose.

Account Lockout

A cracked user account password jeopardizes the security of the entire network. The account lockout policy is designed to lock an account out of the computer if a user (or intruder attempting to crack the network) enters an incorrect password a specified number of times, thereby limiting the effectiveness of dictionary-based password crackers. The account lockout policy contains the following settings:

- **Account Lockout Duration:** Specifies the number of minutes that an account remains locked out. Every account except for the default Administrator account can be locked out in this manner. You can set this value from 0 to 99999 minutes (or about 69.4 days). A value of 0 means that accounts that have exceeded the specified number of failed logon attempts are locked out indefinitely until an administrator unlocks the account.

- **Account Lockout Threshold:** Specifies the number of failed logon attempts that can occur before the account is locked out. You can set this value from 0 to 999 failed attempts. A value of 0 means that the account will never be locked out. Best practices recommend that you should never configure a setting of 0 here.

- **Reset Account Lockout Counter After:** Specifies the number of minutes to wait after which the account lockout counter is reset to 0. You can set this value from 1 to 99999.

When you configure this policy, Windows sets default values for the account lockout settings. To configure an account lockout policy, right-click **Account Lockout Threshold**, choose **Properties**, and then specify a value of your choice. As shown in Figure 12-3, Windows suggests default values for the other two policy settings. Click **OK** to define the policy settings and set these defaults. If you want to change the other settings, right-click the appropriate settings, choose **Properties**, and then enter the desired value.

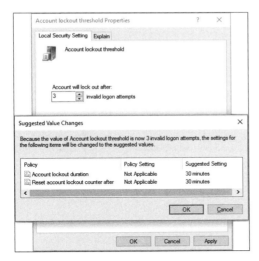

Figure 12-3   Windows Suggests Defaults for the Other Two Lockout Policy Settings

Unlocking an Account

When a user account is locked out because of too many incorrect attempts at entering a password, it is simple for an administrator or a user who is delegated the task to unlock it. Right-click the user account in the Local Users and Groups node of the Computer Management snap-in and choose **Properties**. On the General tab of the user's Properties dialog box, clear the **Account Is Locked Out** check box and then click **OK** or **Apply**.

NOTE   You cannot lock a user account out by selecting this check box; it is provided for unlocking the account only. An account is locked out only by the user entering an incorrect password the specified number of times.

Configuring Local Policies

The Local Policies subnode of Security Settings enables you to configure audit policies, user rights assignment, and security options.

Audit Policies

You have the capability to audit user access to files, folders, and printers by configuring the Audit policy for the local computer. If you need to audit computers that are members of a domain, you can configure the Group Policy in the OU that contains these computers. Otherwise, you can configure the Audit Policy node, which is under Local Policies, as shown in Figure 12-4.

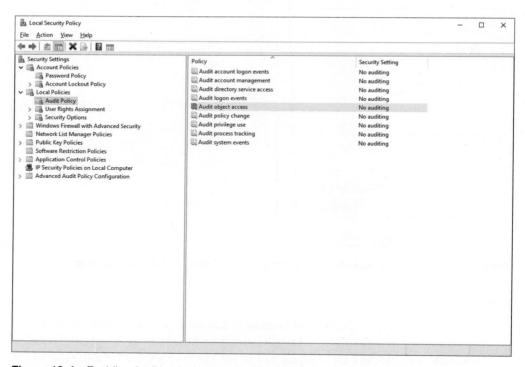

Figure 12-4   Enabling Auditing in the Local Policies Section of the Local Security Policy Console

Using the audit policy settings, you can identify undesirable activities on the computer. For example, if you had a computer whose local user and group configuration was inexplicably changed, you can enable the Audit Account Management policy and select **Success** to determine who made these changes. Figure 12-5 depicts this policy configuration.

Figure 12-5   Enabling Auditing to Trigger an Event Log Entry When an Action Has Completed Successfully, or Has Failed, or Both

Windows 10 enables you to audit the following types of events:

- **Account logon:** Logon by a domain user account at a domain controller. You should track both success and failure.

- **Account management:** Creation, modification, or deletion of computer, user, or group accounts. Also included are enabling and disabling of accounts and changing or resetting passwords. You should track both success and failure.

- **Directory service access:** Access to an AD DS object as specified by the object's SACL. This category includes the four subcategories mentioned earlier in this section; enabling directory service access from the Group Policy Management Editor enables all four subcategories. Enable this category for failures (if you record success, a large number of events will be logged).

- **Logon events:** Logon or logoff by a user at a member server or client computer. You should track both success and failure (success logging can record an unauthorized access that succeeded).

- **Object access:** Access by a user to an object such as a file, folder, or printer. You need to configure auditing in each object's SACL to track access to that object. Track success and failure to access important resources on your network.

- **Policy change:** Modification of policies including user rights assignment, trust, and audit policies. This category is not normally needed unless unusual events are occurring.

- **Privilege use:** Use of a user right, such as changing the system time. Track failure events for this category.

- **Process tracking:** Actions performed by an application. This category is primarily for application developers and does not need to be enabled in most cases.

- **System events:** Events taking place on a computer, such as an improper shutdown or a disk with very little free space remaining. Track success and failure events.

Group Policy or Local Security Policy enables you to configure success or failure for these types of actions. In other words, you can choose to record successful actions, failed attempts at performing these actions, or both. For example, if you are concerned about intruders that might be attempting to access your network, you can log failed logon events. You can also track successful logon events, which is useful in case the intruders succeed in accessing your network. For purposes of auditing files, folders, or printers, you need to enable object access auditing.

There is an additional policy that is more applicable to domain controllers than it is for Windows 10 client computers—that is, the Audit Account Logon Events. This, although similar to Audit Logon Events, will trigger an event log entry only when a user logs on to a computer but has been authenticated by another computer. You might want to use this and the Audit Logon Event policies together on your domain controllers to get an idea of how your AD DS site configuration is affecting your logon traffic, but it will not give you much to go on for a Windows 10 computer that is not part of a domain.

NOTE For more information on auditing and new features in Windows 10 and Windows Server 2016, refer to "Security Auditing" at https://technet.microsoft.com/itpro/windows/whats-new/whats-new-windows-10-version-1507-and-1511#security-auditing.

Security Options

The Security Options subnode within the Local Policies node includes a large set of policy options, as shown in Figure 12-6, that are important in controlling security aspects of the local computer. The list that follows describes several of the more important options that you should be familiar with.

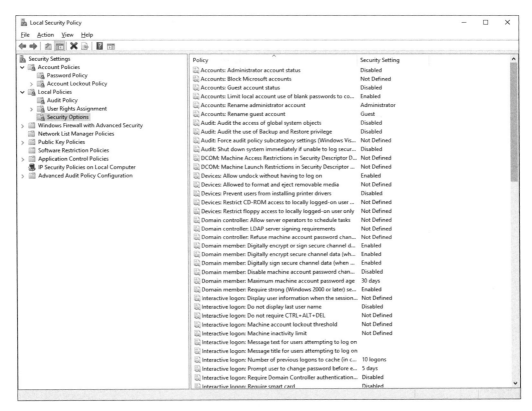

Figure 12-6 Security Options Subnode Containing a Comprehensive Set of Policy Settings That Help Enhance the Security of a Windows 10 Computer

- **Accounts: Block Microsoft Accounts:** Introduced in Windows 8, you can prevent users from adding Microsoft accounts. By selecting Users Can't Add Microsoft Accounts, you can prevent users from adding Microsoft accounts, switching local accounts to a Microsoft account, or connect a domain account to a Microsoft account. By selecting Users Can't Add or Log On with Microsoft Accounts, you can prevent existing Microsoft account users from logging on. Be aware that this option might make it impossible for an existing administrator to log on if the administrator is using a Microsoft account. Microsoft recommends that you keep this policy disabled or not configured.

- **Accounts: Rename Administrator Account:** This option renames the default administrator account to a value you specify. Intruders cannot simply look for "Administrator" when attempting to crack your network.

- **Interactive Logon: Do Not Display Last User Name:** Enable this option to prevent the username of the last logged-on user from appearing in the logon dialog box, thus preventing another individual from seeing a username. This can also help to reduce lockouts.

- **Interactive Logon: Do Not Require CTRL+ALT+DEL:** When enabled, a user is not required to press Ctrl+Alt+Delete to obtain the logon dialog box. Disable this policy in a secure environment to require the use of this key combination. Its use prevents rogue programs such as Trojan horses from capturing usernames and passwords.

- **Interactive Logon: Require Windows Hello for Business or Smart Card:** When enabled, users must employ a smart card to log on to the computer.

- **User Account Control:** Several policy settings determine the behavior of the UAC prompt for administrative and nonadministrative users, including behavior by applications that are located in secure locations on the computer, such as %ProgramFiles% or %Windir%. We discuss UAC in the next section.

> **NOTE**   For more information on the policy settings in the Security Options subnode, refer to "Security Options" at https://technet.microsoft.com/en-us/itpro/windows/keep-secure/security-options.

Configuring Remote Wipe

An issue with mobile devices is that their portability and convenience also make them easily lost or stolen. A lost computer in the wrong hands means not just the loss of the device, but possibly the loss of much more valuable information that the device contains. Not only could the computer contain sensitive and confidential information, it will typically also contain credentials, cached network information, and login accounts to a variety of cloud-based and business resources.

Remote Business Data Removal can remove or make corporate data inaccessible on the remote computer. It wipes only data that came from company resources, while leaving the user's personal content alone. This capability makes it easier for enterprises to allow knowledgeable workers to use their own devices for business tasks and still maintain control over company resources.

When it becomes clear that a mobile device is lost and will not be recovered in a timely manner, the safest course of action would be to ensure that the entire device is reset to factory settings and wiped clean of any personal or business information it may contain.

Microsoft's Exchange ActiveSync system, used for mobile phones and now available for Windows 10 and Windows 10 Mobile, has had support for remote wiping a device since its release. When used on mobile phones, including Windows 10

Mobile phones, it clears all data on the device. Administrators can perform a remote wipe on a managed device from the Exchange Administration Center (EAC), and users can even issue wipe commands themselves from the Outlook Web App user interface.

When used on Windows 10 Mobile and Windows 10, however, ActiveSync's remote wipe features does not delete all the data on the computer—only email, contacts, and calendar information stored in the Mail application.

A more comprehensive remote wipe capability is available using Microsoft Intune. You learn about Microsoft Intune, including configuration options for remote wipe, in Chapter 13, "Microsoft Intune."

Managing Data Synchronization

In today's modern workforce, employees often need to work from anywhere on any device. At the same time, it is becoming increasingly important that organizational data is strictly managed, both to protect secure assets and to comply with complex regulatory requirements and business policies. These competing trends are difficult to reconcile without complexity and pain for users.

Assume that an organization requires all documents that are considered records or work products to be managed exclusively on domain-managed file shares. Servers are kept in a secure data center; file shares are encrypted and backed up on a regular basis. User access is carefully managed through provisioning of users and ACLs, all access is monitored through security logs, and audit reports are carefully checked for compliance with HIPAA, Sarbanes-Oxley, and other regulations by auditing firms.

But now Fred in the Marketing department is headed out to a conference on the other side of the country. His presentation is not finished, and he needs some accounting documents and reference material from the server, as well as the presentation he has been working on, all maintained on the file share server. He has several hours of travel through airports and on shuttles to work on his files, but that means making a copy of the files on his laptop. If he finishes the work and emails the documents to himself, there are now at least three versions: the originals from the file share, the versions he emailed to himself, and the versions that he updated at the last minute before his meeting. In addition, he just ran afoul of company policy by sending internal accounting information through insecure email.

Plenty of other scenarios are possible, typically involving the need to centrally manage data and to allow users to work offline or on the road. Recall from Chapter 11, "Configuring and Securing Mobile Devices," that Windows 10 now has the capability to synchronize offline folders with file shares. Starting with Windows Server 2012 R2, you can also now support Work Folders, another technique to allow users to access company data offline in a secure manner, while automatically supporting synchronization and centralized management. Work Folders is supported in Windows 10, but also using mobile devices, including Android and iOS.

Work Folders

When you use Work Folders to store files, you're able to access the files from all your devices, even when offline. Work Folders is supported in Windows 7 and later, and you can use the Work Folders app to access files on an iOS or Android device.

Work Folders is supported as a role on Windows Server, version 2012 R2 and later. The role requires the IIS Hostable Core feature as well as File and Storage Services. Typically you use file shares with Work Folders, but it is not required; you can use any available storage area as a Work Folder. After the role is installed on Windows Server, you set up a sync share using the New Sync Share Wizard, as shown in Figure 12-7. When you create the sync share, you can configure access permissions and even set device security, such as encryption or requiring Lock screen passwords for devices.

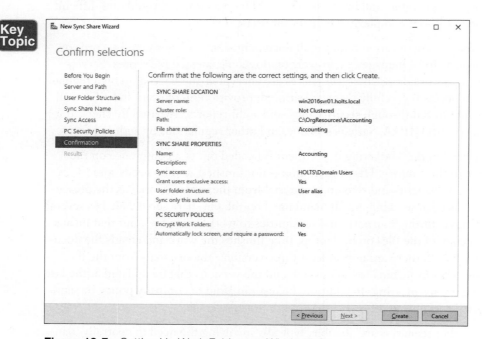

Figure 12-7   Setting Up Work Folders on Windows Server

You should be aware of the following software and infrastructure requirements for using Work Folders:

- A server running Windows Server 2012 R2 or later.

- A volume with an NTFS formatted file system for file storage.

- An SSL certificate for the server. It must include as Alternative Subject Names the URLs for the server or servers where Work Folders are hosted, and it must have the common name workfolders.*domainname* (where *domainname* is the name of your private or public domain). The SSL certificate must be applied to the IIS hosted core instance running on the Work Folders server.

- A DNS name configured for workfolders.*domainname*, pointing to all servers where Work Folders are hosted.

- Providing Internet access to Work Folders requires infrastructure supporting Internet hosting, including a certificate from a public CA, a server accessible from the Internet, and a public domain name and DNS.

- Clients must be running Windows 7 or later, Android version 4.4 or later, or iOS version 8 or later. Windows 7 must be the Professional, Enterprise, or Ultimate edition, and must be joined to the domain.

Use the following procedure to set up Work Folders on a Windows 10 computer:

Step 1.   From the Search bar or Cortana, type **Work Folders** and then click **Work Folders**. You can also find it from Control Panel under System and Security.

Step 2.   Click the **Set Up Work Folders** link.

Step 3.   Enter your organizational email address. You can also enter the URL for the Work Folders by clicking the **Enter a Work Folders URL Instead** link.

Step 4.   When authenticated, the Confirm Work Folders location page is displayed, as shown in Figure 12-8. You can change the Work Folders location at this point, but you will not be able to change it later.

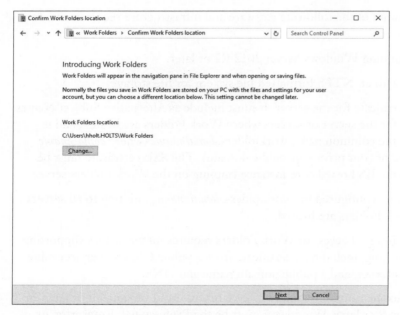

Figure 12-8   Confirming the Local Storage Location for Work Folders

Step 5.   If you have set security policies, on the server, a warning is displayed. You must check the **Accept These Policies on My PC** check box to proceed. Check the box if necessary, and then click the **Set Up Work Folders** button.

Step 6.   After the wizard completes, it will start synching your local Work Folders location with the Work Folders storage location on the server.

Your Work Folders location begins synching with the server right away. You can set up Office apps to use Work Folders. To do that, use the **Add a Place** option from the **File Open** menu, and select **Work Folders**. This makes it convenient for opening and saving files in Work, Excel, and other Office apps.

With Work Folders configured, the Control Panel app provides information on your server storage and the synchronization status, as shown in Figure 12-9. From this interface you can check for any file errors or issues synching your files, and the most recent sync date and time. You can also use the Sync Now link to immediately synchronize your files.

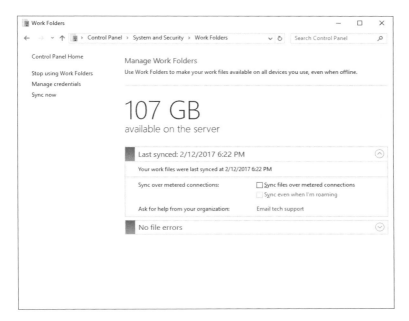

Figure 12-9   Work Folders Status Page

If Work Folders are configured to require encryption, the files in the Work Folders location will be encrypted. You can tell if the files are encrypted because the file-names will be green in File Explorer when viewing the folder. If the policy has not been set, you can encrypt the files in your Work Folders manually.

NOTE   You should be aware that Work Folders is a remote access and synchronization solution, not a collaboration tool. Each user you configure to use Work Folders has his or her own private workspace on the server and can sync files with multiple devices. However, you cannot create a Work Folders location that is shared by multiple users.

Managing Broadband Connectivity

From Chapter 6, "Windows 10 Networking," you should have a good understanding of setting up and managing Internet connections, TCP/IP connectivity and troubleshooting, managing Wi-Fi connectivity, and other network connection technologies in Windows 10. The term *broadband* is generally used for almost any type of Internet connection with speeds better than dial-up; however, we use broadband in this context to describe any over-the-air networking connection, such as cellular, satellite, or other wide-area data service. Broadband is used interchangeably with metered connection because these types of networks almost universally are limited, and charges are based on usage, typically in the amount of data transferred.

Smartphones and most mobile devices support the use of broadband data connections typically referred to as 3G, 4G, 4G LTE, EDGE, or something similar. These are broadband networks, for the purposes of this discussion. Windows 10 supports broadband connections in every edition, but it will be encountered most frequently on Windows 10 Mobile devices. Many Microsoft Surface devices offer built-in broadband connections, enabled by a subscription from a local mobile phone provider. For instance, the Surface 3 offers 4G LTE using a data plan from AT&T or T-Mobile.

Metered Networks

Windows 10 includes many features for working with and managing broadband connections and can automatically detect when you are connected to broadband, switch to Wi-Fi when it is available, and limit the use of a broadband connection to save money on charges. You learned about some of these features in previous chapters.

For instance, in Chapter 1, "Introducing Windows 10," you learned about the toggle that prevents Windows from downloading drivers and updates when you are using a metered connection. In Chapter 6, "Windows 10 Networking," you learned how to set a network connection's properties to manually tell Windows that the connection is a metered connection, and in the discussion about preferred wireless networks, you learned how Windows prioritizes when to use a broadband connection or not. You also learned in Chapter 11, "Configuring and Securing Mobile Devices," how to set offline file policies to configure whether offline file synchronization would occur if the device is connected to a broadband network.

Broadband Tethering

Windows 10 devices, including laptops and many hybrid devices, do not actually have broadband connections available to them. There are a couple of ways to add broadband to any device. Many providers offer devices that you connect through a USB port and connect your device to their mobile broadband network. But the most popular way is to use a mobile phone's tethering feature to connect your device to the phone's mobile network. This is also known as a mobile hotspot, and most modern phones have this feature, but it typically needs to be enabled by your mobile provider.

A hotspot is very easy to set up and use. Figure 12-10 shows a hotspot setup page for an Android phone. After the hotspot is configured and enabled, you connect to it like any other Wi-Fi connection. When you do so, you should be sure to configure the connection as a metered connection, as described in Chapter 6. Windows has no way to know that the network connection on the other end (the actual Internet network) is actually a broadband connection.

Figure 12-10   Configuring Tethering on an Android Smartphone

To connect to the broadband hotspot, or tether your Windows 10 device to it, click the **Network** icon from Action Center. As shown in Figure 12-11, the new hotspot connection is available as a wireless network. Click the **Connect** button and type in the password you configured on the phone when prompted.

Figure 12-11   Connecting to Your Mobile Phone Hotspot as You Would Any Other Wi-Fi Connection

You can view further details of your tethered connection by clicking **All Settings** from the Action Center, selecting **Network and Internet**, and then clicking the **Wi-Fi** menu. Your current connection should show up as Connected and Secured. Click the network icon to view additional details, as shown in Figure 12-12. From this page, you can also change the toggle for **Set as a Metered Connection** to **On**, so that Windows knows this is a broadband connection and will limit its Internet usage while you are using that connection.

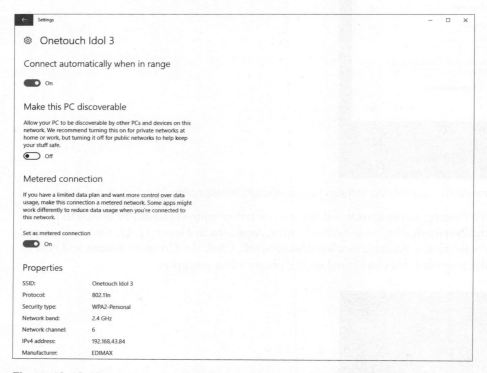

Figure 12-12   Details for an Android-Based Broadband Hotspot Connection

Ensuring that Windows knows you are using a metered connection has the following effect:

- Disables automatic downloading of Windows updates.

- Disables automatic downloading of app updates.

- Disables peer-to-peer uploading of updates.

- Tiles may not update.

- Store apps behave differently, typically turning off background data updates.

Exam Preparation Tasks

Review All the Key Topics

Review the most important topics in the chapter, noted with the Key Topics icon in the outer margin of the page. Table 12-2 lists a reference of these key topics and the page numbers on which each is found.

Table 12-2   Key Topics for Chapter 12

Key Topic Element	Description	Page Number
List	Security policy settings	595
Figure 12-2	Shows available password policies	597
List	Describes available auditing policies	601
Paragraph	Remote Wipe functions	604
Figure 12-7	Configuring Work Folders on Windows Server	606
Step List	Enabling Work Folders on Windows 10	607
Figure 12-11	Setting up broadband tethering	611

Complete the Tables and Lists from Memory

Print a copy of Appendix B, "Memory Tables" (found on the book's website), or at least the section for this chapter, and complete the tables and lists from memory. Appendix C, "Memory Tables Answer Key," also on the website, includes completed tables and lists to check your work.

Definitions of Key Terms

Define the following key terms from this chapter and check your answers in the glossary:

account lockout policy, Admin Approval mode, broadband, Local Security Policy, metered connection, password policy, Remote Wipe, Work Folders

This chapter covers the following subjects:

- **Microsoft Intune Administration:** In this section you are introduced to some of the administration features in the Microsoft Intune portal. You need to know how to create users and groups, as well as groups for the devices you manage. This section also covers device enrollment and management, remote computer management, and the connector site system role.

- **Microsoft Intune Monitoring:** When you are using Intune to manage your organization's Windows 10 devices, you need to understand how to monitor those devices and manage the policies for them.

- **Deploying Software Updates:** You can use Microsoft Intune to deploy software updates for the devices you are managing. In this section you learn about using reports to identify updates, configuring deadlines for update installations, and even how to deploy updates for third-party applications.

This chapter covers the following objectives for the 70-697 exam:

Deploy software updates by using Microsoft Intune: Use reports and In-Console Monitoring to identify required updates, approve or decline updates, configure automatic approval settings, configure deadlines for update installations, deploy third-party updates.

Manage devices with Microsoft Intune: Provision user accounts, enroll devices, view and manage all managed devices, configure the Microsoft Intune subscriptions, configure the Microsoft Intune connector site system role, manage user and computer groups, configure monitoring and alerts, manage policies, manage remote computers.

CHAPTER 13

Microsoft Intune

In recent years, more and more businesses have been moving applications, platforms, and software to the "cloud." This provides many advantages for organizations. Instead of managing a data center with expensive hardware and monitoring backups and storage, using cloud applications allows them to leverage economies of scale and purchase only the amount of storage and back-office processing power they need. Microsoft's cloud offerings include Microsoft Intune, a unique Software-as-a-Service (SaaS) application used by businesses to manage their Windows devices, including security, applications, updates, and more.

Intune helps companies minimize the complexity of managing a large base of mobile devices and a geographically dispersed workforce by using the cloud to manage devices wherever they are, helping to keep corporate information secure. Intune works with not only Windows Mobile devices, but also Android and iOS devices. It provides a self-service portal for users to enroll their devices and install company software. Administrators and support technicians can use Intune to deploy certificates, VPN configurations, and email profiles onto enrolled devices. They can also use the portal to keep those devices locked down and encrypted, and even fully erase the data on devices when they are lost or stolen.

Organizations can also use Intune to manage desktops and laptops in the organization using the same management console used for mobile devices. Intune can manage Windows PCs as well as UNIX/Linux servers and any version of Windows from XP to Windows 10. Intune can monitor devices and help protect them against malware infections and software vulnerabilities by keeping patches up-to-date. Administrators can maintain an inventory of all of the organization's computers and enforce system policies, deliver software, and generate reports of any issues on devices detected by the Intune device monitoring features.

In this chapter you learn about Intune, many of its features, and how to manage devices and collect vital information about organization assets using the Intune portal interfaces. You also learn how to deploy software, manage policies and security settings, and organize and administer devices with Intune.

"Do I Know This Already?" Quiz

The "Do I Know This Already?" quiz allows you to assess whether you should read this entire chapter or simply jump to the "Exam Preparation Tasks" section for review. If you are in doubt, read the entire chapter. Table 13-1 outlines the major headings in this chapter and the corresponding "Do I Know This Already?" quiz questions. You can find the answers in Appendix A, "Answers to the 'Do I Know This Already?' Quizzes."

Table 13-1   "Do I Know This Already?" Foundation Topics Section-to-Question Mapping

Foundation Topics Section	Questions Covered in This Section
Microsoft Intune Administration	1–8
Microsoft Intune Monitoring	9–11
Deployment Software Updates	12–13

CAUTION   The goal of self-assessment is to gauge your mastery of the topics in this chapter. If you do not know the answer to a question or are only partially sure of the answer, you should mark that question as wrong for purposes of the self-assessment. Giving yourself credit for an answer you correctly guess skews your self-assessment results and might provide you with a false sense of security.

1. To utilize Microsoft Intune for managing computers and devices, what other Microsoft cloud product will you need to use?

   a. Office 365 and TeamViewer

   b. TeamViewer and the Microsoft System Center Configuration Manager (SCCM)

   c. Office 365 and Azure AD

   d. Azure AD and TeamViewer

   e. Azure AD, TeamViewer, SCCM, and Office 365

2. What is the purpose of the roles you assign to users in the Office 365 portal?

   a. Users need to be in the correct role to enroll devices.

   b. The role will determine the type of device a user is assigned.

   c. Users are assigned roles to have administrative rights in the Office 365 portal.

   d. Roles are assigned in Azure AD, not Office 365.

3. You have added several users to your account using the Office 365 portal, but no users are showing up in the Intune console Groups menu. What went wrong?

   a. Users will show up in Intune only when they enroll a device or when you link a user to a device.

   b. You forgot to add an Intune license.

   c. Your users were not added to the correct group.

   d. Users were created without an email address.

   e. You need to copy the users to Intune.

4. You have added an APNs certificate to your Intune console. What type of devices does this enable you to enroll?

   a. Windows computers

   b. Windows phones

   c. Android devices

   d. iOS and Mac devices

   e. Any mobile device

5. What types of devices can you enroll with Microsoft Intune?

   a. Windows 10 and Windows 10 mobile

   b. Any Windows device

   c. Windows and Apple devices

   d. Windows, Android, iOS, and Mac devices

   e. Android, Windows Mobile, and iOS devices

6. A user has lost his mobile phone, and reports that he will not be able to find the device. The device is managed in the organizational Microsoft Intune portal. What should you do?

   a. Use Exchange ActiveSync to clear the device.

   b. Use Intune to wipe the device.

   c. Delete the device from Intune.

   d. Reset the passcode on the device.

   e. Lock the device from Intune.

7. Where are user groups for Microsoft Intune managed?

   a. At the Intune portal

   b. In your on-premises Active Directory

   c. In Office 365 portal

   d. In Azure AD portal

   e. In TeamViewer

8. What do you need to enable users of managed Windows 10 computers to request remote assistance from the Microsoft Intune Center?

   a. A full Office 365 license

   b. A TeamViewer account

   c. Remote Desktop connections in the Intune Console

   d. All of these answers are correct.

9. What are the available severity levels for Intune alerts?

   a. Critical and Warning

   b. Critical, Informational, and Enabled

   c. Critical, Warning, and Informational

   d. Critical, Error, Warning

   e. Critical, Disastrous, Warning, Informational

10. Device enrollment policies are used for what types of devices?

    a. Windows and Windows Mobile

    b. iOS and Mac

    c. Android and iOS

    d. All of these answers are correct.

11. You want to make sure that all devices managed in Intune use screen locks and time out to the screen lock after 15 minutes. What types of policies should you configure?

    a. Configuration policies

    b. Device compliance policies

    c. Conditional access policies

    d. Corporate device enrollment policies

    e. Resource access policies

12. You can use Microsoft Intune to manage what types of updates?

   a. Windows 8.1 and later updates

   b. Microsoft updates

   c. Third-party updates

   d. Microsoft and third-party updates

13. To help plan the budget for hardware upgrades next year, you would like to find out the number of Windows computers you have with older CPUs. What type of report would you run from Intune to help you get this information?

   a. Update reports

   b. Mobile device inventory reports

   c. Detected software reports

   d. Computer inventory reports

   e. Device history reports

Foundation Topics

Microsoft Intune Administration

You have learned a few of the features of Microsoft Intune in previous chapters. Recall, for instance, the methods available for sideloading apps using Microsoft Intune, from Chapter 5, "Installing and Managing Software."

In this chapter, you get a more comprehensive view of Microsoft Intune and its capabilities. For the 70-697 exam, you need to be familiar with Microsoft Intune administration and management of users and devices. This section covers provisioning and management of user accounts and devices, configuring the Intune connector site system role, and some tasks for managing remote computers.

User Accounts, Device Enrollment, and Device Management

Microsoft Intune is a member of Microsoft's cloud service offerings and is integrated with Office 365 and Azure AD. One of the more recent innovations introduced to Intune is integration of groups with Azure AD, so Intune no longer has independent groups; it uses Azure AD groups instead. This provides a number of advantages. You can use the same group experience across all of Enterprise Mobility (Microsoft Intune), Security, and Azure AD apps. Azure AD groups support Intune deployments to users and devices.

Managing accounts and devices requires the use of at least two Microsoft administration portals, and typically a third if you plan to utilize user groups in Intune:

- The Office 365 Admin center, at https://portal.office.com.

- The Intune administration console, at https://manage.microsoft.com.

- The Intune dashboard and group management section of Azure at https://portal.azure.com.

The Intune administration console is used for most of the management, including setting up and managing policies, devices, apps, and so on. You use the Office 365 Admin center to add and manage users and accounts. The Office 365 Admin center has links at the bottom of the left menu for navigating to Intune and Azure AD portals. User groups are now fully integrated with Azure AD.

User Accounts

Adding users for Intune starts at the Office 365 Admin center, where user accounts are created before they can be used for Intune. The main page, shown in Figure 13-1, includes a Users section and an Add a User link. Click the **Add a User** link to display the page shown in Figure 13-2.

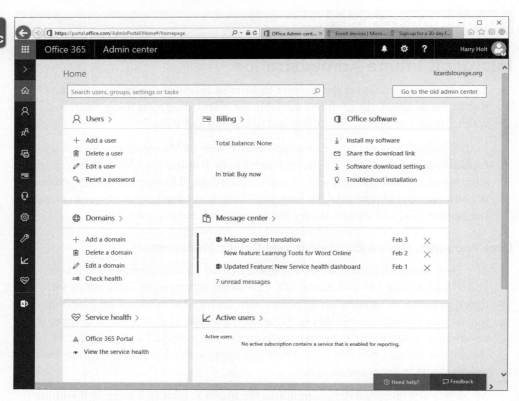

Figure 13-1   Using Office365 Admin Center to Add Users for Intune

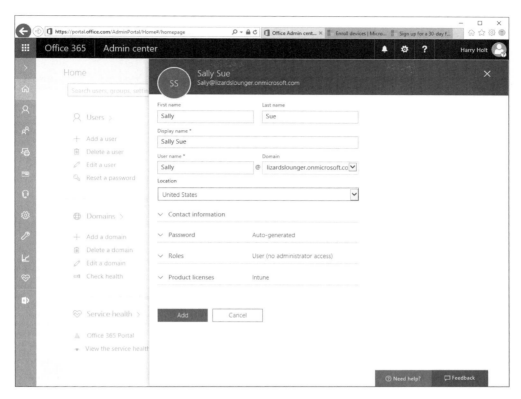

Figure 13-2   Adding a User in the Office 365 Admin Center

As shown in Figure 13-2, the username is part of your company's domain. When you click the **Create** button, you can choose to send the temporary Intune password to the user's organizational email account, or select another email address. You can expand the links for other details to make any changes you want before creating the account, such as Contact information, the initial password for the user, and any roles. By default the user will have only basic access to Office 365, but if you want the user to have administrative access to the Office 365 portal, you can assign a different role. You are also setting the user's product licenses, which you can change by clicking the **Product Licenses** link. If you do not have an Office 365 subscription, this defaults to the Intune license, which will be the only one available. Users will need to be assigned an Intune license to enroll their devices.

If you have many users to add, you can create a CSV file to import a list of users. From the Office 365 Admin center, select **Users**, click the **More** link, and then select **Import Multiple Users**. This displays the page shown in Figure 13-3. You can download a template for the CSV file from the links provided, either with headers only, or with headers and some sample user information to get you started with the required format.

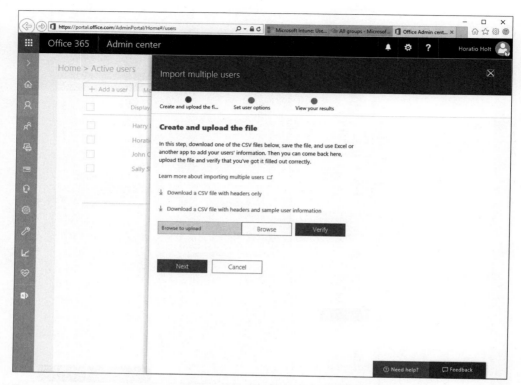

Figure 13-3 Importing Multiple Users into the Office 365 Console Using CSV Files

You manage your users from this interface as well. Clicking the **Users** link from Figure 13-1 displays the list of users you have provisioned. From that page you can perform tasks such as deleting a user, resetting a password, or changing the user's role or contact information.

From the Office 365 portal, you can navigate to the Intune portal by clicking the **Admin Centers** menu and selecting the **Intune** link, which opens the Microsoft Intune portal and displays the Dashboard page, as shown in Figure 13-4.

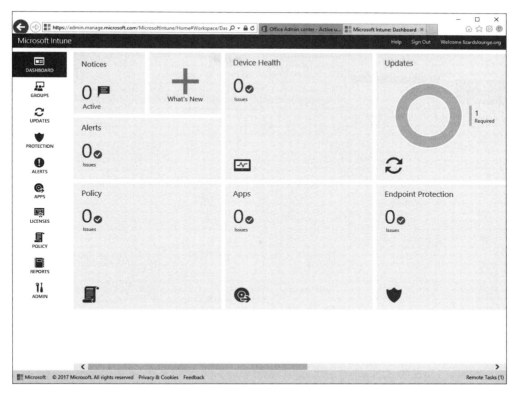

Figure 13-4   Microsoft Intune Dashboard

The Intune Dashboard is the top-level management interface for the Intune portal. Notice from Figure 13-4 that a menu is presented on the left side for various Intune functions. Microsoft is busy making a lot of updates to its cloud-based portal applications based on user feedback, so the UI can change frequently. Currently many of the features are available by clicking one of the dashboard tiles. For instance, clicking the APPS tile will navigate to the Apps Management menu, which we first encountered in Chapter 5. The portal will also update your location in the menu. Clicking one of the major menu items will take you to an overview for that menu and display a submenu for navigating various features and functions.

To view the Intune users, click the **GROUPS** menu and then select **Users**. Intune displays a page similar to Figure 13-5. The users you added using the Office 365 portal do not initially show up on this list. Instead, you will see only users who have enrolled their devices or users you have manually linked to an enrolled device.

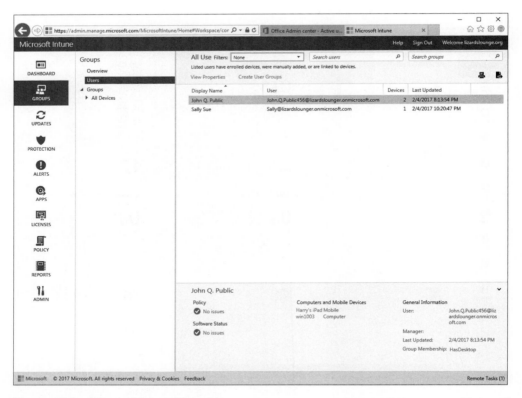

Figure 13-5   Microsoft Intune Users Menu

Because the main management interface for users is over in the Office 365 portal, user administration tasks are available for users in the Intune portal. You can view users' properties and group memberships. As mentioned earlier, you do not manage groups in the Intune portal—instead, you manage them in Azure. The one thing you can manage through Intune is the links between users and devices. Users can have multiple devices, but each device can be linked to only one user. In Figure 13-5, you can see at the bottom of the page that John Q. Public is linked to two devices: an iPad device and a computer.

NOTE   Microsoft frequently reviews feedback from users of its portal and cloud products, and often makes changes to the user interface and navigation features, as well as integrating functionality to improve the user experience. For the 70-697 exam, you will not be expected to know all the menus and locations of functionality in these portals. Instead, you should focus on understanding the features available and how they can help you manage devices and improve the security of your organization. To check up on the latest changes to Microsoft Intune, see "What's New in Microsoft Intune" at https://docs.microsoft.com/en-us/intune/whats-new/whats-new-in-microsoft-intune.

Enrolling Devices

You can manage both mobile devices and Windows PCs with Microsoft Intune, and Intune can perform the role of the Mobile Device Management (MDM) authority for your organization. Before enrolling devices, ensure that Intune is set as the MDM authority.

To set the MDM authority, or ensure that Microsoft Intune is set as your authority, log in to the Intune console, select the **Admin** menu, and then select **Mobile Device Management**. You should see the page shown in Figure 13-6, with the Mobile Device Management Authority setting showing the Set to Microsoft Intune checked. If not, you can choose **Set MDM Authority** from the Tasks list, and confirm that you want to set Intune as the authority.

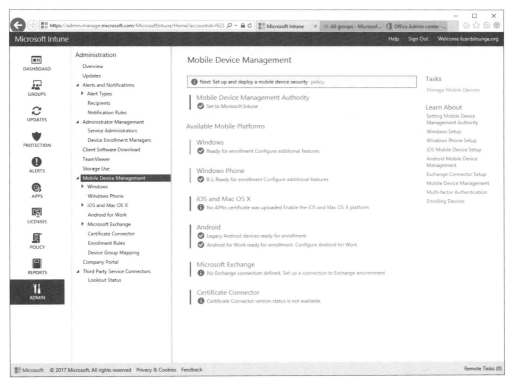

Figure 13-6 Microsoft Intune Can Be Set as Your Mobile Device Management (MDM) Authority

You can enroll an Android device using the Intune Company Portal app, which is available on Google Play. Users can install the app and then log in with the Office 365 account name and password you set up in the Office 365 Admin portal.

The Company Portal app will be given the following privileges on the Android device:

- Erase All Data
- Change the Screen-Unlock Password
- Set Password Rules
- Monitor Screen-Unlock Attempts
- Lock the Screen
- Set Lock-Screen Password Expiration
- Set Storage Encryption
- Disable Cameras
- Disable Some Screen Lock Features

Enrolling an Apple iOS or Mac device requires a few additional steps, because it will require setting up Intune with an Apple Push Notification Service (APNs) certificate, signed by Apple, to enable iOS or Mac enrollment. Use the following steps to enable enrollment for iOS devices:

Step 1.   From the Microsoft Intune portal, select **Admin**, and then expand **Mobile Device Management**, click **iOS and Mac OS X**, and select **Upload an APNs Certificate**.

Step 2.   From the menu shown in Figure 13-7, click **Download the APNs Certificate Request**.

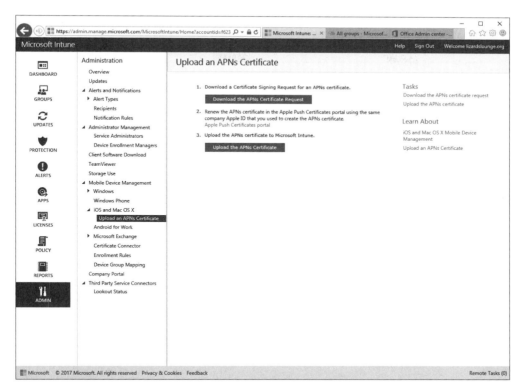

Figure 13-7   Managing APNs Certificates Using the Intune Administration Menu

Step 3.   Save the CSR file to your local machine.

Step 4.   Go to the Apple Push Certificates Portal at https://idmsa.apple.com/ IDMSWebAuth/ and log in using your company's Apple ID.

Step 5.   Select the **Create a Certificate** button.

Step 6.   From the upload screen, browse for the CSR file you saved in Step 3.

Step 7.   On the next screen, select **Download** to download the signed certificate, and save it to your local machine.

Step 8. Return to the Microsoft Intune portal, and click the **Upload the APNs Certificate** button.

Step 9. Browse to the .PEM file you downloaded from Apple in Step 7 and enter your Apple ID; then click **Upload**.

After completing these steps and installing your APNs certificate, you are ready to enroll iOS and Mac OS X devices in Intune. You should see a screen similar to Figure 13-8.

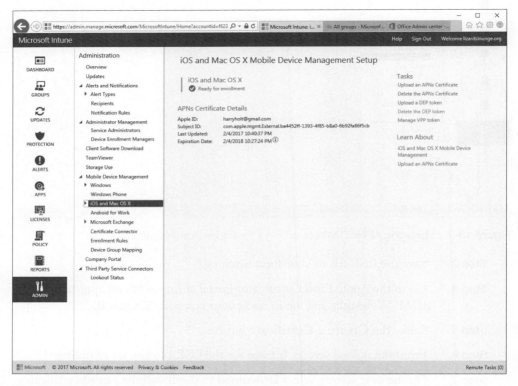

Figure 13-8   After Installing an APNs Certificate in Intune, You Are Ready to Enroll iOS Devices

To enroll an iOS device, you use the Microsoft Intune Company Portal app from the Apple store. Install the app on the iOS device and then log in. The process for enrolling the device is similar to the Android process. The main difference is that you will be required to accept the APNs certificate and install it as part of the Management Profile on the device trust store, as shown in Figure 13-9.

Figure 13-9   Installing the Intune Organizational Management Profile on an iOS Device

You can also enroll Windows computers and devices to Microsoft Intune. Just like mobile devices, users must be set up in Office 365 portal and assigned an Intune license before they can enroll a computer. The first step is to download the client software for Microsoft Intune. You can then deploy it to client computers. This can be done manually on each computer, or you can deploy the software using Group Policy or custom scripts.

Use the following procedure to manually enroll a Windows 10 computer with your organization's Intune management portal.

Step 1.   Log in to the computer using the organizational account credentials or a local account with rights to install new software.

Step 2.   Extract the .ZIP file to the local computer. The file includes the setup executable and an ACCOUNTCERT file. Be sure not to rename or remove the ACCOUNTCERT file. It should be in the same directory as the setup executable.

Step 3.   The computer will be automatically enrolled.

After the client software is installed, you should see the device show up in the Intune portal.

Note that there are two ways to enroll a Windows 10 computer. The preceding procedure installs the Intune client, and the computer will be enrolled as a "Computer" device. You can also enroll the device using the Windows settings, and the device will be enrolled as a "Device" instead of as a "Computer." This is useful only if you are not using on-premises Active Directory. Use this procedure to enroll the computer as a device:

Step 1.   Access the Action Center and select **All Settings**.

Step 2.   From the Settings page, select **Accounts**.

Step 3.   Select the **Access Work or School** option, and then click **Connect**.

Step 4.   Enter the email for your Intune user account and then click **Next**. The Microsoft Intune sign-in page is displayed.

Step 5.   Enter the credentials for your Intune or Office 365 user account, and then click **Sign In**.

Step 6.   When the You're All Set! page is displayed, click **Close**.

Enrolling as a device is more appropriate for users who want to use their personal devices while gaining access to organizational resources such as email, SharePoint, or Office 365. This is also the preferred method for organizations that are using Microsoft cloud-based solutions for infrastructure management. If you have an investment in on-premises Active Directory, Exchange, the Microsoft System Center Configuration Manager (SCCM), and other tools, you should use the Intune client software if you want to manage devices with Intune.

Viewing and Managing Devices

You can view all enrolled devices from the Microsoft Intune portal. To view devices, click the **Groups** menu, and then select **All Devices**. The list of devices will be displayed, as shown in Figure 13-10.

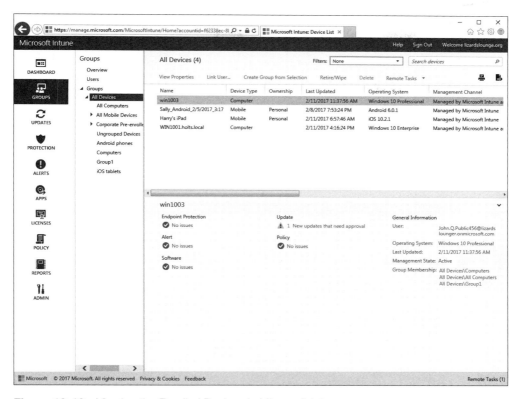

Figure 13-10 Viewing the Enrolled Devices in Microsoft Intune

This is the interface for managing all your enrolled devices. Many attributes are displayed for each device, such as the name of the device as configured locally, the type of device, the operating system, and other basic information. You can view more details by selecting the device and clicking the **View Properties** menu. The properties available will depend on the type of device. For Windows 10 computers, the following categories of properties will be available on a tabbed menu, similar to Figure 13-11.

- **General:** Basic information about the device and status, such as updates, endpoint protection status, the user linked to the device, and the date and time when the last update was applied. This tab also provides links to retire or wipe the device and to link the device to a user.

- **Updates:** Windows updates for the computer. From this menu you can approve updates, check installed or failed updates, and do other tasks related to applying updates to the device.

- **Malware:** Lists any malware that has been detected on the device.

- **Alerts:** View any device-related alerts that may need administrator attention.

- **Hardware:** Displays detailed hardware information about the device, including any attached network interfaces, printers, and peripherals.

- **Software:** Lists all software installed on the computer and the current version. The list will include Windows operating system components and any Windows Store apps.

- **Policy:** Displays the list of Intune policies that have been applied to the device.

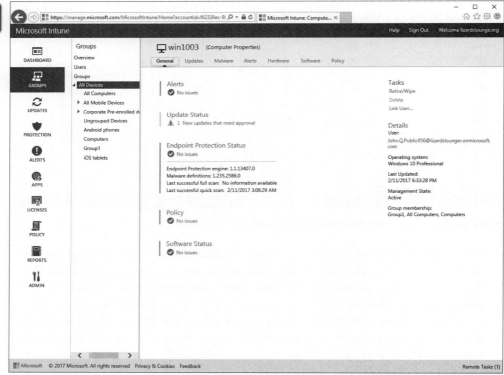

Figure 13-11   Computer Properties Page for Devices in Microsoft Intune

If a device has been lost or stolen, or you simply want to stop managing the device from Intune for any reason, you can use the Retire/Wipe link to close out the device. Clicking the link displays the dialog shown in Figure 13-12. Select whether you want to clear out only company data or completely wipe everything from the device and restore it to factory settings; then click the **Yes** button. If the device is turned on and connected to the Internet, it will take less than 15 minutes to start wiping the device.

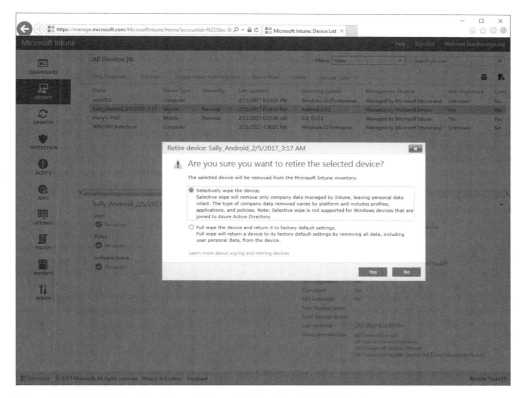

Figure 13-12   Confirm the Type of Remote Wipe for a Mobile Device

There are also a few additional tasks you can perform on selected devices using the Remote Tasks drop-down menu. The following tasks are available. Some tasks are available only for computer device types, whereas others are available for mobile device types.

- **Run a Full Malware Scan (Computer):** Runs the installed malware scanner on the computer, performing a full scan. On Windows 10 computers, Windows Defender will run a full scan.

- **Run a Quick Malware Scan (Computer):** Tells the computer to run a quick malware scan using the installed antimalware software. On Windows 10 computers, Windows Defender will run a quick scan.

- **Restart Computer (Computer):** Performs a soft reboot of the operating system.

- **Update Malware Definitions (Computer):** Causes the computer to check the Internet for any new malware definitions and install any new ones available.

- **Refresh Policies (Computer):** Causes the computer to check for any policy updates and apply them immediately.

- **Refresh Inventory (Computer):** Tells the Intune client on the device to refresh the inventory of hardware and software and report back to the Intune portal.

- **Remote Lock (Mobile):** Causes the device to enable the screen lock immediately.

- **Passcode Reset (Mobile):** Resets the passcode used to unlock the device screen. This works differently depending on the device. On an iOS device, the passcode is removed and must be added back to the device. On Android, a new temporary passcode is set, and the user will need to change it.

The Microsoft Intune Connector Site System Role

You can use a hybrid solution for managing your mobile devices. Large organizations that are currently using SCCM may want to leverage the management capabilities of the current infrastructure and be able to remotely manage all their mobile devices using an Intune subscription.

By integrating SCCM functions with the Intune management portal, administrators can configure a "single pane of glass" management interface. That is, they will have a single administration UI for managing all the organization's devices, even while some functionality is supported by SCCM and others by Intune. Centralizing administration views in this way can go a long way to simplifying and streamlining administration tasks.

Organizations that currently are not using SCCM for device management should avoid the hybrid model and leverage the Intune standalone instead. Several new features are coming to Intune, and should be available by the publication date of this text. These features make using a hybrid model with SCCM unnecessary and redundant:

- Programmatic access (API), including an SDK and PowerShell management options.

- Custom reporting.

- Role-based Access Control.

- Scalable support for more than 50,000 mobile devices.

- Manage both traditional PC clients and Intune-managed devices from the same console.

As you will see, configuring a hybrid MDM solution is an involved process that requires careful planning and execution. The details of these tasks are out of scope of this text and not needed for the 70-697 exam. Instead, you should only be concerned with knowing what technologies are involved in configuring the connector and the purpose for using a hybrid solution, as described in the list that follows:

Step 1. **Create an MDM Collection:** This is a collection of users you create in SCCM to specify all the users that can enroll devices.

Step 2. **Configure Domain Name Requirements:** Users must be able to enroll using a publicly resolvable email address or UPN. If your company does not have a public domain name, you must create an alternate login ID for your users in Azure AD.

Step 3. **Configure the Intune Subscription:** In SCCM, you must configure your Intune subscription information. This includes specifying the user collection you created in Step 1, and specifying a site code and company contact, and other information. You will use your Intune subscription credentials, which will be managed by SCCM.

Step 4. **Create the Service Connection Point:** You first install the service connection point site system role using the normal process for installing server roles. After it is installed, you use SCCM to create a Site System Server using the available wizard. This will be the back-end communication channel between your on-premises SCCM installation and the Microsoft Intune management site.

Step 5. **Enable Platform Enrollment:** Configure the device enrollment types. You can set up iOS, Windows, and Android enrollment. Just like with Intune standalone, you will need to configure an Apple APNs certificate for iOS enrollment. Windows enrollment requires the creation of DNS records to point to the SCCM enrollment server.

Step 6. **Verify MDM Configuration:** After all these configuration tasks are complete, check the logs for any issues and start enrolling devices.

After you have configured SCCM and Intune as a hybrid MDM, you will not be able to manage devices from the Intune website anymore. The single pane of glass management interface has become the only interface available. If you want to disconnect SCCM and start using Intune standalone, you need to contact Microsoft support to help you with that transition, so it's very important to plan your road map for device management in advance.

> **NOTE**   For more information about configuring SCCM and hybrid MDM, see "Setup Hybrid Mobile Device Management (MDM) with System Center Configuration Manager and Microsoft Intune" at https://docs.microsoft.com/en-us/sccm/mdm/deploy-use/setup-hybrid-mdm.

Manage User and Computer Groups

Devices are organized and managed using device groups. Do not confuse device groups with user groups, which are managed in Microsoft Azure AD. Device groups are managed in Intune, including some built-in groups. By default, all devices are members of the All Devices group. Also, Windows computers will automatically be added to the All Computers group, and any iOS, Android, or Windows Mobile device will be added to the All Mobile Devices group.

You can add your own custom groups for managing devices, based on your own criteria, and newly enrolled devices will be added to these groups based on the criteria you define. The type of criteria you can use includes the device type (computer or mobile), an organization unit from your directory, or the Active Directory domain that the device is joined to. From the menu previously shown in Figure 13-10, you can select several devices and then click the **Create Group from Selection** link to create a custom group. Instead of using general criteria for the devices added, you will be adding specific devices to the group. If you want to add other devices later, you will need to edit the group and add those devices to the list.

To create a user group, click the **Users** option from the **Groups** menu, and then click the **Create User Groups** link from the menu. This will redirect you to the Azure portal where user groups are managed, as shown in Figure 13-13. Click the **Add** button at the top to create a new group. Each group will have a Name, an optional Description, and a Membership Type, which can be either Assigned or Dynamic. The Membership Type determines how members are added to the group. For a Dynamic group, you create a rule based on the Azure AD attributes of your users. For instance, you could assign members automatically if they are members of a certain department, have a specific job title, or other criteria. If you create a group with an Assigned Membership Type, you will be manually adding and removing members to the group.

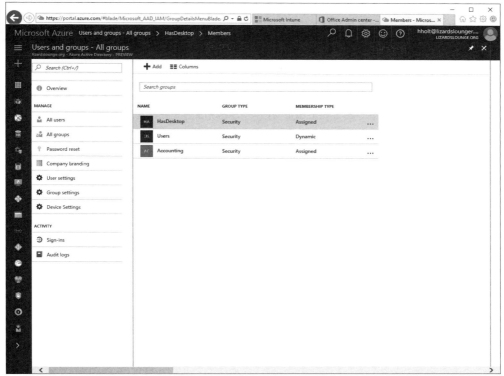

Figure 13-13   Managing User Groups in the Azure AD Portal

You can view the group membership of a user in Intune. Select **Users** from the Groups menu, and select a user from the list. The user details at the bottom of the page include a Group Membership section that lists the groups that the user belongs to. Clicking the link for any of the groups listed will direct you to the group in the Azure portal.

> **NOTE**   This section describes user and computer groups as they work in Intune and Azure AD currently. However, Microsoft is in the process of migrating all groups, including device groups, to Azure, so this information will change after the migration occurs. For more information, see https://docs.microsoft.com/en-us/intune/deploy-use/categorize-devices-with-device-group-mapping-in-microsoft-intune.

Manage Remote Computers

You learned earlier in the chapter how to enroll Windows 10 computers for Microsoft Intune. You can enroll any Windows computer with Intune that uses Microsoft Vista or later, and manage those computers from the Intune console. The computer must be running a supported edition, using Professional or higher. You cannot enroll Home or Basic editions. These computers will show up in your Intune console as Computer device types, and will automatically be added to the All Computers group.

After you have installed the Intune client as described earlier, and the computer is successfully enrolled, a new icon will show up in the system tray. Click the icon and select **Microsoft Intune Center** to display the page shown in Figure 13-14. These are options for users on an enrolled Windows computer. They can download any applications you have made available on the Intune portal, check for updates, use their installed antimalware tool, or send a request for Remote Assistance to the organization's administrators.

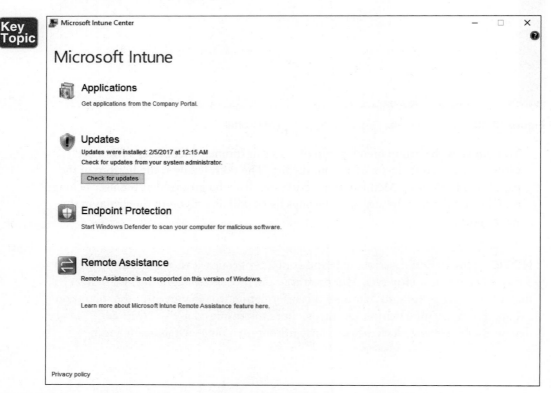

Figure 13-14 Microsoft Intune Center on Windows Computers with the Intune Client Installed

In Figure 13-14, you may notice the message Remote Assistance Is Not Supported on This Version of Windows. To use Remote Assistance through the Intune Center, you need to sign up for a TeamViewer account and connect your TeamViewer subscription account to Intune.

To enable TeamViewer, navigate to the Admin menu of the Microsoft Intune portal, click **TeamViewer** from the menu, and then select the **Enable** link. After your TeamViewer account is enabled, users will have a Request Remote Assistance link in their Intune Center console. When they click the link, the support technicians monitoring the TeamViewer console will get a notification that a user is requesting assistance and can then connect to a remote desktop session to render assistance. Configuring and using TeamViewer for desktop support are far outside the scope of this text, but you should know what it is used for and how to enable the connector in Intune.

Microsoft Intune Monitoring

Devices and computers that are managed by Intune return detailed information about their hardware properties, updates, and other information. You can configure Intune to provide monitoring information and trigger alerts for events that you want to be notified about.

Configure Monitoring and Alerts

Alerts are used to keep you in touch with what's happening in Microsoft Intune and the devices and computers that are enrolled. Alerts are generated based on alert types, which are preconfigured rules built in to Intune. You can configure the State and Severity for each alert. State is whether the alert type is enabled or disabled. There are three levels of Severity that you can set:

- **Critical:** Indicates a serious issue that requires investigation as soon as possible.

- **Warning:** Indicates an issue that is not serious but might become serious without attention or intervention.

- **Informational:** Indicates information that is not critical.

Some alert types might have some additional configuration properties, such as a percentage of devices affected before the alert is triggered. You manage alerts from the Intune Alerts menu. From the Overview page, you can view a summary of any alerts that have been triggered. Alerts are categories for you in a hierarchy, with All Alerts at the top. Other major categories include Endpoint Protection, Monitoring, Notices, Policy, Remote Assistance, System, and Updates.

To configure alert types, access the Overview page from the Alerts menu and select **Configure Alert Type Settings**. Intune displays a page similar to Figure 13-15. To modify alert type settings, select the alert type from the list. You can enable or disable the alert from the menu at the top, or choose the **Configure** link to configure settings for the alert to change the state or select the severity you want for the alert.

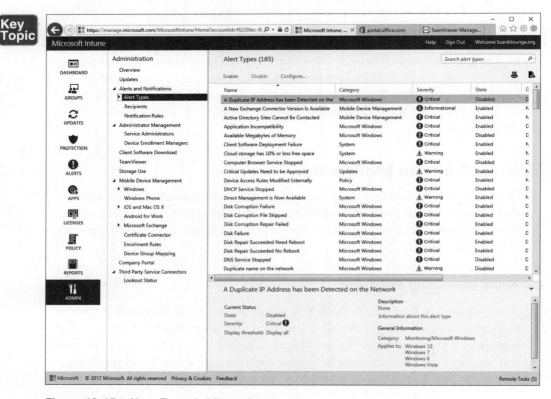

Figure 13-15   Alerts Types in Microsoft Intune

Some alerts also allow you to select a display threshold. This setting allows you to configure a percentage of devices so that the alert type is triggered only after the threshold has been reached. Other alerts may have additional settings that you can configure. For instance, the Available Megabytes of Memory alert, shown in Figure 13-16, can be set with a Frequency and Threshold. The frequency tells Intune how often to check the available memory, in seconds, and the threshold is the amount of available memory below which an alert would be triggered.

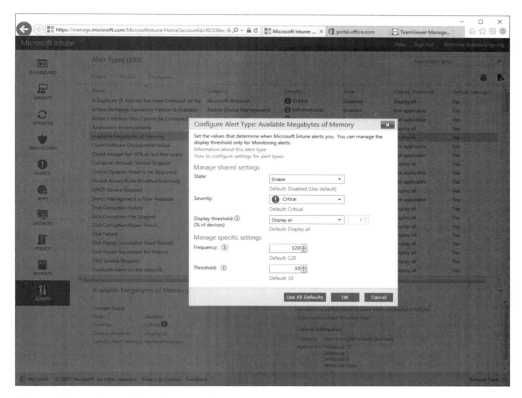

Figure 13-16 Some Alert Types in Microsoft Intune Have Additional Attributes That Can Be Configured

You can also configure Microsoft Intune to send email notifications when an alert is triggered. You first need to set up recipients for alerts. To configure emails for alerts, use the following procedure:

Step 1.   Select the **Admin** menu and then click **Recipients**.

Step 2.   Click the **Add Link** to add a recipient. You must enter the email in the Email Address field and the Confirm Email Address field, and then click **OK**. Add as many recipients as needed using this procedure.

Step 3.   Select the **Notification Rules** option from the **Admin** menu.

Step 4.   Select the type of alert rule to configure from the list, shown in Figure 13-17. You can use the All Alerts rule to set recipients for all alert types.

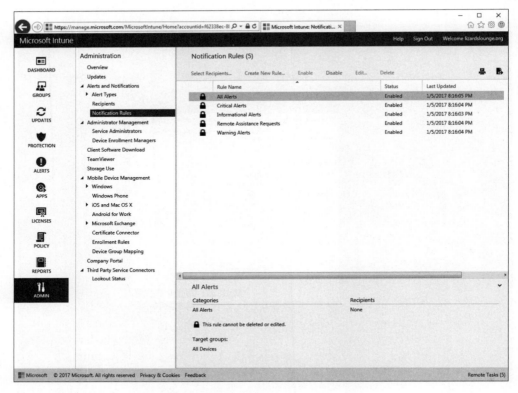

Figure 13-17   Notification Rules in Microsoft Intune

Step 5.   Click the **Select Recipients** link from the top to display the list of email recipients you configured in Step 2.

Step 6.   Check the box next to the email address of the recipients you want to receive notifications, and then click **OK**.

Step 7.   For more detailed control of who should get an email notification for more specific alert types, use the **Create New Rule** link to set up your own rule. You can select from any of the categories of alert types.

An email will be sent to all the email addresses you selected.

Managing Policies

Microsoft Intune allows you to use policies, which are groups of settings that control features on devices and computers. You create policies using built-in templates with specific settings. You can deploy policies to device groups or user groups.

Policies fall into a few broad categories:

- **Configuration policies:** Use configuration policies to manage security settings and features on enrolled devices.

- **Device compliance policies:** If you use conditional access policies, you can use compliance policies to set the rules and settings for defining device compliance before allowing the device to access organizational resources. Even if you do not use conditional access, you can use compliance policies to monitor devices and mediate any issues.

- **Conditional access policies:** These policies secure email and other organizational resources based on the conditions you set.

- **Corporate device enrollment policies:** These policies are used for setting up iOS and Mac device management. You learned about setting up APNs for iOS and Mac device enrollment earlier in this chapter.

- **Resource access policies:** These policies work together to help users get access to files and other organizational resources.

If you use Group Policy in your organization, and you have Windows PCs joined to your domain using Group Policy objects, some of the Intune policies may control the same settings and features. When conflicts occur, the domain-level Group Policy will always take precedence over Intune policy, unless the PC cannot contact a domain controller for some reason, in which case the Intune policy will be applied.

Conditional access policies can be set to allow access to Dynamics CRM Online, Exchange, SharePoint Online, or Skype for Business Online. You need an online subscription to the specific service to use these policies. For Exchange, either you need a subscription to Exchange Online, or you must configure a connection between Microsoft Intune and your Exchange server.

Configuration policy templates fall under several categories. Follow this procedure to create a configuration policy:

Step 1. In the Microsoft Intune administration policy, select **Configuration Policies** from the Policy menu, and then click the **Add** link.

Step 2. Select the policy you want to configure, and whether to use the recommended settings or custom settings. For some policies, only the custom settings are available. Click **Create Policy**.

Step 3. Enter a name and, optionally, a description for the policy.

Step 4. Configure the required settings and then click **Save Policy**.

Step 5. In the dialog box that appears, choose **Yes** to deploy the policy immediately, or **No** to create the policy without deploying. You can deploy the policy later.

After you have created the policy, you can deploy it by selecting the policy and choosing the Manage Deployment link, displaying the dialog box shown in Figure 13-18. You can select from your configured user groups or device groups. A mix of groups is allowed, so you can choose groups from one category or both.

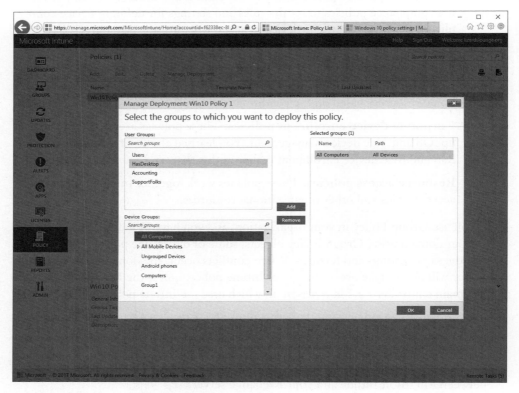

Figure 13-18   Managing Policy Deployment

When a policy is deployed, Intune begins to try notifying the device that it should check in with Intune for policy updates. If the device does not check in, Intune makes three more attempts to contact the device. The device gets its policy updates on the next check-in with Intune.

NOTE   For details about the Microsoft Intune configuration policies that you can set and the devices they apply to, see the "Microsoft Intune Configuration Policy Reference" at https://docs.microsoft.com/en-us/intune/deploy-use/microsoft-intune-policy-reference.

To configure compliance policies, select **Compliance Policies** from the menu, click the **Add** link, and then give your compliance policy a name. You can toggle various settings off and on for the compliance settings you want to enforce. Some of the important compliance policies that you can set are listed in Table 13-2.

Table 13-2   Microsoft Intune Compliance Property Settings

Category	Setting	Description
System Security	Require a password to unlock mobile devices	Set to yes or no.
System Security	Allow simple passwords	Set to yes or no.
System Security	Minimum password length	Can be set between 4 and 14.
System Security	Required password type	Set to alphanumeric or numeric.
System Security	Minutes of inactivity before a password is required	Causes the screen to lock after the time you set. Set to 1 minute, 5 minutes, 15 minutes, or 1 hour.
System Security	Encryption	Requires encryption to be enabled on the device. Applies to Windows Phone, Android, and Samsung KNOX.
Device Health	Require devices to be reported as healthy	Applies to Windows 10 Desktop and Mobile.
Device Health	Require that devices prevent installation of apps from unknown sources	Applies to Android only.
Device Health	Device must not be jailbroken or rooted	Applies to iOS and Android.
Device Properties	Minimum Windows Version	Specify a minimum Windows version.
Device Properties	Minimum Windows Phone or Windows 10 Mobile version	Specify a minimum version for Windows Phone or Windows 10 Mobile devices.

Deploying Software Updates

You can use Microsoft Intune to manage updates for the Windows computers enrolled with Microsoft Intune. Using Intune for managing updates is similar to using an on-premises Windows Server Update Services (WSUS) server to manage updates for your Windows PCs.

After you have at least one device enrolled as a Computer device type in Intune, updates will be available in the Intune portal. Selecting the Updates menu item will display a large list of updates available, as shown in Figure 13-19. Updates are available for Windows versions back to Windows XP and are categorized in groups, such as Critical Updates, Security Updates, Service Packs, and so on.

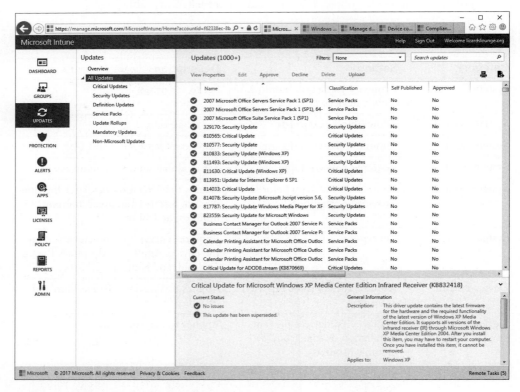

Figure 13-19 Windows Updates for Deployment in Microsoft Intune

You can modify the updates you see in the Intune console so that you see updates only for the products you care about. For instance, if you do not have any Windows XP computers to manage, and only use one version of Office across all of your computers, you can hide those updates that do not apply to you. You can accomplish this from the Updates section of the Admin menu. You can select from the product categories, such as Windows, Works, Office, developer tools, and others. You can also select which updates to see based on the update classification, which includes security updates, tools, service packs, and other classifications.

From this section you can also set up what are called *Automatic Approval Rules* for your updates. Click the **New** button in the Automatic Approval Rules section to create a rule. For the rule, you select the product categories, update classifications, and the user and device deployments groups for your rule. Any updates that show up in Intune that apply to the rule you configure will automatically be approved for deployment to your computers.

For instance, you might want to make sure that any critical updates are not held up waiting for your approval, so you can create a rule that all Windows updates classified as critical will automatically be approved for your All Computers group. These updates will then be approved and deployed as soon as they are available.

Updates that do not fall into the automatic approval rules you set will need to be manually approved before they are deployed to your Windows devices. You can make those decisions by viewing the properties of the update, testing it on your reference computers, and approving the update for deployment when you decide it's ready for production. From the Updates menu, shown in Figure 13-19, select any update and then click the **Properties** link to view the details of the update. This will display details of the update, the operating system or software it applies, and includes links to the KB article for the update and whether the update has been superseded by any subsequent updates. The Properties page also includes links to approve or decline the update.

From the Updates section of Intune, you can use the Filters drop-down at the top of the list to see just the updates you care about. For instance, select **New Updates to Approve** to see the updates that are waiting for your approval. You can also view updates by classification using the menu selections on the left.

Use the following steps to approve an update:

Step 1.   Select the **Approve** link either from the list or the Properties page for the update.

Step 2.   Select the user groups and device groups where you want the update to be deployed. You can select any combination of user and device groups. Click the **Next** button.

Step 3.   In the Approval Setting page, select the approval type. The options are Required Install or Available Install.

Step 4.   Choose the deadline for the update. The options are None (the update will be installed on a normal Windows update scheduler), As Soon as Possible, One Week, Two Weeks, One Month, or Custom. The Custom option allows you to select a specific date and time by which the update must be installed.

Step 5.   Click **Finish** to complete the approval process.

Updates that have deadlines and require restarts will cause a forced restart at the time of the deadline, regardless of when the update was actually installed. This is the same behavior as the update deadline used in WSUS.

Third-Party Updates

You can include third-party updates and manage them in Microsoft Intune just like you do Windows updates. From the Updates menu, select the **Overview** section and click the **Add Updates** button. This launches the Microsoft Intune Software Publisher app, as shown in Figure 13-20. If the software is not installed on your computer, it will be downloaded and installed.

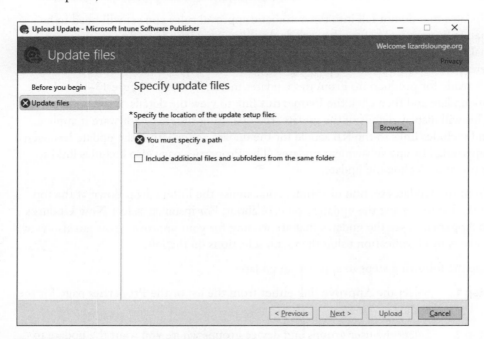

Figure 13-20   Using the Microsoft Intune Software Publisher

Use the following procedure to upload your update file:

Step 1.   Click the **Browse** button to locate the update, and then click the Upload button. You can upload an MSI, MSP, or EXE file. Click **Next**.

Step 2.   Enter the publisher name, the app name, the classification, and a description. The classification can be Critical, Security, Update Rollups, or Service Packs. Click **Next**.

Step 3.   On the Requirements page, select the architecture (32-bit or 64-bit), and the operating system. Only Windows operating systems are supported. Choose **Any** if the update applies to any Windows version. Click **Next**.

Step 4.   Choose from either default detection rules or add your own detection rule. You can add a rule based on whether a specific file exists, a Registry key, or an MSI product code. Click **Next**.

Step 5. On the Prerequisites page, you can specify any other software that your update is dependent on. It can be other software managed in Intune, or you can specify a rule. The rules offer the same options as the detection rules in Step 4. If your update has no dependencies, select **None**. Click **Next**.

Step 6. The next page gives you an option to provide command-line arguments for your update installer. Enter any arguments needed or select **No**. Click **Next**.

Step 7. The next page allows you to select return codes to determine whether the update was successful. Enter any return codes you want Intune to evaluate during the installation, or select **No** and then click **Next**.

Step 8. On the summary page, review your selections and then click **Upload** to send the update to Intune.

Your update will quickly appear in the Updates section of the Intune console. You can then perform approvals or use a rule to automatically deploy the update, just like the Microsoft updates.

Reports and In-console Monitoring

You have learned how to view properties of your devices, set up alerts and notifications, and check on the health of your enrolled devices.

You can also use the console to check alerts. Any triggered alerts will show up in the Alerts menu of the Intune console. Alerts are categorized by the types of alerts, such as Endpoint Protection, Notices, Policy, and Updates, among others. So if you are not receiving emails for alerts, you can still check the console for any alerts that have been triggered and take action.

Another tool for managing your devices is to use reports. You can use reports to get information about software, hardware, and licenses in your organization, and help you decide your resource needs and plan your budgets for future expenditures. Reports fall into several categories, as described in Table 13-3.

Table 13-3 Microsoft Intune Reports

Report Type	Description
Update Reports	Shows the software updates that have been deployed to computers and any that failed, are pending, or needed.
Detected Software Reports	Shows software installed on your computers.
Computer Inventory Reports	Information about all your managed computers.

Report Type	Description
Mobile Device Inventory Reports	Information about the mobile devices you are managing in Intune.
License Purchase Reports	Shows the software titles for all licensed software, based on their licensing agreements.
License Installation Reports	Compares installed software on computers with your license agreement coverage, based on the software agreements in the Microsoft Volume Licensing Service Center (VLSC). It also shows software products managed outside of the VLSC.
Terms and Conditions Reports	Shows information about users with apps installed from your lists of compliant and noncompliant apps.
Certificate Compliance Reports	Shows which certificates have been issued to users and devices.
Device History Reports	A historical log of retire, wipe, and delete actions in Intune.
Heath Attestation Reports	Shows the health of mobile devices.
Mac OS X Hardware Report	Shows hardware details for all enrolled Mac OS X devices.
Mac OS X Software Report	Shows software that is installed on all Mac OS X devices.

Create a report in Intune from the Reports menu of the console. Choose the report type you want, select the criteria for the report, and then click the **View Report** button. The report will be displayed in a new browser window. You can sort the report by any column by clicking on the column header.

Exam Preparation Tasks

Review All the Key Topics

Review the most important topics in the chapter, noted with the Key Topics icon in the outer margin of the page. Table 13-4 lists a reference of these key topics and the page numbers on which each is found.

Table 13-4   Key Topics for Chapter 13

Key Topic Element	Description	Page Number
Figure 13-1	Adding users for Intune using the Office 365 portal	620
Step List	Enabling enrollment for iOS and Mac devices	626

Key Topic Element	Description	Page Number
Figure 13-9	Enrolling an iOS device with Microsoft Intune	629
Step List	Enrolling a Windows computer with Microsoft Intune	629
Figure 13-11	Viewing device properties in the Intune portal	632
Step List	Configuring the Microsoft Intune connector site system role	635
Figure 13-13	Managing user groups in Azure AD	637
Figure 13-14	The Microsoft Intune Center	638
Figure 13-15	Microsoft Intune alert types	640
Step List	Creating Intune configuration policies	643
Table 13-2	Important Microsoft Intune compliance properties	645
Step List	Approving updates in Intune	647
Step List	Uploading third-party updates for management by Intune	648

Complete the Tables and Lists from Memory

Print a copy of Appendix B, "Memory Tables" (found on the book's website), or at least the section for this chapter, and complete the tables and lists from memory. Appendix C, "Memory Tables Answer Key," also on the website, includes completed tables and lists to check your work.

Definitions of Key Terms

Define the following key terms from this chapter, and check your answers in the glossary.

APNs, Azure, device enrollment, hybrid, MDM, Microsoft Intune, Office 365, single pane of glass, SCCM, WSUS

This chapter covers the following subjects:

- **Configuring Data Encryption Using Encrypting File System (EFS):** This section shows you how to secure data on your Windows 10 computer by using encryption to prevent others from viewing specific files or folders. You also learn how to back up your EFS keys and configure recovery agents in case your keys are lost.

- **Configuring Disk Quotas:** This section shows you how to specify quotas that limit the amount of disk space used by users storing files on your Windows 10 computer.

- **Configuring File Access Auditing:** Auditing lets you record actions that take place on your computer, including attempts to access files, folders, and printers. This section shows you how to use Group Policy to set up a policy that effectively tracks these types of activities.

- **Configuring Shared Resources:** This section shows you how to configure your computer to share resources such as folders and printers, and how to set up a standard set of permissions that control access to these resources from computers on the network. We also discuss how to configure and manage printer settings including Location Aware Printing technology, which enables you to automatically associate configured printers with the network where the printer is available.

This chapter covers the following objectives for the 70-697 and 70-698 exams:

Configure file and folder access: Encrypt files and folders by using EFS, configure disk quotas, configure file access auditing, configure authentication and authorization.

Configure shared resources:

- Configure shared folder permissions, configure HomeGroup settings, configure libraries, configure shared printers, configure OneDrive.

- Configure file and printer sharing and HomeGroup connections; configure folder shares, public folders, and OneDrive; configure file system permissions; configure OneDrive usage; troubleshoot data access and usage.

CHAPTER 14

Configuring File and Folder Access

From the earliest version of Windows NT right up to the present, Windows has had a system of access permissions in place that determine who has access to what and what they can do to it. You learned about how to use NTFS security permissions to specify who has access to files and folders and what they can do with them in Chapter 7, "Windows 10 Security." More recent versions of Windows have enabled users to protect data even further with encryption methods that can help to prevent those who might have circumvented other access controls from viewing or modifying confidential information. Windows can also track the usage of disk space by individuals using the computer and place a disk quota on the maximum amount of storage a particular user can access. Included also is a system of auditing access attempts to files and folders so that individuals in charge of security are able to track all types of access on the network and take appropriate measures to protect sensitive information. This chapter looks at these and other methods of sharing and protecting resources on computers and their networks.

One of the major reasons for connecting computers in a network is to share resources such as folders, files, and printers. Resources can exist on computers that are not connected to a network; and these resources may need to be secured, protected, and accessed by different users as well. Windows 10 comes with a host of tools designed to secure and manage resources wherever they may be found. Nowadays, resources can even exist remotely on the cloud; Windows 10 includes the OneDrive feature that enables you to share images, documents, and so on among computers, smartphones, and other devices in different physical locations. Microsoft expects you to be knowledgeable about all these features when taking the 70-697 and 70-698 exam.

In a modern workplace, workers require access to information created by others in the company and work they produce must be made available to their coworkers and superiors. Therefore, such resources must be shared so that others can access them. But lots of confidential information is also out there, and it must be protected from access by those who are not entitled to view it. At home, family members need to share things such as photos, videos, and music. But parents have sensitive information, such as family finances, that must be protected as well.

"Do I Know This Already?" Quiz

The "Do I Know This Already?" quiz allows you to assess whether you should read this entire chapter or simply jump to the "Exam Preparation Tasks" section for review. If you are in doubt, read the entire chapter. Table 14-1 outlines the major headings in this chapter and the corresponding "Do I Know This Already?" quiz questions. You can find the answers in Appendix A, "Answers to the 'Do I Know This Already?' Quizzes."

Table 14-1 "Do I Know This Already?" Foundation Topics Section-to-Question Mapping

Foundation Topics Section	Questions Covered in This Section
Configuring Data Encryption Using EFS	1–2
Configuring Disk Quotas	3
Configuring File Access Auditing	4
Configuring Shared Resources	5–10

CAUTION The goal of self-assessment is to gauge your mastery of the topics in this chapter. If you do not know the answer to a question or are only partially sure of the answer, you should mark that question as wrong for purposes of the self-assessment. Giving yourself credit for an answer you correctly guess skews your self-assessment results and might provide you with a false sense of security.

1. You want to encrypt the Confidential folder. This folder is located on the D:\ volume, which is formatted with the FAT32 file system. You access the folder's Properties dialog box and click the Advanced button. But the option to encrypt the folder is not available. What do you need to do to encrypt this folder? (Each correct answer presents a complete solution to the problem. Choose two.)

   a. Format the D:\volume with the NTFS file system.

   b. Use the Convert.exe utility to convert the D:\ volume with the NTFS file system.

   c. Move the Confidential folder to the C:\ volume, which is formatted with the NTFS file system.

   d. Decompress the Confidential folder.

2. You are the desktop support specialist for your company. A user named Peter has left the company, and you have deleted his user account. Later you realize that he had encrypted his Work folder on his Windows 10 computer, and you must regain access to this folder. What should you do?

    a. Log on to Peter's computer with your user account and decrypt the file.

    b. Log on to Peter's computer with the default administrator account and decrypt the file.

    c. Re-create Peter's user account, log on with this account, and decrypt the file.

    d. You cannot access this folder; it is permanently lost.

3. Your company has hired several college students for the summer as interns. They will be storing files on the D: drive of a Windows 10 computer. You have created user accounts for each student and added these accounts to a group named Interns. You want to ensure that these students do not store a large amount of data on the D: drive, so you decide to limit each user to 500 MB space on the D: drive. What should you do? (Each correct answer presents part of the solution. Choose two.)

    a. Ensure that the D:\ drive is formatted with the NTFS file system.

    b. Ensure that the D:\ drive is formatted with the FAT32 file system.

    c. In the Add New Quota Entry dialog box, select the **Do Not Limit Disk Usage** option and specify the 500 MB limit and the Interns group.

    d. In the Add New Quota Entry dialog box, select the **Limit Disk Space To** option and specify the 500 MB limit and the Interns group.

    e. In the Add New Quota Entry dialog box, create a separate disk quota for each user in the Interns group that specifies the Do Not Limit Disk Usage option and the 500 MB limit.

    f. In the Add New Quota Entry dialog box, create a separate disk quota for each user in the Interns group that specifies the Limit Disk Space To option and the 500 MB limit.

4. You are responsible for maintaining data security on a Windows 10 Pro computer used by your boss. He has stored a large number of documents containing sensitive corporate information that only a limited number of individuals are permitted to access. He would like to know when others attempt to access this information. To this extent, you have enabled object access auditing on his computer.

A couple of weeks later, your boss informs you that he has noticed a couple of files have been altered in an inappropriate fashion. He has checked the Security log on his computer, but no information is available to suggest who is accessing these files, so he asks you to rectify this problem. What should you do?

    a. You also need to enable auditing of logon events in the Local Security Policy snap-in on your boss's computer.

    b. You also need to access File Explorer on your boss's computer. From this location, ensure that the appropriate auditing entries have been enabled for the folder in which the sensitive documents are located.

    c. You need to ask your boss to check events recorded in the System log of his computer.

    d. You should move the folder containing the sensitive documents to a server located in a secured room, and on which auditing has been enabled.

5. You want users at other computers on your network to be able to access folders located in the libraries of your Windows 10 computer without the need to perform additional sharing tasks, so you open the Advanced Sharing Settings dialog box. Which option should you enable?

    a. File and Printer Sharing

    b. Public Folder Sharing

    c. Password Protected Sharing

    d. Media Streaming

6. Which of the following are true about hidden administrative shares? (Choose three.)

    a. These shares are suffixed with the $ symbol and are visible in any Explorer window.

    b. These shares are suffixed with the $ symbol and are visible only in the Shares node of the Computer Management snap-in.

    c. These shares are suffixed with the $ symbol and can be accessed from the Network and Sharing Center.

    d. You can access these shares by entering the UNC path to the share in the Run command.

    e. These shares are created by default when Windows 8.1 is first installed, and they cannot be removed.

7. Which of the following are valid permissions you can set for shared folders? (Choose three.)

    a. Full Control

    b. Modify

    c. Change

    d. Read and Execute

    e. Read

8. Which of the following is not true about file libraries in Windows 10?

    a. Libraries are virtual folders that are actually pointers to the Documents, Pictures, Music, and Videos folder locations on the computer.

    b. Each library consists of a user-specific folder and a public folder.

    c. You can add additional folders to any library at any time in Windows 8.1.

    d. You are limited to the four default libraries; it is not possible to designate additional libraries in Windows 10.

9. You have shared your printer so that others can access it on the network. You want Kristin, who works at another computer on the network to be able to pause, resume, restart, and cancel all documents, but you do not want her to be able to modify printer properties or permissions. What printer permission should you grant her user account?

    a. Print

    b. Manage This Printer

    c. Manage Documents

    d. Full Control

10. Your laptop now automatically uses the Richardson office printer when you are visiting the Richardson office and the color laser printer near your office when you are at headquarters. Recently, the color printer was moved to another floor and a newer printer installed in its place. You have installed the new printer drivers and tested it, but whenever you return to headquarters, it prints to the printer that is now on another floor. What is the best way to fix this issue?

    a. Delete the original color printer.

    b. Turn off location-aware printing.

    c. Use the Printer Troubleshooting tool

    d. Select the newer printer specifically for a print job. It will then become your default printer and Windows will use it each time you print after that.

Foundation Topics

Configuring Data Encryption Using Encrypting File System (EFS)

You often hear news reports that mention thefts of laptop computers containing valuable data. In one such case, a computer stolen from a doctor's car in Toronto contained the records of thousands of patients, exposing them to misuse and potential identity theft. The computer was protected with a password but the data was not encrypted. Windows 10 includes the following two systems of data encryption, designed to protect data not only on your laptop when you are in a place such as an airport or hotel where a thief can grab it when you're momentarily distracted, but also at any other place where an unauthorized individual might attempt to either connect to it across the network or physically access it:

- First introduced with Windows Vista, BitLocker Drive Encryption encrypts a computer's entire system partition. You learned about BitLocker and Bit-Locker To Go in Chapter 8, "Windows 10 Data Security."

- First introduced with Windows 2000 and refined with each successive iteration of Windows, the Encrypting File System (EFS) can be used to encrypt files and folders on any partition that is formatted with the NTFS file system. We discuss EFS in this section.

EFS enables users to encrypt files and folders on any partition that is formatted with the NTFS file system. The encryption attribute on a file or folder can be toggled the same as any other file attribute. When you set the encryption attribute on a folder, all its contents—whether subfolders or files—are also encrypted.

The encryption attribute, when assigned to a folder, affects files the same way that the compression attribute does when a file is moved or copied. Files that are copied into the encrypted folder become encrypted. Files that are moved into the encrypted folder retain their former encryption attribute, whether or not they were encrypted. When you move or copy a file to a file system that does not support EFS, such as FAT16 or FAT32, the file is automatically decrypted.

> **TIP** Remember that the file system must be set to NTFS if you want to use EFS, and no file can be both encrypted and compressed at the same time. On the exam, you may be presented with a scenario where a user is unable to use EFS or file compression on a FAT32 volume. The correct answer to such a problem is to convert the file system to NTFS, as described later in the section "Preparing a Disk for EFS."

Encrypting File System Basics

EFS uses a form of public key cryptography, which utilizes a public and private key pair. The public key or digital certificate is freely available to anyone, whereas the private key is retained and guarded by the user to which the key pair is issued. The public key is used to encrypt data, and the private key decrypts the data that was encrypted with the corresponding public key. The key pair is created at the first time a user encrypts a file or folder using EFS. When another user attempts to open the file, that user is unable to do so. Therefore, EFS is suitable for data that a user wants to maintain as private, but not for files that are shared.

Windows 10 has the capability to encrypt files directly on any NTFS volume. This ensures that no other user can use the encrypted data. Encryption and decryption of a file or folder are performed in the object's Properties dialog box. Administrators should be aware of the rules to put into practice to manage EFS on a network:

- Only use NTFS as the file system for all workstation and server volumes.

- Keep a copy of each user's certificate and private key on a USB flash drive or other removable media.

- Remove the user's private key from the computer except when the user is actually using it.

- When users routinely save documents only to their Documents folder, make certain their documents are encrypted by having each user encrypt his or her own Documents folder.

- Use two recovery agent user accounts that are reserved solely for that purpose for each Active Directory Domain Services (AD DS) organizational unit (OU) if computers participate in a domain. Assign the recovery agent certificates to these accounts.

- Archive all recovery agent user account information, recovery certificates, and private keys, even if obsolete.

- When planning a network installation, keep in mind that EFS does take up additional processing overhead; plan to incorporate additional CPU processing power in your plans.

A unique encryption key is assigned to each encrypted file. You can share an encrypted file with other users in Windows 10, but you are restricted from sharing an entire encrypted folder with multiple users or sharing a single file with a security group. This is related to the way that EFS uses certificates, which are applicable individually to users, and how EFS uses encryption keys, which are applicable individually to files. Windows 10 continues the capability introduced with Windows Vista to store keys on smart cards. If you are using smart cards for user logon, EFS automatically locates the encryption key without issuing further prompts. EFS also provides wizards that assist users in creating and selecting smart card keys.

You can use different types of certificates with EFS: third-party–issued certificates, certificates issued by certificate authorities (CAs)—including those on your own network—and self-signed certificates. If you have developed a security system on your network that utilizes mutual authentication based on certificates issued by your own CA, you can extend the system to EFS to further secure encrypted files. For more information on using certificates with EFS, refer to the Windows 10 Help and Support Center.

NOTE   For more information on the technology behind EFS, refer to "How EFS Works" at https://technet.microsoft.com/en-us/library/cc962103.aspx.

Preparing a Disk for EFS

Unlike versions of Windows prior to Vista, the system and boot partition in Windows 10 must be formatted with NTFS before you can install Windows 10, as you learned in Chapter 9, "Managing User Data." However, a data partition can be formatted with the FAT or FAT32 file systems. But you must ensure that such a partition is formatted with NTFS before you can encrypt data using EFS. If it is not, you can convert the hard disk format from FAT to NTFS or format the partition as NTFS. There are two ways to go about this:

- Use the command-line Convert.exe utility to change an existing FAT16 or FAT32 partition that contains data to NTFS without losing the data.

- Use the graphical Disk Management utility to format a new partition, or an empty FAT partition, to NTFS. If the volume contains data, you will lose it. (You can also use the command-line Format.exe utility to format a partition as NTFS.)

The Convert.exe utility is simple to use and typically problem-free, although you should make certain to back up the data on the partition before you convert it as a precaution. Perform the following steps to use this utility:

Step 1.   Log on to the computer as an administrator. Know which drive letter represents the partition that you plan to convert, because only the partition that contains the encrypted files needs to be formatted with NTFS. For example, if users store all their data on drive D: and want to encrypt those files, you convert drive D: to NTFS.

Step 2. From the taskbar Search text box, ensure that Apps is selected, type **cmd** into the Search box, and press Enter.

Step 3. The command prompt window opens. At the prompt, type **convert d: /fs:ntfs**.

Step 4. The conversion process begins. If you are running the Convert.exe utility from the same drive letter prompt as the partition you are converting, or a file is open on the partition, you are prompted with a message that states Convert Cannot Gain Exclusive Access to D:, So It Cannot Convert It Now. Would You Like to Schedule It to Be Converted the Next Time the System Restarts (Y/N)? Press **Y** at the message.

Step 5. Restart the computer. The disk converts its format to NTFS. This process takes considerable time to complete, but at completion, you can access the Properties dialog box for the disk you've converted and note that it is formatted with the NTFS file system.

Encrypting Files

You can use either the **cipher** command-line utility or the advanced attributes of the file or folder to encrypt a file. To use the cipher utility for encrypting a file named Myfile.txt located in the C:\mydir folder, the full command to use is as follows:

```
cipher /e c:\mydir\myfile.txt
```

To change the Advanced encryption attribute of a file, open File Explorer and navigate to the file. Right-click the file and select **Properties**. On the General tab, click the **Advanced** button in the Attributes section. The Advanced Attributes dialog box opens, as shown in Figure 14-1.

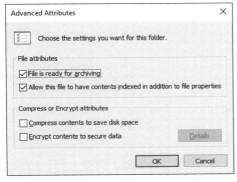

Figure 14-1 Advanced Attributes Dialog Box Enabling You to Either Compress or Encrypt a File

Select the **Encrypt Contents to Secure Data** check box and click **OK**. Then click **OK** again to close the file's Properties dialog box. You are given a warning dialog that lets you choose between encrypting just the file that you had selected or both the file and its parent folder. Select one of the options and click **OK**.

> **NOTE**   Note that the compression and encryption attributes are mutually exclusive. In the Advanced Attributes dialog box, if you select the Compress Contents to Save Disk Space check box, the check mark disappears from the Encrypt Contents to Secure Data check box. These two attributes are mutually exclusive—you can select only one.

After a file has been encrypted, you can view its encryption attribute details by again right-clicking the file, selecting **Properties**, and then clicking the **Advanced** button on the General tab. In the Advanced Attributes dialog box, click the **Details** button. The User Access To (file) dialog box opens, as shown in Figure 14-2.

Figure 14-2   Adding Other Users to Encrypted File Access List

You can see who is able to open the encrypted file, and you can add other user accounts to share the encrypted file and view the designated data recovery agent, if any. Click the **Add** button to share the encrypted file. A dialog box listing all the EFS-capable certificates for users opens. If a user has never been issued a certificate, the user's account does not appear in this dialog box.

> **TIP** If the desired user has not been issued an EFS certificate, she needs only to log on to the computer and encrypt a different file. This automatically creates a certificate that will be visible the next time you attempt to share an encrypted file.

After a file is encrypted, an unauthorized user attempting to open the file is given an error message that says the user does not have access privileges. If an unauthorized user tries to move or copy an encrypted file, the user receives an Access Is Denied error message.

Backing Up EFS Keys

What if a user were to encrypt a file using EFS and then the user's account were to become corrupted or be deleted for any reason? Or what if the user's private key were to become corrupted or lost? You would be unable to decrypt the file, and it would be permanently inaccessible. Windows 10 offers the capability for backing up EFS certificates and keys to reduce the likelihood of this occurring. Use the following procedure to back up EFS keys:

Step 1. From the User Access dialog box previously shown in Figure 14-2, click **Back Up Keys**.

Step 2. The Certificate Export Wizard starts. Click **Next**.

Step 3. On the Export File Format page, the Personal Information Exchange– PKCS #12 (.PFX) format is selected by default. If desired, select the **Include All Certificates in the Certification Path if Possible** and **Export All Extended Properties** options, and then click **Next**.

Step 4. On the Password page, type and confirm a password. This is mandatory, and you should choose a hard-to-guess password that follows the usual complexity guidelines. Then click **Next**.

Step 5. On the File to Export page, type the name of the file to be exported, and then click **Next**. By default, this file is created in the user's Documents library with the .pfx extension.

Step 6. Review the information on the completion page, and then click **Finish**.

Step 7. You are informed the export was successful. Click **OK**.

Step 8. You should move this file to a location separate from the computer, such as a USB key that you store securely (such as in a locked cabinet).

Decrypting Files

The process of decryption is the opposite of encryption. You can either use the **cipher** command or change the Advanced attribute for encryption on the file.

To use the **cipher** command to decrypt the file, access the taskbar Search text box, type **cmd** into the Search box, and then press Enter. At the command prompt, type **cipher /d c:\myfolder\myfile.txt** and press Enter. The file will be decrypted.

To use the Advanced Attributes method, open File Explorer and navigate to the file. Right-click the file and select **Properties**. On the General tab, click the **Advanced** button. In the ensuing Advanced Attributes dialog box, clear the **Encrypt Contents to Secure Data** check box. Click **OK**, and then click **OK** again.

If you are not the person who originally encrypted the file, or if you are not the designated recovery agent, you will receive an error for applying attributes that says the access is denied.

EFS Recovery Agents

What if the user's keys, even though backed up, were to become lost or corrupted? Without some type of recovery capability, such a file would become permanently inaccessible. EFS in Windows 10 uses the concept of *recovery agents* as a means to recover encrypted data in such a situation.

Designated recovery agents are user accounts authorized to decrypt encrypted files. When a user account is designated as a recovery agent, you essentially are granting it a copy of the key pair. If you lose the key pair, or if they become damaged, and if there is no designated recovery agent, there is no way to decrypt the file and the data is permanently lost. By designating a recovery agent before a user first uses EFS, you can ensure that encrypted files and folders remain accessible by someone responsible for their maintenance.

Windows 10 can include two levels of EFS recovery agents:

- **Local computer:** By default, the local administrator account created when you first install Windows 10 is the recovery agent. Note that this account is not the account whose name you specify during Windows 10 installation; it is a built-in account that can be accessed from the Local Users and Groups node of the Computer Management snap-in. The account is disabled by default, but you can enable it from its Properties dialog box by clearing the **Account Is Disabled** check box.

- **Domain:** When you create an AD DS domain, the first domain administrator account is the designated recovery agent. You can use Group Policy to designate additional recovery agents, and you can delegate the responsibility of EFS recovery to other users if desired.

You can use Group Policy to designate additional recovery agents. A user must have an appropriate certificate before he can be designated as a recovery agent. Use the following procedure:

Step 1. Open Group Policy and navigate to the Computer Configuration\Windows Settings\Security Settings\Public Key Policies\Encrypting File System node.

Step 2. Right-click this node and choose **Add Data Recovery Agent**.

Step 3. The Add Recovery Agent Wizard starts with a Welcome page. Click **Next**.

Step 4. On the Select Recovery Agents page shown in Figure 14-3, select a user from the Recovery Agents list and then click **Next**. (If necessary, click **Browse Folders** to locate a certificate for the desired user.)

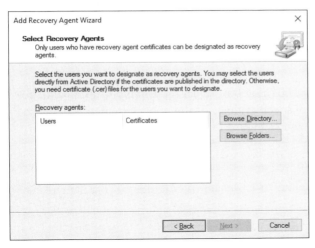

Figure 14-3 Add Recovery Agent Wizard Enabling You to Designate Additional Users as EFS Recovery Agents

Step 5. You are informed that you have successfully completed the wizard. Review the information about the designated recovery agents, and then click **Finish**.

NOTE For more information on backing up keys and designating recovery agents in EFS, refer to "How to Back Up the Recovery Agent Encrypting File System (EFS) Private Key in Windows" at http://support.microsoft.com/kb/241201 and "Create and Verify an Encrypting File System (EFS) Data Recovery Agent (DRA) Certificate" at https://technet.microsoft.com/en-us/itpro/windows/keep-secure/create-and-verify-an-efs-dra-certificate.

Configuring Disk Quotas

First introduced in Windows 2000 and improved with each successive version of Windows is the concept of disk quotas. This feature allows an administrator to set a limit on the amount of disk space used by an individual user. You can send a warning to users when they reach a certain level of disk usage, and you can write an event to the event log if a user attempts to exceed his quota. When you have enabled disk quotas, Windows 10 also collects disk usage statistics for all users enabled on the volume, thus allowing the administrator to keep track of disk usage. Thereby, the administrator can manage disks more efficiently and prevent users from "hogging" disk space.

File Explorer enables you to enable quotas on a per-volume, per-user basis. Use the following procedure to enable disk quotas:

Step 1.   In File Explorer, right-click the volume (partition) on which you want to enable disk quotas, and then select **Properties**.

Step 2.   In the Properties dialog box, click the **Quota** tab, and then click the **Show Quota Settings** command button to display disk quota information.

Step 3.   On the Quota Properties dialog box, select the **Enable Quota Management** check box. Then specify values for the quota parameters described in Table 14-2 and shown in Figure 14-4.

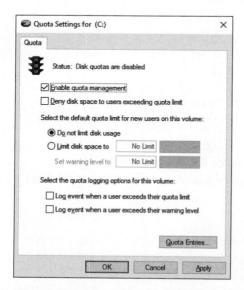

Figure 14-4   Enabling Disk Quotas for Individual Users on Given Disks

Step 4.   To configure quota entries for specific users, click the **Quota Entries** command button. From the Quota Entries dialog box, you can view the status of all quotas configured on the volume, including the username, amount of space used, quota limit, warning level, and percentage used.

Step 5.   To add a quota entry, click **Quota > New Quota Entry**, type the username to whom the quota will apply in the Select Users dialog box, and then click **OK**. Then in the Add New Quota Entry dialog box (see Figure 14-5), select **Limit Disk Space To**, specify the desired limit and warning levels, and then click **OK**. Repeat as needed to add quotas for other users.

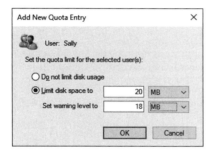

Figure 14-5   Add New Quota Entry Dialog Box Enabling You to Add a Disk Quota for a Single User

Step 6.   After making any changes and closing the Quota Entries dialog box, click **OK** or **Apply**. A Disk Quota message box (see Figure 14-6) warns you that the disk will be rescanned and that this may take several minutes.

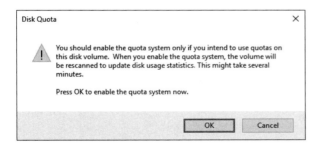

Figure 14-6   Warning That the Disk Volume Will Be Rescanned to Update Disk Usage Statistics

Step 7.   Click **OK** to close this message box and start the scan.

Table 14-2 describes the options that are available on the Quota tab of the disk's Properties dialog box mentioned in Step 3.

Table 14-2   Disk Quota Configuration Options

Option	Description
Enable Quota Management	Enables quota management and enables the other options so that you can configure them.
Deny Disk Space to Users Exceeding Quota Limit	When users exceed their quota, they receive an Out of Disk Space message and they cannot write further data.
Do Not Limit Disk Usage	Select this option when you do not want to limit the amount of disk space used.
Limit Disk Space To	Configures the disk space limit per user.
Set Warning Level To	Configures the amount of disk space that a user can write before receiving a warning.
Log Event When a User Exceeds Their Quota Limit	Writes an event to the Windows system log on the computer running disk quotas whenever a user exceeds her quota limit.
Log Event When A User Exceeds Their Warning Level	Writes an event to the Windows system log on the computer running disk quotas anytime a user exceeds his quota warning level, not his actual quota.

When the disk quota system is active, a user checking the properties of the volume where it is enabled sees only the amount of space permitted on the quota; the available space is the permitted space minus the space already used. If a user tries to copy a file that is larger than the allowed space, he receives a message that the file cannot be copied. In addition, an event is written to the Event log if you have selected the appropriate check box described in Table 14-2. You can view usage statistics by clicking the **Quota Entries** button.

> **NOTE**   You can enable quotas only on volumes formatted with the NTFS file system. Only administrators can enable quotas, but they can permit users to view quota settings.

Some Guidelines for Using Quotas

The following are a few guidelines for using disk quotas:

- When installing applications, use the default Administrator account rather than your own user account. That way, the space used by the applications will not be charged against your quota if you have one.

- If you want to use disk quotas only to monitor disk space usage, specify a soft quota by clearing the **Deny Disk Space to Users Exceeding Quota Limit** check box in File Explorer. That way, users are not prevented from saving important data.

- Set appropriate quotas on all volumes that a user can access. Provide warnings to the users, and log events when they exceed their quota limit and/or warning level.

- Be aware that use of hard quotas might cause applications to fail.

- Monitor space used and increase the limits for those users who need larger amounts of space.

- Set quotas on all shared volumes, including public folders and network servers, to ensure appropriate use of space by users.

- If a user no longer stores files on a certain volume, delete her disk quota entries. You can do this only after her files have been moved or deleted, or after someone has taken ownership of them.

NOTE You should be aware that NTFS file compression actually has no particular effect on the amount of quota space available to such a user. Disk quotas are calculated based on the amount of space occupied by uncompressed folders and files, regardless of whether files are compressed or not compressed.

Configuring Object Access Auditing

Users on a network are naturally curious about the myriad of volumes, folders, and files that they find. They like to "poke around" to see what's there. And some can have malicious thoughts, so sensitive information might be accessed, modified, or even deleted. Corporate security policies generally stipulate that records must be kept of who attempts to access or modify such sensitive information. For this purpose, Microsoft has included object access auditing in its operating systems ever since the early days of Windows NT.

Object access is just one kind of a large list of events that Windows enables you to audit. Windows enables you to audit user access to files, folders, and printers by configuring the Audit policy for the local computer. If you need to audit computers that are members of an AD DS domain, you can configure the Group Policy in the domain or OU that contains these computers. Otherwise, you can configure the Local Group Policy setting for object access auditing. We discussed auditing in more detail in Chapter 12, "Managing Mobile Devices."

To configure object access auditing, you must configure two pieces of information:

- Enable success or failure auditing for object access.

- Specify the folders, files, or printers for which access is to be audited.

Enabling Object Access Auditing

Use the following procedure to enable object access auditing on a Windows 10 computer:

Step 1. From the Search box or Cortana, type **gpedit.msc** into the text box and select **Edit Group Policy** from the results. This opens the Local Group Policy Editor MMC snap-in.

Step 2. Navigate to the Computer Configuration\Windows Settings\Security Settings\Local Policies\Audit Policy node. You receive the series of policy options shown in Figure 14-7.

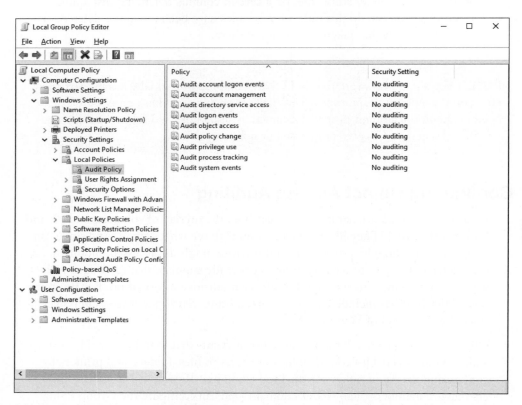

Figure 14-7 Audit Policy Subnode in the Local Group Policy Editor Enabling You to Audit Several Types of Actions on Your Windows 10 Computer

Step 3. Double-click **Audit Object Access**. You receive the Audit Object Access Properties dialog box shown in Figure 14-8.

Figure 14-8   Enabling Auditing to Trigger an Event Log Entry When an Action Has Completed Successfully, or Has Failed, or Both

Step 4.   To audit successful and/or failed attempts at accessing files, folders, or printers, select **Success** and/or **Failure** as required. Select the **Explain** tab of the Properties dialog box to obtain more information on what the setting does.

Step 5.   Click **OK** or **Apply**.

NOTE   Additional audit policies are available in the Advanced Audit Policy subnode of Group Policy, available from the Computer Configuration\Windows Settings\ Security Settings\Local Policies\Audit Policy node. For more information on advanced audit policy settings as a whole, refer to "Advanced Security Audit Policy Settings" at https://technet.microsoft.com/en-us/itpro/windows/keep-secure/ advanced-security-audit-policy-settings.

Specifying Objects to Be Audited

To track object access or directory service access, you must configure the system access control list (SACL) for each required object. Use the following procedure:

Step 1.   In File Explorer, right-click the required file, folder, or printer and choose **Properties**.

Step 2.   Select the **Security** tab of the object's Properties dialog box.

Step 3.   Click **Advanced** to open the Advanced Security Settings dialog box, and then select the **Auditing** tab.

Step 4.   You are warned that you must be an administrator or have the appropriate privileges to view the auditing properties of the object. Click **Continue** to proceed, and then click **Yes** in the UAC prompt if you receive one.

Step 5.   Click **Add** to display the Auditing Entry dialog box. To add users or groups to this dialog box, click **Select a Principal**.

Step 6.   Type the required user or group into the Select User or Group dialog box, and then click **OK**.

Step 7.   On the Auditing Entry dialog box that appears (see Figure 14-9), select the types of actions you want to track, and then click **OK**.

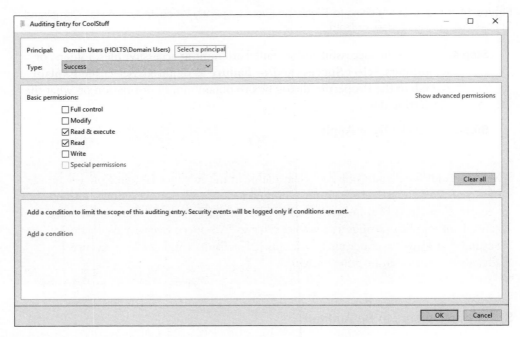

Figure 14-9   Configuring the SACL for a User or Group

Step 8.   The completed auditing entries appear in the Advanced Security Settings dialog box, as shown in Figure 14-10. Click **OK** twice to close these dialog boxes.

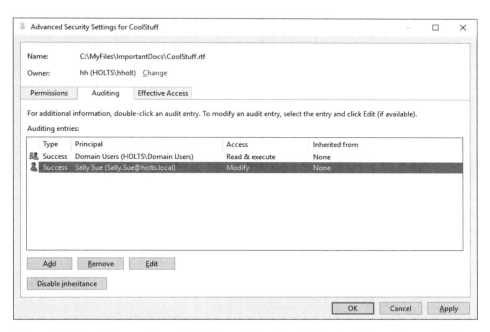

Figure 14-10   Advanced Security Settings Dialog Box Displaying Information on the Types of Object Auditing Actions That Have Been Specified

After you have configured object access auditing, attempts to access audited objects appear in the Security Log, which you can view from Event Viewer in the Administrative Tools folder. For more information on any audited event, right-click the event and choose **Event Properties**. For more information on Event Viewer and viewing the logs it contains, refer to Chapter 19, "Monitoring and Managing Windows."

TIP   Ensure that the security log has adequate space to audit the events that you configure for auditing, because the log can fill rapidly. The recommended size is at least 128 MB. You should also periodically save the existing log to a file and clear all past events. If the log becomes full, the default behavior is that the oldest events will be overwritten (and therefore lost). You can also configure the log to archive when full and not to overwrite events, but new events will not be recorded. Loss of recorded events could be serious in the case of high-security installations.

> **NOTE**   You can also use the Auditpol.exe command-line tool to perform audit policy configuration actions. For information on the subcommands available for this command, open a command prompt and type **auditpol /?**. For additional information on this command, refer to "Auditpol" at http://technet.microsoft.com/en-us/library/cc731451.aspx. The information refers to Windows 8.1 and Windows Server 2012, but no changes to the auditpol command were made for Windows 10.

Configuring Shared Resources

Sharing is a basic concept of networking in any computer environment. Simply put, sharing means making resources available on a network. Typically, this means a folder on one computer is made accessible to other computers that are connected to the first computer by a network. The purpose of sharing folders is to give users access to network applications, data, and user home folders in one central location. You can use network application folders for configuring and upgrading software. This serves to centralize administration because applications are not maintained on client computers. Data folders allow users to store and access common files, and user home folders provide a place for users to store their own personal information. You can also share other resources, such as printers, so that users can print to a printer not directly attached to their computer.

You can share folders according to either or both of two file sharing models:

- **Public Folder Sharing:** The simplest means of sharing folders, this model involves the use of a shared folder located within each of the Windows libraries. However, you cannot limit access to items in these public folders; you can only enable or disable public folder sharing for all libraries from the Advanced Sharing Settings dialog box in the Network and Sharing Center, previously introduced in Chapter 6, "Windows 10 Networking."

- **Standard Folder Sharing:** Enables you to utilize a standard set of permissions that determine user access to files and folders across the network, in a similar fashion to that used in previous Windows versions. More secure than public folder sharing, you can enable or disable standard folder sharing on a per-computer basis.

Using the Network and Sharing Center to Configure File Sharing

As introduced in Chapter 6, the Network and Sharing Center enables you to perform actions related to sharing of resources on your computer with others on the network. Click **Change Advanced Sharing Settings** to obtain the Advanced

Sharing Settings dialog box shown in Figure 14-11. Among other networking options, you can specify the file sharing options described in the list that follows.

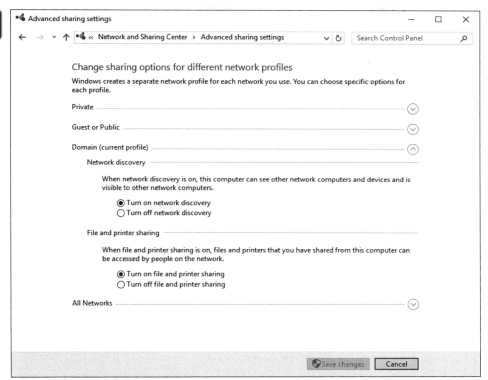

Figure 14-11   Advanced Sharing Settings Dialog Box Enabling You to Configure Several Global File and Folder Sharing Settings

- **File and Printer Sharing:** Enables the Standard Folder Sharing model, thereby allowing others on the network to access shared files on your computer and print from printers attached to your computer.

- **Public Folder Sharing:** Enables the Public Folder Sharing model, thereby allowing others on the network to access files in your Public folders of each Windows library (Documents, Pictures, Videos, and Music).

- **Media Streaming:** Enables others on the network to access shared music, pictures, and videos on the computer and enables your computer to access these types of shared information on the network.

- **File Sharing Connections:** Enables you to select the level of encryption used to protect file sharing connections. You should keep the default of 128-bit encryption selected unless you need to share files with devices that understand a lower level of encryption only.

Sharing Files, Folders, and Printers

Shared folders are folders on the local hard drive that other users on a network can connect to. For the exam, it is critical that you understand how to manage and troubleshoot connections to shared resources, how to create new shared resources, and how to set permissions on shared resources. The process that Windows 10 uses to share folders is that an administrator selects a folder, regardless of its location in the local folder hierarchy, and shares it through the Sharing tab of the folder's Properties dialog box.

Administrators may find that the Computer Management snap-in is helpful in file and folder security management. To open this snap-in in Windows 10, right-click **Start** and choose **Computer Management** from the menu that appears. You can also open Computer Management from within Administrative Tools, which is found in the System and Security category of Control Panel. If you have enabled the Administrative Tools feature on the Start menu, click the tile for **Computer Management** from this location. To manage file and folder security, expand the **Shared Folders** node in the left pane. Select the **Shares** subnode to see the shared folders, as shown in Figure 14-12. The hidden administrative shares are followed by a dollar sign ($) and cannot be modified. From the remaining shared folders, select one to double-click and view the security settings on the folder.

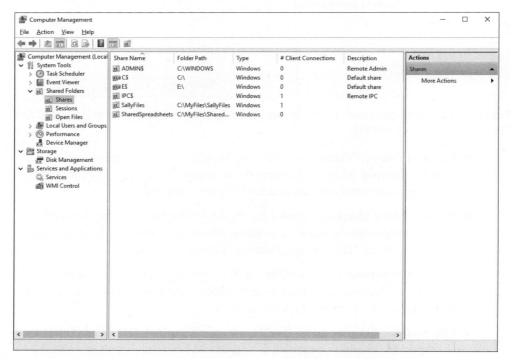

Figure 14-12 Viewing Shares on Your Computer from the Shared Folders Node of the Computer Management Snap-In

Aside from the default administrative shares, there are no folders that are automatically shared with the network. To share files with other users across the network, you must manually do so for each folder containing the files that you want to share. To share a folder with other network users, you can open any File Explorer window and then use the following procedure:

Step 1. In a File Explorer window, navigate to the folder, right-click it, select **Share With**, and then click **Specific People**. The File Sharing dialog box opens, as shown in Figure 14-13.

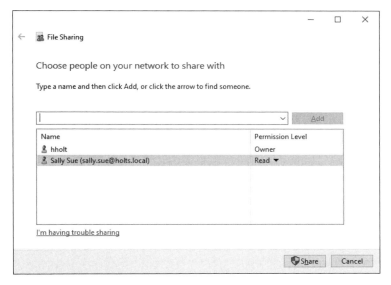

Figure 14-13 File Sharing Dialog Box Enabling You to Choose Those You Want to Share a File With

Step 2. Type the name of a user with whom you want to share the folder, and then click **Add**. The name appears in the Name list with a default permission level of Read (for example, Sally Sue in Figure 14-13).

Step 3. To share with another user, repeat Step 2 as many times as required. When finished, click **Share**. If you receive a User Account Control (UAC) prompt, click **Yes**.

Step 4. When the file is shared, you receive a message informing you that your folder is shared. This message enables you to email the link to the users with whom you shared the folder or copy it to other programs or documents. Click **Done**.

To add people to the sharing list, repeat this procedure and select **Change Sharing Permissions** from the File Sharing dialog box. Then type the name of the required user and click **Add**. To remove a shared folder, right-click the folder and select **Share With > Stop Sharing**.

Configuring Shared Folder Permissions

Windows 10 shares folders to others as Read, which means that the users you specify can view but not modify available files. The Advanced Sharing feature in Windows 10 enables you to modify these properties when necessary.

When granting full access to your local files to other users across a network, your computer becomes vulnerable to both unintentional and intentional attacks. Not only can the data be viewed for malicious purposes, such as corporate spying, it can be altered or destroyed on purpose or accidentally. For this reason alone, you should always grant the most restrictive permissions necessary for a network user to conduct work on those files. Granting just enough permission without being too lenient requires careful consideration. If you are too stringent, users can't get their jobs done. If you are too lenient, the data is at risk.

Use the following procedure to modify shared folder properties:

Step 1.   In a File Explorer window, right-click the shared folder and choose **Properties**.

Step 2.   Click the **Sharing** tab (see Figure 14-14).

Figure 14-14   Sharing Tab of a Folder's Properties Dialog Box Enabling You to Modify Shared Folder Properties

Step 3.   Click **Advanced Sharing**. If you receive a UAC prompt, click **Yes**. The Advanced Sharing dialog box shown in Figure 14-15 appears. This dialog box provides you with the shared folder options introduced in Table 14-3.

Figure 14-15   Advanced Sharing Dialog Box Enabling You to Configure Several Properties of Shared Folders

Table 14-3   Shared Folder Options in Windows 10

Option	Description
Share This Folder	Click to start sharing the folder.
Share Name	This is the folder name that remote users will employ to connect to the share. It will appear in a user's File Explorer window, or the user can access it by typing **\\computername\sharename** at the Run command. (Press the Windows key +R to open the Run command, or select it from the Start right-click menu.)
Comments	This information is optional and identifies the purpose or contents of the shared folder. The comment appears in the Map Network Drive dialog box when remote users are browsing shared folders on a server.
User Limit	This sets the number of remote users who can connect to a shared resource simultaneously, reducing network traffic. For Windows 10, the limit is 20 (it was 10 on Windows Vista and older client versions of Windows).
Permissions	Permissions can be assigned to individual users, groups, or both. When a folder is shared, you can grant each user and each group one of the three types of permissions for the share and all of its subdirectories and files, or choose to specifically deny them those permissions.
Caching	Enables offline access to a shared folder.

Step 4.   To add an additional share name, click **Add** under the Share Name section. (If this command button is dimmed, ensure that the Share This Folder option is selected and click **Apply**.) An additional share name enables users to access the shared folder under this name.

Step 5.   To change the maximum number of simultaneous users, type the required number or use the arrows to select a number. This number cannot be higher than 20 on a Windows 10 computer.

Step 6.   To change shared folder permissions, click **Permissions**. This displays the Permissions For (folder name) dialog box shown in Figure 14-16. By default, the creator of the share receives Full Control permission, and other users receive the Read permission. Click **Add** to add an additional user or group, and then modify this user's permissions as desired. Click **OK** when finished. The available shared folder permissions are as follows:

- **Read:** Users are allowed to view but not modify files.

- **Change:** Users are allowed to view and modify files, but not change the attributes of the shared folder itself.

- **Full Control:** Users are allowed to perform any task on the folder or its constituent files, including modifying their individual attributes and permissions used by others accessing them.

Figure 14-16   Permissions For (Folder Name) Dialog Box Enabling You to Configure Permissions That Apply to Users Accessing the Folder Across the Network

TIP   If you select permissions from the Deny column, you are explicitly denying access to that user or group. Such an explicit denial overrides any other permissions allowed to this group. Remember this fact if users experience problems accessing any shared resources across the network.

Step 7.   To modify settings that affect how users view and access shared folder contents, click **Caching** (as shown earlier in Figure 14-15) and configure the settings in the Offline Settings dialog box as required.

Step 8.   To set granular security permissions on the folder, click the **Security** tab and modify the settings in the dialog box shown in Figure 14-17 as required. These permissions apply to everyone accessing the folder either locally or across the network; more restrictive permissions configured here override those configured from the Sharing tab. We discuss these settings in detail later in this chapter.

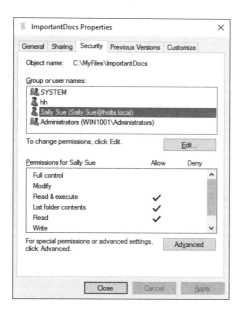

Figure 14-17   Security Tab of a Folder's Properties Dialog Box Enabling You to Configure Granular Permissions for Users and Groups Accessing the Folder

Step 9.   When you are finished, click **Close** to close the folder's Properties dialog box. You can also click **Apply** to apply your changes and continue making modifications.

Use of the Public Folder for Sharing Files

Windows 10 provides the Public folder as a location for sharing files as a default. By default, Public Folder Sharing is turned off. To use this folder for sharing files, access the Advanced Sharing Settings dialog box shown previously in Figure 14-11 and specify the desired option in the Public Folder Sharing section. You have the following options at C:\Users\Public:

- **Turn on Sharing So Anyone with Network Access Can Read and Write Files in the Public Folders:** Shares the folder with Full Control shared folder permission. If password protected sharing is turned on, a password is required.

- **Turn off Public Folder Sharing (People Logged On to This Computer Can Still Access These Folders):** Disables sharing of the Public folder.

By default, this folder is located at C:\Users\Public and becomes visible when you select the **Turn on Sharing** option. You can configure additional security options on this folder by accessing the Sharing tab of its Properties dialog box from this location and following the procedure outlined earlier in this section.

Mapping a Drive

Mapping a network drive means associating a shared folder on another computer with a drive letter available on your computer. This facilitates access to the shared folder. Proceed as follows to map a drive on a Windows 10 computer:

Step 1. Right-click **Start** and choose **File Explorer**.

Step 2. Select **This PC**.

Step 3. From the ribbon menu, select the **Computer** tab, and then click the **Map Network Drive** button.

Step 4. In the Map Network Drive Wizard, select the drive letter to be assigned to the network connection for the shared resource. Drive letters being used by local devices are not displayed in the Drive list. You can assign up to 24 drive letters.

Step 5. Enter the UNC path for the server and share name you want to map. For example, to connect to the shared folder HRPolicies on a computer named WIN2016SVR01, type **\\win2016svr01\HRPolicies**, as shown in Figure 14-18. You can also click **Browse** to find the shared folder, and then select the desired path.

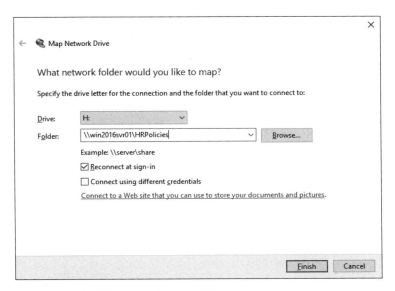

Figure 14-18 Mapping a Network Drive

Step 6. Select a connection option, as follows:

- **Reconnect at Sign-In:** This option is enabled by default and creates permanent connections. It reconnects the user to the shared folder each time the user logs on unless the user manually disconnects from the resource.

- **Connect Using Different Credentials:** Enables you to connect to a shared folder using a different user account. This option is useful if you are at another user's computer and need to connect to a resource to which the currently logged-in user does not have the appropriate access.

Step 7. Click **Finish**.

Command-Line Administration of Shared Folders

Windows 10 provides the **net share** command that you can use to manage shared resources. This is useful if you need to use scripts for automating administrative tasks. The syntax is as follows:

```
net share [sharename] [/parameters]
```

In this command, *sharename* is the name of the shared resource, and */parameters* refers to any of a series of parameters that you can use with this command. Table 14-4 describes several of the more common parameters used with this command.

Table 14-4 Several Common Parameters Used with the **net share** Command

Parameter	Description
/users:*number*	Specifies the maximum number of users who can access the shared resource at the same time. Specify Unlimited to allow the licensed limit of users.
/cache:*option*	Enables offline caching, according to the value of *option*: **Documents:** Specifies automatic reintegration of documents. **Programs:** Specifies automatic reintegration of programs. **Manual:** Specifies manual reintegration. **BranchCache:** Enables BranchCache and manual caching of documents on the shared folder. **None:** Advises the client that caching is inappropriate.
/delete	Stops sharing the specified resource.
/remark:*"text"*	Adds a descriptive comment. Enclose the comment (*text*) in quotation marks.

Note that you can also use this command without any parameters to display information about all the shared resources on the local computer.

Media Streaming

Turning media streaming on enables users and devices on the network to access music, pictures, and videos in Windows Media Player and from devices attached to the computer, such as digital cameras, portable device assistants (PDAs), smartphones, and so on. In addition, the computer can locate these types of shared files on the network. To turn media sharing on, access the Media Streaming section of the Advanced Sharing Settings dialog box and click **Choose Media Streaming Options**. In the Choose Media Streaming Options for Computers and Devices dialog box that appears, click **Turn on Media Streaming**. You can then customize media streaming options, including selecting a media library and choosing what types of media will be accessible according to star ratings and parental control settings.

NOTE   For further information on media streaming, consult the Windows 10 Help and Support Center.

Configuring File Libraries

First introduced in Windows 7, a *library* is a set of virtual folders that are shared by default with other users of the computer. By default, Windows 10 includes six libraries (Camera Roll, Documents, Pictures, Saved Pictures, Music, and Videos). Documents and Pictures libraries are automatically pinned to the File Explorer folder on the taskbar, so you can access those libraries by right-clicking the taskbar folder icon. You can also access the libraries by clicking **View** on the File Explorer toolbar; then, on the expanded toolbar that appears, click **Navigation Pane > Show Libraries**. This adds a Libraries entry to the folder list of the File Explorer window. Click this entry to view the libraries, as shown in Figure 14-19. The subfolders you see here are actually pointers to the folder locations on the computer. You can also think of them as the results of search queries. From the Libraries folder, you can create a new library by right-clicking **Libraries** in the folder list and choosing **New > Library** in the toolbar and providing a name for your new library.

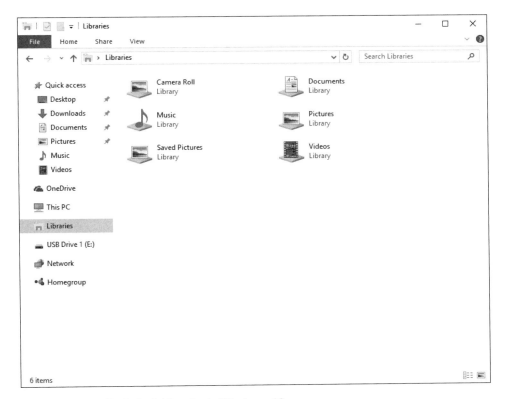

Figure 14-19   Six Default Libraries in Windows 10

Each library contains a user-based subfolder, located by default at C:\Users\
%username%, as well as a public subfolder from C:\Users\Public, which you can
view by right-clicking the library and choosing **Properties**. From the dialog box,
shown in Figure 14-20, you can add folders by clicking the **Add** button and navigating to the desired folder; this can even include shared folders located on other
computers on the network. You can also add folders to a library from any Explorer
window by right-clicking the folder and choosing the Include in Library option
from the pop-up window.

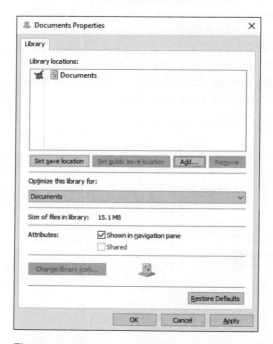

Figure 14-20   Library Properties Dialog Box Allowing You to Add Folders to a Library and
Change Other Properties

The Properties dialog box shown in Figure 14-20 enables you to change several
other properties of the selected library. The check mark indicates the default save
location used by programs such as Microsoft Office. To change this location, select
the desired location and click the **Set Save Location** button. You can add additional
folders to the library by clicking **Add** and selecting the desired folder, similar to that
discussed in the previous paragraph. To remove a folder from the library, select it
and click **Remove**.

HomeGroup

First introduced in Windows 7 is the concept of a homegroup, which is a small group of Windows 7, 8.1, or 10 computers connected together in a home or small office network that you have designated in the Network and Sharing Center as a home network. Computers running any edition of Windows 7, 8.1, or 10 can join a homegroup, but you must have Pro, Enterprise, or Ultimate 7 to create a homegroup. Computers running Windows Vista or earlier cannot join a homegroup. To create or join a homegroup, you must set your computer's network location profile setting (discussed in Chapter 16, "Configuring and Maintaining Network Security") to **Private**. Refer to the section "Configuring Network Discovery" in Chapter 16 for more information.

Creating a Homegroup

You can create a homegroup from the HomeGroup applet, which is accessed from the Network and Internet category of Control Panel by clicking **HomeGroup**. You can also access this applet by accessing the Search bar or Cortana and typing **homegroup** into the Search field, or by clicking **HomeGroup** from the Network and Sharing Center. From the Share with Other Home Computers dialog box shown in Figure 14-21, click **Create a Homegroup**, and then click **Next**. As shown in Figure 14-22, the Create a Homegroup Wizard enables you to select the type of resources you want to share with other computers. For each resource listed here, select **Shared** or **Not Shared** as required. After making your selections and clicking **Next**, the wizard provides you with a password that you can use to add other computers to the homegroup (see Figure 14-23). Make note of this password so that you can join other computers to the homegroup, and then click **Finish**.

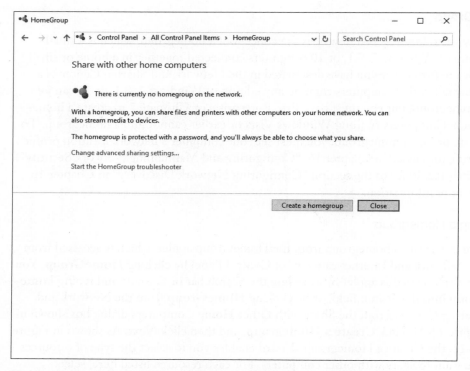

Figure 14-21   The Homegroup Applet Displaying Option to Create a Homegroup

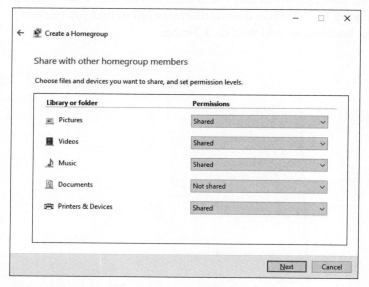

Figure 14-22   Determining the Type of Resources You Want to Share on the Homegroup

Figure 14-23   Password That Enables You to Join Other Computers to the Homegroup

Joining a Homegroup

After you have created a homegroup, when you move to another computer on the network, the computer recognizes the homegroup and the Share with Other Home Computers dialog box informs you of this (see Figure 14-24). Click **Join Now** to join the homegroup, select the libraries you want to share, and then type the homegroup password when requested.

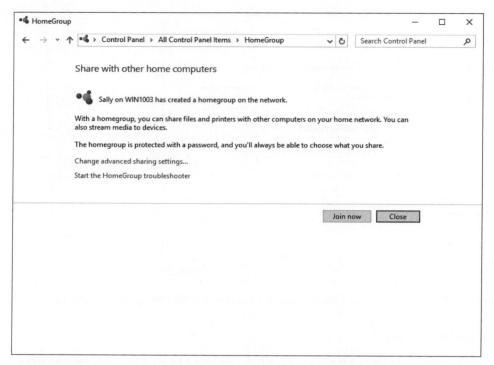

Figure 14-24   If a Homegroup Exists on the Network, You Are Prompted to Join It

NOTE   If your computer is joined to a domain, you can still join a homegroup. However, you cannot share libraries or printers to the homegroup, and you cannot create a homegroup. This feature enables you to bring a portable computer home from work and access shared resources on your home network. Furthermore, it is possible to use Group Policy to prevent domain computers from being joined to a homegroup.

After you've joined a homegroup, you receive the Change Homegroup Settings dialog box shown in Figure 14-25 when you access the HomeGroup option in the Control Panel Network and Internet category. From here you can change the types of libraries and printers that are shared with other homegroup computers. You can also perform any of the other self-explanatory actions shown in Figure 14-25 under Other Homegroup Actions. Selecting the Change Advanced Sharing Settings option takes you to the Advanced Sharing Settings dialog box previously shown in Figure 14-11.

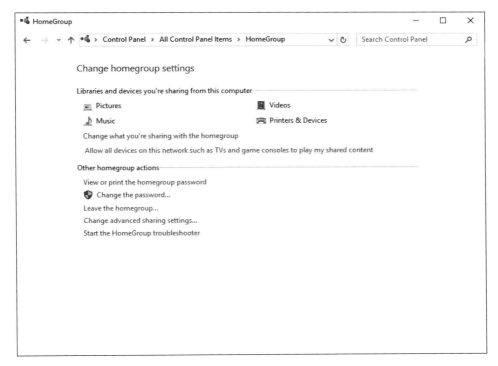

Figure 14-25   Change Homegroup Settings Dialog Box Enabling You to Change Which Items You Share on the Homegroup, or Perform Other Configuration Actions

Selecting the Allow All Devices on This Network Such as TVs and Game Consoles to Play My Shared Content option displays the dialog box shown in Figure 14-26. The list includes all computers and other media devices found on the network, including media players, electronic picture frames, and others. You can allow or block media access to each device individually by selecting the drop-down lists provided, or you can allow or block all devices by choosing from the appropriate command buttons.

Figure 14-26 Choose Media Streaming Options for Computers and Devices Dialog Box Enabling You to Choose Which Devices Are Allowed to Access Shared Media

You can also modify the file sharing options for subfolders located within any of your shared libraries. To do this, navigate to the desired library and select the folder. From the Share With section of the Share tab, choose one of the following:

- **Homegroup (View):** Shares the file or folder with Read permission to all users in the homegroup.

- **Homegroup (View and Edit):** Shares the file or folder with Full Control permission to all users in the homegroup.

- **Specific People:** Displays the Choose People on Your Network to Share With dialog box previously shown in Figure 14-13. Type the name of the user with whom you want to share the folder, and then click **Add**.

OneDrive

In Windows 10, you can share files and folders in OneDrive just like any other folder on your local computer. If you have joined a HomeGroup, you can share your OneDrive (or any folders in it) with users on your homegroup. All the options are the same as any other folder, so you can share as view, as view and edit, or select specific users in your homegroup to share with.

You learned other aspects of OneDrive—how to set it up and configure OneDrive settings, in Chapter 9, "Managing User Data." Refer to the "Supporting Data Storage" topic in Chapter 9 for the details on OneDrive.

Troubleshooting Data Access and Usage

Sharing files and folders with other computers on your network, whether using a central server or a distributed set of Windows computers, is a convenient and efficient way of managing data. Ensuring that users have the level of permissions that they need can become a complex and frustrating task, however, especially when the number of users and computers grows. To deal with these issues, you need an understanding of how permissions work in a Windows network, as well as how NTFS permissions work with share permissions to secure files and folders.

Effective Permissions

Users who belong to more than one group may receive different levels of permission. Both shared folder and NTFS permissions are cumulative. Your effective permissions are a combination of all permissions configured for your user account and for the groups of which you are a member. In other words, the effective permission is the least restrictive of all permissions that you have. For example, if you have Read permissions for a given file, but you are also a member of a group that has Modify permissions for the same file, your effective permissions for that file or folder would be Modify.

However, there is one important exception to this rule. If you happen to be a member of yet another group that has been explicitly denied permissions to a resource (the permission has been selected in the Deny column), then your effective permissions will not allow you to access that resource at all. Explicit denial of permission always overrides any allowed permissions.

Putting the two types of permissions together, the rules for determining effective permissions are simple:

- At either the shared folder or NTFS permissions level by itself, if a user receives permissions by virtue of membership in one or more groups, the *least restrictive* permission is the effective permission. For example, if a user has Read permission assigned to his user account and Full Control permission by virtue of membership in a group, he receives Full Control permission on this item.

- If the user is accessing a shared folder over the network and has both shared folder and NTFS permissions applied to it, the *most restrictive* permission is the effective permission. For example, if a user has Full Control NTFS permission on a folder but accesses it across the network where she has Read shared folder permission, her effective permission is Read.

- If the user is accessing a shared folder on the computer where it exists, shared folder permissions do not apply. In the previous example, this user would receive Full Control permission when accessing the shared folder locally.

- If the user has an explicit denial of permission at either the shared folder or NTFS level, he is denied access to the object, regardless of any other permissions he might have to this object.

> **TIP** It is important to remember that specifically denying permission to a file within a folder overrides all other file and folder permissions configured for a user or for a group that may contain that user's account. There is no real top-down or bottom-up factor to consider when it comes to denying permissions. If a user is a member of a group that has been denied a permission to a file or folder, or if a user's individual account has been denied a permission to a particular resource, that is what counts. If you are denied access to a folder, it does not matter what permissions are attached to a file inside the folder, because you cannot get to it.

Practical Guidelines on Sharing and Securing Folders

When you share folders, it is important to control how they are used. To control the use of shared folders, you should be aware of how shares are applied in Windows 10. The following facts should be kept in mind.

- **Denying permissions overrides all other shared permissions that may be applied to a folder:** If a user is part of a group that is denied permission to access a particular resource, that user will not be able to access that resource, even if you grant her user account access to the share.

- **Multiple permissions accumulate:** You may be a member of multiple groups, each with a different level of permissions for a particular shared resource. Your effective permissions are a combination of all permissions configured for your user account and the groups of which you are a member. As a user, you may have Read permissions for a folder. You may be a member of a group with Change permissions for the same folder. Your effective permissions for that folder would be Change. If you happen to be made a member of yet another group that has been denied permissions to a folder, your effective permissions will not allow you to access that folder at all. That is the one important exception to this rule.

- **Copying or moving a folder alters the shared permissions associated with that folder:** When you copy a shared folder, the original shared folder is still shared, but the copied folder is not. When you move a shared folder to a new location anywhere, that folder is no longer shared by anyone.

- **When you share a folder that is located on an NTFS volume, you still need to consider the NTFS permissions that apply to that folder:** There may already be NTFS permissions in place on a folder that you are in the process of sharing. You will need to consider how your NTFS and shared folder permissions combine. (See the next item.) If there aren't any NTFS permissions on that folder, you may need to configure NTFS permissions for your shared folder, or it is possible that no one will be able to access it.

- **When shared folder and NTFS file and folder permissions combine, the most restrictive permissions apply:** When both NTFS and shared folder permissions apply to the same folder, the more restrictive permission is the effective permission for that folder. Do not lose sight of the fact, however, that shared folder permissions have no effect on users who are logged in to the computer locally.

- **When a folder resides on an NTFS volume:** You need at least the NTFS Read permission to be able to share that folder at all.

Configuring Shared Printers

If you have turned on file and printer sharing from the Advanced Sharing Settings dialog box, you can share any printer attached to your computer so that others on the network can print documents to it. Use the following steps to share a printer:

Step 1. From the Search bar or Cortana, type **printers**, and then select **Devices and Printers**. You can also access the Hardware and Sound category in Control Panel and select **Devices and Printers**.

Step 2. In the Devices and Printers Control Panel applet, right-click your printer and choose **Printer Properties**.

Step 3. Click the **Sharing** tab to display the dialog box shown in Figure 14-27.

Figure 14-27 Sharing a Printer

Step 4.   Click **Change Sharing Options** to enable the sharing options on this dialog box.

Step 5.   Click **Share This Printer** and either accept the share name provided or type a different name. This name identifies the printer to users on other computers.

Step 6.   If users are running older Windows versions, click **Additional Drivers** to install drivers for these Windows versions. Select the required drivers from the Additional Drivers dialog box that appears, and then click **OK**.

As with shared folders, you can assign share permissions for printers. Select the **Security** tab of the printer's Properties dialog box to configure the options shown in Figure 14-28. By default, the Everyone group receives the Print permission and the Administrators group receives the Print, Manage This Printer, and Manage Documents permissions. Table 14-5 describes the printer permissions, including Special Permissions.

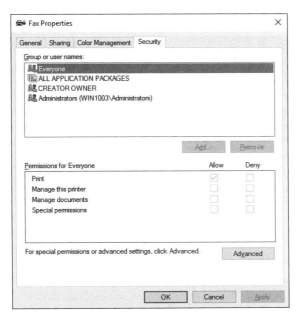

Figure 14-28 Changing Permissions for Shared Printers

Table 14-5 Printer Permissions in Windows 10

Parameter	Description
Print	Users can connect to a given printer to print documents and control print job settings for their own documents only. This can include pausing, deleting, and restarting only their own documents in the print queue.
Manage This Printer	Users can assign forms to paper trays and set a separator page. In addition, they can change the printing order of documents in the queue, pause, resume, and purge the printer, change printer properties, and delete the printer itself or change printer permissions. Users with this permission can also perform all tasks related to the Manage Documents permission.
Manage Documents	Users can pause, resume, restart, and cancel all documents. They can also set the notification level for finished print jobs and set priority levels and specific printing times for documents to print.
Special Permissions	Enables the assignment of granular permissions, including Read Permissions, Change Permissions, and Take Ownership. To configure special permissions, click the **Advanced** button.

> **NOTE**   For more information on configuring printer permissions, refer to "Set or Remove Permissions for Printer Use" at https://technet.microsoft.com/en-us/library/cc719924(v=ws.10).aspx.

Configuring Location Aware Printing

Location Aware Printing, first introduced in Windows 7, enables you to automatically print to a printer on the network your computer is currently connected to. For example, if you have a portable computer that you use both at home and in the office, you can print to the office computer when you are at work. Returning home in the evening, you print a document, and this print job automatically goes to the home printer without your having to change the default printer, thereby simplifying this task and reducing problems from attempting to print to the wrong printer.

Location Aware Printing in Windows 10 obtains network names from several sources, including the Active Directory Domain Services (AD DS) domain name at work and the SSID of your home wireless network. The Manage Default Printers dialog box then enables you to associate a default printer with each network to which you connect, and Windows automatically specifies the assigned printer as the default when you connect to its network.

To use Location Aware Printing, you need to be running Windows 10 Pro, Education, or Enterprise edition. The feature is not available in Windows Mobile or the Home edition of Windows 10.

Use the following procedure to set up Location Aware Printing:

Step 1.   Access the Action Center and select **All Settings**.

Step 2.   Click the **Devices** option and then select **Printer & Scanners** from the Settings menu.

Step 3.   From the Printers & Scanners settings page in Figure 14-29, click the **Let Windows Manage My Default Printer** toggle to **On**.

Step 4.   Each time you use a printer on a specific network, Windows automatically uses it as the default whenever you connect to that network.

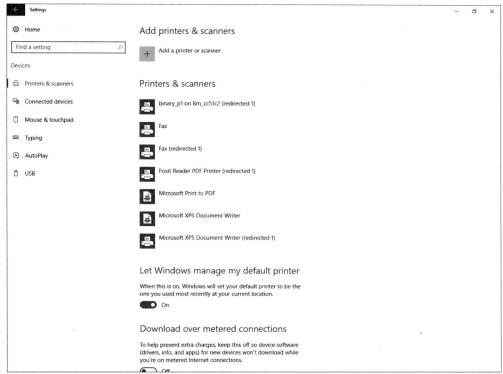

Figure 14-29   Printers & Scanners Settings Page Enabling You to Work with Printers and Tell Windows Whether to Automatically Manage Your Default Printer

If you want to change the default printer for a network, you can select a default printer while you are connected to that network. Access the Devices and Printers Control Panel applet, right-click the printer, and then select **Set as Default Printer** from the pop-up menu.

To stop Windows from changing your default printer every time you use a specific printer, you can turn off the Let Windows Manage My Default Printer setting. You can then manually manage your default printer, and it will not change even if you connect to a different network. With the setting turned off, you also have a new option in the Printers & Scanners settings page. It will identify the current default printer with the word Default just under the name of the printer. To change the default, select the printer you want to use, and then click the **Manage** button. From the Settings page of the printer, click the **Set as Default** button to make that printer your default.

Exam Preparation Tasks

Review All the Key Topics

Review the most important topics in the chapter, noted with the Key Topics icon in the outer margin of the page. Table 14-6 lists a reference of these key topics and the page numbers on which each is found.

Table 14-6   Key Topics for Chapter 14

Key Topic Element	Description	Page Number
Figure 14-1	Shows how to use EFS to encrypt files or folders.	661
Step List	Shows how to back up EFS keys.	663
Step List	Shows how to configure disk quotas.	666
Table 14-2	Describes available disk quota configuration options.	668
Step List	Shows how to enable object access auditing.	670
Step List	Shows how to specify objects to be audited.	672
Figure 14-11	Advanced Sharing Settings dialog box enables you to configure several global file sharing and network discovery options.	675
Figure 14-15	Advanced Sharing dialog box allows you to set share permissions, user limits, and other options.	679
Table 14-3	Describes available folder sharing options.	679
Figure 14-16	Specifying shared folder permissions.	680
Paragraph	Describes the concept of libraries.	685
Paragraph	How to create a HomeGroup.	687
List	Describes the interaction between share permissions and NTFS permissions.	693
Table 14-5	Printer permissions in Windows 10.	697
Figure 14-29	The Printers & Scanners settings page allows you to set whether you want Windows to manage your default printer.	699

Complete the Tables and Lists from Memory

Print a copy of Appendix B, "Memory Tables" (found on the book's website), or at least the section for this chapter, and complete the tables and lists from memory. Appendix C, "Memory Tables Answer Key," also on the website, includes completed tables and lists to check your work.

Definitions of Key Terms

Define the following key terms from this chapter, and check your answers in the glossary.

administrative shares, auditing, certificate, decryption, disk quotas, encryption, Encrypting File System (EFS), hidden shares, library, public folder sharing, recovery agent, shared folder permissions, shared folders, system access control list (SACL)

This chapter covers the following subjects:

- **Configuring Remote Authentication:** To secure sensitive and valuable organizational resources, it is vital that users connecting from remote locations using the Internet or dial-up connections are positively authenticated. In this section you learn about processes and technologies available for securely authenticating the users requesting access to your network and computers.

- **Configuring Remote Desktop Settings:** This section describes new and improved methods of connecting to and managing computers remotely. You learn about time-saving management options that enable you to perform a large range of management tasks on remotely located computers directly from your Windows 10 computer.

- **Configuring VPN Authentication and Settings:** In this section you learn about how to set up dial-up and VPN connections for access to organization resources from the Internet and other remote locations.

- **Configuring Remote Management:** Microsoft now includes many tools that administrators can use for remotely managing Windows computers and servers. In this section you learn how to identify the appropriate tools for remote management, and how to use administrative tools, such as MMC console applets, PowerShell remoting, and Remote Assistance, to manage and administer computers and settings remotely.

This chapter covers the following objectives for the 70-697 and 70-698 exam:

Configure remote connections: Configure remote authentication; configure Remote Desktop settings; configure VPN connections and authentication; enable VPN reconnect; configure broadband tethering; configure app-triggered VPN, traffic filters, and lockdown VPN; configure DirectAccess.

Configure remote management: Choose the appropriate remote management tools; configure remote management settings; modify settings remotely by using the Microsoft Management Console (MMC) or Windows PowerShell; configure Remote Assistance, including Easy Connect; configure Remote Desktop; configure Remote PowerShell.

CHAPTER 15

Configuring Remote Access

Chapter 7, "Windows 10 Security," introduced you to the various tools and technologies available in Windows 10 for ensuring that only authenticated users gain access to computers and the resources they contain. In this chapter, we continue the discussion of computer management by looking at the methods available for accessing and managing computers across the network, and in particular the methodologies used for managing computers in remote locations. We take a look at accessing and managing computers through a virtual private network (VPN), using new technologies such as Remote Desktop Gateway and DirectAccess, and the authentication techniques you need to be aware of.

You also learn about technology that enables you to manage computers from afar and make connections to these computers from diverse locations. You will see that you can be in a distant location, such as home or hotel, and perform almost anything that you could do directly from the computer console. When that emergency occurs late at night, you can diagnose many problems and perform fixes without the need to travel to the office.

"Do I Know This Already?" Quiz

The "Do I Know This Already?" quiz allows you to assess whether you should read this entire chapter or simply jump to the "Exam Preparation Tasks" section for review. If you are in doubt, read the entire chapter. Table 15-1 outlines the major headings in this chapter and the corresponding "Do I Know This Already?" quiz questions. You can find the answers in Appendix A, "Answers to the 'Do I Know This Already?' Quizzes."

Table 15-1   "Do I Know This Already?" Foundation Topics Section-to-Question Mapping

Foundation Topics Section	Questions Covered in This Section
Configuring Remote Authentication	1–3
Configuring Remote Desktop Settings	4–6
Configuring VPN Authentication and Settings	7–11
Configuring Remote Management	12–14

CAUTION   The goal of self-assessment is to gauge your mastery of the topics in this chapter. If you do not know the answer to a question or are only partially sure of the answer, you should mark that question as wrong for purposes of the self-assessment. Giving yourself credit for an answer you correctly guess skews your self-assessment results and might provide you with a false sense of security.

1.   Which of the following remote access authentication protocols should you avoid because it sends credentials in unencrypted form?

    a. PAP

    b. CHAP

    c. EAP-TTLS

    d. MS-CHAPv2

2.   Which of the following remote authentication protocols uses a secure tunnel and can be used with 802.1X authentication as well as RADIUS servers?

    a. CHAP

    b. PAP

    c. Smart cards

    d. EAP-TTLS

3.   Which of the following is a valid remote access network authentication protocol used by Windows 10 and other recent Windows versions?

    a. Charon

    b. Styx

    c. Nix

    d. Kerberos

    e. Hydra

4.   You are working from home on your Windows 10 Pro computer and need to access your work computer, which is also running Windows 10 Pro by means of your cable Internet connection. What tool should you use to make this connection?

    a. Hyper-V

    b. Remote Assistance

    c. Remote Desktop

    d. Virtual private network

5. Yesterday evening, you worked on an important project from home on your wife's home computer, which runs Windows 10 Home. Your children interrupted you, and you forgot to upload your work to your work computer. The work computer runs Windows 7 Professional. Needing the upgraded project files, you attempt to connect to your home computer but are unable to do so. What do you need to do to make this connection?

   a. Download the Remote Desktop Connection Software application from Microsoft and install it on your home computer.

   b. Upgrade your work computer to Windows 10 Pro or Enterprise.

   c. Upgrade your home computer to Windows 10 Pro.

   d. Use Remote Assistance to make the connection.

6. Which of the following remote access protocols does not provide data encryption on its own?

   a. PPTP

   b. L2TP

   c. SSTP

   d. IKEv2

7. You have created a VPN connection but now need to enable the use of File and Printer Sharing for Microsoft Networks so that you can print a report on the office network that your manager needs to have by 8:00 tomorrow morning. You right-click the connection and choose **View Connection Properties**. Which tab contains the option that you must configure?

   a. General

   b. Options

   c. Security

   d. Networking

   e. Sharing

8. You are downloading a large file to your laptop at the airport Wi-Fi connection while waiting for your flight to be called. You are concerned that you might need to interrupt the download and want to be able to resume the download at your destination hotel room, so you have enabled VPN Reconnect. What protocol does this feature use?

   a. PPTP

   b. L2TP/IPsec

   c. SSTP

   d. IKEv2

9. You have set up a new Windows Server 2016 computer on which you want to enable users to connect remotely for Remote Desktop sessions. What role will you be configuring?

   a. VPN Reconnect

   b. DirectAccess

   c. Remote Desktop Services

   d. Internet Connection Sharing

10. You have decided to configure a DirectAccess server for your mobile work-force to use when they need files from the servers, access to the network print-ers, and other needs. You are ready to start rolling out a pilot and need to order the laptops for the mobile staff. What is the best client operating system to use?

    a. Windows 10 Mobile

    b. Windows 10 Home

    c. Windows 10 Pro

    d. Windows 10 Enterprise

11. Which of the following are valid commands that you can enter at a PowerShell interface? (Choose all that apply.)

    a. **Get-process**

    b. **Value-output**

    c. **Select-object**

    d. **Format-data**

    e. **Folder-create**

12. You are helping a worker in your organization with a configuration issue and decided to run some PowerShell cmdlets you have to check some items on the remote computer. When you run the command, specifying the remote com-puter name, the command fails to connect to the remote computer and dies with the error WinRMOperationTimeout. What is the most likely cause of failure?

    a. You do not have administrative access to the remote computer.

    b. The remote computer is not in the PowerShell list of TrustedComputers.

    c. PowerShell Remoting is not enabled.

    d. The command syntax was incorrect.

13. You want to be able to use all the tools in the Computer Management administrative tool to manage a remote computer. Which of the following firewall application settings do you need to enable? (Select all that apply.)

   a. Remote Event Log

   b. Remote Scheduled Tasks Management

   c. Windows Firewall with Advanced Security

   d. Remote Service Management

14. You are working from home on your Windows 10 computer and experience a problem that you cannot fix. You want to contact a user on another Windows 10 computer that you believe can help you correct your problem. What tool should you use?

   a. Hyper-V

   b. Remote Assistance

   c. Remote Desktop

   d. Virtual Private Network

Foundation Topics

Configuring Remote Authentication

Microsoft has built several remote management tools into Windows 10 and Windows Server 2016 that allow you to connect to computers located across the hall or across the continent. You can use these tools to save precious minutes out of a busy day, or an entire trip lasting days, to manage and troubleshoot resources located on these computers. Users in other locations can connect to your computer, and you can offer suggestions or train them in procedures that correct problems or make their day's work go more smoothly.

Whenever you connect a computer or network to the public Internet, it becomes a target for a vast array of criminals and nefarious actors hoping to exploit resources that do not belong to them. Authenticating over a remote connection is necessary for a wide range of functionality, but it is also a potential attack vector for malicious activity. It is important that users and administrators, as well as business process services, are able to use remote connections for access to resources; however, those connections must be secure, authentication must be robust, and unauthorized access must be detected and stopped.

Remote Authentication Planning

The methods of authentication used for remote workers and administrators depend entirely on the infrastructure of the network, the services available, the type of remote access required, and the sensitivity of the data being exposed over the remote connection. This chapter covers some details on configuring different types of remote connections, include Remote Desktop, Remote Management, VPNs, and broadband connections. You should be aware of the authentication types, and variations, used for these different types of services.

You should also be familiar with the authentication methods previously discussed in Chapter 7, "Windows 10 Security," which can also come into play when managing remote authentication, and often are configured through Group Policies to enforce more stringent requirements on top of the specific protocol connections. For instance, in a domain environment, you can require dual-factor authentication for all connections, or only for remote connections. Or you may require that any computers connecting to your network remotely have their own certificate previously issued by the domain CA, and disallow any connections that do not present recognized certificates.

Throughout this text, including this chapter and others, you learn about various types of remote connection technologies and ways of authenticating users and computers. It would be impractical to list every combination available for use in a Windows environment, and especially in a mixed computing environment with Windows servers and workstations playing various roles. Table 15-2 lists some of the connection types and the most common authentication technologies that can play a role. Details of each are found throughout the text, referenced in the last column.

Table 15-2   Remote Connection Types and Common Remote Authentication Technologies

Connection Type	Authentication Technologies	Chapter References
Remote Desktop	Network Level Authentication, smart cards, certificates, NTLM, Kerberos	Chapter 7, Chapter 14
VPN	Smart cards, machine certificate, CHAP, EAP, PEAP, PAP, PSK	Chapter 6, Chapter 15 (see Table 15-3)
Remote Management	Kerberos, NTLM, certificates	Chapter 15

Be sure that you can distinguish between connection security and remote authentication. Table 15-2 lists authentication methods, including certificates—it should be noted that certificates play a part in authentication as well as connection security. (Certificates can be used both to authenticate the certificate owner as well as negotiate end-to-end encryption between trusted certificate owners.)

Remote Access Authentication Protocols

Authentication is the first perimeter of defense that a network administrator can define in a remote access system. The process of authenticating a user is meant to verify and validate a user's identification. If the user provides invalid input, the authentication process should deny the user access to the network. An ill-defined authentication system, or lack of one altogether, can open the door to mischief and disruption because the two most common methods for remote access are publicly available: the Internet and the public services telephone network.

Remote authentication protocols fall into two main categories, Extensible Authentication Protocol (EAP) methods and non-EAP methods. Non-EAP methods are not considered secure, and Microsoft recommends those with TLS-based confidentiality such as PEAP or EAP-TTLS. Table 15-3 discusses the authentication protocols supported in Windows 10 and Windows Server 2016.

Table 15-3   Authentication Protocols for Remote Access

Acronym	Name	Usage	Security
CHAP	Challenge Handshake Authentication Protocol	Client requests access. Server sends a challenge to client. Client responds using MD5 hash value. Values must match for authentication.	Non-EAP. One-way authentication. Server authenticates client.
MS-CHAPv2	Microsoft Challenge Handshake Authentication Protocol version 2	Requires both the client and the server to be Microsoft Windows based. Does not work with LAN Manager. Client requests access, server challenges, client responds with an MD5 hash value and piggybacks a challenge to server. If a match is found, server responds with a success packet granting access to client, which includes an MD5 hash response to the client's challenge. Client logs on if the server's response matches what client expects. Note that the older MS-CHAP authentication protocol is no longer supported as of Windows 7.	Non-EAP. Mutual (two-way) authentication.

Acronym	Name	Usage	Security
EAP-TTLS	Extensible Authentication Protocol Tunneled Transport Layer Security	Developed for PPP and can be used with IEEE 802.1X. Is capable of heading other authentication protocols, so improves interoperability between RAS systems, RADIUS servers, and RAS clients. First supported natively in Windows 8.1 and Windows Server 2012.	EAP method. Provides additional authentication types based on plug-in modules, enables enhanced interoperability and efficiency of authentication process.
PEAP	Protected Extensible Authentication Protocol with Transport Layer Security	A highly secure password-based authentication protocol combination that utilizes certificate-based authentication.	EAP method. Uses certificate-based encryption.
PAP	Password Authentication Protocol	Client submits a clear-text user identification and password to server. Server compares to information in its user database. If a match, client is authenticated.	Non-EAP. Clear-text, one-way authentication. Least secure method.
Smart cards	Certificates	User must have knowledge of PIN and possession of smart card. Client swipes card, which submits smart card certificate, and inputs PIN. Results are reviewed by server, which responds with its own certificate. If both client and server match, access is granted. Otherwise, error that credentials cannot be verified.	Certificate-based, two-way authentication.

NOTE   When using certificate authentication, the client computer must have a way of validating the server's certificate. To ensure absolutely that this validation will work, you can import the server's certificate into the client's Trusted Publishers list. If there is no way for a client to validate the server's certificate, an error displays stating that the server is not a trusted resource.

NTLM and Kerberos Authentication

As noted in Table 15-2, Kerberos and NTLM authentication are used in many scenarios. These are the default authentication technologies used to authenticate a user, using a username and password, to a Windows computer. Kerberos is available only in Active Directory domains, and NTLM is generally always used between computers that are not domain joined.

NTLM authentication includes several discrete authentication protocols—namely, LAN Manager, NTLM version 1 (NTLMv1), and NTLM version 2 (NTLMv2). When NTLM is used, the resource computer either contacts a domain authentication service for the user's account or looks up the user in the local account database. NTLM credentials consist of a domain name or server name, a username, and information that can be used to confirm the user's password (typically a password hash). Older LAN Manager and NTLMv1 protocols are more vulnerable than newer protocols used in recent versions of Windows.

Kerberos authentication works with an AD domain by the use of *tickets* issued by domain controllers based on the credentials passed from a client. The ticket is then used to authenticate the user to other domain-managed computers and resources. In this way, both the computer requesting authentication and the computer granting access first check in with the server to confirm authentication.

Kerberos provides several advantages over NTLM authentication:

- Always includes server authentication
- Stronger cryptography
- Faster performance on repeated connections, using a single ticket
- Can fall back to NTLM authentication when Kerberos authentication is not available

Generally, the use of Kerberos or NTLM will be decided by the Windows security providers available, the domain controllers when they are available, and the policies put in place at the domain level.

Keep in mind that when using remote connections, especially when directly connecting to Remote Desktop computers over the Internet or an untrusted network, Kerberos cannot be used, because there will be no connection between the remote computer and the domain controllers on the remote network. So in those scenarios NTLM authentication will be used.

> **NOTE** For more information about NTLM Authentication, refer to "NTLM Overview" at https://technet.microsoft.com/en-us/windows-server-docs/security/kerberos/ntlm-overview and the links provided in that document. You can learn more about Kerberos authentication by referring to "Kerberos Authentication Overview" at https://technet.microsoft.com/en-us/windows-server-docs/security/kerberos/kerberos-authentication-overview.

Remote Authentication Group Policies

Several Group Policies can be utilized to control remote authentication protocols in Windows 10. You will find these policies in the Local Group Policy Editor under Computer Configuration\Windows Settings\Security Settings\Local Policies\Security Options, as shown in Figure 15-1. The following are several of the more important policy settings that you should be familiar with:

- **Network Security: Configure Encryption Types Allowed for Kerberos:** This setting allows you to specify which encryption types can be used for domain-based Kerberos authentication. By default, all supported encryption types are allowed.

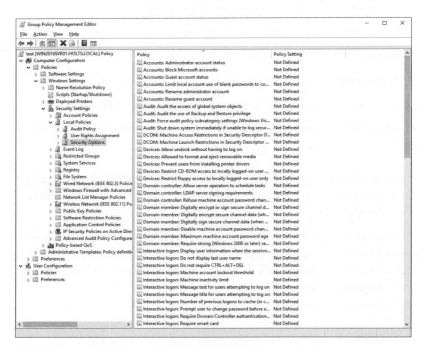

Figure 15-1 Network Security Group Policy Settings in Windows 10

- **Network Security: Minimum Session Security for NTLM SSP Based (Including Secure RPC) Clients:** This setting ensures that NTLM authentication can occur only over strong (128-bit) encryption. This is the recommended setting and is the default policy for Windows 7, Windows 8, Windows 8.1, Windows 10, Windows Server 2008 R2, and Windows Server 2012/R2/2016.

- **Network Security: Restrict NTLM: Audit Incoming NTLM Traffic:** If enabled, the server logs events for NTLM pass-through authentication requests that would be blocked when the Network Security: Restrict NTLM: Incoming NTLM Traffic policy is set to Deny All Domain Accounts. Events are logged to the Operational log under the Applications and Services Log/Microsoft/Windows/NTLM.

- **Network Security: Restrict NTLM: Incoming NTLM Traffic:** You can block NTLM authentication for all accounts or for domain accounts. Note that blocking NTLM authentication on a computer that is not domain joined will disable authentication entirely, because only domain accounts can use Kerberos authentication.

Configuring Remote Desktop Settings

Windows 10 continues to improve upon the Remote Desktop and Remote Assistance tools first introduced with Windows XP and upgraded with each iteration of the Windows operating system. The Remote Server Administration Tools (RSAT) for Windows 10 download enables you to manage roles and features installed on servers running Windows Server 2003 or later from your Windows 10 desktop. Also offered are the new Windows Remote Management service and (introduced with Vista) the Windows PowerShell command-line interface.

CAUTION Only limited management of servers running older versions of Windows Server is possible when using RSAT for Windows 10. In the original and R2 versions of Windows Server 2008, you can perform most administrative actions, but you cannot install or remove server roles or features. Support for Windows Server 2003 is generally limited to most Active Directory and network management tools.

For more information on server components that can be managed using RSAT in Windows 10, refer to "Description of Remote Server Administration Tools for Windows 10" at https://support.microsoft.com/en-us/help/2693643/remote-server-administration-tools-rsat-for-windows-operating-systems.

Windows 10 incorporates the Remote Desktop Protocol (RDP), which was originally introduced with Terminal Services and included with Windows XP Professional. The protocol allows any user to use the Remote Desktop application to run a remote control session on a Windows Terminal Server or a Windows computer that has been configured to provide Remote Desktop services. RDP is also used when a Remote Assistance session is conducted, as described in the previous section.

When Windows 10 is configured to be a Remote Desktop host, there is a restriction for usage that does not apply to a Terminal Services computer. This restriction is that only one user can ever execute an interactive session on the computer at any one time. So if you run a Remote Desktop session, and a user is already logged on to the Remote Desktop server, that user will be logged off (at your request) for your own session to run. However, that user's session will be saved so that he can resume it later.

Establishing a Remote Desktop Connection with Another Computer

Any version of Windows 10 can be a Remote Desktop client; however, only the Pro, Education, or Enterprise edition of Windows 10 can be a Remote Desktop host (server). You can run a Remote Desktop session with another computer running Windows 10 or any older Windows version back to Windows XP. Use the following instructions to make a Remote Desktop connection:

Step 1.   In the Search bar or Cortana, type **remote** into the Search field, and then select **Remote Desktop Connection** from the program list. This opens the Remote Desktop Connection dialog box, as shown in Figure 15-2.

Figure 15-2   Remote Desktop Connection Dialog Requiring You to Know the Name and/or IP Address of the Target Computer

The Computer list shows only Windows Terminal Servers. Windows 10 computers do not advertise the Remote Desktop service, so you are required to know the full name or IP address of the computer, unless you have connected to it before. The Remote Desktop client will save a list of the 10 most recent connections.

Step 2. Type the name or IP address of the Windows XP, Vista, Windows 7, Windows 8.1, or Windows 10 computer and click **Connect**. You should see a message box informing you that you are connecting, followed by a remote session with a logon screen prompting you for a user ID and password.

Step 3. Click the **Show Options** button. The General tab for the connection's Properties dialog box opens. You can save the current logon settings or open a file containing previously saved settings, as well as change the computer name in this dialog box.

Step 4. Click the **Display** tab. If your session is running slowly, you can increase performance by reducing the number of colors and size of the screen.

Step 5. Click the **Local Resources** tab. You can choose whether to map sounds, disk drives, printers, clipboard, and serial ports. You can also select how the key combination Alt+Tab works when executing that key combination while in the remote session. By clicking the **More** button, you can choose to use smart cards and specified ports on this computer to be used within the remote session.

Step 6. Click the **Programs** tab. If you would like to configure a connection that starts a single application, rather than *all* the applications, you can type the command line in this screen so that it executes automatically.

Step 7. Click the **Experience** tab. This tab enables you to enable or disable various display behaviors shown in Figure 15-3 to enhance the computer's performance according to the connection speed as selected from the drop-down list provided.

Figure 15-3   Experience Tab of the Remote Desktop Connection Dialog Box Enabling You to Select the Performance Options Applicable to the Remote Session

Step 8.   Click the **Advanced** tab. You can choose from three options that describe the behavior if authentication fails: Warn Me (the default), Connect and Don't Warn Me, or Do Not Connect. You can also configure Remote Desktop Gateway settings that apply for connections to remote computers located behind firewalls.

Step 9.   Click the **Hide Options** button to return to the original logon screen. Type the information for your username and password, and click **OK** to start the session.

Step 10.   If someone else is already logged on to the computer, you will be asked whether you should log off the existing user. Click **Yes**. The session begins.

NOTE   A Universal Windows Platform (UWP) app version of Remote Desktop is also available for Windows 10. This is a free app that you can download by accessing the Windows Store. After you've downloaded and installed this app, you can connect to a remote computer by accessing the app from the Start menu, selecting the **Add** button, choosing **Desktop**, and typing the name or IP address of the desired computer in the PC Name text box provided. Save the connection and you can click it to connect. To connect to other computers on your corporate network without setting up a VPN, add a Gateway Server in the app settings.

Configuring the Server Side of Remote Desktop

The Server Side of the Remote Desktop connection refers to the computer to which you are making the connection. Before you can use Remote Desktop, you must enable the computer to which you want to connect to receive Remote Desktop connections. This computer must be running the Pro, Education, or Enterprise edition of Windows 10. You can do this from the Remote tab of the System Properties dialog box, as follows:

Step 1. Access the Remote tab of the System Properties dialog box. To do so, right-click the **Start** menu, select **System**, and then click the **Remote Settings** link. This displays the dialog box shown in Figure 15-4.

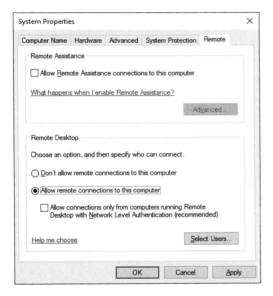

Figure 15-4   Remote Tab of the System Properties Dialog Box Used to Enable Remote Connections

Step 2. Select the **Allow Remote Connections to This Computer** option.

Step 3. You receive a message box warning you that users cannot connect if the computer is in Sleep or Hibernation mode. If you want to change this behavior, select the **Power Options** link provided. When finished, click **OK**.

Step 4. If desired, select the check box labeled **Allow Connections Only from Computers Running Remote Desktop with Network Level Authentication (Recommended)**. This option enables users with computers running Remote Desktop with Network Level Authentication to connect to your computer. This is the most secure option if people connecting to your computer are running Windows 7, 8.1, or 10. If you do not select this option, users with any version of Remote Desktop can connect to your computer, regardless of Windows version in use.

Step 5.   Click **OK** or **Apply**.

You also need to specify the users that are entitled to make a remote connection to your computer. By default, members of the Administrators and Remote Desktop Users groups are allowed to connect to your computer. To add a nonadministrative user to the Remote Desktop Users group, click the **Select Users** button in the Remote tab previously shown in Figure 15-4. This opens the Remote Desktop Users dialog box shown in Figure 15-5. Click **Add**, and in the Select Users dialog box that appears, type the name of the user to be granted access, and then click **OK**. The Select Users dialog box also enables you to add users from an Active Directory Domain Services (AD DS) domain if your computer is a domain member.

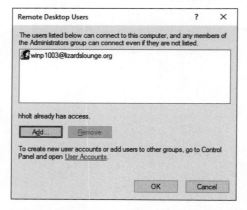

Figure 15-5   Remote Desktop Users Dialog Box Enabling You to Grant Remote Desktop Access to Nonadministrative Users

Selecting a Nondefault Port

You can configure the listening port, from the default TCP 3389, to another port of your choice. When you do so, only the people who specify the port can connect and then run a remote session. In Windows 10, you are able to adjust the port only by editing the Registry:

Step 1.   Open the Registry Editor, supply your UAC credentials, and navigate to the HKEY_LOCAL_MACHINE\System\CurrentControlSet\Control\ TerminalServer\WinStations\RDP-Tcp key.

Step 2.   Select the **PortNumber** value, click the **Edit** menu, and then select **Modify**.

Step 3.   Click **Decimal** and type in the new port number.

Step 4.   Click **OK** and close the Registry Editor.

On the client computer, you then make a connection by opening the Remote Desktop Connection dialog box as previously described and shown in Figure 15-2. In the Computer text box, type the name or IP address of the Remote Desktop host computer, concatenated with a colon and the port number. For example, if you edited the Registry of the host computer named NANC511 with an IP address of 192.168.0.8 and changed the port number to 4233, then you would type either **NANC511:4233** or **192.168.0.8:4233** into the Computer text box of the Remote Desktop Connection dialog box.

Keep in mind that a Remote Desktop connection functions across any TCP/IP link, whether dial-up, local, or otherwise. When you configure a host computer, be sure to add users to the Remote Desktop users group and to create an exception for Remote Desktop traffic for the Windows Firewall. You should also create the exception on the client computer. Refer to Chapter 16, "Configuring and Maintaining Network Security," for information on configuring Windows Firewall.

Configuring VPN Authentication and Settings

Connectivity is the most valuable capability in a computer. By connecting to other computers, a computer can access other information, applications, and peripheral equipment. Businesses have long since discovered that their employees will work longer hours and greatly increase their productivity when they are able to connect to the company's network from remote sites. For this reason, they provide Remote Access Service (RAS) servers with VPN servers and Internet connections, and may offer dial-up networking with modems when needed. When connecting to a corporate network using VPN (or dialing up with a modem), the user can open files and folders, use applications, print to printers, and pretty much use the network just as if he or she were connected to the network through its network adapter.

When you configure a VPN connection in Windows 10, it will typically negotiate protocols with the server automatically. You can configure which protocols to use manually. Organizations need to protect the entire connection for remote users on VPN connections, including routing information for the internal network. The encryption, therefore, is performed at the network level between the two endpoints, namely the Windows 10 client and the device or server at the other end.

The following are standard protocols used to create a VPN connection:

- **Point-to-Point (PPP) VPN Protocol:** The oldest of the protocols, it uses Microsoft Point-to-Point Encryption (MPPE) to secure the connection data. It uses 128-bit keys and is considered to have weaker security than others.

- **Point-to-Point Tunneling Protocol (PPTP):** A protocol used to transmit private network data across a public network in a secure fashion. PPTP supports multiple networking protocols and creates a secure VPN connection.

- **Layer 2 Tunneling Protocol (L2TP):** Similar to PPTP, it improves security by including support for IPsec. Used with IP Security (IPsec), it creates a secure VPN connection encrypted with either 3DES or AES, which can use up to 256 bit keys.

- **Secure Socket Tunneling Protocol (SSTP):** A newer tunneling protocol that uses Secure Hypertext Transfer Protocol (HTTPS) over TCP port 443 and is able to transmit traffic across firewalls and proxy servers that might block PPTP and L2TP traffic. SSTP uses Secure Sockets Layer (SSL) for transport-level security that includes enhanced key negotiation, encryption, and integrity checking.

- **Internet Key Exchange Version 2 (IKEv2):** A tunneling protocol that uses IPsec Tunnel Mode over UDP port 500. This combination of protocols also supports strong authentication and encryption methods.

Understanding Remote Access

When you set up a new connection or network in Windows 10, the Connect to a Workplace option allows you to set up dial-up networking connections using a modem or any other type of connection—between two different computers, between a computer and a private network, between a computer and the Internet, and from a computer through the Internet to a private network using a tunneling protocol. You can share both dial-up connections and connections configured as VPN connections using Internet Connection Sharing (ICS). All these functions and features offer different ways of connecting computers across large geographical distances.

When a computer connects to a remote access server, it performs functions nearly identical to logging on locally while connected to the network. The major difference is the method of data transport at the physical level, because the data is likely to travel across a rather slow telephone line for dial-up and some Internet connections. Another difference between a local network user and a remote access user is the way that the user's identification is authenticated. If using Remote Authentication Dial-In User Service (RADIUS), the RADIUS server takes on the task of authenticating users and passing along their data to the directory service(s) in which the users' accounts are listed.

Don't confuse remote access with remote control. Remote access is the capability to connect across a dial-up or VPN link, and from that point forward, to be able to gain access to and use network files, folders, printers, and other resources identically to the way a user could do on a local network computer. Remote control, on the other hand, is the capability to connect to a computer remotely, and then, through the use of features such as Remote Desktop or Remote Assistance discussed earlier in this chapter, control the computer as if you were at the console.

Establishing VPN Connections and Authentication

We've already touched on VPN connections. The way a VPN works is rather interesting. The private network is connected to the Internet. One method for establishing a VPN or DirectAccess services is for an administrator to set up a VPN server or appliance that sits between the private network and the Internet (also known as *dual-homed*). When a remote computer connects to the Internet, whether via dial-up or other means, the remote computer can connect to the VPN server by using TCP/IP. Then the tunneling protocols encapsulate the data inside the TCP/IP packets that are sent to the VPN server. After the data is received at the VPN server, it strips off the encapsulating headers and footers and then transmits the packets to the appropriate network servers and resources.

The tunneling protocols, although similar and all supported by Windows 10 and Windows Server 2016, act somewhat differently. PPTP incorporates security for encryption and authentication in the protocol by using Microsoft Point-to-Point Encryption (MPPE). SSTP encrypts data by encapsulating PPP traffic over the Secure Sockets Layer (SSL) channel of the HTTPS protocol. IKEv2 encapsulates datagrams by using IPsec ESP or AH headers. L2TP does not provide encryption on its own. Instead, you must use IPsec to secure the data.

To establish the VPN client connection on Windows 10, use the following procedure. To follow along with this exercise and to test it, you should have a client computer and a VPN server that can both connect to the Internet. These two computers should not be connected in any other way than through the Internet.

Step 1.   Open the Network and Sharing Center by searching for it in the Search bar or Cortana under Settings, or by right-clicking the network icon in the Notification area and selecting **Open Network and Sharing Center**.

Step 2.   Click **Set Up a New Connection or Network**.

Step 3.   The Set Up a Connection or Network page shown in Figure 15-6 offers several connection options. Select **Connect to a Workplace** and then click **Next**.

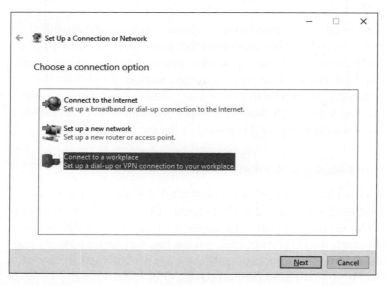

Figure 15-6   Set Up a Connection or Network Dialog Box Enabling You to Connect to Several Types of Networks

Step 4.   You are given the option for selecting a dial-up or a VPN connection. Click **Use My Internet Connection (VPN)**.

Step 5.   On the Connect to a Workplace page (see Figure 15-7), type the name of the organization and the Internet address (FQDN, IPv4 address, or IPv6 address). You can select to use a smart card if it is required, and if you check the Remember My Credentials box, your authentication information for the connection will be saved by Credential Manager. The Allow Other People to Use This Connection check box will configure the connection for use with Internet Connection Sharing (ICS). When you have finished with the options, click **Create**.

Figure 15-7   Internet Address and Destination Name of the Network You Want to Access

Step 6.   Windows displays the Networks Settings pane after it creates the connection. Click the new connection and then click the **Connect** button that appears to start the connection.

Step 7.   On the Network Authentication prompt, type the username and password you will use to access the network. If this is a domain-based network, type the domain name with the username in the box, as depicted in Figure 15-8. Click **OK** to connect.

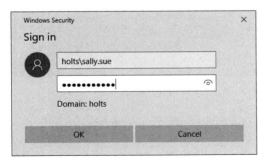

Figure 15-8   Entering Authentication Credentials for Connecting to the VPN

Step 8. To connect later to your connection, access the Action Center, click **Start > Settings**, and then select **Network & Internet**. The network status page is displayed by default, showing your current connection. To connect to your VPN connection, click the **VPN** menu option and then click the VPN connection to use, which displays the connection options as shown in Figure 15-9. Click the **Connect** button to connect to the network.

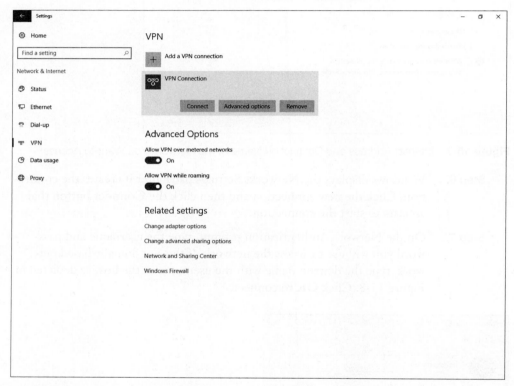

Figure 15-9 Connecting to a VPN Connection from the Network Settings Page

After you have set up a VPN connection, you can modify its properties if required. From the Network Connections Control Panel applet, right-click the connection and choose **Properties**. The connection's Properties dialog box consists of the following tabs, each with different types of configurations:

- **General:** This tab enables you to specify the hostname or IP address of the destination, and the need to connect to a public network such as the Internet before attempting to set up the VPN connection.

- **Options:** This tab provides access to disable credential saving and a setting to determine how long to allow an idle connection before closing the network (or hanging up). The PPP Settings button enables you to use Link Control Protocol (LCP) extensions and software compression, or to negotiate multilink (use of multiple dial-up lines for increased transmission speed) for single-link connections.

- **Security:** As you can guess, the Security tab lets you select the type of VPN (automatic, PPTP, L2TP/IPsec, SSTP, or IKEv2), the authentication protocols to use, including EAP (for smart cards, certificates already on this computer, or trusted root certification authorities), CHAP, MS-CHAPv2, PAP, and so on. You can also configure encryption to be optional, required, or required at maximum strength.

- **Networking:** This tab enables you to specify the use of TCP/IPv4 and TCP/IPv6, as well as File and Printer Sharing for Microsoft Networks, and the Client for Microsoft Networks. Click **Install** to install additional features, including network clients, services, and protocols. To install these features, you should have an installation disc.

- **Sharing:** This tab lets you configure ICS to share the connection with other computers on your local network. You can also select options to establish dial-up connections when other computers attempt to access the Internet, or allow other users on the network to control or disable a shared connection. Click **Settings** to configure ICS.

VPN Connection Security

As already mentioned, any of PPTP, L2TP, SSTP, or IKEv2 enable you to set up a tunneled connection from a remote location across the Internet to servers in your office network and access shared resources as though you were located on the network itself. Recall that PPTP, SSTP, and IKEv2 include built-in security for encryption and authentication, whereas L2TP does not. You must use IPsec to secure data being sent across an L2TP connection.

An issue that you should be aware of concerns the encryption levels used by client and server computers when establishing a VPN connection. If these encryption levels fail to match, you might receive an error code 741 accompanied by the message stating The Local Computer Does Not Support the Required Encryption Type or an error code 742 with the message The Remote Server Does Not Support the Required Encryption Type. This problem occurs if the server is using an encryption level different from that of your mobile computer. Older servers might be using Rivest Cipher 4 (RC4) encryption at a level of either 40 bits or 56 bits. By default,

Windows Vista and later clients, including Windows 10, use 128-bit encryption. You can try modifying the encryption level on the client to resolve this:

Step 1.   From the Network and Sharing Center, click **Change Adapter Settings** to access the Network Connections dialog box.

Step 2.   Right-click the desired VPN connection and select **Properties**.

Step 3.   On the Security tab of the VPN Connection Properties dialog box shown in Figure 15-10, select **Maximum Strength Encryption (Disconnect if Server Declines)** and then click **OK**.

Step 4.   Attempt your connection again.

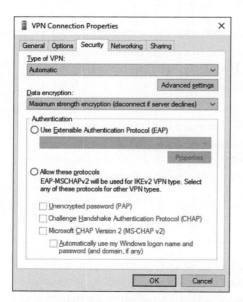

Figure 15-10   Security Tab of the Connection's Properties Dialog Box Enabling You to Specify the Level of Encryption Used in a VPN Connection

Enabling VPN Reconnect

First introduced in Windows 7 is the VPN Reconnect feature, which utilizes IKEv2 technology to automatically reestablish a VPN connection when a user has temporarily lost her Internet connection. This avoids the need to manually reconnect to the VPN and possibly having to restart a download. VPN Reconnect can reestablish a connection as long as eight hours after the connection was lost. A user could be connected to an airport Wi-Fi connection when his flight is called for boarding; when he lands at his destination, he can reconnect and finish his download.

Use the following procedure to set up VPN Reconnect:

Step 1.   Access the Security tab of the connection's Properties dialog box as previously shown in Figure 15-10.

Step 2.   Click the **Advanced Settings** button.

Step 3.   In the Advanced Properties dialog box shown in Figure 15-11, click the **IKEv2** tab and ensure that Mobility is selected, and then select a value (30 minutes by default) in the Network Outage Time dialog box.

Step 4.   Click **OK**, and click **OK** again to close the connection's Properties dialog box.

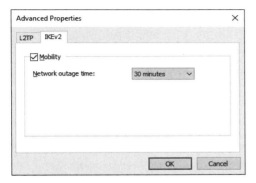

Figure 15-11   Choosing a Reconnection Time of Up to Eight Hours from the Advanced Properties Dialog Box

App-Triggered VPN, Traffic Filters, and Lockdown VPN

You have seen how to set up and configure VPN connections on Windows 10 computers and devices. The interfaces you used work with the underlying Windows VPN platform. Many users of enterprise VPN solutions may also use third-party VPN clients that administrators distribute to their users or preconfigure on their devices. For the 70-698 exam, and in order to support VPNs as a technology professional, you need to be familiar with VPN technologies and the features and functions available on Windows 10 for managing VPN connections and ensuring security.

Windows 10 includes a built-in VPN plug-in for managing VPN connections, which you learned about previously in this chapter for setting up a VPN connection. It also includes a UWP VPN plug-in platform, which you have seen at work previously in Figure 15-8 and Figure 15-9. These plug-ins are built on top of the Windows VPN platform. In this section you learn more about the VPN platform clients and some additional features that you can configure.

Table 15-4 summarizes some of the general aspects and capabilities of VPN technologies used on Windows 10. The built-in plug-in and the UWP VPN plug-in platform are both built on top of the Windows VPN platform.

Table 15-4   VPN Platforms for Windows 10 Computers

Characteristics	Built-in Plug-in	UWP VPN Plug-in Platform	Third-Party Win32 App
Description	Uses desktop Windows and control panel applets for management and configuration.	Based on UWP APIs. Third parties can create app-containerized plug-ins.	Win32 NDIS kernel.
Protocols	Native protocols: L2TP, PPTP, SSTP, IKEv2.	Native protocols: L2TP, PPTP, IKEv2.	May use native protocols or third-party or proprietary protocols.
Platform	Windows 10 desktop or laptop computer.	Available on all Windows 10 devices.	Only for desktop.
Features	All Windows 10 VPN features.	All Windows 10 VPN features.	Does not take advantage of new VPN features.

App-Triggered VPN

There are a number of new features in Windows 10 to auto-trigger VPN. With auto-triggered VPN, users do not have to manually connect when VPN is needed to access organizational resources. There are three types of auto-trigger rules:

- **App trigger:** You can configure VPN profiles in Windows 10 to connect to VPN automatically whenever one of the apps you specify is launched. Desktop or UWP apps can be configured to automatically trigger a VPN connection.

- **Name-based trigger:** You can configure a name-based rule so that if a request for a resource using a specific domain name is detected, it triggers a VPN connection.

- **Always on:** If you configure a VPN connection as Always On, the VPN profile will make a connection based on any of three events: user sign-in, a network change, or the device screen is turned on or activated.

For any of these trigger types, you can also configure the trusted network detection feature, which will tell the VPN profile not to connect if the device is already on a trusted network. Using the combination of a VPN trigger and trusted network detection, users can use their device in the office connected to the private trusted network and travel to other locations with Internet access, and always have access to secured private organizational resources using secure communications automatically.

You can configure VPN profiles for devices in your organization using a number of tools, including System Center Configuration Manager (SCCM), Microsoft Intune, and other enterprise management tools. Use the following procedure to configure app-triggered VPN in Microsoft Intune:

Step 1. From the Policy menu in the Microsoft Intune portal, select **Configuration Policies**, and then click **Add**.

Step 2. Expand the Windows section, select the VPN Profile (Windows 10 Desktop and Mobile and later) template, and then click **Create Policy**.

Step 3. Enter a Name for the policy, a VPN Connection Name, a Connection Type, and add a server for the connection, as shown in Figure 15-12. The VPN connection also requires an Authentication method, and, depending on the connection type you select, may also require some XML code for EAP.

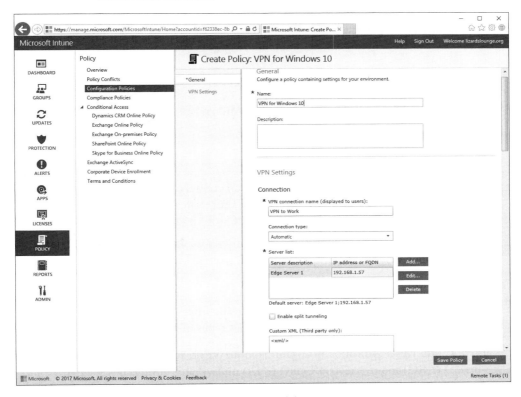

Figure 15-12 Configuring a VPN Policy in Microsoft Intune

Step 4. In the Associated Apps section, click the **Add** button, and then select the app type (Desktop or Universal), and enter the app identifier, as shown in Figure 15-13. Click **OK**.

Figure 15-13 Adding an App Filter in a Microsoft Intune VPN Policy

Step 5. Repeat Step 4 for all the apps you want to trigger the VPN connection.

Step 6. When you are satisfied with the VPN policy settings, click the **Save Policy** button.

The app identifier you use when configuring an app-triggered VPN, as shown previously in Figure 15-13, is a property that uniquely identifies an app. For Windows UWP apps, you use the Package Full Name. Desktop apps can be identified using the Product ID or GUID.

NOTE You learned about Microsoft Intune and Mobile Device Management (MDM) in Chapter 13, "Microsoft Intune." Review the section "Managing Policies" for details about Intune policies and how to create and deploy policies for your managed devices.

NOTE If you need to use EAP XML for a VPN connection, refer to the article "EAP Configuration" at https://msdn.microsoft.com/en-us/windows/hardware/commercialize/customize/mdm/eap-configuration for a technique for automatically generating the XML file required.

Traffic Filters

Windows 10 provides the capability to add traffic filters to any native Windows VPN profile. Filters allow you to control what types of traffic are allowed over the VPN. There are two types of traffic filter rules:

- **App-based rules:** You can specify a list of applications so that only traffic originating from those apps is allowed over the VPN interface.

- **Traffic-based rules:** You can use rules based on ports, IP addresses, and protocols to specify that only traffic matching the rules is allowed over the VPN interface.

You can combine many sets of rules, both app-based and traffic-based, to specify the types of traffic allowed. For instance, you can specify that your in-house accounting application must be allowed through the VPN, and access only port 3850, and that all other apps on a device can use only port 443.

You can create traffic filters for a VPN connection using the VPN policy in Microsoft Intune. The Corporate Boundaries section of the VPN policy allows you to configure rules that specify the type of network traffic. See Figure 15-14 for the dialog you would use to add a traffic filter rule to the profile.

Figure 15-14   Configuring Traffic Filters in a Microsoft Intune VPN Policy

LockDown VPN

The LockDown VPN feature in Windows 10 allows you to enforce a VPN profile on a device that allows network traffic only over the VPN interface. Users of the device would not be able to connect to the Internet or any other local network without connecting to the VPN connection you specify. LockDown VPN has the following characteristics:

- The device tries to keep the VPN always connected.

- Users of the device cannot disconnect the VPN.

- Users of the device cannot delete or modify the VPN profile.

- The VPN LockDown profile uses forced tunnel connection.

- If the device cannot connect to the VPN, all network traffic is blocked.

- You can create only a single VPN LockDown profile on a device.

- The VPN LockDown profile is limited to using only the IKEv2 connection type.

You can only configure the LockDown VPN feature using an MDM solution, such as Microsoft Intune, by deploying a ProfileXML configuration profile. There is no way to configure this type of VPN profile using PowerShell or Group Policy.

Configuring DirectAccess

Microsoft has introduced some new technologies to enable remote access requirements that make it easier to configure and manage for administrators and the mobile workforce. Microsoft introduced DirectAccess and Remote Desktop Gateway (RD Gateway) for Windows Server 2008 R2. The RD Gateway component of RDS enables employees on the public Internet to securely access Windows desktops and applications that are hosted in a Microsoft Azure cloud service. You will not need to know the details of server-side configuration of these technologies for the 70-698 exam, but you should be familiar with the features of RDS and DirectAccess, how they work, and when they should be used in an organization.

Remote Desktop Services (RDS)

Remote Desktop Services (RDS) is a platform for building virtualization services for customers, including delivering individualized application, secure mobile, and remote desktop access, and enabling users to run applications and the desktop from the cloud.

RDS can be deployed on-premises with Windows Server 2016, or by using Microsoft Azure for cloud deployments. RDS can be used to set up session-based virtualization or virtual desktop infrastructure (VDI), or both. You can publish desktops to provide users with a full desktop experience with applications installed and managed centrally in an enterprise environment. Using RemoteApps, you can specify individual applications hosted on the virtualized machines, while users use their own desktops to run the applications as if they were locally installed.

DirectAccess

DirectAccess, first introduced as a feature with Windows 7 and Windows Server 2008 R2, enables users to directly connect to corporate networks from any Internet connection. When enabled, a user can access network resources as though he were actually at the office. DirectAccess uses IPv6 over IPsec to create a seamless, bidirectional, secured tunnel between the user's computer and the office network, without the need for a virtual private network (VPN) connection.

The benefits of DirectAccess include the following:

- **Improved mobile workforce productivity:** Users have the same connectivity to network resources whether they are in or out of the office. Users can be connected through any Internet connection, such as a client's office, a home, a hotel, an airport Wi-Fi connection, and so on.

- **Improved management of remote users:** You can apply Group Policy updates and software updates to remote computers whenever they are connected by means of DirectAccess.

- **Improved network security:** DirectAccess uses IPv6 over IPsec to enable encrypted communications and secured authentication of the computer to the corporate network even before the user has logged on. IPv6 also provides globally routable IP addresses for remote access clients. Encryption is provided using Data Encryption Standard (DES), which uses a 56-bit key, and Triple DES (3DES), which uses three 56-bit keys.

- **Access control capabilities:** You can choose to allow only specific applications or subnets of the corporate network or to allow unlimited network access by DirectAccess users.

- **Simplified network traffic:** Unnecessary traffic on the corporate network is reduced because DirectAccess separates its traffic from other Internet traffic. You can specify that DirectAccess clients send all traffic through the Direct-Access server.

Windows Server 2008 R2 and later includes the required server functionality to operate DirectAccess. Optionally, you can also include Microsoft Forefront Unified Access Gateway (UAG). This option provides enhanced security within and outside the corporate network, enabling DirectAccess for IPv4-only applications and resources on the network. Security is improved on the DirectAccess server, and built-in wizards and tools simplify deployment and reduce configuration errors.

Windows 10 DirectAccess client computers must be running Windows Enterprise edition; it is not available in Windows 10 Home or Windows 10 Pro. DirectAccess can be deployed using either basic or advanced deployments. In the basic deployment scenario, a single DirectAccess server is used, with no need for infrastructure settings such as a certificate authority or Active Directory security groups. You should be aware of the following prerequisites for deploying a basic DirectAccess server:

- The server must be running Windows Server 2008 R2 or later.

- Windows firewall must be enabled on all profiles.

- Basic deployment of DirectAccess is supported only when all client computers are running Windows 10, Windows 8, or Windows 8.1.

- ISATAP is not supported. You must use native IPv6.

- Two-factory authentication is not supported; domain credentials are required for authentication.

- DirectAccess will be deployed to all mobile computers in the current domain.

- The DirectAccess server is the Network Location Server.

- Changing policies outside of the DirectAccess management console or Power-Shell is not supported.

> **NOTE** For more details on deploying DirectAccess using the basic deployment method, access the article "Install and Configure Basic DirectAccess" at https://technet.microsoft.com/windows-server-docs/networking/remote-access/directaccess/single-server-wizard/install-and-configure-basic-directaccess and follow the references for the steps involved.

Deploying DirectAccess with advanced settings has more infrastructure requirements, but provides greater flexibility in how DirectAccess is configured and managed in a large enterprise. The requirements for deploying DirectAccess using the advanced scenario include the following:

- Public key infrastructure (PKI) must be deployed in the domain.

- Windows firewall must be enabled on all profiles.

- Windows Server 2008 R2 or later must be used.

- DirectAccess clients must be running either Windows Server 2008 R2 or later, Windows 7 Enterprise or Ultimate, Windows 8 or 8.1 Enterprise, Windows 10 Enterprise LTSB, or Windows 10 Enterprise.

- Changing policies by using a feature other than the DirectAccess management console or Windows PowerShell is not supported.

- Separating NAT64/DNS64 and IPHTTPS server roles on another server is not supported. These roles must be run on the DirectAccess server.

> **NOTE** For more details on deploying DirectAccess using the advanced deployment method, access the article "Deploy a Single DirectAccess Server with Advanced Settings" at https://technet.microsoft.com/en-us/windows-server-docs/networking/remote-access/directaccess/single-server-advanced/deploy-a-single-directaccess-server-with-advanced-settings.

After your infrastructure and servers have been configured for DirectAccess, including the Group Policy Objects for DirectAccess clients, the clients will have DirectAccess capability after they have updated Group Policy settings. To update them right away, run the **gpupdate /force** command-line command from an administrative command prompt.

Configuring Remote Management

Performing administration and management tasks on a number of Windows servers and Windows 10 clients can be a challenge even in a small organization. As the number of computers grows, the task can become daunting without the capability to remotely manage computers from a central location.

Microsoft has provided a number of network technologies and tools to assist administrators in the many management and support tasks needed to keep their systems secure and performing correctly. In this section you learn some principles to guide you in selecting the right tools for the job in your organization. You also learn about the remote management command-line tools that you can use to automate administration tasks across a set of computers, saving you a significant amount of time. You need to know how to configure these tools ahead of time so that you can perform any management tasks from a central location.

In this section you also learn about Remote Assistance, and how users can request help when needed. Instead of traveling to their location, Remote Assistance enables you to help them from a remote location.

Choosing the Right Tools

The capability to remotely manage computers and servers is vital in large enterprises. If you must physically visit a computer to perform routine administrative tasks, you will either need a large staff of technicians or you will get so far behind that you can end up with security vulnerabilities. Microsoft continues to expand and improve the capabilities of remote management tools with each iteration of Windows, and with Windows 10, remote management capabilities are continuing to improve.

You learned about the Remote Server Administration Tools (RSAT) in Chapter 4, "Managing Windows in an Enterprise," and how to install the tools on a Windows 10 computer to manage servers, domains, Group Policies, and other remote management tasks. You also learned in Chapter 13, "Microsoft Intune," about using cloud services such as Microsoft Intune and Office 365 to remotely manage devices and computers.

In this chapter you were introduced to Remote Desktop configuration and how to use Remote Desktop to connect to remote computers. Remote Desktop allows you to log on to any computer in your enterprise that includes a full GUI desktop, and perform any administration task.

In this section you learn about some additional tools that allow you to not only remotely administer servers and computers, but to perform administration tasks on groups of computers all at once, and tools that enable you to write scripts to automate routine administration and management tasks using the command line.

Table 15-5 lists some of the remote management tools available in Windows 10 or Windows Server 2016.

Table 15-5   Remote Management Tools

Tool Name	Description	Command Line or GUI
Remote Desktop	Connect to a computer remotely and log in to the GUI as if you are in front of the computer console. Cannot be used on Windows Server Core.	GUI
MMC	Microsoft Management Console (MMC) has many snap-ins that can connect to remote computers for managing settings.	GUI
WinRM	Windows Remote Management (WinRM) is a platform for remote management. It enables the use of WinRS, event forwarding for MMC Event Viewer, and Windows PowerShell remoting.	Command line platform
WinRS	WinRS, or Windows Remote Shell, allows you to manage and execute programs remotely. Requires WinRM enabled on the remote computer.	Command line
PowerShell Remoting	PowerShell remoting features allow you to remotely run PowerShell commands. Require WinRM enabled on the remote computer.	Command line

The tool to use depends entirely on the administration scenario. If you need to check the Windows Event log for many computers, you can use the MMC and Event Viewer to collect logs from many computers into a single view on your local computer. Performing complex configuration tasks or troubleshooting an issue on one or a few computers is probably best handled using Remote Desktop or Remote Assistance.

You should consider using Group Policy Objects for many configuration tasks when you need to modify or enforce a specific configuration on a group of computers. When using a GPO is not practical or the settings you want are not available, using a command-line tool or script enabled by WinRM may be the best choice. WinRM and PowerShell Remoting will also be your tool of choice for administration of remote Windows Server Core installations. Because Windows Server Core does not include a desktop GUI, you will not be able to use Remote Desktop. If you plan on significant use of command-line tools for remote management, be aware that WinRM must be enabled on each computer.

Windows Remote Management (WinRM)

Microsoft has provided Windows Remote Management (WinRM) to assist you in managing hardware on a network that includes machines that run a diverse mix of operating systems. WinRM is the Microsoft implementation of the WS-Management Protocol, which was developed by an independent group of manufacturers as a public standard for remote computer management. You can use WinRM to monitor and manage remote computers.

WinRM is a series of command-line tools that operate from an administrative command prompt. Use the following procedure to set up the Remote Management Service:

Step 1.   Right-click **Start** and choose **Command Prompt (Admin)**.

Step 2.   Accept the UAC prompt, type **winrm quickconfig**, and then press Enter.

Step 3.   You receive the output shown in Figure 15-15. Type **y** twice as shown in the figure to enable the granting of remote administrative rights to local users, create a WinRM listener on HTTP, and enable a firewall exception that allows WinRM packets to pass.

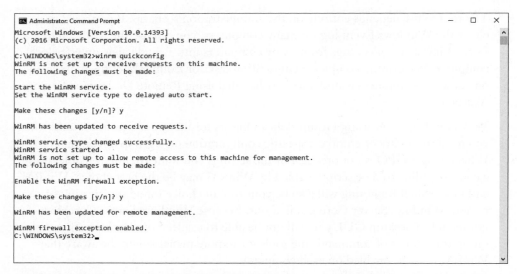

Figure 15-15 Enabling WinRM from an Administrative Command Prompt or an Administrative Windows PowerShell Session

You can also configure WinRM by means of Group Policy. This enables you to enable WinRM for all computers in the same AD DS site, domain, or organizational unit (OU). Access the Computer Configuration\Administrative Templates\ Windows Components\Windows Remote Management node. This node contains two subnodes: WinRM Client and WinRM Service. The WinRM Client policies deal with permitted authentication methods and available trusted hosts, whereas the WinRM Service policies deal with how the service listens on the network for requests, as well as client authentication methods that it will accept and whether unencrypted messages are permitted. You can also enable or disable an HTTP listener. For more information on the available policies in each of these subnodes, double-click any policy and consult the Help text provided. If you use Group Policy, remember to enable rules for Windows Firewall. You need to enable two inbound rules: the Windows Remote Management service rule and the Network List Manager Policies rule. You can learn about details of working with Windows Firewall in Chapter 16, "Configuring and Maintaining Network Security."

After you've set up WinRM, you are able to use either of two tools included in the Remote Management Service: Windows Remote Shell and Windows PowerShell. We take a quick look at each of these tools in turn. See the next section for use of Windows PowerShell.

> **NOTE** For more information about Windows Remote Management, refer to "About Windows Remote Management" at http://msdn.microsoft.com/en-us/library/aa384291(VS.85).aspx.

Using Windows Remote Shell

Windows Remote Shell (WinRS) enables you to execute command-line utilities or scripts against a remote computer. For example, you can run the **ipconfig** command on a remote computer named Server1 by typing the following command:

```
winrs -r:Server1 ipconfig
```

You can specify the NetBIOS name of a computer located on the local subnet or the fully qualified domain name (FQDN) of a computer on a remote network. You can also specify user credentials under which the WinRS command will be executed, by using the following command:

```
Winrs -r:Server1 -u:user_name -p:password command
```

In this command, *user_name* is the username in whose context you want to run the command, *password* is the password associated with this username, and *command* is the command to be run. You can use this syntax to remotely execute any command that you can normally run locally using the **cmd.exe** command prompt. If you don't specify the password, Windows Remote Shell prompts you for the password. You can also use http:// or https:// against the computer name in the **-r** parameter to specify an HTTP or Secure HTTP connection to a remote computer specified by its URL or IP address.

> **NOTE** For more information on using WinRS, open a command prompt and type **winrs /?**. You can also reference the "winrs" article at https://technet.microsoft.com/en-us/windows-server-docs/management/windows-commands/winrs.

Using Windows PowerShell and MMCs for Remote Management

Windows PowerShell, currently in version 5.1 for Windows 10, is a task-based command-line scripting interface that enables you to perform a large number of tasks and is particularly useful for remote management. PowerShell includes the Integrated Scripting Environment (ISE), which assists you in the task of writing, testing, and executing scripts. You can control and automate the administration of remote Windows computers and their applications. Installed by default in Windows 7 and later, as well as Windows Server version 2008 R2 and later, PowerShell also enables you to perform automated troubleshooting of remote computers. You can even read from and write to the Registry as though its hives were regular drives; for example, HKLM for HKEY_LOCAL_MACHINE and HKCU for HKEY_CURRENT_USER.

> **NOTE**   You can also use PowerShell 5.0 on computers running Windows 7 (with Service Pack 1)/Server 2008 R2 with Service Pack 1/2012 or newer. Any scripts you write using PowerShell 5.0 can then be run on computers using any of these operating systems. To install PowerShell 5.0, download the Windows Management Framework 5.0, which includes PowerShell, PowerShell Desired State Configuration (DSC), WMI, WinRM, and other tools.

PowerShell and PowerShell ISE

Windows PowerShell borrows from the functionality of the object-oriented Microsoft .NET programming model. Objects used by this mode have well-defined properties and methods; for example, a file object has properties such as its size, modification date and time, and so on. All commands issued to PowerShell are in the form of a command-let, or *cmdlet*, which is an expression of the form *verb-object*: for example, **Get-process**. You can run a cmdlet on its own or build these tools into complex scripts that enable you to perform almost unlimited tasks against any computer on the network. The following are several verbs used in many cmdlets:

- **Get:** Retrieves data

- **Set:** Modifies or establishes output data

- **Format:** Formats data

- **Select:** Selects specific properties of an object or set of objects. Also finds text in strings, files, or XML documents

- **Out:** Outputs data to a specific location

You can start a PowerShell session from the command line by typing **powershell**, or from the PowerShell ISE in the Start menu, or by searching for **powershell** in the Search bar or Cortana. Starting PowerShell ISE from the Start menu icon will start a PowerShell command session with helpful tools for writing and testing scripts, similar to that shown in Figure 15-16.

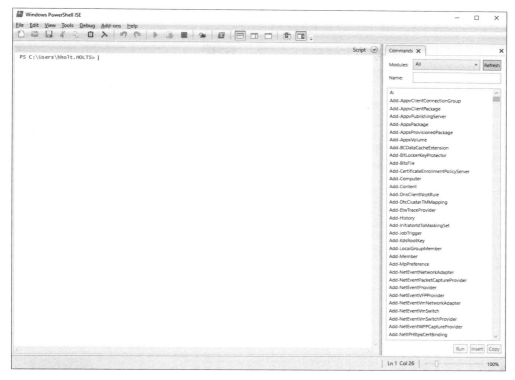

Figure 15-16   Executing a Large Number of Cmdlets from a PowerShell Session

Help functions are provided for all available cmdlets, but you must run the Update-Help command as an administrator to download the help files and install them for use on the PowerShell command line. After you have the help files loaded, you can type **help** *verb-**, where *verb* is an available PowerShell verb, including (but not restricted to) those mentioned in the previous paragraph.

You can also get help on PowerShell objects by typing **help** **-object*, where *object* is a PowerShell object. See the next paragraph for an example of obtaining help for the **content** object.

A new feature in PowerShell 3.0 and later is the **-Online** option of the **help** command. This is useful if the help files are not installed, or when you do not want to install the help files on the local computer. The **Get-Help -Online** feature opens the online version of the help topic directly in the default web browser. For instance, running the PowerShell command **Get-Help Get-Process -Online** will display the help in Edge, as shown in Figure 15-17.

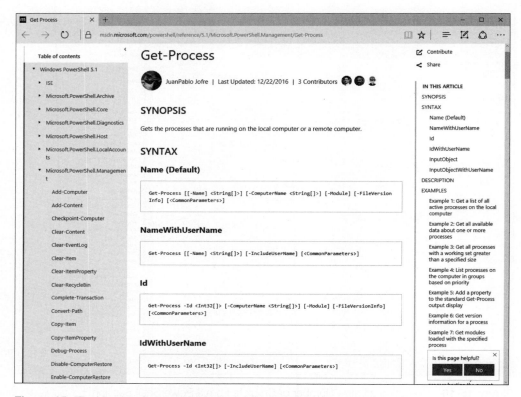

Figure 15-17   Viewing Online Help for PowerShell Cmdlets

When you write a cmdlet, you can populate the **HelpUri** property of your cmdlet class so that others that use the script can obtain help information from the Internet or the local intranet on the organization's servers.

PowerShell 3.0 and later includes the PowerShell Integrated Scripting Environment (ISE), which is a PowerShell graphical user interface (GUI) that enables you to run commands and write, edit, run, test, and debug scripts in the same window. Access this tool from either the Administrative Tools menu or the PowerShell ISE link when searching for **powershell** in the Search bar or Cortana. PowerShell ISE also includes debugging, multiline editing capabilities, selective execution, and many other components that aid you in writing and debugging complex scripts. An example of PowerShell ISE is shown previously in Figure 15-16.

The PowerShell ISE also includes the Intellisense feature to help you put together PowerShell commands. Start typing in the ISE prompt, and whenever you type a dash (–), the ISE will pop up a list of possible commands, or parameters. You can also take advantage of Intellisense to help you complete commands by typing a few characters and then pressing the Tab key. Intellisense will try to guess the command you want and fill in the rest. If more than one command matches the first few characters you type, Intellisense will assume that you want the first command alphabetically.

To run a PowerShell command against a remote computer, use the following command:

```
Icm computername {powershell-cmd}
```

In this command, **Icm** is a short-hand alias for the **Invoke-Command** cmdlet, *computername* is the name of the computer you are running the command against, and *{powershell-cmd}* is the command being run.

PowerShell Remoting

You can use PowerShell to automate management tasks on any computer in your network or with connectivity. PowerShell Remoting works with WinRM to enable scripting support for remote management tasks.

You can enable PowerShell Remoting on any Windows computer with PowerShell 3.0 or later installed using the **Enable-PSRemoting** command from an Administrative PowerShell command prompt. Because PowerShell Remoting relies on WinRM, the cmdlet will also perform the WinRM autoconfiguration tasks and enable other features required. The cmdlet performs all the following setup tasks:

- Starts the WS-Management service and sets the startup type to Automatic

- Creates a listener to accept remote requests for PowerShell Remoting commands

- Enables firewall exceptions for WS-Management

- Registers and enables the PowerShell session configurations

- Modifies the security descriptor for all session configurations to enable remote access

- Restarts the WS-Management service

After configuring PowerShell Remoting, you can use PowerShell Remoting commands to manage remote computers in a trusted domain. If you want to manage remote computers in other domains, or computers that are not domain joined, you will also need to add the remote computer to the list of trusted hosts. To do so, you use the **winrm** command. For example, to add a remote computer named Win-10Pro01 to the list of trusted hosts on the local computer, open an administrative command prompt and type the following:

```
winrm set winrm/config/client @{TrustedHosts="Win10Pro01"}
```

You can then use PowerShell Remoting commands on Win10Pro01. You need to repeat the command for any remote computers that are not part of the local domain.

This is a very powerful remote management tool. For instance, suppose you want to check the free disk space on a remote computer. You can query the status of any WMI object using the PowerShell Get-WMIObject cmdlet. You can use the following command to get free space on all the logical disks:

```
Invoke-Command {Get-WMIObject win32_logicaldisk}
```

The output, as shown in Figure 15-18, displays the disks available on the remote computer, the total size, and the free space. You could write a PowerShell command script to read a list of remote computers, run the command on each one, and create a file you can check each week to check for potential storage issues on all the computers you manage.

You can perform this type of query on any WMI object, and there are many related to hardware devices, operating system parameters, Windows objects, and Registry settings. You can get a complete list using Get-WMIObject -List. As you can see, using PowerShell with its Remoting capabilities provides a wealth of administration tooling for managing Windows computers.

There are also many PowerShell cmdlets that you can run on remote computers even if they have not been configured for WinRM. The **Get-WmiObject** cmdlet described earlier is one example of these types of commands. Other examples include **Restart-Computer**, **Test-Connection**, and **Get-EventLog**.

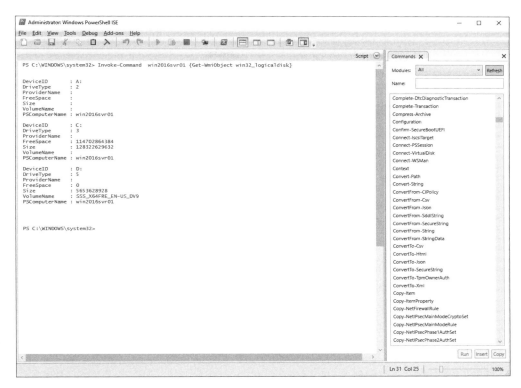

Figure 15-18   Query Information About Logical Disks on Remote Computers Using PowerShell Remoting

NOTE   For more information on all aspects of Windows PowerShell, start with the "Windows PowerShell Reference" at https://msdn.microsoft.com/en-us/library/ms714469(v=vs.85).aspx, and the resource links available from there. For more details on PowerShell Remoting, refer to the article "Running Remote Commands" at https://msdn.microsoft.com/en-us/powershell/scripting/core-powershell/running-remote-commands.

Using MMC Snap-ins for Remote Management

Microsoft's Windows Remote Management framework is also used to enable many of the Microsoft Management Console snap-ins to work remotely for many administrative tasks. For instance, the Computer Management snap-in works well for managing Windows services, for scheduling tasks, and for performing Disk Management tasks on any remote computer where WinRM has been enabled.

Recall from the previous section that enabling WinRM, using either PowerShell or the **WinRM quickconfig** command, will enable the firewall rules for WinRS and PowerShell Remoting. Many of the MMC snap-ins use different protocols and ports and need their own firewall rules before they will work remotely. The rules for these tools need to be enabled using the following procedure:

Step 1.   Right-click the **Start** button and select **Control Panel**.

Step 2.   In the Search Control Panel box, type **firewall**, and then click **Allow an App or Feature Through Windows Firewall**.

Step 3.   Click the **Change Settings** button.

Step 4.   Make sure the check box is selected next to the apps with the following names, as desired for the remote management tasks you want to enable:

- **Performance Logs and Alerts:** Allows viewing performance information from the Performance Monitor snap-in.

- **Remote Event Log Management:** Allows viewing and managing Windows logs using the Event Viewer snap-in.

- **Remote Scheduled Tasks Management:** Allows viewing, managing, and running scheduled tasks using the Scheduled Tasks snap-in.

- **Remote Service Management:** Allows viewing, starting, stopping, and changing startup configuration of Windows services using the Services snap-in.

- **Remote Volume Management:** Allows using the Disk Management snap-in to manage disks and volumes on remote computers.

- **Windows Firewall Remote Management:** Allows the use of the Windows Firewall with Advanced Security snap-in to manage firewall rules and settings.

Step 5.   Click the **OK** button to save your settings.

The computer is now ready to allow MMC snap-ins to connect from remote computers. To connect to a remote computer from a network-enabled MMC snap-in, right-click the snap-in name in the left pane, and then select **Connect to Another Computer**. In the resulting dialog box, type the name of the remote computer into the **Another Computer** box, and then click **OK**.

Some snap-ins, such as the Event Viewer, allow you to specify an account name to use when authenticating to the remote computer, as shown in Figure 15-19. This may be needed in a workgroup environment or when connecting to a computer joined to a different domain.

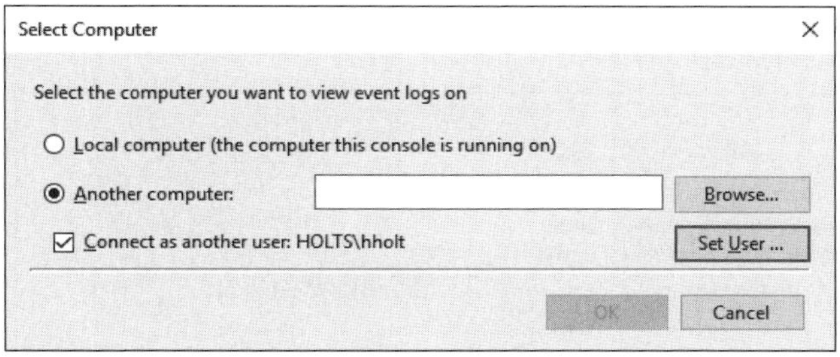

Figure 15-19 Connecting to a Remote Computer from the Event Viewer MMC Snap-in

Remote Assistance

First introduced with Windows XP, Remote Assistance allows a user running a Windows 10 computer on a network to request assistance online; it also allows for an expert to offer assistance remotely. Regardless of how the session is initiated, the result is that the expert can remotely view the user's console and provide assistance to the user by taking control of the session, or the expert can view the session and give specific directions on how to fix the problem the user is experiencing. Beginning with Windows 7, Remote Assistance includes the Easy Connect option, which uses the Peer Name Resolution Protocol (PNRP) to send the Remote Assistance invitation across the Internet. Easy Connect provides a password that you must provide separately to the other individual (for example, by making a phone call).

The requirements for Remote Assistance are that both computers must be configured to use it. If using an AD DS domain, Group Policy for Remote Assistance must also allow the user to accept Remote Assistance offers and must list from which experts the users can accept offers. An Active Directory network also requires both users to be members of the same or trusted domains.

Windows Firewall can affect whether a user can receive Remote Assistance offers or use Remote Desktop. To configure Windows Firewall to use either or both of these features, follow these steps:

Step 1. Use any of the methods previously described in Chapter 16, "Configuring and Maintaining Network Security," to open Windows Firewall.

Step 2. In the Windows Firewall applet, select **Allow an App or Feature Through Windows Firewall** from the task list on the left side of the applet.

Step 3.   On the Allow Apps to Communicate Through Windows Firewall dialog box shown in Figure 15-20, click **Change Settings** and then select the **Remote Assistance** and **Remote Desktop** check boxes under the Private and/or Domain columns.

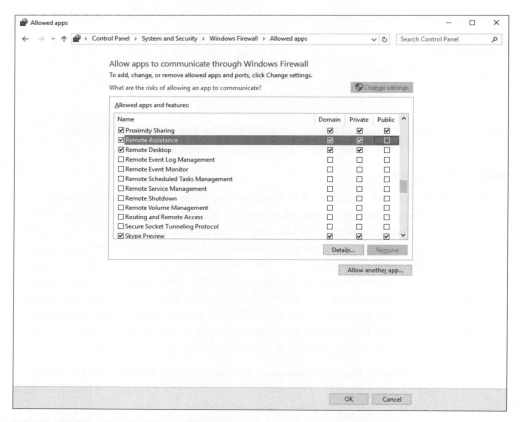

Figure 15-20   Allowing Remote Assistance and Remote Desktop to Communicate Through Windows Firewall

Step 4.   Click **OK** to close the applet.

CAUTION   Select only these options under the Public column if you need to accept requests from individuals on public networks; deselect these options after you've completed the action. If you have made changes to the port number of any service, you need to use Windows Firewall with Advanced Security to enable a firewall rule allowing that port to pass. You learn how to do this in Chapter 16.

Use the following steps to configure Windows 10 to accept Remote Assistance Offers:

Step 1.   Right-click **Start** and choose **System**. You can also open the Search bar or Cortana, type **system** into the Search box, and then select **System** from the list of settings that appears. This opens the Control Panel System applet.

Step 2.   Click the **Remote Settings** link. If you receive a User Account Control (UAC) prompt, click **Yes** to proceed.

Step 3.   Select the **Remote** tab of the System Properties dialog box, as shown in Figure 15-21.

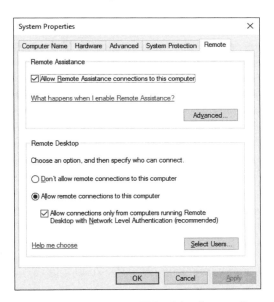

Figure 15-21   Remote Tab of the System Properties Dialog Box Enabling You to Configure Remote Assistance and Remote Desktop Settings

Step 4.   Select the **Allow Remote Assistance Connections to This Computer** option in the Remote Assistance section.

Step 5.   Click the **Advanced** button to display the Remote Assistance Settings dialog box shown in Figure 15-22 and select the **Allow This Computer to be Controlled Remotely** check box.

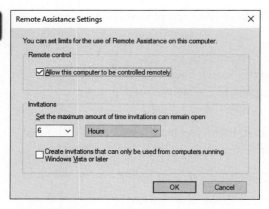

Figure 15-22   Configuring Remote Assistance Settings

Step 6.   If you want to allow connections only from computers running Windows Vista or later, or Windows Server 2008 R2 or later, select the check box labeled **Create Invitations That Can Only Be Used from Computers Running Windows Vista or Later**.

Use the following steps to send a Remote Assistance invitation to receive help from an expert user:

Step 1.   Access the System and Security category of Control Panel and select **Launch Remote Assistance** in the System section.

Step 2.   This action displays the Windows Remote Assistance dialog box shown in Figure 15-23, which enables you to either ask for help or help someone else. To ask for help, click **Invite Someone You Trust to Help You**.

Step 3.   Select one of the three options on the following page, shown in Figure 15-24:

- **Save This Invitation as a File:** Creates an invitation file in the Microsoft Remote Control Incident (MsRcIncident) format. You can use this method with Web-based email programs by sending it as an attachment.

- **Use Email to Send an Invitation:** Available only if you have configured an email account in the Mail app or installed another email client.

- **Use Easy Connect:** Uses the Peer Name Resolution Protocol to send the invitation across the Internet. The other person must also be using a Windows 7, 8.1, or 10 computer.

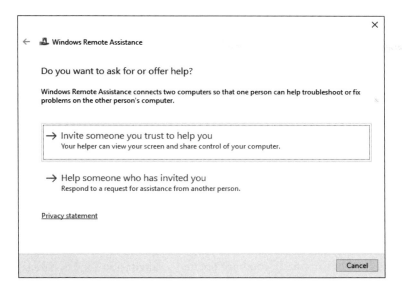

Figure 15-23   Windows Remote Assistance Enabling You to Either Ask for Help or Help Someone Else

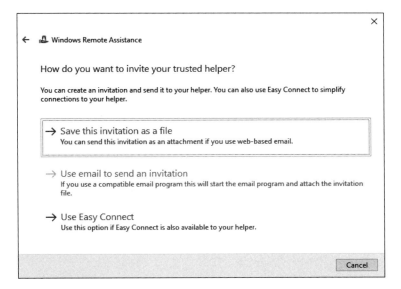

Figure 15-24   Remote Assistance Allows You to Send Invitations Three Ways

Step 4.   The next step depends on the option you've selected from Figure 15-24:

- If you save the invitation as a file, you are prompted for a name and location to save the file.

- If you use email, your email program opens and provides a prepared message including an invitation attachment. Supply the email address of the expert who will be helping, and then send the message.

- If you use Easy Connect, you receive a password that you need to provide to the expert by another means, such as by phone. You can also click **Chat** to start an online chat session. See the next section for more information on Easy Connect.

Depending on from whom you are requesting information and how you are requesting it, you should make a selection that will best reach the expert user. Whichever method you select for use, you can password-protect the session; the Easy Connect option has already done that for you. If you have created an invitation for assistance and want to cancel it before it expires, you can use the View Invitation Status option and cancel the invitation.

After the expert receives the email or the invitation file, he can open Remote Assistance on his computer and select the **Help Someone Who Has Invited You** option previously shown in Figure 15-23. He can then open the invitation file that the other person has sent and begin offering assistance to the user. He sees a Remote Assistance Expert console that provides a real-time view of the user's session. This is called a *shadow session*. If remote control has been enabled, the expert can click the Take Control button, notifying the user that the expert is asking to share control of the keyboard and mouse. The user can prevent a remote control session by pressing the Esc key, pressing Ctrl+C, or clicking the Stop Control button in the chat window.

NOTE   For more information about using Remote Assistance, including a detailed step-by-step procedure, refer to "User Remote Assistance to Let Someone Fix Your PC" at https://support.microsoft.com/en-us/instantanswers/018e0e28-050c-0f1b-1562-b15aaad6ab7d/use-remote-assistance-to-let-someone-fix-your-pc.

TIP   You can ask a user who is experiencing problems to make a recording of the steps she has taken. To do so, ask her to type **psr** into the Search bar or Cortana in Windows 10 or the Start Menu Search text box in Windows Vista or 7. Then select **Steps Recorder** or **psr.exe**. This opens the Steps Recorder. She can click **Start Record**, perform the steps that are creating the problem, and then click **Stop Record**

when she's finished. At that time she can click **Add Comment** and then save the recording as a zip file that she can attach to the Remote Assistance request email message.

Configuring and Using Easy Connect

As already introduced, Easy Connect provides a simple way to create a Remote Assistance session between two computers running Windows 7 or later without the need for sending an invitation file. The user receives a password that she needs to provide to the expert by another means such as by phone.

After the user has selected the Use Easy Connect option, the expert receives a Remote Assistance dialog box asking him to type the password that Remote Assistance provided to the other person. Using the supplied password, the expert can initiate the session, and the user's computer validates the password and invitation before the user is prompted to start the session.

The following are several problems that might be encountered when attempting to use Easy Connect:

- **The user's computer is running an older Windows version:** For Easy Connect to be available, both computers must be running Windows 7 or later.

- **Limited access to the Internet:** If access to the Internet is limited on either computer, Easy Connect is disabled. Some corporate networks might limit Internet access.

- **A router in the network doesn't support Easy Connect:** Easy Connect uses the Peer Name Resolution Protocol (PNRP) when transferring the assistance request over the Internet. Microsoft provides a utility for determining whether routers are configured for PNRP. You should install PNRP on any router running a version of Windows Server, or enable PNRP on the router being used.

Exam Preparation Tasks

Review All the Key Topics

Review the most important topics in the chapter, noted with the Key Topics icon in the outer margin of the page. Table 15-6 lists a reference of these key topics and the page numbers on which each is found.

Table 15-6   Key Topics for Chapter 15

Key Topic Element	Description	Page Number
Table 15-3	Authentication protocols for Remote Access	709
List	Remote Authentication Group Policies	712
Step List	Outlines the procedure used for creating a Remote Desktop connection	714
List	Connection protocols for VPN connections	720
Figure 15-7	Creating a VPN connection	723
Step List	Configuring VPN Reconnect	727
Step List	Configuring app-triggered VPN connections using Microsoft Intune	729
Figure 15-14	Configuring traffic filters using Microsoft Intune VPN policies	731
List	The services and settings configured when enabling PSRemoting	743
Figure 15-22	Configuring Remote Assistance	750
Step List	Requesting help using Remote Assistance	750

Complete the Tables and Lists from Memory

Print a copy of Appendix B, "Memory Tables" (found on the book's website), or at least the section for this chapter, and complete the tables and lists from memory. Appendix C, "Memory Tables Answer Key," also on the website, includes completed tables and lists to check your work.

Definitions of Key Terms

Define the following key terms from this chapter, and check your answers in the glossary.

Challenge Handshake Authentication Protocol (CHAP), Easy Connect, EAP-TTLS, Internet Key Exchange version 2 (IKEv2), Layer 2 Tunneling Protocol (L2TP), Microsoft Challenge Handshake Authentication Protocol version 2 (MS-CHAPv2), Password Authentication Protocol (PAP), Point-to-Point Protocol (PPP), Point-to-Point Tunneling Protocol (PPTP), Protected Extensible

Authentication Protocol-Transport Layer Security (PEAP-TLS), Remote
Assistance, Remote Desktop, Remote Desktop Gateway (RD Gateway), Secure
Socket Tunneling Protocol (SSTP), virtual private network (VPN), Windows
PowerShell

This chapter covers the following subjects:

- **Configuring Windows Firewall:** This section introduces you to the Windows Firewall Control Panel applet and shows you how to create exceptions that allow specified programs or ports to communicate through the firewall. It then continues with the Windows Firewall with Advanced Security Microsoft Management Console snap-in, and shows you how to create and modify the various types of rules available with this tool.

- **Configuring IPsec Security Rules:** This section continues from the previous one, showing you how to create connection rules for Windows Firewall that allow connections only for specific users or computers on the network.

- **Configuring Network Discovery:** In this section you learn about Network Discovery, network profiles, and how to configure discovery for a Windows 10 computer. The capability of Windows 10 to connect to Wi-Fi networks comes with security risks. This section looks at technologies used to ensure that private information remains private even when it is transmitted over the air where it can be picked up by anyone.

This chapter covers the following objectives for the 70-697 and 70-698 exams:

Configure networking: Configure and support IPv4 and IPv6 network settings; configure name resolution; connect to a network; configure network locations; configure network discovery; configure Wi-Fi settings; configure Wi-Fi Direct; troubleshoot network issues; configure VPN, such as app-triggered VPN, traffic filters, and lockdown VPN; configure IPsec; configure Direct Access.

Configure and maintain network security: Configure Windows Firewall, configure Windows Firewall with Advanced Security, configure connection security rules (IPsec), configure authenticated exceptions, configure network discovery.

Configure networking: Configure Windows Firewall, configure Windows Firewall with Advanced Security.

Configuring and Maintaining Network Security

In Chapter 6, "Windows 10 Networking," you learned how to set up and maintain wireless networks. The explosion of wireless networks, with many hotels and restaurants offering free Wi-Fi connections, has made it easy for cyber-criminals to go about the business of intercepting and stealing information for financial gain, political purposes, and many other nefarious endeavors. In fact, the year 2013 started out with a report that the Japanese Ministry of Agriculture, Forestry, and Fishery was hacked with the theft of more than 3,000 documents, including some of their negotiating strategies. Late in 2013, the Target department store chain was hacked, with the compromise of as many as 40 million customers in the United States and Canada. More recently, the Democratic National Committee and campaign managers were hacked and their emails released on the Internet, leading the government to conclude that Russia interfered with the 2016 national election. Anyone who works with or supports a modern computer network must be able to ensure that the network maintains an adequate level of security, so Microsoft expects you to know basic security practices as a component of the 70-697 and 70-698 exams.

"Do I Know This Already?" Quiz

The "Do I Know This Already?" quiz allows you to assess whether you should read this entire chapter or simply jump to the "Exam Preparation Tasks" section for review. If you are in doubt, read the entire chapter. Table 16-1 outlines the major headings in this chapter and the corresponding "Do I Know This Already?" quiz questions. You can find the answers in Appendix A, "Answers to the 'Do I Know This Already?' Quizzes."

Table 16-1 "Do I Know This Already?" Foundation Topics Section-to-Question Mapping

Foundation Topics Section	Questions Covered in This Section
Configuring Windows Firewall	1–5
Configuring IPsec Security Rules	6–7
Configuring Network Discovery	8–10

CAUTION   The goal of self-assessment is to gauge your mastery of the topics in this chapter. If you do not know the answer to a question or are only partially sure of the answer, you should mark that question as wrong for purposes of the self-assessment. Giving yourself credit for an answer you correctly guess skews your self-assessment results and might provide you with a false sense of security.

1. You want to configure Windows Firewall settings on your notebook computer so that others are unable to access anything on your computer. Which type of network location should you enable?

    a. Work

    b. Home

    c. Public

    d. Private

2. Which of the following actions can you perform from the Windows Firewall Control Panel applet on your Windows 10 computer? (Choose three.)

    a. Specify ports that are allowed to communicate across the Windows Firewall.

    b. Specify programs that are allowed to communicate across the Windows Firewall.

    c. Set the firewall to block all incoming connections, including those in the list of allowed programs.

    d. Configure logging settings for programs that are blocked by the firewall.

    e. Specify a series of firewall settings according to the type of network to which you are connected.

3. You open the Windows Firewall with Advanced Security snap-in and notice that a large number of firewall rules have already been preconfigured. Which of the following rule setting types does *not* include any preconfigured firewall rules?

    a. Inbound rules

    b. Outbound rules

    c. Connection security rules

    d. Monitoring rules

4. You want to configure Windows Firewall so that Windows Media Player can receive data only from connections that have been authenticated by IPsec. What setting should you configure?

   a. Run the New Inbound Rule Wizard, specify the path to Windows Media Player on the program page, and then specify the Allow the Connection if It Is Secure option.

   b. Run the New Outbound Rule Wizard, specify the path to Windows Media Player on the program page, and then specify the Allow the Connection if It Is Secure option.

   c. Run the New Connection Security Rule Wizard, specify the path to Windows Media Player on the program page, and then specify the Allow the Connection if It Is Secure option.

   d. Merely select Windows Media Player from the Allowed Programs and Features list in the Windows Firewall Control Panel applet.

5. You have configured a new inbound rule that limits connections by a specific application on your computer to only those connections that have been authenticated using IPsec. The next day when you start your application, you realize that you should have configured this rule as an outbound rule. What should you do to correct this error with the least amount of effort?

   a. Access the Scope tab of the Properties dialog box for your rule and change the scope from Inbound to Outbound.

   b. Access the Advanced tab of the Properties dialog box for your rule and change the interface type from Inbound to Outbound.

   c. Select the rule from the list of inbound rules in the Details pane of Windows Firewall with Advanced Security and drag the rule to the Outbound Rules node in the console tree.

   d. You must deactivate or delete the inbound rule you configured and then use the New Outbound Rule Wizard to set up a new rule that is specific to your application.

6. You want Windows Firewall with Advanced Security to display a notification when a program is blocked from receiving inbound connections. What should you do?

   a. Right-click **Windows Firewall with Advanced Security** at the top of the console tree and choose **Properties**. From the tab corresponding to the required profile, click **Customize** under Settings. Then ensure that the Display a Notification drop-down list is set to **Yes**.

   b. Right-click the **Inbound Rules** node in the console tree and choose **Properties**. From the tab corresponding to the required profile, click **Customize** under Settings. Then ensure that the Display a Notification drop-down list is set to **Yes**.

   c. Right-click the **Monitoring** node in the console tree and choose **Properties**. From the tab corresponding to the required profile, click **Customize** under Settings. Then ensure that the Display a Notification drop-down list is set to **Yes**.

   d. Right-click the **Firewall** subnode below the Monitoring node in the console tree and choose **Properties**. From the tab corresponding to the required profile, click **Customize** under Settings. Then ensure that the Display a Notification drop-down list is set to **Yes**.

7. You are configuring a firewall rule to allow only the Accounting group to connect to network shares on a computer. What Action in General settings should you select before specifying the group in the Remote Users setting?

   a. Allow the connection

   b. Allow the connection if it is secure

   c. Block the connection

   d. Block edge traversal

8. In which Network Profiles can you turn off Network Discovery? (Select all that apply.)

   a. Private

   b. Guest or Public

   c. Domain

   d. All Networks

9. You are configuring Network Discovery, turning it on for a network. You have also configured Network Discovery to perform automatic setup of network-connected devices. Which network profile are you configuring?

    a. Private

    b. Guest or Public

    c. Domain

    d. All Networks

10. You are offsite with a coworker and want to collaborate by creating an ad-hoc network to connect your individual Windows 10 laptops to each other. Which wireless security type will be used when the two computers establish a connection?

    a. WEP

    b. WPA-Enterprise

    c. WPA2-Enterprise

    d. WPA-Personal

    e. WPA2-Personal

Foundation Topics

Configuring Windows Firewall

Originally called the Internet Connection Firewall (ICF) in Windows XP prior to SP2, Windows Firewall is a personal firewall, stopping undesirable traffic from being accepted by the computer. Using a firewall can avoid security breaches as well as viruses that utilize port-based TCP or UDP traffic to enter the computer's operating system. For computers that use broadband Internet connections with dedicated IP addresses, the Windows Firewall can help avoid attacks aimed at disrupting a home computer. When you take your laptop to a Wi-Fi–enabled public location, such as an airport, hotel, or restaurant, the firewall protects you from individuals who might be probing the network to see what they can steal or infect. Even people with dial-up Internet connections can benefit from added protection. The Windows Firewall is enabled by default when you install Windows 10, as it was in all Windows operating systems since Vista.

Windows Firewall is a stateful host-based firewall that you can configure to allow or block specific network traffic. It includes a packet filter that uses an access control list (ACL) specifying parameters (such as IP address, port number, and protocol) that are allowed to pass through. When a user communicates with an external computer, the stateful firewall remembers this conversation and allows the appropriate reply packets to reach the user. Packets from an outside computer that attempts to communicate with a computer on which a stateful firewall is running are dropped unless the ACL contains rules permitting them.

Windows Vista introduced considerable improvements to its original implementation in Windows XP SP2, including outbound traffic protection, support for IP Security (IPsec) and IP version 6 (IPv6), improved configuration of exceptions, and support for command-line configuration. Microsoft has improved Windows Firewall even further in more recent versions of Windows. The following are some of the important recent features. Of particular note are the new PowerShell cmdlets introduced for Windows 10 and Windows Server 2016.

- **Support for Internet Key Exchange version 2 (IKEv2) for IPsec transport mode:** Additional scenarios have been supported, including IPsec end-to-end transport mode connections. Included is expanded support for interoperability with other operating systems using IKEv2 for end-to-end security and the support for Suite B requirements described in Request for Comment (RFC) 4869.

- **Windows Store app network isolation:** You can fine-tune network access in Windows Firewall to provide added control of Windows Store apps. You can enforce network boundaries that allow compromised apps to access only networks to which they have been explicitly granted. Doing so significantly reduces the scope of their impact on other networks, the system, and the network. You can also isolate apps and protect them from malicious access across the network.

- **New Windows PowerShell cmdlets for Windows Firewall:** You can use PowerShell for configuration and management of Windows Firewall, IPsec, and related features. Full configuration capabilities are now available.

You can perform basic configuration of Windows Firewall from a Control Panel applet. You can also perform more advanced configuration of Windows Firewall, including the use of security policies from a Microsoft Management Console (MMC) snap-in. We look at each of these in turn.

Basic Windows Firewall Configuration

The Windows Firewall Control Panel applet, found in the System and Security category and shown in Figure 16-1, enables you to set up firewall rules for each of the network types: Private, Guest or Public, and Domain.

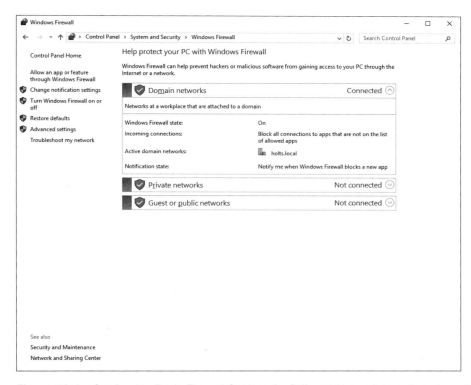

Figure 16-1 Configuring Basic Firewall Settings for Different Network Locations from the Windows Firewall Control Panel Applet

NOTE If your computer is joined to an Active Directory Domain Services (AD DS) domain, you will see the Domain Networks location as shown in Figure 16-1. If your computer is not joined to a domain, you will not see this network. Settings in this location can be configured through exclusively using domain-based Group Policy so that users cannot modify firewall settings locally.

You can enable or disable the Windows Firewall separately for each connection. In doing so, you are able to use Windows Firewall to protect a computer connected to the Internet via one adapter, and not use Windows Firewall for the adapter connected to the private network. Use the following instructions to perform basic firewall configuration:

Step 1.   Open the Windows Firewall applet by using any of the following methods:

- Right-click **Start** and choose **Control Panel**. Then click **System and Security > Windows Firewall**.

- In the Search bar or Cortana, type **firewall** into the Search field. From the list of programs displayed, click **Windows Firewall**.

- Open the Network and Sharing Center and select **Windows Firewall** from the list in the bottom-left corner.

Step 2.   From the left pane, select **Turn Windows Firewall On or Off**. If you receive a User Account Control (UAC) prompt, click **Continue**. This displays the Customize Settings for Each Type of Network dialog box, shown in Figure 16-2.

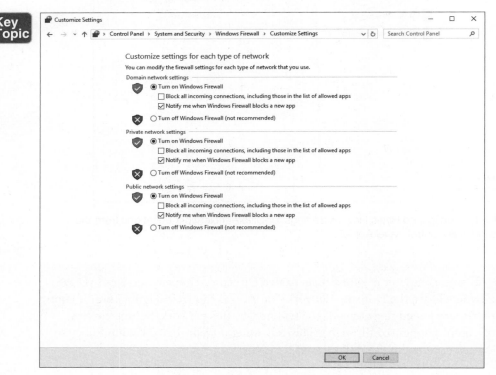

Figure 16-2   Customize Settings for Each Type of Network Dialog Box Enabling You to Turn the Firewall On or Off and to Block Incoming Connections

Step 3.   If you are connected to a corporate network with a comprehensive hardware firewall, select **Turn Off Windows Firewall (Not Recommended)** under the Private Network Location Settings section. If you connect at any time to an insecure network, such as an airport or restaurant Wi-Fi hotspot, select the **Block All Incoming Connections, Including Those in the List of Allowed Programs** option under Public Network Settings. This option disables all exceptions you've configured on the Exceptions tab.

WARNING Don't disable the firewall unless absolutely necessary, even on the Private Network Settings section. Never select the Turn Off Windows Firewall option in Figure 16-2 unless you're absolutely certain that your network is well protected with a good firewall. The only exception should be temporarily to troubleshoot a connectivity problem. After you've solved the problem, be sure to reenable the firewall immediately.

Step 4. To configure program exceptions, return to the Windows Firewall applet and click **Allow an App or Feature Through Windows Firewall**.

Step 5. From the list shown in Figure 16-3, select the programs or ports you want to have access to your computer on either of the Private or Public profiles. Table 16-2 describes the more important items in this list. Clear the check boxes next to any programs or ports to be denied access, or select the check boxes next to programs or ports to be granted access.

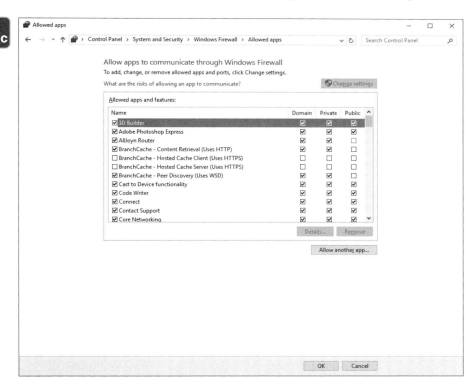

Figure 16-3 Allow Apps to Communicate Through Windows Firewall Dialog Box Enabling You to Specify Which Programs Are Allowed to Communicate Through the Firewall

Table 16-2   Key Windows Firewall Configurable Exceptions

Exception	Description	Enabled by Default?
Core Networking Network Discovery	Each option works with the other to enable your computer to connect to other network computers or the Internet	Yes; network discovery for home or work only
Distributed Transaction Coordinator	Coordinates the update of transaction-protected resources such as databases, message queues, and file systems	No
File and Printer Sharing	Enables your computer to share resources such as files and printers with other computers on your network	Yes
HomeGroup	Allows communication to other computers in the homegroup	Yes, for Private only when joined to a homegroup
iSCSI Service	Used for connecting to iSCSI target servers and devices	No
Key Management Service	Used for machine counting and license compliance in enterprise environments	No
MSN Money MSN News MSN Sports MSN Weather Mail and Calendar Microsoft Edge, People, Photos, and Messaging	Allows these default Windows apps to communicate on the Internet; others might also be listed, including some games	Yes
Media Center Extenders	Allows Media Center Extenders to communicate with a computer running Windows Media Center	No
Netlogon Service	Maintains a secure channel between domain clients and a domain controller for authenticating users and services	Only on a computer joined to an Active Directory domain
Network Discovery	Allows computers to locate other resources on the local network	Yes, for Private only
Performance Logs and Alerts	Allows remote management of the Performance Logs and Alerts service	No
Remote Assistance	Enables an expert user to connect to the desktop of a user requiring assistance in a Windows Feature	Yes, for Private only
Remote Desktop	Enables a user to connect with and work on a remote computer	No

Exception	Description	Enabled by Default?
Remote (*item*) Management	Enables an administrator to manage items on a remote computer, including event logs, scheduled tasks, services, and disk volumes	No for all these tasks
Routing and Remote Access (RRAS)	Enables remote users to connect to a server to access the corporate network (used on RRAS server computers only)	No
Store and Store Purchase App	Enables access to the App Store, and, separately, access to purchase apps from the Store	Yes
Windows Remote Management	Enables you to manage a remote Windows computer	No

Step 6.   To add a program not shown in the list, click **Allow Another App**. From the Add an App dialog box shown in Figure 16-4, select the program to be added and then click **Add**. If necessary, click **Browse** to locate the desired program. You can also click **Network Types** to choose which network type is allowed by the selected program.

Figure 16-4   Add an App Dialog Box Enabling You to Allow Specific Programs Access Through the Windows Firewall

Step 7.   Use the Allow Apps to Communicate Through Windows Firewall dialog box (refer to Figure 16-3) to view the properties of any program or port on the list; select it, and click **Details**.

Step 8.   To remove a program from the list, select it and click **Remove**. You can do this only for programs you have added using Step 6.

Step 9.   If you need to restore default settings, return to the Windows Firewall applet previously shown in Figure 16-1 and click **Restore Defaults**. Then confirm your intention in the Restore Default Settings dialog box that appears.

Step 10.   If you are experiencing networking problems, click **Troubleshoot My Network** to access the network troubleshooter, which automatically attempts to detect and correct any network issues.

Step 11.   When you are finished, click **OK**.

TIP When allowing additional programs to communicate through the Windows Firewall, by default these programs are allowed to communicate through the private network profile only (or the domain profile for domain-joined computers). You should retain this default unless you need a program to communicate through the Internet from a public location. From the Public column of the dialog box shown in Figure 16-3, you should select the boxes next to any connections that link to the Internet. You should clear the boxes next to any connections to a private network.

Configuring Windows Firewall with Advanced Security

First introduced in Windows Vista and enhanced in more modern versions of Windows, the Windows Firewall with Advanced Security snap-in enables you to perform a comprehensive set of configuration actions. You can configure rules that affect inbound and outbound communication, and you can configure connection security rules and the monitoring of firewall actions. Inbound rules help prevent actions such as unknown access or configuration of your computer, installation of undesired software, and so on. Outbound rules help prevent utilities on your computer from performing certain actions, such as accessing network resources or software without your knowledge. They can also help prevent other users of your computer from downloading software or inappropriate files without your knowledge.

Use any of the following methods to access the Windows Firewall with Advanced Security snap-in:

- Access the Search bar or Cortana, type **security** into the Search field of the Start menu, and then select **Windows Firewall with Advanced Security** from the Apps list.

- From the task list on the left side of the Windows Firewall applet (refer to Figure 16-1), select **Advanced Settings**.

- If you have enabled the Administrative Tools option from the Start menu as described in Chapter 4, "Managing Windows in an Enterprise," click the **Windows Firewall with Advanced Security** tile on the Start menu.

After accepting the UAC prompt (if you receive one), you see the snap-in shown in Figure 16-5.

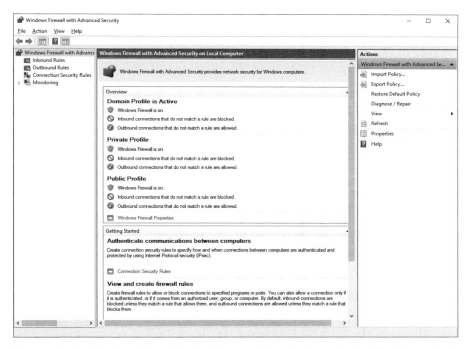

Figure 16-5   Windows Firewall with Advanced Security Snap-in Enabling You to Perform Advanced Configuration Options

When the snap-in first opens, it displays a summary of configured firewall settings. From the left pane, you can configure any of the following types of properties:

- **Inbound Rules:** Displays a series of defined inbound rules. Enabled rules are shown with a green check mark icon. If no icon is visible, the rule is not enabled. To enable a rule, right-click it and select **Enable Rule**; to disable an enabled rule, right-click it and select **Disable Rule**. You can also create a new rule by right-clicking **Inbound Rules** and selecting **New Rule**. We discuss creation of new rules later in this section.

- **Outbound Rules:** Displays a series of defined outbound rules, also with a green check mark icon for enabled rules. You can enable or disable rules and create new rules in the same manner as with inbound rules.

- **Connection Security Rules:** By default, this branch does not contain any rules. Right-click it and choose **New Rule** to create rules that are used to determine limits applied to connections with remote computers.

- **Monitoring:** Displays a summary of enabled firewall settings and provides links to active rules and security associations. This includes a domain profile for computers that are members of an AD DS domain. The following three links are available from the bottom of the Details pane:

    - **View Active Firewall Rules:** Displays enabled inbound and outbound rules.

    - **View Active Connection Security Rules:** Displays enabled connection security rules that you have created.

    - **View Security Associations:** Displays IPsec main mode and quick mode associations.

Configuring Multiple Firewall Profiles

A *profile* is simply a means of grouping firewall rules so that they apply to the affected computers dependent on where the computer is connected. The Windows Firewall with Advanced Security snap-in enables you to define different firewall behavior for each of the following three profiles:

- **Domain Profile:** Specifies firewall settings for use when connected directly to an AD DS domain. If the network is protected from unauthorized external access, you can specify additional exceptions that facilitate communication across the LAN to network servers and client computers.

- **Private Profile:** Specifies firewall settings for use when connected to a private network location, such as a home or small office. You can open up connections to network computers and lock down external communications as required.

- **Public Profile:** Specifies firewall settings for use when connected to an insecure public network, such as a Wi-Fi access point at a hotel, restaurant, airport, or other location where unknown individuals might attempt to connect to your computer. By default, network discovery and file and printer sharing are turned off, inbound connections are blocked, and outbound connections are allowed.

To configure settings for these profiles from the Windows Firewall with Advanced Security snap-in, right-click **Windows Firewall with Advanced**

Security at the top-left corner and choose **Properties**. This opens the dialog box shown in Figure 16-6.

Figure 16-6   Windows Firewall with Advanced Security on Local Computer Properties Dialog Box Enabling You to Configure Profiles Specific for Domain, Private, and Public Networks

You can configure the following properties for each of the three profiles individually from this dialog box:

- **State:** Enables you to turn the firewall on or off for the selected profile and block or allow inbound and outbound connections. For inbound connections, you can either block connections with the configured exceptions or block all connections. Click **Customize** to specify which connections you want Windows Firewall to help protect.

- **Settings:** Enables you to customize firewall settings for the selected profile. Click **Customize** to specify whether to display notifications to users when programs are blocked from receiving inbound connections or allow unicast responses. You can also view but not modify how rules created by local administrators are merged with Group Policy-based rules.

- **Logging:** Enables you to configure logging settings. Click **Customize** to specify the location and size of the log file and whether dropped packets or successful connections are logged (see Figure 16-7).

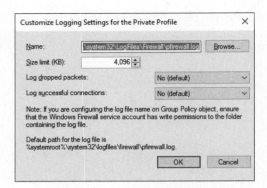

Figure 16-7 Customizing Logging Settings for Each of the Windows Firewall Profiles

In addition, you can configure IPsec settings from the IPsec Settings tab (refer to Figure 16-6), including defaults and exemptions. IPsec authentication rules enable you to configure bypass rules for specific computers that enable these computers to bypass other Windows Firewall rules. Doing so enables you to block certain types of traffic while enabling authenticated computers to receive these types of traffic. Configuring IPsec settings is covered later in the "Configuring IPsec Security Rules" section of this chapter.

Configuring New Firewall Rules

By clicking **New Rule** under Inbound Rules or Outbound Rules in the Windows Firewall with Advanced Security snap-in (refer to Figure 16-5), you can create rules that determine programs or ports that are allowed to pass through the firewall. Use the following procedure to create a new rule:

Step 1. Right-click the desired rule type in the Windows Firewall with Advanced Security snap-in and choose **New Rule**. This starts the New (Inbound or Outbound) Rule Wizard, as shown in Figure 16-8. (We chose a new inbound rule, so our example shows the New Inbound Rule Wizard.)

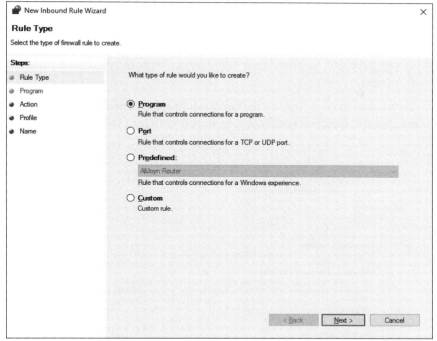

Figure 16-8 New (Inbound or Outbound) Rule Wizard Starts with a Rule Type Page Enabling You to Define the Type of Rule You Want to Create

Step 2.   Select the type of rule you want to create:

- **Program:** Enables you to define a rule that includes all programs or a specified program path.

- **Port:** Enables you to define rules for specific remote ports using either the TCP or UDP protocol.

- **Predefined:** Enables you to select from a large quantity of predefined rules covering the same exceptions described previously in Table 16-2 and shown in Figure 16-3. Select the desired exception from the drop-down list.

- **Custom:** Enables you to create rules that apply to combinations of programs and ports. This option combines settings provided by the other rule-type options.

Step 3.   After you've selected your rule type, click **Next**.

Step 4.   The content of the next page of the wizard varies according to which option you've selected. On this page, define the program path, port number and protocol, or predefined rule that you want to create, and then click **Next**.

Step 5.   On the Action page, specify the action to be taken when a connection matches the specified conditions, as shown in Figure 16-9.

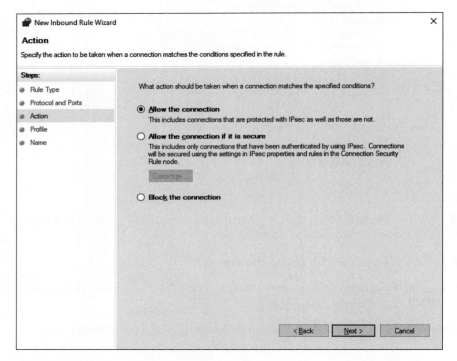

Figure 16-9   Action Page Enabling You to Specify the Required Action Type

Step 6.   If you choose the Allow the Connection if It Is Secure option, click **Customize** to display the dialog box shown in Figure 16-10. From this dialog box, select the required option as explained on the dialog box and click **OK**. If you desire that encryption be enforced in addition to authentication and integrity protection, select the **Require the Connections to Be Encrypted** option and also select the provided check box if you want to allow unencrypted data to be sent while encryption is being negotiated.

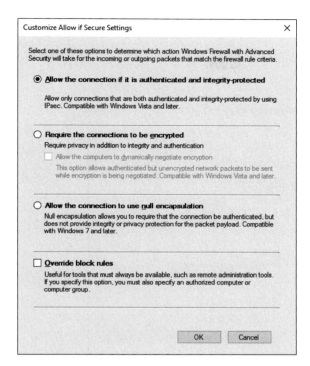

Figure 16-10 Customize Allow if Secure Settings Dialog Box Enabling You to Select Additional Actions to Be Taken for Packets That Match the Rule Conditions Being Configured

Step 7.   Click **Next** to display the Users page, shown in Figure 16-11. This page enables you to limit the users that are allowed to connect using this rule. By default, all users are authorized to connect. To limit authorized users, select the check box labeled **Only Allow Connections from These Users** and click **Add** to display the Select Users or Groups dialog box, which enables you to select one or more users to be allowed access. To prevent users that are otherwise authorized to use the connection, select the check box labeled **Skip This Rule for Connections from These Users** and click **Add** to display the Select Users or Groups dialog box and specify the desired users. The latter option is useful if you want to prevent access by a specific user while allowing access by other users of the group to which the first user belongs.

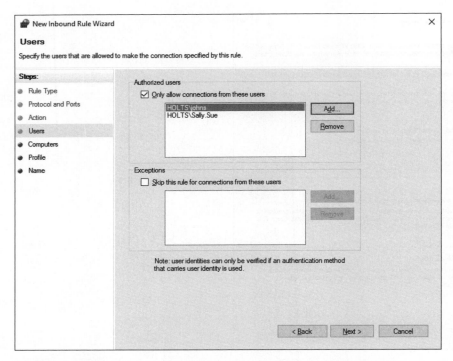

Figure 16-11   Specifying Users Who Are Allowed to Create the Connection Specified by the Rule

Step 8.   Click **Next** to display the Computers page. Options on this page are similar to those for users in Figure 16-11 and enable you to limit the computers that are allowed to use the rule you're creating.

Step 9.   Click **Next** to display the Profile page. On this page, select the profiles (**Domain**, **Private**, and **Public**) to which the rule is to be applied. Then click **Next**.

Step 10.   On the Name page, specify a name and optional description for your new rule. Click **Finish** to create the rule, which will then appear in the Details pane of the Windows Firewall with Advanced Security snap-in.

Configuring IPsec Security Rules

IPsec is a set of industry standard cryptography protection protocols and services. IPsec can be used to protect any TCP/IP protocol, with the exception of Address Resolution Protocol (ARP).

Windows Firewall with Advanced Security supports IPsec, which allows you to require authentication from any device. When authentication is required, devices that are unable to be authenticated will be blocked from communicating with your secured computer or device. You can also require encryption on any network connection to ensure transport security.

The connection security rules in Windows Firewall with Advanced Security are configured using a set of conditions and actions that are applied to network connection attempts that match the condition. The action applied can be to allow, block, or require the connection to be protected using IPsec.

Configuring New Connection Security Rules (IPsec)

Creating a new connection security rule is similar to that for inbound or outbound rules as discussed in the previous section, but the options are slightly different. From the Windows Firewall with Advanced Security dialog box previously shown in Figure 16-5, right-click **Connection Security Rules** and choose **New Rule** to display the New Connection Security Rule Wizard, as shown in Figure 16-12.

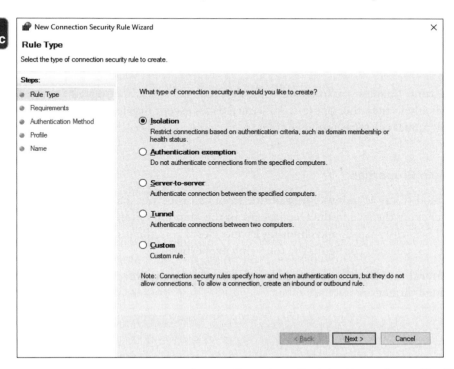

Figure 16-12 New Connection Security Rule Wizard Enabling You to Create Five Types of Connection Security Rules

Connection security rules manage authentication of two machines on the network and the encryption of network traffic sent between them using IPsec. Security is also achieved with the use of key exchange and data integrity checks. As shown in Figure 16-12, you can create the following types of connection security rules:

- **Isolation:** Enables you to limit connections according to authentication criteria that you define. For example, you can use this rule to isolate domain-based computers from external computers, such as those located across the Internet. You can request or require authentication and specify the authentication method that must be used.

- **Authentication Exemption:** Enables specified computers, such as DHCP and DNS servers, to be exempted from the need for authentication. You can specify computers by IP address ranges or subnets, or you can include a predefined set of computers.

- **Server-to-Server:** Enables you to create a secured connection between computers in two endpoints that are defined according to IP address ranges.

- **Tunnel:** Enables you to secure communications between two computers by means of IPsec tunnel mode. This encapsulates network packets that are routed between the tunnel endpoints. You can choose from several types of tunnels; you can also exempt IPsec-protected computers from the defined tunnel.

- **Custom:** Enables you to create a rule that requires special settings not covered explicitly in the other options. All wizard pages except those used to create only tunnel rules are available.

Modifying Rule Properties

You can modify any Windows Firewall rule from its Properties dialog box, accessed by right-clicking the rule in the Details pane of the Windows Firewall with Advanced Security snap-in and choosing **Properties**. From the dialog box shown in Figure 16-13, you can configure the following properties:

- **General tab:** Enables you to edit the name and description of the rule or change the action.

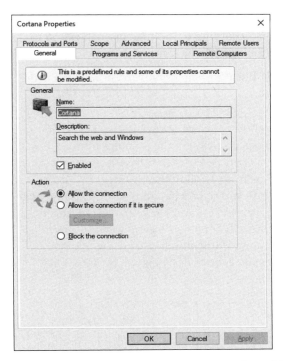

Figure 16-13   Properties Dialog Box for a Firewall Rule Enabling You to Modify Rules Criteria for Rules You Have Created or Default Rules Supplied in Windows Firewall with Advanced Security

- **Programs and Services tab:** Enables you to define which programs and services are affected by the rule.

- **Remote Computers tab:** Enables you to specify which computers are authorized to allow connections according to the rule, or enables you to specify computers for which the rule will be skipped.

- **Protocols and Ports tab:** Enables you to specify the protocol type and the local and remote ports covered by the rule.

- **Scope tab:** Enables you to specify the local and remote IP addresses of connections covered by the rule. You can specify Any Address or select a subnet or IP address range.

- **Advanced tab:** Enables you to specify the profiles (domain, private, or public) to which the rule applies. You can also specify the interface types (local area network, remote access, and/or wireless) and whether edge traversal (traffic routed through a NAT device) is allowed or blocked.

- **Local Principals tab:** Enables you to specify which local users or groups are authorized to allow connections according to the rule, or enables you to specify users or groups for which the rule will be skipped.

- **Remote Users tab:** Similar to the Local Principals tab, except it works with users or groups at remote computers.

NOTE   For additional information on all aspects of using the Windows Firewall with Advanced Security snap-in, refer to "Windows Firewall with Advanced Security" at https://technet.microsoft.com/en-us/itpro/windows/keep-secure/windows-firewall-with-advanced-security and the links and references in the article. For details on planning security in your organization using Windows Firewall with Advanced Security rules and IPsec encryption, start with "Windows Firewall with Advanced Security Design Guide" at https://technet.microsoft.com/en-us/itpro/windows/keep-secure/windows-firewall-with-advanced-security-design-guide.

Configuring Notifications

You can configure Windows Firewall with Advanced Security to display notifications when a program is blocked from receiving inbound connections according to the default behavior of Windows Firewall. When you have selected this option and no existing block or allow rule applies to this program, a user is notified when a program is blocked from receiving inbound connections.

To configure this option, right-click **Windows Firewall with Advanced Security** at the top of the left pane in the Windows Firewall with Advanced Security snap-in, and then choose **Properties**. This opens the dialog box previously shown in Figure 16-6. Select the tab that corresponds to the profile you want to configure, and then click the **Customize** command button in the Settings section. From the Customize Settings for the (selected) Profile dialog box shown in Figure 16-14, select **Yes** under Display a Notification and then click **OK** twice.

Figure 16-14 Configuring Windows Firewall to Display Notifications

Group Policy and Windows Firewall

Group Policy in Windows Firewall enables you to configure similar policies to those configured with the Windows Firewall with Advanced Security snap-in. Use the following procedure to configure Group Policy for Windows Firewall:

Step 1. From the Search bar or Cortana, type **gpedit.msc**, and then click **gpedit.msc** in the Programs list. If you receive a UAC prompt, click **Continue**.

Step 2. Navigate to the Computer Configuration\Windows Settings\Security Settings\Windows Firewall with Advanced Security\Windows Firewall with Advanced Security node. The right pane displays the Windows Firewall with Advanced Security settings, as shown in Figure 16-15.

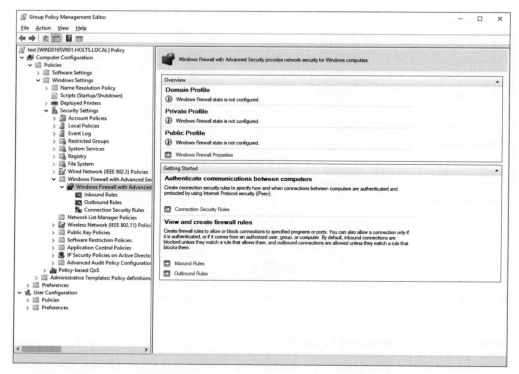

Figure 16-15 Using Group Policy to Configure Windows Firewall with Advanced Security Options

Step 3. Scroll the Details pane to select links for inbound rules, outbound rules, and connection security rules. These links open subnodes in the console tree.

Step 4. Unlike the Group Policy with Windows Firewall snap-in, no default rules are present. To add rules, right-click in the Details pane and select **New Rule**. This starts the New Rule Wizard, which enables you to create rules using the same options already discussed in this section.

After you have added firewall rules in Group Policy, you can filter the view according to profile (domain, private, or public) or by state (enabled or disabled).

> **TIP** A Group Policy feature first introduced in Windows Vista enables you to configure common policy settings for all user accounts on a computer used by more than one user. This includes Windows Firewall as discussed here, as well as UAC and all other policy settings. In addition, you can configure separate policies for administrators or nonadministrators. If necessary, you can even configure local group policies on a per-user basis.

Configuring Authenticated Exceptions

Windows Firewall with Advanced Security enables you to configure exceptions for users and computers accessing your computer through firewall rules that are included by default or created by an administrator. Use the following procedure to configure authenticated exceptions:

Step 1.   From the Windows Firewall with Advanced Security snap-in, select the inbound or outbound rule you want to configure.

Step 2.   Double-click the rule to display the Properties dialog for the selected rule.

Step 3.   Select the Configuration tab from the rule properties. You can create authenticated exceptions for Remote Users, Remote Computers, or Local Principals. Local Users are defined using the Local Principals tab. Select the appropriate tab.

NOTE   Note that you cannot set an exception for Remote Users on an inbound rule. The reason for this should be fairly obvious: Because the outbound rules are only for network connections initiated on the local computer, a remote user would never apply. You can set exceptions for a remote computer because a local user might initiate a connection to that remote computer. Inbound rules do not have a Remote Users tab on their Properties dialog.

Step 4.   To create an exception for a remote computer or remote user account, the Action for the rule must be set to **Allow the Connection if It Is Secure**. Windows enforces this restriction so that a rule does not request authentication credentials if they would be transferred over an unsecure network connection. If you attempt to do so, you will encounter an error, such as displayed in Figure 16-16.

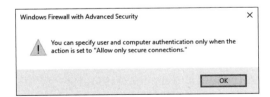

Figure 16-16   Windows Will Not Allow Authentication Exceptions for a Rule Over an Unsecure Connection

Step 5.   For authenticated users, select the check box labeled **Only Allow Connections from These Users**. After the box is checked, the Add button is enabled. The tab for Remote Computers is similar, but the check box refers to computers instead of users.

Step 6. Click the **Add** button and specify the user or group accounts in the **Select Users or Groups** dialog box. When you are finished selecting user and group objects, click **OK** to add them to the **Authorized Users** list, as shown in Figure 16-17. If you are working with the Remote Computers tab, the process is the same, but you can select only from **Groups** and **Built-in Security Principals**.

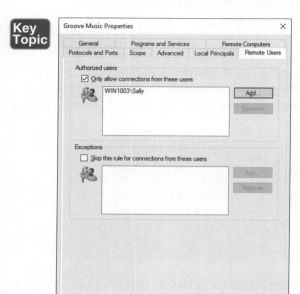

Figure 16-17   Selecting Authenticated Users Allowed to Use a Network Connection

Step 7. The Exceptions section is used to exclude any Authorized users or computers that may be selected from a group. For example, if you include the group Human Resources in the Authorized users list, all members of the group will be allowed to use the connection; however, you want to exclude the Human Resources receptionist, which is also a member of the group. You would check the **Skip This Rule for Connections from These Users** box, and add the receptionist to the Exceptions list.

Configuring Network Discovery

Network Discovery was introduced in Windows Vista to improve the security of the operating system by enabling better control over how Windows computers communicate and find each other over a network. Network Discovery is enabled by default on Windows 10 when it is connected to a private network and turned off when it detects that it is connected to a public or unidentified network. You can configure settings for each network profile that is created.

Windows Vista and Windows 7 included three types of network profiles called Public, Home, and Work. This was a little confusing for users, as the Home and Work profiles essentially worked the same. Network discovery was enabled for both and turned off for the Public network. Beginning with Windows 8, an improved profile model was introduced by creating a separate profile for each network you use. Windows 10 now describes your network as a Private network or a Public or Guest network. Domain-joined computers will use the Domain network when they are connected to the domain network.

In Windows 10, Network Discovery is configured from the Advanced Sharing options of the Network and Sharing Center. Access the Advanced Sharing Settings by clicking the **Change Advanced Sharing Options** link in the Network and Sharing Center, as illustrated in Figure 6-13 in Chapter 6, "Windows 10 Networking." Typically a Windows 10 computer starts with three network profiles, called Private, Guest or Public, and All Networks, as shown in Figure 16-18.

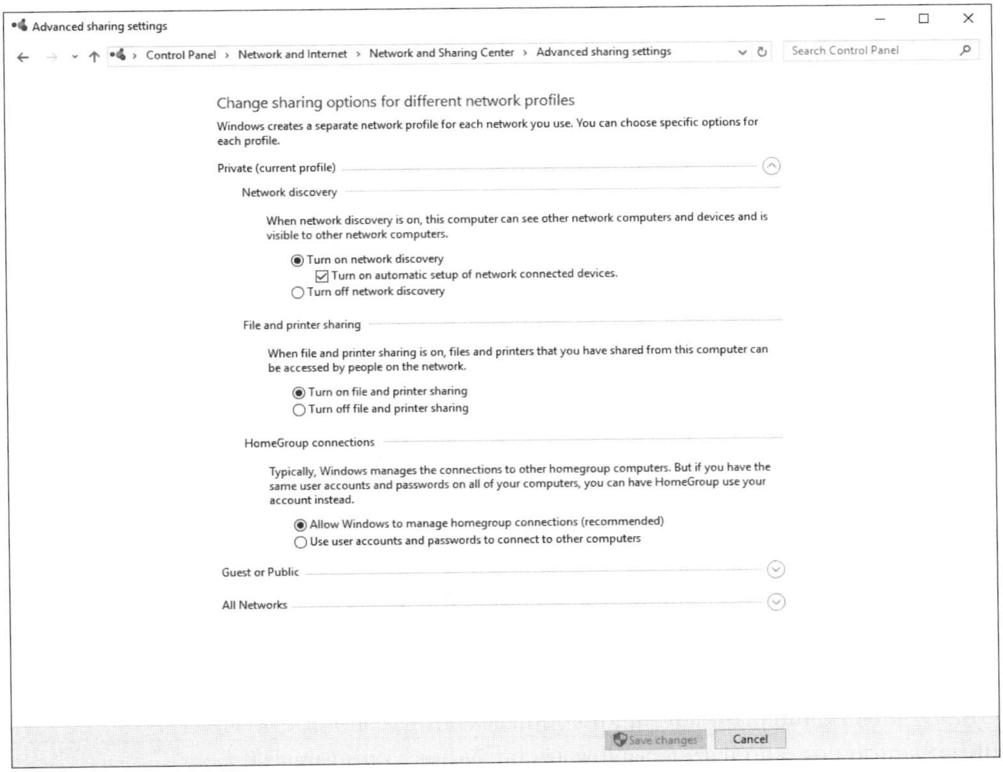

Figure 16-18 Typical Network Profiles in the Advanced Sharing Settings Dialog Box

If you join the Windows 10 computer to an Active Directory domain, a Domain profile is added, as shown in Figure 16-19.

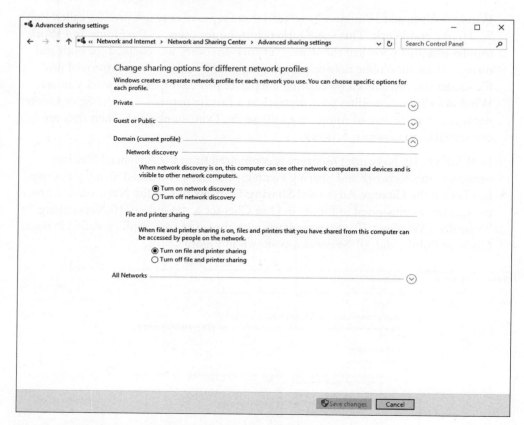

Figure 16-19   All Network Settings on a Domain-Joined Windows 10 Computer

The configuration options differ slightly for each profile type created by Windows. The individual options were covered in Chapter 6. Table 16-3 lists the options for each type of network profile.

Table 16-3   Network Discovery and Sharing Options for Windows 10 Network Profiles

Network Profile	Sharing Option	Description
Private	Network discovery	Can be turned on or off. When turned on, can also configure whether to turn on automatic setup of network-connected devices.
Private	File and printer sharing	Can be turned on or off.

Network Profile	Sharing Option	Description
Private	HomeGroup connections	Options: Allow Windows to manage homegroup connections. Use user accounts and passwords to connect to other computers.
Guest or Public	Network discovery	Can be turned on or off. Automatic setup of network-connected devices is not available.
Guest or Public	File and printer sharing	Can be turned on or off.
Domain	Network discovery	Can be turned on or off. Automatic setup of network-connected devices is not available.
Domain	File and printer sharing	Can be turned on or off.
All Networks	Public folder sharing	Can be turned on or off. This setting applies to all profiles.
All Networks	Media streaming	Media streaming options available for music, pictures, and videos. This setting applies to all profiles.
All Networks	File sharing connections	Select between strong (128-bit) encryption and weaker (40- or 56-bit) encryption. Strong encryption is recommended but may not work for some devices or older computers. This setting applies to all profiles.
All Networks	Password protected sharing	Can be turned on or off. This setting applies to all profiles. Not available on domain-joined computers. If the computer is joined to a domain, password protected sharing is always enabled.

Managing Wireless Security

Wireless connectivity creates a tempting attack vector for criminals looking for access to valuable private information. Wireless networks are ubiquitous today, and corporations are rolling out wireless infrastructure in their offices to provide convenience for employees and save costs. It is important to ensure not only that the information moving through the network is secure, but that unauthorized outside entities stay off your network and cannot access any resources for their own purposes.

Windows 10 supports the complete range of wireless security protocols, supported in Windows 7 and Windows 8.1, from Wired Equivalent Privacy (WEP) to Wi-Fi Protected Access (WPA2), Protected Extensible Authentication Protocol (PEAP), and its combination with Microsoft Challenge Handshake Authentication Protocol version 2 (MS-CHAPv2) and Extensible Authentication Protocol Transport Layer Security (EAP-TLS). WPA is no longer available as a connection type using the GUI Wi-Fi configuration dialogs starting with Windows 8.1. If your router supports only WPA, you can still configure Windows 10 to use it using the **netsh** command-line utility.

Windows 10 will use WPA2-Personal for maximum security when communicating by means of an ad hoc wireless network (direct communication with another wireless computer without use of an access point). This helps to protect against common vulnerabilities associated with such unprotected networks. Table 6-7 in Chapter 6 lists the types of wireless security available in Windows 10 and the encryption (of each) that can be used. Refer to that table for details.

NOTE   WPA2-Enterprise security provides the highest level of wireless networking authentication security. It requires authentication in two phases: first, an open system authentication and, second, authentication using EAP. It is suitable for domain-based authentication and on networks using a Remote Authentication Dial-In User Service (RADIUS) authentication server. In environments without the RADIUS server, you should use WPA2-Personal security

The WPA and WPA2 protocols can use either TKIP or AES for encryption. These are strong encryption protocols, and AES is considered especially secure. WPA2 still supports TKIP but uses AES by default instead of TKIP.

WARNING   Microsoft, and most network security professionals, recommend against using WEP. Because of the limitations of WEP's encryption, a hacker can capture enough frames in a fairly short amount of time to determine the shared keys or shared secret key used between access point and stations, and decrypt the packets. WPA and WPA2 are more secure and not as vulnerable to sniffing and intrusion.

When Windows 10 connects to a new wireless network, it prompts you to decide whether you want to turn on sharing for that network. Selecting No, Don't Turn On Sharing or Connect to Devices tells Windows to configure the connection as a Public network. As covered in the previous section, Network Discovery will be disabled by default on Public networks so that your computer will not advertise its presence to other computers on the network.

You can examine the connection properties, including the security and encryption types, for any wireless network your computer is connected to. To do so, right-click the **Start** button and select **Network Connections**. When the window is displayed, right-click the wireless network connection and select **Status**, and then click **Wireless Properties**. Select the **Security** tab to view the security settings.

The result will be similar to Figure 16-20. If you know the Security types available on the network, you can change the current setting from the **Security Type** drop-down. Similarly, if you want to select a different encryption type, choose from the options available in the **Encryption Type** drop-down. When you click the **OK** button, Windows temporarily disconnects from the access point and attempts to reconnect using the settings you selected. In Windows 10, only AES is available for WPA2.

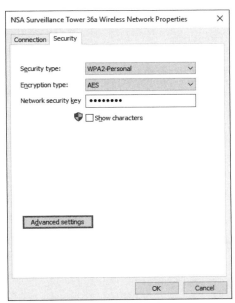

Figure 16-20   Configuring Security Settings for a Wireless Network Connection

Exam Preparation Tasks

Review All the Key Topics

Review the most important topics in the chapter, noted with the Key Topics icon in the outer margin of the page. Table 16-4 lists a reference of these key topics and the page numbers on which each is found.

Table 16-4   Key Topics for Chapter 16

Key Topic Element	Description	Page Number
Step List	Shows how to perform basic Windows Firewall configuration	763
Figure 16-2	Customizing Windows Firewall settings for each network type	764
Figure 16-3	Allowing apps to communicate through Windows Firewall	765
List	Describes available Windows Firewall with Advanced Security rule types	769
List	Describes types of available Windows Firewall with Advanced Security profiles	770
Figure 16-8	Creating new firewall rules of different types	773
Figure 16-12	Shows different types of firewall connection security rules	777
Step List	Shows how to configure authenticated exceptions	783
Figure 16-17	Selecting authenticated users allowed to use a network connection	784
Table 16-3	Network discovery settings and sharing options for Windows 10 network profiles	786
Figure 16-20	Configuring security settings for a wireless network connection	789

Complete the Tables and Lists from Memory

There are no memory tables in this chapter.

Definitions of Key Terms

Define the following key terms from this chapter, and check your answers in the glossary.

AES, authenticated exceptions, firewall profile, firewall rule, Internet Protocol Security (IPsec), network discovery, TKIP, WEP, WPA-2, Windows Firewall, Windows Firewall with Advanced Security

This chapter covers the following subjects:

- **Remote Desktop Services and RemoteApp:** This section provides an overview of Remote Desktop Services (RDS) and goes into detail with RemoteApp, a technology that enables administrators to make programs that are accessed remotely through RDS appear as though they are running on the end user's computer. You learn about configuring Group Policy Objects (GPOs) to support RemoteApp packages, how to subscribe to Azure RemoteApp and desktop connections, and how to import and export RemoteApp configurations in Microsoft Azure.

- **Microsoft Azure RemoteApp:** Microsoft Azure is a cloud offering from Microsoft that provides organizations with management tools and a virtual server hosting platform. In this section you get a brief overview of Azure services and learn how to configure RemoteApp, desktop connections settings, and how Azure can be used to support iOS and Android devices.

This chapter covers the following objectives for the 70-697 exam:

Deploy and manage Azure RemoteApp: Configure RemoteApp and Desktop Connections settings, configure Group Policy Objects (GPOs) for signed packages, subscribe to the Azure RemoteApp and Desktop Connections feeds, export and import Azure RemoteApp configurations, support iOS and Android, configure remote desktop web access for Azure RemoteApp distribution.

CHAPTER 17

Managing Mobile Apps

Microsoft's cloud offerings include Microsoft Intune, which you learned about in Chapter 13, "Microsoft Intune," as well as Office 365 and Microsoft Azure. You learned a few of the features of Microsoft Azure in Chapter 13—specifically, using Azure AD to manage user groups. Azure has many more capabilities for helping organizations manage their assets. This chapter focuses on mobile apps and how to deploy and manage RemoteApp features.

RemoteApp makes use of Remote Desktop Services (RDS) to allow users to access cloud-based applications and use them as if they were locally installed applications. Instead of being presented in a full Remote Desktop session, RemoteApp is integrated with the client desktop, running in its own window. Multiple RemoteApp programs typically share the same RDS session.

Using RemoteApp provides system administrators with a number of advantages in certain scenarios. When you manage applications centrally and allow users to access them remotely, application administration is greatly simplified. Deployment of Line-of-Business (LOB) programs is faster and easier than deploying to multiple, often remotely located client computers, and enables the use of custom applications by users who do not have assigned devices.

In this chapter, you get a more comprehensive view of Microsoft Azure and its capabilities for hosting mobile applications using Remote Desktop sessions. For the 70-697 exam, you need to be familiar with Microsoft RemoteApp and Desktop Connections capabilities, configurations, and how to manage and deploy applications for Windows computers as well as iOS and Android devices.

"Do I Know This Already?" Quiz

The "Do I Know This Already?" quiz allows you to assess whether you should read this entire chapter or simply jump to the "Exam Preparation Tasks" section for review. If you are in doubt, read the entire chapter. Table 17-1 outlines the major headings in this chapter and the corresponding "Do I Know This Already?" quiz questions. You can find the answers in Appendix A, "Answers to the 'Do I Know This Already?' Quizzes."

Table 17-1 "Do I Know This Already?" Foundation Topics Section-to-Question Mapping

Foundation Topics Section	Questions Covered in This Section
Remote Desktop Services and RemoteApp	1–5
Microsoft Azure RemoteApp	6–9

CAUTION   The goal of self-assessment is to gauge your mastery of the topics in this chapter. If you do not know the answer to a question or are only partially sure of the answer, you should mark that question as wrong for purposes of the self-assessment. Giving yourself credit for an answer you correctly guess skews your self-assessment results and might provide you with a false sense of security.

1. Which of the following server roles are involved in hosting RemoteApp applications? (Select all that apply.)
   a. Hyper-V
   b. RD Connection Broker
   c. Remote Desktop Licensing
   d. Active Directory Federation Services
   e. IIS Web Server

2. Which Remote Desktop Services component is used to host and stream applications to RemoteApp clients?
   a. RD Connection Broker
   b. RD Gateway
   c. RD Virtualization Host
   d. RD Session Host

3. What type of certificate is initially installed for RemoteApp services?
   a. Self-signed certificate
   b. Public CA certificate
   c. RemoteApp certificate
   d. Application Signing certificate

4. You are adding a certificate to your RemoteApp servers so that users' computers trust the applications you publish for them. Which role service requires the publisher's certificate?

    a. RD Connection Broker–Enable Single Sign On

    b. RD Connection Broker–Publishing

    c. RD Web Access

    d. RD Gateway

5. You have some Windows 10 computer users that would like to use the RemoteApp applications you have published without using a client application. What service needs to be configured?

    a. RD Connection Broker

    b. RD Gateway

    c. Virtual Desktop Session Manager

    d. RD Web Access

6. You have configured Azure RemoteApp to serve applications to 200 users with a dozen servers hosting and streaming the applications, and want to deploy a high availability configuration so that users can connect to the applications consistently. You are deploying several load-balanced RD Connection Broker servers. What single-instance component in Azure will be used to coordinate the brokers and connections?

    a. RD Session Host

    b. Shared database server

    c. RD Gateway

    d. RD Web Access console

7. You are deploying applications in Azure RemoteApp. You want to make sure your users can save Visio diagrams to the on-premises network share and use a central office plotter in the Engineering department. What kind of collection should you create?

    a. Central database collection

    b. Cloud collection

    c. Office 365 collection

    d. Hybrid collection

8. You have several users who want to access the in-house Line-of-Business application from their iPads, but the application runs only on Windows. So you have published the application as a RemoteApp. What do the iPad users need to install?

   a. They need the application sideloaded.

   b. Microsoft Remote Desktop from the iTunes store.

   c. Microsoft RemoteApp client from the iTunes store.

   d. Your self-signed certificate.

9. Your users are accessing your RemoteApp server to run your applications using Android and iOS devices. What credentials should they use to log in?

   a. Their Apple or Google account

   b. Their Windows account

   c. Their Azure AD account

   d. The credentials for your on-premises Active Directory

Foundation Topics

Remote Desktop Services and RemoteApp

You learned about Remote Desktop in Chapter 15, "Configuring Remote Access," as well as how to use the Remote Desktop client and Remote Desktop Protocol (RDP) for accessing remote servers and computers for administration and configuration. Microsoft has continued to improve RDP and the clients and server services that use it through the various iterations of Windows and Windows Server versions.

On the server side, Remote Desktop Services (RDS) is a bundled set of services that provide desktop virtualization, RD Gateway, RemoteApp, and other Desktop-as-a-Service (DaaS) capabilities based on RDP technologies. Microsoft has also deployed RDS in the cloud, and customers can use their Azure subscription to access many of the same capabilities available for on-premises deployments. One of the services of RDS is RemoteApp, which leverages RDP protocols to allow users to run applications deployed to RDS servers and platforms on their local devices.

Configuring RemoteApp

RemoteApp technology was first introduced with Windows Server 2008 R2 and supported in later versions of Windows Server. Using on-premises Windows

Servers, administrators are able to deploy mobile applications by installing the Remote Desktop Services (RDS) role (formerly the RD Session Host Server role). Users can then access the applications deployed for RemoteApp using their own computers or devices.

In Windows Server, applications are installed on the RDS server just like on any local desktop computer. For instance, the full version of the Microsoft Office desktop suite could be installed on the RDS server. Users would then be able to use any of the applications over an RD session without installing them locally.

RemoteApp requires a number of roles and features installed on Windows Server. Features will be installed automatically when you select the RD services you want to include, as shown in Figure 17-1.

The other roles required to support the RDS role are described in the list that follows.

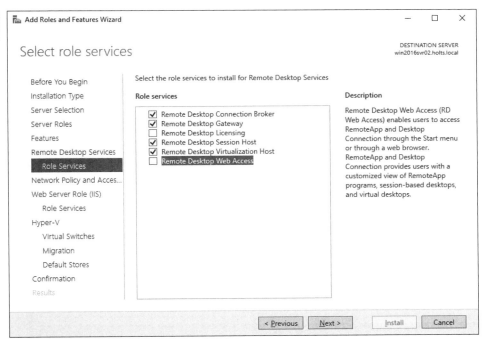

Figure 17-1   Installing Roles for RemoteApp on Windows Server 2016

- **Hyper-V** is required for the Virtual Desktop Infrastructure (VDI). RemoteApp can make use of VDI for virtualizing the Remote Desktop sessions where your RemoteApp applications are hosted. If you choose to use session-based RemoteApp hosting, Hyper-V is not required.

- **Remote Desktop Services (RDS)** is a set of related services including RD Connection Broker, RD Session Host, and RD Virtualization Host used to support remoting capabilities using the RDP protocol.

- **Hyper-V management tools**, including Hyper-V for Windows PowerShell and Hyper-V GUI management tools, provide the needed administration tools for virtual services.

- **Remote Desktop Licensing Diagnoser tools** can be used to help diagnose various aspects of RDS deployment.

- **IIS Web Server** is required if you want to use Remote Desktop Web Access.

After you have installed the roles, you then need to run the Add Roles and Features Wizard again, but instead of using the typical Role-Based or Feature-Based Installation, this time select the **Remote Desktop Services (RDS) Installation** type, as shown in Figure 17-2.

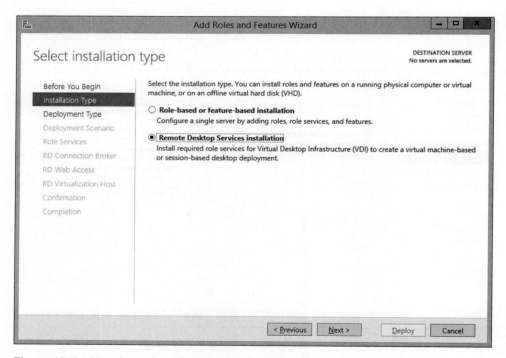

Figure 17-2   New Quick Start RDS Deployment Simplifies the Implementation of RemoteApp Services in Windows Server 2016

When you have completed your selections in the wizard, the required services for RemoteApp will be installed. New for Windows Server 2016 is the Quick Start deployment for RDS, as shown in Figure 17-3. This simplified deployment allows you to deploy RDS on a single server and creates a collection and publishes RemoteApp programs.

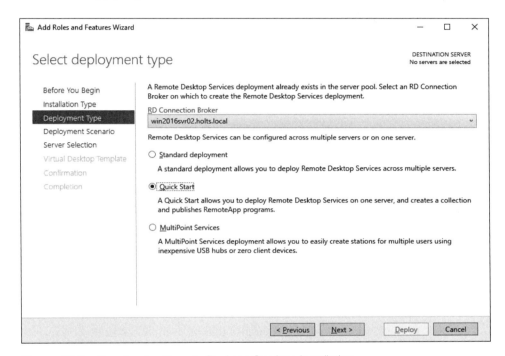

Figure 17-3   Running the Remote Desktop Services Installation

After the installation is completed, you can start managing RemoteApp and Desktop Services from Server Manager, as shown in Figure 17-4. From this page, you can add RD Licenses; add or manage the RD Gateway; manage your RD Session Hosts and RD Virtualization Hosts; and perform other tasks.

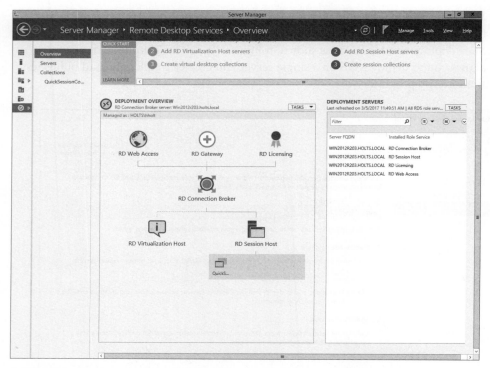

Figure 17-4   Remote Desktop Services Manager in Windows Server

Figure 17-4 depicts the components involved in supporting RemoteApp. In this test deployment, all the components have been installed on a single server, as you can see by checking the Deployment Servers section. In a production deployment supporting many users, components would be spread across many servers, with multiple services supporting a single component for redundancy and high availability.

- **RD Web Access** or Remote Desktop Web Access enables users to access RemoteApp (and desktop connection) using the Start menu on their device or using a web browser. It provides a customized view of the RemoteApp programs you publish.

- **RD Connection Broker** is used to provide access to RemoteApp. It supports load balancing and reconnection to existing sessions. It is also used to aggregate RemoteApp sources from multiple RD Session Host servers when the servers host different applications.

- **RD Gateway** provides the capability to make your RemoteApp and Remote Desktop sessions available over the public Internet. This is an optional component, and in Figure 17-4, no RD Gateway is deployed in the infrastructure, so access to RemoteApp from the Internet is not enabled.

- **RD Licensing** is used to track licenses for the applications and desktop services you provide to users. Each host session requires a Client Access License (CAL) for the users who access it for Remote Desktop or RemoteApp applications.

- **RD Virtualization Host** is used for a virtual machine-based (VM-based) deployment for the Virtual Desktop Infrastructure (VDI). When deploying RDS, you can choose either VM-based deployment or session-based deployment. In Figure 17-3, the session-based deployment was chosen because it is more appropriate for supporting RemoteApp services. VM-based deployments are more often used for providing full-featured virtual desktops for users.

- **RD Session Host** is used for hosting the RD session and the applications (specifically, the application collections) that are running in RemoteApp. This is the service that users are connected to when they are running a RemoteApp application. You can add multiple RD Session Hosts to the infrastructure, and then add multiple application collections to each. The RD Connection Broker will keep track of the hosts and the applications available to RemoteApp users.

NOTE   A detailed description of Remote Desktop Services infrastructure and procedures for implementation is beyond the scope of this text and the 70-697 exam. In fact, thorough coverage of the topic would require an entire book of its own. To find out more about the topic and requirements, start with "Welcome to Remote Desktop Services" at https://technet.microsoft.com/en-us/windows-server-docs/compute/remote-desktop-services/welcome-to-rds.

Configuring Group Policy Objects (GPOs) for Signed Packages

In Chapter 5, "Installing and Managing Software," you learned about signing apps for deployment using sideloading. Recall that LOB apps must have a digital signature, and the signing authority must be trusted by the device so that the app can be installed and run. You have learned a bit about certificate authority (CA) services throughout the text, for instance for Secure Boot in Chapter 2, "Implementing Windows," driver signing in Chapter 3, "Post-Installation Configuration," certificate-based authentication and working with an Active Directory certificate authority in Chapter 7, "Windows 10 Security," and other uses of certificates throughout the text. You should be familiar with the concepts.

When you publish applications through the RemoteApp RDS services, the applications that users run should also be signed. Signing an application for RemoteApp is the same process you learned about for signing apps for sideloading in Chapter 5.

If you are publishing LOB applications in RemoteApp, the applications should be signed, but they can be signed by your own internal enterprise CA. You can use Group Policy Objects to deploy trusted certificates and signed packages for RemoteApp and RDS.

By default when you install RDS and RemoteApp, a self-signed certificate is generated for connections and the RD Web. When users attempt to access applications, a certificate warning is displayed, similar to Figure 17-5. Users can select Connect and go ahead and use the application, but this presents some issues. First, users should be cautious about accessing anything over the public Internet and should avoid any security issues that Windows warns them about. You want your users to be cautious about such things to avoid truly nefarious websites and applications that can compromise their computer and your organization. In addition, because users are educated to avoid connecting to sites that may have compromised security, you will inevitably be fielding many phone calls and support requests when users see these warnings.

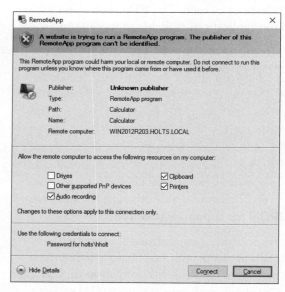

Figure 17-5   Warning That the Certificate Used for a RemoteApp Application Is Not Trusted

If you have deployed a public key infrastructure (PKI) in your organization or your Azure tenant, you can create a Group Policy Object (GPO) to distribute the CA certificate as a trusted publisher to all the computers in the domain. Use the following procedure to ensure that your domain computers trust the certificate you are using:

Step 1.   Use the Certificates MMC to locate your organization's CA certificate, as outlined in Chapter 7. Refer to Figure 7-34. You may need to perform this step from the CA server.

Step 2.   Double-click the certificate to view the certificate information, and then click the **Details** tab.

Step 3.   Click the **Copy to File** button. Windows displays the Certificate Export Wizard. Click **Next**.

Step 4.   On the file format page, select **DER encoded (.CER)**. Click **Next**.

Step 5.   Browse to a location on the local PC to save the file, and enter a filename to use. Click **Next**.

Step 6.   Click **Finish** to save the file.

Step 7.   From the Group Policy Management console, select a GPO or create a new one.

Step 8.   Right-click the GPO and select **Edit**. The Group Policy Management Editor is displayed.

Step 9.   Navigate to Computer Configuration\Policies\Windows Settings\ Security Settings\Public Key Policies, as shown in Figure 17-6.

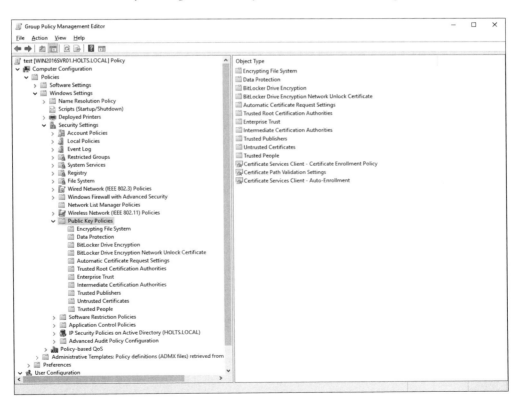

Figure 17-6   Using the Public Key Policies GPO to Distribute Certificates to Domain-Joined Computers

Step 10.   Right-click the **Trusted Root Certification Authorities** node and select **Import**.

Step 11.   Make sure that Local Machine is selected in the Store Location area, and then click **Next**.

Step 12.   Click **Browse** to locate the certificate file you saved in Step 6. Click **Next**.

Step 13.   On the Certificate Store page, make sure that **Trusted Root Certification Authorities** is selected, as shown in Figure 17-7, and then click **Next**.

Figure 17-7   Adding Your Certificate to the Trusted Root Certification Authorities Policy

Step 14.   Click **Finish** to import the certificate.

Save your GPO and apply it to the OU in the Active Directory where the computer accounts are located. The next time those computers refresh their group policies, they will download the certificate and install it in their own Trusted Root Certification Authorities store.

Configuring Remote Desktop Web Access for Azure RemoteApp Distribution

The next step is to use a signed certificate for your published applications. First, request a certificate from your organization's CA. The process is the same as the Requesting Certificates procedure outlined in Chapter 7. Request a computer certificate for your RD Session Host where the applications are published. You then need to export the certificate using Steps 2–6 in the preceding procedure, but on Step 4 you must select the **Personal Information Exchange–PKCS #12** option and export the private key. You will be asked for a password to secure the private key, as shown in Figure 17-8. After you have the .PFX file saved to disk, you can use it to sign your RemoteApp applications.

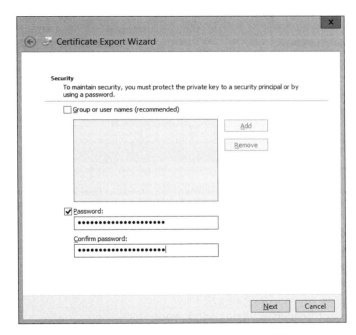

Figure 17-8 Requirement to Supply a Password When Exporting a Certificate with a Private Key

Use the following procedure to sign your published RemoteApps using this .PFX certificate.

Step 1.   From Server Manager, select **Remote Desktop Service**, then **Overview**. This displays the screen shown previously in Figure 17-3.

Step 2.   From the top of the Deployment Overview section, click **Tasks** and then select **Edit Deployment Properties** to display the Deployment Properties dialog. Select **Certificates**. The page shown in Figure 17-9 is displayed.

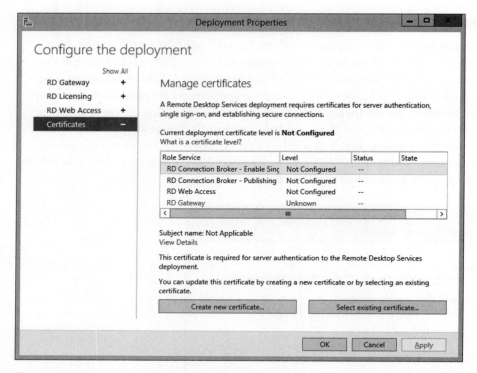

Figure 17-9   RemoteApp Deployment Properties Dialog Allowing You to Add Private Key Certificates to the Services

Step 3.   Select the **RD Connection Broker–Publishing** service, and then click **Select Existing Certificate**.

Step 4.   Click the **Browse** button to locate the .PFX file you saved, enter the private key password, and then click **OK**.

Step 5.   On the Deployment Properties dialog, click **Apply**.

Step 6.   After the configuration is saved, the RD Connection Broker–Publishing displays Trusted in the Level column, as shown in Figure 17-10.

Your RemoteApp applications are now signed. When users access the application, they will no longer get a scary message about an unknown publisher. Instead, as shown in Figure 17-11, your own domain is shown as the publisher, and users know they can trust your application.

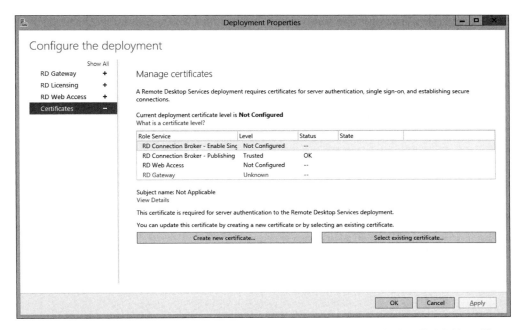

Figure 17-10   Certificate from Your CA Added to the RD Connection Broker–Publishing, Showing It Is Trusted

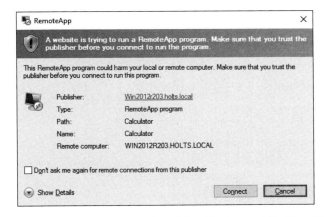

Figure 17-11   After You Install Certificates and Enable a Trust, Your Applications Are Signed and Trusted

Subscribing to Azure RemoteApp and Desktop Connection Feeds

To use Azure RemoteApp, or RemoteApp in an on-premises environment, users of Windows 10 PCs need to install the RemoteApp client. The client can be downloaded from https://www.microsoft.com/en-us/cloud-platform/azure-remoteapp-client-apps, but if you are deploying RemoteApp in your organization, you should deploy the client to Windows computers using your management solution, such as System Server Configuration Manager (SCCM), Microsoft Intune, or other means. The Windows client is supported on Windows 7 and later computers.

On Windows 10, downloading the client from the Microsoft site presents the confirmation shown in Figure 17-12. Click **Install** to install the application.

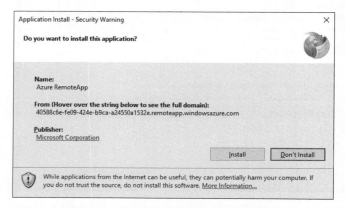

Figure 17-12   Downloading and Installing the RemoteApp Client on Windows

Use the following procedure to configure the Azure RemoteApp client and subscribe to desktop connection feeds:

Step 1.   On the Azure RemoteApp welcome page, shown in Figure 17-13, click **Get Started**.

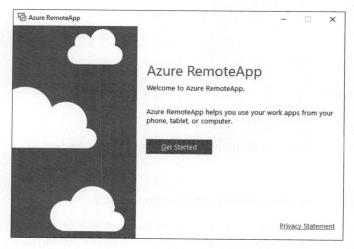

Figure 17-13   Running the Azure RemoteApp Client for the First Time

Step 2. From the Microsoft Azure sign-in page, provide your Azure AD credentials, and then click **Sign In**.

Step 3. The Azure RemoteApp client is displayed, as shown in Figure 17-14. The applications that you have published are now available on the Start menu of the computer.

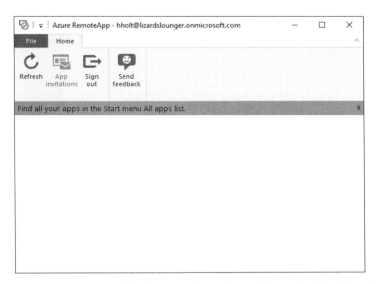

Figure 17-14   After Signing In to Azure RemoteApp, the Client Loads Your Applications to the Start Menu of the Local Computer

Step 4. Access the **Start** button, and click the application to run it. It will run as if the application was locally installed on the computer.

With RD Web Access, users can also sign in to the RemoteApp URL using a web browser to access their applications, as shown in Figure 17-15. Typically, users need to sign in with their domain credentials on the website. However, you can implement Single Sign On (SSO) for your users of the RD Web Access interface by installing a trusted certificate for the RD Web Access server.

The procedure is the same as described previously, but instead of adding the certificate to the RD Connection Broker–Publishing, add the certificate to the RD Connection Broker–Enable Single Sign On. Users can then access the RD Web Access URL and will automatically be authenticated.

Figure 17-15 Accessing RemoteApp Applications Using a Web Browser and the RD Web Access Service

Microsoft Azure RemoteApp

You have learned a few of the features of Microsoft Azure. Recall, for instance, managing user groups and attributes from Chapter 13, "Microsoft Intune." Azure is integrated with Microsoft's other cloud offerings, including Office 365 and Intune.

Azure provides a lot of capabilities for distributing mobile apps to user computers and devices. The Azure App Service platform enables app hosting for mobile apps that you develop, and can speed development and deployment of those apps for mobile devices and phones. These services are out of scope of this chapter and the 70-697 exam. The type of services covered here is based on Remote Desktop Services, part of the Microsoft Virtual Desktop Infrastructure (VDI), which provides users a way to run full-featured desktop applications remotely using their computer or mobile device.

Configuring RemoteApp and Desktop Connection Settings

The hub of connections to RemoteApp and other RDS services is the RD Connection Broker. The Connection Broker can be on the same server as the RDS server or on another server in the network. For high availability, you can configure multiple, load-balanced Connection Broker servers, and the connections coming in will be distributed so that no one server gets too overloaded with connection requests. If one Connection Broker goes down, you still have one or more available to handle requests.

You can leverage the Microsoft Azure platform to configure a high-availability RD Connection Broker cluster, using an Azure SQL Database as the back end. Follow this procedure to configure a highly available Connection Broker configuration in Microsoft Azure. The details of these steps are beyond the scope of this text and the exam, but we outline the high-level process in the following procedure:

Step 1.   Create two Azure virtual machines (VMs) with Microsoft Server 2016.

Step 2.   Configure load balancing between the servers. Your load-balancing configuration can use Azure Load Balancer (if your RDS services will also be hosted in Azure) or Windows Server 2016 Software Load Balancer if you will be using on-premises servers.

Step 3.   Create a new Azure SQL Database.

Step 4.   Install Microsoft ODBC Driver 13.1 for SQL Server on both VMs you created in Step 1.

Step 5.   Create the RDS 2016 environment with one Connection Broker. In the Connection Broker topology, select **Configure High Availability**.

Step 6.   In the RD Connection Broker configuration page, choose **Shared Database Server**, enter the cluster name for the Connection Broker cluster, and input the connection string for the shared database.

Step 7.   In the Connection Broker topology, choose **Add RD Connection Broker Server** and add the second Connection Broker.

You now have a highly available RD Connection Broker configuration, deployed in the cloud. Your clients can connect to the Azure Connection Broker and be connected to your RemoteApp servers, which can be on-premises or in the cloud.

Azure RemoteApp Collections

In Azure, RemoteApps are supported using two kinds of Azure RemoteApp collections:

- **Cloud collections** are hosted in the cloud and store data for those programs in the cloud. You can use cloud collections for applications that do not require resources in the private, on-premises organizational network.

- **Hybrid collections** are also hosted and store data in the cloud, but also enable users to access resources on the private organizational network. If your applications use things such as on-premises file shares or databases, they need to be configured as part of a hybrid collection.

When you sign up for Azure RemoteApp, the portal will make a default image available for your RemoteApp hosting, using Office 365. With this image available, you can allow any of your users access to Office 365 applications using RemoteApp, without the need to install the applications on their device.

Use the following procedure to create a collection in Azure RemoteApp:

Step 1.   From the Azure portal, select **App Services**, and then select the **Remote-App** menu in the left navigation tree.

Step 2.   Click **Create a RemoteApp** collection from the menu, and then select **Quick Create**.

Step 3.   Enter a name for the new collection, the region where you want to host the collection, and the billing plan you want to use.

Step 4.   From the Template Image drop-down list, select the image to use. You can use the Office 365 image, as mentioned, or one of the other Office images available. If you want to install and use your own applications, select a server image, such as Windows Server 2012 R2. You can customize it and add your own applications.

Step 5.   Click the **Create RemoteApp Collection** button.

It can take up to an hour for Azure to create your collection.

Publishing RemoteApp Applications

After your Azure RemoteApp collection has been created, you will need to share the apps with your users by publishing the collection. Use the following procedure to publish apps in your collection:

Step 1.   Access the RemoteApp section from the Azure portal and select your collection.

Step 2.   Click the **Publishing** tab at the top, click the **Publish** button at the bottom of the screen, and then select **Publish Start Menu Programs**.

Step 3.   Select the applications from the collection that you want to publish, and then click **Complete**. Wait for the application to finish publishing.

Step 4.   Select the **User Access** tab at the top of the screen.

Step 5.   In the box provided, enter usernames (email addresses) for your users.

Step 6.   After all the users you want to access the application have been added, click **Save**.

To use RemoteApp applications, users need to install the Microsoft Remote Desktop client app on the users' devices. This is the only software required on the local device for accessing any RemoteApp application. You use the app for Mac OS X, iOS, Android, Windows Phone, and Windows RT.

NOTE   The Microsoft Remote Desktop client app, needed for RemoteApp, can be downloaded from the app store for the device. For Android devices, use the Google Play store, the iTunes Store for iOS and Mac devices, and the Windows Store for Windows Phone and Windows 10 Mobile. Windows PCs require the RD client. Links to the client for all devices are available at https://www.microsoft.com/en-us/cloud-platform/azure-remoteapp-client-apps.

An Azure RemoteApp application is available for Windows computers (Windows 7 and later are supported), Windows Mobile devices, Mac OS X, iOS, and Android. Users start the application and then sign in to their organization's Azure account using their Azure credentials.

Support for iOS and Android

Users of iOS and Android devices need to install the Microsoft Remote Desktop client from their respective app stores to access your RemoteApp collections and applications. When your users start up the Remote Desktop client on their device, they can sign in using their Azure Active Directory (Azure AD) credentials and access the applications you have published. Provide the following procedures for your end users to follow from the device. The process is the same on iOS and Android.

Step 1.   Open the Microsoft Remote Desktop app.

Step 2.   Click the **Add** button (the plus symbol in the upper-right corner).

Step 3.   From the menu, select **Azure RemoteApp**. The Azure RemoteApp screen is displayed, as shown in Figure 17-16.

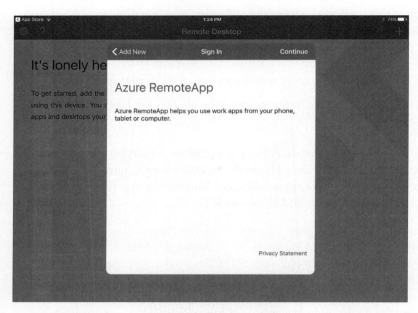

Figure 17-16   Adding the Azure RemoteApp Connection in the Microsoft Remote Desktop App

Step 4.   On the Azure RemoteApp screen, select **Continue**.

Step 5.   On the Sign In screen, enter your Azure AD credentials provided by your administrator.

Step 6.   After you sign in, the applications available to you are displayed, as shown in Figure 17-17. Click the application you want to run.

The applications users access in this way will run just as if they were on a Windows PC running the application locally. Touchscreen functionality is enabled for certain functions, such as dragging windows, selecting sections of the application, accessing the menu, and so on. Users can also access the Remote Desktop menu at the top of the screen to switch between a mouse pointer-style interface and touchscreen, as shown in Figure 17-18. The menu also provides functions to end the session, return to the home screen, or start a new session.

Figure 17-17 Applications Published in Azure RemoteApp Are Available to Users of iOS and Android Devices

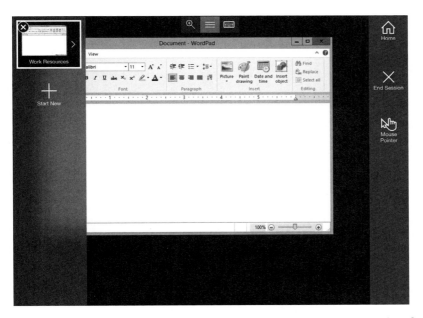

Figure 17-18 Accessing the RemoteApp Control Options in a RemoteApp Session

> **NOTE** Microsoft has discontinued Azure RemoteApp, and stopped receiving new customers as of October 1, 2016. Existing customers will be supported until August 31, 2017. Microsoft recommends that current customers and others interested in this type of functionality transition to Citrix XenApp "express." As of March 2017, the Microsoft Exam objectives for exam 70-697 still require knowledge of Azure RemoteApp, and the exams have not been updated to remove questions related to the topic. We have provided information in this chapter to help you prepare for the exam in case you are tested on the objects. For more information, see "Application Remoting and the Cloud" at https://blogs.technet.microsoft.com/enterprisemobility/2016/08/12/application-remoting-and-the-cloud/.

Exam Preparation Tasks

Review All the Key Topics

Review the most important topics in the chapter, noted with the Key Topics icon in the outer margin of the page. Table 17-2 lists a reference of these key topics and the page numbers on which each is found.

Table 17-2 Key Topics for Chapter 17

Key Topic Element	Description	Page Number
Figure 17-1	Installing roles for RemoteApp	797
List	Remote Desktop services deployed to support RemoteApp	800
Step List	Deploying certificates for RemoteApp signing using Group Policy Objects	802
Step List	Configure private keys for signing published RemoteApp applications	805
Step List	Configuring high-availability configuration for RemoteApp using Azure	811
Step List	Creating an application collection in Azure RemoteApp	812
Step List	Using the Microsoft Remote Desktop app for Android and iOS for RemoteApp	813
Figure 17-17	Accessing RemoteApp applications from Android and iOS	815

Definitions of Key Terms

Define the following key terms from this chapter, and check your answers in the glossary.

application signing, APNs, Azure RemoteApp, cloud collection, DaaS, hybrid collection, PKCS #12, RD Connection Broker, RD Gateway, RD Session Host, RD Web Access, RDS, RemoteApp client, VDI

This chapter covers the following subjects:

- **Implementing Apps:** The primary purpose of deploying Windows in an organization is to support apps that users need to perform their duties. This section teaches you how to implement the Windows Store for Business, a private store similar to the public Windows Store that you can use to make volume-purchased apps available to your users as well as your own Line-of-Business (LOB) apps. This section also discusses Windows 10 startup options and managing the startup for Windows features.

- **Desktop Application Compatibility:** Many applications currently in use today were originally written for Windows 7 or older versions of Windows. Some of these might not work properly with Windows 10. This section describes methods you can use to make these applications work properly. It also discusses Windows Installer, default program settings, and App-V applications.

- **User Experience Virtualization:** User Experience Virtualization (UE-V) is a technology available in Windows 10 that allows you to maintain users' application and Windows settings and customizations across devices and logins. Learn about the capabilities of UE-V and how to configure UE-V in your organization.

- **Using Microsoft Intune for Desktop Apps:** When you manage Windows computers with Microsoft Intune using the Intune client, you can make desktop applications available to your users, or automatically deploy them on your managed computers.

This chapter covers the following objectives for the 70-697 and 70-698 exams:

Implement apps: Configure desktop apps, configure startup options, configure Windows features, configure Windows Store, implement Windows Store apps, implement Windows Store for Business, provision packages, create packages, use deployment tools, use the Windows Assessment and Deployment Kit (ADK).

Support desktop apps: Support considerations include the following: desktop app compatibility using Application Compatibility Toolkit (ACT) including shims and compatibility database; desktop application coexistence using Hyper-V, Azure RemoteApp, and App-V; installation and configuration of User Experience Virtualization (UE-V); deploy desktop apps by using Microsoft Intune.

CHAPTER 18

Managing Desktop Applications

We have finished looking at configuration and troubleshooting of hardware devices attached to or included with your computer. Having done so, it is now time to turn to the software applications installed on the computer. With each new version of Windows comes updated applications, including Internet Explorer, now in version 11, expected to be the last version of Internet Explorer, and the new default browser, Windows Edge. However, organizations and individuals have invested big money in applications that were run on older computers running operating systems such as Windows Vista, 7, and 8.1. A new operating system brings with it the potential for compatibility issues, in which software written for older operating systems might not run properly, or stop responding (hang), or not even start. For the 70-697 and 70-698 exams, it is important that you know how to configure applications so that they work properly on Windows 10.

Windows 10 brings an entirely new suite of small-scale applications written for Universal Windows Platform (UWP), which users can purchase and download from the new Windows Store and that are designed to work with Windows 10 computers, Windows 10 Mobile for phones, tablets, and even Xbox. Although some of these apps can enhance productivity in a corporate environment, downloading and using many of them can become a major distraction for users during the work day. For organizations, Microsoft now offers the Windows Store for Business. This is a private store, available only on Windows 10 devices, that you can use to acquire apps, volume purchase apps for your organization's employees, and even restrict your users and devices to using only the Store for Business on their connected devices. You learn about the Store for Business, how it integrates with other cloud services, such as Azure and Microsoft Intune, and learn how to manage the store and your private store apps.

There are some other tools that you need to learn about that help manage applications for Windows 10. You learn about the Application Compatibility Toolkit (ACT), and you return to the Microsoft Intune management tool to learn about how it can help you distribute desktop apps. You also learn about some additional features of the Windows Assessment and Deployment Kit (ADK).

"Do I Know This Already?" Quiz

The "Do I Know This Already?" quiz allows you to assess whether you should read this entire chapter or simply jump to the "Exam Preparation Tasks" section for review. If you are in doubt, read the entire chapter. Table 18-1 outlines the major headings in this chapter and the corresponding "Do I Know This Already?" quiz questions. You can find the answers in Appendix A, "Answers to the 'Do I Know This Already?' Quizzes."

Table 18-1 "Do I Know This Already?" Foundation Topics Section-to-Question Mapping

Foundation Topics Section	Questions Covered in This Section
Implementing Apps	1–3
Desktop Application Compatibility	4–8
User Experience Virtualization	9–10
Using Microsoft Intune for Desktop Apps	11–12

CAUTION The goal of self-assessment is to gauge your mastery of the topics in this chapter. If you do not know the answer to a question or are only partially sure of the answer, you should mark that question as wrong for purposes of the self-assessment. Giving yourself credit for an answer you correctly guess skews your self-assessment results and might provide you with a false sense of security.

1. Fast Startup in Windows 10 makes use of what technology?
   a. Sleep Mode
   b. Hibernation
   c. SSD
   d. PowerShell

2. To deploy Windows Store for Business, what type of accounts do you need to configure for your users?
   a. Office 365 accounts
   b. Microsoft accounts
   c. Azure Active Directory accounts
   d. Microsoft Intune accounts

3. Your organization has deployed the Windows Store for Business, and a lot of applications are being added. You would like to delegate some other employees to manage the applications, but not users or the store settings. Which role should you assign? (Each answer represents a complete solution. Choose two.)

   a. Admin

   b. Billing Administrator

   c. Purchaser

   d. User Administrator

   e. Global Administrator

4. You want to advertise a Windows Installer package named Program.msi to all users of the computer. Which of the following commands should you type?

   a. **msiexec /am Program.msi**

   b. **msiexec /au Program.msi**

   c. **msiexec /jm Program.msi**

   d. **msiexec /ju Program.msi**

5. You have obtained a minor compatibility fix that is designed to enable an engineering program to work with Windows 10 while the developers update the program as a more permanent solution. What is this compatibility fix generally known as?

   a. Compatibility mode

   b. Filter

   c. Shim

   d. Hotfix

6. You would like all file types that currently open in Internet Explorer to open with Firefox instead. What should you do? (Each correct answer represents a complete solution. Choose two.)

    a. From the Programs applet in Control Panel, select **Set Your Default Programs** and then select **Associate a File Type or Protocol with a Program**. From the list that appears, select the extensions that currently open in Internet Explorer and click **Change Program**. In the Open With dialog box that appears, select **Firefox**.

    b. From the Programs applet in Control Panel, select **Default Programs**, and then select **Set Your Default Programs**. From the list that appears, select **Firefox**, and then click **Set This Program as Default**.

    c. From the Programs applet in Control Panel, select **Default Programs**, and then select **Set Program Access and Computer Defaults**. In the dialog box that appears, select **Custom**, and then select **Mozilla Firefox**.

    d. From a File Explorer list, right-click any file with an .htm or .html extension and choose **Open With > Choose Default Program**. Then select **Firefox** from the list that appears.

7. You are working with a financial application your company has used successfully on Windows 7 computers for more than seven years. The application does not respond when accessed on a Windows 10 Pro computer. What compatibility option should you try in order to get this program working?

    a. Run This Program in Compatibility Mode For (and select Windows 7)

    b. Reduced Color Mode

    c. Disable Display Scaling on High DPI Settings

    d. Run This Program as an Administrator

8. You are implementing App-V in your enterprise. Where are the programs stored?

    a. On a server file share

    b. On the client computers

    c. On the App-V publishing server

    d. On the App-V management server

9. Which of the following settings are synchronized by default on a UE-V enabled system? (Select all that apply.)

   a. Microsoft Office 2016

   b. Start menu settings

   c. All applications in the Program Files folder

   d. Internet Explorer 11

   e. Windows accessories

10. When you deploy UE-V in your organization, which of the following steps should you perform first?

   a. Create the settings storage location.

   b. Deploy the UE-V agent.

   c. Deploy the Group Policy Object with UE-V settings.

   d. Create settings location templates.

11. What tool is used to place applications available for installation into Microsoft Intune?

   a. Intune Portal upload tool

   b. Intune Software Publisher

   c. PowerShell Intune cmdlets

   d. Windows Update

12. You have published several applications to the Intune Portal and sent some emails to a few users asking them to test the installations and make sure the applications are installed correctly. They all responded that the applications were not available from the Portal when they logged in. What do you need to do to make sure the applications are available for installation?

   a. Create new Azure AD user accounts for the users.

   b. Deploy the applications to a user group.

   c. Add the users to Office 365.

   d. Deploy the applications to the device group.

   e. Give the users your administrator credentials.

Foundation Topics

Implementing Apps

You have learned about the Windows Store and the Universal Windows Platform (UWP) apps in earlier chapters, mainly in Chapter 5, "Installing and Managing Software." The material in the "Windows Store and Cloud Apps" section was specific to the 70-697 exam; however, it will be covered in the 70-698 exam, so you should review that material for both exams.

In this section, we cover material more specific to the 70-698 exam. You will need to review Chapter 5 for some of the objectives related to Windows Store and UWP. The following objectives are fully covered in Chapter 5, so the topic coverage is not included in this chapter:

- Configure Windows Store

- Implement Windows Store apps

- Provision packages

- Create packages

- Use deployment tools

Startup Options and Windows Features

One of Microsoft's objectives when developing Windows 10 was to improve the boot and startup times for the Windows operating system. If you have been using Windows 10, you are probably impressed by how fast it starts up, and it is clear that Microsoft succeeded in its goal of making Windows boot much faster than in previous versions.

Windows 10 includes a feature called Fast Startup, which leverages Hibernate to enable startup faster than is typically required for a normal cold boot. This feature was called Fast Boot in Windows 8 and 8.1. Typically, Fast Startup is enabled by default in Windows 10. You can check the option in Control Panel.

Step 1.   From Control Panel, access **Power Options**.

Step 2.   From the Power Options Control Panel applet, select **Choose What the Power Buttons Do**.

Step 3.   In the Shutdown Settings section, look for the Turn On Fast Startup option, as shown in Figure 18-1.

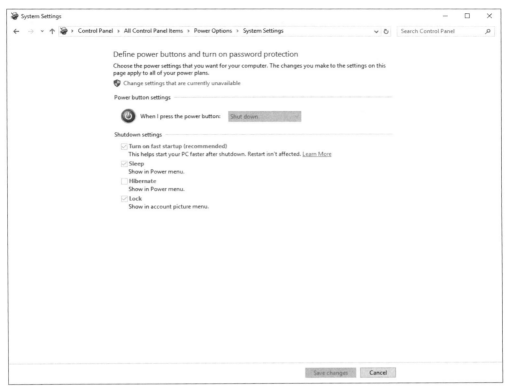

Figure 18-1   Enabling or Disabling the Fast Startup Option in the Control Panel Power Settings

Step 4.   To enable the option, click the **Change Settings That Are Currently Unavailable** link, and then check the **Turn On Fast Startup (Recommended)** option.

This option stores your computer's state by storing certain settings from the computer's memory into a file called hiberfil.sys in the root of the C: drive. When you start up the computer, it loads up the file in what is called Hybrid Startup mode.

Applications that are configured to start up during Windows boot can also affect the startup speed of the computer. You can view and manage the startup applications from the Task Manager. Use the steps that follow to view the startup applications.

Step 1.   Right-click the taskbar and select **Task Manager** from the pop-up menu (or press Ctrl+Shift+Esc).

Step 2.   Click the **More Details** option at the bottom of the Task Manager window.

Step 3.   From the Details view, select the **Startup** tab.

The Startup tab of Task Manager displays your startup applications, similar to Figure 18-2. The screen lists all the applications that will start up during Windows boot, along with the Publisher, the Status, and the Startup impact.

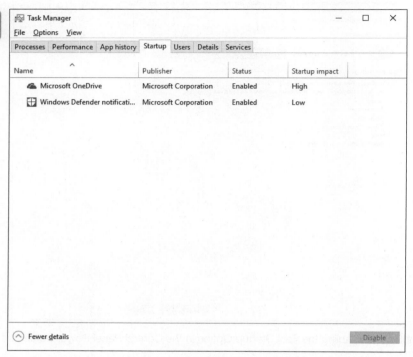

Figure 18-2 Startup Tab of the Task Manager Details View Allowing You to View and Manage Startup Applications

Notice from Figure 18-2 that impact shown for OneDrive is High. This indicates that OneDrive can significantly impact the startup speed of the system. From the dialog box you can select **Microsoft OneDrive** from the list and then click the **Disable** button. OneDrive will then not start up during the Windows boot. You can still use and access OneDrive after the system boots, or when you need to use it, but it will automatically start and sync up your OneDrive files. You can start it later from the Start menu to reenable the file sync.

Windows Store for Business

Introduced for Windows 10 and Windows 10 Mobile is the Windows Store for Business. It is designed for businesses that want to purchase and deploy store apps for their users from a central location. In this way it provides value to organizations by enabling volume purchases of apps and a central point for managing distribution.

You can also use the Windows Store for Business for deploying Line-of-Business (LOB) apps that you have developed for employees.

Windows Store for Business requires Windows 10 on a computer or mobile device, and users need Microsoft Azure AD accounts, which you create in the Azure AD. You can optionally use Microsoft Intune to manage distribution of the apps to users and devices. You learned about Microsoft Intune in Chapter 13, "Microsoft Intune."

Signup and User Configuration

To get started using Windows Store for Business, sign up at https://businessstore.microsoft.com. If you already have an Azure account, after you agree to the terms of service, your account will be set up. The first person to sign in must be a Global Admin of the Azure AD tenant. You can then access the main page of the store, which will be similar to Figure 18-3.

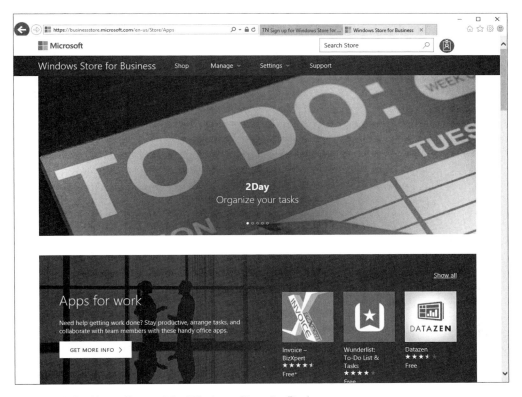

Figure 18-3 Home Page of the Windows Store for Business

When you sign up, you can then assign roles to other employees in the Azure AD to administer the Windows Store for Business. The store is integrated with Azure AD,

Office 365, and, if you are using Microsoft Intune, it can integrate with that management tool as well. You learned about these cloud services in Chapter 13.

You can assign roles to other users in your organization to help administer the store and the apps you make available through purchase or upload. From the store portal shown in Figure 18-3, click the **Settings** menu and then select **Permission**. When you first sign up, the only user will be yourself, and as mentioned, you will have the Global Admin role. To add other users, click the **Add People** link. This displays the page shown in Figure 18-4.

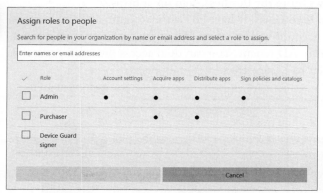

Figure 18-4   Assigning User Roles in Windows Store for Business

Using the Assign Roles to People page, click in the Search box to find a user. Recall that users must exist in your tenant Azure AD, and you can search by name or email address. Select the user you want from the search list, and the user will be added to the box. You can select multiple users if you want to assign the same role to several people. Check the box for the role to assign, and then click the **Save** button.

The Store for Business administrators will have permissions to configure a number of settings in the store.

- **Account information:** Manage the organization account and payment information, and configure whether to make offline-licensed apps available through the Store for Business account.

- **Device Guard signing:** Use the Device Guard signing portal to add unsigned apps to a code integrity policy. You can also sign code integrity policies.

- **LOB publishers:** You can assign developers in your organizations to become LOB publishers. Your list of LOB publishers can be activated or invited. LOB publishers can add custom-developed apps to your store.

■ **Management tools:** View the management tools integrated with Azure AD. You can choose one for management app updates and distribution, as shown in Figure 18-5. If you used Microsoft Intune as an MDM as described in Chapter 13, it is available to activate as the management tool in your integrated Windows Store for Business account.

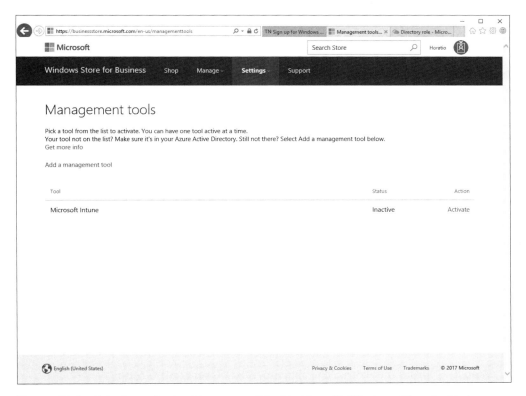

Figure 18-5   Selecting a Device Management Tool to Use with Windows Store for Business

■ **Permissions:** Manage permissions for organizational employees.

■ **Private store:** Update the name for the private store. The name will be displayed on a tab in the Store.

Device Guard is a set of features designed to improve security of connected devices using virtualization-based security options. Implementing Device Guard locks down devices so that only the software or programs from trusted software publishers is allowed to run on the device. To use LOB applications on these devices requires signing the applications so that they are trusted on the device and will be allowed to run. You learned about Device Guard in Chapter 7, "Windows 10 Security."

NOTE   To learn more about Device Guard signing for Windows Store for Business, see "Device Guard Signing" at https://technet.microsoft.com/en-us/itpro/windows/manage/device-guard-signing-portal.

Note that the preceding roles are Windows Store for Business roles. Permissions for each role are shown in Figure 18-4. Users in your Azure AD will automatically be assigned permissions in the store, as detailed in Table 18-2.

Table 18-2   Global User Account Permissions in Windows Store for Business

Permission	Global Administrator	User Administrator	Billing Administrator
Assign Roles	Yes	Yes	No
Modify Company Profile	Yes	No	No
Manage Store for Business Settings	Yes	No	No
Acquire Apps	Yes	No	Yes
Distribute Apps	Yes	No	Yes
Sign Policies and Catalogs	Yes	No	No

Global user roles are assigned in Azure AD. Use the following procedure to assign Global roles in Azure AD:

Step 1.   Log in to the Azure portal at https://portal.azure.com.

Step 2.   Select **Azure Active Directory** from the menu.

Step 3.   From the Azure AD submenu, select **Users and Groups**.

Step 4.   Select **All Users**, and then select the user you want to configure. You can use the Search box at the top of the All Users list to find a user.

Step 5.   From the user menu shown, select **Directory Role**.

Step 6.   From the Directory role page, use the option buttons to select whether the user is a normal User, a Global Administrator, or a Limited Administrator.

Step 7.   If you select Limited Administrator, a list of options appears. You can select multiple administration roles. The two that apply to the Store for Business are the Billing Administrator role and the User Administrator role.

Step 8.   After making your selections, click the **Save** button.

When a user has an applicable Global rule in your Azure AD, she can sign into the Windows Store for Business and perform the functions based on her role, as described in Table 18-2.

Working with Store for Business Apps

Similar to the Window Store, the Windows Store for Business has thousands of apps that you can acquire and make available to your users. The apps are UWP apps, designed for Windows 10, Windows Phone, Surface Hub, Windows IoT, and HoloLens. Some apps may have been written for Windows 8 or Windows 8.1, but are compatible with Windows 10. When you add an app to your inventory, it will be assigned to a specific platform, or be available for all devices.

There are two licensing models for the apps you can add to your Windows Store for Business:

- **Online licensing:** This is the traditional model also used in Windows Store. Users connect to the Store for Business to get an app and license, based on their Azure AD accounts. You can distribute these apps by assigning them to your users, adding it to the private store for users to download, or distribute them through a management tool.

- **Offline licensing:** For apps that are available for offline licensing, you can download the apps and deploy them using your private network. This allows you to deploy these apps on devices that cannot access the store. To distribute these apps, you can either use a provisioning package in a deployment image or use a management tool such as Microsoft Intune.

Some apps in the Store for Business are free, and some require a licensing fee. To acquire apps that require a fee, add payment information to your Store for Business account, or you can provide a payment method when you acquire the app. Use the following procedure to acquire apps from the Store:

Step 1. Log in to your Store for Business portal with an account that has permissions to acquire apps.

Step 2. Select the **Shop** menu, or use the Search bar to find an app, and then click the app you want to purchase.

Step 3. From the app description page, select the license type.

Step 4. Free apps are added to your Inventory when you select Get the App. For paid apps, select the quantity of the app you want and click **Next**. If your account does not have a payment method configured, you will be prompted for payment.

Step 5.   After the app has been acquired, it appears in your Inventory. Select **Inventory** from the Manage menu to see your apps. Your Inventory is displayed, as shown in Figure 18-6.

Step 6.   To add the app to your private store, click the **Actions** column for the app and then select **Add to Private Store**.

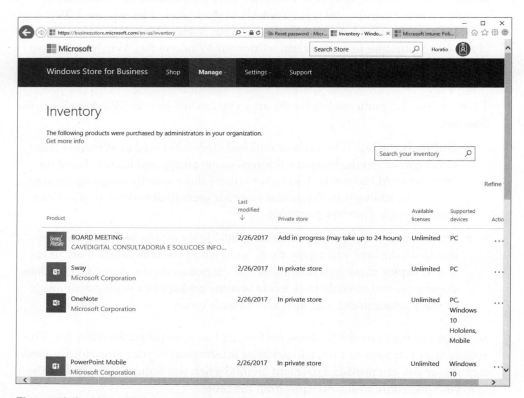

Figure 18-6   Your Windows Store for Business Inventory

From the Inventory page shown in Figure 18-6, you can start assigning apps to users. To do so, click the **Actions** column for the app and then select **Assign to People**. Type the name of a user into the box provided, as shown in Figure 18-7. You can continue to add names for all the people you want to assign the app to. When you are finished, click the **Assign** button.

Figure 18-7   Assigning an App to Users in the Store for Business

Client Configuration

By default, when users log in to their computers using their Azure AD credentials, the Store for Business private store will be available as a tab on the Store when they open it, as shown in Figure 18-8. Users who are using a device that is not connected to the Azure AD, or who are using a local account, can still access the private store by using the Add Work or School Account option and signing in with their Azure AD credentials, as shown in Figure 18-9.

Figure 18-8   Private Store Tab on the Windows 10 Store App

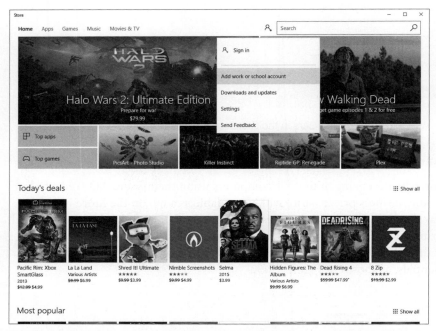

Figure 18-9   Adding a Work or School Account to the Windows 10 Store App

You can configure your devices to limit access only to your organization's private store. If you are using Microsoft Intune to manage your devices, you can configure a policy to enforce the store setting. Use a Custom Configuration policy and configure the **ApplicationManagement/RequirePrivateStoreOnly** policy setting, as shown in Figure 18-10.

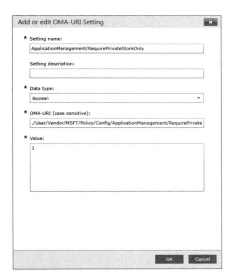

Figure 18-10   Allowing Only the Private Store Using Microsoft Intune Policy

You can also enforce the setting to allow only your private store by using Group Policy Objects. The GPO setting is found in Computer Configuration\ Administrative Templates\Windows Components\Store. Enable the policy called **Only Display the Private Store Within the Windows Store App**, as shown in Figure 18-11 to allow only the private store. You can then attach the GPO to any OU in your Active Directory.

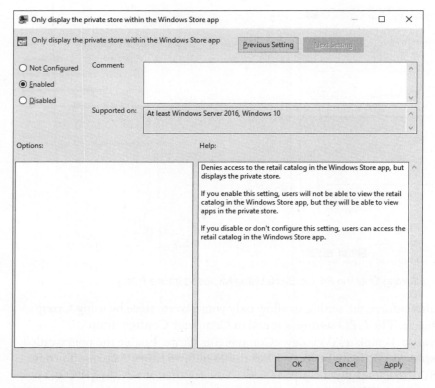

Figure 18-11   Allowing Only the Windows Store Using Windows Group Policy Objects

> **NOTE**   For more information about Windows Store for Business and how to manage your private store and apps, start with the references in the article "Windows Store for Business" at https://technet.microsoft.com/en-us/itpro/windows/manage/windows-store-for-business.

Windows Assessment and Deployment Kit (ADK)

You learned some of the features and applications available in the Windows Assessment and Deployment Kit (ADK) in previous chapters of this text. Table 18-3 is provided here as a reference to the tools provided in the ADK that you have learned about and the chapter where it is covered. This section focuses on how the ADK can help you to implement apps and administer them on Windows 10.

Table 18-3 Tools and Features of the ADK and Where They Are Covered

Topic	Chapter
Windows System Image Manager	Chapter 2, see "Performing an Unattended Installation of Windows 10"
Installing the ADK	Chapter 2, see "Performing an Unattended Installation of Windows 10"
Windows Imaging and Configuration Designer (ICD)	Chapter 4, see "The Windows Imaging and Configuration Designer (ICD)"
Provisioning Packages	Chapter 4, see "The Windows Imaging and Configuration Designer (ICD)"
User State Migration Tool (USMT)	Chapter 9, see "Migrating User Profiles"

A lot of functionality is available in the ADK. You can review Chapter 2 for information about installation of the ADK and the options available to install on a reference computer or an administration computer. Several additional tools are discussed in this chapter. If you are preparing for the 70-698 exam, you should also review the topics in other chapters, and the topics in the following list are also required for the 70-697 exam:

- **Application Compatibility Tools:** You learn about these tools in the next section, "Desktop Application Compatibility." The Microsoft SQL Server 2012 Express database is also available in the ADK and can be used for storing your application compatibility settings.

- **Microsoft User Experience Virtualization (UE-V) Template Generator:** You learn about UE-V in this chapter in the "User Experience Virtualization" section. The template is a useful tool for managing UE-V.

- **Microsoft Application Virtualization (App-V) Sequencer:** You learn about App-V in the next section, "Desktop Application Compatibility."

Desktop Application Compatibility

As noted in Chapter 2, "Implementing Windows," when you move to a new operating system, you should look at software compatibility while you are in the planning, development, and testing phases of the new operating system. Windows 10 is no different in this matter. Many applications that were originally developed for Windows Vista, 7, or 8.1 might not run properly on Windows 10; antivirus applications developed for older Windows operating systems in particular are often incompatible.

In this section you learn how to use the Application Compatibility Toolkit (ACT) to identify incompatible applications and develop a strategy to deal with them. You also learn about some strategies for supporting incompatible applications, and tools for handling application coexistence when it can be problematic.

Application Compatibility Toolkit (ACT) and Compatibility Database

ACT is a Microsoft resource that helps administrators resolve compatibility of their applications with Windows 10. ACT is included with the Windows ADK and provides compatibility fixes, modes, and help messages; tools for created customized fixes and help messages; compatibility databases; and a query tool you can use to search for installed compatibility fixes on local computers.

Using the Application Compatibility Toolkit (ACT)

ACT helps organizations to produce a comprehensive inventory of fixes and compatibility modes. It also identifies which applications might require additional testing or the use of a shim, which is a minor system compatibility fix that assists in enabling older applications to work properly with Windows 10.

ACT 6.1 is included with the Windows Assessment and Deployment Kit (ADK), which you can download from https://msdn.microsoft.com/en-us/windows/hardware/commercialize/adk-install. If you installed the ADK as described in Chapter 2, using the defaults as previously shown in Figure 2-9, you will need to return to the installation wizard to complete the installation and configuration of ACT. Use the following procedure:

Step 1. In the taskbar Search text box or Cortana, type **adk** and then select **adksetup.exe**.

Step 2. You are informed that the features installed are up-to-date and given additional options. Click **Change** and then click **Continue**.

Step 3. From the Select the Features You Want to Change dialog box, select **Application Compatibility Toolkit (ACT)** and **Microsoft SQL Server 2012 Express**, and then click **Change**.

Step 4. If you receive a UAC prompt, click **Yes**.

Step 5. Wait while installation of ACT takes place. Click **Close** when finished.

After you've installed the ACT, you can access the Compatibility Administrator by typing **compatibility administrator** into the Search bar or Cortana and selecting this item from the list that appears. As shown in Figure 18-12, the Compatibility Administrator comes loaded with fixes and settings for hundreds of applications that Microsoft has tested. You can apply compatibility fixes and compatibility modes to any application and then save the information you've configured to an SQL database, either on a computer running SQL server or by using SQL Express, available for installation of the ADK.

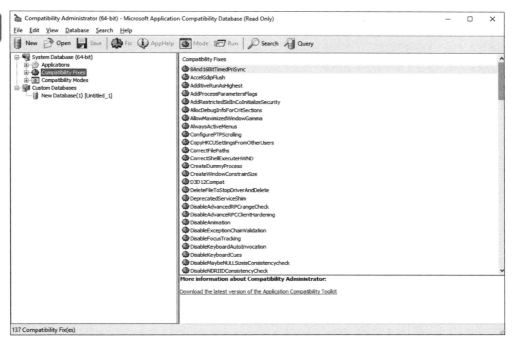

Figure 18-12   Compatibility Administrator Helps You to Configure the Compatibility of Hundreds of Applications Originally Written for Older Windows Versions

Note that there are two versions of the Compatibility Administrator, a 32-bit and a 64-bit version. You need to use the 32-bit version for 32-bit applications, and the 64-bit version for 64-bit applications. You also need to maintain separate databases for each.

You can search for fixes that are currently installed using the Search tool. To find applications that have fixes, ensure that you are using the right version of the Compatibility Administrator (32-bit or 64-bit) for the applications you want to search:

Step 1.   From the Compatibility Administrator window, click the **Search** button.

Step 2.   Click the **Browse** button and select the directory to search.

Step 3.   Select at least one of the search options: **Entries with Compatibility Fixes**, **Entries with Compatibility Modes**, and/or **Entries with AppHelp**.

Step 4.   Click the **Find Now** button to start the search. Any results will show up in the lower window, as shown in Figure 18-13.

Step 5.   Click the **Export** button to save your search results to a text file. You can also double-click one of the files to view details of the fix from the database.

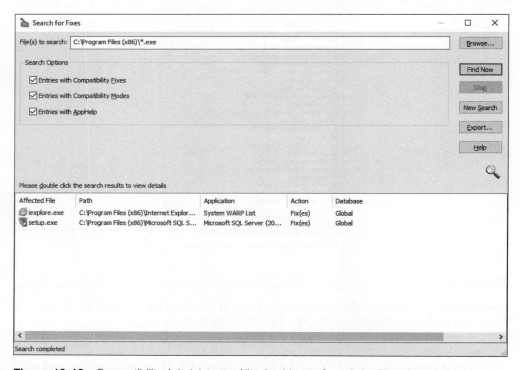

Figure 18-13   Compatibility Administrator Allowing You to Search for Fixes for Applications Installed on the Local Computer

A lot of fixes are included with the ACT. These fixes are small pieces of code that capture API calls and translate them to current Windows API calls so that the application works the same way it did on older versions. You can search for applications with fixes using the Compatibility Administrator. Expand the Applications node from the left pane to find the application by name. Select the application to view the fixes available, as shown in Figure 18-14.

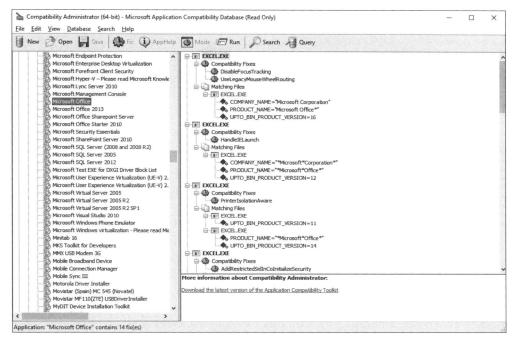

Figure 18-14   Compatibility Administrator Allowing You to Find Existing Fixes Available for Many Applications

You can enable and disable any fix using the Administrator tool. It may be necessary to disable a fix; for example, if a vendor has released a new version of the application, you will need to disable the fix to test the application and confirm that the new version is correct. To disable a fix, select the application from the list in the left pane, click the **Database** menu, and then select **Disable Entry**. You can enable a fix using the same procedure.

More details in the usage and configuration of ACT are beyond the scope of the 70-697 exam and are not included here.

> **NOTE**   To learn more about using the tool to manage and create fixes, follow the references in the article "Managing Application-Compatibility Fixes and Custom Fix Database" at https://technet.microsoft.com/en-us/itpro/windows/plan/managing-application-compatibility-fixes-and-custom-fix-databases?f=255&MSPPError=-2147217396.

NOTE   Most of the functionality available in previous versions of the ACT has been replaced with Upgrade Analytics, part of the Microsoft Operations Management Suite of tools. Learn more about the Upgrade Analytics solutions by following the links in the "SUA User's Guide" at https://technet.microsoft.com/en-us/itpro/windows/plan/sua-users-guide.

Using Windows Installer

Windows Installer is an application installer and configuration service that Microsoft has provided with Windows versions dating back to Windows XP and Windows Server 2003. It enables you to install, configure, update, and patch applications efficiently, thereby reducing total cost of ownership (TCO). Currently in version 5.0, Windows Installer running on a Windows 10 or Windows Server 2016 computer supports the installation of applications on all versions of Windows, including approved apps on Windows 10. Windows Installer offers a method of installing applications in a consistent manner. Using this method, a manufacturer can provide a way to package an application so that administrators can create scripted packages and deploy the application to Windows computers throughout a network.

Windows Installer enables administrators to deploy software so that it is always available to users and repairs itself if needed. The software is always available to a user, regardless of what happens. If a user's computer fails, a support person needs only to provide a replacement computer with Windows 10 installed. The user starts the computer and logs on, and the required software packages are automatically installed. Should necessary files become corrupted or deleted, they are automatically reinstalled the next time the user requires the application.

Recent improvements in the functionality of Windows Installer include the following:

- Windows Installer 3.0 and later can install multiple patches with a single transaction that integrates the progress of installation, rollbacks, and reboots. This includes that application of patches in a specified sequence.

- Windows Installer 4.5 and later can use transaction processing in installing multiple packages. In other words, if the entire installation cannot complete successfully or is canceled by the user, Windows Installer rolls back changes and restores the computer to its original status. This ensures that all packages in a multipackage transaction are installed or none of them are installed.

- Windows Installer 5.0 can enumerate all components installed on the computer. In addition, packages can be used to customize the services on a computer. Developers can modify packages for installing an application according to per-user or per-computer scenarios.

■ Windows Installer 5.0 enables administrators to author packages to secure new accounts, Windows services, files, folders, and Registry keys. You can use a security descriptor that specifies permissions denial or inheritance from a parent source, or specifies permissions of a new account.

Windows Installer uses the following file types:

■ Application installation files use the .msi file extension. These are the basic files that install all programs.

■ Transform files use the .mst extension. These files are created to "transform," or script, the way the installation takes place.

■ Patch files use the .msp extension. These files apply hotfixes or other patches that correct bugs or security problems with the associated application.

In an Active Directory Domain Services (AD DS) environment, Windows Installer takes advantage of Group Policy Objects (GPOs) for deployment purposes. You can use a GPO to deploy applications in any of the following ways:

■ **Publish a Package to Users:** Provides users who receive this GPO with the capability to install the application through the Control Panel Programs applet. The application will also be installed when the user attempts to open a file whose extension is associated with the application.

■ **Assign a Package to Users:** Automatically provides the application within the Start screen of any computer that the user logs on to. The application installs upon the activation of the icon in the Start screen or when the user attempts to open a file whose extension is associated with the application.

■ **Assign a Package to Computers:** Installs the application automatically upon startup.

CAUTION Never assign a Windows Installer Application to both a user and a computer. If you do so, and the two GPOs use different transforms, the operating system will install and uninstall the application every time it is accessed.

When you right-click any .msi file, you see the options shown in Figure 18-15 pertaining to file installation actions, as described in the list that follows.

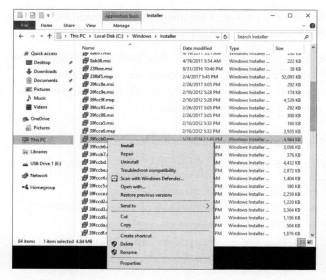

Figure 18-15   Windows Installer Options Pertaining to Application Installation Actions

- **Install:** The default. Installs the application using default parameters.

- **Repair:** Attempts to repair an unsuccessful installation. Use this option when you've had a problem.

- **Uninstall:** Use this option to remove the application, especially when the application installs improperly.

- **Troubleshoot Compatibility:** Starts a wizard that enables you to test program compatibility settings before installing the program.

From the command line, you can use the Msiexec.exe file along with the .msi package name to install, uninstall, or repair the package, as well as to advertise or create an installation package. (Advertising a program does not install it on a computer—it makes the application available for the user to install.) You can use any of the following actions with Msiexec.exe from a command prompt:

- To install an application, type **msiexec /I** *filename*.**msi**, where *filename* is the name of the application.

- To remove an application, type **msiexec /X** *filename*.**msi**.

- The repair parameters can assist when troubleshooting a Windows Installer problem. To repair the application, type **msiexec /F** [*parameter*] *filename*.**msi**, where [*parameter*] refers to an option listed in Table 18-4 describing the repair action to be performed.

- To advertise an application, type **msiexec /J** [*parameter*] *filename***.msi**. There are two parameters for advertising: **m** advertises to all users on the computer, whereas **u** advertises only to the current user.

- Administrative installation packages are required for deploying applications from network shares. To create an administrative package for deployment, type **msiexec /A filename.msi**.

Table 18-4   Msiexec.exe Repair Parameters

Parameter	Function	Troubleshooting Usage
a	Reinstalls all the files for the application	Use when the application does not completely install.
c	Reinstalls any missing file or one whose checksum is invalid	Use when you receive file missing error messages.
d	Reinstalls any missing file or an invalid version of a file	Use after installing a different application that overwrites shared files and you receive errors or experience problems.
e	Reinstalls any missing file, or an equal or older version of a file	Use when you have rolled back another application's installation and then you receive error messages.
m	Rewrites the Registry entries of the application that are attached to the computer (HKEY_LOCAL_MACHINE)	Use when the application displays the same error for all users who use the computer.
o	Reinstalls any missing file or an older version of a file	Use when you have rolled back another application's installation and then you receive error messages.
p	Reinstalls any missing file	Use when the application does not finish copying files.
s	Re-creates application shortcuts	Use when you use a Start screen or desktop icon and the application does not open, but you can run the application from the command line or Run dialog box.
u	Rewrites the Registry entries of the applications that are attached to the user (HKEY_USERS or HKEY_CURRENT_USER)	Use when the application works for one user but does not work for another, even though they are using the same computer.

Parameter	Function	Troubleshooting Usage
v	Caches a package locally (overwriting any existing cached package) and then runs the application from the source	Use when you install from a network location that is connected by a slow or unpredictable network link, or when the application has failed during the file copy process. The **v** option should be used only for reinstall—do not use this option for the first installation.

NOTE   For additional parameters used with Msiexec.exe, open a command prompt and type **msiexec /?**. Also refer to "Command-Line Options" at https://msdn.microsoft.com/en-us/library/aa367988.aspx.

The Windows Installer service runs on each computer and depends upon the Remote Procedure Call (RPC) service. The Windows Installer service, by default, does not start up automatically when you boot Windows 10. Instead, it starts up whenever an .msi package is run. The service works in conjunction with the Msiexec.exe executable file, which interprets the information in the .msi file.

NOTE   You can use Msiexec.exe to repair .msi packages. If you have trouble with an .msi package, you can run the Msiexec.exe file from the command line to repair the package. You can also use Msiexec.exe to control the installation process through its optional command-line switches, whether you run it from the command line or use it in a script.

Understanding MSI Features and Support

Before Windows Installer standards were published for use by third-party manufacturers, each manufacturer developed a proprietary method of installation. These methods used different installation executables and assorted parameters and had varying degrees of scripting capabilities. A few companies developed software that could create a standard installation package, but they did not manage problems with files overwriting newer versions of the same file (the old DLL hell), and most had no method for rolling back versions nor provided a granular deployment method.

Windows Installer uses a standard set of installation rules. Compliant applications must handle versioning rules to prevent overwriting newer files, maintain a record of any changes made to Windows—both file changes and Registry keys—and be capable of functioning with the Msiexec.exe file and Windows Installer service.

The .msi file acts as a relational database in which the fields in the file contain the instructions that can effectively deploy an application. When an installation begins, the Windows Installer service and Msiexec.exe cooperatively convert the .msi data into an installation/uninstallation script.

A management application programming interface (API) is part of Windows Installer. This API tracks the installed applications, noting which features and components are selected and the path chosen by the installer. The API is able to determine which component is not functioning properly and is able to selectively reinstall the component, which avoids having to reinstall the entire application.

You can customize how an application is installed by creating a transform file, which has the extension of .mst. The transform file answers the questions that the installation process asks, such as the path for the application, the component selection, and other configuration options.

> **NOTE**   For more information on Windows Installer, refer to "Windows Installer" at https://msdn.microsoft.com/en-us/library/windows/desktop/cc185688(v=vs.85).aspx and links found in the document.

Implementing Shims

A *shim* is a minor system compatibility fix that assists in enabling applications originally written for older Windows versions to work with a newer operating system such as Windows 10. Applications communicate with Windows by calling functions built in to the operating system via an internal structure called the *application programming interface* (API). As the Windows operating system evolves from one version to the next (and even with updates to the same version), modification of these functions to suit all applications in use could limit the ability to improve Windows functionality or require considerable additional software code. This could lead to a "bloated" operating system.

By using a shim, the import address table redirects application programming interface (API) calls to the shim, whose code implements modifications that enable the application to work properly with Windows 10. An example would be the redirection of application output to a user-specific folder rather than a general folder, thereby enabling you to configure a more restrictive access control list (ACL) than would be otherwise needed. You can also use shims to locate system files that have been moved to a new location because of a change in Windows architecture; however, you cannot use a shim to circumvent built-in Windows security mechanisms.

CAUTION   You should regard shims as a temporary fix for your applications, to be used only until an updated version of the application becomes available.

Microsoft creates shims on a per-application basis and packages them in custom shim database files with the .sdb extension. You can install these files using the sdbinst.exe command-line tool, which is found in the %systemroot%\system32 folder on a 32-bit computer and in the %systemroot%\sysWOW64 folder on a 64-bit computer, as well as using the Compatibility Administrator, which you learned about earlier in this chapter. Open an administrative command prompt and type the following:

```
Sdbinst filename.sdb [-?] [-q] [-u filepath] [-g GUID] [-n "name"]
```

In this command, the parameters are as follows:

- *filename.sdb*: The path and name of the shim database you are installing
- [**-?**]: Displays help information
- [**-q**]: Quiet mode (automatically accepts prompts)
- [**-u** *filepath*]: Uninstalls the database specified by the file path
- [**-g** *GUID*]: Specifies the database to be installed using a GUID
- [**-n** "name"]: internal name of file (for uninstall only)

The workflow recommended by Microsoft for implementing shims includes the following steps:

Step 1.   Create a new compatibility database (*.sdb) using the Compatibility Administrator, which is a component of the Application Compatibility Toolkit (ACT).

Step 2.   Select the application and then select the required compatibility fixes or shims.

Step 3.   Test the application with the compatibility fix or shim.

Step 4.   Save the compatibility database and deploy using the **sdbinst.exe** command.

NOTE   For more information on using shims, refer to "Managing Application-Compatibility Fixes and Custom Fix Databases" and the references provided at https://technet.microsoft.com/en-us/itpro/windows/plan/managing-application-compatibility-fixes-and-custom-fix-databases.

Configuring File Associations and Default Program Settings

By default, when you open a file with a known extension, Windows opens this file with an application known as the *default program*. For example, Windows opens image files with the new Windows 10 Photos app by default. If you have more than one image viewer program installed on your computer, such as Irfan View, Breeze Browser, Adobe Bridge, or others including the older Windows Photo Viewer, you can choose which program opens the image by default when you double-click an image file with a given extension such as .jpg or .tif. Windows stores information in the Registry for all file types for which a default association has been defined or for which you have created a default program setting.

Modifying Default Program Settings

To modify default program settings or create new settings, use the following steps:

Step 1.   Open Control Panel from the Start menu Windows System category and choose the **Programs** category.

Step 2.   Click **Default Programs** to see the options shown in Figure 18-16.

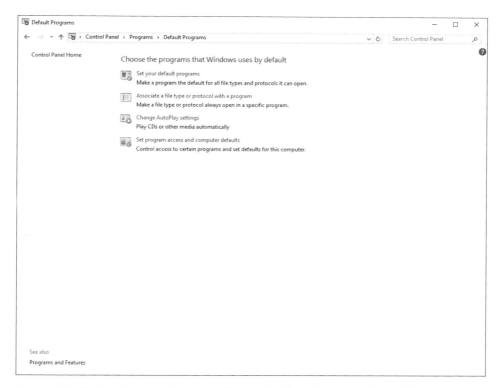

Figure 18-16   Control Panel Programs Applet Enabling You to Set Default Programs or Associate File Types with the Desired Program

Step 3.   Click **Set Your Default Programs**, and in the Set Your Default Programs window, select the program whose options you want to configure. You receive the options shown in Figure 18-17.

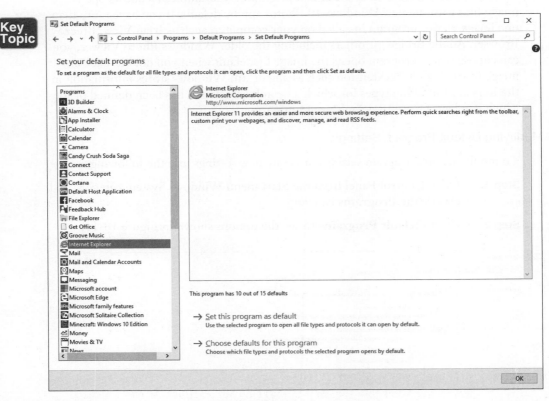

Figure 18-17   Set Your Default Programs Window Enabling You to Select a Program That Will Act as the Default for All File Types and Protocols That It Can Open

Step 4.   To use the selected program to open all file types and protocols it is capable of opening, click **Set This Program as Default**. To select from a list of file types and protocols, click **Choose Defaults for This Program**.

Step 5.   The Set Associations for a Program window shown in Figure 18-18 provides a list of file types the chosen program can open. Select the file extensions you want to have the program open. To choose all file types, select the **Select All** check box. To remove file types, deselect their check boxes. When finished, click **Save**.

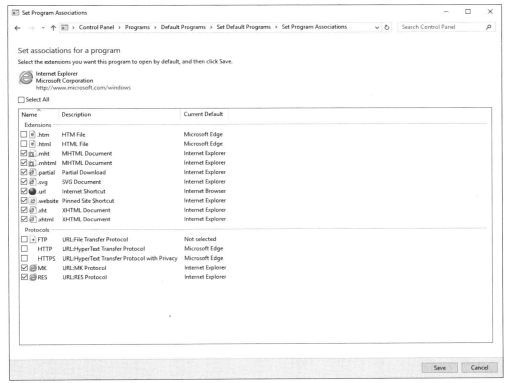

Figure 18-18 Selecting a Program as the Default for Its File Types

Step 6.   You are returned to the Set Your Default Programs window. If desired, select another program to modify its file associations. When finished, click **OK** to return to the Default Programs applet.

Associating File Extensions with Specific Programs

The Default Programs applet also lets you associate a file extension with a program. Use the following steps:

Step 1.   From the Default Programs applet, click **Associate a File Type or Protocol with a Program**. You receive the Associate a File Type or Protocol with a Specific Program window shown in Figure 18-19.

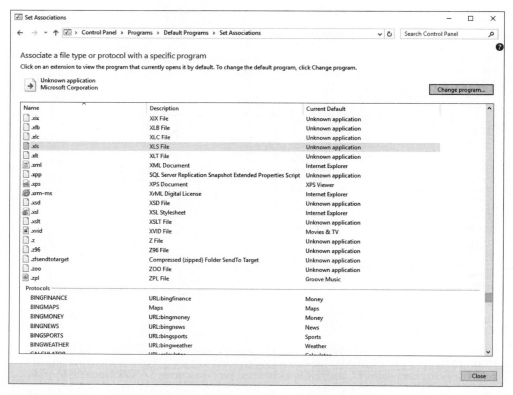

Figure 18-19   Associate a File Type or Protocol with a Specific Program Window Enabling You to Choose the Default Program to Be Used with a File Using a Given Extension

Step 2.   Scroll this list and select the extension whose default program you want to modify; for example, .xls. Then click **Change Program**.

Step 3.   If you want to change the default program, click **More Apps** to expand the list of available programs, as shown in Figure 18-20.

Step 4.   Select the desired program and then click **OK**. The list updates to reflect the change you've made.

Step 5.   Repeat for any other extensions you want to modify. When finished, click **Close** to return to the Default programs applet.

If Windows cannot associate the selected file extension with a program, you are given the option of trying an app on the computer or locating one from the Windows Store. Selecting an app on the computer brings up a list similar to that shown in Figure 18-20. Select a program you think might be able to open the file extension.

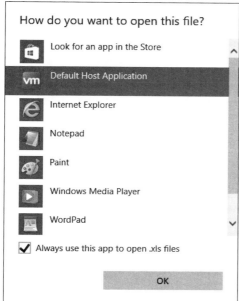

Figure 18-20   List of Programs That Are Capable of Opening a File with the Given Extension

NOTE   You can also modify a file association from any File Explorer window. Right-click a file with the extension you want to modify and choose **Open With**. You receive a dialog box similar to that shown in Figure 18-20, which enables you to accept the current default or choose a new one.

CAUTION   It is possible that the selected application will be unable to open a file with the extension you have selected. If you receive an error message when attempting to open such a file, return to the Set Associations window, click **Change Program** again, and either select another program on the computer or attempt to locate one online.

Configuring Application Compatibility Mode

As in previous Windows versions, Windows 10 provides the Application Compatibility mode that assists you in troubleshooting applications that do not run properly in Windows 10. In general, applications originally written for Windows 7 or

Windows 8.1 should work in Windows 10. Applications written for older versions of Windows might not run properly, might stop responding (hang), or might refuse to start at all. If these applications worked properly in previous Windows versions, this could indicate a compatibility issue with Windows 10. Application Compatibility mode emulates the environment found on versions of Windows as far back as Windows 95. This mode also provides several other options that might enable a program to run. Use the following procedure to configure Application Compatibility mode:

Step 1.   Right-click the shortcut to the program from the Start menu or desktop and choose **Properties**.

Step 2.   Select the **Compatibility** tab to display the options listed in Table 18-5 and shown in Figure 18-21.

Table 18-5   Application Compatibility Options

Option	Description
Run compatibility troubleshooter	Starts a troubleshooting routine that attempts to discern the cause of compatibility problems. You are presented with options to try a set of recommended compatibility settings or troubleshoot the program further based on problems suggested in Figure 18-22.
Run this program in compatibility mode for	Select the Windows version from the drop-down list that you know the program works properly on.
Reduced color mode	Uses a limited set of colors to run the program. Some older programs are designed to run in this color space.
Run in 640×480 screen resolution	Runs this program in a smaller window. Try this option if the graphical user interface (GUI) appears jagged or is rendered poorly.
Disable display scaling on high DPI settings	Shuts off automatic font resizing if you are using large-scale font sizes. Try this option if large-scale fonts interfere with the program's appearance.
Run this program as an administrator	Some programs require Administrator mode to execute properly. You will receive a User Account Control (UAC) prompt when this option is selected. This option is not available to nonadministrative users.
Change settings for all users	Enables you to choose settings that will apply to all users on the computer.

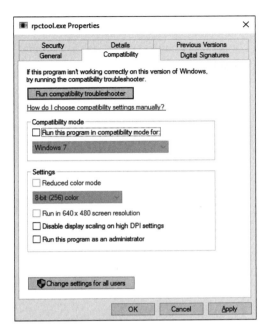

Figure 18-21 Compatibility Tab of an Application's Properties Dialog Box

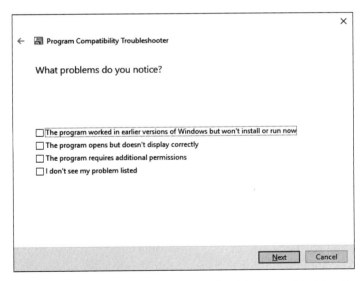

Figure 18-22 Program Compatibility Troubleshooter Enabling You to Choose from Several Possible Compatibility Problems

Step 3.　Select one or more of these options and then click **Apply**.

Step 4.　Test the program to see if it works properly. If necessary, repeat Steps 3 and 4 until the program does work properly.

CAUTION　You should not use the Program Compatibility options with older anti-virus programs, disk utilities, or system programs. Such programs might cause data loss or create a security risk.

Desktop Application Coexistence

During deployment planning for rolling out Windows 10 in your organization, you will need to make an effort to identify any applications that may not be compatible with Windows 10. You may also encounter scenarios that require an older version of an application to run on the same computer with the newer version. Because many applications update the older version instead of leaving it in place, you need to find a way to isolate the older and newer versions.

In some circumstances, you may have applications that will not work even with Compatibility mode. It might be an older application that is still needed or that the organization is heavily invested in. You might run into applications that a small group in your organization needs but that cannot run in Windows 10.

Eliminating these programs from your organization can be problematic. Even if it is a small group of users who rely on it, their business processes might rely on that application for day-to-day operations. It might be an application developed in-house that will take a significant effort to update. Or it might have been developed by a third-party vendor that is no longer in business.

Supporting applications that need to coexist with other applications, or need to be accessible from Windows 10 but cannot run in Windows 10 natively, can be supported in one of three ways.

- **Use Client Hyper-V:** You can use Windows Client Hyper-V for any of these scenarios. Users can run an older version of Windows as a VM under Hyper-V and access their application in the virtual desktop. Older applications can be supported the same way, even if compatible with Windows 10. You can run the older application in a Windows 10 VM, while the newer application is available directly on the host. You learned about Hyper-V in Chapter 10, "Windows Hyper-V."

- **RemoteApp:** Another option for handling incompatible applications is to run them as a RemoteApp on a Windows Server. This is a good option for running multiple versions of an application, but it may be problematic if the application is incompatible with Windows 10, because you would need to use older versions of Windows Server. An application that will not run on Windows 10 cannot be hosted in RemoteApp on Windows Server 2016. So consider the road map for your server infrastructure in this case. You learned about RemoteApp in Chapter 17.

■ **App-V:** App-V is a virtualization technology that allows you to virtualize applications and run them side by side on the same computer. Similar to RemoteApp, users can access an application in App-V from anywhere and use it as if it is installed locally on their device. You will learn about App-V next in this section.

Managing App-V Applications

In recent years, as the workers have become more mobile and require access to their files and applications anywhere at any time, Microsoft has developed technologies to help make mobility easier for workers and the IT professionals that support them. Virtualization technologies and cloud computing are part of this mobility evolution. Microsoft Application Virtualization (App-V) is Microsoft's application virtualization and streaming solution.

App-V enables centralized management of application management and deployment. User applications and their application settings are maintained centrally and are managed using Active Directory and Group Policies. Only the App-V client is required on local Windows platforms, allowing users to access their applications from any organization client over the network, or when offline if the application has been run previously from that client computer. The application is never installed locally.

Overview of App-V

With App-V 5.1, virtual applications work more like traditional, locally installed applications. Applications are isolated as in older versions, but now separate App-V applications can be enabled to communicate with each other, allowing integrations between them when required.

To take advantage of centralized management and distribution of App-V applications, Windows Configuration Manager 2012 or App-V v5 server is required. On the server side, App-V includes an App-V Management Server along with a database to provide the overall management of the infrastructure, an App-V Publishing Server for hosting and streaming functionality for the virtual applications, and an App-V Reporting Server and database that provides App-V reporting services. Using these components allows an administrator to manage the applications and sessions, and publish applications for users to the Publishing Server. Users access their applications using an App-V client.

The App-V client is configured to connect to the server to stream the content or, optionally, download to a local drive. Note that App-V applications can run without a centrally managed infrastructure. The applications still run in isolation and are not installed locally, but applications cannot be updated and per-user authorization is not possible.

Application Virtualization, and virtualization in general, is a complex and involved topic, with its own field of study. For the 70-697 exam, you need not be an expert in virtualization technologies, but you should be able to identify App-V as a concept and know some basics of working with the App-V client on Windows 10.

The App-V client is distributed as part of the Microsoft Desktop Optimization Pack (MDOP). Windows 10 and Windows 8.1 already have all the software required for the App-V 5.1 client. For Windows 7 and Windows Server 2012, the following software is required:

- Microsoft Windows .NET Framework 4.5 (full package).

- Windows PowerShell 3.0 or later.

- The App-V Sequencer client may be needed to manage App-V packages.

NOTE   For more information on deploying the App-V client, see "Planning for the App-V 5.1 Sequencer and Client Deployment" at https://technet.microsoft.com/en-us/itpro/mdop/appv-v5/planning-for-the-app-v-51-sequencer-and-client-deployment and links found in the document.

NOTE   Managing and maintaining an enterprise App-V infrastructure are out of the scope of Exam 70-697 and this book. For details on the infrastructure configuration and management, start with the "Microsoft Application Virtualization 5.1 Administrator's Guide" at https://technet.microsoft.com/en-us/itpro/mdop/appv-v5/microsoft-application-virtualization-51-administrators-guide.

You can manage the App-V client and configuration from the client computer using the client management console, by using PowerShell, or using Group Policy.

The App-V Management Console

The App-V client provides a management application that can be used to perform some basic tasks for the App-V applications published for the user. Start the App-V client by clicking the Microsoft App-V Client UI tile from the Start menu, or typing **App-V** into the Search box or Cortana, and then clicking the **Microsoft Application Virtualization Client** link. From this screen, shown in Figure 18-23, you can work with the available App-V applications and App Connection Groups.

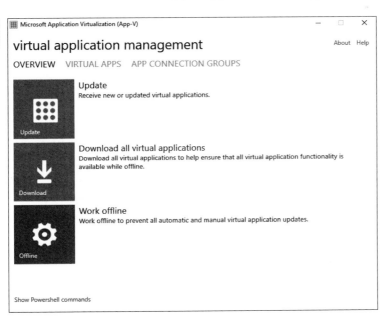

Figure 18-23 Managing App-V Applications from the App-V Client Management Console

The App-V client management console has the following features:

- **Overview tab:**

  - The Update tile is used to refresh an App-V application or receive a new package.

  - Use the Download tile to download all the packages published to the user.

  - Work Offline is used to disable all automatic and manual updates of App-V applications.

- **Virtual Apps tab:** Displays all the packages published to the user. You can select a package from the list to view the included applications and display information about package use and how much of the package has been downloaded to the computer. You can also use the Repair function to repair a misbehaving App-V package, but note that this will delete any user settings for that package.

- **App Connection Groups tab:** Clicking this tab displays all the connection groups available. Recall that a Connection Group is used to allow communication and integration between virtual applications. Select a group to view which packages are included.

App-V Command-Line Utilities

With App-V version 5.1, Microsoft has provided a suite of PowerShell scripts for managing applications, packaging, updates, and other tasks. These scripts require PowerShell version 3.0 or later. PowerShell version 3.0 was included with Windows 8, and PowerShell version 5.1 is included with Windows 10. Note the link at the bottom of the App-V management console screen from Figure 18-21 called Show PowerShell commands. Clicking the link displays the available commands for managing App-V applications on the client. Table 18-6 describes each command and how it is used.

The [*path*] parameter in these commands refers to the location of the App-V package. Typically this will be an HTTP URL such as http://appv-server/apps/MyApplication.appv; however, the path could also be the name of a file on a file share or even the local computer.

Table 18-6   PowerShell Commands for Managing App-V Clients

Command	Purpose
Get-AppvClientPackage	Returns a list of all App-V packages currently on the system. The following switch parameters are available to filter the results: **-Name**, **-Version**, **-PackageId**, and **-VersionId**.
Mount-AppvClientPackage	Downloads a package published for the user into the App-V cache.
Set-AppvPublishServer	Use to enable or disable automatic and manual updates of App-V applications.
Mount-AppvClientConnectionGroup	Download and/or repair Application Connection Groups available to the user.
Get-AppvPublishingServer	Display the current path(s) or URL(s) used for locating and downloading App-V applications. Returns the descriptive location name and a numeric **ServerId** for each publishing server.
Add-AppvPublishingServer	Add a new publishing location for App-V applications. The following parameters are required: **-Name** *LocationName* **-URL** *path or url*.

Command	Purpose
Sync-AppvPublishingServer	Checks the server and adds or removes packages and connection groups based on entitlements for the user. The parameter **-ServerId** can be used to select a specific server to sync.

NOTE   For more details about these commands, open a PowerShell version 3.0 prompt from a Windows computer with App-V 5.1 client installed, and type **Get-Help** followed by the name of command.

User Experience Virtualization

If you have used any Windows computer for a long period of time, you likely know how frustrating it is when the computer either dies or the hard drive becomes unrecoverable. Even if you have saved all your files and backups, you will have to reconfigure all your applications and their custom settings, the appearance of your system, and other settings to get back to the way you are used to working. Even if you have not, as an IT professional you know how frustrating it can be for your users.

It is also difficult if you work on different devices, because you need to duplicate your setup or deal with the defaults on any device you do not use the most.

With User Experience Virtualization (UE-V), you can capture all your customized settings for Windows and your application and store them on your private network on a server file share. When you log on to a device, your settings are applied. UE-V can apply custom settings on any device you use, and even on virtual desktop (VDI) sessions when you log on.

UE-V consists of both a server and client component. The client component is included with Windows 10 Enterprise edition. Table 18-7 describes at a high level the components involved in UE-V and the purpose of each.

Table 18-7   Components of UE-V

Component	Purpose
UE-V Service	The UE-V Windows service runs on every device that needs to synchronize user settings. It monitors applications and Windows settings and synchronizes any changes between devices.
Settings packages	Configuration settings are stored in settings packages managed by the UE-V service. The packages are locally stored and then copied to the file share storage location.

Component	Purpose
Settings storage location	The storage location is a network file share that users have access to.
Settings location templates	Location templates are XML files used by UE-V to determine how to monitor and synchronize application settings and synchronize settings between devices.
Universal Windows applications list	The applications list is used by UE-V to determine which applications are enabled for synchronization. The list typically includes most Windows applications.

Some settings are synchronized by default on UE-V–enabled systems:

- Microsoft Office 2016, 2013, and 2010
- Internet Explorer 10 and 11
- Windows accessories (WordPad, NotePad)
- Desktop background
- Ease of Access
- Desktop settings (Start menu, taskbar, folder options, desktop icons, and regional and language settings)

Settings for applications are synchronized (saved and copied to the storage location) when you close the application. Settings for Windows are synchronized when you log off the device or when the device screen is locked.

Getting Started with UE-V

UE-V requires Windows 10 Enterprise or Windows 8 or 8.1 Enterprise or Pro edition for client computers. Clients must also have PowerShell 3.0 or later and .NET Framework 4.5 or later. It also requires Windows Server 2012 or later on the server side.

You will need to perform some configuration on the server and enable UE-V on client devices. Note that these are only basic high-level tasks. You should deploy UE-V in a lab environment and test it to make sure it meets your organization's requirements, and carefully plan the implementation if it does.

Select a centrally located computer and create the storage location. You should create a security group specifically for all UE-V users. Grant the group permission to create a directory, and grant full permission to all subdirectories. You should grant Full control at the share level to your UE-V group, and Read and Create Folders permissions to the UE-V group at the NTFS level. If you are using System Center

Configuration Manager (SCCM) in your organization, you can install and use the UE-V Configuration Pack to configure settings.

You can also configure UE-V using Group Policy Objects. Settings are available as administrative templates for computers and for users. Policy settings are available for configuring the UE-V services as well as specific settings for desktop applications and UWP apps. In Group Policy Management Editor, navigate to Computer Configuration\Administrative Templates\Windows Components\Microsoft User Experience Virtualization to edit the GPOs for UE-V, as shown in Figure 18-24.

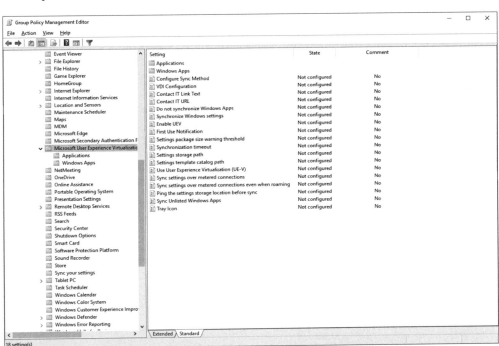

Figure 18-24   Configuring UE-V Using Group Policy Objects

The most important of the UE-V Group Policies are as follows:

- **Enable UEV:** This policy allows you to enable or disable the UE-V feature and services.

- **First Use Notification:** Enable this policy setting to enable a notification in the system tray that appears the first time the UE-V agent is run.

- **Settings Storage Path:** Use this policy to configure the UNC path name for the UE-V storage location. The share must be accessible by all UE-V users.

- **Settings Template Catalog Path:** If you use custom settings location templates, you can enable this policy and configure the UNC path name where the templates are stored.

- **Tray Icon:** This setting enables an icon in the system tray to display notifications for UE-V on users' computers.

- **Do Not Synchronize Windows Apps:** This policy defines whether UE-V synchronizes settings for Windows Store and UWP apps. By default, app settings are synched. You can enable this policy to turn off synchronization for apps.

Group Policy folders under Microsoft User Experience Virtualization, Applications, and Windows Apps contain a long list of applications that are synchronized by default. You can customize which applications and apps are synchronized by enabling or disabling the policy for each policy in these folders. If you do not configure these policies, the applications and apps will be synchronized by default.

Custom Settings Location Templates

UE-V will synchronize many applications based on the default templates that are included. If you want to use UE-V to synchronize other applications, such as third-party or LOB applications, you need to create custom location templates to support those applications.

The Windows Assessment and Deployment Kit (ADK) includes as an installation option the UE-V Template Generator, a tool that you can use to create custom settings location templates. After the generator is installed, you can start it using the icon on the Start menu, or by searching for **ue-v** in the Search bar or Cortana. The UE-V Template Generate screen will be similar to Figure 18-25.

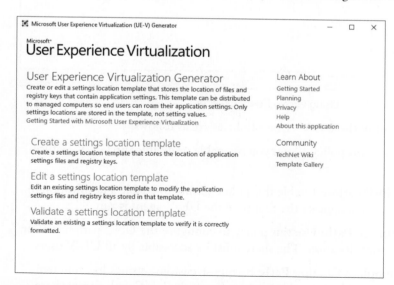

Figure 18-25   UE-V Settings Location Template Generator Tool

Use the following procedure to create a custom settings location template:

Step 1. From the UE-V settings location template generator, click **Create a Settings Location Template**.

Step 2. On the Specify Application page, click the **Browse** button to find the application .exe or shortcut (.lnk). Click **Next**.

Step 3. Wait for the application to start, and then close the application. The template generator will run in the background and detect where the application stores its settings. After the application is closed, click the **Next** button to continue.

Step 4. On the Review Locations page, check the Registry and Files locations that were detected. You can uncheck the boxes for any location you do not want to include in the synchronization. Click **Next**.

Step 5. On the Edit Template page, shown in Figure 18-26, you can review the location settings detected and modify them if needed. Click the Registry tab to see Registry locations, and the Files tab to view the files used for the application's settings. When you are satisfied, click **Create**.

Step 6. Select a location and save your XML template file.

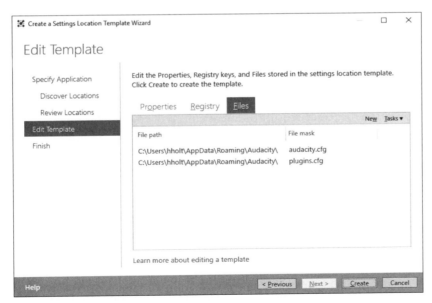

Figure 18-26 Editing a Location Template Using the UE-V Generator Tool

You should test your template before deploying it to the organization. If you need to make changes after testing, you can use the UE-V template generator to edit the template and save your changes.

You can deploy your template using SCCM, Group Policy, or using the UE-V settings template catalog, which is a share location you set up on the server when deploying UE-V for your organization. Templates deployed to the settings template catalog location are automatically updated by the UE-V service.

NOTE   For more information about UE-V, planning for deployment in an organization, and details for server and client configurations, start with the article "User Experience Virtualization (UE-V) for Windows 10 Overview" at https://technet.microsoft.com/en-us/itpro/windows/manage/uev-for-windows.

Using Microsoft Intune for Desktop Apps

In Chapter 13, "Microsoft Intune," you learned how to use the Microsoft Intune cloud-based management tool as a Mobile Device Management (MDM) solution, as well as how to enroll devices and Windows computers. You also learned about adding apps to Microsoft Intune and side-loading apps to configured devices.

For Windows 10 computers that you manage with Microsoft Intune and the Intune client, you can also manage desktop applications and deployment for your managed computers. The process is similar to deploying apps and deep linking apps, which you learned about in Chapter 13.

You can deploy applications that use Windows Installer (.exe or .msi files) by publishing the application files to Microsoft Intune. Publishing your applications is the first step. The process is the same as publishing a UWP (.appx) application. To install applications on PCs, they must be capable of silent installation without user interaction. Apps that cannot perform silent installation on computers will fail.

Use the following steps to publish desktop apps to Intune:

Step 1.   Log in to the Intune portal, select the **Apps** menu, and then select **Apps** from the submenu. All your current apps are displayed.

Step 2.   Click the **Add App** link. This launches the Intune Software Publisher Wizard.

Step 3.   On the Software Setup page, in the Select How This Software Is Made Available to Devices box, select **Software Installer**. For the Select the Software Installer File Type, select **Windows Installer**. Click the

Browse button and select the application setup file. If other files in the folder are required, check the **Include Additional Files and Folders from the Same Folder** check box. Click **Next**.

Step 4. On the next page, enter the publisher in the Publisher box, if it is not filled in automatically. You can optionally select an image to use for the application's icon. Click **Next**.

Step 5. On the Requirements page, you must select an architecture (32-bit or 64-bit) and an operating system if the application has minimum Windows version requirements. Select **Any** for these fields if the software runs on any version. Click **Next**.

Step 6. On the Detection rules page, you can tell Intune how it can tell if the software is already installed on a computer. This is useful for automatic deployment. Choose from either **Default Detection Rules** or add your own detection rule. You can add a rule based on whether a specific file exists, a Registry key, or an MSI product code, as shown in Figure 18-27. Click **Next**.

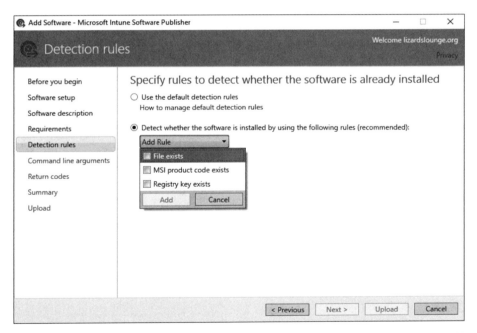

Figure 18-27   Selecting Software Detection Tools in the Intune Software Publishing Wizard

Step 7.   If the application installer needs any command-line arguments when it runs, you can provide them on the Command-Line Arguments page. If it does not, select **No**. If it does, select **Yes** and enter the arguments in the box provided. For instance, if the application is an .msi, you can add the **/s** parameter so that it will install silently.

Step 8.   The Return Codes pages allows you to select return codes to determine whether the installation was successful. Enter any return codes you want Intune to evaluate during the installation, or select **No** and then click **Next**.

Step 9.   Review the Summary page to make sure all your selections are correct, and then click the **Upload** button to upload your application installer to Intune.

After the upload of your application setup program is complete, the application appears in the list of apps on the Intune portal. The next step is to make your desktop application available for users to install. From the Intune portal list of apps, select the new application and click the **Manage Deployment** link to get started.

You can select the user groups that will be allowed to install the software, or select from device groups where you want the software deployed. You can use any combination of user and device groups for the deployment. When you click **Next**, you can select the Deployment Action for the groups you selected. For devices, you can only select **Required Install**. That means that Intune will automatically download the installer and install the application on those devices. For user groups, you can select **Required Install** or **Available Install**.

If you simply want to make the application available for users to download and install when they need it, you can select Available Install for the user group. Recall from Chapter 13 that user groups are managed in Azure AD. When you are finished with your selections, click the **Finish** button on the Manage Deployment Wizard.

Users can access the Microsoft Intune Center from the Windows 10 system tray icon, and click the **Get Applications from the Company Portal** link. The link will bring up the default browser so that the user can access the portal. After logging in, the user can view the apps available, as shown in Figure 18-28. Applications the user selects to install will be installed silently on the local computer.

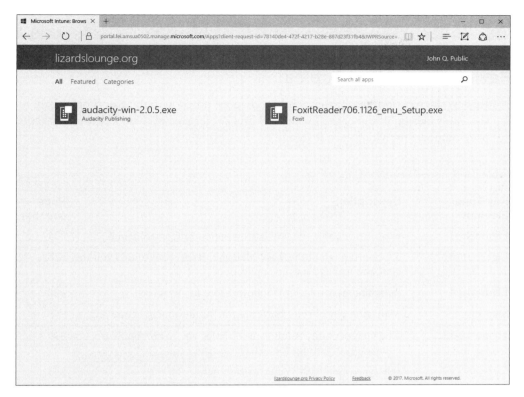

Figure 18-28 User Installation of Desktop Applications That You Make Available in the Microsoft Intune Portal

NOTE For more information on installing desktop applications in Microsoft Intune, see "Add Apps for Windows PCs That Run the Intune Software Client" at https://docs.microsoft.com/en-us/intune/deploy-use/add-apps-for-windows-pcs-in-microsoft-intune.

Exam Preparation Tasks

Review All the Key Topics

Review the most important topics in the chapter, noted with the Key Topics icon in the outer margin of the page. Table 18-8 lists a reference of these key topics and the page numbers on which each is found.

Table 18-8   Key Topics for Chapter 18

Key Topic Element	Description	Page Number
Figure 18-1	Enable or disable the fast startup option in Control Panel	825
Figure 18-2	The startup tab of the Task Manager details view allows you to view and manage startup applications	826
Figure 18-4	Assigning user roles in Windows Store for Business	828
Step List	Managing global rules for Store for Business using Azure AD	830
Figure 18-12	The Compatibility Administrator helps you to configure compatibility settings for older programs	839
List	File types used with Windows Installer	843
List	Describes available methods of software deployment using Group Policy	843
List	Describes types of actions you can perform using Msiexec.exe	844
Figure 18-17	Shows you how to set up default file types and protocols to be opened by a program	850
Figure 18-18	Shows you how to select file extensions to be opened by a program by default	851
Figure 18-20	Selecting a default program to be used with a specific file extension	853
Table 18-5	Application Compatibility Options	854
Figure 18-23	Manage App-V applications from the App-V client management console	859
Table 18-6	PowerShell commands for managing App-V clients	860
Table 18-7	Components of UE-V	861
Figure 18-24	UE-V Group Policies	863
Step List	Publishing an application to Microsoft Intune	866

Complete the Tables and Lists from Memory

Print a copy of Appendix B, "Memory Tables" (found on the book's website), or at least the section for this chapter, and complete the tables and lists from memory. Appendix C, "Memory Tables Answer Key," also on the website, includes completed tables and lists to check your work.

Definitions of Key Terms

Define the following key terms from this chapter, and check your answers in the glossary.

application compatibility, Application Compatibility Manager, Application Compatibility Toolkit (ACT), App-V, Assessment and Deployment Kit (ADK), default program, fast startup, .msi file, .msp file, .mst file, online licensing, offline licensing, private store, settings location template, shim, UE-V, Windows Store for Business

This chapter covers the following subjects:

- **Monitoring Windows 10:** This section shows you how to work with Event Viewer and configure event log subscriptions that enable you to collect events from multiple computers in one place. It continues by describing the capabilities of Performance Monitor. It introduces the concept of performance objects and counters and describes the more important objects and counters that you should be familiar with. It then shows you how to log information using data collector sets that can be stored for later analysis and display. Task Manager was completely redesigned with Windows 8.1, providing users with an easy view of process performance information and making it easier to locate processes that consume large amounts of computer resources or that are not responding, and there are a few changes for Windows 10. This section shows you how to configure the options presented by Task Manager.

- **Configuring Advanced Management Tools:** This section provides you with an overview of the Microsoft Management Console (MMC), the Services utility, Task Scheduler, and Windows PowerShell and how they help provide efficiency gains for managing daily or repeated tasks.

This chapter covers the following objectives for the 70-698 exam:

Monitor Windows: Configure and analyze Event Viewer logs, configure event subscriptions, monitor performance using Task Manager, monitor performance using Resource Monitor, monitor performance using Performance Monitor and Data Collector Sets, monitor system resources, monitor and manage printers, configure indexing options, manage client security by using Windows Defender, evaluate system stability using Reliability Monitor, troubleshoot performance issues.

Configure advanced management tools: Configure services, configure Device Manager, configure and use the MMC, configure Task Scheduler, configure automation of management tasks using Windows PowerShell.

CHAPTER 19

Monitoring and Managing Windows

When you first set up a brand new Windows 10 computer with a baseline set of applications, you will generally find that it performs very capably. As you install additional applications, store data, and work with the computer, its performance can slow down. Factors that affect a computer's performance include memory, processor, disks, and applications. Windows 10 contains an extensive suite of system and performance monitoring tools that enable you to monitor system performance and diagnose problems that might be occurring, even very subtly, within your computer. Many of these tools can be found in the Computer Management snap-in, which we introduced in Chapter 1, "Introducing Windows 10," and have covered in several subsequent chapters. These tools include Event Viewer, Performance Monitor, Reliability Monitor, Action Center, and Task Manager, all of which enable you to monitor and troubleshoot computer performance. This chapter looks at using these tools to troubleshoot system errors, monitor system performance, and optimize your computer to keeping it working at a level close to that observed when you first set it up.

"Do I Know This Already?" Quiz

The "Do I Know This Already?" quiz allows you to assess whether you should read this entire chapter or simply jump to the "Exam Preparation Tasks" section for review. If you are in doubt, read the entire chapter. Table 19-1 outlines the major headings in this chapter and the corresponding "Do I Know This Already?" quiz questions. You can find the answers in Appendix A, "Answers to the 'Do I Know This Already?' Quizzes."

Table 19-1 "Do I Know This Already?" Foundation Topics Section-to-Question Mapping

Foundation Topics Section	Questions Covered in This Section
Monitoring Windows 10	1–8
Configuring Advanced Management Tools	9–11

CAUTION   The goal of self-assessment is to gauge your mastery of the topics in this chapter. If you do not know the answer to a question or are only partially sure of the answer, you should mark that question as wrong for purposes of the self-assessment. Giving yourself credit for an answer you correctly guess skews your self-assessment results and might provide you with a false sense of security.

1. You want to reduce the number of events viewed in the System log of Event Viewer because you've found that you waste a lot of time going through thousands of minor events when trying to locate important events that can pinpoint problems. What should you do?

    a. Filter the log to display only Critical, Warning, and Error events.

    b. Filter the log to display Error, Warning, and Information events.

    c. Configure the log to overwrite events after 48 hours.

    d. Create an event log subscription.

2. You are responsible for eight computers that are configured as a workgroup located in a small medical office. You want to collect event logs from all these computers onto a single computer so that you can spot problems more rapidly. What should you configure on this computer?

    a. A source-initiated event subscription

    b. A collector-initiated event subscription

    c. A filter that views logs by event source

    d. A filter that views logs by user and computer

3. Which of the following commands do you have to run on all computers involved in an event log subscription before setting up the subscription? (Choose two.)

    a. **Winrm**

    b. **Wdsutil**

    c. **Wecutil**

    d. **Logman**

4. You are working at your computer, and a program you're using has hung and you cannot exit the program. Which utility can you use to terminate the program? (Choose two; each is a complete solution.)

    a. Reliability Monitor

    b. Resource Monitor

    c. Performance Monitor

    d. Task Manager

    e. Event Viewer

5. Which of the following actions can you perform from the simplified interface in Task Manager? (Choose all that apply.)

    a. Close an unresponsive program.

    b. Start a new program.

    c. Open the folder in which a running executable file is located.

    d. Display summary performance statistics on a running program.

    e. Perform an Internet search on a selected program.

6. Your Windows 10 Pro computer has been starting slowly as of late, and you suspect that unnecessary apps are starting automatically at startup. What should you do to locate these apps and ensure that they do not run at startup?

    a. In the simplified interface in Task Manager, right-click the required apps and choose **Properties**. Then clear the check box labeled **Run at Startup**.

    b. In the advanced interface in Task Manager, select the **Startup** tab. Then right-click the required apps and choose **Disable**.

    c. In the advanced interface in Task Manager, select the **Services** tab. Then right-click the required services and choose **Disable**.

    d. In the System Configuration utility, select the **Startup** tab. Then right-click the required apps and choose **Disable**.

7. You want to receive a message when your computer's processor time exceeds 85 percent. What feature of Performance Monitor should you configure?

    a. Event Trace Data Collector Set

    b. Event log

    c. Performance Counter Alert Data Collector Set

    d. System Diagnostics Data Collector Set

8. You think your computer might need more RAM, and you're wondering how much memory is committed to either physical RAM or running processes. What counter should you check in Performance Monitor?

   a. Memory\Pages/sec

   b. Memory\Available Bytes

   c. Memory\Committed Bytes

   d. Processor\% Processor Time

   e. System\Processor Queue Length

9. You are considering disabling some services on your Windows 10 computer, but want to ensure that you do not disable important services that other services depend on for their functionality. Where should you check for the required information?

   a. The Dependencies tab of the service's Properties dialog box, accessed from the Services snap-in

   b. The General tab of the service's Properties dialog box, accessed from the Services snap-in

   c. The General tab of the System Configuration tool

   d. The Services subnode of the Software Environment node in the System Information tool

10. You suspect that the Indexing service on your Windows 10 computer is not performing properly, so you perform a search on several items you know are present on the computer. After several minutes, the computer has not located these items. What should you do?

    a. In the Indexing Options applet, click **Modify**. Then in the Indexed Locations dialog box, choose a location on a partition with lots of free space, and then click **OK**.

    b. In the Indexing Options applet, click **Advanced**. Then in the Advanced Options dialog box, click **Rebuild**.

    c. In the Indexing Options applet, click **Advanced**. Then in the Advanced Options dialog box, specify a location on a partition with lots of free space, and then click **Select New**.

    d. In the Indexing Options applet, click **Advanced**. Then in the Advanced Options dialog box, select the **File Types** tab and clear the check boxes for file extensions you're sure are not in use.

11. What PowerShell cmdlets prefix convention is used to retrieve information about a specific function?

    a. **Get-**

    b. **Invoke-**

    c. **Disable-**

    d. **Enable-**

Foundation Topics

Monitoring Windows 10

Your Windows systems and devices include many tools for monitoring the health of the hardware, operating system, device drivers, and application performance. Tools have been added and matured through the evolution of Windows operating system versions. In this section you learn about many of these tools and some basics of how to use them to monitor the health of your systems and to gather clues to troubleshoot issues or improve performance.

Event Viewer

One of Windows 10's standard troubleshooting tools is Event Viewer, which has been around since the days of Windows NT but has been upgraded with each new Windows release. Event Viewer is incorporated into the Computer Management console, as well as being available from the Advanced Tools window. You can rely on this utility to be able to see errors and system messages. This tool enables you to view events from multiple event logs on the local computer or another computer to which you can connect, save event filters as custom views for future use, schedule tasks to run in response to events, and create and manage event log subscriptions.

You can open Event Viewer by using any of the following methods:

- In Windows 10, right-click **Start** and choose **Event Viewer** from the menu that appears.

- From the Start menu, expand the Windows Administrative Tools folder, and select **Event Viewer**.

- Access the Search bar or Cortana and type **event** into the Search field. Select **Event Viewer** from the list.

- From the Search bar or Cortana, type **msconfig** into the Search field. Then click **System Configuration** in the list. From the Tools tab of System Configuration, select **Event Viewer**, and then click **Launch**.

- Access the Action Center and click **All Settings** to open the Settings. Type **event** into the Search bar, and then click **View Event Logs**.

If you receive a User Account Control (UAC) prompt, click **Yes** or supply administrative credentials. The Event Viewer snap-in opens and displays a summary of recent administrative events in the Details pane, as shown in Figure 19-1.

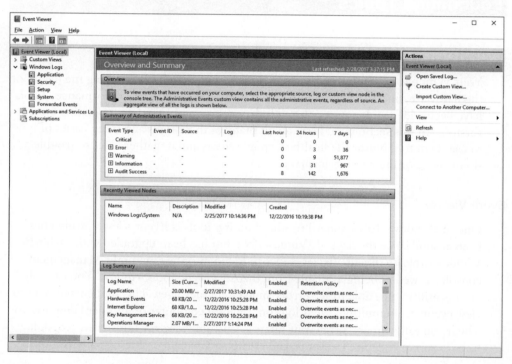

Figure 19-1   Event Viewer Recorded Events That Have Occurred on Your Computer

The sections that follow provide more detail with regard to several aspects of working with Event Viewer.

Viewing Logs in Event Viewer

To view the actual event logs, expand the Windows Logs subnode. Windows 10 records events in the following types of logs:

- **Application:** Logs events related to applications running on the computer, including alerts generated by data collector sets.

- **Security:** Logs events related to security-related actions performed on the computer. To enable security event logging, you must configure auditing of the types of actions to be recorded.

- **Setup:** Logs events related to setup of applications.

- **System:** Contains events related to actions taking place on the computer in general, including hardware-related events (see Figure 19-2).

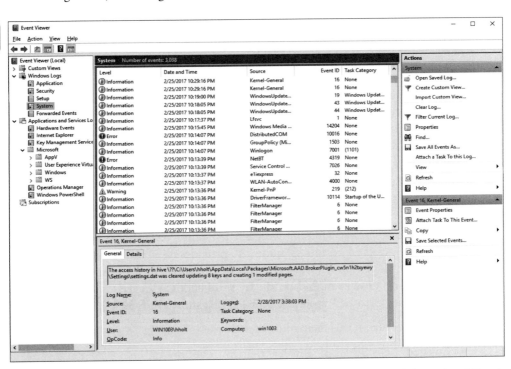

Figure 19-2 Most Event Viewer Logs Record Errors, Warning Events, and Informational Events

- **Forwarded Events:** Contains events logged from remote computers. To enable this log, you must create an event subscription.

- **Applications and Services logs:** Contained in its own subnode, these logs store events from single applications or components, as opposed to events with potential systemwide impact. Logs may include categories such as Distributed File Service (DFS) replication, hardware events, Internet Explorer events, Key Management service events, Windows Assessment Console events, and Windows PowerShell events. You will also see a folder labeled Microsoft with logs for various Microsoft applications and services.

> **NOTE**   If you are looking at Event Viewer on a server, you may observe additional event logs added by applications such as Active Directory and DNS. Installed applications on servers and even on Windows 10 might add additional event logs to Event Viewer.

Most logs in Event Viewer record the three types of events—errors, warnings, and informational events—as previously seen in Figure 19-2. Error messages are represented by a red circle with a white exclamation mark in the center. Information messages are represented by a balloon with a blue "i" in the center, and warning messages are represented by a yellow triangle with a black exclamation mark in the center. Although not always true, an error is often preceded by one or more warning messages. A series of warning and error messages can describe the exact source of the problem, or at least point you in the right direction. To obtain additional information about an event, select it. The bottom of the central pane displays information related to the selected event. You can also right-click an event and select **Event Properties** to display information about the event in its own dialog box that can be viewed without scrolling.

Customizing Event Viewer

If you have selected many auditable events, the Event Viewer logs can rapidly accumulate a large variety of events. Windows 10 provides capabilities for customizing what appears in the Event Viewer window. To customize the information displayed, right-click **Event Viewer** in the console tree and choose **Create Custom View**. This displays the Create Custom View dialog box shown in Figure 19-3.

Options available from this dialog box include the following:

- **Logged:** Select the time interval that you want to examine.

- **Event Level:** Choose the type(s) of events you want to view. Select **Verbose** to view extra details related to the viewed events.

- **By Log:** Select the Windows logs or Applications and Services logs you want to include.

- **By Source:** Select from an extensive range of Windows services, utilities, and components whose logs you want to include.

- **Task Category:** Expand the drop-down list and select the categories you want to view.

- **Keywords:** Select the keywords that you want to include in the customized view.

- **User and Computer(s):** Select the usernames of the accounts to be displayed and the names of the computers to be displayed. Separate the names in each list by commas.

- **XML tab:** Enables you to specify an event filter as an XML query.

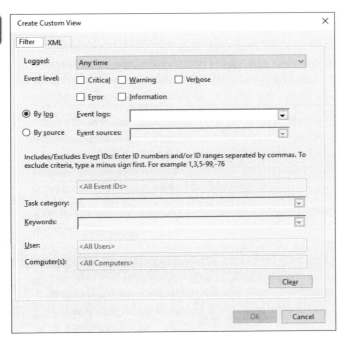

Figure 19-3 Creating Custom Views That Filter Event Logs According to Several Categories

When you have made your selections, click **OK** and type a name for the custom view in the Save Filter to Custom View dialog box that appears. After you have saved the custom view, you can see this view by expanding the Custom Views node in the console tree to locate it by the name you provided.

Creating Tasks from Events

Event Viewer in Windows 10 also enables you to associate tasks with events. Event Viewer integrates with Task Scheduler to make this action possible. To do so, right-click the desired event and choose **Attach Task to This Event**. Follow the instructions in the Create Basic Task Wizard that opens, as shown in Figure 19-4. Actions that you can take include starting a specified program, sending an email, and displaying a message.

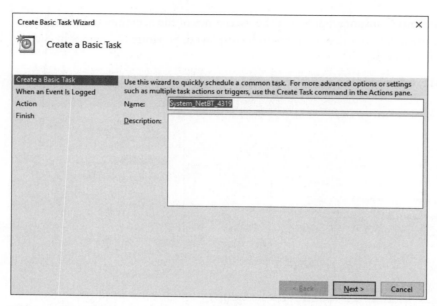

Figure 19-4   Create Basic Task Wizard Enabling You to Specify an Action That Will Be Taken Each Time a Specific Event Takes Place

NOTE   For more information on Event Viewer, start with "Event Viewer" and references contained therein at https://msdn.microsoft.com/en-us/library/aa745633(v=bts.10).aspx.

Using Event Log Subscriptions

Event Viewer includes a Subscriptions feature that enables you to collect event logs from a number of computers (referred to as *source computers*) in a single, convenient location on a computer termed the *collector computer* that helps you keep track of events that occur on these computers. You can specify the events that will be collected and the local log in which they will be stored. After activating the subscription, you can view these event logs in the same manner as already discussed for local event logs.

The Event Subscriptions feature works by using Hypertext Transfer Protocol (HTTP) or Secure HTTP (HTTPS) to relay specified events from one or more originating (source) computers to a destination (collector) computer. It uses the Windows Remote Management (WinRM) and Windows Event Collector (Wecsvc) services to perform these actions. To configure event log subscriptions, you must configure these services on both the source and collector computers.

You can configure Event Subscriptions to work in either of two ways:

- **Collector-initiated:** The collector computer pulls the specified events from each of the source computers. This type is typically used where there are a limited number of easily identified source computers.

- **Source-initiated:** Each source computer pushes the specified events to the collector computer. This type is typically used where there are a large number of source computers that are configured using Group Policy.

Configuring Computers to Forward and Collect Events

You learned about Winrm, which is required for event forwarding, in Chapter 15, "Configuring Remote Access." You need to run the **Winrm** and **Wecutil** commands at both the source and collector computers. To do so, log on to each source computer with an administrative user account (it is best to use a domain administrator account when configuring computers in an Active Directory Domain Services [AD DS] domain). Add the computer account of the collector computer to the local Administrators group on each source computer. In addition, type the following command at an administrative command prompt or PowerShell window:

```
Winrm quickconfig
```

Also log on to the collector computer with an administrative account, open an administrative command prompt or PowerShell window, and type the following command:

```
Wecutil qc
```

Having run these commands, the computers are now ready to forward and collect events. Note that in a workgroup environment, you can use only collector-initiated subscriptions. In addition, you need to perform the following additional steps:

- You must add a Windows Firewall exception for Remote Event Log Management at each source computer. If you want to configure source-initiated subscriptions, you may also need to configure an exception for the receiving computer, if the source computers are in a different domain. We discussed configuring Windows Firewall in Chapter 16, "Configuring and Maintaining Network Security."

- You must add an account with administrative privileges to the Event Log Readers group at each source computer, and specify this account in the Configure Advanced Subscription Settings dialog box mentioned in the next section.

- At a command prompt on the collector computer, type **winrm set winrm/ config/client @{TrustedHosts="<*sources*>"}**. In this command, <*sources*> is a list of the names of all workgroup source computers separated by commas.

> **NOTE**   For more information on the **wecutil** command, refer to "wecutil" at https://technet.microsoft.com/en-us/windows-server-docs/management/ windows-commands/wecutil.

Configuring Event Log Subscriptions

After you have completed the preceding procedures at all source and collector computers, you are ready to configure event log subscriptions at the collector computer by using the following procedure:

Step 1.   In the console tree of Event Viewer, right-click the type of log you want to configure a subscription for and choose **Properties**.

Step 2.   Select the **Subscriptions** tab of the Properties dialog box that appears.

Step 3.   If the Windows Event Collector Service is not running, Event Viewer displays a message box asking you to start this service. Click **Yes** to proceed.

Step 4.   Click **Create** to create your first event subscription. This displays the Subscription Properties dialog box shown in Figure 19-5.

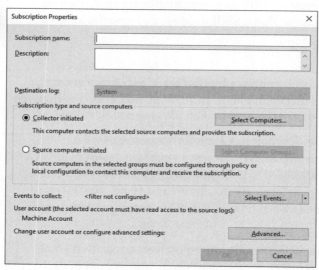

Figure 19-5   Subscription Properties Dialog Box Enabling You to Configure an Event Log Subscription

Step 5.   Configure the following properties for your event log subscription and then click **OK** when finished:

- **Subscription Name:** Provide an informative name that you will use to locate your event log subscription later. If desired, type an optional description in the field provided.

- **Destination Log:** Displays the log type, according to the Windows log you right-clicked in Step 1 of this procedure.

- **Subscription Type and Source Computers:** Select **Collector Initiated** and click the **Select Computers** button to specify the computers from which you want to collect event data. Or select **Source Computer Initiated** to specify groups of computers that have been configured through Group Policy to receive the subscription from the computer at which you are working. In either case you can also select computers from an AD DS domain.

- **Events to Collect:** Click **Select Events** to display the Query Filter dialog box, which provides the same options as shown previously in Figure 19-3 and enables you to select the event types that will be included in the subscription.

- **Advanced:** Click **Advanced** to display the Advanced Subscription Settings dialog box shown in Figure 19-6, which enables you to select the user account that has access to the source logs and optimize event delivery. To specify a user other than the one indicated, click **Specific User**; then click the **User and Password** button and type the required user/password information. Choose **Normal** to provide reliable event delivery without conserving bandwidth. Select **Minimize Bandwidth** to control the use of bandwidth but reducing the frequency of event delivery. Select **Minimize Latency** to ensure the most rapid delivery of events.

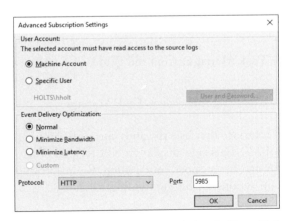

Figure 19-6 Advanced Subscription Settings Dialog Box Enabling You to Specify User Account and Event Delivery Settings

NOTE   If you select a different user account from the Advanced Subscription Settings dialog box, the account you select must be a member of the local computer's Event Log Readers group or the Administrators group.

Monitoring Computer Performance

Windows 10 includes several tools that are used for monitoring, optimizing, and troubleshooting performance. These include Task Manager, Resource Monitor, and Performance Monitor.

Task Manager

The Task Manager has had a complete redesign in Windows 8.1 and Windows 10 from its design in Windows 7 and previous versions. The new design optimizes the use of Task Manager for the most common actions performed by users. Most specifically, users tend to utilize this tool to close misbehaving applications or to locate and kill processes that are using excessive quantities of computer resources. At the same time, designers wanted to ensure that no other uses of Task Manager were removed despite their not being as frequently used.

Task Manager provides data about currently running processes, including their CPU and memory usage, and enables you to modify their priority or shut down misbehaving applications. You can use any of the following methods to start Task Manager:

- In Windows 10, right-click the **Start** button and choose **Task Manager** from the menu that appears.
- Access the Search bar or Cortana, and type in **task manager**. Then select **Task Manager** from the list.
- Press Ctrl+Shift+Esc.
- Press Ctrl+Alt+Delete and select **Task Manager** from the Windows Security dialog box.
- Right-click a blank area on the taskbar, and then select **Task Manager**.

Task Manager opens with a simplified interface that lists the apps currently running on your computer, as shown in Figure 19-7. This view displays a Not Responding message beside any running application that has stopped functioning. Right-clicking an app enables you to perform a series of actions, including the following:

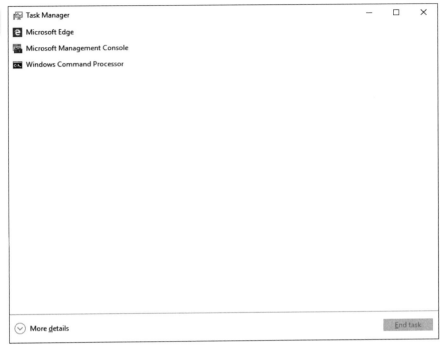

Figure 19-7 Task Manager in Windows 10 Providing a List of Apps That Are Currently Running on Your Computer

- **Switch To:** Brings the focus on the desktop to the selected app.

- **End Task:** Enables you to shut down an unresponsive app (same as clicking the End Task command button).

- **Run New Task:** Brings up the Create New Task dialog box (similar to the Run dialog box on previous Windows versions), which enables you to start a program or open a folder, a document, or a web page from the Internet. You can also create the task with administrative privileges.

- **Always on Top:** Keeps the Task Manager window displayed on top of any other windows that might otherwise cover it.

- **Open File Location:** Opens a File Explorer window focused on the folder in which the selected app is located.

- **Search Online:** Opens Internet Explorer to your default search engine and performs an Internet search on the selected app.

- **Properties:** Displays a Properties dialog box for the selected app.

Click **More Details** to open the advanced interface of Task Manager, as shown in Figure 19-8. By default, the advanced interface displays the Processes tab, which provides information on resources (CPU, memory, disk, and network) consumed by processes running on the computer. This information is grouped according to process type (applications, background processes, and Windows processes) and is color coded, with darker colors representing resources being utilized more intensively. If an application is using an extreme amount of a given resource, the column header and the responsible application are strongly highlighted, drawing your attention to this occurrence. You can expand a process to locate multiple instances of the process by clicking the triangle to the left of the desired process. You can modify the properties of a running application or terminate an ill-behaved process or one that is consuming a large amount of resources. (Right-click the process and choose **End Task**.) You can also obtain information from the Internet about an unfamiliar process by right-clicking it and choosing **Search Online**. This runs your default search engine in Internet Explorer to locate information on the selected process.

Task Manager						
File Options View						
Processes Performance App history Startup Users Details Services						
Name	6% CPU	51% Memory	0% Disk	0% Network		
Apps (4)						
e Microsoft Edge	0%	13.3 MB	0 MB/s	0 Mbps		
> Microsoft Management Console	0%	18.0 MB	0 MB/s	0 Mbps		
> Task Manager	3.8%	10.0 MB	0 MB/s	0 Mbps		
> Windows Command Processor	0%	0.5 MB	0 MB/s	0 Mbps		
Background processes (35)						
Application Frame Host	0%	4.6 MB	0 MB/s	0 Mbps		
Browser_Broker	0%	2.6 MB	0 MB/s	0 Mbps		
COM Surrogate	0%	1.8 MB	0 MB/s	0 Mbps		
> COM Surrogate	0%	2.5 MB	0 MB/s	0 Mbps		
O Cortana	0%	73.5 MB	0 MB/s	0 Mbps		
Device Association Framework ...	0%	1.4 MB	0 MB/s	0 Mbps		
> FileZilla Server (32 bit)	0%	4.2 MB	0 MB/s	0 Mbps		
Host Process for Setting Synchr...	0%	3.2 MB	0 MB/s	0 Mbps		
⌄ Fewer details					End task	

Figure 19-8 Advanced Interface of Task Manager Displaying All the Processes Running and Providing Summary Performance Information on Each Item

TIP You can sort processes according to the amount of a specific resource they're consuming by clicking the title (CPU, Memory, Disk, or Network) of the desired resource. Doing so can help you to locate an ill-behaved process. For example, by clicking Memory, you can see which processes are using the most RAM.

The remaining six tabs perform the following tasks:

- **Performance:** Provides a limited performance monitoring function as shown in Figure 19-9, showing processor, memory, disk, and network statistics. This tab is ideal for providing a quick snapshot of computer performance. Select any of the objects in the left column to display its statistics. You can also access the Resource Monitor application described earlier in this chapter.

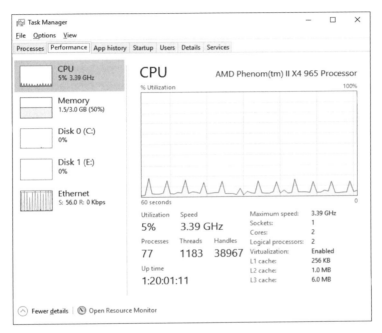

Figure 19-9 Performance Tab of Task Manager Providing a Simple Performance Graph Focused on the Selected Performance Object

- **App History:** Provides history information on CPU, network, metered network, and tile updates history for each app on the computer since the last time usage history was deleted. Click **Delete User History** to restart collection of history data.

- **Startup:** Provides information on processes configured to start when you restart your computer. Information provided includes the publisher name, the status of the program (enabled or disabled), and the startup impact. To prevent an application from starting on the next boot, right-click it and choose **Disable**, or select it and click the **Disable** command button. On a disabled task, this button changes to **Enable**.

- **Users:** Displays the users that have sessions, active or disconnected, running on the local computer.

- **Details:** Provides detailed information on all instances of all processes running on the computer and enables you to end specific processes.

- **Services:** Provides information on services installed on the computer. You can view which services are running or stopped, the service group to which they belong, and descriptive information about each service. You can start a stopped service or stop a running service by right-clicking the service name and selecting **Start** or **Stop**. You can also determine whether a service is associated with a particular process by right-clicking the service name and selecting **Go to Details**. This opens the Details tab and highlights the selected process.

You can access additional options from the menu bar of Task Manager. In particular, you can start a new process from the File menu. Doing so is equivalent to using the Run dialog box and is useful if the Explorer process has terminated or is misbehaving. The Options menu allows you to keep the Task Manager window always visible on the desktop. The View menu allows you to adjust the refresh rate of the graph on the Performance tab. It also allows you to modify what data is displayed on the Processes and Users tabs.

Resource Monitor

Resource Monitor provides a summary of CPU, disk, network, and memory performance statistics, including mini-graphs of recent performance of these four components. In Windows Vista, Resource Monitor was combined with Performance Monitor in a single MMC snap-in; Windows 10 (as was the case with Windows 7 and Windows 8.1) separates these two applications into their own interfaces. Use any of the following procedures to open Resource Monitor:

- If you've enabled Administrative Tools on the Start menu, click the **Resource Monitor** icon.

- From the Search bar or Cortana, type **resource** into the Search field, and then select **Resource Monitor** from the displayed apps.

- From the taskbar Search field or Cortana, type **msconfig** into the Search field. Then click **System Configuration** in the Programs list. From the Tools tab of System Configuration, select **Resource Monitor** and then click **Launch**.

- Open Task Manager and click **Open Resource Monitor** from the Performance tab.

After you've opened Resource Monitor, you can click the downward-pointing arrow on the right side of any of the four headings to display additional information about a component similar to that shown for CPU in Figure 19-10.

Figure 19-10 Expanding Each Component in Resource Monitor to Obtain a Summary of Its Performance Information

For each of the four components, the information provided on the Overview tab includes the application whose resource usage is being monitored (known as the image) and the process identifier number (PID) of the application instance. The following additional information is provided on the Overview tab for each of the four components:

- **CPU:** A brief description of the monitored application, the number of threads per application, the CPU cycles currently used by each application instance, and the average CPU resulting from each instance as a percentage of total CPU usage.

- **Memory:** Current hard faults per second and memory usage information in KB for committed, working set, sharable, and private memory components.

- **Disk:** The file being read or written by each application instance, the current read and write speeds in bytes/minute, and the total disk input/output (I/O) in bytes/minute, the I/O priority level, and the response time in milliseconds.

- **Network:** The IP address of the network component with which the computer is exchanging data, the amount of data (bandwidth) in bytes per second (sent, received, and total) by each instance.

To filter the display of disk, network, and memory usage according to process, select the check box or boxes in the Image column of the CPU section, as previously shown in Figure 19-9. To change the size of the graphical displays on any tab, select **Large**, **Medium**, or **Small** from the Views drop-down list above the graphical displays.

By selecting the tab associated with each component, you can view additional details about the component selected.

CPU Tab

The CPU tab provides graphical displays of the total CPU percentage utilization, as well as values for each processor or core and the Service CPU Usage. If you want to display information for certain processors or cores only, you can do so by selecting **Monitor > Select Processors** and choosing the desired processor(s) from the dialog box that appears. Tabulated information includes CPU usage by all processes and services running on the machine. You can filter the display in the information tables of any tab by selecting the check boxes for the desired processes in the Processes section, similar to the action previously described for the Overview tab. When you are filtering the results on any tab, the graphical displays include an orange line that represents the proportion of each activity type represented by the selected processes; tabulated displays show an orange information bar that informs you which processes are included.

Memory Tab

The Memory tab provides graphical displays of the Used Physical Memory, Commit Charge, and Hard Faults/sec memory counters. Besides a tabular view of memory usage by processes running on the computer, this tab includes a bar graph representation that shows the relative amount of memory apportioned to Hardware Reserved, In Use, Modified, Standby, and Free. The amount of memory that's available to programs includes the total of standby and free memory. Free memory includes zero page memory.

Disk Tab

Graphs included on the Disk tab include total disk usage over a 60-second period plus the queue length for each disk as well as the total queue length. Processes with disk activity are tabulated, along with bytes/sec values for disk reads, writes, and total access. Disk activity by process and available storage by logical disk volume are also tabulated.

Network Tab

The Network tab includes graphical display of network activity, as well as the number of TCP connections and the percentage utilization of network connections across each network adapter in the computer. Tabulated information includes the processes with network activity, for which the number of bytes/sec sent, received, and total are shown. Tables of network activity, TCP connections, and listening ports are also shown; similar to other tabs, you can filter these displays by selecting the check boxes in the top section of the tabular display.

TIP   You can use Resource Monitor to end unresponsive processes in a manner similar to that of Task Manager. Such a process is displayed in red in the top section of the Overview tab. Right-click the process in the tabular display and choose **End Process**. A message box warns you that you will lose any unsaved data and that ending a system process might result in system instability. Click **End Process** to end the process or click **Cancel** to quit.

NOTE   For more information on using Resource Monitor, see "Resource Availability Troubleshooting Getting Started Guide" at http://technet.microsoft.com/en-us/library/dd883276(WS.10).aspx. The article refers to Windows 7 and Windows Server 2008, but the information is applicable to Windows 10.

Performance Monitor

The Windows 10 Performance console includes the following monitoring tools:

- **Performance Monitor:** Provides a real-time graph of computer performance, either in the current time or as logged historical data.

- **Data Collector Sets:** Records computer performance information into log files. Data collectors are grouped into groups that you can use for monitoring performance under different conditions.

- **Reports:** Creates a report of performance report data.

Performance Monitor, which is shown in Figure 19-11, provides a real-time graph of computer performance and enables you to perform tasks such as the following:

- Identify performance problems such as bottlenecks.

- Monitor resource usage.

- Track trends over time.

- Measure the effects of changes in system configuration.

- Generate alerts when unusual conditions occur.

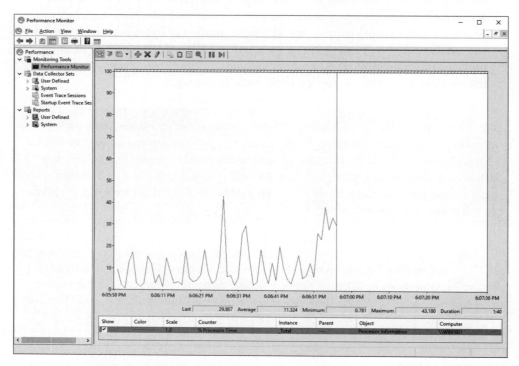

Figure 19-11   Performance Monitor Displays a Real-Time Graph of Activity for Selected Objects and Counters

Before you learn more about the Performance Monitor tool, you need to be familiar with the following terms, which are used in a specific manner when referring to performance metrics:

- **Object:** A specific hardware or software component that the Performance Console is capable of monitoring. It can be any component that possesses a series of measurable properties. Windows 10 comes with a defined set of objects; applications such as Internet Information Services (IIS) installed on Windows 10 may add more objects to the available set.

- **Counter:** One of a series of statistical measurements associated with each object.

- **Instance:** Refers to multiple occurrences of a given object. For example, if your computer has two hard disks, two instances of the PhysicalDisk object will be present. These instances are numbered sequentially, starting with 0 for the first occurrence. An instance labeled **_Total** is also present, yielding the sum of performance data for each counter. Note that not all objects have multiple instances.

Information on objects and counters is displayed in the following format: *Object (_instance)\Counter*. For example, Processor (_0)\%Processor Time measures the %Processor time on the first processor. The instance does not appear if only a single instance is present.

Performance Monitor enables you to obtain a real-time graph of computer performance statistics. Use the following procedure:

Step 1. Access the Search bar or Cortana and type **performance** into the Search field. Then click **Performance Monitor** in the Programs list. If you have the administrative tools displayed on the Start menu, you can select **Performance Monitor** from this location. You can also start Performance Monitor from the Computer Management console or from the Tools tab of System Configuration by selecting **Performance Monitor** and then clicking **Launch**.

Step 2. If you receive a User Account Control (UAC) prompt, click **Yes** or supply administrative credentials.

Step 3. In the Performance console, click **Performance Monitor**. As previously shown in Figure 19-11, Performance Monitor displays the Processor\%Processor Time counter.

Step 4. To add objects and counters, click the green **+** icon on the toolbar.

Step 5. In the Add Counters dialog box that appears (see Figure 19-12), ensure that the Select Counters from Computer drop-down list reads <Local computer> for monitoring the local computer performance. Then select the desired object and instance from the lists directly below the Select Counters list.

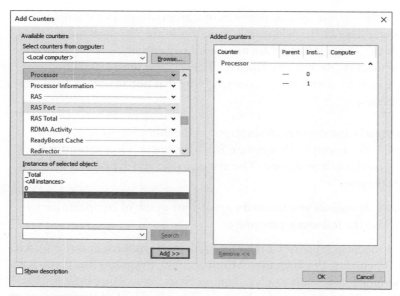

Figure 19-12   Selecting from a Large Number of Objects from the List in the Add Counters Dialog Box

Step 6.   Expand the desired object to display a list of available counters from which you can select one or more counters, as shown in Figure 19-13. To add counters to the graph, select the counter and click **Add**.

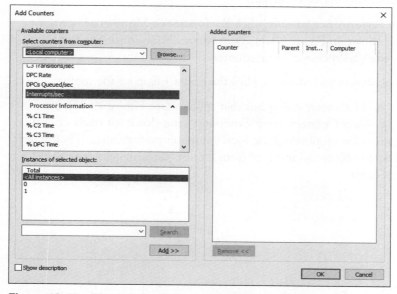

Figure 19-13   Expanding a Performance Object Enables You to Select from the Available Counters for That Object

Step 7. Repeat Steps 5 and 6 to add more counters. You learn about suitable counters in the following sections.

Step 8. When you are finished, click **OK**.

TIP You can highlight individual counters in Performance Monitor. To highlight an individual counter in the Performance Monitor display, select it from the list at the bottom of the Details pane and click the highlight icon (looks like a highlighter pen) in the taskbar. You can also press the **Backspace** key to highlight the counter. The highlighted counter appears in a heavy line. You can use the up- or down-arrow keys to toggle through the list of counters and highlight each one in turn. This feature helps you to find the desired counter from a graph that includes a large number of counters.

NOTE For more information on Performance Monitor, refer to "Performance Monitor Getting Started Guide" at http://technet.microsoft.com/en-ca/library/dd744567(WS.10).aspx. Although the article was written for Windows 7, the information still applies to Performance Monitor in Windows 10.

Data Collector Sets

A data collector set is a set of performance objects and counters that enable you to log computer performance over time while you are performing other tasks. Such logging is important because changes in computer performance often occur only after an extended period of time. Best practices state that you should create a *performance baseline*, which is a log of computer performance that you can save for comparing with future performance and tracking any changes that might have occurred over time. In this way you can identify potential bottlenecks in computer performance and take any required corrective measures. You can also monitor the effectiveness of any changes you make to a computer's configuration.

The Data Collector Sets feature was formerly known as Performance Logs and Alerts in Windows versions prior to Vista.

Creating Data Collector Sets

Data collector sets are binary files that save performance statistics for later viewing and analysis in the Performance Monitor snap-in; you can also export them to spreadsheet or database programs for later analysis. Windows 10 creates a series of data collector sets by default. The default data collector sets enable you to log default sets of performance counters for various purposes, including system diagnostics, LAN diagnostics, system performance, wireless diagnostics, event trace sessions, and startup event trace sessions. To view these sets, expand the branches under the Data Collector Sets node of Performance Monitor. Right-click any available data collector set and choose **Properties** to view information on the selected data collector set.

You may also create your own user-defined data collector set. Use the following procedure to create a data collector set:

Step 1. In the console tree of the Performance Monitor snap-in, select and expand **Data Collector Sets**.

Step 2. Select **User Defined**.

Step 3. To create a new data collector set, right-click a blank area of the Details pane and select **New > Data Collector Set**. The Create New Data Collector Set Wizard starts.

Step 4. Provide a name for the new data collector set. Select either **Create from a Template (Recommended)** or **Create Manually (Advanced)**, and then click **Next**. If you select the Create Manually (Advanced) option, refer to the next procedure for the remainder of the steps you should perform.

Step 5. If you select the Create from a Template option, you receive the dialog box shown in Figure 19-14, which enables you to use one of the following templates:

- **Basic:** Enables you to use performance counters to create a basic data collector set, which you can edit later if necessary.

- **System Diagnostics:** Enables you to create a report that contains details of local hardware resources, system response times, and local computer processes. System information and configuration data are also included.

- **System Performance:** Enables you to create a report that provides details on local hardware resources, system response times, and local computer processes.

- **WDAC Diagnostics:** Provides trace detailed debug information for Windows Data Access Components (WDAC) components using BidTrace.

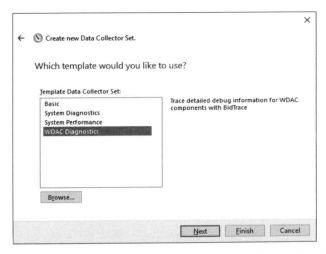

Figure 19-14   Create New Data Collector Set Wizard Enabling You to Use Several Templates

Step 6.   Select the desired template and click **Browse** to locate a template file (XML format) if one exists. Then click **Next**.

Step 7.   Select a location to which you would like the data to be saved (or accept the default location provided), and then click **Next**.

Step 8.   You receive the Create the Data Collector Set? page shown in Figure 19-15. To run the set as a different user, click **Change** and then select the desired user. To start logging now or configure additional properties, select the option provided. Then click **Finish**.

Figure 19-15   Create the Data Collector Set? Page Enabling You to Run the Set as Another User or Open the Properties of the Data Collector Set

To create a custom data collector set, use the **Create Manually (Advanced)** option in Step 4 of the previous procedure and then use the following steps to complete the procedure:

Step 1.   After selecting the **Create Manually (Advanced)** option and clicking **Next**, you receive the screen shown in Figure 19-16, which enables you to specify the following options:

- **Performance Counter:** Enables you to select performance objects and counters to be logged over time. Click **Next** to specify the performance counters to be logged and the desired sampling interval.

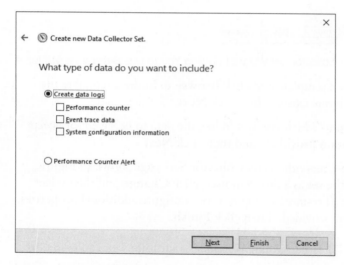

Figure 19-16   Creating Several Types of Logs or Alerts from the Create Manually Option in the Create New Data Collector Set Wizard

- **Event Trace Data:** Enables you to create trace logs, which are similar to counter logs, but they log data only when a specific activity takes place, whereas counter logs track data continuously for a specified interval.

- **System Configuration Information:** Enables you to track changes in Registry keys. Click **Next** to specify the desired keys.

- **Performance Counter Alert:** Enables you to display an alert when a selected counter exceeds or drops beneath a specified value. Click **Next** to specify the counters you would like to alert and the limiting value (see Figure 19-17 for an example).

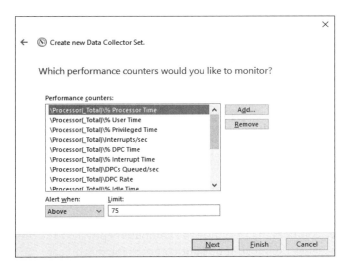

Figure 19-17   Creating an Alert That Informs You When the Processor\% Processor Time Value Exceeds 75 Percent

Step 2.   If you used the Create Data Logs option, select a location to save the log files and then click **Next**. After clicking Next, or if you used the Performance Counter Alert option instead, you receive the same dialog box shown previously in Figure 19-15. Make any changes needed and click **Finish**.

Using Performance Monitor to Create a Data Collector Set

Perhaps the simplest method to create a data collector set is to use a set of counters you have already configured in Performance Monitor. The following steps show you how:

Step 1.   After creating a performance graph as described earlier in this section, right-click **Performance Monitor** in the console tree and select **New > Data Collector Set**. The Create New Data Collector Set Wizard starts, as previously described.

Step 2.   Provide a name for the data collector set and then click **Next**.

Step 3.   Accept the location to which the data is to be saved, or type or browse to the location of your choice, and then click **Next**.

Step 4.   In the Create the Data Collector Set? page, select any required options and then click **Finish**.

The data collector set is created and placed in the User Defined section. If you select the option to start the data collector set now, logging begins immediately and continues until you right-click the data collector set and choose **Stop**.

You can view data collected by the data collector set in Performance Monitor. From the view previously shown in Figure 19-10, select the **View Log Data** icon (the second icon from the left in the toolbar immediately above the performance graph). In the Source tab of the Performance Monitor Properties dialog box that appears, select the **Log Files** option and click **Add**. Select the desired log file in the Select Log File dialog box that appears, click **Open**, and then click **OK**. This displays the selected log in the performance graph.

Optimizing and Troubleshooting Memory Performance

The Memory object includes counters that monitor the computer's physical and virtual memory. Table 19-2 discusses the most important counters for this object.

Table 19-2   Important Counters for the Memory Object

Counter	What It Measures	Interpretation and Remedial Tips
Pages/sec	The rate at which data is read to or written from the paging file	A value of 20 or more indicates a shortage of RAM and a possible memory bottleneck. To view the effect of paging file performance on the system, watch this counter together with LogicalDisk\% Disk Time. Add RAM to clear the problem.
Available Bytes (KBytes, MBytes)	The amount of physical memory available	A value consistently below 4 MB indicates a shortage of available memory. This might be due to memory leaks in one or more applications. Check your programs for memory leaks. You may need to add more RAM.
Committed Bytes	The amount of virtual memory that has been committed to either physical RAM or running processes	Committed memory is in use and not available to other processes. If the amount of committed bytes exceeds the amount of RAM on the computer, you may need to add RAM.
Pool Nonpaged Bytes	The amount of RAM in the nonpaged pool system memory (an area holding objects that cannot be written to disk)	If this value exhibits a steady increase in bytes without a corresponding increase in computer activity, check for an application with a memory leak.

Counter	What It Measures	Interpretation and Remedial Tips
Page Faults/sec	The number of data pages that must be read from or written to the page file per second	A high value indicates a lot of paging activity. Add RAM to alleviate this problem.

In addition to these counters, the Paging File\% Usage counter is of use when troubleshooting memory problems. This counter measures the percentage of the paging file currently in use. If it approaches 100%, you should either increase the size of the paging file or add more RAM.

Lack of adequate memory may also have an impact on the performance of other subsystems in the computer. In particular, a large amount of paging, or reading/writing data from/to the paging file on the hard disk, results in increased activity in both the processor and disk subsystems. You should monitor counters in these subsystems at the same time if you suspect memory-related performance problems. You learn more about monitoring counters later in the section "Optimizing and Troubleshooting Processor Utilization."

The paging file is an area on the hard disk that is used as an additional memory location for programs and data that cannot fit into RAM (in other words, virtual memory). By default, the paging file is located at *%systemdrive%\pagefile.sys* and has a default initial size of the amount of RAM in the computer plus 300 MB, and a default maximum size of three times the amount of RAM in the computer.

To improve performance on a computer equipped with more than one physical hard disk, you should locate the paging file on a different hard disk than that occupied by the operating system. You can also increase the size of the paging file or configure multiple paging files on different hard disks. Any of these configurations help to optimize performance by spreading out the activity of reading/writing data from/to the paging files. Note that you should retain a paging file on the system/boot drive to create a memory dump in case of a crash. This memory dump is useful for debugging purposes.

Use the following procedure to modify the configuration of the paging file:

Step 1. In the Search bar or Cortana, type **performance** and then select **Adjust the Appearance and Performance of Windows** from the list of options that appears. This opens the Performance Options dialog box.

Step 2. Select the **Advanced** tab.

Step 3. In the Virtual Memory section of this tab, click **Change**.

Step 4.   As shown in Figure 19-18, the Virtual Memory dialog box displays the disk partitions available on the computer and the size of the paging file on each. To add a paging file to a drive, first clear the **Automatically Manage Paging File Size for All Drives** dialog box. Select the drive and choose **Custom Size** to specify an initial and maximum size in MB or **System Managed Size** to obtain a default size. To remove a paging file, select the drive holding the file and click **No Paging File**. Note that some programs may not work properly if you choose the **No Paging File** option. Then click **Set**.

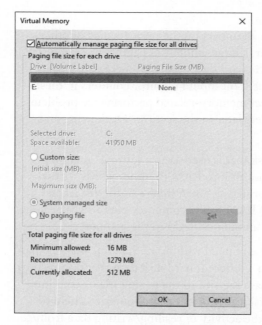

Figure 19-18   Modifying Paging File Properties from the Virtual Memory Dialog Box

Step 5.   Click **OK** three times to apply your changes and to close the Performance Options and System Properties dialog boxes.

Step 6.   Click **Restart Now** to restart your computer if so prompted.

Optimizing and Troubleshooting Processor Utilization

The processor is the "heart" of the system because it executes all program instructions, whether internal to the operating system or in user-executed applications. The Processor object contains counters that monitor processor performance. Table 19-3 discusses the most important counters for this object.

Table 19-3   Important Counters for the Processor Object

Counter	What It Measures	Interpretation and Remedial Tips
% Processor Time	The percentage of time the processor is executing meaningful actions (excludes the Idle process)	If this value is consistently greater than 85%, the processor could be causing a bottleneck. You should check the memory counters discussed previously; if these are high, consider adding more RAM. Otherwise, you should consider adding a faster processor (or an additional one if supported by your motherboard).
Interrupts/sec	The rate of service requests from I/O devices that interrupt other processor activities	A significant increase in the number of interrupts, without a corresponding increase in system activity, may indicate some type of hardware failure. Brief spikes are acceptable.

You should also look at the System\Processor Queue Length counter. If the value of this counter exceeds 2, a processor bottleneck may exist, with several programs contending for the processor's time.

Almost every computer today has more than a single processor "core," and these will show up as several processors in the performance counters list. Note that you can use the _Total counter, which provides statistics of all processors combined, or you can select individual processors, which are listed numerically as processor 0, 1, 2, and so on. Including the _Total counter and the individual processors can help you determine if any older, single-threaded applications or processes are causing an issue. Many older applications still in use today do not take advantage of multiple processors and can use only a single processor or core for all their work. If you notice that a single processor is at high utilization, while others are low or idle, you likely have such an application, and it is very busy.

As mentioned in Table 19-3, memory shortages may frequently manifest themselves in high processor activity. It is usually much cheaper and easier to add RAM to a computer than to add a faster or additional processor. Consequently, you may want to consider this step first when you are experiencing frequent high processor activity.

Optimizing and Troubleshooting Disk Performance

Disk performance is measured by two processor objects: The PhysicalDisk counters measure the overall performance of a single physical hard disk rather than individual partitions. LogicalDisk counters measure the performance of a single partition or volume on a disk. These counters include the performance of spanned, striped, or RAID-5 volumes that cross physical disks.

PhysicalDisk counters are best suited for hardware troubleshooting. Table 19-4 describes the most important counters for this object.

Table 19-4   Important Counters for the PhysicalDisk Object

Counter	What It Measures	Interpretation and Remedial Tips
% Disk Time	The percentage of time that the disk was busy reading or writing to any partition	A value of over 50% suggests a disk bottleneck. Consider upgrading to a faster disk or controller. Also check the memory counters to see whether more RAM is needed.
Avg. Disk Queue Length	The average number of disk read and write requests waiting to be performed	If this value is greater than 2, follow the same suggestions as for % Disk Time.
Average Disk Sec/ Transfer	The length of time a disk takes to fulfill requests.	A value greater than 0.3 may indicate that the disk controller is retrying the disk continually because of write failures.

LogicalDisk counters are best suited for investigating the read/write performance of a single partition. Table 19-5 describes the most important counters for this object.

Table 19-5   Important Counters for the LogicalDisk Object

Counter	What It Measures	Interpretation and Remedial Tips
% Disk Time	The percentage of time that the disk is busy servicing disk requests	A value greater than 90% may indicate a performance problem except when using a RAID device. Compare to Processor\% Processor Time to determine whether disk requests are using too much processor time.
Average Disk Bytes/Transfer	The amount of data transferred in each I/O operation	Low values (below about 20 KB) indicate that an application may be accessing a disk inefficiently. Watch this counter as you close applications to locate an offending application.
Current Disk Queue Length	The amount of data waiting to be transferred to the disk	A value greater than 2 indicates a possible disk bottleneck, with processes being delayed because of slow disk speed. Consider adding another faster disk.
Disk Transfers/sec	The rate at which read or write operations are performed by the disk	A value greater than 50 may indicate a disk bottleneck. Consider adding another faster disk.
% Free Space	Percentage of unused disk space	A value less than about 15% indicates that insufficient disk space is available. Consider moving files, repartitioning the disk, or adding another disk.

TIP You should log disk activity to a different disk or computer. The act of recording performance logs places an extra "hit" on performance for the disk on which logs are recorded. To obtain accurate disk monitoring results, record this data to a different disk or computer.

Monitoring System Resources

You have learned about several tools in this chapter for monitoring resources and performance of your Windows computers. If you are using an MDM tool such as Microsoft Intune, you can also configure alerts to monitor computers for resource issues. You learned about using Intune alerts in Chapter 13, "Microsoft Intune." Figure 19-19 shows some of the many alert types available in Intune for monitoring resources. Alert types are available for monitoring memory, disk, CPU utilization, and others.

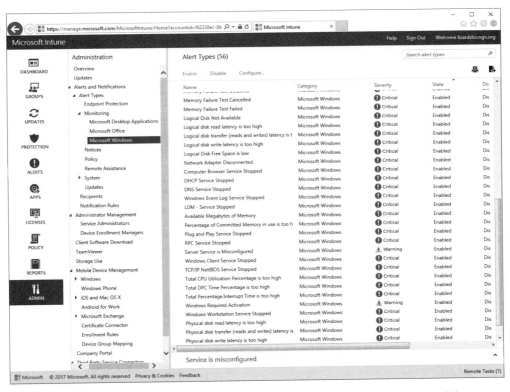

Figure 19-19 Some Alert Types Available for Monitoring Computers Using Microsoft Intune

You can perform several tasks associated with performance monitoring and optimization from the command line. The following are several available tools:

- **Logman:** Manages data collector logs. You can start, stop, and schedule the collection of performance and trace data.

- **Relog:** Creates new performance logs from data in existing logs by modifying the sampling rate and/or converting the file format.

- **Typeperf:** Displays performance data to the command prompt window or to a log file.

You can also use the **Perfmon** command to start the Performance Monitor from a command line. For information on running these tools, type the command name followed by **/?** at a command prompt.

Monitoring and Managing Printers

We have already shown you how to share printers and assign permissions to them in Chapter 14, "Configuring File and Folder Access." This chapter also discusses location-aware printing, which enables you to send documents to a conveniently located printer by adjusting whether to allow Windows to manage your default printer. You also learned about print sharing, configuring printer access security, and manually managing default printers.

Windows also includes the Printer Management tool in Windows 10. If you have enabled Administrative tools in the Start menu, you can click the **Printer Management** icon in the folder to open Print Management, which displays the console shown in Figure 19-20. You can also open the Print Management console from the Search bar or Cortana by searching for **print**, and then selecting **Print Management** from the list.

From the Print Management console, you can view all the printers and printer drivers. You can also add all the print servers available on your network, view the drivers and printers connected to those, and manage the printer queues and jobs. In Figure 19-20, you can see under Custom Filters that the console has provided a way to view at a glance how the printers are doing. In the figure, there are 14 printers, 12 drivers, no printers that are down (not ready), and no printers with jobs. So it's easy to see what is going on with printing in your environment.

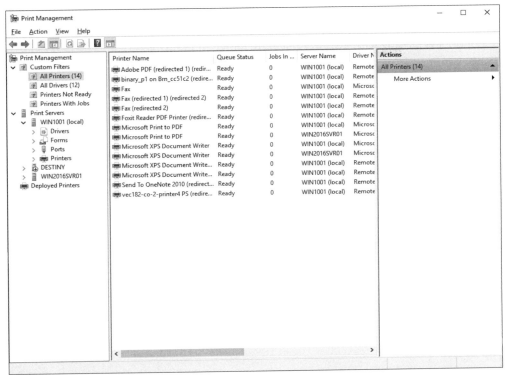

Figure 19-20   Monitor and Manage Your Printers Using the Print Management Console

A print server is available by default on any Windows 10 computer or Windows Server. So when you see Print Servers in your Print Management console, it is really referring to any computer that does not have printing disabled. To add a print server, right-click the **Print Servers** node and select the **Add/Remote Servers** menu option. From the dialog box, you can browse for a computer on your network or type the computer name into the box. Click **Add to List** to add the computer to the list. When you click **OK**, the computer will show up under the Print Servers node. Refer to Figure 19-20, which has three print servers connected.

You can manage any printer from this interface, as long as you have permissions. You can select one of the folders in Custom Filters or the Printers node under one of the Print Servers to see the printers. You can right-click one of the folders to view the context menu. This provides many of the same options available from the Control Panel Printers and Scanners applet for managing printers, such as viewing the printer queue, setting sharing, and accessing the device properties pages. If you had administration permissions on a Windows Active Directory, you also have the option to Deploy with Group Policy. As shown in Figure 19-21, this form provides an automatic way to deploy the printer connection to an existing Group Policy Object.

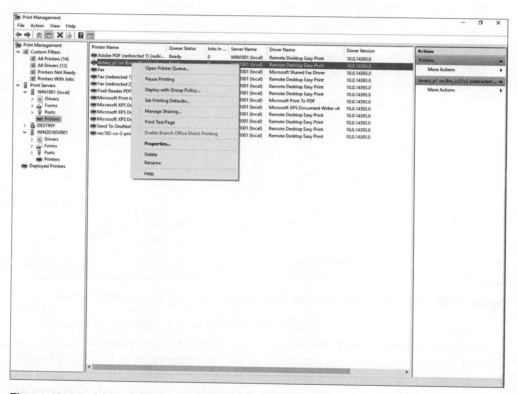

Figure 19-21   Deploying Printer Connections Using Group Policy Objects from the Print Management Console

You can also manage the print drivers that are installed on any of the print servers. You can right-click the **Drivers** node and then select **Add Driver**. This starts the Add Driver Wizard, which will walk you through the driver installation, as shown in Figure 19-22. Select the driver from the list provided, or if you have a driver from the manufacturer, click the **Have Disk** button to select it. You can perform this type of printer driver installation for any print server, which includes any remote servers you have added to the console's Print Servers list. You need administrative access to the computer to perform this action.

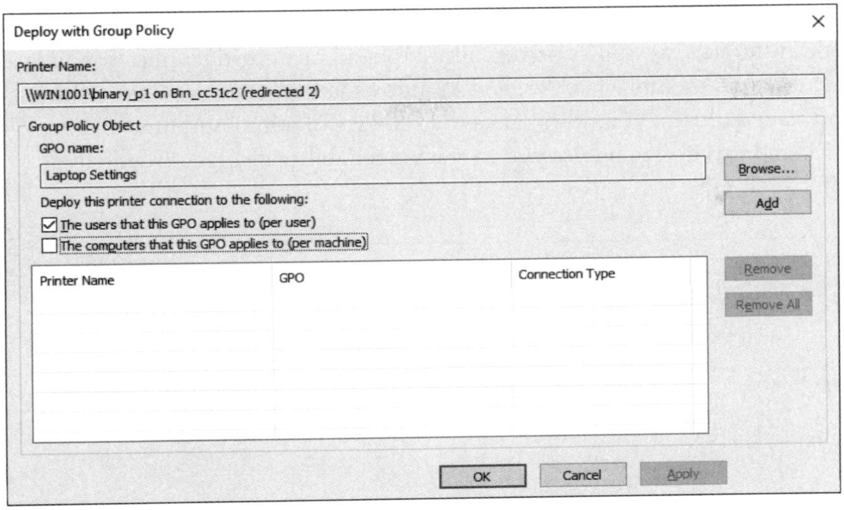

Figure 19-22 Installing Printer Drivers

If you want to remove a printer driver, expand the node under Print Servers for the computer you want to work with and then select the **Drivers** node. All drivers installed on that computer are listed in the center pane. Right-click the driver you want to remove and select **Remote Driver Package**. You need administrative access to the computer to remove a printer driver.

As with many management tools for Windows 10, Microsoft has provided the capability to work with printers using PowerShell. The PrintManagement module includes many cmdlets for managing printers, allowing you to view printer status, add and remove printers and printer drivers, and work with printer jobs. Most of the tasks you can perform using the Print Management console can also be performed using PowerShell.

NOTE For more information about using PowerShell and the PrintManagement module for monitoring and managing printers, see "PrintManagement Module" at https://technet.microsoft.com/itpro/powershell/windows/print/index.

Reliability Monitor

First introduced with Windows Vista, Reliability Monitor utilizes the built-in Reliability Analysis Component (RAC) to provide a trend analysis of your computer's system stability over time. As shown in Figure 19-23, Reliability Monitor provides the System Stability Chart, which correlates the trend of your computer's stability against events that might destabilize the computer. Events tracked include Windows

Updates; software installations and removals; device driver installations, updates, rollbacks, and removals, as well as driver failure to load or unload; application hangs and crashes; disk and memory failures; and Windows failures, such as boot failures, crashes, and sleep failures. Windows ranks the stability of your computer on a scale from 1 to 10, and this chart enables you to track a reliability change directly to a given event.

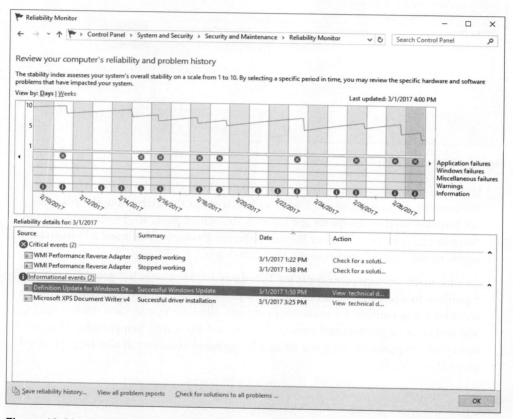

Figure 19-23   Reliability Monitor Providing a Trend Analysis of Your Computer's Stability

Reliability Monitor is integrated with Problem Reports and Solutions to improve the correlation of system changes, events, and possible problem resolutions.

NOTE   To display data in the System Stability Chart, you must run your computer for at least 24 hours after first installation of Windows 10. For the first 28 days, Reliability Monitor uses a dotted line on the Stability Chart graph, indicating that the data is insufficient to establish a valid baseline for this index.

Use the following steps to run Reliability Monitor:

Step 1. Ensure that you are logged on as an administrator or have administrator credentials available.

Step 2. In the Search bar or Cortana, type **reliability** into the Search text box. Then click **View Reliability History** in the list. If you receive a UAC prompt, supply administrative credentials if needed and click **Yes**.

Step 3. Wait while Reliability Monitor generates its report. As shown previously in Figure 19-23, events that cause the stability index to drop are marked in one of the event rows. Click a date containing one of these marks and then expand the appropriate section to obtain more information for the following categories:

   - **Application Failures:** Software programs that hang or crash. Information provided includes the name of the program, its version number, the type of failure, and the date.

   - **Windows Failures:** Problems such as operating system crashes, boot failures, and sleep failures. Information provided includes the type of failure, the operating system and service pack version, the Stop code or detected problem, and the failure date.

   - **Miscellaneous Failures:** Other types of failures, such as improper shutdowns. Information includes the failure type, details, and date.

   - **Warnings:** Other problems such as unsuccessful application reconfiguration or update installation. Information includes the type of reconfiguration attempted.

   - **Information:** Includes the successful installation of various updates and definition packs, as well as successful installation or uninstallation of software programs.

Step 4. To view a comprehensive list of problems, click the **View All Problem Reports** link at the bottom of the dialog box. The list displayed includes the various types of failures noted here.

Step 5. To export an XML-based reliability report, click **Save Reliability History**, specify a path and filename, and then click **Save**.

Step 6. To check for solutions to problems, click **Check for Solutions to All Problems**. Reliability Monitor displays a Checking for Solutions message box as it goes to the Internet and attempts to locate solutions to your problems. You may need to click **Send Information** to send additional information to the Microsoft Error Reporting Service.

Configuring Advanced Management Tools

Windows 10 contains several additional tools that you can use to manage your computer's performance. These include the System Configuration Utility, the Action Center, and the Services console.

Microsoft Management Console (MMC)

As with previous versions of Windows, the Microsoft Management Console (MMC) is still a powerful tool used by administrators to manage local and remote servers including Server Core installations. Custom read-only MMC consoles can be created with specific snap-ins containing only those tools required for the specific delegate function. Windows 10 includes version 3.0 of the MMC, which has been around since Windows XP SP3 and Windows Server 2003 SP2, and includes the following features:

- **Action pane:** The Action pane is located on the right side of the console. It lists all actions available to users.

- **Improved dialog boxes:** The Add/Remove snap-in dialog has been updated to allow for better snap-in organization.

- **Improved error handling:** This version of MMC provides additional error-handling notices and provides the ability to take specific actions when the errors occur.

The Microsoft Management Console is available and can be accessed by launching the MMC.exe application. If you are using a client workstation such as Windows 10, a wide array of MMC snap-ins are installed as part of the Remote Server Administration Tools package.

MMC Options for Delegation

MMC 3.0 provides the capability to create custom or limited views for the specific MMC snap-ins. After snap-ins have been configured and added to the console, the console can be saved as an .MSC file, which you can use to reload your view of administrative tools or distribute to other administrators and users.

MMC offers the following console configuration modes and options:

- **Author Mode:** Grants users full access to all MMC functionality, which includes the ability to add or remove snap-ins, create new windows, create taskpad views and tasks, and view all areas of the console tree. This is the mode that is enabled by default for all new consoles. Typically, consoles are set up by an administrator and then locked down by changing the mode to one of the user access modes.

- **User Mode–Full Access:** Prevents users from adding or removing snap-ins or changing snap-in properties. Users have full access to the tree.

- **User Mode–Limited Access, Multiple Window:** Prevents users from accessing areas of the tree that are not visible in the snap-in console windows.

- **User Mode–Limited Access, Single Window:** Opens the snap-in console in single-window mode and prevents users from accessing areas of the tree that are not visible in the single snap-in console window.

- **Do Not Save Changes to This Console:** Regardless of what is changed, the console is not saved. Changes will be lost the next time it opens.

- **Allow the User to Customize Views:** When checked, this option allows the user to customize console views, including enabling filters.

You can configure Console Options via the Options menu item of the MMC File menu, as shown in Figure 19-24.

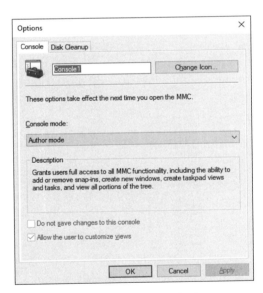

Figure 19-24   MMC Console Options

After you create a custom MMC console, you can lock it down using the appropriate console option and/or filters using the View menu; save the console as an .MSC file and distribute it accordingly. Delegates will be able to manage local or remote servers assuming the following criteria have been met:

- Delegates have been granted proper access to the server or resources.

- Windows Firewall has been configured to accept MMC connections.

Windows Services

Windows services run in the background and enable significant and important functions on your computer—in fact, nearly all actions performed on the computer depend upon one or more services. Many applications install their own services when you install them. Many services are configured to start automatically at system startup; although many of these are essential to proper computer operation, having nonessential services starting can degrade computer performance noticeably.

You can configure service startup and properties from the Services snap-in. This tool is a component of the Computer Management snap-in and can also be accessed in its own console by right-clicking the **Start** button and selecting **Computer Management**. You have seen this console before; for example, in Chapter 9, "Managing User Data," you used the Disk Management tool to configure storage and disks. The Computer Management console, shown in Figure 19-25, lists all services installed on the computer and indicates their status and startup type. You can also access the services console as a standalone by accessing the Search bar or Cortana, typing in **services**, and clicking **Services** from the list.

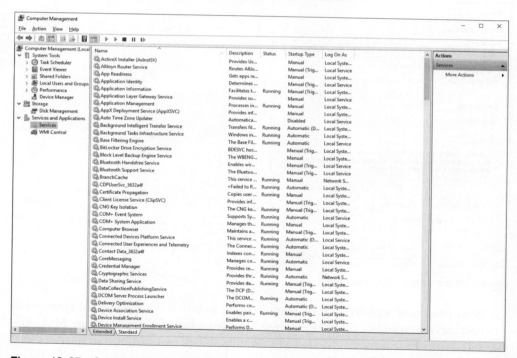

Figure 19-25 Services Console Enabling You to Observe the Status of Services Running on Your Computer

You can modify the properties of any service, including its startup type as required. Right-click the desired service and choose **Properties** to bring up its Properties dialog box shown in Figure 19-26. This allows you to configure the following properties of each service:

- **General tab:** You can set the startup type to Automatic, Automatic (Delayed Start), Manual, or Disabled. By disabling services that consume extra computer resources on startup, you can sometimes improve computer performance. Certain services should also be disabled for improving computer security. However, you must ensure that all essential services remain set to Automatic. Set nonessential services that perform useful tasks to Manual startup.

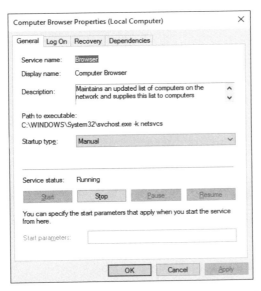

Figure 19-26   Configuring Service Properties from Each Service's Properties Dialog Box

- **Log On tab:** Enables you to change the account used by services when logging on. In nearly all cases, you should leave this set to its default Local System Account.

- **Recovery tab:** Enables you to specify actions to be taken if the service fails, such as restarting the service, restarting the computer, running a program, or taking no action.

- **Dependencies tab:** Lists the services that this service depends on as well as the system components that depend on this service running properly. There are no configurable options on this tab, but the information displayed can be useful in troubleshooting failures.

System Configuration Utility

The System Configuration Utility enables you to disable common services and startup programs to selectively troubleshoot which items are preventing a normal startup.

To start the System Configuration Utility, type **msconfig** into the taskbar Search bar or Cortana field, then click **System Configuration** in the list. If you receive a UAC prompt, click **Yes** or supply administrative credentials. You receive the dialog box shown in Figure 19-27.

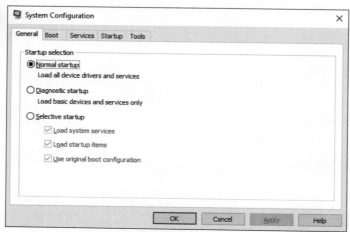

Figure 19-27 System Configuration Utility Enabling You to Troubleshoot Problems That Prevent Windows from Starting Normally

The sections that follow describe the functions available on each tab.

General Tab

The General tab allows you to choose Normal Startup, which loads all drivers and services configured to start automatically; Diagnostic Startup, which loads basic drivers and services; or Selective Startup, which enables you to select the following options:

- **Load System Services:** Starts all services that are configured for automatic startup.

- **Load Startup Items:** Starts applications that have been configured to start at boot or logon time.

- **Use Original Boot Configuration:** Remains selected unless you modify default settings on the Boot tab.

Boot Tab

The Boot tab provides several boot options that are useful if you encounter problems starting your computer normally. The following boot options are available:

- **Safe Boot:** Provides four options for booting your computer into Safe Mode. The Minimal option brings up the Windows GUI with only critical system services loaded, and networking disabled. The Alternate Shell option boots to the command prompt and disables both the GUI and networking. The Active Directory Repair option boots to the GUI and runs Active Directory as well as critical system services. The Network option boots to the Windows GUI with only critical services loaded, and enables networking.

- **No GUI Boot:** Starts Windows without displaying the Windows splash screen.

- **Boot Log:** Boots according to the other options selected and logs information from the boot procedure to *%systemroot% \Ntbtlog.txt*.

- **Base Video:** Uses standard VGA drivers to load the Windows GUI in minimal VGA mode.

- **OS Boot Information:** Displays driver names as the boot process loads them.

On a multiboot computer, the display window contains entries for the different operating systems present. To choose which operating system boots by default, select the desired entry and click **Set as Default**. Use the Timeout setting to specify the number of seconds that the boot menu is displayed on a multiboot computer. In addition, the Make All Boot Settings Permanent option disables tracking of changes made in the System Configuration Utility. This option disables the ability to roll back changes by selecting the **Normal Startup** option from the General tab.

Services Tab

The Services tab lists all Windows services available on the computer, including those installed by other applications running on the computer. You can enable or disable individual services at boot time when you think that running services might be causing boot problems. Clear the check box for those services you want to disable for the next boot, or click the **Disable All** command button to disable all non-essential services.

To show only services installed by non-Microsoft programs, select the **Hide All Microsoft Services** check box. This enables you to more rapidly locate non-Microsoft services that might be contributing to boot problems.

CAUTION Ensure that you do not disable essential services. You might encounter system stability problems or other malfunctions if you disable too many services. Ensure that services you disable are not essential to your computer's operation. The Disable All option does not disable secure Microsoft services required at boot time.

Startup Tab

In previous Windows versions, the Startup tab listed all applications that are configured to start automatically when the computer starts up. In Windows 10 this option has been removed and replaced with a link to Task Manager; clicking this link opens the advanced version of Task Manager to the Startup tab.

Tools Tab

Shown in Figure 19-28, the Tools tab enumerates all diagnostic applications and other available tools. It provides a convenient location from which you can start a program; to do so, select the desired program and click **Launch**.

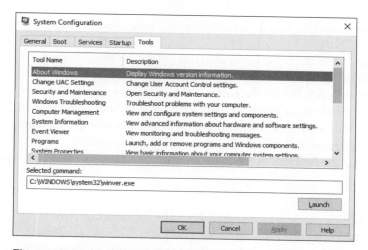

Figure 19-28 Tools Tab Enabling You to Start a Program from a Comprehensive List of Windows Diagnostic Utilities

NOTE For more information on using System Configuration in Windows 10, refer to "MSConfig the System Configuration Tool" at https://answers.microsoft.com/en-us/windows/wiki/windows_10-update/msconfig-the-system-configuration-tool/273dea8e-4cbe-47e9-8489-f400e879ce17.

Configuring Indexing Options

Windows 10 helps you locate information on your computer by building an index of all the most commonly used file types on your computer. By default, Windows indexes all folders included in libraries, email, and offline files. Data that you're not likely to search, such as program files and system files, are not indexed.

Use the following procedure to configure indexing options:

Step 1. Access Control Panel, select either **Large Icons** or **Small Icons** under View, and then select **Indexing Options** from the list of applets displayed. You can also access the Search bar or Cortana, type in **indexing**, and then click **Indexing Options** from the list. Either of these procedures opens the Indexing Options applet, as shown in Figure 19-29.

Figure 19-29   Indexing Options Applet Enabling You to Configure How Windows Indexes Files on Your Computer

Step 2. As shown, the locations included in the index are displayed. To modify these locations, click **Modify**.

Step 3. You receive the Indexed Locations dialog box shown in Figure 19-30. To add or remove selected locations, select or clear the check boxes provided. To include or exclude folders within a location displayed, click this location to expand it, and then select or deselect the desired folders. To show additional locations (such as program files and system files), click **Show All Locations**. When finished, click **OK**.

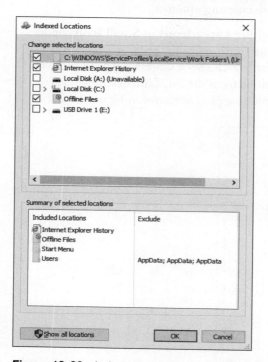

Figure 19-30 Indexed Locations Dialog Box Enabling You to Modify Drives, Folders, and Files Included in the Index

Step 4. For additional indexing options, click **Advanced** to display the Advanced Options dialog box shown in Figure 19-31. Select from the following options as desired:

- **Index Encrypted Files:** Includes files and folders encrypted with the Encrypting File System (EFS) or BitLocker in the index. Microsoft recommends that you enable BitLocker on the system drive if you select this option.

Figure 19-31   Advanced Options Dialog Box Enabling You to Configure Additional Indexing Settings

- **Treat Similar Words with Diacritics as Different Words:** Recognizes words with accents or other diacritical marks as different (for example, resume versus résumé).

- **Rebuild:** If the index is unable to find a file that you're sure is in an indexed location, you might need to re-create the index by selecting this button. This action might take several hours, during which searches might be incomplete.

- **Index Location:** Use this option to change the default location of the index; for example, if you need to free up space on a given disk or partition. This action restarts the indexing service, and the change will not take place until after the service has restarted.

- **File Types Tab:** Enables you to add new file types to the index according to file extension (see Figure 19-32). You can also remove existing file types by clearing their check boxes.

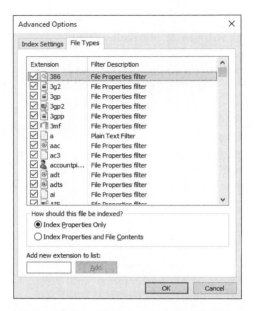

Figure 19-32   File Types Tab Enabling You to Specify Which File Extensions Are Indexed

> **Step 5.**   When finished, click **OK** to close the Advanced Options dialog box, and then click **Close** to close the Indexing Options applet.

NOTE   For more information on indexing features in Windows, refer to "Windows Indexing Features" at https://technet.microsoft.com/en-us/library/dd744700(v=ws.10).aspx. Though written for Windows 7, the procedures described also apply to Windows 10.

Task Scheduler

Task Scheduler is an MMC snap-in that allows you to schedule and automate tasks to perform a specific action at a specific time. You can also use it to trigger an event as a follow-up to another event occurring. For example, suppose you need to restart your computer every day at 2 a.m.. One option is to set your alarm clock every morning at 2 a.m. just to restart the server. On the other hand, using a scheduled task to run automatically seems a bit easier.

There are a few components associated with Task Scheduler:

- **Triggers:** A trigger is a set of criteria that when met executes a specific task. Triggers can be based on a schedule, a logon event, a startup event, during a period of inactivity, upon session connect/disconnect, workstation lock/unlock, and the like.

- **Actions:** An action refers to an event that occurs after a trigger is set. Actions include starting a program such as a script, sending an email, displaying an alert, and so on.

- **Conditions:** Allows you to specify how the actions should be taken. Conditions include items such as idle times, current power state, and if the task should stop if the computer is on battery power, for instance.

- **Settings:** Specifies additional settings, such as what to do if the task fails or if the schedules are missed due to the computer being offline.

The layout of Task Scheduler is similar to that of other MMC snap-ins, as shown in Figure 19-33.

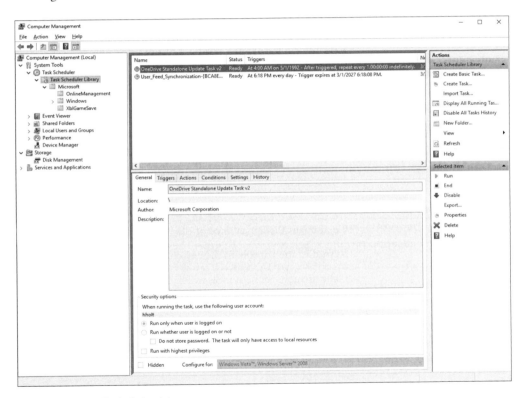

Figure 19-33   Task Scheduler

Right away you will notice from Figure 19-33 that some scheduled tasks are already defined. If you have set up OneDrive, there is a task to check for OneDrive updates every day. Internet Explorer has created a task called User_Feed_Synchronization to synchronize all your RSS feeds. You can expand the folders to explore other tasks that Windows or other software may have created for you. Figure 19-33 includes an

OnlineManagement folder, added by the Microsoft Intune client, which you learned about in Chapter 13. Under the Windows folder are lots of other folders for applications that need to perform scheduled tasks to keep your applications functioning properly.

The Task Scheduler Library contains the hierarchy where all your scheduled tasks are stored. You can create your own custom folders for storing and organizing your tasks. In the center pane, notice the list of active tasks. Highlight the task to configure triggers, actions, conditions, and so on. On the far right pane, you see a list of actions. Table 19-6 outlines the available actions.

Table 19-6   Task Scheduler Actions

Action	Description
Create Basic Task	Basic wizard used to create a task specifying only basic settings, which includes only the trigger and action.
Create Task	Full wizard, which allows you to create a task specifying security settings, triggers, task recovery options, scheduling, conditions, and so on.
Import Task	Allows the importing of a task from a saved .XML file.
Display All Running Tasks	Shows all running tasks, when they started, how long they ran, the current state, and the location of the task.
Disable All Task History	When clicked, task history is disabled. Click again to reenable.
New Folder	Creates a folder to store or group configured tasks.
View	Customizes the appearance of the Task Scheduler console.
Refresh	Refreshes the console to display changes in events or tasks.
Help	Calls the console help tool, which displays links to Task Scheduler information available on TechNet.

Scheduling a Task with Task Scheduler

To schedule a task with Task Scheduler, perform the following steps:

Step 1.   Open Task Scheduler from the Computer Management snap-in or via Administrative Tools.

Step 2.   On the right pane, click **Create Basic Task**. The Create Basic Task Wizard appears, as shown in Figure 19-34.

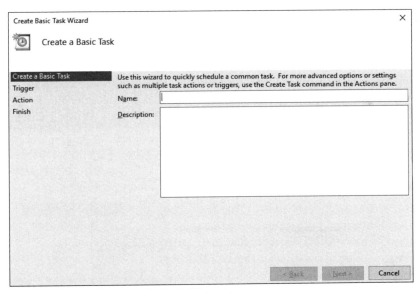

Figure 19-34   Create Basic Task Wizard

Step 3.   Type a name for the task and an optional description, and click **Next**.

Step 4.   For this example, we create a task called Run Task Manager, which opens Task Manager at logon. Select the **When I Log On** option button for the trigger, as shown in Figure 19-35. Click **Next** to continue.

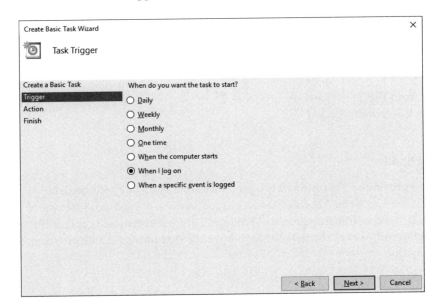

Figure 19-35   Create Basic Task Wizard: Configure Trigger

Step 5.   For the Action, select **Start a Program**.

Step 6.   Browse to the path of the program or script; in this case Taskmgr.exe, and click **Next**.

Step 7.   Confirm your task settings and click **Finish**. As shown in Figure 19-36, if you would like to review the properties of the task, select the check box labeled **Open the Properties Dialog for This Task When I Click Finish**.

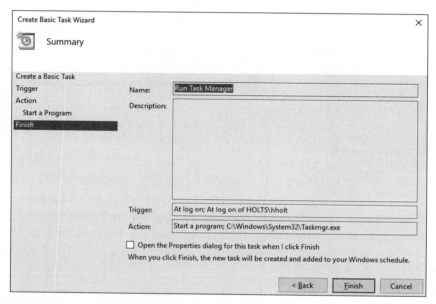

Figure 19-36   Create Basic Task Wizard: Finish

Step 8.   Refresh the Task Scheduler console to see your newly created task in the Task Scheduler Library.

Windows PowerShell

As you learned previously, PowerShell is a powerful command-line tool available since Windows Server 2008. Microsoft has included Version 5.1 with the release of Windows 10. In an upcoming update for Windows 10, PowerShell will replace the command shell (**cmd.exe**) as the default shell; it is now that powerful and with that much functionality.

You have learned a number of uses for PowerShell in previous chapters, beginning with some introductory material in the very first chapter, "Introducing Windows 10," where you learned how to configured PowerShell as the default shell right away. For review, some of the uses of PowerShell that have been covered are summarized in Table 19-7.

Table 19-7   PowerShell Functionality Mentioned in Previous Chapters of This Book

PowerShell Information	Chapter
Replace command prompt with PowerShell	Chapter 1
Use PowerShell to work with Windows Images	Chapter 2
Use PowerShell to customize Start menu and taskbar layouts	Chapter 3
Install PowerShell cmdlets for Remote Management Server Tools	Chapter 4
You can use PowerShell for provisioning packages to images	Chapter 5
Use PowerShell to configure Device Guard policies	Chapter 7
Use PowerShell to reset a computer's Active Directory domain account	Chapter 7
Use PowerShell to configure storage and Storage Spaces	Chapter 9
Using PowerShell and PowerShell Remoting for remote management	Chapter 15
Introduction to the PowerShell ISE	Chapter 15
Manage Windows Firewall with PowerShell	Chapter 16
Use PowerShell to manage App-V clients	Chapter 18

These topics cover only some of the tasks you can perform with PowerShell. Because PowerShell is a scripting language, you can automate these tasks and many more. Microsoft has provided the capability to send and execute PowerShell cmdlets to remote computers using WinRM, as we discussed in Chapter 15.

If you have configured computers for remote management, you can use one of the most powerful cmdlet remote administration tools for PowerShell, which is the **PSSession** cmdlet. This cmdlet functions similar to a Telnet session in that you connect directly to the remote server. When connected, you virtually have full access to run all commands as if you were sitting in front of the computer console. Some of the more common remote administration cmdlets are outlined in Table 19-8.

Table 19-8 PowerShell Basic Cmdlets for Remote Administration

Cmdlet	Description	Examples
Get	Used to retrieve or get information about a specific function	**Get-Process:** To retrieve or get a list of processes running on a computer. **Get-Service:** To retrieve or get a list of services running on a computer. **Get-EventLog:** Enables you to manage event logs and retrieve events contained within those event logs. **Get-WmiObject:** Retrieves information from the Windows Management Instrumentation (WMI), such as specific hardware or software information.
Invoke	Allows you to run a single command on one or more computers. As commands are executed, a remote session is established and disconnected upon completion. This cmdlet is particularly helpful for automating some manual tasks.	For commands: **Invoke-Command** -ComputerName *[Computer1, Computer 2]* -ScriptBlock {command} For scripts: **Invoke-expression c:\testscript\ testscript.ps1**
PSSession	Similar to a Telnet session, **PSSession** creates a persistent connection to a remote computer. From here you can execute virtually any command that you could if you were logged on locally. Commands can be executed until you exit the session using the **Exit-PSSession** command.	**New-PSSession**: **New-PSSession** -ComputerName *[remote computer]* **Get-PSSession:** List active sessions **Enter-PSSession:** Switch between sessions **Exit-PSSession:** Exit a session

NOTE For a full amount of reference material for PowerShell, start with the "Windows PowerShell Owner's Manual" available at https://technet.microsoft.com/en-us/library/ee221100.aspx.

Exam Preparation Tasks

Review all the Key Topics

Review the most important topics in the chapter, noted with the key topics icon in the outer margin of the page. Table 19-9 lists a reference of these key topics and the page numbers on which each is found.

Table 19-9   Key Topics for Chapter 19

Key Topic Element	Description	Page Number
Figure 19-2	Viewing error, warning, and information messages in Event Viewer	879
Figure 19-3	Filtering event logs	881
Figure 19-5	Creating an event log subscription	884
Figure 19-7	The Task Manager presents a simplified view of apps running on the computer, and enables you to shut down misbehaving apps	887
Figure 19-8	The advanced interface of Task Manager presents a color-coded view of apps, background processes, and Windows processes, highlighting those processes that are using the most resources	888
Figure 19-10	Using Resource Monitor to monitor your computer's resource utilization	891
Step List	Shows you how to use Performance Monitor	895
Step List	Shows you how to create a Data Collector Set	898
Table 19-2	Describes the important counters for the Memory performance object	902
Table 19-3	Describes the important counters for the Processor performance object	905
Figure 19-19	Monitoring computers using Microsoft Intune alerts	907
Figure 19-20	Using the Printer Management console to monitor and managing printers	909
Figure 19-27	Using the System Configuration Utility to troubleshoot Windows startup issues	918
Table 19-6	Task Scheduler actions	926
Step List	Lists the tasks required to schedule a basic task	926
Table 19-7	Where to find tasks you can perform with PowerShell throughout this book	929
Table 19-8	Basic PowerShell cmdlets for remote administration	930

Complete the Tables and Lists from Memory

Print a copy of Appendix B, "Memory Tables" (found on the book's website), or at least the section for this chapter, and complete the tables and lists from memory. Appendix C, "Memory Tables Answer Key," also on the website, includes completed tables and lists to check your work.

Definitions of Key Terms

Define the following key terms from this chapter, and check your answers in the glossary.

alert, data collector sets, event log subscription, Event Viewer, indexing, Microsoft Management Console (MMC), Msconfig, paging file, performance counter, performance object, Performance Monitor, Print Management, Reliability Monitor, Resource Monitor, System Configuration Utility, Task Manager, Task Scheduler

This chapter covers the following subjects:

- **Configuring a USB Recovery Drive:** A USB recovery drive enables you to boot your computer and perform a repair should your computer become non-functional. This section shows you how to create a USB recovery drive.

- **System Restore and Restore Points:** This feature enables you to restore your computer to a previous point in time. You need to know how to recover your computer from problems caused by improper configuration, malware, or other situations. You can also refresh the Windows 10 operating system back to its factory settings. Push Button Reset is especially useful for Windows mobile and tablet computers. Windows 10 enables you to configure several options related to restore points, including the drives from which data is restored, the space used by restore points, and the ability to manually create or delete restore points.

- **Resolving Hardware and Device Issues:** This section discusses the use of Device Manager to resolve driver problems, including conflicts.

- **Driver Rollback:** When a faulty driver has been installed that results in problems with some hardware component, you can roll back the driver to a previous version. This section shows you how to perform driver rollback.

This chapter covers the following objectives for the 70-697 and 70-698 exams:

Configure system recovery: Configure a recovery drive, configure system restore, perform a refresh or recycle, perform a driver rollback, configure restore points, resolve hardware and device issues, interpret data from Device Manager, perform recovery operations using Windows Recovery.

CHAPTER 20

Configuring System Recovery Options

As users work with their Windows 10 computers, increasingly large amounts of programs, data, and other items accumulate on the hard drive. As you learned in Chapter 19, "Monitoring and Managing Windows," the computer's performance tends to slow down for a variety of reasons. Now we go a step further— any of a number of factors can cause a computer to become unresponsive and result in the need for system recovery actions. Windows 10 offers several technologies for repairing and recovering computers that are responding slowly or that have stopped responding entirely. As a desktop support technician or network administrator, it is important that you are capable of performing system recovery, both for the real world and for the 70-697 and 70-698 exams.

"Do I Know This Already?" Quiz

The "Do I Know This Already?" quiz allows you to assess whether you should read this entire chapter or simply jump to the "Exam Preparation Tasks" section for review. If you are in doubt, read the entire chapter. Table 20-1 outlines the major headings in this chapter and the corresponding "Do I Know This Already?" quiz questions. You can find the answers in Appendix A, "Answers to the 'Do I Know This Already?' Quizzes."

Table 20-1 "Do I Know This Already?" Foundation Topics Section-to-Question Mapping

Foundation Topics Section	Questions Covered in This Section
Configuring a USB Recovery Drive	1–2
System Restore and Restore Points	3–9
Resolving Hardware and Device Issues	10
Driver Rollback	11

CAUTION   The goal of self-assessment is to gauge your mastery of the topics in this chapter. If you do not know the answer to a question or are only partially sure of the answer, you should mark that question as wrong for purposes of the self-assessment. Giving yourself credit for an answer you correctly guess skews your self-assessment results and might provide you with a false sense of security.

1. You want to ensure that you can fully restore your computer to its operating system in the event of a hardware failure. Which of the following should you do to accomplish this objective with the least amount of administrative effort?

    a. Create a system recovery disc.

    b. Create a system state backup.

    c. Create a USB recovery drive.

    d. Create a Complete PC Backup.

2. Which of the following items are included in a backup created by the System Restore applet in Windows 10? (Choose all that apply.)

    a. Registry

    b. DLL cache folder

    c. User profiles

    d. User libraries

    e. Installed application executables

    f. COM+ and WMI information

3. You have downloaded and installed an application that you thought would improve your productivity, but you discover that this application has over-written several drivers and other essential files. You would like to return your computer to its status as of the day before you downloaded the application. What should you do to accomplish this task with the least amount of effort?

    a. Roll back the affected drivers.

    b. Restore your user profile to that of the most recent backup created before the application was downloaded.

    c. Restore your operating system from a system image backup.

    d. Use System Restore and specify the desired date.

4. You want to fully restore your computer to the manufacturer's default functionality because of a virus infestation that has affected multiple locations on the hard drive. Which type of recovery should you use for this restore?

   a. Windows Complete PC Backup

   b. Push-button reset

   c. Windows Backup and Restore

   d. System Repair Disc

   e. System Restore

5. Which of the following actions will enable you to choose Advanced Startup Options on a Windows 10 Pro computer that has no other operating system installed on it? (Each correct answer presents a complete solution. Choose three.)

   a. Restart your computer and press F8 after the POST sequence has completed.

   b. From the Settings app, select **Update & Security**. Then from the Windows Update window, click **Recovery** and then click **Restart Now** under Advanced Startup.

   c. From the logon screen, click the Power icon in the bottom-right corner of this screen and then hold the Shift key down while clicking **Restart**.

   d. Press Ctrl+Alt+Delete and select the **Change PC Settings** option. Then from the PC Settings window, click **General** and then click **Restart Now**.

   e. Boot your computer from the Windows 10 installation DVD. When the language preferences screen appears, click **Next**, and then click **Repair Your Computer**.

6. You use a USB recovery drive to start your computer and choose the Troubleshoot option. Which of the following recovery options can you select to repair your computer? (Choose three.)

   a. Refresh Your PC

   b. Reset Your PC

   c. Advanced Options

   d. Device Driver Rollback

   e. Recovery Console

7. You install a new video driver and reboot your computer. The display shows a large number of horizontal lines and nothing is legible, so you are unable to log on. You reboot your computer, access the Choose an Option screen, and select **Troubleshoot** to select troubleshooting options. What should you do to correct this problem with the least amount of effort?

    a. From the Troubleshoot screen, select **Refresh Your PC**.

    b. From the Troubleshoot screen, select **Reset Your PC**.

    c. From the Troubleshoot screen, select **Advanced Options**. Select **Startup Settings** and then select **Enable Low-Resolution Video**. Then perform a device driver rollback.

    d. From the Troubleshoot screen, select **Advanced Options**. Select **Startup Settings** and then select **Enable Safe Mode**. Then perform a device driver rollback.

    e. Use the system repair disc to reboot your computer and then select the **System Restore** option.

8. Your computer's hard disk has failed, and you have installed a new 1.5 TB hard disk. You are lucky enough to have created a system image backup a week ago. What should you do to get your computer up and running again with the least amount of effort and without losing your installed applications?

    a. Start your computer with a USB recovery drive and choose the option to use a system image you created earlier to recover your computer.

    b. Start your computer with a USB recovery drive and choose the option to reinstall Windows.

    c. Start your computer with a USB recovery drive and choose the **System Restore** option.

    d. Start your computer with a Windows 8.1 DVD and perform an in-place upgrade of Windows.

9. You have downloaded an interesting application from the Internet, but are afraid that it might contain a malicious component. Some of your friends have suggested that you not install this application, but you'd really like to give it a try. What should you do before installing the application so that you can recover your computer if necessary by using the least amount of effort?

    a. Use System Restore to manually create a restore point.

    b. Boot your computer to Safe Mode and install the application; then try running the application before booting back to a regular startup.

    c. Use File History to create a backup of all your data files before installing the application.

    d. Use Windows Backup and Restore to create a system image backup.

10. You had a problem with your computer a few days ago and are afraid it may happen again. But you have not been able to find a solution and do not have any notifications that a solution has been found. Where can you go to check for a solution right away?

   a. Action Center

   b. Device Manager

   c. Security and Maintenance

   d. System Information

11. An update that you downloaded from the Internet has resulted in your sound card not working. Checking Device Manager, you discover that the sound card is using a problematic driver. What should you do to correct this problem most rapidly?

   a. Roll back the affected driver.

   b. Download and install a new driver from the sound card manufacturer's website.

   c. Use System Restore and specify a date before the download occurred.

   d. Use a system repair disc to repair your computer.

Foundation Topics

Configuring a USB Recovery Drive

You can use a USB recovery drive to boot your computer to the Windows Recovery Environment discussed later in this chapter should you need to recover from a serious error or to restore Windows on your computer. This procedure relies on a recovery image found on many computers that can be used to refresh your computer. This image is typically stored on a dedicated recovery partition, and is generally 3–6 GB in size.

Use the following procedure to create a USB recovery drive:

Step 1. Click **Start** and scroll the app list to expand Windows System. Then choose **Control Panel > System and Security > Save Backup Copies of Your Files with File History**.

Step 2. In the File History applet, select the **Recovery** option.

Step 3. You receive the Advanced Recovery Tools dialog box shown in Figure 20-1. Click **Create a Recovery Drive**. If you receive a UAC prompt, click **Yes**.

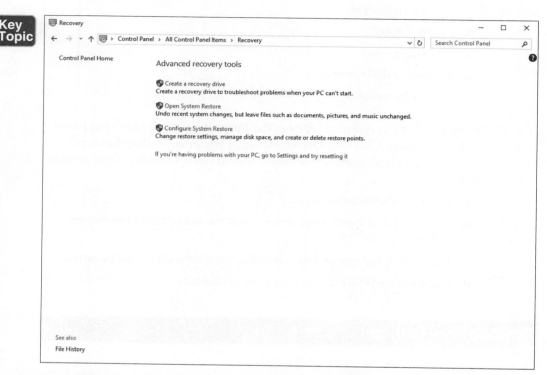

Figure 20-1 Recovery Applet Includes Three Advanced Recovery Tools

Step 4. The Recovery Drive Wizard starts with the Create a Recovery Drive page shown in Figure 20-2. If your computer has a recovery partition, the check box shown will be available. Ensure that it is selected, and then click **Next**.

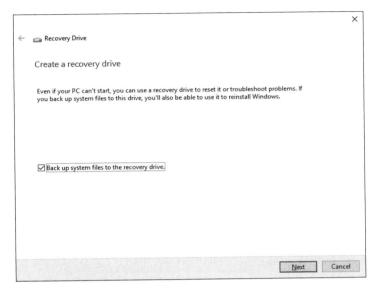

Figure 20-2   Creating a Recovery Drive

> **Step 5.**   After a few seconds, the Select the USB Flash Drive page appears, as shown in Figure 20-3. If more than one drive is available, select the desired drive and then click **Next**.

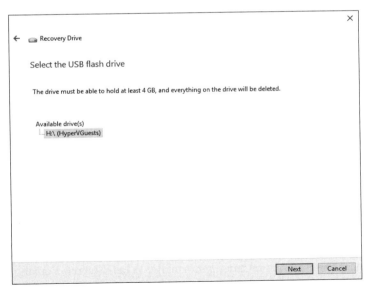

Figure 20-3   Selecting a USB Drive for Creating the Recovery Drive

Step 6. You are warned that everything on the selected drive will be deleted. If you need to back up any files, click **Cancel** and copy these files before proceeding. When ready, click **Create** to proceed.

Step 7. The wizard tracks the process of formatting the drive, copying utilities, and completes the process. When informed that the recovery drive is ready, click **Finish**.

CAUTION Make sure that nothing of importance is stored on the flash drive before using it to create a recovery drive! The procedure given here will erase everything stored on the USB recovery drive, so copy any important data from the drive to another location before creating the USB recovery drive.

NOTE For more information on creating a recovery drive, refer to "Create a USB Recovery Drive" at https://support.microsoft.com/en-us/help/17422/windows-8-create-usb-recovery-drive.

Performing Recovery Operations Using Windows Recovery

Windows now includes many recovery operations you can use to repair a troubled system, and these operations are easier to perform and more reliable when you have prepared for issues by creating a USB recovery drive. The USB recovery drive is used to automatically recover a computer that will not start normally by loading a Startup Repair routine that provides several recovery options. The following are some of the problems that Startup Repair can attempt to repair:

- Missing, corrupted, or incompatible device drivers
- Missing or corrupted system files or boot configuration settings
- Improper or corrupted Registry keys or data
- Corrupted disk metadata, such as the master boot table, boot sector, or partition table

Startup Repair provides a diagnostics-based, step-by-step troubleshooting tool that enables end users and tech support personnel to rapidly diagnose and repair problems that are preventing a computer from starting normally. When Startup Repair determines the problem that is preventing normal startup, it attempts to repair this problem automatically. If it is unable to do so, it provides support personnel with diagnostic information and suggests additional recovery options.

Use the following procedure to run the USB recovery drive and invoke Startup Repair:

Step 1. Insert the USB recovery drive and restart your computer. If necessary, press a key to boot the computer from the USB recovery drive as opposed to the hard disk. If your BIOS does not support booting from a USB drive, you need to boot from the Windows 10 installation DVD and then insert the USB recovery drive.

Step 2. If you are booting from the USB recovery drive, the Choose Your Keyboard Layout screen appears. Select your desired layout.

Step 3. The Windows 10 logo and progress indicator appears. Then the Choose an Option dialog box, shown in Figure 20-4, appears.

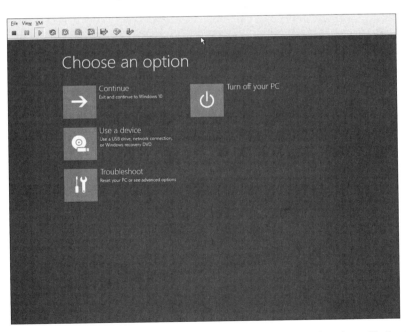

Figure 20-4 Choose an Option Screen Appearing After Booting with the USB Recovery Drive

Step 4. Select **Troubleshoot** and then from the Troubleshoot screen, select **Advanced Options**. The Advanced Options screen shown in Figure 20-5 is displayed. Select **Startup Repair**.

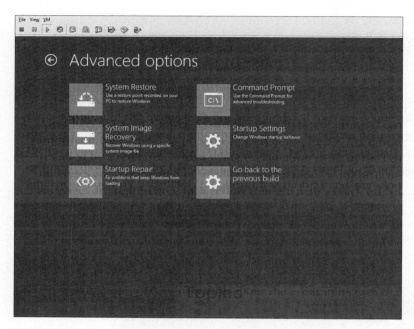

Figure 20-5   The Advanced Options Screen for Windows 10 Recovery

Step 5.   On the Startup Repair screen, you are asked to choose a target operating system. Choose the one you want to repair, or the Windows 10 selection if there is only one available.

Step 6.   The computer displays Diagnosing Your PC for a few minutes while it checks for issues.

Step 7.   If Windows finds a problem that it can fix, it prompts you to restart the computer.

Step 8.   Startup Repair searches for problems. If it does not detect any problem, it informs you and offers links to Shut Down the computer or to Advanced Options, which displays the options from Figure 20-5. It also displays the location of the log file created during the diagnosis procedure.

Step 9.   If Startup Repair detects and repairs a problem, it displays a message informing you that it repaired the problem successfully.

Step 10.   When you are finished, click **Shut Down** to shut down your computer normally. You can then start the computer from the normal boot drive.

System Restore and Restore Points

First introduced with Windows XP, System Restore enables you to recover from system problems such as those caused by improper system settings, faulty drivers, and incompatible applications. It restores your computer to a previous condition without damaging any data files, such as documents and email. System Restore is useful when problems persist after you have uninstalled incompatible software or device drivers, or after downloading problematic content from a website, or when you are having problems that you cannot diagnose, but that have started recently.

During normal operation, System Restore creates snapshots of the system at each startup and before major configuration changes are started. It stores these snapshots and manages them in a special location on your hard drive. It also copies monitored files to this location before any installation program or Windows itself overwrites these files during application or device installation. These snapshots include backups of the following settings:

- Registry

- DLL cache folder

- User profiles

- COM+ and WMI information

- Certain monitored system files

System restore points are not the same as data backup. System Restore can restore applications and settings to an earlier point in time, but it does not back up or restore any personal data files. Use the File History application to back up personal data files or recover any that have been deleted or damaged.

Configuring System Restore

You can run System Restore from the System Properties dialog box. The following steps show you how:

Step 1. Access the Control Panel System applet from the System and Security category. In Windows, you can also right-click **Start** and choose **System> About**, and then click **System Info** under Related Settings. You can also click **Open System Restore** in the Recovery applet previously shown in Figure 20-1 (skip to Step 3).

Step 2. On the left pane of the System applet, select **System Protection**.

Step 3. If you receive a UAC prompt, click **Yes**. This opens the System Protection tab of the System Properties dialog box, as shown in Figure 20-6.

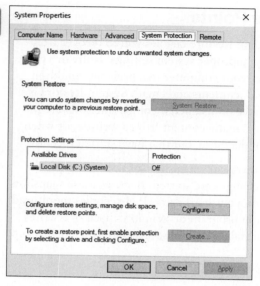

Figure 20-6   System Protection Tab of the System Properties Dialog Box with a System Restore Option

Step 4.   Click **System Restore** to open the System Restore dialog box, as shown in Figure 20-7. You can also access this dialog box by typing **restore** into the taskbar Search text box, and clicking **Create a Restore Point**.

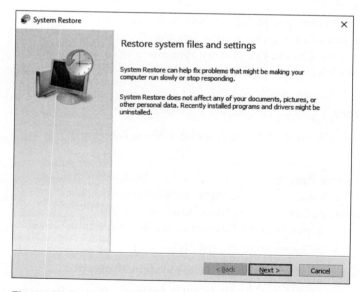

Figure 20-7   System Restore Dialog Box Enabling You to Restore System Files and Settings

TIP   If your computer has System Protection turned off, the System Restore button will be grayed out, and you cannot select it. Turn on System Protection by clicking the **Configure** button shown in Figure 20-6, select **Turn on System Protection**, and then click **OK**.

TIP   If the System Restore dialog box informs you that no restore points have been created, click **Cancel** to return to the System Protection tab and then click **Create** to create a restore point. When informed that the restore point was created successfully, click **Close**. We discuss creating and configuring restore points later in this chapter.

Step 5.   Click **Next** to display the Restore Your Computer to the State It Was in Before the Selected Event page.

Step 6.   If you want to restore your computer to the date and time mentioned, leave the default of Recommended Restore selected, and then click **Next** to skip to Step 8 of this procedure. To choose a different restore point, select **Choose a Different Restore Point**, and then click **Next** to display the Restore Your Computer to the State It Was in Before the Selected Event page shown in Figure 20-8.

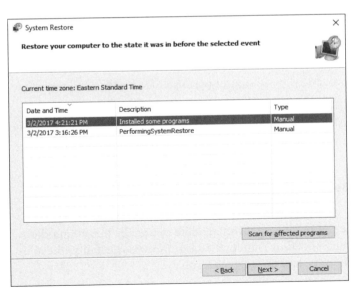

Figure 20-8   System Restore Enabling You to Select the Date and Time to Which You Want to Restore Your Computer

Step 7.   Select a date and time to which you want to restore your computer, and then click **Next**.

Step 8.   In the Confirm Your Restore Point dialog box shown in Figure 20-9, note the warning to save open files and then click **Finish** to perform the restore.

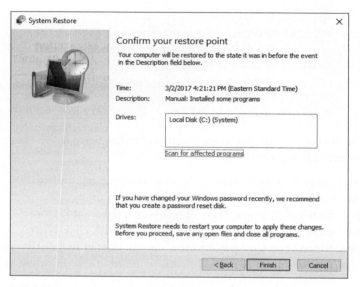

Figure 20-9   Confirming Your Choice of Restore Point

Step 9.   You receive a message box informing you that System Restore may not be interrupted and cannot be undone if being performed from Safe Mode. Click **Yes** to proceed. The computer performs the restore, and then shuts down and restarts.

Step 10.   Log back on as an administrator. You receive a System Restore message box informing you that the restore completed successfully. Click **Close**.

Performing a Refresh or Recycle

Included in Windows 10 is the push-button reset, which enables users to repair issues with their PCs in a quick and easy manner, while optionally preserving their files, data, and user settings. Added in Windows 10 is improved reliability, the ability to recover from failed resets, and imageless recovery.

There are three options available to users for the push-button reset:

- **Refresh Your PC:** Allows you to reinstall the Windows 10 OS while preserving all user accounts, files in libraries and user folders, and Windows Store apps.

- **Reset Your PC:** Reinstalls the original Windows 10 image, but also completely clears all user accounts, passwords, data, and settings. This is especially useful if you are selling or recycling your computer.

- **Bare Metal Recovery:** Restores the partition layout for the system disk and reinstalls the OS and any preinstalled customizations from external media.

These push-button processes are especially useful on smaller devices, such as small form-factor devices running Windows 10 Mobile, which may not have traditional optical drives and removable hard drives, making it a challenge to reinstall or to ensure that user data is cleared when the device is reassigned or ready to decommission. They also often come with hardware-specific devices and drivers. With push-button refresh, the original OEM system image is restored, including all the device-specific hardware drivers included. No need to hunt down driver discs or locate them on manufacturer websites.

Refreshing Your Computer

The push-button refresh preserves data and user customizations; however, Windows Store apps and installed applications are not retained, and most settings for those applications will be lost. For instance, the following system folders are reset to the original state, and any settings or data in the folders will be lost:

- ProgramData
- Program Files
- Program Files (x86)
- AppData folders in User's folders
- Windows

All folders other than AppData under User profiles are preserved after the refresh, including Documents and the Desktop, but any files or folders users may have created outside of the \Users folders will be lost. Similar to a reinstall of Windows, the refresh creates a Windows.old folder in the system partition and moves many folders there, such as ProgramData and Users. Preinstalled Windows Store apps are recovered after the refresh, but user-acquired Windows apps from the Windows Store are not preserved. User-installed desktop apps are lost; a list of these apps is created and stored in a file on the desktop.

Use the following procedure to perform a push-button reset to refresh a Windows 10 PC:

Step 1.   From the Windows Settings screen, select **Update & Security**, and then select the **Recovery** menu to display the screen shown in Figure 20-10.

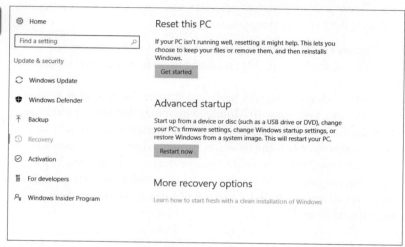

Figure 20-10   Recovery Screen Allowing You to Reset Your PC, Go Back to an Earlier Build, Access Advanced Startup, and Access Other Recovery Options

Step 2.   On the Recovery page, click the **Get Started** button under Reset this PC. The screen displays the options shown in Figure 20-11.

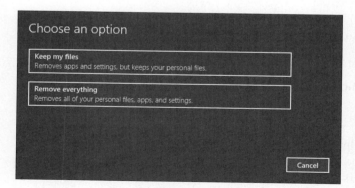

Figure 20-11   Update and Recovery Screen Providing Two Options for Restoring Your Computer

Step 3.   Select **Keep My Files** to refresh your PC without affecting your files. Windows displays a Getting Things Ready screen for a few minutes.

Step 4. The Your Apps Will Be Removed warning screen shown in Figure 20-12 lists the apps that will be removed and lets you know that the list will be saved to the desktop. Click **Next** to proceed.

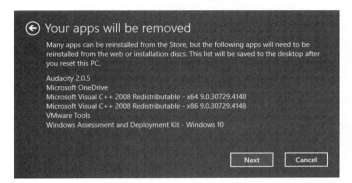

Figure 20-12 Refresh Your PC Screen

Step 5. The next Refresh Your PC screen (see Figure 20-13) describes what will happen next. Make a note of these items, and then click **Reset** to proceed. Windows displays a Getting a Few Things Ready message and a progress indicator, and then restarts, displaying the Installing Windows progress screen shown in Figure 20-14 as the user files are preserved, folders are created, and the image is refreshed. After another restart, Windows 10 starts normally with the operating system refreshed.

Figure 20-13 Screen Describing What Happens During the Refresh

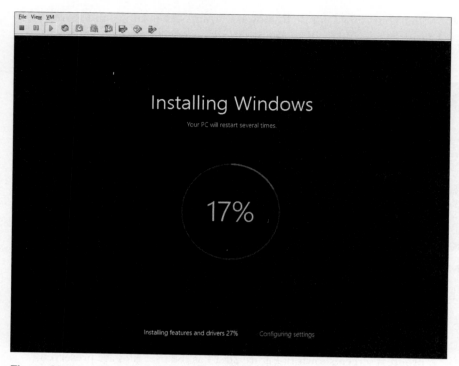

Figure 20-14 Windows Refreshing Your Computer

NOTE You might be prompted to insert the Windows installation DVD or media. This is typical on a computer without a recovery partition (as described in Chapter 2, "Implementing Windows"). Cancel the refresh, insert the Windows 10 media, and restart your computer to try again.

Resetting Your Computer to Original Installation Condition

This process performs a complete reinstall of Windows, without preserving user accounts, data, or settings. It is otherwise similar to what is described in the preceding section. The complete reset takes less time to prepare, because Windows does not need to save user files or create the Windows.old folder. Use the following procedure to perform a push-button reset to completely reset a Windows 10 PC:

Step 1. Use Steps 1 and 2 of the previous procedure to access the Recovery screen previously shown in Figure 20-11.

Step 2. Select **Remove Everything** to remove everything and reinstall Windows.

Step 3.   If you have more than one drive, Windows prompts you whether you want to remove all files from all drives, or only the system drive. Select either the **Only the Drive Where Windows Is Installed** option, or the **All Drives** option.

Step 4.   You receive two options as shown in Figure 20-15, providing you with the options Just Remove My Files and Remove Files and Clean the Drive. The options are similar to the choice when formatting an NTFS volume: the quick reset simply deletes the file table, whereas a thorough reset formats the entire drive, writing zeros to every sector. Select the most appropriate option according to your needs. If you are retiring the computer or assigning it to someone else, you should clean the drives.

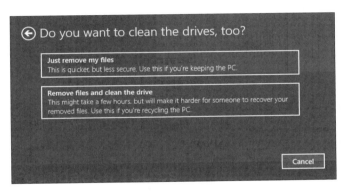

Figure 20-15   Two Options for Fully Cleaning Your Drive

Step 5.   The Ready to Reset This PC page shown in Figure 20-16 displays the actions that will take place. If you need to copy files to your File History drive, click **Cancel** and perform this task (which is described in Chapter 21, "Configuring File Recovery"). Click **Reset** to proceed.

Figure 20-16   Ready to Reset Your Computer to Its Initially Installed Condition

Step 6.   The reset proceeds and the computer restarts. The time required depends on the option you selected in Step 4. When finished, log back on.

> **NOTE**   Although a drive format does not perform a highly secure erase, it does make it much more difficult for the next user of the device to recover sensitive data from the drive.

> **NOTE**   For more information and details on the refresh and reset process, the folders preserved and refreshed during a push-button refresh, and how to customize the refresh process, review the MSDN article "How Push-Button Reset Features Work" at https://msdn.microsoft.com/en-us/windows/hardware/commercialize/manufacture/desktop/how-push-button-reset-features-work.

Advanced Startup Options

The Update and Recovery screen previously shown in Figure 20-4 also enables you to perform several Advanced startup actions, as described briefly in this section. The options enable you to perform any of the following:

- **Continue:** Restarts your computer into Windows 10 without performing any troubleshooting actions.

- **Use Another Operating System:** Enables you to boot your computer from an alternative version of Windows if one is available.

- **Troubleshoot:** Enables you to refresh or reset your PC (as described earlier in this section) or boot into one of several advanced options described later in this section.

- Turn off your PC.

> **TIP**   If you are at the logon screen, you can click the Power icon in the bottom-right corner of this screen and then hold down the Shift key while clicking **Restart**.

> **TIP**   You can also access Windows RE by booting your computer from the Windows 10 installation DVD. When the language preferences screen appears, click **Next**, and then click **Repair Your Computer**.

Windows RE contains its own set of drivers and files apart from the main Windows installation; therefore, software problems within Windows do not affect starting this option, enabling you to begin troubleshooting effectively when you are unable to start your computer using any of the other options. You are returned to the Choose an Option screen previously shown in Figure 20-4, from which you can perform tasks as outlined earlier in this section.

Selecting **Troubleshoot** from Figure 20-4 and then **Advanced Options** on the Troubleshoot screen that appears enables you to choose from the options shown previously in Figure 20-5, which enable you to perform the following actions:

- **System Restore:** Enables you to perform System Restore, as described earlier in this chapter.

- **System Image Recovery:** Enables you to attempt recovering your computer from a system image created previously.

- **Startup Repair:** Attempts to repair problems with your computer without additional user intervention. You will need to log on with an administrative account and supply your password. After a minute or so, you receive a message informing you of any changes that were made, or that Startup Repair couldn't repair your PC.

- **Command Prompt:** Boots to a command prompt. This is useful if you cannot obtain a normal GUI.

- **UEFI Firmware Settings:** Enables you to modify United Extensible Firmware Interface (UEFI) settings. This option is not available if your computer is using a legacy BIOS instead of UEFI.

- **Go Back to the Previous Build:** If your computer has had a major update recently that has caused issues, you can revert to the previous build of Windows 10. This option is available only if you have updated the computer within the past 10 days.

- **Startup Settings:** Enables you to restart your computer and access additional advanced startup options, as follows:

    - **Enable Low-Resolution Video Mode:** The Enable Low-Resolution Video option starts Windows 8.1 at the lowest video resolution of 640×480. This is useful if you have selected a display resolution and refresh rate that is not supported by your monitor and video card, or if you have installed a driver that is incompatible with your video card. You can go to the Display Properties dialog box, select an appropriate video option, and then reboot to Normal mode.

- **Enable Debugging Mode:** Debugging mode provides advanced troubleshooting options for experienced developers and administrators. It sends kernel debug information to another computer via a serial cable.

- **Enable Boot Logging:** The Enable Boot Logging option starts Windows 10 normally while creating the \windows\ntbtlog.txt file, which lists all drivers that load or fail to load during startup. From the contents of this file, you can look for drivers and services that are conflicting or otherwise not functioning. After using this mode, reboot to Safe Mode to read the ntbtlog.txt file and identify the problematic driver.

- **Enable Safe Mode:** Safe Mode starts your computer with a minimal set of drivers (mouse, VGA, and keyboard), so that you can start your computer when problems with drivers or other software are preventing normal startup. It is useful if your computer has stopped responding or is running very slowly or if the computer fails to respond after new hardware or software is installed. You can perform actions such as uninstalling problematic software, disabling hardware devices in Device Manager, rolling back drivers, or using System Restore to roll back the computer to an earlier point in time. You can also choose Safe Mode with Networking, which starts network drivers as well as the other basic drivers, and Safe Mode with Command Prompt, which starts the computer to a command prompt. This can be useful if you cannot obtain a normal GUI.

- **Disable Driver Signature Enforcement:** This option permits you to install unsigned drivers or drivers that are improperly signed. After you reboot normally, driver signatures are again enforced, but the unsigned driver is still used.

- **Disable Early-Launch Antimalware Protection:** Select this option to prevent the startup of early launch antimalware drivers. This allows drivers that might contain malware to be installed.

- **Disable Automatic Restart on System Failure:** This option prevents Windows 10 from automatically restarting if a problem is causing your computer to enter an endless loop of failure, restart attempt, and failure again.

> **NOTE**   You can use Safe Mode and System Restore together to correct problems. If you are unable to start your computer properly but are able to start in Safe Mode, you can perform a System Restore from Safe Mode to restore your computer to a functional state.

CAUTION   Safe Mode has its limitations. Safe Mode does not repair problems caused by lost or corrupted system files or problems with basic drivers. In these cases, you may be able to use the Windows Recovery Environment.

NOTE   For more information on startup repair options, refer to "Windows RE Troubleshooting Features" at https://msdn.microsoft.com/en-us/windows/hardware/commercialize/manufacture/desktop/windows-re-troubleshooting-features.

Performing a System Image Recovery

Windows 10 enables you to perform a system image backup, which includes all files necessary to fully restore your computer in the event of a hardware failure. You have already learned how you can recover your computer using settings available from the push-button refresh feature. If you have not set up these options and are faced with a catastrophic disk failure, you can still use the system image recovery to restore your computer.

If you are using this method to restore your computer, you first need to access the Windows 10 Startup Troubleshoot options. There are three methods that can be used, depending on the current state of the system you want to repair:

- If the system is able to run Windows 10, access the Recovery option described earlier in this chapter and shown in Figure 20-10, and click the **Restart Now** button. Your system will restart to the screen shown in Figure 20-5.

- If you have a USB recovery drive, insert the drive and boot the computer using the USB recovery drive. You may need to access the BIOS or EFI boot options to enable the computer to boot from the USB recovery drive.

- If the system is not running and you do not have a USB recovery drive, use a Windows 10 installation DVD to start the computer.

Use the following steps:

Step 1.   From the startup options screen as depicted previously in Figure 20-4, select **Troubleshoot**. The Troubleshoot screen in Figure 20-17 is displayed.

Figure 20-17 Windows 10 Startup Troubleshoot Options

Step 2.   Click **Advanced Options** to display the Advanced Options page previously shown in Figure 20-5.

Step 3.   Select the **System Image Recovery** option.

Step 4.   The computer proceeds with the recovery by restarting and preparing
system image recovery. If there is more than one local Administrator
account, Windows may prompt you to select the one to use, and to enter
the password.

Step 5.   The Re-image Your Computer options shown in Figure 20-18 enable
you to select the system image to use. If the image is on an attached disk,
Windows will automatically locate the latest one. Otherwise, use **Select a
System Image** backup to attach or insert the disk with the system image
and click **Next**.

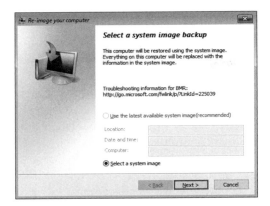

Figure 20-18   Selecting the System Image Backup to Use for Recovery

Step 6.   From the Re-image Your Computer dialog box shown in Figure 20-19, click **Install Drivers** if you need to reinstall drivers for required disks or **Advanced** to specify additional options for restarting the computer and checking for disk errors. When finished, click **Next** to continue.

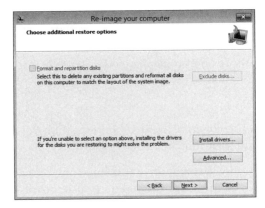

Figure 20-19   Re-image Your Computer Dialog Box Providing Several Additional Restore Options

Step 7.   Review the options provided and click **Back** if you need to make any changes. Then click **Finish** to proceed with re-imaging your computer.

Step 8.   You are warned that all data on the drives to be restored will be replaced with data from the image. Click **Yes** to continue.

Step 9.   A message box charts the progress of re-imaging your computer, and then the computer restarts. After you log back on, a Recovery message box informs you that recovery has completed and offers an option to restore user files. Click **Restore My Files** to do so or **Cancel** to quit.

Configuring Restore Points

Earlier in this chapter, you learned how to use System Restore to restore your computer to an earlier point in time. Windows automatically creates restore points when certain actions take place. Each of these restore points contains a complete set of information required to restore the computer to that respective point in time. On computers with over 64 GB hard disk space, restore points can occupy up to 5 percent of space to a maximum of 10 GB, whichever is less. With less than 64 GB hard disk space, restore points can occupy up to 3 percent of disk space.

Windows automatically creates restore points before certain actions take place:

- **Application Installation:** Assuming that the app installer is compliant with System Restore, Windows creates a restore point that enables you to restore the computer to its previous state should problems occur during or after the application installation.

- **Automatic Windows Update Installation:** After Windows Update downloads updates and before they are installed, an update is created so that you can restore the computer to its previous state should a problem occur with any update.

- **System Restore:** Windows creates a restore point before restoring the computer to a previous state. This facilitates your selecting a different restore point, should you find the selected restore point to be inappropriate. When the computer restarts, you receive an option to revert to the previous condition should the restore not work properly.

In addition, Windows 10 automatically creates a restore point after 7 days if no other restore points have been created within that time interval.

By default, System Protection is enabled for the %systemdrive% volume only. You can manually create a restore point for any volume at any desired time. Use the following procedure:

Step 1.   Access the System Protection tab of the System Properties dialog box as described earlier in this chapter and shown in Figure 20-6.

Step 2.   To configure a restore point for any volume on your computer, select it from the list and click **Configure** to receive the dialog box shown in Figure 20-20.

Step 3.   Click **Turn On System Protection** and then click **Apply**.

Step 4.   Adjust the slider under Disk Space Usage to specify the maximum amount of disk space that will be used.

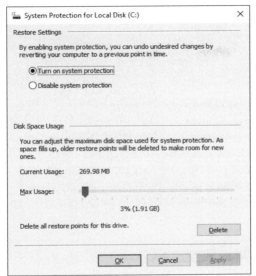

Figure 20-20   Enabling and Configuring System Protection on Any Volume on Your Computer

Step 5.   If you want to delete old restore points for this drive to free up disk space, click **Delete** and then confirm your intention by clicking **Continue** in the message box that appears. Note that this cannot be undone.

Step 6.   When finished, click **OK** to return to the System Protection tab.

Step 7.   Repeat Steps 2 to 6 as required to configure System Restore for other drive volumes on your computer.

You can also manually create a restore point from the System Protection tab previously shown in Figure 20-6. Click the **Create** button and then in the System Protection tab shown in Figure 20-21, type a descriptive name for the restore point and then click **Create**.

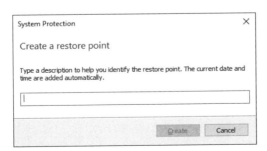

Figure 20-21   Manually Creating a Restore Point at Any Time

> **TIP** The **Restore-Computer** PowerShell cmdlet also enables you to restore your computer to a restore point that you specify as a parameter to this cmdlet. This command restarts the computer and then performs the restore. It is supported only on client operating systems Windows Vista and later. For more information, including available parameters and options, refer to "Restore-Computer" at https://msdn.microsoft.com/en-us/powershell/reference/5.1/microsoft.powershell.management/restore-computer.

> **NOTE** For more information on restore points, refer to "Restore Points" at https://msdn.microsoft.com/en-us/library/windows/desktop/aa378910(v=vs.85).aspx.

Resolving Hardware and Device Issues

Even with all the improvements Microsoft has made in device and driver management in recent Windows versions, problems still occur. Drivers use system resources, including IRQ lines, I/O ports, DMA channels, and physical memory addresses. If two hardware components attempt to use the same location of any of these resources, a conflict results, and these components will not work. For example, you install a new scanner and discover that your network adapter does not work. Such a situation happens more often when using a non-PnP device. In such a situation, you should check resource assignments for conflicts. It is frequently necessary to modify settings on the non-PnP device, for example, with the aid of jumpers or DIP switches. Some devices may have configuration settings available in the computer BIOS, such as built-in devices. Reconfigure the device with the aid of manufacturer instructions, which may be located on a label placed on the device or manufacturer's documentation.

In this section, we take a look at troubleshooting driver resource conflicts and resolving other driver issues.

Using Device Manager to Resolve Driver Conflicts

You can use Device Manager, shown in Figure 20-22, to determine whether a resource conflict exists by changing the view. Device Manager offers several view types that assist in monitoring, as described in Table 20-2.

Table 20-2   Device Manager Views

View	What It Displays
Devices by type	Displays devices by the type of installed device, such as monitor or mouse. This is the default view. If you have multiple monitors, for example, you see each of the monitors displayed below the Monitor node.
Devices by connection	Displays devices according to the type of connection, For example, all the disk drives and CD or DVD drives connected to the IDE controller are displayed under the IDE connection node.
Resources by type	Displays devices according to resource type. Resources DMA, I/O, IRQ, and memory. For example, Figure 20-22 shows devices listed in the order of the I/O resources it uses.
Resources by connection	Displays resources according to their type of connection. This also serves to indicate which resources are currently available.

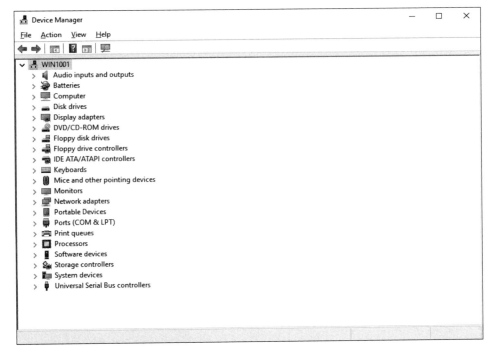

Figure 20-22   Device Manager Providing an Organized View of Devices by the I/O Resources They Consume

The View menu also offers two customization options that affect what you see. To expand the views to show non–PnP devices, select **Show Hidden Devices**. To modify what items Device Manager shows, select **Customize**. This displays the Customize View dialog box shown in Figure 20-23, which enables you to select the items shown by Device Manager.

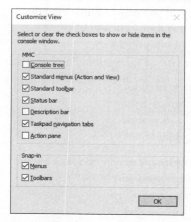

Figure 20-23   Selecting Which Items Are Displayed in the Device Manager Window

To view resources being used by a specific device, access the Resources tab of the device's Properties dialog box. As shown in Figure 20-24, this tab displays a list of all resources in use and reports conflicts that might be occurring. To change resource settings, clear the **Use Automatic Settings** check box and then click **Change Setting**. In the dialog box that appears, select a setting that does not conflict with other settings. Device Manager informs you if these settings conflict with any other devices; if so, modify the settings so that no conflicts occur, and then click **OK**.

Figure 20-24   Resources Tab of a Device's Properties Dialog Box Displaying All Resources in Use and Informing You of Any Conflicts That Might Be Occurring

Use of Security and Maintenance to View Device-Related Problems

The Windows 10 Action Center also often displays notifications about device-related issues, and will notify you when an applicable fix is found. You can check for solutions manually by accessing the Security and Maintenance page of Control Panel and clicking the **Check for Solutions** link in the Maintenance section, as shown in Figure 20-25.

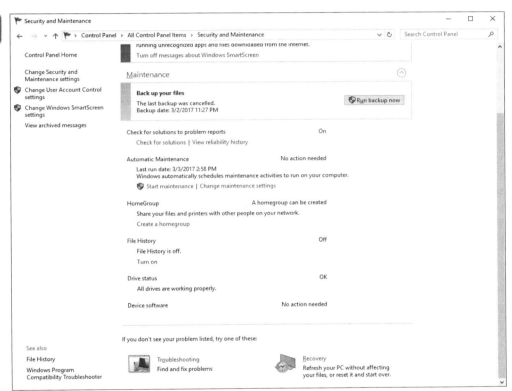

Figure 20-25 Windows 10 Maintenance Section Allowing You to Check for Solutions

When a problem occurs, Windows searches for problems on the Internet. The user is notified when a solution to a device-related problem is found. A web link is supplied and notification is suppressed after the user has installed the application. Action Center can also display notifications alerting you to problems and solutions related to devices that don't post drivers at Windows Update. The user is alerted to the need to download and install a driver update and a link is provided, specifying the device and providing links to the latest signed driver from the manufacturer's site.

Use of System Information to View Device-Related Problems

The System Information utility is another place you can check devices and locate potential problems. In the Search bar or Cortana, type **msinfo** into the Search field, and then click **System Information**. Expand the Hardware Resources section and select a category to obtain information, as shown in Figure 20-26. Note that the information displayed in the Conflicts/Sharing subnode does not necessarily indicate problems, because some resources can be shared without creating a problem. Also note the Forced Hardware node, which displays information about devices whose default configuration has been modified by the user. Information in this node can be useful when troubleshooting resource conflicts.

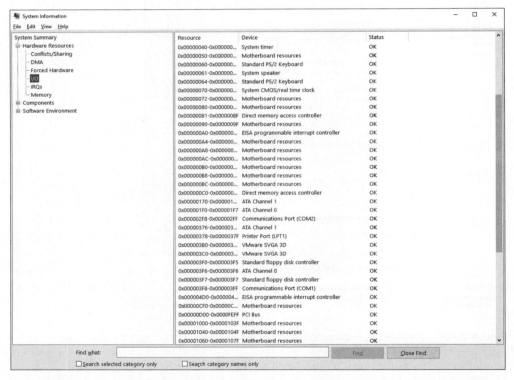

Figure 20-26   System Information Displaying Details About Hardware Resources, Including Resource Conflicts and Sharing

Rolling Back Drivers

Device drivers are software utilities that enable hardware components to communicate with the operating system. All components that you see in Device Manager utilize drivers, including disk drives, display adapters, network interface cards, removable media (floppy, CD-ROM, DVD-ROM, and so on) drives, keyboards, mice, sound cards, USB controllers, and so on, for this purpose. External components such as printers, scanners, and so on also use drivers. With each new version of the operating system, it becomes necessary for hardware manufacturers to produce new drivers. Drivers written for older operating systems such as Windows XP, Vista, and Windows 7 might work with Windows 10 but can result in reduced device functionality, or they might not work at all. You need to be able to install, configure, and troubleshoot drivers for various components for the 70-697 and 70-698 exams and for real-world computer support tasks.

In versions of Windows prior to Windows XP, this was almost impossible to do. As was the case in Windows Vista, Windows 7, and Windows 8.1, Windows 10 maintains a copy of the previous driver each time a new one is updated. If, at any time, you want to restore the previous version, simply roll back the driver. Driver problems can occur occasionally when a manufacturer releases a new driver that has not been thoroughly tested and Windows Update automatically downloads and installs the driver without your intervention.

Although you can use System Restore to restore your computer to a point prior to installation of the problematic driver, it is normally much simpler to roll back the driver. To do so, open Device Manager, right-click the device, and choose **Properties**. From the Driver tab of the device's Properties dialog box shown in Figure 20-27, click **Roll Back Driver** and then click **Yes** in the Driver Package rollback message box that appears. If this option is unavailable (dimmed), Windows does not have a previous version of the driver. If necessary, you can restart your computer in Safe Mode and then employ this procedure to roll back a troublesome driver.

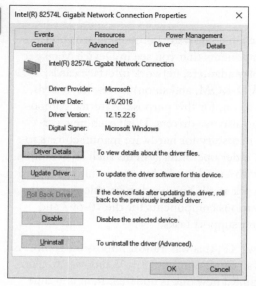

Figure 20-27 Driver Tab of a Device's Properties Dialog Box Enabling You to Roll Back the Driver

You can roll back all device drivers except for printers. You might receive a UAC prompt before either updating a driver or rolling it back to a previous version.

In some cases, your computer might not even start after installing a problem driver and rebooting. You can try the following options:

- System Restore resets the PC to a recent restore point. This is especially helpful if you have created a restore point in advance.

- Automatic Repair looks for common issues, including recent device changes, and attempts to resolve the issue automatically.

- You can also use System Image Recovery if you have a recent image available.

- If you are unsure which driver is causing the issue, you can use your PC's Startup and Recovery dialog, as discussed earlier, to enable options such as boot logging, Safe Mode, and disable automatic restart on system failure to gather more information about the problem.

NOTE   For more information on device drivers, including updating and rollback, refer to Chapter 3, "Post-Installation Configuration." The section "Configure Devices and Device Drivers" discusses rolling back device drivers.

> **TIP** It is usually helpful to create a restore point before installing the new driver. This enables you to restore your computer to its status as of before the driver installation, using the System Restore feature. Use of System Restore for performing these actions was covered earlier in this chapter.

Exam Preparation Tasks

Review All the Key Topics

Review the most important topics in the chapter, noted with the Key Topics icon in the outer margin of the page. Table 20-3 lists a reference of these key topics and the page numbers on which each is found.

Table 20-3   Key Topics for Chapter 20

Key Topic Element	Description	Page Number
Figure 20-1	The Recovery applet includes three advanced recovery tools	940
Figure 20-6	System Protection provides several options for restoring your operating system to a previous point in time	946
Figure 20-10	The Recovery screen provides several recovery options for your PC	950
List	The Advanced options from the Troubleshoot section of Window PE recovery	955
Figure 20-20	Configuring system protection for disk volumes	961
Table 20-2	Describes available view options in Device Manager	963
Figure 20-25	The Windows 10 Maintenance section of the Security and Maintenance Control Panel applet	965
Figure 20-27	You can roll back a driver from the Driver tab of the device's Properties dialog box	968

Definitions of Key Terms

Define the following key terms from this chapter, and check your answers in the glossary.

device driver, push-button reset, Safe Mode, startup repair, System Protection, System Restore, USB recovery drive, Windows Recovery Environment

This chapter covers the following subjects:

- **Restoring Previous Versions of Files and Folders:** When a file or folder has become corrupted, improperly modified, or deleted, you can restore it from a backup to undo any harmful changes. In this topic we cover how to restore files and folders when they are lost or corrupted. Windows 10 provides a number of protection mechanisms for files, including File History.

- **Configuring File History:** Microsoft has created the new File History feature in Windows 10 as the primary application for backing up files and folders on your computer. Backups of data files are very important because you could lose valuable information should your hard disk fail. This section shows you how to configure the options available in File History.

- **Recovering Files from OneDrive:** OneDrive provides integrated cloud storage for Windows 10, as covered in Chapter 9, "Managing User Data." This section shows you how to recover files and previous versions of files stored on the OneDrive service.

This chapter covers the following objectives for the 70-697 exam:

Configure file recovery: Restore previous versions of files and folders, configure file history, recover files from OneDrive, configure Windows Backup and Restore, perform a backup and restore with WBAdmin.

CHAPTER 21

Configuring File Recovery

Backing up and restoring crucial data is an important responsibility for an individual charged with this duty. Without some sort of backup strategy in place, loss of critical data could threaten the very existence of an organization. At the very least, it can make a computer unusable. Windows 10 offers a backup utility called File History that simplifies the task of backing up files stored in the usual data folder locations. In this chapter, you learn about the various strategies used to back up your data, as well as restoring data from various locations, including your computer and Windows OneDrive.

"Do I Know This Already?" Quiz

The "Do I Know This Already?" quiz allows you to assess whether you should read this entire chapter or simply jump to the "Exam Preparation Tasks" section for review. If you are in doubt, read the entire chapter. Table 21-1 outlines the major headings in this chapter and the corresponding "Do I Know This Already?" quiz questions. You can find the answers in Appendix A, "Answers to the 'Do I Know This Already?' Quizzes."

Table 21-1 "Do I Know This Already?" Foundation Topics Section-to-Question Mapping

Foundation Topics Section	Questions Covered in This Section
Restoring Previous Versions of Files and Folders	1–5
Configuring File History	6–10
Recovering Files from OneDrive	11–12

CAUTION The goal of self-assessment is to gauge your mastery of the topics in this chapter. If you do not know the answer to a question or are only partially sure of the answer, you should mark that question as wrong for purposes of the self-assessment. Giving yourself credit for an answer you correctly guess skews your self-assessment results and might provide you with a false sense of security.

1. You have selected the option to let Windows choose what will be backed up. Which of the following are backed up using this option? (Choose all that apply.)

   a. Windows libraries

   b. Desktop folders

   c. Data folders on portable hard drives

   d. Windows system image

2. You have run a backup from the Backup and Restore applet, but a few days later you realize that the backup does not include all the files and folders you should have backed up. You return to the Backup and Restore applet and notice that the Set Up Backup option is no longer available. What should you do?

   a. Click **Manage Space** and add the required files and folders.

   b. Click **Change Settings** and add the required files and folders.

   c. Select the **Create a System Image** option.

   d. Select the **Back Up Computer** option.

3. You have configured Windows Backup to back your files and folders up on a monthly basis, but you decide you need to perform a weekly backup, so you access the Backup and Restore applet. You cannot find an option to change the backup schedule. What option should you select first?

   a. Turn Off Schedule

   b. Manage Space

   c. Set Up Backup

   d. Change Settings

4. Which of the following commands would you use to perform a backup of the C: drive to a portable hard drive configured as the E: drive?

   a. **Ntbackup backup -backuptarget:e: -include:c:**

   b. **Ntbackup backup -backuptarget:c: -include:e:**

   c. **Wbadmin start backup -backuptarget:e: -include:c:**

   d. **Wbadmin start backup -backuptarget:c: -include:e:**

5. Which of the following files and folders are backed up by default when using the new File History feature? (Choose all that apply.)

   a. Libraries

   b. Operating system files

    c. Contacts

    d. Application files

    e. Folders placed on the desktop

6. By default, which of the following locations can you use to hold backup copies of data created by File History? (Choose three.)

    a. Network folders

    b. CD-ROM and DVD-ROM drives

    c. Internal hard drives configured using the Storage Space feature

    d. USB thumb drives

    e. External hard drives

7. You are about to make a lot of changes to some important documents on your computer, and you want to make sure you have a good backup of the files. You know that File History is enabled, but how would you ensure that your current files are backed up?

    a. Restore the backup and watch for messages asking if you want to copy and replace files in the same location.

    b. Open File History from the Control Panel and select **Run Now**.

    c. Use the Search option and specify each file that you want to check.

    d. Simply browse the backed-up files and verify that all required files are present.

8. You would like to configure File History to store only the most recent version of each file in order to conserve disk space. What option should you configure from the Advanced Settings dialog box?

    a. Under the Keep Saved Versions setting, choose the **Until Space Is Needed** option.

    b. Under the Save Copies of Files setting, choose the **Most Recent Version Only** option.

    c. Click **Clean Up Versions** and select the **All but the Latest One** option, and then click **Clean Up** to proceed.

    d. Click **Clean Up Versions** and select a one-month interval, and then click **Clean Up** to proceed.

9. You have stored your work documents in the D:\workarea folder on your Windows 10 Pro computer. You would like to ensure that File History backs up all documents in this folder. What should you do? (Each correct answer represents a complete solution. Choose two answers.)

   a. From File Explorer, add the D:\workarea folder to the Documents library.

   b. From the File History applet, click **Add** and add the D:\workarea folder.

   c. From the File History applet, click **Select Folder** and then select the D:\workarea folder in the Select Folder dialog box that appears.

   d. From File Explorer, create a new library named **Workarea**.

   e. From the Backup menu of the modern settings screen, select **More Options**; then use **Add a Folder** to manually add the D:\workarea folder to File History.

10. You are working on an important report that your boss needs first thing tomorrow morning and discover that an entire section that took you several days to prepare is missing. What should you do to get this section back with the least amount of effort and ensure that you do not lose your most recent changes?

    a. Access the Previous Versions tab of the report's Properties dialog box and select a version from a couple of days ago. Then click **Copy**.

    b. Access the File History and select a version from a couple of days ago. Then click **Restore**.

    c. Restore from File History a backup created a couple of days ago. When prompted, select the **Restore To** option.

    d. Restore from a backup created a couple of days ago and select the option to restore to another location.

11. You have been working on several documents on your Windows 10 PC's OneDrive storage and have been cleaning up old documents to conserve space. You then emptied the Recycle Bin to recover the space. The next day you realized you had deleted two important files that you needed. How would you recover your lost files?

    a. Check the Recycle Bin on your PC.

    b. Check the Recycle Bin on OneDrive.com.

    c. Look in the Restore Personal Files dialog in your PC's File History.

    d. Check the Volume Shadow storage for the deleted files.

12. Your OneDrive storage space is 7 GB, and you recently deleted about 4 GB of files to make room for some new files. How long will the deleted files be kept in the OneDrive Recycle Bin?

    a. 30–45 days

    b. 15–30 days

    c. One week

    d. 3 days

Foundation Topics

Restoring Previous Versions of Files and Folders

First introduced with Windows XP Professional and continued through Windows 10 is the concept of volume shadow copies, or Volume Shadow Storage (VSS), which creates shadow copies of files and folders as you work on them so that you can retrieve previous versions of files that you might have corrupted or deleted.

The shadow copy feature, first introduced with Windows XP and Windows Server 2003, has been renamed to File History starting with Windows 8.1 and Windows Server 2012 R2 and continued in Windows 10 and Windows Server 2016. This feature creates copies of files in real time as you work on them. Volume shadow copies enable users to work with files on the volume being backed up during the backup process, without the risk of having the backup program skip the open files. Using this technology removes the need for applications to be shut down to ensure a successful, complete backup.

How to Restore Damaged or Deleted Files

You have a number of options for protecting your files and making sure you can restore damaged files, older versions in case you made changes and want to view or restore the previous version, or even if your hard drive dies and you need to restore them all. The capability to recover files regardless of the reason requires some planning and foresight. You should be aware that many things can happen to damage your files or cause a problem with the device where you typically store them, so you need to plan for any eventuality

We discuss several options for protecting your files in this chapter so that they can be restored. All of them require you to configure a process to make copies of the files. In many organizations, even smaller ones, you may create policies to ensure that users maintain important work files on a file share or other enterprise storage location, so that administrators can maintain backups and restore files for users when needed. Even in those cases, you will inevitably end up working with files locally that need to be protected.

In this chapter you learn about File History, which you can use to not only back up local files, but maintain a versioned history of them that you can restore. You also learn about using the Windows 7 Backup and Restore tool, which was dropped in Windows 8.1, but has been restored for Windows 10 computers. If you make use of OneDrive, you also need to know how to recover files lost from the cloud storage service, and that topic is also addressed.

Using Windows Backup to Protect Your Data

Much to the chagrin of many Windows users, Microsoft removed the Backup and Restore utility in Windows 8. Although not used by a large proportion of Windows users, for many home and small businesses, the Backup and Restore utility was the tool of choice for keeping their files backed up and secure, and for recovering from computer disasters.

Microsoft listened to the needs of these users and included the utility in Windows 10. It is even called Backup and Restore (Windows 7), to emphasize that it is the same tool that was included in Windows 7, and promotes the tool as a way to restore any backups you created using Windows 7. The Backup and Restore (Windows 7) Control Panel applet provides a comprehensive tool for performing all backup and restore actions. In this chapter, we take a look at the various backup options. As in Windows 7, the Backup and Restore applet enables you to restore any backup data on a disk or a portion thereof from a variety of media, including tapes, shared network drives, CD-ROM drives, USB flash drives, and so on. You should look at using restore points, image backups (covered in Chapter 20, "Configuring System Recovery Options"), and File History (covered in the next section of this chapter) to maintain file and system backups going forward.

Configuring Windows Backup for the First Time

Use the following steps to set up Windows Backup and Restore for first use:

Step 1. Click **Start**, scroll to and expand **Windows System**, click **Control Panel > System and Security > Backup and Restore (Windows 7)**. You can also click **Start**, type **backup** into the Start Menu Search field, and then select **Backup and Restore (Windows 7)** from the programs list. As shown in Figure 21-1, the Backup and Restore applet opens and informs you that Windows Backup has not been set up.

Step 2. Click **Set Up Backup**. A Starting Windows Backup message box appears. After a few seconds, the Set Up Backup Wizard starts with the Select Where You Want to Save Your Backup page shown in Figure 21-2.

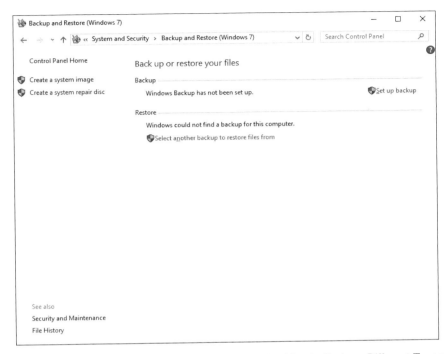

Figure 21-1   Backup and Restore Applet Enabling You to Perform Different Types of Backup Procedures

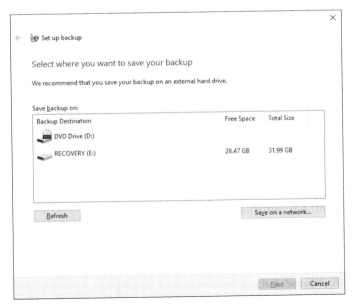

Figure 21-2   Selecting a Location Where Your Backup Will Be Stored

Step 3. Select a suitable destination for your backup and then click **Next**. Microsoft recommends that this be on an external hard disk. Be aware that you might need a large number of DVD-ROM discs to back up a system configured with a large number of applications and data, should you select this option.

NOTE The wizard alerts you if the selected drive does not have enough space to store a system image. If you receive this message, select a different backup destination. You can still back up selected files and folders to a disk that does not have sufficient space for a system image.

Step 4. To back up to a network location, select **Save on a Network**. From the Select a Network Location page shown in Figure 21-3, type the UNC path to the network share plus a username and password with administrative credentials on the remote share. Then click **OK**. If you are on an Active Directory Domain Services (AD DS) domain and using an account with Domain Administrator or Backup Operator privileges, you should not need to enter any credentials here.

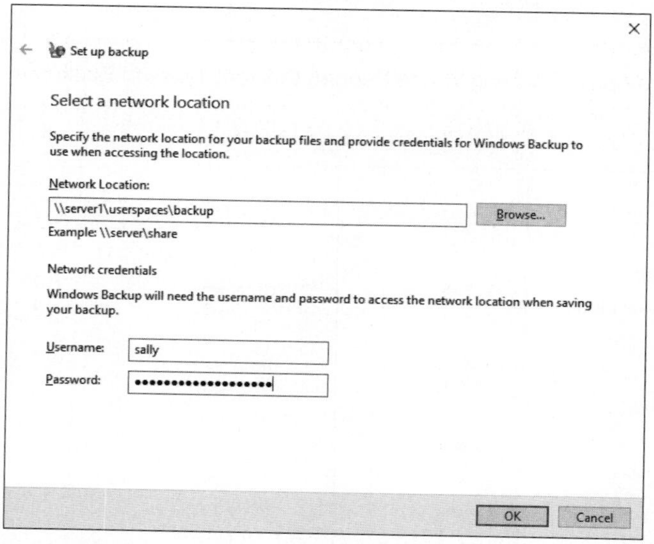

Figure 21-3 Specifying a Location and Credentials for a Network-Based Backup

Step 5. The What Do You Want to Back Up? page shown in Figure 21-4 enables you to choose what libraries and folders will be backed up, or you can select the default of **Let Windows Choose**. This default backs up all personal data and also creates a complete system backup. Make a choice and then click **Next**.

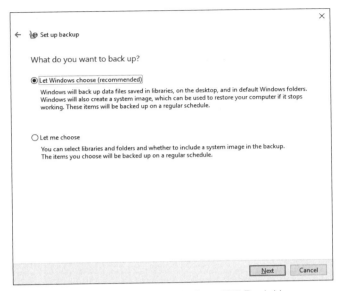

Figure 21-4 Choosing What Windows Will Back Up

Step 6. If you select the **Let Me Choose** option, you receive the page shown in Figure 21-5, from which you can select what libraries, folders, files, and drives are to be backed up. You can expand any entry in this list to choose the specific items to be backed up. To create a system backup, select the check box labeled **Include a System Image of Drives**. When finished, click **Next**.

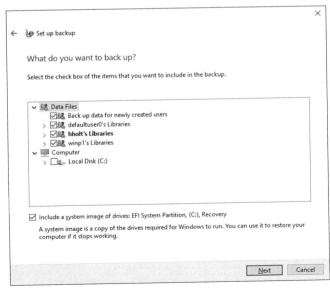

Figure 21-5 Choosing the Items to Be Backed Up

Step 7.   The Review Your Backup Settings page summarizes the items you have selected for backup. If you need to make changes, click the back arrow in the top-left corner of the dialog box. If you want to change the backup schedule, which is every Sunday at 7:00 p.m. by default, click the link provided. (We discuss scheduling backups later in this chapter.) When finished, click **Save Settings and Run Backup** to close the wizard and perform a backup.

Having set up your backup, the Backup and Restore applet now shows information about the backup and charts its progress, as shown in Figure 21-6.

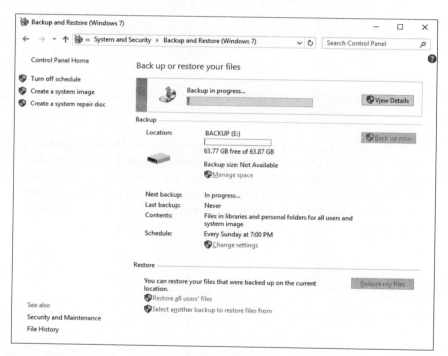

Figure 21-6   Backup and Restore Applet Displaying the Progress of the Current Backup and Enabling You to View Its Details and Modify the Backup Settings

Managing and Troubleshooting Your Backups

After you have configured your initial backup, the Backup and Restore applet appears similar to that previously shown in Figure 21-6, enabling you to perform various management tasks, as follows:

- **Back Up Now:** Performs an incremental backup of files and folders according to settings you have configured in the Backup and Restore Wizard. An *incremental backup* procedure backs up only those files and folders that have changed since the previous backup. This procedure also marks these files as having been backed up.

- **Manage Space:** Displays the Manage Windows Backup Disk Space dialog box shown in Figure 21-7. As shown, this dialog box provides a summary of the space used by backups. Click **Browse** to modify the backup location used. Click **View Backups** to display the dialog box shown in Figure 21-8, which lets you delete older backups to free up space on the backup volume. Click **Change Settings** to display the dialog box shown in Figure 21-9, which enables you to conserve disk space by keeping only the latest system image.

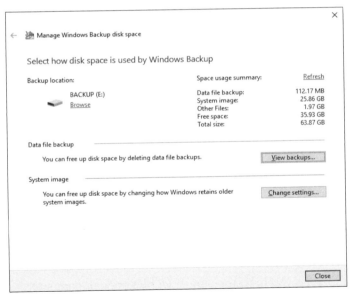

Figure 21-7   Manage Windows Backup Disk Space Dialog Box Enabling You to Configure Several Settings Related to Space Used by Windows Backup

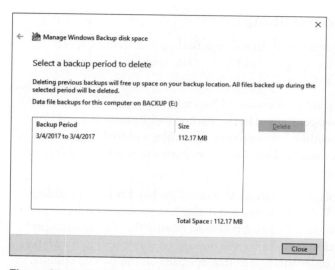

Figure 21-8   Deleting Older Backups if Required to Free Up Disk Space for New Backups

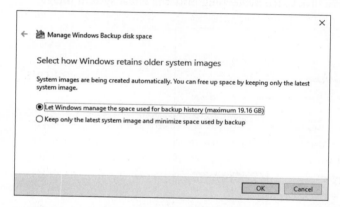

Figure 21-9   Conserving Disk Space by Choosing the Option to Keep Only the Latest System Image

- **Change Settings:** Restarts the Set Up Backup Wizard so that you can modify all settings used by the default backup routine.

- **Restore My Files:** Enables you to restore any or all files on your computer.

Within the backup volume you've specified, the Backup and Restore applet creates a folder named by your computer's name. On a network location accessed by more than one computer, you see folders named for each computer. The Backup and Restore applet automatically creates a subfolder structure within the computer folder that contains a subfolder for each backup you've performed, as well as a couple of system files. These subfolders are named Backup Set *yyyy-mm-dd hhmmss*, where *yyyy-mm-dd hhmmss* refers to the date and time (24-hour clock) at which the backup was performed. For example, a backup performed on April 26, 2017, at 3:13:30 p.m. created a folder named Backup Set 2017-04-26 151330. Each of these backup set subfolders contains a series of similarly named .zip files that hold the backed-up data, plus a Catalogs folder that includes Windows Backup Catalog (.wbcat) files that contain pointers to the appropriate .zip files for each of the individual files backed up during this backup operation. If you desire, you can locate backed-up files directly from their respective compressed folders from this information without using the Backup and Restore applet directly.

If a problem arises during backup, the Backup and Restore applet informs you and provides options for resolution. The following are several problems that this applet will alert you to:

- **Insufficient Backup Disk Space:** Backup and Restore provides a Check Backup Disk Space message informing you that the disk your backups are saved on doesn't have enough free space.

- **Unavailable Network Location:** If the backup server is unavailable or offline, Backup and Restore informs you. Check that the server is operational and that network connectivity is okay.

- **Open Files Might Be Skipped:** If Backup is unable to copy all files in the source locations, Backup and Restore provides a Check Your Backup Results message that informs you some files were skipped.

To troubleshoot any of these messages, click **Options** to display a dialog box such as that shown in Figure 21-10, which provides one or more options for troubleshooting the problem. Click **Show Details** to obtain more information on the problem that occurred, and click any of the available options to troubleshoot the problem.

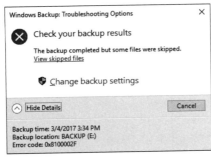

Figure 21-10   Troubleshooting Options When a Problem Occurs During Backup

> **NOTE** For additional troubleshooting scenarios that you might encounter, refer to "Troubleshooting Backup and Recovery" at http://technet.microsoft.com/en-us/library/cc731602.aspx. The article is based on Windows 7, but it is the same utility that is included in Windows 10.

Scheduling Your Backups

By default, Backup and Restore (Windows 7) schedules your backup to take place every Sunday at 7 p.m. After you have created your first backup using the procedure outlined in the previous section, you can modify the backup schedule by performing the following procedure:

Step 1. Use the previous procedure to open the Backup and Restore Control Panel applet.

Step 2. Click **Change Settings** to reopen the Set Up Backup Wizard.

Step 3. Click **Next** repeatedly until you reach the Review Your Backup Settings page, and then click **Change Schedule**.

Step 4. On the How Often Do You Want to Back Up? page shown in Figure 21-11, select the desired options. If you select Weekly, select the desired day; if you select Monthly, select the desired day of the month from the drop-down list provided.

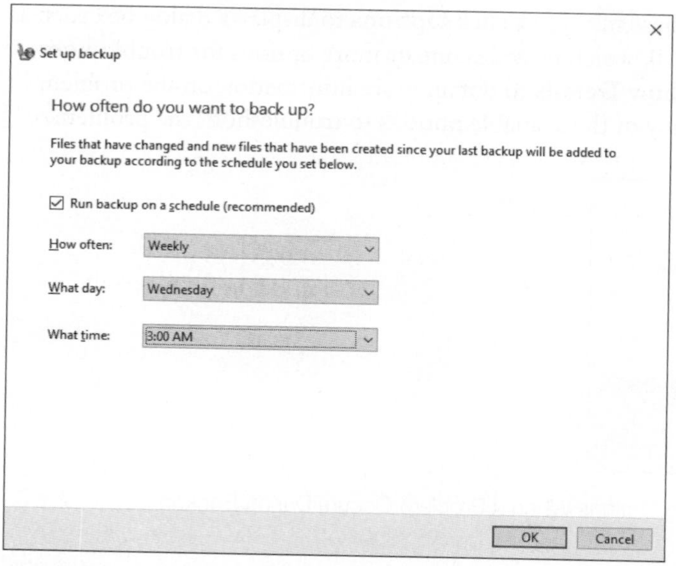

Figure 21-11   Selecting the Day and Time at Which Your Backup Will Be Performed

Step 5. From the What Time drop-down list, select the hour at which the backup is to commence. Ensure that this is set to a time when your computer will be turned on.

Step 6. When finished, click **OK**. The Backup and Restore applet displays your configured day and time.

> **NOTE** If you do not want Windows to automatically perform scheduled backups, click the **Turn Off Schedule** link found on the left side of the Backup and Restore applet. This applet now indicates that no schedule exists. Click the **Turn On Schedule** link that appears to restore scheduled backups.

Recovering Files with Backup and Restore (Windows 7)

After you have configured Backup and Restore (Windows 7), and have backup sets, you can restore files using the utility. You can also restore files from a backup set that you create with Windows 7. This is particularly useful if you have upgraded your computer to Windows 10 or have a new Windows 10 computer and would like to restore all your files. Instead of copying the files from the old computer, you can use your Windows 7 backup to restore your files.

From the Backup and Restore (Windows 7) Control Panel applet previously shown in Figure 21-6, you can use the Restore My Files button to select files to restore from a backup you have created from your current computer. Note from the previously shown Figure 21-1, if you haven't set up backups for your current computer, you can still restore files from an older backup by clicking the Select Another Backup to Restore Files From. This link is available even if you have not configured the utility to create backups on your current computer.

Use the following procedure to restore your files:

Step 1. If you need to select another backup, click the **Select Another Backup to Restore Files From** link in the Backup and Restore (Windows 7) applet. Windows searches for a backup on nonsystem drives attached to your computer. The page shown in Figure 21-12 is displayed. If your backup is on a network share, click the **Browse Network Location** button to locate the server and fileshare and select it.

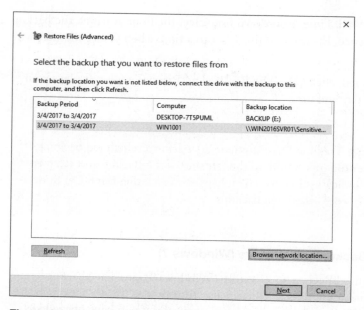

Figure 21-12   Selecting the Backup to Use, or Choosing to Browse the Network for a Backup Set

Step 2.   After you select the backup you want to use, click the **Next** button.

Step 3.   The Restore Files dialog is displayed, as shown in Figure 21-13.

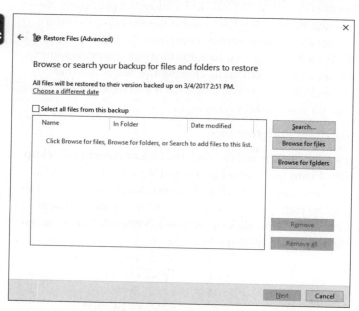

Figure 21-13   Restore Files Dialog Box Enabling You to Select the Files and Folders You Want to Restore

Step 4. To restore a file, click **Browse for Files**, or to restore a complete folder, click **Browse for Folders**. You see the dialog box shown in Figure 21-14.

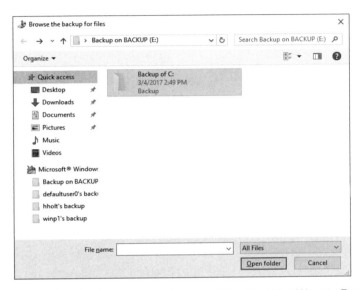

Figure 21-14 Browsing for Files or Folders That You Want to Restore

Step 5. Use this dialog to find the files or folders you want to restore, and double-click the desired item or items. You are returned to the Restore Files dialog box with the items you selected added to the list.

Step 6. If you are unsure of the location of an item you want to restore, click the Search button and type in all or part of the filename or folder name to look for. Select the item and click **OK** to return to the previous dialog box.

Step 7. When you are finished selecting files or folders, click **Next**.

Step 8. The Where Do You Want to Restore Your Files? page shown in Figure 21-15 allows you to select a location to save the restored files. Select a location and then click **Restore** to restore the files.

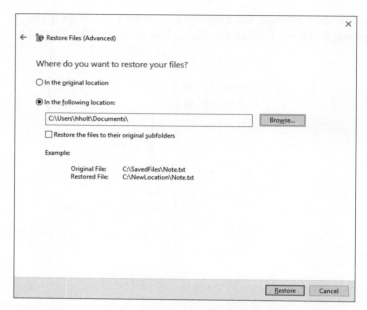

Figure 21-15 Where Do You Want to Restore Your Files? Page Enabling You to Select a Location to Save the Restored Files

Step 9.   If the restore encounters a conflict with a file that already exists on your computer, you receive a dialog box asking how to handle the conflict. Select the appropriate response.

Step 10.   Windows displays a message box that charts the progress of file restoration. When completed, it informs you. Click **Finish**.

If you are restoring files from a current backup that your computer created recently, you can select the Restore My Files button (refer to previously shown Figure 21-6). Restoring files uses the same process; simply start from Step 2 in the procedure outlined earlier.

Using Wbadmin to Recover Data

You can use the **Wbadmin** command to recover files and folders that you have previously backed up using this command, as explained earlier in this chapter. Use the following syntax:

```
wbadmin start recovery -version:<VersionIdentifier>
  -items:{<VolumesToRecover> | <AppsToRecover> |
  <FilesOrFoldersToRecover>} -itemtype:{Volume | App | File}
  [-backupTarget:{<VolumeHostingBackup> |
  <NetworkShareHostingBackup>}]
```

In this command:

- The **-version:**<*VersionIdentifier*> parameter refers to a version identifier of the backup to recover in MM/DD/YYYY-HH:M format.

- The **-items:**{<*VolumesToRecover*> | <*AppsToRecover*> | <*FilesOrFolders ToRecover*>} parameter specifies a comma-delimited list of volumes, applications, files, or folders to be recovered, according to the item type you specify.

- The **-itemtype:**{**Volume** | **App** | **File**} parameter specifies the type of items to be recovered.

- The **-backuptarget** parameter specifies the storage location containing the backup that you want to recover.

For example, to recover a backup of volume e: that was taken at 8:00 a.m. on February 28, 2016, use the following command:

```
wbadmin start recovery -version:02/28/2016-08:00 -itemType:Volume
    -items:e:
```

NOTE Additional parameters are available; for a complete description of this command and its available parameters, refer to "Wbadmin Start Recovery" at https://msdn.microsoft.com/en-us/library/cc742070(v=ws.10).aspx.

Configuring File History

Chapter 20, "Configuring System Recovery Options," introduced you to the new File History backup application first included with Windows 8.1 and continued in Windows 10, which enables you to back up files and folders located within your libraries, contacts, favorites, and desktop, as well as create a USB recovery drive. We also looked at the options available in Windows 10 for restoring or recovering your computer when problems prevent it from starting up normally. Now we turn our attention to ensuring that important data on your computer is backed up and that you can recover this data from any type of misadventure, such as improper deletion or modification, corruption, and so on.

Windows 7 has used the Backup and Restore applet in Control Panel as the central location for performing all types of backup and restore operations. Although this tool was restored in Windows 10 after its removal in Windows 8.1, Microsoft recommends using the new File History feature that enables an automatic backup of all files located in your libraries, contacts, favorites, and the desktop. Remember that libraries are collections of files and folders that hold documents, music, pictures, and videos in a centralized location that is shared across the network by default. We

990 MCSA 70-697 and 70-698 Cert Guide

introduced the concept of libraries in Chapter 14, "Configuring File and Folder Access."

Microsoft created the File History feature with the following ideas in mind:

- File History facilitates the process of protecting data so that users can set it up and become confident that their personal information is being protected.

- File History supports backing up data to external hard drives, USB thumb drives, and network folders.

- File History reduces the complexity of configuring and running a backup program.

- File History acts as an automatic, silent service that works in the background to protect data without the need for user interaction.

- File History supports laptops and other mobile devices much better than previous backup solutions, working with situations such as changing power states and connection to and disconnection from different networks.

- File History provides an easy-to-do restore experience that facilitates the process of locating, previewing, and restoring files and folders.

Setting Up File History

In Windows 7, a front end was available called Previous Versions, which allowed you to select any file and revert to a previous version created with the Volume Shadow Copy Service. The File History feature in Windows 10 behaves differently. Although File History still uses the Volume Shadow Copy Service, it does not directly use the shadow copies, but instead copies files in the user's directory to a second drive. VSS allows File History to make backups of your files even while you are working on them.

Microsoft recommends that you use a portable hard drive or network location with File History. This ensures that your files and folders are protected against a catastrophic failure of some type. Use the following procedure to set up File History:

Step 1. From the Start button menu, expand Windows System and select **Control Panel > System and Security > File History**. As shown in Figure 21-16, the File History applet opens and informs you that File History is off. If there are files that are encrypted with Encrypting File System (EFS), on a network location, or on a drive that is not formatted with the NTFS file system, these files are not backed up.

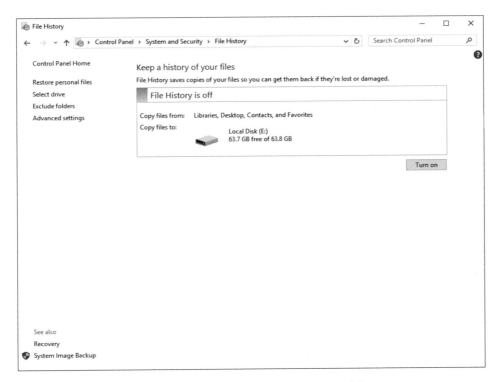

Figure 21-16 The File History Applet Displaying File History Is Off

Step 2. Click **Turn On**. File History asks you whether you want to recommend the drive to other members of your homegroup. After you choose **Yes** or **No**, File History informs you that it is saving copies of your files for the first time.

Step 3. If you want to change the location where your backups are stored, click **Select Drive**. You receive the Select a File History Drive dialog box shown in Figure 21-17. Select the desired external hard drive or USB thumb drive or click **Add Network Location** to save your files to a location on the network. Then click **OK**.

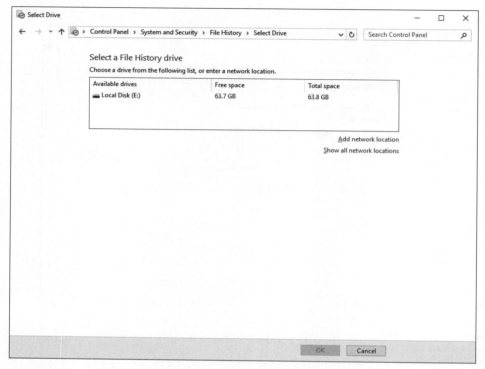

Figure 21-17   Selecting a Drive to Be Used by File History

Step 4.   If you want to exclude folders in the default locations from being backed up, click **Exclude Folders** to display the Exclude from File History dialog box. As shown in Figure 21-18, this dialog box initially shows you that no locations are excluded. Click **Add** to specify a location to be excluded.

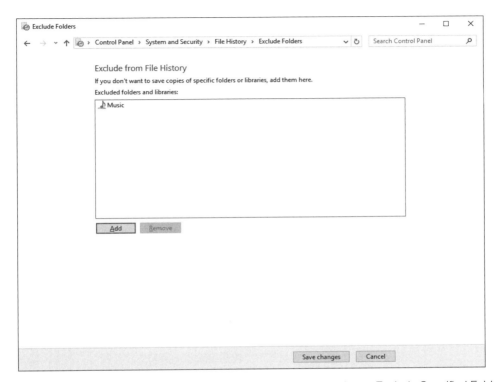

Figure 21-18 Exclude from File History Dialog Box Enabling You to Exclude Specified Folders from Being Backed Up

Step 5. In the Select Folder dialog box, double-click the library in which the folder to be excluded is located, select the desired folder, and then click **Select Folder**.

Step 6. Repeat as needed to exclude additional folders. When finished, click **Save Changes** to return to the File History applet.

Step 7. To configure additional File History options, click **Advanced Settings** to display the dialog box shown in Figure 21-19.

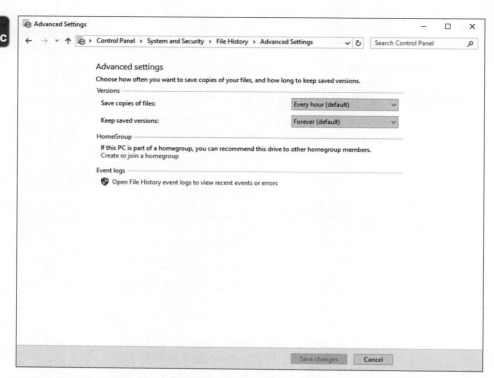

Figure 21-19   Advanced Settings Dialog Box Enabling You to Specify Additional Options Related to How File History Keeps Copies of Your Files

Step 8.   Select from the following options as desired:

- **Save Copies of Files:** Specify the interval at which File History saves copies of files. You can select options from every 10 minutes to daily (every hour by default).

- **Keep Saved Versions:** By default, File History keeps saved versions forever. You can choose several options from 1 month to 2 years, or you can choose the **Until Space Is Needed** option to limit the number of older saved versions of files.

- **Clean Up Versions:** To delete older versions of files and folders, click **Clean Up Versions**. This deletes files older than a specified age (one year by default), except the most recent version of a file or folder that has not changed within the interval chosen. Select a desired interval (or select the **All but the Latest One** option to keep only the most recent version of files) and then click **Clean Up** to proceed or **Cancel** to exit.

- **HomeGroup:** If your computer is part of a homegroup, you receive an option to recommend the drive to other homegroup members. Select the check box provided to do so. If your computer is not part of a homegroup, you receive an option to create or join a homegroup. Click **Create or Join a Homegroup** to specify a homegroup that will be recommended to other computers on the homegroup. This displays the Share with Other Home Computers dialog box previously shown in Figure 14-21 in Chapter 14 that enables you to create a new homegroup or join an existing one. We discussed homegroups in Chapter 14.

- **Event logs:** Click **Open File History Event Logs to View Recent Events or Errors** to open Event Viewer to a sublocation under Applications and Services Logs where errors, warnings, or informative messages are logged. We discussed Event Viewer in Chapter 19, "Monitoring and Managing Windows."

Step 9.   When finished, click **Save Changes** to return to the File History applet.

Step 10.   Click **Run Now** to create the backup copies. File History records the status of saving copies of your files and displays the date and time files were copied when it finishes.

TIP   You can also access File History from the modern settings screens. Click **Start > Settings**; then click **Update & Security** and select an option under Back Up Using File History. From here you can add a drive to File History, and select the **More Options** link to receive the page shown in Figure 21-20, which enables you to Back Up Now, change the backup schedule, select a different drive to be used, and other options.

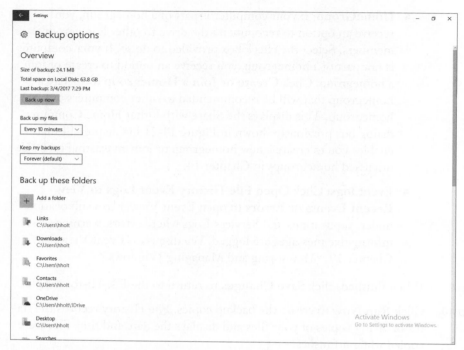

Figure 21-20 File History Start Screen App Enabling You to Turn File History on, Select a Drive, and Perform a Backup

Adding Additional Folders to File History

If you want to add a folder that is not located in one of the default locations used by File History, you can perform one of the following actions:

- **Add It to an Existing Library:** From a File Explorer window, right-click the desired folder and choose **Include in Library**, and then specify the desired library.

- **Create a New Library:** From the context menu displayed, choose **Create New Library**. This automatically creates a new library named after the selected folder and displays this library in the list displayed on the left side of the File Explorer window.

- **Manually Add the Folder to File History:** From the modern settings screen shown in Figure 21-20, use the **Add a Folder** button to select any folder on your computer and add it to File History backup.

> **NOTE** For additional information on using the File History feature, see the Windows Help topic "Back Up and Restore Your Files" at https://support.microsoft.com/en-us/help/17143/windows-10-back-up-your-files.

Restoring Files Using File History

Having backed up files and folders with File History, you can recover previous versions of files should problems such as data corruption, deletion, or improper modification occur. Use the following procedure:

Step 1. Open File History using any of the procedures given previously.

Step 2. From the options provided on the left side of the File History applet, click **Restore Personal Files**. You receive the Home–File History dialog box shown in Figure 21-21.

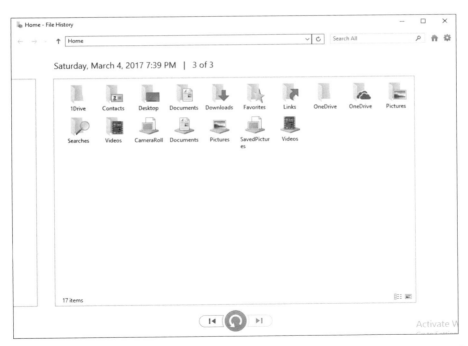

Figure 21-21 Home–File History Dialog Box Displaying the File Folders and Libraries Being Backed Up with File History

Step 3. Double-click the desired folder and library to see its contents.

Step 4. If necessary, double-click a subfolder to access the desired file. You see a window similar to the one in Figure 21-22.

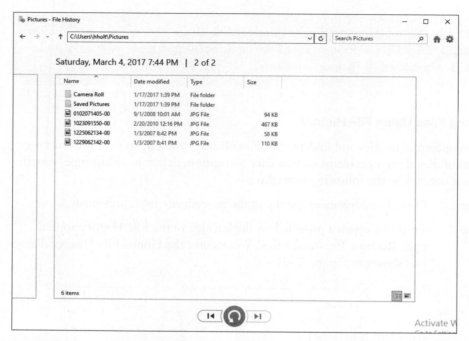

Figure 21-22   File History Displays Files Available for Recovery

Step 5.   Select the desired file and click the large green button to restore it.

Step 6.   If the file already exists, you receive the Replace or Skip Files dialog box shown in Figure 21-23 providing options to replace, skip, or compare the files.

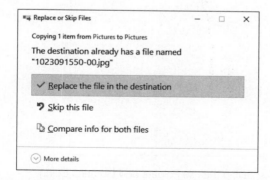

Figure 21-23   Options for Replacing or Skipping an Existing File

Step 7.   Repeat these steps to recover additional files if necessary.

File History does not require system protection to work; however, it does not back up files in all locations on the hard drive, but only those in the libraries folders, or in contacts, favorites, on the desktop, or in your OneDrive folder.

Note that as shown in Figure 21-21, only files in certain folders are available in your File History. As described earlier in this chapter, you need to configure File History to back up files in other locations by adding folders to your libraries or adding folders using the modern settings page for File History.

> **TIP**   You can use the Restore function to restore multiple previous versions of a file; for example, if you need to track changes to a document that have been made by several individuals. From the File History dialog box, select a file, right-click the **Restore** button, choose the **Restore To** option, and use the File Explorer dialog to create a folder to which you want to copy the document. Repeat this process as often as required, creating new folders with descriptive names for each previous version you want to restore. You can also rename each previous version with an appropriate descriptive name as you restore it, so that you do not need to create multiple folders.

Creating a System Image

The File History applet provides an option to create a system image, which enables you to fully restore your computer in the event of a hardware failure. You can also use this procedure to back up your data at the same time. Use the following procedure:

Step 1.   From the bottom-left corner of the File History applet (refer to Figure 21-16), click **System Image Backup**. If you receive a UAC prompt, click **Yes**. On the Backup and Restore page, click the **Create a System** image link.

Step 2.   The Where Do You Want to Save the Backup? screen shown in Figure 21-24 enables you to save the backup to a hard disk or to one or more DVDs. Make a selection and then click **Next**.

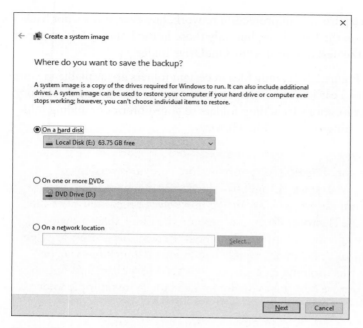

Figure 21-24   Saving a System Image Backup to a Hard Drive, a Set of DVDs, or a Network Location

Step 3.   The Confirm Your Backup Settings page shows which disks will be backed up, and to what location. Verify that these are correct and then click **Start Backup** to perform the backup.

Step 4.   Windows displays a progress chart as the backup is performed. When you are informed that the backup is completed, click **Close**.

Step 5.   The Create a System Image applet now displays the date and time that the complete system image backup was performed.

NOTE   You can also use the Microsoft Diagnostics and Recovery Toolset (DaRT) to perform system and data backup and recovery on Windows 10 computers. DaRT is a component of the Microsoft Desktop Optimization Pack (MDOP), which is available through Software Assurance or Microsoft Volume Licensing. As an advanced tool available only through these premium sources, DaRT is beyond the scope of the 70-697 and 70-698 exams. For more information, refer to "Diagnostics and Recovery Toolset 10" at https://technet.microsoft.com/en-us/itpro/mdop/dart-v10/index.

> **CAUTION**   Creation of shadow copies, which is required for File History to back up open files, requires that the Volume Shadow Copy Service be started. By default this service is set for Manual startup, which means that the service will be started as required. If the service is set to Disabled, shadow copies will not be created. If the service is not started, Windows will not create File History for any open files.

Recovering Files from OneDrive

We introduced Microsoft OneDrive in Chapter 9, "Managing User Data." One-Drive is free cloud storage for your Windows 10 devices that integrates seamlessly with other local and network storage available in Windows.

OneDrive and the Recycle Bin

The Microsoft OneDrive includes a Recycle Bin that can be used to recover any deleted files. You should be aware of the retention policies for your OneDrive Recycle Bin:

- Deleted files are kept for a maximum of 30 days. That means that no more than 30 days after the file is deleted, it will be removed.

- If the Recycle Bin reaches 10% of the total space for the OneDrive (which is 0.7 GB for the free 7 GB storage), files are deleted after 3 days, oldest files first, until the Recycle Bin storage reaches less than 10% of the total space.

In Windows 10, the local PC's Recycle Bin is also used for OneDrive. If you delete a file in OneDrive storage, it is moved to the PC's Recycle Bin for easy recovery. This works regardless of whether the files are online only or available offline.

You can recover deleted files from either the local PC Recycle Bin or the OneDrive.com Recycle Bin. If you empty the Recycle Bin on your local PC, you may still be able to recover your files from OneDrive.com using the following procedure:

Step 1.   From a web browser, sign in to your OneDrive account at OneDrive.com.

Step 2.   In the left menu, find the Recycle Bin link and click it. Any deleted files in your OneDrive Recycle Bin will show up in the list, as shown in Figure 21-25.

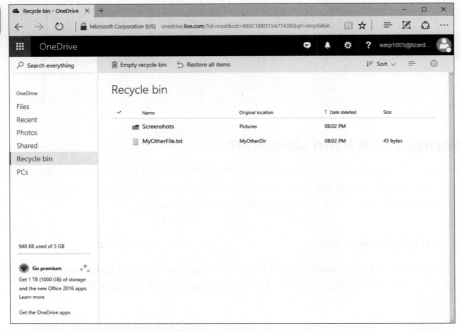

Figure 21-25   Deleted Files in the OneDrive Recycle Bin

Step 3.   To restore all the files, select the **Restore All Items** link at the top of the page. Or, enable the check box to the left of each file by clicking it and then select **Restore**.

Step 4.   Check your OneDrive storage on Windows. The files should be restored there as well. It may take a few minutes for your OneDrive storage to sync if you are using a slow network connection. Note that you can also choose which files to sync with your computer, so make sure that you have not excluded files from synchronizing.

OneDrive Version History

Similar to the File History in Windows 10, OneDrive maintains multiple versions of your Office documents automatically. Each time you edit a document from One-Drive, whether directly from the OneDrive storage or OneDrive.com, a new version of the document is created. OneDrive will keep track of up to 25 previous versions of each file. Note that the previous versions can be accessed only from OneDrive.com.

To access prior versions, sign in to your OneDrive.com account, locate your document, and right-click it. If changes have been made to the document since it was first added to that OneDrive folder, you will see a version history selection, as shown in Figure 21-26. Select the menu item to open the current document and view the previous versions.

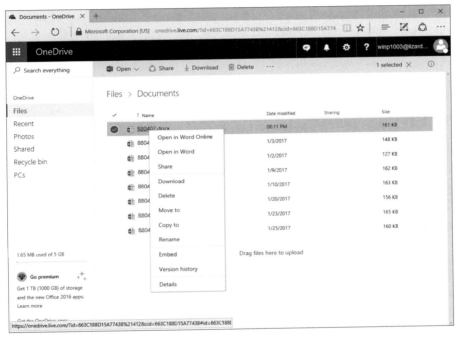

Figure 21-26   OneDrive Maintains Version History of Office Documents

Older versions of the document are displayed on the screen, along with the date and time each version was saved. When you select a previous version, OneDrive will display the person that made the change (in case the file is shared with others). You will also have the option to restore the file to the previous version, or download the version to save on your PC.

NOTE   Version history works only for MS Office files such as Word documents, Excel spreadsheets, and PowerPoint presentations. Version history is not maintained for other file types such as images and text files.

Exam Preparation Tasks

Review All the Key Topics

Review the most important topics in the chapter, noted with the Key Topics icon in the outer margin of the page. Table 21-2 lists a reference of these key topics and the page numbers on which each is found.

Table 21-2   Key Topics for Chapter 21

Key Topic Element	Description	Page Number
Step List	How to set up Backup and Restore (Windows 7)	976
Figure 21-5	Choosing items to back up in Backup and Restore	979
Figure 21-7	Managing backup disk space used by the Backup and Restore (Windows 7) utility	981
Figure 21-10	Troubleshooting backup issues	983
Figure 21-13	Selecting files to restore from a Windows backup	986
Step List	Shows you how to set up File History	990
Figure 21-19	File History provides several advanced options that specify how copies of files are retained	994
Step List	Restoring files from File History	997
Figure 21-25	Recovering files from OneDrive	1002

Definitions of Key Terms

Define the following key terms from this chapter, and check your answers in the glossary.

backup, File History, OneDrive, shadow copies, **wbadmin**, Windows 7 Backup and Restore applet

CHAPTER 22

Final Preparation

The first 21 chapters of this book cover the technologies, protocols, design concepts, and considerations required to be prepared to pass the Microsoft Certified Solutions Associate (MCSA) Configuring Windows Devices 70-697 and Installing and Configuring Windows 10 70-698 exams. Although these chapters supply the detailed information, most people need more preparation than just reading the first 21 chapters of this book. This chapter details a set of tools and a study plan to help you complete your preparation for the exams.

This short chapter has two main sections. The first section lists the exam preparation tools useful at this point in the study process. The second section lists a suggested study plan now that you have completed all the earlier chapters in this book.

NOTE   Note that Appendix B, "Memory Tables," and Appendix C, "Memory Tables Answer Key," exist as soft-copy appendixes on the website for this book, which you can access by going to www.pearsonITcertification.com/register, registering your book, and entering this book's ISBN: 9780789758804.

Tools for Final Preparation

This section lists some information about the available tools and how to access the tools.

Pearson Test Prep Practice Test Software and Questions on the Website

Register this book to get access to the Pearson Test Prep practice test software (software that displays and grades a set of exam-realistic, multiple-choice questions). Using the Pearson Test Prep practice test software, you can either study by going through the questions in Study Mode or take a simulated (timed) 70-697 or 70-698 exam.

The Pearson Test Prep practice test software comes with two full practice exams. These practice tests are available to you either online or as an offline Windows application. To access the practice exams that were developed with this book, please see the instructions in the card inserted in the sleeve in the back of the book. This card includes a unique access code that enables you to activate your exams in the Pearson Test Prep software.

Accessing the Pearson Test Prep Software Online

The online version of this software can be used on any device with a browser and connectivity to the Internet, including desktop machines, tablets, and smartphones. To start using your practice exams online, follow these steps:

Step 1.   Go to http://www.PearsonTestPrep.com.

Step 2.   Select **Pearson IT Certification** as your product group.

Step 3.   Enter your email/password for your account. If you don't have an account on PearsonITCertification.com or CiscoPress.com, you will need to establish one by going to PearsonITCertification.com/join.

Step 4.   In the My Products tab, click the **Activate New Product** button.

Step 5.   Enter the access code printed on the insert card in the back of your book to activate your product.

Step 6.   The product will now be listed in your My Products page. Click the **Exams** button to launch the exam settings screen and start your exam.

Accessing the Pearson Test Prep Software Offline

If you wish to study offline, you can download and install the Windows version of the Pearson Test Prep software. There is a download link for this software on the book's companion website, or you can enter this link into your browser:

http://www.pearsonitcertification.com/content/downloads/pcpt/engine.zip

To access the book's companion website and the software, follow these steps:

Step 1.   Register your book by going to PearsonITCertification.com/register and entering the ISBN: 9780789758804.

Step 2.   Respond to the challenge questions.

Step 3.   Go to your account page and select the **Registered Products** tab.

Step 4.   Click the **Access Bonus Content** link under the product listing.

Step 5. Click the **Install Pearson Test Prep Desktop Version** link under the Practice Exams section of the page to download the software.

Step 6. After the software finishes downloading, unzip all the files on your computer.

Step 7. Double-click the application file to start the installation, and then follow the onscreen instructions to complete the registration.

Step 8. After the installation is complete, launch the application and select the **Activate Exam** button on the My Products tab.

Step 9. Click the **Activate a Product** button in the Activate Product Wizard.

Step 10. Enter the unique access code found on the card in the sleeve in the back of your book and click the **Activate** button.

Step 11. Click **Next** and then the **Finish** button to download the exam data to your application.

Step 12. You can now start using the practice exams by selecting the product and clicking the **Open Exam** button to open the exam settings screen.

Note that the offline and online versions will sync together, so saved exams and grade results recorded on one version will be available to you on the other as well.

Customizing Your Exams

When you are in the exam settings screen, you can choose to take exams in one of three modes:

- Study Mode
- Practice Exam Mode
- Flash Card Mode

Study Mode allows you to fully customize your exams and review answers as you are taking the exam. This is typically the mode you would use first to assess your knowledge and identify information gaps. Practice Exam Mode locks certain customization options because it is presenting a realistic exam experience. Use this mode when you are preparing to test your exam readiness. Flash Card Mode strips out the answers and presents you with only the question stem. This mode is great for late stage preparation when you really want to challenge yourself to provide answers without the benefit of seeing multiple-choice options. This mode will not provide the detailed score reports that the other two modes will, so it should not be used if you are trying to identify knowledge gaps.

In addition to these three modes, you will be able to select the source of your questions. You can choose to take exams that cover all the chapters, or you can narrow your selection to a single chapter or the chapters that make up specific parts in the book. All chapters are selected by default. If you want to narrow your focus to individual chapters, deselect all the chapters, and then in the Objectives area select only those on which you want to focus.

You can also select the exam banks on which to focus. Each exam bank comes complete with a full exam of questions that cover topics in every chapter. The two exams printed in the book are available to you as well as two additional exams of unique questions. You can have the test engine serve up exams from all four banks or just from one individual bank by selecting the desired banks in the exam bank area.

There are several other customizations you can make to your exam from the exam settings screen, such as the time of the exam, the number of questions served up, whether to randomize questions and answers, whether to show the number of correct answers for multiple answer questions, or whether to serve up only specific types of questions. You can also create custom test banks by selecting only questions that you have marked or questions on which you have added notes.

Updating Your Exams

If you are using the online version of the Pearson Test Prep software, you should always have access to the latest version of the software as well as the exam data. If you are using the Windows desktop version, every time you launch the software, it checks to see whether there are any updates to your exam data and automatically downloads any changes that were made since the last time you used the software. This requires you to be connected to the Internet at the time you launch the software.

Sometimes, due to many factors, the exam data may not fully download when you activate your exam. If you find that figures or exhibits are missing, you may need to manually update your exams.

To update a particular exam you have already activated and downloaded, select the **Tools** tab and select the **Update Products** button. Again, this is only an issue with the desktop Windows application.

If you want to check for updates to the Pearson Test Prep practice test software, Windows desktop version, simply select the **Tools** tab and select the **Update Application** button. This will ensure you are running the latest version of the software engine.

Premium Edition

In addition to the free practice exams provided on the website, you can purchase additional exams with expanded functionality directly from Pearson IT Certification. The Premium Edition of this title contains an additional two full practice exams and an eBook (in both PDF and ePub format). In addition, the Premium Edition title also has remediation for each question to the specific part of the eBook that relates to that question.

Because you have purchased the print version of this title, you can purchase the Premium Edition at a deep discount. There is a coupon code in the book sleeve that contains a one-time-use code and instructions for where you can purchase the Premium Edition.

To view the Premium Edition product page, go to www.informit.com/title/9780134643793.

Memory Tables

Like most Cert Guides from Pearson, this book purposely organizes information into tables and lists for easier study and review. Rereading these tables can be very useful before the exam. However, it is easy to skim over the tables without paying attention to every detail, especially when you remember having seen the table's contents when reading the chapter.

Instead of just reading the tables in the various chapters, this book's Appendixes B and C give you another review tool. Appendix B lists partially completed versions of many of the tables from the book. You can open Appendix B (a PDF is available on the book website after registering) and print the appendix. For review, you can attempt to complete the tables. This exercise can help you focus on the review. It also exercises the memory connectors in your brain; plus it makes you think about the information without as much information, which forces a little more contemplation about the facts.

Appendix C, also a PDF located on the book website, lists the completed tables to check yourself. You can also just refer to the tables as printed in the book.

Chapter-Ending Review Tools

Chapters 1 through 21 each have several features in the "Exam Preparation Tasks" section at the end of the chapter. You might have already worked through these in each chapter. It can also be useful to use these tools again as you make your final preparations for the exam.

Suggested Plan for Final Review/Study

This section lists a suggested study plan from the point at which you finish reading through Chapter 21 until you take the MCSA 70-697 or 70-698 exam. Certainly, you can ignore this plan, use it as is, or just take suggestions from it.

The plan uses three steps:

Step 1.   **Review key topics and "Do I Know This Already?" (DIKTA) quiz questions:** You can use the table that lists the key topics in each chapter, or just flip the pages looking for key topics. Also, reviewing the DIKTA questions from the beginning of the chapter can be helpful for review.

Step 2.   **Complete memory tables:** Open Appendix B from the book website and print the entire thing, or print the tables by major part. Then complete the tables.

Step 3.   **Use the Pearson Test Prep practice test software to practice:** The Pearson Test Prep practice test software can be used to study using a bank of unique exam-realistic questions available only with this book.

Summary

The tools and suggestions listed in this chapter have been designed with one goal in mind: to help you develop the skills required to pass the MCSA 70-697 and 70-698 exams. This book has been developed from the beginning to not just tell you the facts but to also help you learn how to apply the facts. No matter what your experience level leading up to when you take the exams, it is our hope that the broad range of preparation tools, and even the structure of the book, helps you pass the exams with ease. We hope you do well on the exams!

Answers to the "Do I Know This Already?" Quizzes

Chapter 1

1. **D.** Windows 10 Education includes all features of Windows 10 Enterprise and differs only in that it is available with Microsoft's Academic Volume Licensing for schools, universities, and colleges. All the features mentioned in the other answer choices here are available in Windows 10 Education.

2. **A, D.** You must have the Pro or Enterprise version of Windows 10 to join a Windows Server domain or encrypt files using EFS. You can run Windows Firewall or use more than one monitor on a computer running any version of Windows 10.

3. **B.** To obtain a menu with administrative tools and utilities, you need to right-click the Start button. When you click Start, you see an alphabetical list of installed programs, a menu that contains tiles, and (in behind) the Windows desktop.

4. **A, B, C, D, E, F.** You can perform all these tasks and several others from the new Windows settings screen, which you can access by clicking **Start** and then clicking the small gear wheel icon near the bottom-left corner of the Start menu.

5. **C.** File History and the Backup and Restore utilities are included under the System and Security Control Panel category. It makes sense to find it there, because a secure system strategy includes ensuring that user files are backed up in case of a system or hard drive failure or other issues. Note also that it is easy to find any Control Panel applet by using the Search Control Panel box in the upper-right corner of the Control Panel applet.

6. **C.** An update roll-up is a packaged set of updates that fix problems with specific Windows components or software packages such as Microsoft Office. A critical security update is a single update that Microsoft issues to fix a problem that is critical for a computer's security. An optional update is a potentially useful non-security-related update. A service pack is a comprehensive operating system update that often adds new features or improvements to existing features.

7. A, F. You should click **Change Active Hours** from the Windows Update app in Windows Settings, and then specify the start and end times when you normally use your computer. You can also access Group Policy, enable the Configure Automatic Updates policy, and select the **4–Auto Download and Schedule the Install** option. You should then specify a convenient time (default is 3:00 a.m.). None of the other options listed in the question enable automatic installation of updates.

8. D. You should enable the Select When Quality Updates Are Received option and set the deferral interval to 30 days. Quality updates refer to the updates generally published on Patch Tuesday, usually for driver, security, or other similar update types. The Automatic Updates Detection Frequency policy specifies the length of time in hours used to determine the waiting interval before checking for updates at an intranet update server; this does not defer receiving of updates. Disabling the Allow Automatic Updates Immediate Installation policy does not help in this scenario. Feature updates are often referred to as upgrades, and they add new features, such as the upgrade from version 1511 to version 1607 in Windows 10; this is not the type of update specified in this scenario.

9. C. The Specify Intranet Microsoft Update Service Location policy enables you to specify a WSUS server on your network that client computers can access to receive software updates without accessing the Internet. With the other policies mentioned, client computers will still attempt to access the Internet for updates.

10. B. The Update History option displays a list of updates installed on your computer. From this location, you can click any update to provide detailed information, including a More Info link to Microsoft websites that provide additional details. The Restore Hidden Updates found in older Windows versions is no longer present in Windows 10. None of the other options mentioned here provide this information.

11. B. Windows Store apps can be updated only by using the Windows Store app. Windows Automatic Update is not aware of Store apps and will not update them.

12. C. You can use PowerShell to view app information and error logs. The Store app does not have an interface to view detailed error information, and errors will not be logged in the Event Viewer logs. There is no Control Panel applet for managing Store apps.

Chapter 2

1. **A.** Windows 10 requires a 1 GHz processor. A higher processor speed will increase the speed of application execution but is not required for running Windows 10.

2. **D.** A 64-bit Windows 10 installation requires at least 20 GB of hard drive space on the system partition. You need additional hard drive space for your applications and data, but not for the Windows installation. Note that a 32-bit Windows 10 installation requires at least 16 GB of hard drive space.

3. **A, C, D.** Most 32-bit programs can run efficiently on a 64-bit machine; programs specifically designed to run on a 64-bit machine won't work on 32-bit Windows; and 64-bit device drivers are required on 64-bit machines. But device drivers written for 32-bit Windows will not work on a 64-bit machine.

4. **A, B, C, D, F.** You should have all these items on hand before beginning a Windows 10 installation. The Windows 10 installation media is on DVD and not CD, so you do not need a CD-ROM drive. You can install from the network or from a bootable USB drive.

5. **A, E.** When installing Windows 10 from a DVD-ROM, you can configure the username and password and membership in an Azure Active Directory. You configure local domain membership, language, time, currency format, and computer name and background color after installation of Windows 10 is completed.

6. **A.** Windows SIM (Windows System Image Manager) is used to perform these actions. Windows AIK is the Automated Installation Kit, which was used to customize the installation and deployment of Windows Vista/7. Windows Assessment and Deployment Kit (ADK), which includes Windows SIM, is the Windows Deployment Kit for Windows 10, which replaces the Windows AIK. Sysprep is a utility that prepares a computer running Windows with a set of installation applications for imaging and deployment to multiple target computers.

7. **A.** When setting up a multiple-boot system, you should install the oldest operating system first. In this scenario, you would install Windows 7, then Windows 8.1, and finally Windows 10.

8. **D.** The setupact.log file records modifications performed on the system during Setup. The netsetup.log file reports the results of a computer attempting to join a workgroup or domain. The setuperr.log file records errors generated by hardware or driver issues during Windows installation. The setupapi.log file records data about Plug and Play devices and drivers, or about application installation.

9. B. An upgrade installation maintains all Windows settings, personal files, and applications from the previous Windows installation, whereas a clean installation of Windows 10 requires that you reinstall all programs and re-create all Windows settings. Clean installations do not maintain any settings, files, or applications from the previous Windows installation (except for files stored on a different partition). An upgrade installation does not require that you reinstall all programs and re-create all Windows settings.

10. C, D, E, F, G. You need to ensure that all hardware is listed in the Windows Certification Program, check for available BIOS upgrades, scan your computer for viruses and then remove or disable your antivirus program, and then install the latest updates for Windows 8.1. The Windows Anytime Upgrade was used with Windows 7 to upgrade to a higher edition; it has been replaced by the Add features command in the Charms bar and is not associated with upgrading an older Windows operating system. The Windows Upgrade Assistant was available for upgrades to Windows 8.1; it does not apply to Windows 10 upgrades.

11. A. The simplest way is to insert the Windows 10 DVD and upgrade directly to Windows 10 Pro. It is not necessary to upgrade to Windows 8.1 or any other edition of Windows 7. You could upgrade to Windows 8.1 and then to Windows 10, but this would require additional licensing costs and take much more time.

12. B. When you perform a clean installation of Windows 10 over Windows 7 on the same partition without formatting this partition, a Windows.old folder is created, and the Windows 7 system files are placed in this folder. You would need to perform the clean installation on a different partition to create a dual-boot system.

13. C. The files are placed in the \Users\Fred\Documents folder. The Windows.old folder stores other Windows 7 files, and nonaccessible links are created to the My Documents folder for application APIs. This is also true when upgrading a Windows 8/8.1 computer. It should not be necessary to restore these files from backup; however, it is good practice to back them up before upgrading in case some type of failure occurs during the upgrade process.

14. A. The upgrade of Windows 10 Home to Windows 10 Pro is accomplished easily by manually entering a product key after the purchase. This is true whether or not you've purchased the upgrade license; if you haven't purchased the license, you can click Go to Store to purchase one. The Activation screen is accessed from the Search utility (Cortana) and not the Settings utility. You do not need to insert the Windows 10 DVD.

15. A, B, C, E. VHDs enable all these advantages, with the exception of using devices with less disk space. Often, using VHDs will require additional disk space, not less.

16. C. VHDs can be fixed, so the entire space allocated is initialized; dynamic, so that space is utilized as needed but not initially; and differencing, using a child block as changes are made to the parent image. VHD and VHDX are formats, not types. Limited and expanding are not VHD types, nor is expandable or variable.

17. C. To install Windows Features, access the Control Panel, select **Programs**, and then select **Turn Windows Features On or Off**. You can download only apps from the Windows store, not features, and these features are not available for download from Microsoft's website. The Apps & Features page of the modern settings is used to manage UWP and Windows Store apps, not features. However, a link at the bottom of the page under Related Settings opens the Control Panel Programs and Features applet. The System Control Panel applet cannot be used to install features.

18. B. You can use the DISM tool to install Windows Features in online or offline images, using the **Enable-Feature** option. DiskPart is used to manage disk partitions. BCDedit is used to modify the boot configuration. Sysprep is used to generalize a Windows image, but cannot be used to install features. Windows PE is the Preinstallation Environment and is not a command-line tool.

19. A. You should used fixed VHDs for deploying Windows images in a production environment. Fixed VHDs provide improved performance over dynamic VHDs, which need to continually allocate new space as they are used. Differencing VHDs are used primarily for testing or development and are not appropriate for general use in most cases. Expandable is not a VHD type. VHDX is used for Hyper-V, is a format, not a type, and cannot be used for native boot.

20. A, B, D, E. All these best practices apply and should be taken into account during your planning. A VHD is a single large file, so if it becomes corrupted, recovering mission-critical data may not be possible. You should always plan for additional storage for apps, data, and temporary files. The page file is created outside the VHD, so the host storage volume should have sufficient space, and generalizing the image using Sysprep allows Windows to initialize properly on different computers. You should use fixed VHDs for production environments and differencing VHDs for use in development and testing, so answer C is incorrect.

Chapter 3

1. **B.** You can drag the top and/or the left edge of the Start menu to customize the size of the menu. Tablet mode will make the Start menu larger, but will take over the desktop and might not show any additional applications. You cannot expand the Start menu from the left or the bottom. You can toggle the Show More Tiles option on the modern Settings page, but that will only widen the menu and will not show additional applications. Dragging the top and right edge to resize the menu is the best option.

2. **B.** You must store the Start menu configuration in an .XML file and store it on a server file share accessible by all computers that need the custom Start menu. The policy will point to the location and name of this file. All customizations are contained in a single file, so a folder full of files is not needed. You cannot store the settings in a domain object. You use a PowerShell command to create the .XML file with the configuration, not to apply it on the workstation computers.

3. **D.** You can toggle the setting to automatically hide any notifications when you are plugged into a presentation display. Changing the system icons will not affect notifications, and your screen will not be locked during the presentation, so notifications will still appear. You can turn off notifications from senders currently sending notifications, but others could still appear. Quiet Hours will also turn off notifications, but they will turn off immediately and stay off until you toggle it back on, so you could miss important notifications before and after your presentation; therefore, D is the best option.

4. **B.** These Cortana options can be toggled on or off. The Microphone setting allows you to configure the microphone and speech system. Other Privacy Settings is a link to the modern Settings privacy options. Cortana language is a selection of available languages, and Bing SafeSearch is a link to Bing.com's search settings.

5. **B, C, E, F.** The Edge browser offers a simplified browser that does not include the capability of using RSS feeds, compatibility view, or the ability to directly access the Internet Options dialog box. Further, you cannot pin websites to the taskbar, but you can pin websites to the Start menu to create tiles that automatically open the pinned websites. Both Edge and IE support Adobe Flash and tabbed browsing.

6. **B.** You should set Internet Explorer Standards Mode for Local Intranet, which will ensure all internal web applications that users access will be viewed in Internet Explorer using IE 7 compatibility. If you turn on Standards Mode for all websites, some Internet sites will not work properly. Turning off the Compatibility View button will ensure there is no way to view the local web

applications properly. Microsoft lists will not include your internal applications, and Quirks Mode will likely not resolve all the compatibility issues.

7. A, B, C, D, E, F. You can access Device Manager using any of these methods.

8. B. A disabled device is indicated in Device Manager by a red "X" appearing over the device icon. A black exclamation point icon on a yellow triangle background appearing next to the device icon indicates that a device is functioning but experiencing problems. A yellow question mark indicates that the device is not properly installed or is in conflict with another device in the system. A blue "i" on a white field indicates that the device has been configured manually with resource configurations.

9. D. First introduced in Windows 8.1, the Events tab of the device's Properties dialog box displays a time-based list of actions that have occurred with regard to the device. None of the other tabs mentioned here provide this information.

10. B. By uninstalling a device driver, you remove the driver completely from the computer. You should do this only after you have removed the device, because Windows will otherwise redetect the device at the next reboot and reinstall the driver. You should also select the **Delete the Driver Software for This Device** check box. None of the other options provided will remove the driver completely.

11. B. The sigverif.exe utility is used to determine whether any unsigned drivers are present. The sfc.exe utility is the System File Checker, which checks the digital signature of system protected files. Msinfo32.exe is the System Information utility, which provides a large amount of information on hardware and software on the computer but does not provide driver signature information. Gpedit.exe is the Local Group Policy Editor, which is used to apply policies to a computer or a series of computers.

12. B. If the device worked before you updated its driver, you can roll back the driver to restore the previous driver that worked with the device. A further update might solve the problem but would not likely be available because you already updated the driver. Uninstalling or disabling the driver would not work.

13. A. If the installation of a new device on your computer results in another device not working, this indicates that the two devices are attempting to use the same resource (such as an IRQ). Any of the other options provided could result in the new device (the NIC) not working, but other devices would still work.

14. D. The Conflicts/Sharing subnode of the Hardware Resources category in System Information provides information on device-related problems but does not provide tools for correcting these problems. Device Manager enables you to correct these problems. Sigverif.exe provides information on unsigned

drivers but does not provide information on device-related problems. Action
Center provides information on some device problems plus a link for corrective actions.

15. D. Creating a Restore Point will enable you to restore the computer to the
point in time before the driver was installed. Although you can also do this
with a system image, it is a much longer task and requires more resources than
necessary.

16. C. Only drivers that have an Advanced tab have driver-specific settings that
can be changed through the Device Manager. The Details tab displays such
settings, but they cannot be changed in that dialog.

Chapter 4

1. A, B, D, E. The logical components of AD DS include forests, trees, domains,
and OUs. Sites and global catalogs are physical components.

2. B. By default, AD DS allows a normal user account to join up to 10 computers to the domain without any additional privileges. Members of the Domain
Administrators group and users with the Create Computer Objects in the
Active Directory are not restricted to 10 computers and can add computers
to the domain as needed. Follow this procedure in Windows 10 to join the
domain.

3. C. After you've joined a domain, to use your local account again, you need
to use domain syntax for your login name. This is in the form *domain\user*.
You can also use your User Principal Name (UPN), which is
user@domain.name. So, for instance, if Sally.Sue is a member of the *test.local*
domain, she can use either **TEST\Sally.Sue** or **Sally.Sue@test.local**. For
local computer accounts, the domain name is the name of the computer.

4. A, B, C. Remote Server Administration Tools (RSAT) is a collection of tools
that are useful for managing Server Core as well as Full GUI installations.
RSAT includes Server Manager, MMC snap-ins, PowerShell cmdlets, and
additional command-line tools used to manage remote computers. There is no
such tool as OU Manager.

5. B. After you install Active Directory, the icon for Domain Controllers is different from the blank folder icon for the other containers because it is a special
container called an organization unit (OU).

6. A. Group Policy lies at the heart of every Active Directory implementation.
It does far more than just define what users can and cannot do with their

computers. It is a series of configuration settings that you can apply to an object or series of objects in Active Directory to control a user's environment in numerous contexts.

7. D. The other tabs are Details, Settings, and Status.

8. A. The ICD tool streamlines the customization and provisioning of Windows images. It is provided for OEMs, system integrators, and IT departments of organizations that provision bring-your-own-device (BYOD) and organizational devices.

9. B. KMS provides advantages for organizations with many devices to manage. Computers do not need to access the Internet for activation, saving bandwidth charges. Organizations may also have isolated devices that do not need Internet access, and these computers can be activated on the internal network instead.

Chapter 5

1. D. You can use any email account to connect to a Microsoft account and log in to Windows. You must activate your account by responding to an email from Microsoft as a verification of your account.

2. A, B, C, D. All these are advantages to using a single Microsoft account for all Windows devices that can use it.

3. C. Using this group policy allows the company to manage all the Microsoft accounts used on computers centrally, without allowing users to create their own.

4. A, D. You can only install Packaged apps from the Windows Store or using sideloading. The Programs and Features applet works only with Windows desktop applications, and "Apploading" does not exist.

5. B. Windows Store apps do not use "active icons"; they display content using their tiles, and can do so even when the app is not running. Apps do not use icons at all, although some apps can optionally show badges in the taskbar, if they are enabled.

6. C. There is no notification in Windows 10 for the availability of an update for individual apps. From the Windows Store settings, you can toggle apps to check and automatically update when an update is available; however, if this toggle is turned off, you need to open the Windows Store and check the number next to your user icon.

7. B. Office 365 is a SaaS (Software as a Service) type of cloud service. PaaS is Platform as a Service (servers); NaaS does not exist; and IaaS is Infrastructure as a Service (networking and servers).

8. A, B, C, D, E. You can manage all these devices using Intune. Windows 10 workstations can be managed with Intune whether they are joined to a domain or not.

9. A, B, C, E. You can use any of these methods to deploy the Office 365 apps to Windows 10 computers. You cannot add the apps to a deployable image, because Office 365 is a per-user cloud application. Images are specific to the device.

10. B, C. Only signed apps can be deployed to Windows 10 devices, and the devices must have sideloading enabled. Apps can be sideloaded; it is not necessary to make your apps available through the Windows Store. You can enable sideloading on Windows devices using group policies if they are domain-joined; however, this is not a requirement because any device can be enabled for sideloading.

Chapter 6

1. A, B, D. All these protocols are components of TCP/IP. Although it is used by TCP/IP-enabled computers, DHCP is not considered to be a component of TCP/IP.

2. C. The default gateway is the IP address of the router that connects your computer's subnet to other subnets on your company's network, as well as the Internet. Although important for your computer's TCP/IP configuration, the other items given here do not address this objective.

3. B. Any IP address in the range 128.0.0.0 to 191.255.255.255 belongs to class B. Class A addresses are in the range 1.0.0.0 to 126.255.255.255; class C addresses are in the range 192.0.0.0 to 223.255.255.255; class D addresses are in the range 224.0.0.0 to 239.255.255.255; class E addresses are in the range 240.0.0.0 to 254.255.255.255.

4. D. CIDR enables you to specify the number of bits that are used for the subnet mask as part of the network address, in this case 24. WINS is not an address notation, but is a protocol used for resolving NetBIOS names to IP addresses. Unicast and multicast are types of IPv6 addresses; this scenario deals with IPv4 addressing.

5. A. A global unicast address is a globally routable Internet address that is equivalent to a public IPv4 address. A link-local unicast address is used for

communication between neighboring nodes on the same link; a site-local unicast address is used for communication between nodes located in the same site; a multicast address provides multiple interfaces to which packets are delivered; and anycast addresses are utilized only as destination addresses assigned to routers. None of these other address types are suitable for direct Internet contact.

6. B. A link-local IPv6 address has an address prefix of fe80::/64. This address is equivalent to an APIPA-configured IPv4 address. The other address types have different network prefixes.

7. D. Teredo is a tunneling communication protocol that enables IPv6 connectivity between IPv6/IPv4 nodes across Network Address Translation (NAT) interfaces, thereby improving connectivity for newer IPv6-enabled applications on IPv4 networks. It uses this prefix. The other address types use different prefixes.

8. C. The DNS tab of the Advanced TCP/IP settings dialog box enables you to specify more than two DNS server addresses. It also allows you to sequence these server addresses in the order of most likely usage. The Internet Protocol (TCP/IP) Properties dialog box (either version 4 or 6) allows you to specify only two DNS server addresses. Another way you could solve this problem would be to add the first two DNS server addresses from this dialog box and then click **Advanced** to add the third DNS server address from the DNS tab as already described. The Alternate Configuration tab enables you to specify an alternate set of TCP/IP addressing parameters for use at a different location, such as when using a portable computer; it does not allow the specification of additional DNS server addresses.

9. A, C. To configure your computer to use DHCP, you should ensure that the Obtain an IP Address Automatically and Obtain DNS Server Address Automatically options are selected. You would specify the other two options if you were configuring your computer to use static IP addressing.

10. B. If your computer is using an IPv4 address on the 169.254.0.0/16 network, it is configured to use APIPA. An address on this network is assigned when the computer is configured to receive an IP address automatically, but is unable to reach a DHCP server. Private IPv4 addressing is in use if the IP address is on any of the 10.0.0.0/8, 172.16.0.0/16, or 192.168.0.0/24 networks. An alternate IP configuration is a separate static IP address that you can configure on a computer that is using DHCP; it would not be using this address.

11. C. You should set the connection as a metered connection. When connected to a metered connection, Windows 10 limits the amount of data used by deferring noncritical updates, updates to Start screen tiles, choosing low-resolution images when available, and other techniques. You can view usage statistics by showing estimated data usage, but not control it. Sharing will affect only local network traffic.

12. B. The conference room is currently the preferred wireless network, because it is the network in range that you last connected to. Your home network was preferred, but it is not in range, and Windows will not attempt a connection there. If you switch your connection to the engineering department, Windows will move that network to the top of the priority list.

13. B. Because only wireless networks currently in range will be displayed in the Network list, out-of-range networks will be hidden. You cannot access wireless profiles from the Network and Sharing dialog, which is used only to manage network adapters and current connections. You can delete the profiles, but you must use the **netsh** command to view the list and delete each profile.

14. D. When you access the network adapter's hardware properties from the Configure button through the connection, the Resources tab is not displayed. If you need to view or modify the resources the device uses, you must use the Device Manager.

15. A, D. 802.11n mode is a wireless property, and Preferred Band allows you to select the frequency for an 802.11n connection. Speed, duplex, transmit, and receive buffers are all properties available only for a wired network adapter.

Chapter 7

1. C. All other options are examples of authorization settings.

2. C. Users can select three gestures in any combination of Taps, Circles, or Straight Lines. You must use exactly three gestures.

3. B, C. Windows 10 does not require Ctrl+Alt+Delete when joined to a domain by default, but you can change this through Group Policies. The Users section of PC Settings only allows users to manage their own account or create new ones. The Users and Groups section of the Computer Management snap-in must be used to change other user account settings. You can disable PIN login using Group Policy for domain-join computers, or set requirements for it, but by default users can use PIN logins for domain-joined computers.

4. C. To switch to a Microsoft account, use the Your Info menu under Accounts Settings and select Sign In with a Microsoft Account instead. You must perform this step before logging out and using your Microsoft account to sign in. The Sign-in Options menu does not provide options for switching your PC sign-in to a Microsoft account, only for adding accounts. By default, you can sign in to domain-joined accounts using a Microsoft account, although Group Policy can be used to block them. You cannot add a domain account to your Microsoft account on the account management web page.

5. B, C. To use Windows Hello, you must have an infrared (IR) camera or a fingerprint reader, and your device must be configured with a PIN. You do not need a Microsoft account to use Windows Hello. A high-resolution camera is not compatible with Windows Hello, because it is easy to defeat with a photograph. There is no need for a strong password for a local or domain account; the password is not needed after Windows Hello has been configured.

6. D. If the network location is set to Public, you cannot join a homegroup. You can join a homegroup even if your computer is joined to an AD DS domain; this facilitates working at home with a laptop that is moved between home and work locations. You can join a homegroup with any edition of Windows 10. A password is automatically created when you create a homegroup; this password is required for another computer to join the homegroup, but you cannot create a homegroup without a password.

7. A, B, D, E. To implement Device Guard, your devices must meet all these requirements. Device Guard will work with the minimum RAM requirements for Windows 10; it does not require 8 GB of RAM.

8. A, B, E. Health attestation will check and evaluate the status and integrity of each of these components, as well as the digital signatures of the secure boot environment. Attestation is not concerned with the status of any EFS folders or the Windows Firewall.

9. B. By default in Windows 10, as was the case in Windows 7, you receive a UAC prompt only if you are using a nonadministrative user account. In Windows Vista, you always received a UAC prompt; in Windows 7/8.1/10, this is true only if you change the UAC settings and select the Always Notify Me When option. You never have to log off from a standard user account and log back on as an administrator; you merely have to supply an administrative password. The latter option occurs only if you've configured the Never Notify Me option in the UAC settings.

10. D. The red title bar and shield indicate that the program is a high-risk program that Windows has blocked completely. You cannot run it in its present form. No command buttons are provided on this message box, so it is impossible to click **Yes** to run the program.

11. C. By enabling the Admin Approval Mode for the Built-In Administrator Account policy in Group Policy, you configure the built-in Administrator account to display UAC prompts in the manner as governed by the User

Account Settings Control Panel applet setting in use. Configuring options in this applet without enabling the Admin Approval Mode for the Built-In Administrator Account policy does not change the behavior of the built-in Administrator account, which by default does not display any UAC prompts.

12. C. You should enable the **Behavior of the Elevation Prompt for Standard Users** policy and then select the **Automatically Deny Elevation Requests** option. This option prevents any applications that require administrative credentials from running. Either of the Prompt for Credentials options would display a UAC prompt that requests an administrative password, but these would still allow these programs to run. Enabling the Only Elevate Executables That Are Signed and Validated policy would perform public key infrastructure signature checks on programs requiring elevated privileges but would still allow programs that pass this check to run.

13. B, C, D. You cannot back up Web Credentials from Credential Manager, and there is no "Windows app" credential type; instead, Windows apps store their credentials as Generic Credentials.

14. C. You can enable Windows Credentials for roaming within the AD domain; however, Web Credentials roam only between devices using the same Microsoft account. On domain-joined computers, Web Credential roaming is disabled.

15. B. Certificates are managed using the Certificates MMC snap-in. The other tools listed do not exist.

16. C. Certificates used for authentication are in the Personal Store of the User Certificates Store set. This is the only location that you can use with storing authentication settings with Credential Manager.

17. E. The Store Passwords Using Reversible Encryption policy weakens security because it stores passwords in a format that is essentially the same as plain text. You should enable this policy only if needed for clients that cannot use normal encryption.

18. B. The Minimum Password Age policy enables you to prevent users from cycling rapidly through passwords and thereby defeating the Enforce Password History policy. When enabled, a user cannot change her password again for the interval specified by this policy.

19. A. Security (NTFS) permissions are cumulative; in other words, a user receives the least restrictive of the permissions that have been applied, so Bob has Full Control permission to the Documents folder.

20. D. Although NTFS permissions are cumulative so that a user receives the least restrictive permission, an explicit denial of permission overrides all allowed

permissions. Therefore, in this scenario, Jim does not have access to the Documents folder.

21. **A.** When a user accesses a folder on the same computer on which it is located using the drive location, the shared folder permission does not apply and the user receives only the NTFS permission that has been assigned to the folder. Therefore, in this scenario, Sharon has Full Control permission on the Documents folder.

22. **C.** When you copy a file or folder from one NTFS volume to another one, the copy inherits the permissions that are applied to the destination location. Therefore, the Accounts folder receives the Read permission that is applied to the D:\Confidential folder.

Chapter 8

1. **C.** You should check the file security and look at the Effective Access permissions for the user. This is the fastest way to determine specific access configured for the user to the file. You can check NTFS and Share permissions and review the access and groups that apply to the file, but checking effective access will perform the task for you faster and more efficiently. Group Policies are unlikely to be an issue with file update permission.

2. **A.** When you move a file from one folder to another folder on the same NTFS volume, the file retains its NTFS permissions. Therefore, in this scenario, Jennifer has Full Control permission to the C:\Confidential\Projects.doc file.

3. **D.** When you move a file or folder to a different partition, it inherits the permissions of the parent folder. The folder will be owned by the Administrator, but will also have all permissions of the parent folder. It will only have the permissions for the E: drive if the folder is moved to the root of E:. Permissions are retained for files and folders moved to the same partition, but not when moving to a different one.

4. **C.** You should use Dynamic Access Control (DAC) in this scenario. Using NTFS permissions can secure files and folders, but would require significant rearrangement of folder structures and ensuring that every document is stored in the correct location. There is also no way to label specific documents as sensitive using NTFS permissions. Share permissions would suffer from the same shortcomings. You can use EFS encryption, but, again, there is no way to specifically identify sensitive documents, and it would require per-user access permissions for each file. DAC is the best option.

5. B, C. To encrypt a file or folder, the file or folder must be located on a volume that is formatted with the NTFS file system. So you need to convert the volume to the NTFS file system or move the folder to another volume that is formatted with the NTFS file system. If you were to format the D:\volume with the NTFS file system, you would destroy the Confidential folder. The folder cannot be compressed because this is also a function of the NTFS file system.

6. B. By default, the administrator account created when Windows 10 is first installed is the default recovery agent for files or folders that have been encrypted on this computer, so you can decrypt the file if you log on with this account. Note that this account is disabled by default, so you need to log on with another account and enable the account first. If you re-create Peter's user account, the new account has a different security identifier (SID) so it does not have the capability of decrypting files encrypted with the old account.

7. C. You should audit the Privilege use category in the Audit Policy node. This category tracks the use of a user right, such as changing the system time or time zone. The Account management category tracks the management of user accounts, including password changes. The Policy change category tracks the modification of policies, such as user rights assignment, trust, and audit policies. The System events category tracks events, such as improper shutdown of a computer or very little free space remaining on a disk.

8. A. In many computers equipped with TPM, you might first need to enable TPM in the BIOS before you can set up BitLocker. You need to enable TPM before you can configure a startup key. You do not need to use Group Policy before enabling TPM. You should contact your hardware manufacturer only if enabling TPM in the BIOS does not work or if the BIOS does not include an option to do so.

9. A. If you use BitLocker To Go to encrypt your USB flash drive containing the BitLocker recovery key, the recovery key may become inaccessible if your computer enters Recovery mode. On a domain computer, it is good practice to save copies of recovery keys to AD DS. It is possible to use BitLocker without additional keys on a computer that is equipped with a TPM, although this is less secure. If your computer is not equipped with a TPM, you must use Group Policy to enable BitLocker first.

10. A, B, C, D, E. All these are possible locations to which a BitLocker recovery key can be saved or backed up.

11. B. The policy Require Additional Authentication at Startup must be enabled before you can enable BitLocker on the system drive if the computer does not have a Trusted Platform Module. The Control Panel applet enables BitLocker on drives, but will not work unless the policy is enabled. Signatures are written to any drive in order to manage them in Disk Management, but this does not affect BitLocker functionality.

12. A. BitLocker does not provide an option for saving the recovery key on a DVD or CD; the only removable storage available is a USB drive. It can also be saved to the domain on a domain-joined computer, to a Microsoft account, a printed hard copy, or a local file.

Chapter 9

1. B, C, G. You can configure primary and extended partitions on a basic disk and create logical drives within an extended partition. The other volume types mentioned here require that you upgrade your basic disk to dynamic storage.

2. C. You should run the **convert gpt** command. This command converts the disk's partition style to GPT (GUID partition table), which enables a volume of more than 2 TB. By default, a disk uses the MBR (master boot record) partition table style, which enables volumes of up to 2 TB. It is not necessary to convert the disk to either basic or dynamic storage (it is basic by default), because you can have a 5 TB primary partition on a basic disk.

3. B. The Tools tab of a volume's Properties dialog box enables you to check the disk for errors, defragment it, or back it up. The General tab provides a pie chart of the disk's space allocation and enables you to specify a volume name and execute the Disk Cleanup utility. The Hardware tab displays hardware information for the computer's disk drives. The Quota tab enables you to configure disk quotas. The Customize tab enables you to optimize folders for specified purposes. None of these other tabs enable you to check your volume for errors.

4. B. This procedure creates a spanned volume, which extends storage on one volume to additional disks without the need for an additional drive letter. A simple volume includes only a single disk. Mirrored and RAID-5 volumes contain 2 and 3–32 disks, respectively, but are created differently.

5. C, D. Mirroring (RAID-1) and striping with parity (RAID-5) are fault tolerant and can withstand failure of a single disk without data loss. Spanning (which is not considered a RAID technology) and striping (RAID-0) are not fault tolerant; loss of a single disk results in loss of the entire volume.

6. A. The maximum space that you can include in a RAID-5 volume is equal to the smallest amount of free space on a single disk multiplied by one less than the total number of disks. Here the smallest amount of free space is 800 GB and the number of disks is 4, so you can have $800 \times 3 = 2400$ GB or 2.4 TB. You require the space equivalent to one disk for parity; without parity you

could have 800 × 4 = 3200 GB or 3.2 TB, but this is not the desired result. In this scenario you could have created a three-disk striped volume without parity of 4.50 TB by using disks 0, 1, and 3 only, but this also is not the desired result. You cannot use all the space available when the sizes of the disks are different, so 5.3 TB is impossible.

7.   D. The **add disk = 1** command in DiskPart creates a mirror on disk 1 of the current volume. This is the only way you can create a fault-tolerant replica of your system and boot volumes. A striped volume is not fault tolerant and cannot be used on the system and boot volumes. A RAID-5 volume is fault tolerant, but you cannot use this technology on the system and boot volumes; further, this technology requires three disks. The **create volume mirror** command is invalid command syntax.

8.   A, B, C. You should have at least 15 percent of free space on your disk so that the Optimize Drives can run in an optimal condition. Any of the first three options will increase the amount of free space.

9.   A, C. You can either specify the volumes to be defragmented, or use the /E parameter to specify the volumes that will not be defragmented. The **defrag /e:** command is incorrect syntax and will produce an error. The **defrag /E c: d:** command will defragment the E: volume but not the C: or D: volumes because it specifies to defragment all volumes except those mentioned.

10.   A. You can create logical groupings of shared folders for facilitating access using a single UNC by using DFS Namespaces. DFS Replication is used to replicate the namespaces or other objects. The description does not apply to disk cleanup. You cannot use storage pools across different servers.

11.   A, B. You can replicate standalone DFS namespaces, as well as AD DS partitions using DFS Replication, when the Active Directory is using a forest functional level of Windows Server 2008 or higher. You cannot use DFS replication to replicate server images or the Registry.

12.   D. You can create a storage space with any size; the pool capacity does not limit this setting. Because space is thin provisioned on the storage space, you can specify a larger amount than you currently have available, and add disks to the storage pool when you want to actually use the space.

13.   B. To use parity, at least three drives are required in the storage pool. A two-way mirror requires a minimum of two drives, and a three-way mirror requires a minimum of five drives.

14. D. You can change the size of the storage space at any time, and as long as you have enough capacity in the storage pool, you can use that space for files. It is not necessary to delete the "music" storage space, because you can overallocate size on storage spaces regardless of the actual physical capacity on the storage pool.

15. C. You will need to log in to the computer with the new account. OneDrive is tightly integrated with Windows 10, and you must be logged in to the correct Microsoft account to use the account's OneDrive. You cannot use OneDrive. com for Windows 10 computer accounts. There is no OneDrive applet in Control Panel, all settings are managed through the OneDrive app, and the OneDrive icon in the Notification area is available only in older versions of Windows.

16. B. Automatically keeping your OneDrive files and local copies up-to-date with any changes requires that you change the OneDrive configuration to make the files available offline. This is the way to sync OneDrive in Windows 10. You can make the entire drive available offline as well, but if you only want to sync "a number of files," you can change this option selectively for specific folders and files. The Windows app allows you to copy files to and from your OneDrive, but it must be done manually. Your OneDrive.com account will not have access to any local computers running Windows 10. The mobile app works only on smartphones and tablets.

17. A, B, C, D. These folders are all default library folders that you can redirect to another location, such as a shared folder on a server. In addition, you can create additional library folders that can be redirected in the same way.

18. B, C, E. Domain-based folder redirection uses a Windows Server 2012 R2 or higher computer configured as a domain controller, plus a server configured with an accessible shared folder. You then create a GPO that specifies folder redirection settings. Note that a server running an older version of Windows Server can also be used, but that some settings offered in Windows Server 2012 R2/2016 might not be available. Neither a router nor a global catalog server is used with folder redirection.

19. B. A mandatory profile is stored on a server using the name NTUser.man. This profile is copied locally to any computer the user logs on to, and any changes are not saved when the user logs off. A roaming profile enables the user to make and save changes. A local profile is stored only on its local computer and is not available across the network. There is no such thing as a permanent profile. (A temporary profile is available and is loaded if an error condition prevents a user from loading her normal profile.)

20. C. You should click **Advanced System Settings** in the System dialog box. In the System Properties dialog box that appears, select the **Advanced** tab and then click **Settings** under User Profiles. Then, in the User Profiles dialog box, select the default profile and click **Copy To**. Type or browse to the desired location and click **OK**. The System Properties dialog box does not have a Profiles tab. It is not necessary to access the Default User settings from %systemdrive%\Users; in fact, this location does not have a Profiles subfolder.

Chapter 10

1. B. The new Hyper-V and Client Hyper-V virtual disk format is VHDX, and these files are created with the .vhdx extension.

2. B, C, D. These are all features of the new VHDX virtual disk format. The original VHD format will support up to 2 TB of space, but the new format files can store up to 64 TB.

3. A, B, D. Any and all of these tools can be used to create virtual hard disks, and they can create both VHD and VHDX files. BCDEdit is used only to edit a physical computer's boot loader, and can add a VHD to the boot loader menu, but cannot edit or modify VHD files.

4. B. The computer appears to meet all the requirements for running Client Hyper-V, including processor support and BIOS features. Hyper-V will not run on 32-bit clients at all, however. Client Hyper-V requires a 64-bit version of Windows 10 Pro, Enterprise, or Education.

5. A. The Client Hyper-V services and management tools are included with Windows 10. It is not installed by default, but can be enabled from the Control Panel's Programs applet by using the Windows Features installation tool.

6. D. The Client Hyper-V configuration settings for virtual machines will always allow you to select the maximum amount of RAM that a VM can be assigned, which is limited to 1 TB. Note that unless the VM operating system can support it and the host actually has that amount of RAM, the memory used by the VM will be less. In most cases, setting the maximum memory to the default of 1 TB simply means the VM is allowed to consume as much memory as is available.

7. C. Because other VMs are using enough processor resources that the application server does not have enough CPU left to run, the best option is to set a higher priority on processor resources to the VM serving the application. That will ensure that as processor resources become scarce, other VMs will be cut back on resources before the application VM.

8. C. Hyper-V can assign virtual processors to each VM based on the total number of physical processor cores available on the host machine. The number of VMs hosted by the Hyper-V host computer does not affect this limit.

9. C. Checkpoints represent a point in time for the state of the virtual machine. When the checkpoint is deleted, the changes are not lost, but are merged into the virtual machine's configuration. Deleting the checkpoint means you cannot revert the machine to that specific point in time.

10. B. The external virtual switch is the type of virtual switch that will automatically provide Client Hyper-V virtual machines access to the host's network and external Internet.

11. A. Because an internal switch does not provide access to any network resources outside the Hyper-V host computer, you will typically need to manually configure the VMs' network settings to enable communications among the VMs and with the host. Another potential method would be to create a single VM with a static IP address and host DHCP and DNS services on that VM to provide the other VMs with automatic network configuration. Note also that autoconfiguration addresses will lock Windows 10 into using only Public network settings, which disables sharing and uses stricter firewall rules.

Chapter 11

1. D. You should select the Always Available Offline option. The Open Sync Center option enables you to configure certain file synchronization options but in itself does not automatically cache available files. The Disk Usage option merely specifies how much disk space can be used by cached files. The Sync Selected Offline Files option enables you to select which files are available offline.

2. C, D. The Optimize for Performance option enables expanded caching of shared programs so that users can run them locally, thus providing enhanced performance. To select this option, you must have the All Files and Programs That Users Open from the Shared Folder Are Automatically Available Offline option selected. The other two options do not optimize performance; in fact, the No Files or Programs from the Shared Folder Are Available Offline option effectively disables Offline Files.

3. B. You should enable the Enable Transparent Caching policy setting. Transparent file caching enables Windows 10 computers to temporarily cache files obtained across a slow WAN link more aggressively, thereby reducing the number of times the client might have to retrieve the file across the slow link. The Configure Background Sync and Slow-Link Mode settings control

synchronization across WAN links but do not enable the transparent caching feature. The Administratively Assigned Offline Files setting specifies network files and folders that are always available offline.

4. C. By default, Sync will not occur when you are on a metered or costed network. You must explicitly turn on the option in settings.

5. A. The only policy that allows you to control the caching of offline files across slow links using a latency value is the Enable Transparent Caching policy. The Configure Slow-Link Mode policy is used to configure UNC paths. The Enable File Synchronization on Costed Networks policy turns caching on or off for metered connections. If you enable the Remove Work Offline Command policy, offline files will be disabled entirely.

6. A. Sleep mode stores the state of your computer in RAM with a small amount of power to keep the RAM alive. Standby mode does not exist in Windows 10. Hibernate saves state to the hard disk, not to RAM. Suspended is not a state.

7. B. The Power Saver power plan uses these settings by default, to save the most amount of power. Note that the Balanced power plan is identified as Energy Star Qualified on some computers.

8. B, C. Either by choosing the Power Saver power plan, or by reducing the maximum power status of the processor from the Processor power management advanced power setting, you can reduce the processor power so that the battery lasts long enough to watch your movie. The Balanced power plan in itself does not accomplish this task. The Sleep setting would make your computer go to sleep during the movie, which is not what you want here. The Multimedia setting controls the sharing of multimedia with others.

9. C, E. You can perform either of these tasks by clicking links available from the battery meter. Presentation mode is not an option. To specify hard disk settings, you must configure a Group Policy setting in the Power Management subnode, or use the Advanced power options. The settings available from the battery icon are specific to the current power plan. You can turn on the Battery Saver feature from the icon as well.

10. D. Windows To Go is a copy of Windows imaged onto a USB device that enables a user to boot any computer with compatible hardware into the operating system on the USB device. It is a complete copy of operating system and application files and not simply a set of user credentials on the USB device. It is not a copy of Windows Mobile; nor is it a copy of Windows 10 located on a network drive.

11. B. Windows To Go is available only for Windows 10 Enterprise or Education, which are required both for creating the Windows To Go workspace and for running Windows To Go on a USB drive.

12. A, C, D, E, F. Wi-Fi Direct enables all these actions with Windows 10 computers. However, connections using Wi-Fi Direct are limited to two computers plus any number of other devices; you cannot connect more than two computers on one Wi-Fi Direct circuit.

Chapter 12

1. E. The Store Passwords Using Reversible Encryption policy weakens security because it stores passwords in a format that is essentially the same as plain text. You should enable this policy only if needed for clients that cannot use normal encryption.

2. B. The Minimum Password Age policy enables you to prevent users from cycling rapidly through passwords and thereby defeating the Enforce Password History policy. When enabled, a user cannot change her password again for the interval specified by this policy.

3. C, E. You should set both the Account Lockout Duration and the Account Lockout Threshold. Both should be set to a value greater than 0. You also do not want to set the account lockout threshold to a very high number. The maximum value is 999, which provides a lot of opportunity to a hacker that is a good guesser or knows the user. A value of 5 is very common, because it provides the user with several chances to remember or correctly type a password, but not too much opportunity for others.

4. C. You should audit the Privilege Use category in the Audit Policy node. This category tracks the use of a user right, such as changing the system time or time zone. The Account Management category tracks the management of user accounts including password changes. The Policy Change category tracks the modification of policies, such as user rights assignment, trust, and audit policies. The System Events category tracks events such as improper shutdown of a computer or very little free space remaining on a disk.

5. C, D. You can use Exchange ActiveSync to remove corporate data and email from the device, or Microsoft Intune to remove corporate data and any personal data as well. Offline File Sync cannot remove data from a device remotely. There is no such thing as Broadband Tethering Remote Wipe. If you had the physical device, it might be nice to clean it with a cloth, but that would not remove data from the device.

6. E. Users can access their Work Folders shared from any of these devices. Windows 7 and later is supported, as well as iOS 8 and later, and Android 4.4 and later.

7. A, D, E. All these are true. Users cannot share their Work Folders with other users; it is limited to access by a single user. On the server side, Windows Server 2012 R2 or later is required.

8. D. A broadband connection is also defined as a metered connection. Although in general usage many consider any high-speed Internet connection, for this text and the 70-697 exam, you should use the metered connection definition. Most wired connections will not be broadband connections. Wireless Wi-Fi connections are not considered broadband. Although an LTE network is a type of broadband connection, not all broadband connections are LTE.

9. B. The best way to limit the use of the connection is to make sure Windows treats the connection as a metered connection. You should not disable your security policies; this will in no way limit network usage. You could turn off file synchronization, but this is only one way your network connection is used, and it will be automatically turned off on a metered connection. The Microsoft Mail app will stop checking for email on a metered connection automatically, so there is no need to turn it off manually.

Chapter 13

1. C. In addition to the Microsoft Intune management portal, you will also use Office 365 for creating and managing user accounts and Azure AD for creating and managing user groups. Although you can integrate TeamViewer and use it for remote assistance, it is not required. You can also integrate your on-premises SCCM server with Intune, but it is not needed, and standalone Intune is recommended for organizations that do not currently make extensive use of SCCM.

2. C. The Office 365 roles are used to allow administrative access to the Office 365 portal. You can delegate global administrative access or customized access for specific tasks such as billing, user management, Exchange access, or others.

3. A. Users will be displayed in the Intune portal only when they are associated with an enrolled device. If you do not assign an Intune license, users will not be able to enroll a device. You cannot create users without an email address, and it must match your organization's host name on the Microsoft.com domain. Users cannot be copied to Intune; they exist only in Office 365 and Azure AD.

4. D. The Apple Push Notification service (APNs) certificates are required only for iOS and Mac devices.

5. D. You can enroll any of these devices with Microsoft Intune for management by Intune.

6. B. You should use Intune to wipe the device. If the user was enrolled in Exchange ActiveSync, you can use that to clear organizational information on the device, but personal user information will be kept intact. There is no delete function for devices in Intune; the Retire/Wipe function is used to remove them. Resetting the passcode may actually clear the passcode on the Lock screen, so that is a bad idea. Locking the device will help secure the device if it cannot be located, but the user stated the device is permanently lost, so it should be wiped.

7. D. User groups for Microsoft Intune are now managed in Azure AD.

8. B. The option to request remote assistance in the Microsoft Intune Center, the Windows client for Intune, can be enabled only by signing up for an account to the TeamViewer tool and configuring the connector in Microsoft Intune.

9. C. The severity levels for Intune alerts are Critical, Warning, and Informational. Enabled is an alert state, not a severity level. There are no Error or Disastrous severity levels.

10. B. You use the device enrollment policies to request and configure APN certificates, which are used only for iOS and Mac devices.

11. B. Screen locks and password requirements for devices are found in the Intune device compliance policies. Configuration policies are used for other general configuration policies. Conditional access policies are used to secure access to organizational resources. Corporate device enrollment policies are used to enable enrollment for iOS and Mac devices. Resource access policies work to help users gain access to organizational resources.

12. D. You can use Intune to manage all kinds of Microsoft updates as well as third-party updates. This includes Windows 8.1 and later but also earlier Windows updates.

13. D. Computer inventory reports will display hardware properties of all managed computers in Intune.

Chapter 14

1. **B, C.** To encrypt a file or folder, the file or folder must be located on a volume that is formatted with the NTFS file system. So you need to convert the volume to the NTFS file system or move the folder to another volume that is formatted with the NTFS file system. If you were to format the D:\volume with the NTFS file system, you would destroy the Confidential folder. The folder cannot be compressed because this is also a function of the NTFS file system.

2. **B.** By default, the administrator account created when Windows 10 is first installed is the default recovery agent for files or folders that have been encrypted on this computer, so you can decrypt the file if you log on with this account. Note that this account is disabled by default, so you need to log on with another account and enable the account first. If you re-create Peter's user account, the new account has a different security identifier (SID), so it does not have the capability of decrypting files encrypted with the old account.

3. **A, F.** You need to ensure that the D:\ drive is formatted with the NTFS file system; if this drive is formatted with the FAT32 file system, you cannot create disk quotas. Then, in the Add New Quota Entry dialog box, create a separate disk quota for each user in the Interns group that specifies the Limit Disk Space To option and the 500 MB limit. The Do Not Limit Disk Usage option does not allow you to set a limit; it merely allows tracking of disk usage without preventing users from exceeding any specified value. It is not possible to set a quota for a group; you need to specify separate quotas for each member of the group.

4. **B.** To fully configure object access auditing, you need to perform two actions: specify auditing in Group Policy and enable auditing for the folder or files whose access is to be tracked. Auditing logon events tracks attempts by others to log on to the boss's computer but does not track access to the sensitive documents. The boss is looking in the right location (the Security log) for audit events; these are not recorded in the System log. It might improve the security of the documents if you move the folder to a secured server, but this does not solve the problem of who is attempting to access them.

5. **B.** By enabling the Public Folder Sharing option, you enable users at other computers to be able to access folders in your libraries. This is known as the Public Folder Sharing model. The File and Printer Sharing option enables you to share folders you have specifically configured for sharing, but you must specifically configure the required folders for sharing. Password Protected Sharing limits the accessibility of shared folders to users who have a username and password. Media Streaming enables sharing of media files with networked devices.

6. B, D, E. Administrative shares are created by default when you first install Windows 10. These shares are suffixed with the $ symbol and are visible from the Shares node of the Computer Management snap-in; they can be accessed by entering the UNC path to the share in the Run command. Because they are hidden, you cannot see them in an Explorer window, nor can you access them from the Network and Sharing Center.

7. A, C, E. You can specify any of Read, Change, or Full Control shared folder permissions. The Modify permissions and the Read and Execute permissions are NTFS security permissions; they are not shared folder permissions.

8. D. It is not true that you are limited to the four default libraries in Windows 10; you can designate additional libraries outside these four defaults at any time. The other four answer options are true for libraries in Windows 10.

9. B. You should grant Kristin's user account the Manage This Printer permission. This permission enables her to do the required tasks. The Print permission only grants the ability to print documents on your printer. The Manage Documents permission enables her also to perform tasks such as modifying printer properties or permissions. Full Control is not included in the printer permissions; it is only a shared folder or NTFS permission.

10. D. The best option is to use the location-aware printing manager to change the default printer associated with the network at headquarters. The issue might resolve itself by deleting the original color printer, but the new printer would not automatically be selected until you print to it. Turning off location-aware printing would allow you to manually select the default printer, but this is not the best option, because you would have to manually manage your printer defaults. The Printer Troubleshooting tool would likely find no issues at all, because printing still works, just not to the desired printer.

Chapter 15

1. A. Password Authentication Protocol (PAP) sends its credentials in clear-text (unencrypted) form, so it is the least secure method of authenticating a remote access connection. All the other protocols mentioned provide some kind of credential security.

2. D. Extensible Authentication Protocol with Tunneled Transport Layer Security, or EAP-TTLS, uses a secure tunneled connection via TLS and can interoperate with 802.1X authentication protocols and RADIUS servers. None of the other protocols use this type of connection security methodology.

3. D. All five answer choices provided here are moons of the dwarf planet Pluto. But, of these, Kerberos is also a secure network access authentication protocol that provides mutual authentication where both the user and the server verify the identity of each other.

4. C. Remote Desktop enables you to connect easily to a remote computer and display its desktop as though you were working directly on the remote computer. Hyper-V enables you to create virtual machines on your Windows 10 or Windows Server 2016 computer. You would use Remote Assistance to invite an expert at another computer to assist you in overcoming some problem or learning how to perform a task. You would use VPN to make a connection to a server on a remote network.

5. C. The computer to which you want to establish a Remote Desktop connection must run the Pro or Enterprise edition of Windows 10. The Remote Desktop Connection Software download enables older computers to make a Remote Desktop connection, but does not enable a computer running Windows 10 Home to receive a Remote Desktop connection from another computer. You can establish a Remote Desktop session with a Windows 7 Professional computer so you do not need to upgrade your work computer to Windows 10. This scenario uses Remote Desktop and not Remote Assistance.

6. B. Although L2TP can provide strong security with IPsec enabled, it has no encryption of its own built in to the protocol. PPTP, SSTP, and IKEv2 provide their own encryption specifications and are part of the standards for these protocols.

7. D. The Networking tab enables you to specify protocols that will be used during your VPN session, including TCP/IPv4, TCP/IPv6, File and Printer Sharing for Microsoft Networks, and the Client for Microsoft Networks. None of the other tabs enable you to configure these options. Note that the Sharing tab enables you to configure Internet Connection Sharing (ICS).

8. D. IKEv2 is the protocol that is used by VPN Reconnect, which was first introduced in Windows 7 and has been continued for Windows 10, that enables you to automatically reestablish a VPN connection if it is temporarily disconnected. None of the other protocols can be used in this situation.

9. C. You should set up the Remote Desktop Services role, and configure the RD Gateway Tools feature. Using RD Gateway will allow remote users a simple way to connect to computers using the Remote Desktop protocol, without the overhead of a VPN. DirectAccess is an option, but would require more resources and is not needed if only Remote Desktop connections will be used. VPN Reconnect is a feature available to clients for VPN connections, and Internet Connection Sharing is only for clients on the local network to share a remote connection.

10. **D.** Using DirectAccess requires Windows 7 Ultimate, Windows 7 Enterprise, Windows 8.1 Enterprise, or Windows 10 Enterprise. It is not available on Windows 10 Pro, Home, or Mobile.

11. **A, C, D.** PowerShell cmdlets take the form verb-object, so Get-process, Select-object, and Format-data are valid cmdlets. Value-output and Folder-create start with nouns, and are not valid.

12. **C.** Because the error was a form of "Timeout," this indicates that the service is not started or the firewall is blocking access. Both of these are configured when PowerShell Remoting is enabled. If there were an authentication issue, some form of Access Denied error should be returned, and this would also be indicated if the computer was not in the list of TrustedComputers, because credentials could not be sent for authentication. PowerShell provides clear indication when the command syntax is incorrect or not recognized.

13. **A, B, D.** All these snap-ins are available in the Computer Management tool except Windows Firewall with Advanced Security, which is a different snap-in.

14. **B.** Remote Assistance enables you to invite an expert at another computer to assist you in overcoming a problem that you are having difficulties with. Hyper-V enables you to create virtual machines on your Windows 10 or Windows Server 2016 computer. You would use Remote Desktop to access another computer, such as your work computer, and work directly on this computer. You would use VPN to make a connection to a server on a remote network.

Chapter 16

1. **C.** The Public network location locks Windows Firewall down so that others cannot access anything on your computer, although it can also limit your access to external resources. The Work and Home network locations allow others to access any items you have configured for sharing on your computer. The Private location is the same as Work and Home.

2. **B, C, E.** You can configure Windows Firewall to specify programs that are allowed to communicate, or you can configure Windows Firewall to block all incoming connections, from the Windows Firewall Control Panel applet. You can also specify firewall settings for home, work, and public networks from this location. However, you must use the Windows Firewall with Advanced Security snap-in to configure ports and logging (the Windows Firewall applet in Windows Vista enabled specifying allowed ports, but this function was removed from this location starting with Windows 7).

3.   C. Windows Firewall with Advanced Security does not include any connection security rules by default. You can use the New Rules Wizard to set up connection security rules, as well as additional rules for the other rule types.

4.   A. You should run the New Inbound Rule Wizard, specify the path to Windows Media Player on the program page, and then specify the Allow the Connection if It Is Secure option. The latter option permits only connections that have been authenticated using IPsec. You need an inbound rule, not an outbound rule. Connection security rules do not permit specifying programs that are allowed to connect. The Allowed Programs and Features list does not enable you to restrict connections to only those that have been authenticated using IPsec.

5.   D. It is not possible to change a rule from Inbound to Outbound from any setting that is available in the rule's Properties dialog box. It is also not possible to drag a rule from one node to another in Windows Firewall with Advanced Security. You must create a new outbound rule to perform this action.

6.   A. The Properties dialog box of Windows Firewall with Advanced Security enables you to perform this action for each of the Domain, Private, and Public profiles. You can access this dialog box by right-clicking **Windows Firewall with Advanced Security** at the top of the console tree and choosing **Properties**. None of the locations mentioned in the other options provide a Properties dialog box.

7.   B. Because authentication credentials will be requested and passed during the setup of the network connection, Windows prevents any authenticated exceptions to be associated with a firewall rule unless it is using a secure connection.

8.   A, B, C. Windows 10 Network discovery can be enabled or disabled on any of the network profiles. Although it is not recommended, you may want to enable this feature even on a network that Windows detects as a public or guest network. Because the All Networks profile contains configuration settings that apply to all other profiles, Network Discovery configuration settings are not included.

9.   A. Configuring network discovery to automatically set up network connected devices is available only on the Private network profile. You can still set up network devices on a Public or Guest network, but because of the risk of compromise, automatically installing devices from an unknown network is not recommended and cannot be enabled. Note that the Domain profile always enables this feature when Network Discovery is turned on.

10.   E. When Windows 10 connects to an ad hoc network, it uses WPA2-Personal by default, which is the strongest authentication and uses the strongest encryption that is available on standard ad hoc network connections.

Chapter 17

1. A, B, C, E. All these server roles are involved in supporting RemoteApp application deployments. Hyper-V is not required unless you are using a virtualized deployment, but all others are required components. Active Directory Federation Services can be involved in all kinds of authentication, but is not associated with RemoteApp.

2. D. Applications are hosted on and streamed from the RD Session Host. The RD Connection Broker is used to coordinate connectivity between clients and RD Session Hosts. The RD Gateway is used only to forward requests from the public Internet to private RDS services. The RD Virtualization Host can be used to host remote desktops, but does not host RemoteApp applications.

3. A. When first deployed, RemoteApp services use a self-signed certificate generated during the installation. A public CA certificate must be obtained from a public CA, such as Verisign or Entrust. There is no certificate type called a RemoteApp certificate. Application signing can be done using a private key from a user certificate or a computer certificate; there is no application signing certificate type.

4. B. When your applications are published by RemoteApp, they use the private key of the certificate installed on the RD Connection Broker–Publishing service. The Certificate for the RD Connection Broker–Enable Single Sign On is used only for signing on to the session host. You can install a certificate on the RD Web Access server, but that will not sign the applications. The RD Gateway ideally should use a public CA certificate, but it cannot be used to provide signing for the published applications.

5. D. You can use the RD Web Access service to allow users to use only a web browser as the client to access your RemoteApp applications. The RD Session Host will still host and stream the application. There is no RD Web Access console, only the IIS manager.

6. B. The only single-instance component in a high availability Azure RemoteApp infrastructure is the shared database server. The database is used to help multiple RD Connection brokers to coordinate and track connections, RD Session Hosts, and clients.

7. D. Only the Hybrid collection can be used to host applications with access to private, on-premises resources. There is no Central Database collection, nor an Office 365 collection, although you can use an Office 365 image in a collection. The cloud collection will not have access to private resources.

8. B. To use RemoteApp from an iPad, users need to download and install the Microsoft Remote Desktop app from the iTunes store. The application does not need to be side-loaded, nor can it be. There is no RemoteApp client for iOS. A self-signed certificate, if it exists, can be added to the iOS trust store, but is not required.

9. C. To use Azure RemoteApp, users will be required to sign in using their Azure AD account. Apple and Google accounts are not used for Azure, and Microsoft accounts are not used for Azure AD or RemoteApp. You can connect your on-premises Active Directory to an Azure AD, but users will still be using the Azure AD credentials for signing in to Azure RemoteApp.

Chapter 18

1. B. Fast Startup mode makes use of hibernation in a Windows computer by saving some settings to the hyberfil.sys file, saving startup time. It does not use Sleep mode. Although an SSD may help a computer start faster, it has nothing to do with the fast startup feature. Fast startup does not use PowerShell to function.

2. C. Any user that you want to access your organization's Windows Store for Business must have an Azure AD account. An Office 365 account is not required. Microsoft accounts are used only for the Windows Store, not the Store for Business. Microsoft Intune accounts are configured in Office 365 and are not the same as the Azure AD accounts needed for the Store for Business.

3. B, C. You can provide users either the Azure AD role Billing Administrator or the Store for Business Purchaser role. The Admin role would provide too many privileges, and the user would be able to change user and store settings. This is also true for the Azure AD Global Administrator. User Administrators cannot manage applications in the Store for Business.

4. C. You would use the command **msiexec /jm Program.msi** to advertise the Program.msi package to all users of the computer. The **msiexec /a** option creates an administrative installation package for deploying the application from a network share; it is not used with the **u** or **m** parameters. The **msiexec /ju** command advertises the package to a specific user of the computer, not to all users.

5. C. Microsoft refers to this type of compatibility fix as a shim. Compatibility mode is a selectable mode that emulates an earlier Windows version or places specified restrictions on desktop properties. A filter is a condition for viewing information on a dialog box or application. A hotfix is a correction for an operating system problem.

6. B, C. You should select **Default Programs** from the Programs applet in Control Panel and then select **Set Your Default Programs**. From the list that appears, select **Firefox**, and then click **Set This Program as Default**. This action automatically changes the default program for all web-based files to Firefox. You could also select **Set Program Access and Computer Defaults**. In the dialog box that appears, select **Custom**, and then select **Mozilla Firefox**. If you select **Associate a File Type or Protocol with a Program**, you could accomplish your task, but you would have to go through a long list of file types and select each one in turn, an action that would be time consuming and error-prone. If you right-click any file with an .htm or .html extension and choose **Open With > Choose Default Program**, and then select **Firefox** from the list that appears, only files with the chosen extension would open with Firefox. You would have to locate files with other extensions that might open in Internet Explorer and also change them, again a cumbersome and error-prone situation.

7. A. You should select **Run This Program in Compatibility Mode For**, and select Windows 7. Because the application has worked successfully on Windows 7, this is the most likely compatibility mode that would enable it to work with Windows 10.

8. C. Applications are stored and streamed from the App-V Publishing Server. You cannot serve App-V applications from a basic file share. App-V applications are not installed on the client computers, only the App-V client. The App-V management server is used to manage the infrastructure, not store and publish applications.

9. A, B, D, E. Settings for all these applications and settings are synchronized by default in UE-V, using default settings location templates. UE-V does not synchronize every program in the Program Files folder, which may contain LOB, third-party, and other applications. Many of these programs require a custom settings location template.

10. A. The first step to deploying UE-V is to create and configure the settings storage location on the central server. You need this share and the UNC available before other tasks. You can then deploy the UE-V agent for computers that do not have it, and create a Group Policy Object to deploy your settings to clients. Creating custom settings location templates is optional.

11. B. You publish applications to Intune using the Intune Software Publisher, which is launched automatically when you add an app from the Intune Portal. There is no Portal upload tool. There are currently no PowerShell cmdlets for publishing software to Intune. You cannot use Windows Update to publish applications to the Intune Portal.

12. B. Before published applications are available to users, they must be deployed from within the Intune Portal. Your users were able to log in to the portal, so they already have Azure AD accounts. Users do not need to be added to Office 365 to access applications you publish. You can deploy applications to a device group instead, but this will automatically push the applications to every device; users will not be able to choose to install them. Do not give your users additional roles in Intune. They could cause problems for you and others, and it does not solve the issue.

Chapter 19

1. A. By filtering the log to display only Critical, Warning, and Error events, you can reduce the number of visible events and more easily locate events of interest. Information events make up the vast bulk of events recorded in the System log and do not represent problematic situations. Configuring the log to overwrite events after 48 hours would reduce the number of events appearing in the log, but might cause loss of events indicating significant problems unless you always look at the logs more frequently. Event log subscriptions collect data from several computers and are not relevant here.

2. B. You should use a collector-initiated event subscription, which pulls events from the specified computers. A source-initiated event subscription is more appropriate where there are a large number of computers configured with Group Policy. A filter that views logs by event source displays logs according to Windows services, utilities, and components; this is not what is needed here. You could use a filter that views logs by user and computer, but this would be less convenient than creating an event log subscription.

3. A, C. You need to run the **Winrm** and **Wecutil** commands. The **Winrm** command initiates the Windows Remote Management service that enables a secure communication channel between source and collector computers. The **Wecutil** command enables you to create and manage subscriptions that are forwarded from remote computers. The **Wdsutil** command enables you to manage a Windows Deployment Services (WDS) server. The **Logman** command enables you to manage data collector sets in Performance Monitor. Neither of the latter two commands is associated with event log subscriptions.

4. B, D. You can use either Resource Monitor or Task Manager to terminate an unresponsive program, although Task Manager is more convenient. To use Resource Monitor, you need to know the process name of the program to be terminated, although this name is often intuitive (for example, WINWORD.EXE for Microsoft Word). The other tools mentioned here do not offer this functionality.

5. A, B, C, E. The simplified interface of Task Manager enables you to perform all these tasks except for displaying performance statistics for a running program. Right-click the desired program and choose the appropriate option from the pop-up menu to perform these tasks. You need to click **More Details** to see the advanced interface of Task Manager to display summary performance statistics on a running program.

6. B. You should access the advanced interface in Task Manager and select the **Startup** tab. Then right-click the required apps and choose **Disable**. There is no Run at Startup check box in the Properties dialog box accessed from the simplified interface in Task Manager. You cannot disable apps from the Services tab in Task Manager; you can only Start, Stop, and Restart them. The Startup tab in System Configuration is used to enable this task; now, it only redirects you to Task Manager. Always keep in mind that Microsoft expects you to know the changed features in the new operating system for the exam.

7. C. You should configure a Performance Counter Alert Data Collector Set. This feature logs conditions that you specify, such as high processor utilization, and alerts you when such conditions occur. An Event Trace Data Collector Set creates trace logs that log data only when a specific activity takes place; however, this type of data collector set does not send messages for specific conditions. An event log is created by Event Viewer and logs a large number of events but not this type of message. A System Diagnostics Data Collector Set creates reports on local hardware resources, system response times, and processes on the computer along with system information and configuration data. It does not provide alerts.

8. C. You should check the Memory\Committed Bytes counter. This counter measures the amount of virtual memory that has been committed to either physical RAM or running processes. Although useful for determining whether additional RAM is needed, the other counters mentioned here do not provide this specific information.

9. A. The Dependencies tab of the service's Properties dialog box, accessed from the Services snap-in, provides you with this information. The General tab of this dialog box does not provide this information. The System Configuration tool would let you disable services but would not provide this information. The Services subnode of the Software Environment node in the System Information tool provides information on all services on the computer, including those that are running or stopped and their startup type, but this location does not provide the required information.

10. B. In the Indexing Options applet, you should click **Advanced**. Then in the Advanced Options dialog box, click **Rebuild**. This action deletes the current index and re-creates a new index. Modifying the locations in the Indexed Locations dialog box modifies where the indexing service searches; it does not enable an improved search for known items. Moving the index to a new location might help, but this should not be the first step in solving this problem. Modifying the file types searched on will not solve this problem.

11. A. The **Get** prefix to cmdlets allows you to retrieve information about a specific function.

Chapter 20

1. C. A USB recovery drive includes all the Windows files that are necessary to restore Windows from a hardware failure. This is the simplest way to accomplish the task required by this scenario. A system recovery disc was available in Windows 7; it enabled you to start the Windows Recovery Environment but did not include all the Windows files required to recover your computing environment completely. The USB recovery drive replaces the system recovery disc in Windows 10. A system state backup was used in Windows 2000/ XP, and a Complete PC Backup was used in Windows Vista for this type of task, but neither is available in Windows 10.

2. A, B, C, F. The System Restore program creates snapshots that include backups of the Registry, DLL cache folder, user profiles, and COM+ and WMI information. In addition, certain monitored system files are backed up. However, user libraries and installed application executables are not backed up.

3. D. The System Restore feature restores your operating system, applications, and settings to the date and time that you have selected. It removes applications, drivers, and similar settings that have changed more recently. Simply rolling back the affected drivers will not fully complete this task. Restoring your profile does not remove bad drivers or applications. Restoring from a system image backup takes considerably more time and effort than using System Restore.

4. B. The Push-Button Reset feature can restore your computer to the original factory image, and performing the reset without preserving your files (by choosing the Remove Everything and Reinstall Windows option) will eliminate the virus infestation. The Windows Complete PC Backup was a feature of Windows Vista, and the Windows Backup and Restore was a feature of Windows 7. These have been replaced in Windows 10 by File History, for recovering individual files and folders and the push-button recovery options

for recovering your operating system. The USB recovery drive enables you to reboot your computer for recovery from a serious error but would not restore to manufacturer's default functionality in this situation. System Restore would roll back recent changes to the operating system volume and any other volumes for which it has been configured; however, viruses that have affected other locations on the hard drive would remain.

5. B, C, E. You can access Advanced Startup Options by selecting **Update & Security** from the Settings app. Then from the Windows Update window, click **Restart Now** under Advanced startup. You can also access these options from the logon screen by clicking the Power icon in the bottom-right corner of this screen and then holding the Shift key down while clicking **Restart**. You can also boot your computer from the Windows 10 installation DVD. When the languages preferences screen appears, click **Next**, and then click **Repair Your Computer**. Windows 10 boots too rapidly to allow you to access startup options by pressing F8, as was possible with older Windows operating systems, except if you have a dual-boot system, in which you can press F8 when the boot loader menu is displayed. The options that appear when you press Ctrl+Alt+Delete do not enable access to startup options.

6. A, B, C. You can select options for **Refreshing Windows** (and preserving files), **Reset Your PC** (deleting all settings) or **Advanced** options (which includes System Restore and System Image Recovery) from the Troubleshoot Options. You can also choose to perform a Windows memory diagnostic or boot to a command prompt. Recovery Console was used in Windows XP, but its function has been replaced with the Command Prompt option that is included under Advanced options.

7. C. You should select **Advanced Options** from the Troubleshoot screen. Select **Startup Settings** and then select **Enable Low-Resolution Video**. Then perform a device driver rollback. This option starts the computer with a basic video driver at 640×480 screen resolution, thereby enabling you to log on and roll back the problematic driver. The Refresh and Reset options would solve the problem, but would take far more effort. Safe Mode might work, but the low-resolution video option is designed for problems of this nature. You do not need to use System Restore to correct this problem.

8. A. The USB recovery drive provides a simple way to start your computer in this scenario and enables you to access a system image. The system image contains everything needed to replace Windows, your programs, and all your files, thereby restoring your computer to its previous condition. The Reinstall Windows option would reinstall Windows, but you would have to reinstall applications and restore files and settings separately. The System Restore option is not available when starting with a USB recovery drive. Performing an in-place

upgrade would also require that you reinstall applications and restore files and settings separately.

9. **A.** You should use System Restore to manually create a restore point. If problems do occur after installing the application, you can use System Restore to restore your computer to the condition that existed immediately prior to the installation. Installing in Safe Mode won't help in any way. Using File History to back up your data would enable you to perform recovery options later, but would take more effort than that of using System Restore. However, you might need to use a system image restore if System Restore does not succeed. Windows Backup and Restore was used in Windows 7 to perform this action, but is no longer available in Windows 10. On the exam, choose the answer that enables you to perform the task at hand most easily.

10. **C.** The Security and Maintenance page of the Control Panel contains a link you can use to tell Windows to search for solutions immediately. Action Center has notifications only if it already found a solution. Device Manager may display an error if a device is malfunctioning, but you cannot search for solutions from there. System Information also informs you only of errors that may exist.

11. **A.** The device driver rollback feature enables you to rapidly restore an older driver to recover device functionality that has been lost. Downloading a new driver or using System Restore would work but would take far more time. Using a USB recovery drive is more drastic and would likely cause other changes as well.

Chapter 21

1. **A, B, D.** The recommended option of letting Windows choose what will be backed up will back up files and folders from all of these locations but will not back up data folders on portable hard drives.

2. **B.** By selecting Change Settings, you can restart the Set Up Backup Wizard, so that you can modify all settings used by the default backup routine. The Manage Space option enables you to manage the space used by backups, including deletion of older backups, but it does not allow you to change the backup configuration. The Create a System Image option enables you to back up all items required to restore Windows operation, but does not necessarily add the files and folders you want. The Back Up Computer option was one of the options available in the Windows Vista Backup and Restore Center, but is no longer present in Windows 10.

3. D. You should select the Change Settings option. This restarts the wizard so that you can change all settings related to the backup, including the schedule. Selecting Turn Off Schedule prevents scheduled backups from occurring. Selecting Manage Space enables you to check the space used by backups and delete old backups. The Set Up Backup option is no longer available after you have run the first backup.

4. C. The **Wbadmin** command-line utility is used in Windows 10 to perform a backup from the command line. You specify the drive to be backed up with the **-include** keyword and the drive on which the backup is to be stored with the **-backuptarget** keyword. The **Ntbackup** utility was used in previous Windows versions to perform backups from the command line, but it is no longer used in Windows 10.

5. A, C, E. File History backs up files and folders stored in libraries, contacts, and desktop folders. File History also backs up favorites as configured in places such as Internet Explorer. However, File History does not back up operating system and application files.

6. A, D, E. File History enables you to back up files and folders to network folders, USB thumb drives, and to external hard drives. You cannot use CD-ROM or DVD-ROM discs, although you could use this option with the Windows 7 Backup and Restore program, which was removed from Windows 8.1 but has been restored to Windows 10. Although the Storage Spaces feature enables you to create a real-time mirror of your data, thereby providing protection against drive failure, File History does not *per se* back up to a Storage Spaces volume.

7. B. You can force Windows to create a backup of your files by selecting Run Now from the File History dialog in Control Panel. You can also check the date and time when the files were last copied. Restoring all the files is time consuming and unnecessary, and may overwrite your current versions if you do not select a separate location. Searching for the files will find only the current version on disk. You can browse the backed-up files in the backup location, but you would need to compare each version to your current files, so forcing a new backup is the best option.

8. C. You should click **Clean Up Versions** and select the **All but the Latest One** option, and then click **Clean Up** to proceed. This action ensures that only the most recent version of each file is retained. Neither the Until Space Is Needed option nor the one-month interval option will necessarily delete all older file versions, although they will free up quite a bit of disk space. The Keep Saved Versions setting does not contain an Until Space Is Needed option.

9. A, D, E. From File Explorer, you should either add the D:\workarea folder to the Documents library, create a new library named Workarea, or use the modern settings screen to manually add the folder. (Note that the new library is automatically named for the folder name, in this case, Workarea.) You cannot add folders to File History by clicking Select Folder; the dialog box that appears only enables you to add libraries to File History. The File History app does not include an Add button that enables you to add a folder—only one that enables you to exclude folders.

10. C. The File History feature retains previous versions of a document and enumerates the available versions in the File History browser. By selecting the Restore To option, you can copy an older version of your report to a different location and then merge the missing section with your current document. If you select the Restore option, the older version will overwrite your current version, losing your most recent changes. Restoring from a backup and selecting the options indicated will work but will take more effort. Previous Versions is no longer available in Windows 10, so that is not an option.

11. B, C. You should check the Recycle Bin on OneDrive.com. Because your files were on the OneDrive storage, the OneDrive.com service will have a copy of the files in its own Recycle Bin, even after you have cleared the Recycle Bin on your PC. After the Recycle Bin on your PC is emptied, you cannot recover files from there. OneDrive files are backed up by File History, so if the folder is selected in File History, you can check there. Volume Shadows are maintained only for local volumes, not OneDrive storage.

12. D. Because the Recycle Bin is using more than 10% of your total storage (in this case, 0.7 GB), the oldest files will start to be deleted in only 3 days. After the Recycle Bin storage falls under 10% of total space, no files will be removed from the Recycle Bin until 30 days after deletion.

Glossary of Key Terms

802.11   A set of protocol standards, defined by IEEE, for wireless digital communications. There have been several defined: 802.11a, 802.11b, 802.11g, 802.11n, and 802.11ac.

access control list (ACL)   The list of permissions granted or denied that is attached to a file or folder.

account lockout policy   A policy setting that locks a user out of a computer if he enters a password incorrectly a specified number of times. This setting is designed to thwart an intruder who uses a password-cracking utility in an attempt to compromise a user account.

Action Center   A Windows 10 tool that provides a common location for all security-related configurations, as well as information on device-related problems.

Active Directory (AD)   The Windows Server 2016 directory service that has been used since its inception in Windows 2000 and forms the basis for centralized network management on enterprise networks. Also known as Active Directory Domain Services (AD DS).

active partition   A partition or volume on a hard disk that has been identified as the primary partition from which the operating system is booted.

Address Resolution Protocol (ARP)   A TCP/IP protocol that is used to resolve the IP address of the destination computer to the physical or Media Access Control (MAC) address.

Admin Approval mode   The default action mode of Windows 10, in which all user accounts—even administrative ones—run without administrative privileges until such privileges are required. When this happens, the user is presented with a UAC prompt.

administrative shares   A series of shares that are automatically created when Windows 10 is first installed. These shares are useful for administrating remote computers on the network.

AES   Advanced Encryption Standard is the strongest encryption available for standardized wireless connections. Developed by the National Institute of Standards and Technology (NIST), AES supports key sizes of 128, 192, or 256 bits.

alert   A notification provided by the Data Collector Sets feature of Performance Monitor that informs you when the value of a counter has exceeded a preconfigured level.

Anycast IPv6 address   A type of IPv6 address that is utilized only for a destination address assigned to a router.

Apple Push Notification services (APNs)   An APN's certificate issued by Apple is required for managing Apple devices.

application compatibility   The process of ensuring that a program or application written for a previous Windows operating system will function properly within Windows 10.

Application Compatibility Manager   A component of the ACT that enables you to collect and analyze compatibility data so that you can remedy any issues before you deploy a new operating system, such as Windows 10.

Application Compatibility Toolkit (ACT)   A Microsoft resource that helps administrators search for and manage compatibility fixes for their applications with Windows 10, thereby helping organizations to produce a comprehensive software inventory.

application signing   Windows looks for a digital signature for the publisher of applications before running the application. Signing the application with a private certificate key enables Windows to check the signature and validate it trusts the publisher. In RemoteApp, you sign applications' user certificates on the RD Session Host, which publishes the applications.

apps   A series of programs included by default with Windows 10 that enables you to access information rapidly from the Internet, or features on your computer such as pictures, music, calendar, maps, Internet Explorer, and so on. You can add additional apps at any time from the Windows Store.

App-V   An application virtualization technology used to stream applications without installing them locally. The only local installation required is the App-V client, which enables virtual applications to run on Windows computers.

Assessment and Deployment Kit (ADK)   The ADK has many tools used for customizing Windows images, test system performance of systems and components, and other tasks.

auditing   A security process that tracks the usage of selected network resources, typically storing the results in a log file.

authenticated exceptions   Windows firewall rules support authenticated exceptions to allow authenticated users or computers to use a network connection that is otherwise blocked.

authentication   A security process that confirms the identity of a user, service, or device.

authorization   The security process and settings that allow access to a specific resource to a specific account.

Automatic Private IP Addressing (APIPA)   The dynamic IPv4 addressing system used when DHCP is unavailable.

Azure   A collection of integrated cloud services offered by Microsoft that is used to build, deploy, and manage applications.

Azure RemoteApp   Microsoft's cloud-based support for hosting RemoteApp applications for use by users on Windows, iOS, and Android devices.

backup   The creation of a copy of programs or data on the computer as a protection against some type of disaster.

Backup and Restore (Windows 7) applet   An application from Windows 7 added to Windows 10 that provides a centralized location and wizards for performing various types of backup and restore procedures.

basic disk   A disk partitioning scheme that uses partition tables supported by many other operating systems and contains primary partitions, extended partitions, and logical drives.

basic input/output system (BIOS)   The firmware application encoded in a computer that initializes the computer before the operating system is loaded. The BIOS manages basic hardware configuration.

battery meter   A small application that runs on mobile computers and displays the percentage of battery power remaining as well as the power plan currently in use.

Bcdboot   A command-line tool that enables you to manage and create new BCD stores and BCD boot entries.

Bcdedit   A command-line tool that enables you to manage boot configuration data (BCD) stores in Windows Vista/7/8/8.1/10/Server 2008/Server 2012/R2/2016.

biometrics   Technologies that measure and analyze human body characteristics, such as DNA, fingerprints, eye retinas and irises, voice patterns, and facial patterns, typically for authentication purposes.

BitLocker   A feature of Windows 10 Pro and Enterprise that enables you to en-crypt the entire contents of your system or data partition. It is useful for protecting data stored on laptops, which are susceptible to theft.

BitLocker To Go   A component of BitLocker that enables you to encrypt the con-tents of a USB flash drive or portable hard drive.

broadband   In the context of Windows connections, broadband is any metered, wireless connection used for Internet access.

CA   See *Certificate Authority*.

cache   A space on the computer's hard disk that is set aside for holding offline cop-ies of shared files and folders from a computer on the network.

certificate   A method of granting access to a user based on unique identification. Certificates represent a distinctive way to establish a user's identity and credentials.

Certificate Authority (CA)   A trusted service that authenticates users and devices and signs certificates for identification and encryption purposes.

Challenge Handshake Authentication Protocol (CHAP)   An authentication pro-tocol that uses a hashed version of a user's password so that the user's credentials are not sent over the wire in clear text.

checkpoint   A point-in-time state of a virtual machine, including hard disk, memory, and hardware configuration information.

classless interdomain routing (CIDR)   A flexible method of stating IP addresses and masks without needing to classify the addresses. An example of the CIDR for-mat is 192.168.1.0/24.

Client Hyper-V   The Microsoft virtualization technology included in Windows 10 Pro, Enterprise, and Education editions.

cloud   Cloud refers to applications, storage, shared resources, and other services available over the Internet. Services that are always available whenever a device is connected to the Internet from anywhere are typically referred to as being "in the cloud."

cloud collection   In Azure RemoteApp, a set of applications that run exclusively on the cloud. They have access only to other cloud-based Azure resources.

Credential Guard   A system that uses virtualization technology to help prevent unauthorized access to the local Windows cache of user and system credentials and password hashes.

credentials   The discrete attributes that make up the total of items required to au-thenticate a user, service, or device. Credentials are typically made up of an account name and password, but can include many other attributes.

DaaS   See *Desktop as a Service*.

Desktop as a Service (DaaS)   A cloud-based desktop virtualization service that provides full desktop experiences to remote users.

data collector sets   A component of the Performance Monitor that records computer performance information into log files. This feature was known as Performance Logs and Alerts in Windows 2000/XP/Server 2003.

Data Execution Prevention (DEP)   A security feature used to prevent buffer overflow exploits by marking memory with nonexecutable or data-only regions and preventing any code execution from those regions.

data recovery agent   A specially configured user account that has the capability to decrypt drives and partitions that have been encrypted using BitLocker.

decryption   Unscrambling the data in an encrypted file through use of an algorithm so that the file can be read.

deep link   The process of adding a store app to the Microsoft Intune portal for deployment to managed devices.

default gateway   The term applied to the router that leads to other networks.

default program   The application that is associated with a file of given extension, so that Windows uses this program to open the file whenever you double-click any file with this extension.

Deployment Image Servicing and Management (DISM)   A command-line tool used for servicing Windows images.

device driver   The specialized software component of an operating system that interfaces with a given hardware component.

device enrollment   The process of connecting a computer or device to Microsoft Intune and allowing the Intune management software to control policies, behavior, and other aspects of the device.

Device Guard   A new Microsoft technology that gives organizations the capability to lock down devices with advanced malware protection against new and unknown attacks.

Device Health Attestation (DHA)   Used to assess device health for Windows PCs and devices, ensuring that security policies are enforced and the device has not been compromised before it is allowed access to organizational resources.

Device Manager   A tool from which you can manage all the hardware devices on your computer. It enables you to view and change device properties, update or roll back drivers, configure settings, and remove devices.

Device Stage   A Windows 10 application that acts as a home page for your hardware devices, listing all devices and enabling you to perform management tasks.

DFS folder   Any shared folder that is contained within a DFS namespace.

DFS Namespace   A DFS technology that enables you to create logical groupings of shared folders on different servers that facilitate the access to data by users on the network. Such groupings are presented to users as a virtual folder tree or namespace.

DFS Replication   A DFS technology that provides an efficient multimaster replication component that synchronizes data between servers with limited bandwidth network links. The contents of folders are synchronized between servers so that users receive the same version of files regardless of which folder target their computer connects to.

differencing VHD   Also known as a child VHD, a VHD that contains only the differences between it and its parent VHD.

DirectAccess   A new feature in Windows Server that enables seamless connectivity to an organization network through the Internet without requiring a VPN.

Disk Management snap-in   A Microsoft Management Console snap-in that enables you to perform all management activities related to disks, partitions, and volumes.

disk quotas   A system of space limits for users on a volume formatted with NTFS. This is set up to ensure that all users have available space on which to store their files, preventing any one user from using all the available space.

DiskPart   A Windows command-line tool that enables you to perform all management activities related to disks, partitions, and volumes. You can use this tool to script actions related to disk management.

Distributed File System (DFS)   A Windows Server 2012 R2 server role that enables administrators to group a large number of shared folders from different servers together in a single tree that enables users to rapidly locate the share they need without searching numerous servers.

domain   A logical grouping of Windows computers, users, and groups that share a common directory database. Domains act as a security boundary and are defined by an administrator.

domain controller (DC)   A server that is capable of performing authentication. In Windows Server 2016, a domain controller holds a copy of the Active Directory database.

Domain Name System (DNS)   A hierarchical naming system that is contained in a distributed database. DNS provides name resolution for IP addresses and DNS names.

driver package   The complete set of files that make up all the components needed for working with a hardware device or peripheral.

driver signing   The digital signature that Microsoft adds to a third-party device driver to validate its usage.

duplex   A term referring to the simultaneity of communications. Simultaneous two-way communication is full duplex, whereas two-way communications that can occur in only one direction at a time are half-duplex.

dynamic disk   A disk partitioning scheme supported by Windows XP/Vista/7/8/ 8.1 as well as Windows Server 2008 R2/2012 R2 that contains dynamic volumes.

Dynamic Host Configuration Protocol (DHCP)   The protocol in the TCP/IP protocol stack that negotiates the lease of an IP address from a DHCP server.

dynamic VHD   A VHD that gradually increases in size toward a configured maximum as data is added to it.

Easy Connect   A feature of Remote Assistance that uses the Peer Network Routing Protocol enabling Remote Assistance connections. It allows the requesting user to use a password that she provides to the technician for connecting to her computer.

Encrypting File System (EFS)   An advanced attribute setting of Windows 2000/ XP/Vista/7/8/8.1/10 and Windows Server 2003/2008 R2/2012/R2/2016 for files and folders on an NTFS-formatted volume that provides certificate-based public key security for those files and folders. EFS encrypts and decrypts files in a manner that is transparent to users.

encryption   Scrambling and rearranging data in a file through use of an algorithm so the file can be read only by individuals or organizations possessing the proper access key.

event log subscription   An Event Viewer feature that enables you to collect event logs from a number of computers in a single, convenient location that helps you keep track of events that occur on these computers.

Event Viewer   An administrative tool that enables an administrator to view and/or archive event logs, such as the operating system, application, setup, and security logs. In Windows 10, this tool also enables you to configure event log subscriptions that collect events from several monitored computers together.

extended partition   One of the primary partitions that can be divided into multiple logical drives.

Extensible Authentication Protocol with Tunneled Transport Layer Security (EAP-TTLS)   A new protocol for Windows Server 2012 R2 and Windows 8.1, and continued in Windows 10 and Windows Server 2016, that uses secure TLS connections to encrypt the authentication traffic during the VPN connection handshake.

fast startup   A setting in Windows 10 that helps make a computer startup faster after shutdown.

feature updates   Updates that contain significant feature additions and changes, as well as security and quality revisions. Previously referred to as upgrades. An example is the upgrade of Windows 10 from version 1511 to version 1607.

Fibre Channel   A special, high-speed network connectivity standard and protocol using optical fiber cables.

File Explorer   The basic window that displays contents of a drive or folder, previously called Windows Explorer.

File History   A feature in Windows 10 that preserves versions of user files in libraries, contacts, and favorites on a separate drive, typically every 10 minutes.

firewall profile   A means of grouping firewall rules so that they apply to the affected computers dependent on where the computer is connected.

firewall rule   A set of conditions used by Windows Firewall to determine whether a particular type of communication is permitted. You can configure inbound rules, outbound rules, and connection security rules from the Windows Firewall with Advanced Security snap-in.

FireWire   Also known as IEEE 1394. FireWire is a fast external bus technology that allows for up to 800 Mbps data transfer rates and can connect up to 63 devices. FireWire devices, although conforming to standards that Windows uses, usually require software from the manufacturer to utilize the specialized capabilities of the hardware.

fixed VHD   A VHD that maintains the same size regardless of how much data is contained in it.

folder redirection   The practice of moving library folders to a different location, which is often a shared folder on a server. Used to facilitate management of storage space on the network and to ensure proper backup of vital data.

forest   A grouping of Active Directory trees that have a trust relationship between them. Forests can consist of a noncontiguous namespace, and unlike domains and trees, do not have to be given a specific name.

global unicast IPv6 address   An IPv6 address that uses a global routing prefix of 45 bits to identify a specific organization's network, a 16-bit subnet ID, and a 64-bit interface ID. These addresses are globally routable on the Internet and are equivalent to public IPv4 addresses.

Group Policy   The Windows Server 2016 feature that allows for policy creation, which affects domain users and computers. Policies can be anything from desktop settings to application assignments to security settings and more.

Group Policy Management Console (GPMC)   An administrative tool used to manage Group Policies. It can be used to create and modify GPOs, check GPO settings, and link GPOs with specific policy settings to an OU or OUs in the Active Directory.

Group Policy Object (GPO)   A collection of policies that apply to a specific target, such as the domain itself (Default Domain Policy) or an organizational unit (OU). GPOs are modified through the Group Policy Management Editor to define policy settings.

hibernation   A condition in which your computer saves everything to the hard disk and then powers down. When you restart your computer from hibernation, all open documents and programs are restored to the desktop.

hidden shares   A shared folder that does not broadcast its presence and is not browsable in the Network folder. A hidden share is indicated by a dollar sign ($) at the end of the folder name.

host   A computing device that has been assigned an IP address.

hybrid   Refers to using both SCCM and Microsoft Intune in concert for mobile device and computer management. Also hybrid MDM.

hybrid collection   In Azure RemoteApp, a set of applications accessible through the cloud that can also access on-premises resources.

hypervisor   An additional layer of software below the operating system for running virtual computers.

indexing   A process in Windows 10 that facilitates the task of users searching data contained in files on the computer so that users can rapidly locate information.

input/output (I/O) port address   A set of wires used to transmit data between a device and the system. As with IRQs, each component has a unique I/O port assigned. There are 65,535 I/O ports in a computer, and they are referenced by a hexadecimal address in the range of 0000h to FFFFh.

Integration Services   A set of applications and software running on a virtual guest that enables the hypervisor to control certain features and performance of the guest operating system.

Internet Connection Sharing (ICS)   The simplified system of routing Internet traffic through a Windows 10 computer so that other computers on the network that are not connected to the Internet can access the Internet.

Internet Control Message Protocol (ICMP)   A TCP/IP protocol that enables hosts on a TCP/IP network to share status and error information. The ping command uses ICMP to check connectivity to remote computers.

Internet Key Exchange version 2 (IKEv2)   A tunneling protocol that uses IPsec Tunnel Mode over UDP port 500. This combination of protocols also supports strong authentication and encryption methods.

Internet Protocol Security (IPsec)   An encryption and authentication protocol that is used to secure data transmitted across a network.

Interrupt Request (IRQ)   A set of wires running between the CPU and devices in the computer; they enable devices to "interrupt" the CPU so that they can transmit data.

IP address   A logical address used to identify both a host and a network segment. Each network adapter on an IP network requires a unique IP address.

IP version 4 (IPv4)   The version of the Internet Protocol that has been in use for many years and provides a 32-bit address space formatted as four octets separated by periods.

IP version 6 (IPv6)   A newer version of the Internet Protocol that provides a 128-bit address space formatted as eight 16-bit blocks, each of which is portrayed as a 4-digit hexadecimal number and is separated from other blocks by colons.

Ipconfig   The command-line utility that provides detailed information about the IP configuration of a Windows computer's network adapters.

ISO   A file format representing an optical disk image such as a DVD or CD.

jumbo frames   The term given to packaging TCP/IP packet data, wrapped by routing headers with a larger amount of data. Typical frames contain 1500 bytes of payload data, whereas jumbo frames can carry up to 9000 bytes of data.

Key Management Service (KMS)   A Windows service used for volume activation. Clients on the network can activate themselves using the KMS over the local network without connecting a directory to Microsoft's servers.

Layer 2 Tunneling Protocol (L2TP)   A protocol used to create VPN tunnels across a public network. This protocol is used in conjunction with IPsec for security purposes.

library   A set of virtual folders that are shared by default with other users of the computer. It is used to group documents of similar type in an easily accessible place.

Line of Business (LOB)   LOB apps are developed in-house for use only within the organization and are not distributed publically or made available on the Windows Store.

link-local IPv6 address   A type of IPv6 address used for communication between neighboring nodes on the same link. Equivalent to IPv4 addresses configured using APIPA.

Link-Local Multicast Name Resolution (LLMNR)   The capability of computers running IPv6 on the local subnet to resolve each other's names without the need for a DNS server. It is enabled by default in Windows 10 IPv6.

Local Security Policy   The security-based Group Policy settings that apply to a local computer and its local users.

local user profile   The collection of Registry settings and files associated with a user's desktop interface that is created the first time a user logs on to a computer. This profile is stored on the local hard disk.

logical drive   A segment of the extended partition that can be assigned a separate drive letter.

mandatory profile   A user profile that is renamed to NTUser.man. This profile is read-only, so that any changes made to the user are never saved when the user logs off. Useful for setting company-specific desktop settings that users are not permitted to modify.

metered connection   Any network connection using a service that is charged based on the amount of data transferred. Many wireless broadband services, smart-phone data plans, and satellite communication services use metered connections. See also *broadband*.

Microsoft account   A cloud service account, previously called a Windows Live account, used to access Windows devices and integrate with cloud services and synchronize multiple devices.

Microsoft BitLocker Administration and Monitoring (MBAM)   A set of server services that enable administrators in an enterprise to manage, monitor, and report on the status of BitLocker encryption on client computers and workstations.

Microsoft Challenge Handshake Authentication Protocol version 2 (MS-CHAPv2)   A Microsoft version of CHAP that uses the same type of challenge/response mechanism as CHAP but uses a nonreversible encrypted password. This is done by using MD4 algorithms to encrypt the challenge and the user's password.

Microsoft Edge   A new, updated Internet browser in Windows 10, which provides enhancements to active Internet browsing, such as Web Note, Reading view, Cortana, and enhanced security measures.

Microsoft Intune   Microsoft's cloud portal for managing devices. Intune can be used to manage Windows mobile devices, Android devices, iOS devices, Windows PCs and computers, and UNIX/Linux servers.

Microsoft Management Console (MMC)   A collection of management tools known as snap-ins that are organized under a single management tool. The tool is used for both local and remote administration.

mirroring   A method of duplicating data between two separate hard disks so that the failure of one disk will not cause the operating system to fail.

Mobile Device Management (MDM)   Using a system to communicate with and manage mobile devices, such as phones and tablets.

Msconfig   The command that opens the System Configuration Utility, which you can use to perform actions such as modifying the startup scheme, the default operating system that boots on a dual-boot computer, services that are enabled, and startup programs that run automatically. You can also launch several computer management tools from this utility.

.msi file   The installation file for an application that uses Windows Installer.

msinfo32   The command that opens the System Information program.

.msp file   The installation file for a patch or hotfix used to update an application that uses Windows Installer.

.mst file   A transform file that performs a scripting-like function for a Windows Installer package.

multicast IPv6 address   An IPv6 address that enables the delivery of packets to each of multiple interfaces.

Network Address Translation (NAT)   A specification in TCP/IP that maps the range of private IP addresses (192.168.0.1–192.168.0.254) to the public IP address of an Internet-facing network adapter.

Network and Sharing Center   A feature of Windows 10 that provides a centralized location from which you can manage all networking tasks, such as connecting to networks and the Internet and sharing files and folders with users at other computers.

Network Discovery   A feature of Windows networking used to allow computers to advertise themselves and locate and connect to other computers and network resources.

NIC   Network Interface Card, or the hardware device used to connect the computer system to a media access layer of a network. Although termed a "card," many NICs are now integrated components of computers and other devices.

NTFS permissions   The security feature available in NTFS that allows you to grant or deny local access rights.

nonuniform memory architecture (NUMA)   A memory allocation technology that groups memory locations and processors into nodes to avoid performance issues caused by multiple processors attempting to access the same memory location, or accessing memory in a location slower to access for the processor that requests it.

Office 365   Microsoft's cloud-based offering for delivering office software and other services to Windows clients.

offline files   A feature built in to all modern Windows versions that enables you to cache locally stored copies of shared files and folders so that you can work with them while offline and resynchronize your changes when you go back online.

offline licensing   Licensing model for store apps that allows you to deploy the apps locally to your systems without accessing the online Windows Store.

OneDrive   A cloud-based, always-available storage and file sharing solution for Windows users.

Online Certificate Status Protocol (OCSP)   A network standard for verifying the status of certificates, retrieving revocation lists, and obtaining the certificate trust change of an X.509 certificate.

online licensing   The traditional licensing model that requires users to authenticate to the online Windows Store or Windows Store for Business to obtain a license and the app.

organizational unit (OU)   An Active Directory container object that allows an administrator to logically group users, groups, computers, and other OUs into administrative units.

paging file   Virtual memory stored on disk that enables Windows 10 to run more applications at one time than would be allowed by the computer's physical memory (RAM).

partition   A configured section of a basic disk that is capable of being formatted with a file system and identified with a drive letter.

Password Authentication Protocol (PAP)   The oldest remote access authentication protocol, which sends the user's credentials over the wire in clear text and can easily be sniffed off of the wire by an attacker.

password policy   A series of Group Policy settings that determine password security requirements, such as length, complexity, and age.

performance counter   A statistical measurement associated with a performance object such as % disk time, queue length, and so on.

Performance Monitor   A Microsoft Management Console (MMC) application that contains several tools for monitoring your computer's performance.

performance object   Hardware or software components that the Performance Monitor can use for tracking performance data.

Personal Identification Number (PIN)   Refers to any of a series of digital confirmation numbers required for use of a device or to supplement authentication of a device user.

Personal Identity Verification (PIV)   A standard developed and published by the National Institute of Standards and Technology to specify the security and encryption attributes of smart cards and their functions.

PKCS #12   A file format for storing many cryptography objects in a file, typically a private key and public key. To export a certificate from a Microsoft CA that includes a private key, the PKCS #12 format is used.

Plug and Play (PnP)   A standard developed by Microsoft and Intel that allows for automatic hardware installation detection and configuration in most Windows operating systems.

Point-to-Point Protocol (PPP)   A dial-up protocol that supports TCP/IP and other protocols with advanced compression and encryption functions.

Point-to-Point Tunneling Protocol (PPTP)   A protocol that is used to create VPN tunnels across a public network and includes encryption and authentication.

power plans   A series of preconfigured power management options that control actions such as shutting off the monitor or hard disks or placing the computer in Sleep mode or hibernation.

PowerShell Remoting   PowerShell Remoting is the framework within PowerShell and enabled by WinRM that allows administrators to run cmdlets and commands on remote computers.

primary partition   A segment of the hard disk. A maximum of four primary partitions may exist on a single basic disk.

Print Management   A Microsoft Management Console (MMC) application that you can use to manage local and remote printers, print servers, jobs, queues, and drivers.

private store   The section of the Windows Store for Business that is private to each organization and includes only the apps that the organization has made available to its users.

Protected Extensible Authentication Protocol-Transport Layer Security (PEAP-TLS)   A remote access authentication and security protocol that provides an encrypted authentication channel, dynamic keying material from TLS, fast reconnect using cached session keys, and server authentication that protects against the setup of unauthorized access points.

provisioned apps   LOB apps that have been added to a Windows image and available to all users of the device.

public folder sharing   A simple Windows 10 folder sharing model that allows others on the network to access files in your Public folders of each Windows library (Documents, Pictures, Videos, and Music).

public key infrastructure (PKI)   A term for the various services and security devices used to implement encryption and identity certificates in an enterprise. The basis for PKI in a Windows Active Directory domain is the Active Directory Certificate Services and related server roles.

Push-Button Reset   A feature in Windows 10 used to refresh the operating system, back to the factory image. Push-Button reset can optionally preserve user data, or it can be used to completely wipe any user files and settings from the device.

quality updates   Traditional operating system updates, generally released on Patch Tuesday (the second Tuesday of each month), although they can be released at any time. They contain items such as security, driver, and critical updates.

RAID-5   A combination of disk striping with parity data interleaved across three or more disks. RAID-5 provides improved disk performance and is fault tolerant.

RD Connection Broker   A component used for RemoteApp that handles connections from remote clients and directs them to the applications or desktops available.

RD Gateway   An RDS component used for forwarding Internet-based clients to internal or private desktop services or RemoteApp applications.

RD Session Host   Used for creating Remote Desktop sessions and hosting and streaming published applications to clients.

RD Web Access   An RDS component that allows clients to connect to the desktop or RemoteApp services using a standard web browser.

recovery agent   A user account that has been granted the authority to decrypt encrypted files.

Reliability Monitor   A monitoring tool that provides a trend analysis of your computer's system stability with time. It shows how events such as hardware or application failures, software installations or removals, and so on affect your computer's stability.

RemoteApp client   Used by Windows computers to access Azure RemoteApp services and applications.

Remote Assistance   A service available in Windows 10 that enables a user to share control of her computer with an administrator or other user to resolve a computer problem.

Remote Desktop   A service available in Windows 10 Pro or Enterprise that allows a single remote control session of a computer running Windows XP, Vista, 7, 8.1, or Windows 10. Remote Desktop uses the Remote Desktop Protocol (RDP), which is the same protocol used in Terminal Services.

Remote Desktop Gateway (RD Gateway)   A Windows Server feature that replaces the Terminal Services feature included with older versions of Windows Server. RD Gateway enables you to connect to remote servers on the corporate network from any computer that is connected to the Internet.

Remote Desktop Services (RDS)   A collection of software and services in Windows Server and Microsoft Azure that support virtual desktops and RemoteApp streaming, and associated services.

remote wipe   The process of deleting all private and personal information on a device connected to the Internet or other network, without any physical or direct access to the device. Remote wipe is enabled at the server managing the device, and the next time the device attempts to connect to a network service it receives a signal and initiates the wipe and reset process.

Resource Monitor   A monitoring tool that provides a summary of CPU, disk, network, and memory performance statistics, including mini-graphs of recent performance of these four components as well as tabulated data pertaining to each.

roaming profile   A user profile that is stored on a shared folder on a server so that a user receives the Registry settings and files for his desktop interface regardless of the computer on which he logs on.

Safe Mode   A method of starting Windows 10 with only the basic drivers enabled, so that you can troubleshoot problems that prevent Windows from starting normally.

Second Level Address Translation (SLAT)   A processor feature, also known as Rapid Virtualization Indexing (RVI), improves processor performance by managing memory with additional indexes or lookup tables.

Secure Boot   Secure Boot is a technology in Windows 10 that protects the pre-OS environment of a computer to ensure that all drivers and system loaders are authenticated and secure.

Secure Socket Tunneling Protocol (SSTP)   A tunneling protocol that uses Secure Hypertext Transfer Protocol (HTTPS) over TCP port 443 to transmit traffic across firewalls and proxy servers that might block PPTP and L2TP traffic.

service pack   A collection of updates and fixes to a software package, usually available via download from the Internet. Service packs are available for download from Microsoft and when using the Microsoft automated update service.

Service Set Identifier (SSID)   A network name that identifies a wireless access point.

settings location template   A template used by UE-V to determine where the settings for a specific application are located so that they can be saved to a central store.

Setup.exe   The application that installs Windows 10 on a new computer or updates an older Windows computer to Windows 10. Also frequently used as a routine for installing applications.

shadow copies   Backup copies of files and folders automatically created by Windows as you work on them, enabling File History to back them up to another location, even while you are working on them.

shared folder permissions   The security feature available when sharing files and folders across a network that allows you to grant or deny access rights to network users.

shared folders   Folders that are made available for access by users who are working at another computer on the network.

shim   A compatibility fix that is used to enable an application originally written for an older Windows version to function properly when running in Windows 10.

sideloading   The process of installing a UWP or other app to a device without installing it through an online vendor's store.

Sigverif.exe   A utility that checks your computer for unsigned device drivers.

single pane of glass   Refers to the concept of using a single UI or user interface with multiple back-end services. The complexity of all the connections and interactions is hidden from the user, simplifying administrative tasks.

site   A physical component of Active Directory that includes computers and other resources at a single geographical location and connected with fast LAN links. Sites are created for the purpose of balancing logon authentication with replication.

site-local IPv6 address   An IPv6 address that is private to the network on which it is located. This type of address cannot be accessed from locations external to its network, such as the Internet.

sleep mode   A condition in which the computer consumes low power but is available for use. Sleep mode saves configuration information to memory and powers down the monitor, disks, and several other hardware components.

Smart Paging   A technique used in Hyper-V that minimizes the risk of running out of memory during virtual machine startup operations by swapping some of the requests for physical memory out to a special file on the disk drive.

SmartScreen   A feature in Windows 10 and Internet Explorer that works in conjunction with dynamically updated online databases to track malicious software and phishing sites to warn users of potential malware and identity theft sites.

Software as a Service (SaaS)   A cloud service that allows users to use software over the Internet without installing it locally. Office 365 is an example of SaaS.

Software License Manager (SLMGR)   A script named slmgr.vbs that can be used to query activation states and manage activation using the command line.

special access permissions   A granular set of NTFS security permissions that enable a single type of access only. Regular NTFS permissions are a combination of special access permissions.

startup repair   A utility that provides a diagnostics-based, step-by-step troubleshooter that enables end users and tech support personnel to rapidly diagnose and repair problems that are preventing a computer from starting normally.

storage pool   A set of physical disk drives grouped together and used as the storage capacity for virtual storage spaces.

storage space   A virtual disk volume, optionally with resiliency, created from a pool of physical disks and used as a single disk drive.

striping   A method of segmenting data and interleaving it across multiple disks, which has the effect of improving disk performance, but is not fault tolerant.

subnet mask   A set of numbers, 32-bits in length, that begins with 1s and ends with 0s in binary notation. The number of 1s represents the number of bits that are considered the subnet address. The bits that are 0s are the host address. Using a subnet mask, you can create more subnets with a smaller number of computers per subnet. All computers on a given subnet must have the same subnet mask. Using dotted decimal notation, a subnet mask is written as 255.255.0.0 (which is the default mask for a Class B address).

Sync Center   A program on mobile computers that synchronizes data with other network devices, including servers, desktop computers, and other portable computers.

synchronization conflicts   Occur when two users have modified a file that is available offline and Windows detects that conflicting modifications have occurred. Windows 10's Sync Center enables you to save either or both of these versions.

synchronizing files   The act of copying files from a shared folder on the network to an offline files cache on a computer or copying the same files back to the shared folder after a user has modified them.

system access control list (SACL)   A list of actions that trigger audit events.

System Center Configuration Manager (SCCM)   A system management product developed by Microsoft for managing large groups of computers.

System Configuration Utility   A tool that enables you to perform actions such as modifying the startup scheme, the default operating system that boots on a dual-boot computer, services that are enabled, and startup programs that run automatically. You can also launch several computer management tools from this utility. Started with the Msconfig.exe command.

System Protection   A troubleshooting tool that provides several options for retaining copies of system files and settings so that you can configure how System Restore works to restore your computer to an earlier point in time.

System Restore   A troubleshooting tool that enables you to restore your computer to an earlier time at which it was operating properly.

Task Manager   A Windows 10 administrative utility that provides data about currently running processes, including their CPU and memory usage, and enables you to modify their priority or to shut down misbehaving applications. You can also manage services, including starting, stopping, enabling, and disabling them, obtain information on network utilization, and display users with sessions running on the computer.

Task Scheduler   Tool used to schedule and automate tasks to perform a specific function at a specific time.

Teredo   A tunneling communication protocol that enables IPv6 connectivity between IPv6/IPv4 nodes across Network Address Translation (NAT) interfaces, thereby improving connectivity for newer IPv6-enabled applications on IPv4 networks.

Temporal Key Integrity Protocol (TKIP)   An encryption standard used for wireless networking. It was the first successor to the weaker WEP encryption standard and incorporates several features to ensure unique encryption keys for every data packet, making it a much more challenging encryption methodology compared to WEP.

tree   A collection of Active Directory domains that form a contiguous namespace. A tree is contained within a forest, and multiple trees can exist within a forest.

UEFI   The Unified Extensible Firmware Interface is a specification designed as a replacement for the older BIOS firmware on PCs. It defines the services and interface points between the computer firmware and the operating system.

USB recovery drive   A USB thumb drive or portable hard drive on which copies of files required to start your computer are used if a problem has prevented your computer from starting properly.

User Account Control (UAC)   A feature in Windows 8.1 that enables you to work with a nonadministrative user account. UAC displays a prompt that requests approval when you want to perform an administrative task. Should malicious software attempt to install itself or perform undesirable actions, you receive a prompt that you can use to prevent such actions from occurring. First introduced in Windows Vista, UAC has been updated in Windows 8.1 to provide new configuration options and reduce the number of prompts.

User Experience Virtualization (UE-V)   A technology that can be used in an organization to save users' Windows and application settings to a central location and synchronize the settings across devices and sessions.

user profile   A series of user-specific settings that are composed of desktop settings, files, application data, and the specific environment established by the user.

Universal Windows Platform (UWP)   A new style of app created by Microsoft. These apps are hosted by the Microsoft Store, or developers can create LOB apps and sideload them to devices. UWP apps work on any type of Windows 10 device, as well as Xbox, and Microsoft Hololens.

Verify.exe   A utility used for low-level debugging of device driver issues.

VFD   Virtual floppy disk, a representation of a floppy disk images store on a disk file.

VHDX   A new format for virtual hard disks optimized for use by Hyper-V virtual machines.

Virtual Desktop Infrastructure (VDI)   A Microsoft technology used to virtualize desktops in a centralized delivery solution. VDI makes use of virtualization technology to store and run desktop workloads in a server-based VM.

virtual hard disk (VHD)   A representation of a hard drive of specific geometry stored in a disk file.

virtual machine   A computer running inside another operating system or hypervisor, sharing the hardware resources of the host and behaving as it would running on a physical computer.

virtual private network (VPN)   A remote access connection technology that uses a protocol such as Point-to-Point Tunneling Protocol or L2TP with IPsec to tunnel through a public network to connect to a private network and maintain a secure connection.

virtual switch   A software representation of a network switch, configured in software and used to connect virtual machines in a Hyper-V environment.

virtualization   The process of creating software representations of physical computer components that behave like their physical counterparts.

VLAN   Virtual LANs are created by use of special routing or virtual switches that tag network packets with VLAN ID numbers, which are then used to divide a network space into individual and separate LAN segments.

volume   A logical drive that has been formatted for use by a file system. Although often considered synonymous with "partition," a volume is most specifically a portion of a dynamic disk, or multiple sections of dynamic disks, that is capable of being formatted with a file system and being identified with a drive letter.

wbadmin   A command-line utility that provides a comprehensive system backup function in a scriptable form.

Wi-Fi Direct   A new industry standard connectivity technology in Windows 8.1 that enables data and content sharing between devices and PCs on a peer-to-peer network that does not require separate Wi-Fi access points.

Wi-Fi Protected Access (WPA and WPA2)   A security protocol developed by the Wi-Fi Alliance to secure wireless networks. WPA2 incorporates stronger AES-based encryption and devices are subject to security certification by the Wi-Fi Alliance. WPA is no longer supported in Windows 10.

Wi-Fi triangulation   A technique that sweeps the current area for Wi-Fi access points and cross-references the information, including the strength of each signal, with a database of locations to determine the location of a computer in range of those access points.

Windows Firewall   The personal firewall software incorporated in Windows 10 that filters incoming TCP/IP traffic. Windows Firewall was first introduced in Windows XP SP2.

Windows Firewall with Advanced Security   A Microsoft Management Console (MMC) snap-in that enables you to configure comprehensive firewall rules specifying conditions for external connection to your computer. Default inbound, outbound, and connection security rules are provided; you can modify these rules or create new rules as required.

Windows Hardware Certification Program   A Microsoft program that identifies all hardware certified to run properly on Windows 10 computers. It replaces the Windows Logo program previously used.

Windows PowerShell   An enhanced task-based command-line scripting interface that enables you to perform a large number of remote management tasks.

Windows Recovery Environment (Windows RE)   A parallel, minimum Windows installation that enables you to boot your computer when your Windows 10 installation will not start by any of the other advanced startup modes. You can perform advanced recovery operations when you have booted into Windows RE.

Windows Server Update Services (WSUS)   A service that can be configured to run on a server, supplying updates, hotfixes, and other patches automatically to computers on a network. WSUS enables you to deploy and manage updates that are downloaded from the Microsoft Windows Update website to WSUS servers running on your own network. Client computers connect to the local WSUS server to download and install updates.

Windows Store for Business   A subscription service for organizations, which they can use to manage and deploy LOB or volume-purchased apps for their employees.

Windows To Go   A bootable version of Windows 10 contained on a USB drive. It includes all operating system files, applications, and Windows settings and can be used to boot a computer with the appropriate hardware into Windows 10, independently of the operating system installed on this computer.

Windows Update   A Windows Settings utility that enables you to maintain your computer in an up-to-date condition by automatically downloading and installing critical updates as Microsoft publishes them.

Windows XP Mode   The basic virtualization technology introduced in Windows Vista for running an instance of Windows XP within a Vista or Windows 7 operating system. Replaced by Client Hyper-V in Windows 10.

Wired Equivalent Privacy (WEP)   A protocol that is used on 802.11-based wireless networks to encrypt data sent between computers on a wireless network or between a computer and its access point. WEP is better security than an open network but is considered less secure than WPA.

wireless access point (WAP)   A router or other device that broadcasts wireless signals to computers on a wireless local area network (WLAN). Also known as an access point or AP. Computers connecting through a WAP are members of an infrastructure (as opposed to ad hoc) wireless network.

wireless local area network (WLAN)   Is synonymous with a local area network (LAN) using wireless equipment and signaling.

wireless network profile   A series of configuration settings that determine the extent of access to external computers according to your computer's location. Windows enables you to create profiles for Home, Work, and Public locations.

Work Folders   A technology introduced for Windows Server 2012 R2 that allows users to sync files on their local device with a secure location on a Windows Server.

Index

Numbers

A

H

M

Q - R

T